Yearbook of American & Canadian Churches 2010

Previous Issues & Editors

Seventy-eighth Issue   Annual

YEARBOOK OF AMERICAN & CANADIAN CHURCHES 2010

Edited by Eileen W. Lindner

Prepared and edited for the
National Council of the Churches of Christ
in the U.S.A.
475 Riverside Drive, New York, NY 10115-0050

Published and distributed
by Abingdon Press
Nashville

Preparation of this *Yearbook* is an annual project of the National Council of the Churches of Christ in the United States of America.

This is the seventy-eighth edition of a yearbook that was first published in 1916. Previous editions have been entitled: *Federal Council Yearbook* (1916–1917), *Yearbook of the Churches* (1918–1925), *The Hand-book of the Churches* (1927), *The New Handbook of the Churches* (1928), *Yearbook of American Churches* (1933–1972), and *Yearbook of American & Canadian Churches* (1973–2009).

Eileen W. Lindner	*Editor*
Marcel A. Welty	*Associate Editor*
Elizabeth During	*Assistant Editor*

Contents

Editor's Preface

This seventy-eighth edition of the *Yearbook of American & Canadian Churches* marks another anniversary that affirms the remarkable service this resource has played in preserving a fascinating record of our ever-changing religious institutions. We are especially conscious of the intense labors of previous editors and contributors who shaped this annual compilation of data in earlier years, and we are grateful to maintain their legacy. This 2010 edition is accessible in both hardcopy and electronically over the Internet using the unique pass code printed on the inside back cover of this volume. Updated information is reflected in the electronic edition twice during the year. In addition, a compact disc exists of data dating from 1916 through 2000, and brings these longitudinal data into ready availability.

Recognizing the Contributions of Many

The field of church statistics is complex and, of necessity, filled with inconsistencies. In recent years, electronic reporting has enabled greater amounts of time at each data collection level to raise questions and to recalculate and refine reports. We at the *Yearbook* are pleased to take our place in this important task of annually capturing a snapshot of American religious life. Reflection upon such findings tells us much about ourselves as well as the institutional religious life in a country which has been referred to as a "nation with the soul of a church."

Our colleagues in the compilation of each edition of the *Yearbook* are the thousands, perhaps tens of thousands, of individuals who keep church records. We rely and build upon the efforts of church pastors, deacons, secretaries and vestrymen and women who carefully review and report church membership statistics and financial giving. We acknowledge the contributions of those at congregational, regional and especially denominational levels who respond with good cheer (most of the time!) and expeditiously (at least at our second request!) in furnishing us with the detailed data we require in the format that we request. We hope that being a part of the record and analysis offered by the *Yearbook* contributes to their sense of satisfaction for a job well done.

For various chapters of the *Yearbook* we are indebted to specific individuals for their assistance in gathering, analyzing and corroborating the information we publish. We thank Eliza Smith Brown for her help in compiling the seminary enrollment data. Mark Duffy has provided updated information regarding church archives and historical records collections. Our colleague Tracy DeLuca, Librarian of the Interchurch Center in New York is a regular and reliable consultant to us. Likewise, Seth Kasten, Librarian at the Burke Library of Union Theological Seminary in New York is ever ready to offer able assistance and counsel. Cathy Lavendar of the United States Census Bureau assured that the Statistical Abstract remains current with *Yearbook* data.

Annual production of the *Yearbook* requires a variety of skills and commitments within our own editorial offices. Associate Editor, Marcel A. Welty gives leadership and prodigious effort to the logistics of researching, requesting, compiling, confirming, correcting, formatting and preparing data for analysis. Elizabeth During returns to the *Yearbook* as Assistant Editor after a leave to finish her doctorate. Her careful attention to detail and efficient research and organization skills make the *Yearbook* possible. Our thanks also to the Rev. Bernard Mayhew, who stepped into a difficult job on short notice and succeeded in keeping us on schedule with his extraordinary diligence and careful attention to detail in a critical time of transition. Almost as closely associated with us as those we see each day are our colleagues and friends of long standing, John and Sylvia Ronsvalle, of the empty tomb, inc. Nationally recognized for their steadfast attention to the patterns of church giving, the Ronsvalles are unfailingly gracious in providing expert assistance and in enabling our own analysis. As we went to press, their excellent analysis of church giving, *The State of Church Giving* through 2007 (Nineteenth edition, October 2009), includes an original survey of 34 churches' overseas mission giving and is highly recommended to those interested in understanding trends in church benevolence.

On behalf of those readers, we extend our gratitude for the wisdom, skill, patience and generosity of those we acknowledge here. No small group of individuals could hope to have the knowledge needed to compile a text as far ranging as the *Yearbook*. Our efforts strengthened by the contributions of all those named above have led to the 78th edition of the *Yearbook of American & Canadian Churches*; we wish to express our deepest thanks to each of them.

The 2010 Edition Features

* Reports on 227 national church bodies which itself is reflective of a remarkably robust immigrant history and the cultural and constitutional freedom of religion so characteristic of the United States.
* Signals that churches reporting in *Yearbook* statistics reflect continued high overall church participation, and account for the religious affiliation of over 163 million Americans.
* Reports on 227 national church bodies including brief histories, leadership and headquarter information and is broadly inclusive of the varieties of American Christianity.
* In this day of increasing awareness of religious pluralism the *Yearbook* offers an updated Directory of Selected Faith Traditions in America.
* Continues to offer an inclusive directory of 234 US local and regional ecumenical bodies with program and contact information.
* Provides listings of theological seminaries and bible schools, religious periodicals and guides to religious research including church archive listings.
* Accurate and timely information through the *Yearbook*'s Internet edition, in its eighth year. As personnel change, area codes and old email addresses are replaced with new ones, and any new information is submitted to the *Yearbook*, our readers are kept current with those changes through two regular electronic updates throughout the year. Access is provided through a unique passcode printed inside the back cover of the *Yearbook*.

The 2010 Edition Updates

* Ranks the 25 largest churches by membership. Only three of the top ten are "mainline" protestant churches. Reports the fastest growing churches in this group as: the Jehovah's Witnesses, Church of God (Cleveland, Tennessee), and the Church of Jesus Christ of Latter-day Saints.
* Analyzes the financial data from 64 churches representing almost 45 million members and almost $36 billion dollars.

The 2010 Edition Trends

* Reports the on the New Immigrant Church and its potential to reshape the religious landscape. (pp. 16–18)
* Notes a continued acceleration of church membership decline in mainline church traditions but a reversal from decline to growth with the Catholic Church. (p. 11)
* Reports on an overall decline in seminary enrollment. (p. 382)
* Despite an overall decline in seminary enrollment, including declines in Hispanic and Asian enrollment, finds African American enrollment has continued to increase.

Eileen W. Lindner
Editor
New York, 2009

I

PERSPECTIVES ON AMERICA'S RELIGIOUS LANDSCAPE

Trends & Developments, 2009

Methodological Considerations

The *Yearbook of American & Canadian Churches* reports annually on data gathered from national religious bodies that reflect the religious affiliations and financial giving patterns of hundreds of millions of Americans. However, these data generally represent information gathered two calendar years prior to the year of publication. For instance, data reported in this 2010 edition of the *Yearbook* reflects information for 2008 that was collected by national church structures in 2009 and reported to the *Yearbook* at the end of 2009 for publication in this 2010 *Yearbook*. This "lag time" often leads our readers to ask if such data is out of date by the time it is printed. In response we would give a qualified "no." Massive national agencies such as the churches reporting through the *Yearbook* move in their institutional lives at nearly imperceptible rates of speed. Moreover, given the vast size and complexity of such diverse organizations, partial data reported more frequently might well have the unintended effect of conveying a sense of "trend" to momentary or regionally isolated patterns of reporting, affiliation and/or financial giving. Now in the 78th edition, the *Yearbook* believes that an annual review of data continues to provide an appropriate interval for tracking the changes in institutional patterns.

No single standard for data collection exists across the variety of ecclesiastical structures reported in the *Yearbook*. Moreover, the definitions of membership and related terms differ widely from one church structure to another. This lack of universal definition and collection methodology has frequently led to questions about the validity and reliability of self-reported data. Recognizing the limitations of the data reported herein, we continue to have confidence in the overall value of trends and other findings based on these figures and this methodology. While church data collection and analytical practices differ across various institutional and organizational margins, they tend to be remarkably consistent within specific organizations over time. (Where we are made aware of changes in a particular church's reporting methods, we will note them for the reader.) This consistency within organizations brings a greater degree of confidence to the relative data of a given church over time. For the same reason the relative size of one church to another as reported here, we believe, provides an accurate picture even while lacking a degree of absolute precision of membership statistics, particularly over time. Thus, we believe that the Southern Baptist Convention is roughly twice the size of The United Methodist Church, for example, and that changes relative to each other over several years are probably an accurate reflection of actual membership trends. Moreover, these data are the most exacting figures presently available, and thus serve as the national standard.

The first eight decades of record keeping represented by the *Yearbook of American & Canadian Churches* is contained on a comprehensive Historic Archive on CD-ROM (which contains membership and financial data from 1916–1999). This CD provides a longitudinal backdrop for the analysis that follows. Only through such a longitudinal study of growth and decline in membership are we able to capture and analyze the emerging patterns. Our annual trends analysis should be regarded as a snapshot taken at a discrete moment in history. The meaning of the figures within that snapshot will best be given definition by the larger and longer context of which they are a part.

The reader is invited to utilize both the current edition and the *Yearbook of American & Canadian Churches'* historic CD to test and amplify the analysis that follows. To obtain the Historic Archive on CD-ROM call 1-888-870-3325 or visit www.electronicchurch.org.

Table 1
LONGITUDINAL INCLUSIVE MEMBERSHIP 1890-2008

Year	Membership	Source	Year	Membership	Source
1890	41,699,342	CRB	1969	128,505,084	YBAC
1906	35,068,058	CRB	1970	131,045,053	YBAC
1916	41,926,852	CRB	1971	131,389,642	YBAC
1926	54,576,346	CRB	1972	131,424,564	YBAC
1931	59,268,764	CH	1973	131,245,139	YBAC
1932	60,157,392	CH	1974	131,871,743	YBAC
1933	60,812,624	CH	1975	131,012,953	YBACC
1934	62,007,376	CH	1976	131,897,539	YBACC
1935	62,678,177	CH	1977	131,812,470	YBACC
1936	55,807,366	CRB	1978	133,388,776	YBACC
1936	63,221,996	CH	1979	133,469,690	YBACC
1937	63,848,094	CH	1980	134,816,943	YBACC
1938	64,156,895	YBAC	1981	138,452,614	YBACC
1940	64,501,594	YBAC	1982	139,603,059	YBACC
1942	68,501,186	YBAC	1983	140,816,385	YBACC
1944	72,492,699	YBAC	1984	142,172,138	YBACC
1945	71,700,142	CH	1985	142,926,363	YBACC
1946	73,673,182	CH	1986	142,799,662	YBACC
1947	77,386,188	CH	1987	143,830,806	YBACC
1948	19,435,605	CH	1988	145,383,739	YBACC
1949	81,862,328	CH	1989	147,607,394	YBACC
1950	86,830,490	YBAC	1990	156,331,704	YBACC
1951	88,673,005	YBAC	1991	156,629,918	YBACC
1952	92,277,129	YBAC	1992	156,557,746	YBACC
1953	94,842,845	YBAC	1993	153,127,045	YBACC
1954	97,482,611	YBAC	1994	158,218,427	YBACC
1955	100,162,529	YBAC	1995	157,984,194	YBACC
1956	103,224,954	YBAC	1996	159,471,758	YBACC
1957	104,189,678	YBAC	1997	157,503,033	YBACC
1958	109,557,741	YBAC	1998	150,105,525	YBACC
1959	112,226,905	YBAC	1999	151,161,906	YBACC
1960	114,449,217	YBAC	2000	152,134,407	YBACC
1961	116,109,929	YBAC	2001	158,952,292	YBACC
1962	117,946,002	YBAC	2002	161,202,780	YBACC
1963	120,965,238	YBAC	2003	163,128,935	YBACC
1964	123,307,449	YBAC	2004	163,438,911	YBACC
1965	124,682,422	YBAC	2005	163,677,894	YBACC
1966	125,778,656	YBAC	2006	163,698,507	YBACC
1967	126,445,110	YBAC	2007*	162,555,074	YBACC
1968	128,469,636	YBAC	2008*	163,325,722	YBACC

*Note: This figure does not include the membership of the Orthodox Church in American, which is reassessing its membership count.

Source Key:
CRB—*Census of Religious Bodies*, Bureau of the Census, Washington
CH—*The Christian Herald*, New York
YBAC—*Yearbook of American Churches*, New York
YBACC—*Yearbook of American and Canadian Churches*, New York

Table 1—Longitudinal Inclusive Membership

This table represents a longitudinal view of aggregated membership totals for all churches reporting to the *Yearbook*. These data do not reflect the entirety of national church membership since some churches either do not gather such data, or do not report them to the *Yearbook*. These figures moreover do not include membership of independent congregations including megachurches. Substantial numbers of church members, therefore, are not accounted for in nationally-gathered membership data. With more than 163 million adherents, the churches collectively continue to maintain a substantial organizational and institutional presence within the United States.

Table 2—US Membership Church Ranking

This table allows comparison in size as determined by membership of the largest twenty-five churches in the nation. Dwarfing any single other church is the Catholic Church, reporting over 68 million adherents. The Church of Jesus Christ of Latter-day Saints is ranked 4th with nearly 6 million members. The remainder of the top 25 are Protestant Churches with two exceptions; the Greek Orthodox Archdiocese, which is ranked 17th, and the Jehovah's Witnesses, which is ranked 22nd, displacing the United Church of Christ in this position.

The patterns of affiliation reflected in this table offer a numerical view and summary of American church history. Protestantism has, since the founding of the republic and until the present moment, enjoyed cultural hegemony accompanied throughout by a consistent substantial Catholic presence.

Four of the twenty-five largest churches are Pentecostal in belief and practice. Strong figures from the Assemblies of God and the Church of God (Cleveland, Tennessee) suggest a continuing increase in numbers of adherents to Pentecostal groups, though it is impossible to state unequivocally from this table since the other two charismatic churches in this ranking have not reported in some years. The four largest Pentecostal churches are: The Church of God in Christ, Assemblies of God, the Pentecostal Assemblies of the World, Inc., and the Church of God (Cleveland, Tennessee), which has moved from 25th to 24th in this ranking.

The ranking of churches on the basis of membership remains relatively stable as indicated by the first column of numbers in Table 2. The last column presents increases (decreases) as a percentage change from the 77th edition's reported membership figures. With the exception of the Catholic Church, United Church of Christ, the American Baptist Churches, and The Episcopal Church, the largest 25 churches are maintaining respective growth (or decline) in membership. The largest percentage change was reported by the United Church of Christ, which diminished its rate of loss from -6.01% to -2.93%. The Catholic Church reversed from a one-year decline of 0.59% to post an increase of 1.49%. The Episcopal Church reports a 2.81% decrease in membership, quickening its losses from its previous -1.76% rate of decline reported in the 2009 edition of the *Yearbook*, but reflecting a slower decline in membership than the 4.15%, decline reported in the 2007 edition. The American Baptist Churches in the U.S.A. doubled its rate of membership decline, going from -0.94% to -2.00%.

The top fifteen churches, those with membership exceeding two million members, are reflective of the constancy of the Historic Black Churches. Six of the fifteen largest churches (The Church of God in Christ, National Baptist Convention USA, National Baptist Church of America Inc., National Missionary Baptist Convention of America, Progressive National Baptist Convention, and African Methodist Episcopal Church) are predominately African American churches. This of course is reflective of the historic strength of the church within the African American community.

In the last quarter century there has been much analysis and debate concerning the decline of "mainline" Protestantism. Whatever the specific rates of growth or decline may be for individual mainline denominations, this ranking illustrates a significant aggregate presence in the American religious landscape. Of the top ten largest churches, three are mainline protestant (United Methodist, Evangelical Lutheran Church in America, and Presbyterian Church (U.S.A.)). In the top twenty-five churches, six are

Table 2
US MEMBERSHIP CHURCH RANKING: Largest 25 Churches

Denomination Name	Current Ranking [2009 Ed.]	Inclusive Membership	Percentage Increase/Decrease 2009/2008
The Catholic Church	1[1]	68,115,001	1.49%
Southern Baptist Convention	2[2]	16,228,438	-0.24%
The United Methodist Church	3[3]	7,853,987	-0.98%
The Church of Jesus Christ of Latter-day Saints	4[4]	5,974,041	1.71%
The Church of God in Christ	5[5]	5,499,875	*0.00%*
National Baptist Convention, U.S.A., Inc.	6[6]	5,000,000	*0.00%*
Evangelical Lutheran Church in America	7[7]	4,633,887	-1.62%
National Baptist Convention of America, Inc.	8[8]	3,500,000	*0.00%*
Assemblies of God	9[10]	2,899,702	1.27%
Presbyterian Church (U.S.A.)	10[9]	2,844,952	-3.28%
African Methodist Episcopal Church	11[11]	2,500,000	*0.00%*
National Missionary Baptist Convention of America'	11[11]	2,500,000	*0.00%*
Progressive National Baptist Convention, Inc.	11[11]	2,500,000	*0.00%*
The Lutheran Church—Missouri Synod (LCMS)	14[14]	2,337,349	-1.92%
The Episcopal Church	15[15]	2,057,292	-2.81%
Churches of Christ	16[16]	1,639,495	*0.00%*
Greek Orthodox Archdiocese of America	17[17]	1,500,000	*0.00%*
Pentecostal Assemblies of the World, Inc.	17[17]	1,500,000	*0.00%*
The African Methodist Episcopal Zion Church	19[19]	1,400,000	*0.00%*
American Baptist Churches in the U.S.A.	20[20]	1,331,127	-2.00%
Baptist Bible Fellowship International	21[21]	1,200,000	*0.00%*
Jehovah's Witnesses	22[23]	1,114,009	2.00%
United Church of Christ	23[22]	1,111,691	-2.93%
Church of God (Cleveland, Tennessee)	24[25]	1,072,169	1.76%
Christian Churches and Churches of Christ	25[24]	1,071,616	*0.00%*
TOTALS		**147,384,631**	**0.49%**

NOTE: Percentage changes in *italic/bold* signify that membership was not updated from previous reported figures.

mainline protestant, though all of them report an overall loss of membership for the latest reporting year. In addition to the three noted above the mainline churches ranked in the top twenty five include The American Baptist Churches, The Episcopal Church, and the United Church of Christ.

Table 3—Membership Gains and Losses
Table 3 offers longitudinal data on rate of growth or loss of church membership of a selected group of large churches for four years, 2005–2008.

The large churches reporting growth measured as a percentage of membership are: the Church of Jesus Christ of Latter-day Saints (1.71%), the Catholic Church (1.49%), and the Assemblies of God (1.27%). These groups appear to show accelerated rates of membership growth. Likewise, among these churches reporting a decline in membership, the rate of decline accelerated in this reporting period. Some will wish to argue that the slowing growth rate is evidence of an increasing secularization of American postmodern society, and its disproportionate impact on liberal religious groups. While such an explanation will satisfy some, caution in drawing such a conclusion is warranted. American society as whole has not experienced the kind and rate of secularization so clearly demonstrated during the last quarter century in Western Europe. Indeed, American church membership trends have defied gravity particularly when the Pentecostal experience is included. Alternative explanations for slowed membership growth must be carefully drawn during the next few years if we are to make sense of the patterns now emerging (see the theme

Last Year's Ranking (2009 Edition)

Denomination Name	Inclusive Membership Figures	Percentage Increase/Decrease 2008– 2009 Editions
The Catholic Church	67,117,016	-0.59%
Southern Baptist Convention	16,266,920	-0.24%
The United Methodist Church	7,931,733	-0.80%
The Church of Jesus Christ of Latter-day Saints	5,873,408	1.63%
The Church of God in Christ	5,499,875	*0.00%*
National Baptist Convention, U.S.A., Inc.	5,000,000	*0.00%*
Evangelical Lutheran Church in America	4,709,956	-1.35%
National Baptist Convention of America, Inc.	3,500,000	*0.00%*
Presbyterian Church (U.S.A.)	2,941,412	-2.79%
Assemblies of God	2,863,265	0.96%
African Methodist Episcopal Church	2,500,000	*0.00%*
National Missionary Baptist Convention of America	2,500,000	*0.00%*
Progressive National Baptist Convention, Inc.	2,500,000	*0.00%*
The Lutheran Church—Missouri Synod (LCMS)	2,383,084	-1.44%
The Episcopal Church	2,116,749	-1.76%
Churches of Christ	1,639,495	*0.00%*
Greek Orthodox Archdiocese of America	1,500,000	*0.00%*
Pentecostal Assemblies of the World, Inc.	1,500,000	*0.00%*
The African Methodist Episcopal Zion Church	1,400,000	-3.01%
American Baptist Churches in the U.S.A.	1,358,351	-0.94%
Baptist Bible Fellowship International	1,200,000	*0.00%*
United Church of Christ	1,145,281	-6.01%
Jehovah's Witnesses	1,092,169	2.12%
Christian Churches and Churches of Christ	1,071,616	*0.00%*
Church of God (Cleveland, Tennessee)	1,053,642	2.04%
TOTAL	**146,663,972**	**-0.49%**

NOTE: Percentage changes in *italic/bold* signify that membership was not updated from previous reported figures.

chapter, p. 16 for a treatment of The New Immigrant Church). Several factors will need to be weighed afresh including the very centrality of the concept of church membership itself. For the age cohorts known as Gen X'ers and Millennials (people now in their 30s and 20s respectively) formal membership may lie outside of their hopes and expectations for their church relationships. For both of these age cohorts membership and commitment to institutions is no longer perceived as a mark of maturity or assumption of generational responsibility. Membership is sometimes perceived as an unnecessary and even undesirable exercise in over-institutionalization. Hence, for some young adults, church attendance, participation in fellowship or mission activities and even financial support of a local congregation does not translate into a desire to formally "join" and be listed among those in membership. The growing prevalence of this practice is reported anecdotally and can often be noted in leafing through local church directories. At the conclusion of the membership directory there typically follows a section labeled as "Friends of the Congregation." If indeed this proves to be a growing tendency among successive generations, church membership as opposed to "affiliation data" may itself need to be reconsidered. Several other factors, emerging patterns of affiliation, and organizational considerations make this demographic inquiry a rich field for further inquiry.

Churches listed here experiencing the highest rate of loss of membership are: the Presbyterian Church (U.S.A.) (-3.28%), which moves this group from 9th to 10th rank, American Baptist Churches (-2.00), The Lutheran Church–Missouri Synod (-1.92%), and the Evangelical Lutheran Church in America (-1.62%).

Table 3

PATTERNS OF U.S. MEMBERSHIP CHANGE OF SELECTED LARGE CHURCHES 2005–2008

Religious Body	2005 Membership Change	Percentage Change	2006 Membership Change	Percentage Change	2007 Membership Change	Percentage Change	2008 Membership Change	Percentage Change
The Catholic Church	-886,008	-1.31	580,191	0.87	-398,000	-0.59	997,985	1.49%
Southern Baptist Convention	2,821	0.02	35,931	0.22	-39,326	-0.24	-38,482	-0.24%
The United Methodist Church	-111,244	-1.36	-79,554	-0.99	-63,723	-0.80	-77,746	-0.98%
Evangelical Lutheran Church in America	-79,653	-1.62	-76,573	-1.58	-64,247	-1.35	-76,069	-1.62%
The Church of Jesus Christ of Latter-day Saints	91,495	1.63	88,644	1.56	94,092	1.63	100,633	1.71%
Presbyterian Church (U.S.A.)	-90,731	-2.84	-73,102	-2.36	-84,328	-2.79	-96,460	-3.28%
The Lutheran Church- Missouri Synod	-22,883	-0.93	-22,867	-0.94	-34,913	-1.44	-45,735	-1.92%
Assemblies of God	51,766	1.86	5,313	0.19	27,091	0.96	36,437	1.27%
American Baptist Churches in the U.S.A.	-28,140	-1.97	-25,422	-1.82	-12,927	-0.94	-62,804	-2.00%

Table 4

U.S. FINANCIAL SUMMARIES 2001–2008

Year	Number Reporting	Full or Confirmed Members	Per Capita Full or Confirmed Members	Inclusive Members	Per Capita Inclusive Members	Total Contributions	Per Capita Full or Confirmed Members	Per Capita Inclusive Members
2001	62	45,359,589	$586.14	49,828,003	$533.58	$31,041,852,581	$684.35	$622.98
2002	59	43,694,611	$615.84	47,773,814	$563.25	$31,465,090,286	$720.11	$658.63
2003	63	44,211,342	$627.07	48,266,164	$574.39	$32,269,713,588	$725.78	$667.34
2004	63	43,823,753	$645.63	47,850,712	$591.30	$33,214,186,254	$757.90	$694.12
2005	65	43,565,587	$665.73	47,922,181	$605.20	$34,170,801,942	$784.35	$713.05
2006	65	42,224,304	$681.45	46,101,429	$624.14	$34,219,114,885	$810.41	$742.26
2007	66	41,881,459	$727.75	45,735,653	$666.42	$35,949,676,148	$858.37	$786.03
2008	64	41,176,007	$738.50	44,960,160	$676.34	$35,922,818,150	$872.42	$798.99

Year	Total Congregational Contributions	Per Capita Full or Confirmed Members	Per Capita Inclusive Members	Totals Benevolences	Per Capita Full or Confirmed Members	Per Capita Inclusive Members	Benevolences as a Percentage of Total Contributions
2001	$26,587,142,109	$586.14	$533.58	$4,510,947,817	$99.45	$90.53	15%
2002	$26,908,804,274	$615.84	$563.25	$4,555,191,495	$104.25	$95.35	14%
2003	$27,723,558,838	$627.07	$574.39	$4,748,202,343	$107.40	$98.38	15%
2004	$28,294,047,495	$645.63	$591.30	$4,921,921,435	$112.31	$102.86	15%
2005	$29,002,718,319	$665.73	$605.20	$5,168,083,623	$118.63	$107.84	15%
2006	$28,773,748,252	$681.45	$624.14	$5,389,573,754	$127.64	$116.91	16%
2007	$30,479,091,937	$727.75	$666.42	$5,470,584,375	$130.62	$119.61	15%
2008	$30,408,578,031	$738.50	$676.34	$5,514,242,844	$133.92	$122.65	15%

Table 4: Financial Trends

Second only to the interest in membership trends is the interest of media and the church world alike in the financial trends reported in the *Yearbook*. While not all churches report their financial information to the *Yearbook*, 64 churches have provided full data for this 2010 edition providing an important glimpse into U.S. church giving. Almost $36 billion dollars are accounted for in the reports of these churches and this is, of course, but a portion of the whole of church giving.

The financial reporting for this 2010 *Yearbook* is based on the financial income reports of the 64 churches reporting essential figures. The records of those 64 reporting churches are detailed in Table 4. The almost 45 million inclusive members contributed a total of almost $36 billion, marking a decrease in the total amount of income to the reporting churches by $26 million.

Given that this figure captures a smaller sample of churches, it is particularly useful to view this decrease in its per capita terms. The $799 contributed per person is an increase of about $13 per person from the previous year. This 1.65% increase in per capita giving is significantly less than the official inflation figure for 2008. It must be remembered that many individuals are contributing to parishes with a declining number of members. In such contexts, this modest increase in per capita giving cannot be expected to offset the financial loss associated with membership decline nor keep pace with rising costs. Moreover, this slight increase in per capita giving was reported as the nation and the world entered into a period of sharp economic decline and uncertainty. This small increase in per capita giving will be a source of some encouragement to some, and will be watched with great interest because of what it might mean for levels of charitable giving in subsequent reporting years.

Benevolence giving for 2008 in our sample of U.S. churches is consistent with the last report at 15%, but remains at the low end in the range of benevolent giving over the period of the last decade. This level of giving for benevolence will be the source of sober reflection for some. The overall increase in giving to the churches, at this reporting, is occurring simultaneously with a nearly stagnant posture in benevolence as a percentage of total giving. The churches that seek generosity from their supporters have not, at least in this sample, matched that generosity with an increase in their own benevolence giving. The practical consequences of such a trend continues to translate in local settings to less support for church-sponsored day care, fewer soup kitchen meals, less emergency help to persons with medical problems, or reduced transportation to the elderly, even as the needs increase.

An interesting comparison can be made with benevolence reported by Canadian churches. While admittedly reporting on a far smaller sample and reflecting a much lower level of total giving, the percentage of benevolence giving for Canadian churches have reported consistently in the 18–20% range, and this year remains at 18%.

No one has given greater attention to church giving patterns than John and Sylvia Ronsvalle. For a fulsome discussion of the giving patterns of churches, see their The State of Church Giving series of publications, by writing: empty tomb, inc. P.O. Box 2404, Champaign, IL 61825, or through www.emptytomb.org.

The New Immigrant Church

Rev. Eileen W. Lindner, Ph.D.

No phrase is more deeply ingrained in the American psyche than our self-understanding as an "immigrant people." Among the most persistent of our communal myths is that of a great melting pot, a polyglot of peoples and religious traditions living in a diverse community, which protects religious freedoms regarding each without fear or favor. As with many cultural myths, the truth of our ethnicity and religious traditions—and the freedom accorded to each—is far more complex and nuanced than our cherished collective memory. To be sure, the American religious landscape has long been replete with religiously diverse topographical features but protestant Christianity long dwarfed all other topographical aspects and has exercised cultural hegemony within the society. For the last twenty years the scholarly work of Diana Eck, Robert Wuthnow and others has called attention to America's growing religious pluralism driven by new patterns of immigration. Until recently focused efforts to understand the scope and variety of this religious pluralism have tended to obscure the larger influx of Christian immigrants and their churches. In our annual quest to offer a snapshot of churches in the United States and Canada, the *Yearbook* this year examines the state of present research and analysis of the New Immigrant Church.

Because the U.S. Census data famously avoids the whole realm of religious affiliation and thereby limits easy access to reliable measures of the religious composition of new arrivals and the General Social Survey (GSS) provides an inadequate measure of smaller religious communities quantitative measures of new immigrants by religious affiliation is difficult to assess. Yet, it can be safely asserted that the largest plurality of immigrants to the U.S. in the last half century and perhaps even the majority, have been Christian in their religious affiliation. A majority of those immigrants have come from nations that are predominately Christian such as Mexico, Central and South America, Eastern Europe, and the Caribbean (see chart on p. 17). Even immigrants from religiously plural nations are more apt, for a variety of reasons, to be Christian such as those immigrants from the Philippines, Korea, the Middle East and sub-Saharan Africa. Contributing to this immigration pattern are factors in the countries of origin of immigrants that constrain the life and witness of Christian communities and thus serve as a motivational factor to emigration. Christians in religiously plural nations of origin often maintain networks and relationships with Christian institutions within the United States, which sometimes provide greater opportunities for immigration. Further evidence of Christian in-migration to the United States has been reflected in the number and diverse traditions that over the last half century have been added to "Religious Bodies" chapter of this *Yearbook*. Such churches as the Korean Presbyterian Church Abroad, the Mar Thoma Church, the Malankara churches, and a variety of Pentecostal churches of Latin American or African origins have been recorded as their institutional presence within the nation stabilized.

The "newness" of New Immigrant Churches is generally demarcated from the passage of Immigration and Nationality Act of 1965, which abolished national quotas that had been enforced since 1924 and effectively shifted the ethnic balance of émigrés from Western Europe to Eastern Europe and Asia. The 1965 law, for example, provided for 300,000 annual visas with 120,000 from the Eastern Hemisphere and limiting immigration to a total of 20,000 from any one country. The implications of such a shift in immigration policy has altered the Christian landscape within the United States and Canada in ways that we are just beginning to understand. Seen from the perspective of new immigrants, religious institutions and practices which accompanied them to North America have adapted in, and been adapted by, their new cultural context. Thus, the in-migration of Christian individuals and their churches has altered not only the demographic composition of Christianity in America but, perhaps more important, has expanded the variety

16

of expressions of the faith itself. In an era in which we have come to expect the inevitable advance of secularism in the U.S., the influx of robust Christian communities among new immigrants once again amends the topographical map of the religious landscape. Impediments to studying the experiences of these churches—language and cultural barriers, absence of data sets and, institutional forms not easily accessible to researchers—must be overcome if we are to obtain a deeper appreciation of how new immigrant churches might yet redefine the shape of Christian life in America.

Highest Immigration to the United States by Country of Birth*: 1961–2008	
Mexico	6,373,466
Philippines	1,931,257
China	1,639,981
India	1,388,825
Africa (All Countries)	1,337,659
Vietnam	1,252,788
Cuba	1,117,424
Dominican Republic	1,060,517
Korea	991,128
Canada	796,641
United Kingdom	756,639
Jamaica	739,334
El Salvador	695,393
Colombia	604,186
Haiti	585,017
Poland	484,301
Germany	466,873
Iran	417,093
Italy	413,192
Guatemala	369,976
Pakistan	339,087
Peru	332,227
All Countries	**32,479,210**

*Data aggregated from U.S.A. Department of Homeland Security, *Yearbook of Immigration Statistics: 2008*

In the last decade marked progress has been made by a series of studies that have addressed questions related to the new immigrant church. Some of these studies have addressed the new immigrant church within the larger framework of immigrant religious communities and others have addressed the immigrant Christian experience directly. Among the studies forming this body of exploration are: The New Ethnic and Immigrant Congregation Project (NEICP), Stephen Warner and Judith Wittner (1998), which examined structural adaptations in diverse non-European immigrant religious communities; Religion, Ethnicity and New Immigrant Research (RENIR), Helen Rose Ebaugh (2000), which examined 13 immigrant congregations in Houston; and Religion and New Immigrants: How Faith Forms Our Newest Citizens, Michael Foley and Dean Hoge, (2007), which surveyed 200 immigrant congregations in the Washington, DC area.

These and other works raise a number of compelling questions for further exploration. At least four implications might fairly be drawn from these studies:

1.   The potential changes to the American religious landscape occasioned
     by the in-migration of new immigrant churches over the last forty
     years has been obscured by greater emphasis to increasing religious
     pluralism and will require closer attention of both secular and church
     related scholars.

2.   Several ethnographic studies have provided deep and rich information
     about the religious practices and social organization of particular con-
     gregations. Institutional and organizational quantitative studies that
     analyze large samples of immigrant churches with measures of mem-
     ber characteristics, organizational structure, religious practices and
     institutional resources. While ethnographic studies offer more detailed
     insight, large quantitative studies will yield greater generalizability.

3.   Future research might well undertake an examination of the forms of
     assimilation—both forced and voluntary—that immigrant churches
     undergo in the North American context. Cultural exchange is a two-
     way street and researchers need to be attentive to the ways in which
     some of the religious beliefs and practices of immigrant churches
     may be adopted by longstanding religious groups.

4.   In late 2010, a long delayed national public policy debate is expected
     related to immigration reform. In anticipation of that debate various
     national denominations and religious coalitions have begun to signal
     their respective stances regarding the direction and scope of such
     reform. Longstanding religious organizations in America approach the
     immigrant churches and immigrant communities with a multifaceted
     agenda. It is likely that this issue may provide an occasion for a
     realignment of religious bodies as each seeks to exercise moral
     authority. Catholics and mainline Protestants have long been advo-
     cates of less restrictive immigration law. More recently the evangeli-
     cal community has demonstrated a less monolithic perspective on the
     question of immigration policy.

On a variety of public policy issues the New Immigrant church may become a factor
in the posture of the faith community on public affairs issues. With the racial, ethnic and
cultural diversity of the immigrant communities more diverse and nuanced views of
matters ranging from abortion to aid and trade policy as well as immigration policy may
find voice as these churches enter into civic engagement in their new culture. As they
do, a new fault line in Christian theology and practice may open within the American
religious landscape.

II

DIRECTORIES

1. United States Cooperative Organizations, National

The organizations listed in this section are cooperative religious organizations that are national in scope. Regional cooperative organizations in the United States are listed in Directory 6, "United States Regional and Local Ecumenical Bodies."

The Alban Institute, Inc.

The Alban Institute is an independent, not-for-profit cradle of learning, grounded in faith and devoted to helping American congregations become greater communities of faithfulness, health, creativity, hospitality and leadership. Alban is the largest congregational resource and advocacy membership organization in the United States, reaching hundreds of thousands of congregants across all faith traditions with our signature of congregation building known as The Alban Way. From Alban's groundbreaking consulting practice, to original research, publications and seminars on leadership, conflict, planning and transitions, The Alban Institute knows what it takes to build vital, enduring communities of faith. Alban draws on a vast reservoir of congregational know-how and wisdom born on the firing line. Clergy and lay leaders seek guidance from the most respected problem solvers, strategists and teachers in the business.

Headquarters

2121 Cooperative Way, Suite 100, Herndon, VA 20171 Tel. (800)486-1318
Media Contact, Director of Research, Dr. Ian Evison

Officers

Pres., The Rev. James P. Wind, Ph.D.

American Bible Society

In 1816, pastors and laymen representing a variety of Christian denominations gathered in New York City to establish an organization "to disseminate the Gospel of Christ throughout the habitable world." Since that time the American Bible Society (ABS) has continued to provide God's Word, without doctrinal note or comment, wherever it is needed and in the language and format the reader can most easily use and understand. The American Bible Society is the servant of the denominations and local churches.

The American Bible Society is committed to promoting personal engagement with the Holy Scriptures with the goal of changed lives. A special emphasis is placed upon advocacy for the Bible cause, partnerships with like-minded churches and para-church organizations, and with provision of Scripture. Today the ABS serves more than 100 denominations and agencies, and its board of trustees is composed of distinguished laity and clergy drawn from these Christian groups.

The American Bible Society played a leading role in the founding of the United Bible Societies, a federation of 140 national Bible Societies around the world that enables global cooperation in Scripture translation, publication and distribution in more than 200 countries and territories. The Bible Society contributes generously to the support provided by the United Bible Societies to those national Bible Societies which request support to meet the total Scripture needs of people in their countries.

The work of the American Bible Society is supported through gifts from individuals, local churches, denominations and cooperating agencies.

Headquarters

National Service Center, 1865 Broadway, New York, NY 10023 Tel. (212)408-1200
Media Contact, Senior Manager, Media Relations, Roy Lloyd, Tel. (212)408-8731 Fax (212)408-1456, rlloyd@americanbible.org

Officers

Chpsn., Rev. R. Lamar Vest
Vice-Chpsn., Dennis Dickerson
Pres., Rev. Dr. Paul G. Irwin
Vice President for Development, Robert L. Briggs
Vice President and Executive Director for Bibles.com, John Cruz

19

Senior Vice President for Domestic Ministries, Rev. Emilio Reyes

Vice President and General Counsel, Peter Rathbun

Vice President for Corporate Services and CFO, Richard Stewart

Dean, Nida Institute for Biblical Scholarship, Dr. Phil Towner

Director of Internal Audit, Donald Cavanaugh

Director for Publishing Services, Bibles.com, Thomas Durakis

Director for Finance and Production Services, Bibles.com., Gary Ruth

DEPARTMENT HEADS

Chief Communications Officer, Denise London

Assistant to Vice President of Finance, Stephen King

Director of Operations, Cheryl Berlamino

Director of Building Management Services, John Colligan

Director of Research, Dr. Joseph Crockett

Chief Technology Officer, Nicholas Garbidakis

Director of Operations, Bibles.com, Dr. John Greco

Editorial and Publications Manager, Charles Houser

Director of Direct Response Programs, H. Lee Manis

Controller, Stephen Sharp

Director of Investments, Nicholas Pagano

Director of Human Resources, Sharon Roberts

Director of Church Relations, David Ramos

Director of Programs, Karina Lucero

Director of Sales and Marketing, Bibles.com, Brian Sherry

Director of Development, Melinda Trine

Director of Relationship Development, Karmen Wynick

American Council of Christian Churches

The American Council of Christian Churches is a Fundamentalist multidenominational organization whose purposes are to provide information, encouragement, and assistance to Bible-believing churches, fellowships, and individuals; to preserve our Christian heritage through exposure of, opposition to, and separation from doctrinal impurity and compromise in current religious trends and movements; to protect churches from religious and political restrictions, subtle or obvious, that would hinder their ministries for Christ; and to promote obedience to the inerrant Word of God.

Founded in 1941, The American Council of Christian Churches (ACCC) is a multi-denominational agency for fellowship and cooperation among Bible-believing churches in various denominations- fellowships, Bible Presbyterian Church, Evangelical Methodist Church, Fellowship of Fundamental Bible Churches (formerly Bible Protestant), Free Presbyterian Church of North America, Fundamental Methodist Church, Independent Baptist Fellowship of North America, Independent Churches Affiliated, along with hundreds of independent churches. The total membership nears 2 million. Each denomination retains its identity and full autonomy, but cannot be associated with the World Council of Churches, National Council of Churches or National Association of Evangelicals.

Headquarters

P.O. Box 5455, Bethlehem, PA 18015 Tel. (610)865-3009 Fax (610)865-3033

Media Contact, Exec. Dir., Dr. Ralph Colas

Officers

Pres., Dr. John McKnight

Vice-Pres., Rev. Randy Ardis

Exec. Sec., Dr. Ralph Colas

Sec., Rev. Jerry L. Johnson

Treas., Mr. Shane Burge

Commissions, Chaplaincy; Education; Laymen; Literature; Missions; Radio & Audio Visual; Relief; Youth

American Friends Service Committee

Founded 1917, Regional offices, 9. Founded by and related to the Religious Society of Friends (Quakers) but supported and staffed by individuals sharing basic values regardless of religious affiliation. Attempts to relieve human suffering and find new approaches to world peace and social justice through nonviolence. Work in 22 countries includes development and refugee relief, peace education, and community organizing. Sponsors off-the-record seminars around the world to build better international understanding. Conducts programs with U.S. communities on the problems of minority groups such as housing, employment, and denial of legal rights. Maintains Washington, D.C. office to present AFSC experience and perspectives to policymakers. The Quaker United Nations offices in New York City and Geneva, Switzerland arrange seminars, testimony before UN committees and behind-the-scence discussions with UN delegates. Seeks to build informed public resistance to militarism. A co-recipient of the Noble Peace Prize. Programs are multiracial, non-denominational, and international.

Headquarters

1501 Cherry St., Philadelphia, PA 19102 Tel. (215)241-7000 Fax (215)241-7275, Website: www.afsc.org

Director of Media Relations, Alexis Moore

Presiding Clerk., Paul Lacey
Treas., James Fletcher
General Secretary, Mary Ellen McNish

The American Theological Library Association

Established in 1946, the American Theological Library Association (ATLA) is a professional association of 1,000 individual, institutional and affiliate members providing programs, products and services in support of theological and religious studies libraries and librarians. ATLA's ecumenical membership represents many religious traditions and denominations.

Headquarters
300 S. Wacker Dr., Suite 2100, Chicago, IL, 60606 Tel. (312)454-5100 Fax (312)454-5505
Media Contact, Sara Corkery, Communications Specialist

Officers
Pres, David R. Stewart, Luther Seminary Library
Vice Pres., Roberta Schaafsma, Perkins School of Theology, Southern Methodist University
Sec., Eileen K. Crawford, Vanderbilt University
Exec. Dir., Dennis A. Norlin, ATLA, 250

American Tract Society

The American Tract Society is a nonprofit, interdenominational organization, instituted in 1825 through the merger of most of the then-existing tract societies. As one of the earliest religious publishing bodies in the United States, ATS has pioneered in the publishing of Christian books, booklets and leaflets. The volume of distribution has risen to over 35 million pieces of literature annually. For free samples or a free catalog contact 1-800-54-TRACT.

Headquarters
P.O. Box 462008, Garland, TX 75046 Tel. (972)276-9408 Fax (972)272-9642
Media Contact, V.P. Evangelism/Outreach, David Leflore

The American Waldensian Society

The American Waldensian Society (AWS) promotes ministry linkages, broadly ecumenical, between U.S.A. churches and Waldensian (Reformed)-Methodist constituencies in Italy and Waldensian constituencies in Argentina-Uruguay. Founded in 1906, AWS aims to enlarge mission discovery and partnership among overseas Waldensian-Methodist forces and denominational forces in the U.S.A.

AWS is governed by a national ecumenical board, although it consults and collaborates closely with the three overseas Waldensian and Waldensian-Methodist boards.

The Waldensian experience is the earliest continuing Protestant experience.

Headquarters
American Waldensian Society, 208 Rodoret Street, South, P.O. Box 398, Valdese, NC 28690 Toll-free Tel. (866)825-3373 Tel. (828)874-3500 Fax (828)874-3560 Voice (828)879-4100 Email: info@waldensian.org, www.waldensian.org
Media Contact, Rev. Francis Rivers Tel. (336)716-4022 Fax (336)716-5075 Email: frivers@wfubmc.edu

Officers
Exec. Dir., The Rev. Francis Rivers PC(USA)
Pres., The Rev. Dr. Gabriella Lettini '09 WC
Vice Pres., Ms. June Rostan '09
Treas., Emile M. Jackumin, Jr. '09 PC(USA)
Sec., Rev. Peter Sulyok, '10 PC(USA)

Appalachian Ministries Educational Resource Center (AMERC)

The mission of AMERC is to promote contextual, cross-cultural education for theological students, faculties, ministers, and other Christian leaders. Working through an ecumenical consortium of theological schools and denominational judicatories, AMERC supports experiential learning about the theological, spiritual, social, economic and environmental aspects of Appalachian culture, especially for rural and small town settings for ministry.

Since 1985 AMERC, has provided quality educational programs and learning experiences for seminaries and other religious leaders interested in ministry in Appalachia and other rural areas. The centerpiece of these programs has been and continues to be in-depth, contextually based dialogue with local people engaged in creative ministries, exploring with them social, economic, political, ecological, cultural, and religious issues. Intense theological reflection is used to understand these issues through the eyes of faith, equipping students and other leaders for ministry in the Appalachian context.

In the new millennium AMERC's form of ministry has changed. AMERC is now supporting its consortium of members by providing program grants, technical and library support, and leadership consultation. The consortium seminaries and other groups, in turn, design and offer an even wider variety of experiential programs in rural and small town ministry in the context of Appalachia. Both seminary, for credit, and continuing education courses are offered. In 2000 AMERC launched its Grants Program for members of the consortium. Since that time AMERC has funded twenty-four winter and summer Travel Seminars, a spring course with an immersion component, a Seminary Faculty Immersion experience and a summer intern program. A consultation and six continuing education events with grants of up to $15,000.

Headquarters

298 Harrison Rd., Berea, KY 40403 Tel. (859)986-8789 Fax (859)986-2576, Email: loliver@amerc.org, Website: www.amerc.org Media Contact, Rev. Dr. Lon D. Oliver, Executive Director

Executive Assistant, Marsha Baker

Officers

Chair, Rev. Dr. Barbara Blodgett, Yale Divinity School

Vice Chair, Rev. Dr. Jackie Johns, Church of God Theological Seminary

Secretary, Ms. Tena Willemsma, Commission on Religion in Appalachia

Treasurer, Mr. Jim Strand, Berea College

The Associated Church Press

The Associated Church Press was organized in 1916. Its membership includes periodicals and Web sites of major Protestant, Catholic, and Orthodox, and ecumenical groups in the U.S. and Canada, and abroad; individual members who supply publishing services on a freelance or student basis; and affiliate members who supply the Christian press with news, information, and vendor services. It is a professional Christian journalistic association seeking to promote excellence among editors and writers, recognize achievements, and represent the interests of the religious press. It sponsors seminars, conventions, awards programs, and workshops for editors, staff people, and business managers. It is active in postal rates and regulations on behalf of the religious press.

Headquarters

Media Contact, Exec. Dir., Mary Lynn Hendrickson, 1410 Vernon St. Stoughton , WI 53589-2248 Tel. (608)877-0011 Fax (608)877-0062, Website: www.theacp.org

Officers

Exec. Dir., Mary Lynn Hendrickson, 1410 Vernon St. Stoughton, WI 53589-2248, Tel.608-877-0011, Fax 608-877-0062, Email: acpoffice@earthlink.net

Pres., Jerry Van Marter, Presbyterian News Service, 100 Witherspoon St., Louisville, KY 40202-1396, Tel. (502)569-5493, Fax (502)569-8073, Email: jvanmart@ctr.pcusa.org

Vice Pres., Terry DeYoung, The Church Herald, 4500-60th St. SE, Grand Rapids, MI 49512-9642, Tel. (616)698-7071, Fax (616)698-6606, Email: tdeyoung@rca.org

Past Pres., Victoria A. Rebeck, The Minnesota Connect, 122 W. Franklin, Ste. 400, Minneapolis, MN 55404-2472, Tel. (612)870-0058 ext. 232, Fax (612)870-1260, Email: victoria.rebeck@mnumc.org

Treas., Silvia Chavez, The Lutheran, 8765 W. Higgins Rd., Chicago, IL 60631-4189, Tel.

(773)380-2543 Fax (773)380-2751, Email: schavez@elca.org

The Associated Gospel Churches

Organized in 1939, The Associated Gospel Churches (AGC) endorses chaplains primarily for strong evangelical Independent Baptist and Bible Churches to the U.S. Armed Forces. The AGC has been recognized by the U.S. Department of Defense for 65 years as an Endorsing Agency, and it supports a strong national defense. The AGC also endorses VA chaplains, police, correctional system and civil air patrol chaplains.

The AGC provides support for its constituent churches, seminaries, Bible colleges and missionaries.

The AGC believes in the sovereignty of the local church, the historic doctrines of the Christian faith and the infallibility of the Bible.

The AGC is a member of the National Conference on Ministry to the Armed Forces (NCMAF) and the Endorsers Conference for Veterans Affairs Chaplaincy (ECVAC).

Headquarters

Media Contact, Pres., Billy Baugham, D.D., National Hdqt., P.O. Box 733, Taylors, SC 29687 Tel. (864)268-9617 Fax (864)268-0166

Officers

Commission on Chaplains, Pres. and Chmn., Billy Baugham, D.D.

Vice-Pres., Rev. Chuck Flesher

Sec.-Treas., Eva Baugham

Executive Committee, Chaplain (Captain) James Poe, USN Member

Association of Catholic Diocesan Archivists

The Association of Catholic Diocesan Archivists, which began in 1979, has been committed to the active promotion of professionalism in the management of diocesan archives. The Association meets annually, in the even years it has its own summer conference, in the odd years it meets in conjunction with the Society of American Archivists. Publications include Standards for Diocesan Archives, Access Policy for Diocesan Archives and the quarterly Bulletin.

Headquarters

Joseph Cardinal Bernardin Archives & Records Center, 711 West Monroe, Chicago, IL 60661 Tel. (312)831-0711 Fax (312)736-0488

Media Contact, Brian P. Fahey

Officers

Episcopal Mod., Most Rev. Thomas J. Paprocki, Auxiliary Bishop, Archdiocese of Chicago

Pres., Emilie Leumas, Archdiocese of New Orleans, 1100 Chartres St., New Orleans, LA 70116-2505

Vice-Pres., Rev. Mr. William Bissenden, Diocese of Bridgeport, 238 Jewett Ave., Bridgeport, CT 06606-2892

Treas., Brian P. Fahey, Diocese of Charleston, 114 Broad St - Rear Building, Charleston, SC 29402

Sec., Janice Cantrell, Diocese of Fort Wayne-South Bend, 915 S. Clinton St., Fort Wayne, IN 46802

Newsletter Editor, Brian P. Fahey, Diocese of Charleston, 114 Broad Street - Rear Building, Charleston, SC 29402

ADRIS-Association for the Development of Religious Information Services

The Association for the Development of Religious Information Services was established in 1971 to facilitate coordination and cooperation among information services that pertain to religion. Its goal is a worldwide network that is interdisciplinary, interfaith and interdenominational to serve both administrative and research applications. ADRIS publishes a blog and provides internet, open data, open source and open standards consulting services.

Headquarters

ADRIS Blog Office, P.O. Box 210735, Nashville, TN 37221-0735 Tel. (615)557-3975 Email: editor@adris.org

Media Contact, Editor., Ed Dodds, P.O. Box 210735, Nashville, TN 37221-0735 Tel. (615)557-3975

AIM: ed1dodds
GoogleTalk: ed.dodds@gmail.com
ICQ: 49457096
Identica: http://identi.ca/eddodds
MSN: dodds@conmergence.com
SIP: ed_dodds_sip
SKYPE: ed_dodds_skype
Twitter: http://twitter.com/ed_dodds
Web: http://www.adris.org
Yahoo: ed_dodds@yahoo.com

Officers

Ed Dodds, P.O. Box 210735, Nashville, TN 37221-0735 Tel. (615)557-3975

Association of Gospel Rescue Missions

The Association of Gospel Rescue Missions (AGRM), formerly the International Union of Gospel Missions, is an association of 300 rescue missions and other ministries that serve more than 7 million homeless and needy people in the inner cities of the U.S., Canada and overseas each year. Since 1913, AGRM member ministries have offered emergency food and shelter,

evangelical outreach, Christian counsel, youth and family services, prison and jail outreach, rehabilitation and specialized programs for the mentally ill, the elderly, the urban poor and street youth. The AGRM operates RESCUE College, an Internet-based distance education program to prepare and train rescue mission workers. The AGRM sponsors Alcoholics Victorious, a network of Christian support groups. AGRM is affiliated with the City Mission World Association, representing over 500 City Mission around the world.

Headquarters

1045 Swif Ave., Kansas City, MO 64116-4127 Tel. (816)471-8020 Fax (816)471-3718

Media Contact, Exec. Dir., Rev. John Ashmen or Phil Rydman

Officers

Exec. Dir., Rev. John Ashmen

Pres., Mr. Rick Alvis, Box 817, Indianapolis, IN 46206 Tel. (317)635-3575

Fax (317)687-3629

Sec., Mr. David Traedwell, 1350 R St NW, Washington DC 20009-4323, Tel. (202)745-7118 Fax (202)232-7072

Vice Pres., Mr. Perry Jones, IIII, 259 S. Pearl St., Albany, NY 12202, Tel. (518)462-0459, Fax (518)462-0489

Association of Statisticians of American Religious Bodies

This Association was organized in 1934 and grew out of personal consultations held by representatives from The Yearbook of American Churches, The National (now Official) Catholic Directory, the Jewish Statistical Bureau, The Methodist (now The United Methodist), Lutheran and the Presbyterian churches.

ASARB has a variety of purposes: to bring together those officially and professionally responsible for gathering, compiling, and publishing denominational statistics; to provide a forum for the exchange of ideas and sharing of problems in statistical methods and procedure; and to seek such standardization as may be possible in religious statistical data. ASARB also conducts the decennial Religious Congregations Membership Study, a county listing of religious groups and their adherents.

Headquarters

Dale Johnson, Church of the Nazarene, 6402 The Paseo, Kansas City, MO 64131 Tel. (800)306-9928

Media Contact, Sec.-Treas., Dale Johnson

Officers

Pres., Mary Gautier, Center for Applied Research in the Apostolate, Georgetown University, Washington, DC 20057 Tel. (202)687-8086 Fax (202)687-8083 Email: gautierm@georgetown.edu

Immediate Past Pres., Rich Houseal, Church of the Nazarene, 6401 The Paseo, Kansas City, MO 64131 Tel. (816)333-7000 Ext. 2473 Fax (816)361-5202 Email: rhouseal@nazarene.org
1st Vice Pres., Major Diana E. Smith, The Salvation Army, 440 West Nyack Road, Box C-635, West Nyack, NY 10994-1739 Tel. (845)620-7382 Fax (845)620-7777 Email: Diana_Smith@use.salvationarmy.org
2nd Vice Pres., John O'Hara, Lutheran Church-Missouri Synod, 1333 S. Kirkwood Road, St. Louis, MO 63122 Tel. (314)965-9917 Fax (314)996-1133 Email: john.ohara@lcms.org

MEMBERS-AT-LARGE
Carl Royster, 21st Century Christian, 2809 12th Ave. S, P.O. Box 40526, Nashville, TN 37204 Tel. (615)383-3842 Fax (615)292-5983 Email: royster@21stcc.com
Destiny Shellhammer, United Church of Christ, 700 Prospect Ave, Cleveland, OH 44111 Tel. (216)736-2149 Fax (216)736-2276 Email: shellhad@ucc.org

The Association of Theological Schools in the United States and Canada
The Association of Theological Schools in the United States and Canada (ATS) is a membership organization of more than 250 graduate schools that conduct post-baccalaureate professional and academic degree programs to educate persons for the practice of ministry and for teaching and research in the theological disciplines. The ATS Commission on Accrediting accredits schools and approves the degree programs they offer.

Headquarters
10 Summit Park Drive, Pittsburgh, PA 15275-1110 Tel. (412)788-6505 Fax (412)788-6510, Media Contact, Dir. of Communications and External Relations, Eliza Brown, Tel. (412)788-6505 x244, Email: brown@ats.edu

Officers
President: John W. Kinney, Dean, Samuel DeWitt Proctor School of Theology of Virginia Union University, Richmond, VA; Vice Vice President: Richard Mouw; President, Fuller Theological Seminary, Pasadena, CA
Secretary: Laura Mendenhall, Senior Philanthropy Advisor, Texas Presbyterian Foundation, Irving, TX
Treasurer: Mary McNamara, Chief Executive Officer, United Theological Seminary of the Twin Cities, New Brighton, MN

Blanton-Peale Institute
Blanton-Peale Institute is dedicated to helping people overcome emotional obstacles by joining mental health expertise with religious faith and values. The Blanton-Peale Graduate Institute provides advanced training in psychoanalysis and pastoral care for ministers, rabbis, sisters, priests and other counselors. The Blanton-Peale Counseling Centers provide counseling for individuals, couples, families and groups. Blanton-Peale promotes interdisciplinary communication among theology, medicine and the behavioral sciences. Blanton-Peale was founded in 1937 by Dr. Norman Vincent Peale and psychiatrist Smiley Blanton, M.D.

Headquarters
3 W. 29th St., New York, NY 10001 Tel. (212)725-7850 Fax (212)689-3212

Officers
Chpsn., Arthur Caliandro
Vice-Chpsn., Elizabeth Peale Allen
Pres., Dr. David Leeming

Bread For The World
Bread for the World is a collective Christian voice urging our nation's decision makers to end hunger at home and abroad. By changing policies, programs and conditions that allow hunger and poverty to persist, we provide help and opportunity far beyond the communities in which we live.

God's grace in Jesus Christ moves us to help our neighbors, whether they live in the next house, the next state or the next continent. Food is a basic need, and it is unjust that so many people do not have enough to eat.

Bread for the World members write personal letters and emails to Congress. We also meet with our representatives in Congress. Working through our churches, campuses, and other organizations, we engage more people in advocacy. Each year, Bread for the World invites churches across the country to take up a nationwide Offering of Letters to Congress on an issue that is important to hungry people.

Bread for the World has two affiliate organizations. Bread for the World Institute does analysis and education on hunger issues. The Alliance to End Hunger engages diverse institutions—Jewish and Muslim groups, charities, universities, corporations, and others—in building the political commitment needed to overcome hunger.

Bread for the World works in a bipartisan way. It enjoys the support of many different church bodies. Bread for the World collaborates with other organizations to build the political commitment needed to overcome hunger and poverty.

Headquarters
50 F St., NW, Ste. 500, Washington, DC 20001 Tel. (202)639-9400 Fax (202)639-9401
Media Contact, Adlai Amor

Campus Crusade for Christ International

Campus Crusade for Christ International is an interdenominational, evangelistic and discipleship ministry dedicated to helping fulfill the Great Commission through the multiplication strategy of "win-build-send." Founded in 1951 on the campus of UCLA, the organization now includes 60 plus ministries and special projects reaching out to almost every segment of society. There are more than 27,000 staff members and 226,000 trained volunteers in 190 countries.

Headquarters
100 Lake Hart Dr., Orlando, FL 32832 Tel. (407)826-2000 Fax (407)826-2120
Media Contact, James Woelbern

Officers
Chmn. & Pres., Steve Douglass
Chief Operating Officer, J. Roger Bruehl
Chief Financial Officer, Roger L. Craft

Center on Conscience & War

CCW(formerly NISBCO), formed in 1940, is a nonprofit organization supported by individual contributions and related to more than thirty religious organizations. Its purpose is to defend and extend the rights of conscientious objectors to war. CCW provides information on how to register for the draft while documenting one's convictions as a conscientious objector, how to cope with penalties if one does not cooperate, and how to qualify as a conscientious objector while in the Armed Forces. It also provides information for counselors and the public about conscientious objection, military service and the operation of the draft. It provides information to and support for conscientious objectors in other countries.

As a national resource center it assists research in its area of interest including the peace witness of religious bodies. Its staff provides referral to local counselors and attorneys and professional support for them. Through publications and speaking, CCW encourages people to decide for themselves what they believe about participation in war and to act on the basis of the dictates of their own informed consciences.

Headquarters
1830 Connecticut Ave. NW, Washington, DC 20009-5732 Tel. (202)483-2220 Fax (202)483-1246
Media Contact, Exec. Dir., J.E. McNeil

Officers
Exec. Dir., J.E. McNeil
Chpsn., Phil Jones

Sec., Theo Sitther
Treas., Tom Hoopes

Center for Parish Development

The Center for Parish Development is an ecumenical, non-profit research and development agency whose mission is to help church bodies learn to become faithful expressions of God's mission in today's post-modern, post-Christendom world. Founded in 1968, the Center brings to its client-partners a strong theological orientation, a missional ecclesial paradigm with a focus on faithful Christian communities as the locus of mission, research-based theory and practice of major change, a systems approach, and years of experience working with national, regional, and local church bodies.

The Center staff provides research, consulting and training support for church organizations engaging in major change. The Center is governed by a 12-member Board of Directors.

Headquarters
1448 East 53rd St., Chicago, IL 60615 Tel. (773)752-1596 Fax (773)752-5093
Media Contact, Office Manager, Beatrice Vansen

Officers
Chpsn., John Rottenberg, 2047 Fawnwood Drive SE, Kentwood, MI 49508
Vice-Chpsn., Stephen B. Bevens, 5401 S. Cornell Avenue, Chicago, IL 60615
Sec., Delton Krueger, 10616 Penn Ave. South, Bloomington, MN 55431
Managing Directors, Raymond Schulte and Dale Ziemer

Chaplaincy of Full Gospel Churches

The Chaplaincy of Full Gospel Churches (CFGC) is a unique coalition of 1500 nondenominational churches and networks of churches united for the purpose of being represented in military and civilian chaplaincies. Since its inception in 1984, CFGC has grown rapidly. Today CFGC represents over 7.5 million American Christians. Additionally, we are connected with another 144 fellowship groups consisting of another 7.5 million members, which gives CFGC the potential of representing a total 15 million.

Churches, fellowships and networks of churches which affirm the CFGC statement of faith that "Jesus is Savior, Lord and Baptizer in the Holy Spirit today, with signs, wonders and gifts following" may join the endorsing agency. CFGC represents its member-networks of churches (consisting of over 90,000 churches nation wide) before the Pentagon's Armed Forces Chaplains Board, the National Conference of Ministry to the Armed Forces, Endorsers Conference for Veterans Affairs

Chaplaincy, Federal Bureau of Prisons, Association of Professional Chaplains, and other groups requiring professional chaplaincy endorsement (State/County/City Correctional, Healthcare, Law Enforcement, Workplace). The organization also ecclesiastically credentials professional counselors.

Headquarters
2715 Whitewood Dr., Dallas, TX 75233-2713
Tel. (214)331-4373 Fax (214)333-4401
Media Contact, Rev. Dr. E. H. Jim Ammerman

Officers
Pres., Rev. Dr. E. H. Jim Ammerman

Christian Council on Persons with Disabilities

Created in 1988, the Christian Council on Persons with Disabilities (CCPD) is a coalition of churches, non-profit organizations and individuals advocating an evangelical perspective concerning people with disabilities and their place in God's world. The coalition provides a national voice for Christians involved in disability ministry, framing the Christian community's response to issues relating to disability.

CCPD provides information and responses on issues specifically relating to the church such as accessibility, disability theology and outreach; as well as disability-related issues of concern to the general public such as genetic research, end-of-life care and cloning.

Advocacy, professional development, networking and education are all part of the coalition's activities. Annual conferences (both national & regional), chapter groups and mentoring programs are part of the coalition's strategy in strengthening the network of disability ministry.

Headquarters
301 E. Pine St. Suite 150, Orlando, FL 32801, Tel. (407)210-3917, Email: ccpd@ccpd.org, Website: www.ccpd.org

Officers
Exec. Dir., Jim Hukill
Pres., Gary Wagner, Of Camp Verde, AZ
Treas., Stan Higgins, of Rohnert Park, CA

Christian Endeavor International

Christian Endeavor International is a Christ-centered, youth-oriented ministry which assists local churches in reaching young people with the gospel of Jesus Christ, discipling them in the Christian faith, and equipping them for Christian ministry and service in their local church, community and world. It trains youth leaders for effective ministry and provides opportunities for Christian inspiration, spiritual growth, fellowship, and service. Christian Endevor International reaches across denomina-

tional, cultural, racial and geographical boundaries. All materials are on the internet at www.teamce.com

Headquarters
424 E. Main St., P.O..Box 377, Edmore, MI 48829, Tel. (989)427-3737 Fax (989)427-5530, Email: contact@teamce.com
Media Contact, Luke Sawyer

Officers
Chief Executive Officer, Timothy Eldred

Christian Management Association

Christian Management Association (CMA) provides leadership training, management resources and strategic networking relationships for leaders and managers of Christian organizations and growing churches. It's membership represents leaders and managers from more than 1,500 Christian organizations and larger churches in the U.S. CMA publishes Christian Management Report magazine, CMA Management Monthly e-newsletter, Total Compensation Survey Report for Christian Ministries, www.CMAonline.org website, CMA Management Tape Library and many other resources. CMA provides management training, resourcing and networking opportunities through its annual conference for Christian organizations and churches, CEO Dialogues one-day roundtables, chapters in selected cities, online Job Market, and many other programs. It also features annually the Best Christian Places to Work finalists and the CMA Management Award. Membership is open to Christian organizations, ministries and churches. Businesses that provide products or services for Christian organizations and churches may apply for a business membership. For complete membership information, go to www.CMAonline.org and click on "Membership."

Headquarters
P.O. Box 4090, San Clemente, CA 92674
Tel: (800)727-4262 Fax: (949)487-0927
John Pearson, CEO, Email: John@CMA online.org
DeWayne Herbrandson, Director of Management Resources, Email: DeWayne@ CMAonline.org
Dick Bahruth, Senior Consultant, Marketing, Email: Dick@CMAonline, org
Marsha Lyons, Director of Conferences & Meetings, Email: Marsha@CMAonline.org
Suzy West, Director of Administration/COO, Email: Suzy@CMAonline.org

Officers
Chairman, Mark G. Holbrook, Pres./CEO, ECCU
Vice-Chairman, C.E. Crouse, Managing Partner, Capin Crouse, LLP

Treas., Robert T. Lipps, Lockton Insurance Brokers of San Francisco

Sec., Mark A. Bankord, Managing Principal/ Chairman, Cap Trust Asset Management

A Christian Ministry in the National Parks

This ministry is recognized by over 40 Christian denominations and extends the ministry of Christ to the millions of people who live, work and vacation in our National Parks. Ministry Staff Members conduct services of worship in the parks on Sundays. The staff are employed by park concessionaires and have full-time jobs in which their actions, attitudes, and commitment to Christ serve as witness. Room and board are provided at a minimal cost; minimum commitment of 90 days needed.

Officers

Dir., The Rev. Richard P. Camp, Jr.

Deputy Director, Gordon Compton

Church Growth Center- Home of Church Doctor Ministries

The Church Growth Center is an interfaith, nonprofit, professional organization which exists to bring transformational change of the Christian church toward the effective implementation of the Lord's Great Commission, to make disciples of all people. This effort is done through consultations, resources, and educational events.

Founded in 1978 by leader Kent R. Hunter, the Church Growth Center offers over 17 different consultation services, including church consultations by experienced consultants, cutting edge resources through The Church Doctor™ Resource Center, and by providing educational events at churches and organizations in the way of providing speakers and resources at seminars, workshops, and conferences. The bi-monthly e-newsletter is the Church Doctor Report.

Headquarters

P.O.Box 145, 1230 U. S. Highway Six, Corunna, IN 46730 Tel. (800)626-8515 Fax (260)281-2167, Website: www.churchdoctor.org

Media Contact, Assistant to President, Cindy Warren

Officers

President, Dr. Kent R. Hunter, D.Min, Ph.D.

Vice Pres., Greg Ulmer

Treas., Rob Olsen

Church Women United in the U.S.A.

Church Women United in the U.S.A. is a racially, culturally, theologically inclusive Christian women's movement, celbrating unity in diversity and working for a world of peace and justice. Founded in 1941, Church Women United is a movement representing Protestant, Roman Catholic, Orthodox and other Christian women; biblically based, shared Christian faith; organized into more than 1200 state and local units working for peace and justice in the United States and Puerto Rico; supported by constituents in state and local units and denominational women's organizations; impassioned by the Holy Spirit to act on behalf of women and children throughout the world; and recognized as a non-governmental organization by the United Nations.

NATIONAL OFFICE

475 Riverside Dr., Ste. 1626, New York, NY 10115 Tel. (800) CWU-5551 OR (212)870-2347 Fax (212)870-2338 — Office manager, Julie Drews, juliedrews@churchwomen.org

LEGISLATIVE OFFICE

CWU Washington Office, 100 Maryland Ave. NE, Rm. 100, Washington, DC 20002 Tel. (202)544-8747, Fax (202)544-9133

Legislative Dir., Wash. Office, Patricia Burkhardt, Email: pburkhardt@churchwomen.org

Officers

Pres., Gail Mengel, Independence, MO

Vice-Pres., Vera Zander, Tucson, AZ

Secretary, Carol Kolsti, Austin, TX

Treasurer, Ann Kohler, Baldwinsville, NY

Regional Coordinators, Central, Susan Decker, Madison, WI; East Central, Margaret Tweet, Rock Island, IL; Mid-Atlantic, Blanche Simmons, Landover, MD; Northeast, Vivian Love-Jones, Newburg, NY; Northwest, Betty Luginbill, Boise, ID; South Central, Martha Moody Boone, Keithville, LA; Southeast, Pat Zangmeister, Tamarac, FL; Southwest, Jenny Ladefaged, Alisa Viego, CA

Churches Uniting in Christ

Churches Uniting in Christ (CUIC) was inaugurated on January 20, 2002, in Memphis Tennessee as a new relationship among nine communions which agreed to start living more fully into their unity in Christ. CUIC is the successor to the Consultation on Church Union (COCU) which was, in 1962 organized to explore the formation of a uniting church. At the 1999 COCU Plenary the nine member communions affirmed eight "Marks" of Churches Uniting in Christ and agreed to move into the new relationship of covenanted communion to be called Churches Uniting in Christ. Following confirmation actions by each of the communions, all nine communions officially constituted Churches Uniting in Christ. The nine member communions are: The African Methodist Episcopal Church, the African Methodist Episcopal Zion Church, the Christian

27

Church (Disciples of Christ), the Christian Methodist Episcopal Church, The Episcopal Church, the International Council of Community Churches, the Presbyterian Church (U.S.A.), the United Church of Christ, and the United Methodist Church. Also participating at present are two Partners in Mission and Dialogue, the Evangelical Lutheran Church in America and the Moravian Church (Northern Province). The Catholic Church participates as an observer. Other communions are exploring various possibilities for relating to CUIC.

CUIC is a bold venture, expressed through the participating communions' covenant to seek to live a new relationship that bears witness to a church that is truly catholic, truly evangelical, and truly reformed. Among the goals for bearing witness to that unity are two very challenging endeavors: to heed the "emphatic call to `erase racism' by challenging the system of white privilege that has so distorted life in this society and in the churches themselves;" and to "provide a foundation for the mutual recognition and reconciliation of ordained ministry by the members of Churches Uniting in Christ by the year 2007. Notably, the commitment to address racism is named as a hallmark of the new relationship and, following the Inaugural ceremony,on Dr. Martin Luther King, Jr. Day, January 21, 2002, the Heads of Communion signed an Appeal to the Churches to work together for the eradication of racism.

The Ecumenical Officers of each of the communions will carry major responsibility for the engagement of their congregations and members in the CUIC relationship. Neighboring congregations are encouraged to celebrate the Eucharist together; invite the participation of each in services of baptism, ordinations and installation as well as other special events in the congregations' lives; and to discover ways in which they might witness together in combating social injustices, especially racism. In addition to the representational Coordinating Council, three task forces will work to enhance the collaborative endeavors of CUIC: Ministry, Racism, and Local and Regional Ecumenism.

Headquarters
475 E. Lockwood Ave, St. Louis MO 63119, Tel. (314)252-3160 Fax (314)252-3162 Email: jamesNTse@gmail.com or cuic@eden.org
Media Contact: Elder James Tse, Email: jamesNTse@gmail.com

Officers
President of the Coordinating Council The Reverend Dr. Suzanne Webb, Christian Church (Disciples of Christ)
Vice Pres., The Rt. Reverend Ronald Cunningham, Christian Methodist Episcopal Church
Sec., Mr. Abraham Wright, International Council of Community Churches

Trea., Elder James N. Tse (Presbyterian Church (U.S.A.))

COORDINATING COUNCIL REPRESENTATIVES FROM MEMBER COMMUNIONS
African Methodist Episcopal Church,
African Methodist Episcopal Zion Church, The Rev. Dr. Harrison Bonner
Christian Church (DISCIPLES OF CHRIST), The Rev. Dr. Suzanne Webb
Christian Methodist Episcopal Church, Bishop Ronald Cunningham
The Episcopal Church (U.S.A.), The Rev. C. Dana Krutz
International Council of Community Churches, Mr. Abraham Wright
Presbyterian Church (U.S.A.), Elder James N. Tse
United Church of Christ, The Rev. Lydia Veliko
The United Methodist Church, Bishop Albert F. Mutti

Evangelical Council for Financial Accountability
Founded in 1979, the Evangelical Council for Financial Accountability has the purpose of helping Christ-centered, evangelical, nonprofit organizations earn the public's trust through their ethical practices and financial accountability. ECFA assists its over 1,400 member organizations in making appropriate public disclosure of their financial practices and accomplishments, thus materially enhancing their credibility and support potential among present and prospective donors.

Headquarters
440 W. Jubal Early Drive Ste. 130, Winchester, VA 22601-6319 Tel. (540)535-0103 Fax (540)535-0533
Media Contact, Pres., Dan Busby

Officers
Pres., Dan Busby

Evangelical Press Association
The Evangelical Press Association is a professional association serving the evangelical periodical publishing industry. EPA provides a variety of services, including training and recognition of outstanding work.

Headquarters
P.O. Box 28129, Crystal, MN 55428 Tel. (763)535-4793 Fax (763)535-4794
Media Contact, Exec. Dir., Doug Trouten

Officers
Pres., Diane McDougall, EFCA Today, P.O. Box 315, Charlottesville, VA 22902
Pres-Elect, Dean Ridings, Navigators, 3820 N. 30th St., Colorado Springs, CO 80904
Treas., Grif Blackstone, Good News in South Florida, P.O. Box 935148, Margate, FL 33093

Sec., D'Arcy Maher, ACSI, P.O. BOX 65130, Colorado Springs, CO 80962-5130
Advisor, Mark Winz, Worldwide Challenge, 100 Lake Hart Drive, #1600, Orlando, FL 32832-0100
Advisor, Marshall Shelley, Leadership, 465 Gundersen Drive, Carol Stream, IL 60188
Exec. Dir., Doug Trouten

Faith & Values Media

(See also National Interfaith Cable Coalition, Inc.)
Faith & Values Media is a nation's largest coalition of Jewish and Christian faith groups dedicated to media production, distribution and promotion. It is a service of the National Interfaith Cable Coalition, Inc., established in 1987.

Faith & Values Media member association includes more than 40 faith groups and religious organizations representing 200,000 congregations and 120 million congregants. Its mission is to use television and other media to promote the vitality of religious experience in everyday life.

Award-winning programming from Faith & Values Media is available on Hallmark Channel and on www.faithstreams.com

Headquarters
74 Trinity Place, Suite 1550, New York, NY 10006 Tel. (212)406-4121 Fax (212)406-4105
Media Contact, Christine Luzano

Officers
Chair, Dr. Daniel Paul Matthews
Vice Chair, Elder Ralph Hardy Jr., Esq.
Secretary, Rabbi Daniel Freelander
Treasurer, Betty Elam

STAFF
President and CEO, Edward J. Murray
Exec. Vice President, Beverly Judge

Federation of Christian Ministries

The Federation of Christian Ministries (FCM)is an ecumenical, faith community founded in 1968. FCM stresses inclusiveness, opening its membership to women and men of varying faith backgrounds who share its vision of an ecumenical, nondenominational community. Its ministers work in many ways: pastoring house churches or congregations/parishes; serving as chaplains in nursing homes, correctional facilities, hospitals; offering healing ministries; promoting groups dedicated to peace and justice. FCM is a member of the International Council of Community Churches and a faith group member of the Association for Clinical Pastoral Education. Its educational branch, Global Ministries University, offers online degree completion, both undergraduate and postgraduate, for adult learners in the field of ministry. Contact: Global MinistriesUniversity.com.

Headquarters
1905 Bugbee Rd., Ionia, MI 48846-9663 Tel. (800)538-8923 or (616)527-0419 Fax (616)527-0419, Email: info@Federationof ChristianMinistries.org
Media Contact: Co-president, Eileen Mackin, Tel. (303)740-7665, cdewall@pcisys.net

Officers
Chairperson(s): Jan & Paul Reithmaier, 7415 K Triwoods Dr., Shrewsbury, MO 63119-4456, Tel. (314)962-6220, p.reith-maier@worldnet.att.net
President(s): Eileen Mackin & Clem DeWall, 11298 E. Maplewood Pl., Englewood, CO 80111-5808. Tel. (303)740-7665, cdewall@pcisys.net.
Treasurer: Roger J. Fecher, 8330 Catamaran Dr., Indianapolis, IN 46236-9585, Tel. (317)826-8940, rjfecher@aol.com.
Secretaries/Central Office: Edward & Judy Kalmanek, 1905 Bugbee Rd., Ionia, MI 48846-9663, Tel. (616)527-0419, ejkalmanek@home.ionia.com.
Development Directors: Frederick A. Mason, 12830 Paulina St. Ste 2E, Calumet Park, IL 60827-5951, Tel. (708)589-3357, Mcrincorg@sbcglobal.net.
Bonnie J. McCulley, 3818 Eagle Ridge Dr., Cape Giradeau, MO 63701-1703, Tel. (573)332-1228, bjmc27@aol.com.
Member at Large: William Manseau, 12 Catherwood Rd., Tewksbury, MA 01876-2620. Tel. (978)851-5547.

REGIONAL VICE PRESIDENTS:
Pacific Region: Peggy & Phil Ripp, 2869 Donizetti Ct., San Jose, CA 95132-2310. Tel. (408)272-8184, philandpeg@sbcglobal.net.
Mountains & Plains: Rebecca David, 624 E. Dover St., Davenport, IA 52803-2611. Tel. (563)323-5740, irishblue03@earthlink.net
Great Lakes: Pamela Spence, P. O. Box 204, Ostrander, OH 43061-0204, Tel (740)666-3204, allespen@midohio.net.
Southern: Eleonora V. Marinaro and David Gaboury, 10231 Oakhill Dr., Port Richey, FL 34668-3291, Tel. (727)697-2763, elly@helpwithdreams.com
Northeast: Michaelita & Thomas Quinn, 93 Post Rd., Danbury, CT 06810-8367. Tel. (203)792-6968, quinnems@aol.com.

Friends World Committee for Consultation (Section of the Americas)

The Friends World Committee for Consultation (FWCC) was formed in 1937. There has been an American Section as well as a European Section from the early days and an

29

African Section was organized in 1971. In 1974 the name, Section of the Americas, was adopted by that part of the FWCC with constituency in North, Central, and South America and in the Caribbean area. In 1985 the Asia-West Pacific Section was organized. The purposes of FWCC are summarized as follows, To facilitate loving understanding of diversities among Friends while discovering together, with God's help, a common spiritual ground; and to facilitate full expression of Friends' testimonies in the world.

Section of the Americas Headquarters
1506 Race St., Philadelphia, PA 19102 Tel. (215)241-7250 Fax (215)241-7285 Email: americas@fwcc.quaker.org www.quaker.org/fwcc/americas/americas.html
Media Contact, Exec. Sec., Margaret Fraser
Latin American Office, Guerrero 223 Pte., Zona Centro, Cd. Mante, TAM 89800 Mexico

The Fund for Theological Education, Inc.
Begun in 1954 with the goal of supporting excellence in the profession of ministry, the Fund for Theological Education has enjoyed a long and rich history, providing gifted women and men with nearly 5000 fellowships and generating innovative new programs for support of persons preparing for ministry and theological teaching. Supported by individuals and grants from a group of U.S. Foundations, FTE envisions new and imaginatve programs to encourage diversity and excellence in the churches and seminaries of North America.

Headquarters
825 Houston Mill Rd., Suite 250, Atlanta, GA 30329 Tel. (404)727-1450 Fax (404)727-1490
Website, www.thefund.org, www.explore ministry .org
Email: fte@thefund.org

Officers
President, Ann Svennungsen
Vice Pres. For Advancement, Jack Gilbert
Dir., Expanding Horizons Partnership, Dr. Sharon Watson Fluker
Dir., Partnership for Excellence, Melissa Wiginton

Glenmary Research Center
The Research Center is a department of the Glenmary Home Missioners, a Catholic society of priests and brothers. The Center was established in 1966 to serve the rural research needs of the Catholic Church in the United States. Its research has led it to serve ecumenically a wide variety of church bodies. Local case studies as well as quantitative research is done to understand better the diversity of contexts in the rural sections of the country. The Center's statistical profiles of the nation's counties cover both urban and rural counties.

Headquarters
1312 Fifth Ave. North, Nashville, TN 37208 Tel. (615)256-1905 Fax (615)251-1472

Officers
Pres., Rev. Daniel Dorsey, P.O. Box 465618, Cincinnati, OH 45246-5618
1st Vice-Pres., Rev. Robert Poandl, P.O. Box 465618, Cincinnati, OH 45246-5618
2nd Vice-Pres., Rev. Dominic Duggins, P.O. Box 465618, Cincinnati, OH 45246-5618
Treas., Ms. Saney Wissel, P.O. Box 465618, Cincinnati, OH 45246-5618
Dir., Kenneth M. Sanchagrin, Ph.D. E-mail, ksanchagrin@glenmary.org Assoc. Dir., Fr. Wil Steinbacher, 1312 5th Ave.N., Nashville, TN 37208 E-Mail, wjsteinba@aol.com

Graymoor Ecumenical & Interreligious Institute (GEII)
Graymoor Ecumenical & Interreligious Institute has its roots in the Graymoor Ecumenical Institute which was founded in 1967 by the Franciscan Friars of the Atonement, to respond to the Friars' historical concern for Christian Unity in light of the theological and ecumenical developments arising from the Second Vatican Council.

In 1991, in response to developments in both the Institute and the wider ecumenical scene, the Graymoor Ecumenical Institute was expanded into an information and service organization with a mission of Christian Unity and interreligious dialogue. Today, the Graymoor Ecumenical & Interreligious Institute employs several means to accomplish this goal. Among these is the annual Week of Prayer for Christian Unity, "a world-wide observance initiated in 1908 by the Rev. Paul Wattson, co-founder of the Society of the Atonement," the theme and text of which are now chosen and prepared by the Pontifical Council for Promoting Christian Unity and representatives of the World Council of Churches. The Institute publishes the monthly journal Ecumenical Trends-to keep clergy and laity abreast of developments in the ecumenical and interreligious movements; provides membership in, and collaboration with, national and local ecumenical and interreligious organizations and agencies; and cooperates with individuals engaged in ecumenical and interreligious work. A new website, www.geii.org has been launched and will continue to be developed as a resource for ecumenical and interreligious research.

Over the years, the Graymoor Ecumenical & Interreligious Institute has sponsored and cosponsored meetings, colloquia, and workshops in areas of ecumenical and interreligious dialogue.

Headquarters

475 Riverside Dr., Rm. 1960, New York, NY 10115-1999 Tel. (212)870-2330 Fax (212)870-2001

Staff

Director, Rev. James Loughran, SA, Tel. (212)870-2330, Email: jlgeii@aol.com
Assoc. Director, Rev. Dr. Timothy MacDonald, SA, Tel. (212)870-2331, Email: tmdgeii @aol.com
Assoc. Dir., Week of Prayer for Christian Unity, Rev. Thomas Orians, SA, Tel. (212)870-2330, Email: togeii@aol.com
Editor, Ecumenical Trends, Rev. James Loughran SA., Graymoor, Route 9, P.O. Box 300, Garrison, NY 10524-0300 Tel. (845)424-3671 ext. 3323, Email: jlgeii@aol.com
Business Manager, Week of Prayer for Christian Unity Office, Mrs. Veronica Sullivan, Graymoor, Rt. 9, P.O. Box 300, Garrison, NY 10524-0300 Tel. (800)338.2620 ext. 2109 or (845)424-2109 Fax (845)424-2163, Email: rsullivan@atonementfriars.org

InterVarsity Christian Fellowship of the U.S.A.

InterVarsity Christian Fellowship is a nonprofit, interdenominational student movement that ministers to college and university students and faculty in the United States. InterVarsity began in the United States when students at the University of Michigan invited C. Stacey Woods, then General Secretary of the Canadian movement, to help establish an Inter-Varsity chapter on their campus. InterVarsity Christian Fellowship-USA was incorporated two years later, in 1941.

InterVarsity's uniqueness as a campus ministry lies in the fact that it is student-initiated and student-led. InterVarsity strives to build collegiate fellowships that engage their campus with the gospel of Jesus Christ and develop disciples who live out biblical values. InterVarsity students and faculty are encouraged in evangelism, spiritual discipleship, serving the church, multiethnicity, righteousness, vocational stewardship and world evangelization. The Urbana triennial missions convention has long been a launching point for missionary service. For more detials on urbana please visit www.urbana.org.

Headquarters

6400 Schroeder Rd., P.O. Box 7895, Madison, WI 53707 Tel. (608)274-9001 Fax (608)274-7882
www.intervarsity.org; info@intervarsity.org
Media Contact, Gordon Govier

Officers

Pres. & CEO, Alec Hill
Vice-Pres., C. Barney Ford; Robert A. Fryling; Karon Morton, Jim Lundgren, Paula Fuller, Jim Tebbe
Bd. Chpsn., Donald Kolowsky
Bd. Vice-Chpsn., E. Kenneth Nielson

Interfaith Impact for Justice and Peace

Interfaith Impact for Justice and Peace is the religious community's united voice in Washington. It helps Protestant, Jewish, Muslim and Catholic national organizations have clout on Capitol Hill and brings grassroots groups and individual and congregational members to Washington and shows them how to turn their values into votes for justice and peace.

Interfaith Impact for Justice and Peace has established the following Advocacy Networks to advance the cause of justice and peace, Justice for Women; Health Care; Hunger and Poverty; International Justice and Peace; Civil and Human Rights. The Interfaith Impact Foundation provides an annual Legislative Briefing for their members.

Members receive the periodic Action alerts on initiatives, voting records, etc., and a free subscription to the Advocacy Networks of their choice.

Headquarters

100 Maryland Ave. N.E., Ste. 200, Washington, DC 20002 Tel. (202)543-2800 Fax (202)547-8107
Media Contact, Jane Hull Harvey

Officers

Chpsn. of Bd., Jane Hull Harvey, United Methodist Church

MEMBERS

African Methodist Episcopal Church
African Methodist Episcopal Zion Church
Alliance of Baptists
American Baptist Churches, USA, Washington Office; World Relief Office
American Ethical Union
American Muslim Council
Center of Concern
Christian Methodist Episcopal (CME) Church
Christian Church (Disciples of Christ)
Church of the Brethren
Church Women United
Commission on Religion in Appalachia
Episcopal Church
Episcopal Urban Caucus
Evangelical Lutheran Church in America
Federation of Southern Cooperatives-LAF
Federation for Rural Empowerment
Graymoor Ecumenical and Interreligious Institute
Jesuit Social Ministries
Maryknoll Fathers and Brothers
Moravian Church in America
National Council of Churches of Christ, Church World Service; Washington Office
National Council of Jewish Women

NETWORK

Peoria Citizens Committee
Presbyterian Church (U.S.A.)
Progressive National Baptist Convention

Presbyterian Hunger Fund
Reformed Church in America
Rural Advancement Fund
Society of African Missions
Southwest Organizing Project
Southwest Voter Registration-Education Project
Toledo Metropolitan Ministries
Union of American Hebrew Congregations
Unitarian Universalist Association
Unitarian Universalist Service Committee
United Church of Christ, Bd. for Homeland Ministries; Bd. for World Ministries; Hunger Action Ofc.; Ofc. of Church in Society
United Methodist Church, Gen. Bd. of Church & Society; Gen. Bd. of Global Ministries Natl. Div.; Gen. Bd. of Global Ministries Women's Div.; Gen. Bd. of Global Ministries World Div.
Virginia Council of Churches
Western Organization of Resource Councils

Interfaith Worker Justice

Interfaith Worker Justice is a network of sixty interfaith groups and people of faith who educate and mobilize the U.S. religious community on issues and campaigns to improve wages, benefits and working conditions for workers, especially low-wage workers. The organization rebuilds relationships between the religious community and organized labor.

The organization supports and organizes local interfaith worker justice groups around the country, publishes Faith Works six times a year providing congregations resources and updates on religion-labor work, coordinates the Poultry Justice project to improve conditions for poultry workers, and promotes healthy dialogue between management and unions in religious owned or sponsored health care facilities.

Headquarters

1020 West Bryn Mawr, 4th floor, Chicago, IL 60660-4627. Tel. (773)728-8400 Fax (773)728-8409
Media Contact, Bob Hulteen, bhulteen@iwj.org

Board of Directors

President: Rev. Nelson Johnson, Pulpit Forum of Greensboro and Faith Community Church
Vice-President: Bishop Gabino Zavala, Archdiocese of Los Angeles
Finance Chair: Rev. Dr. Paul Sherry, National Council of Churches
Fundraising Chair: Rev. Jim Sessions, United Methodist Church
Action Committee Chair: Ms. Edith Rasell, UCC Minister for Labor Relations
Education Committee Chair: Ms. Evely Laser Shlensky,* Commission on Social Action of Reform Judaism (URJ & CCAR)
Board Development Chair: Imam Mahdi Bray, Muslim American Society Freedom Foundation
Dr. Charles Amjad-Ali, Luther Seminary

Mr. Hussam Ayloush, Council on American-Islamic Relations - Southern California
Mr. John Boonstra, Washington Association of Churches
Ms. Linda Chavez-Thompson, AFL-CIO
Ms. Marilyn Clement, Campaign for a National Health Program NOW
Rev. Darren Cushman-Wood, Speedway United Methodist Church
Mr. Robert DeRose, Barkan+Neff
Bishop William DeVeaux, African Methodist Episcopal Church
Dr. Mary Heidkamp, Dynamic Insights International
Ms. Karen Herrling, Catholic Legal Immigration Network, Inc
Ms. Karen McLean Hessel
Rev. Clete Kiley, Bishop's Committee, U.S. Conference of Catholic Bishops
Mr. Jeffry Korgen, The Roundtable
Rabbi Mordechai Liebling, Shefa Fund
Rev. Christopher Lockard, Jesuit Refugee Service
Ms. Linda Lotz, American Friends Service Committee
Rabbi Robert Marx,** Congregation Hakafa
Ms. Cynthia Nance,* University of Arkansas
Rev. J. Herbert Nelson, Liberation Community Church/Mid-South Interfaith Committee for Worker Justice
Rev. Sinclair Oubre, Catholic Labor Network
Mr. Mark Pelavin, Religious Action Center of Reform Judaism
Ms. Rosalyn Pelles, Union Community Fund
Sister Mary Priniski, OP, Catholic Committee of the South
Rev. Meg Riley, Unitarian Universalist Association of Congregations
Rev. Michael Rouse,* St. Catherine AME Zion Church
Mr. Chris Sanders, Political Consultant, UFCW
Mr. Thomas Shellabarger, U.S. Conference of Catholic Bishops
Honorable Charles Steele, Southern Christian Leadership Conference
Rev. Ron Stief, UCC Justice and Witness Ministries Public Life and Social Policy
Mr. Monroe Sullivan, Retired Businessman / Social Activist
Rev. Phil Tom, Urban Ministry Office, Presbyterian Church (U.S.A.)
Rev. Mark Wendorf, McCormick Theological Seminary
Rev. Bennie Whiten, Jr., United Church of Christ
Special Advisors
Bishop Jesse DeWitt,** Retired, United Methodist Church
Rev. Jim Lawson, Holman United Methodist Church
Rev. Joseph Echols Lowery, Southern Christian Leadership Conference

Rev. Addie Wyatt, Vernon Park Church of God
Executive Director
Kim Bobo
* Former Board Officer
** Former Board President

Interreligious Foundation for Community Organization (IFCO)

IFCO is a national ecumenical agency created in 1966 by several Protestant, Roman Catholic and Jewish organizations, to be an interreligious, interracial agency for support of community organization and education in pursuit of social justice. Through IFCO, national and regional religious bodies collaborate in development of social justice strategies and provide financial support and technical assistance to local, national and international social-justice projects.

IFCO serves as a bridge between the churches and communities and acts as a resource for ministers and congregations wishing to better understand and do more to advance the struggles of the poor and oppressed. IFCO conducts workshops for community organizers and uses its national and international network of organizers, clergy and other professionals to act in the interest of justice.

Churches, foundations and individual donors use IFCO services as a fiscal agent to make donations to community organizing projects.

IFCO's global outreach includes humanitarian aid shipments through its Pastors for Peace program to Cuba, Haiti, Nicaragua, Honduras, and Chiapas, Mexico.

Headquarters
402 W. 145th St., New York, NY 10031 Tel. (212)926-5757 Fax (212)926-5842
Media Contact, Dir. of Communications, Gail Walker

Officers
Pres., Rev. Schuyler Rhodes
Vice President & Treasurer, Marilyn Clement

The Kairos Institute, Inc.

The Kairos Institute provides quality support, consultation and in-depth educational opportunities to the professional, medical, mental health and religious communities and promotes assistance, consultation, education and care to families of exceptional children. It's clergy consultation service provides care to many denominations and clergy. "Career Path" offers candidate assessment for ordination and consultation for clergy in transition.

Headquarters
107 Green Ave., Madison, NJ 07940 Tel. (973)966-9099 Fax (973)377-8509

Officers
Executive Director, Kathryn (Penny) Vennard Clark, MSW, LCSW
Clergy Services: The Rev. Dr. Dan Bottorff & The Rev. Dr. Richard Crocker

The Liturgical Conference

The Liturgical Conference works to renew liturgy within the churches for the reunion of the Body of Christ for the life of the world.

As an ongoing movement with the ecumenical church, founded in 1944, it seeks to provide an ecumenical forum for articulating standards of liturgical excellence and for supporting persons who have a common interest and concern for the liturgical life and the liturgical arts of the church. It is the publisher of the journals Liturgy and Homily Service.

Headquarters
P.O.Box 31., Evanston, IL 60201

Officers
Pres., E. Byron Anderson
Vice-Pres., Todd Johnson
Sec., Fritz West
Treas., Lester Ruth

Lombard Mennonite Peace Center

The Lombard Mennonite Peace Center (LMPC) is a nonprofit organization with the mission "to proclaim Christ's good news, the gospel of peace and justice—and to be active in the sacred ministry of reconciliation." With an emphasis on equipping clergy and churches to function in healthy ways, LMPC offers training in conflict transformation and in a family systems approach to church leaders' management of themselves and their congregations.

One- and two-day educational workshops and a five-day "Mediation Skills Training Institute for Church Leaders" are offered throughout the U.S. Ongoing clergy clinics provide church leaders with regular opportunities to reflect on their own functioning. LMPC also provides educational events, consultation and mediation services for congregations and judicatories of all denominations, as well as consultation for individual clergy.

Founded in 1983 as a ministry of a local congregation, LMPC became an independent, 501(c)3 corporation in 1997.

Headquarters
101 W. 22nd St., Suite 206, Lombard, IL 60148 Tel. (630)627-0507 Fax (630)627-0519, Email: admin@LMPeaceCenter.org, Website: www.LMPeaceCenter.org

Officers
Executive Director, Richard G. Blackburn

33

The Lord's Day Alliance of the United States

The Lord's Day Alliance of the United States, founded in 1888 in Washington, D.C., is the only national organization whose sole purpose is the preservation and cultivation of Sunday, the Lord's Day, as a day of rest and worship. The Alliance also seeks to safeguard a Day of Common Rest for all people regardless of their faith. Its Board of Managers is composed of representatives from 25 denominations. It serves as an information bureau, publishes a magazine, Sunday, and furnishes speakers and a variety of materials such as pamphlets, videos, posters, radio spot announcements, cassettes, news releases, articles for magazines and television programs.

Headquarters

Mailing Address: P.O. Box 941745, Atlanta, GA 31141-0745 Tel. (404)693-5530 Website: www.ldausa.org
Media Contact: Tim Norton, tnorton@ldausa.org
Co-Directors: Rev. Timothy A. Norton, tnorton@ldausa.org and Dr. Rodney L. Petersen, petersen@bostontheological.org

Officers

President, Mr. Brian W. Hanse
Presidents Emeriti, Rev. Dr. Roger A. Kvam and Rev. Dr. W. David Sapp

Lutheran World Relief

Lutheran World Relief (LWR) is an overseas development and relief agency based in Baltimore which responds quickly to natural and man-made disasters and supports more than 160 long-range development projects in countries throughout Africa, Asia, the Middle East and Latin America.

As its mission, Lutheran World Relief works with partners in 50 countries to help people grow food, improve health, strengthen communities, end conflict, build livelihoods, and recover from disasters.

Headquarters

700 Light Street, Baltimore, MD 21230-3850 Tel. (410)230-2700 Fax (410)230-2882

Officers

Pres., John A. Nunes

The Mennonite Central Committee

The Mennonite Central Committee is the relief and service agency of North American Mennonite and Brethren in Christ Churches. Representatives from Mennonite and Brethren in Christ groups make up the MCC, which meets annually in June to review its program and to approve policies and budget. Founded in 1920, MCC administers and participates in programs of agricultural and economic development, education, health, self-help, relief, peace and disaster service. MCC has about 1000 workers serving in 55 countries in Africa, Asia, Europe, Middle East and South, Central and North America.

MCC has service programs in North America that focus both on urban and rural poverty areas. There are also North American programs focusing on such diverse matters as community conciliation, employment creation and criminal justice issues. These programs are administered by two national bodies-MCC U.S. and MCC Canada.

Contributions from North American Mennonite and Brethren in Christ churches provide the largest part of MCC's support. Other sources of financial support include the contributed earnings of volunteers, grants from private and government agencies and contributions from Mennonite churches abroad. The total income in FYE2004, including material aid contributions, amounted to $69.4 million (US dollars).

MCC tries to strengthen local communities by working in cooperation with local churches or other community groups. Many personnel are placed with other agencies, including missions. Programs are planned with sensitivity to locally felt needs.

Headquarters

21 S. 12th St., P.O. Box 500, Akron, PA 17501-0500 Tel. (717)859-1151 Fax (717)859-2171
Canadian Office, 134 Plaza Dr., Winnipeg, MB R3T 5K9 Tel. (204)261-6381 Fax (204)269-9875
Media Contact, Larry Guengerich, P.O. Box 500, Akron, PA 17501 Tel. (717)859-1151 Fax (717)859-2171

Officers

Exec. Directors., Intl., Ronald J.R. Mathies; Canada, Donald Peters; U.S.A., Rolando Santiago

National Association of Ecumenical and Interreligious Staff

NAEIS is an association of professional staff in ecumenical and interreligious work. Founded as the Association of Council Secretaries in 1940, the Association was widened to include program staff in 1971, and renamed the National Association of Ecumenical Staff. It has included staff of any faith engaged in interreligious work since 1994. NAEIS provides means for personal and professional growth, and for mutual support, through national and regional gatherings, a newsletter and exchange among its membership.

NAEIS was established to provide creative relationships, mutual support and personal and professional growth of its members.

Headquarters

NAEIS, P.O. Box 95949, Seattle, WA 98145. Email: info@naeis.org

Officers

Pres.: The Rev. C. Dana Krutz, Louisiana Interchurch Conference, 527 North Blvd # 4 Baton Rouge, LA 70802-5720 Tel. (225)344-0134 Email: dankrutz@aol.com

Vice Pres.: The Rev. Scott Anderson, Wisconsin Council of Churches, 750 Windsor St #301, Sun Prairie, WI 53590-2149 Tel. (608)837-3108 Fax:(608)837-3038 Email: sanderson@wichurches.org

Immediate Past Pres.: The Rev. Samuel Muyskens, Interfaith Ministers–Wichita, 820 North Market Street, Wichita, KS 67214-1157 Tel. (512)451-2062 Email: smuyskens@ifmnet.org

Sec.: The Rev. Dr. Clark Lobenstine, Exec. Dir., Interfaith Conference of Metropolitan Washington, 1426 Ninth St. NW, 2nd Floor, Washington, DC 20001-3330, Tel. (202)234-6300 Email: clarkifc@aol.com

Treas.: Alice Woldt, Transitional Exec. Dir., Washington Association of Churches, P.O. Box 95949, Seattle, WA 98145 Email: woldt@thewac.org

The National Association of Evangelicals

The National Association of Evangelicals (NAE) is a voluntary fellowship of evangelical denominations, churches, organizations and individuals demonstrating unity in the body of Christ by standing for biblical truth, speaking with a representative voice, and serving the evangelical community through united action, cooperative ministry and strategic planning.

The association is comprised of approximately 45,000 congregations nationwide from 52 member denominations and fellowships, as well as several hundred independent churches. The membership of the association includes over 250 parachurch ministries and educational institutions. Through the cooperative ministry of these members, NAE directly and indirectly benefits over 30 million people. These ministries represent a broad range of theological traditions, but all subscribe to the distinctly evangelical NAE Statement of Faith. The association is a nationally recognized entity by the public sector with a reputation for integrity and effective service.

The cooperative ministries of the National Association of Evangelicals demonstrate the association's intentional desire to promote cooperation without compromise.

Headquarters

NAE-Washington, 701 G. St., SW, Washington, DC 20024 Tel. (202)789-1011 Fax (202) 842-0392

Media Contact, Galen Carey, (202)789-1011

STAFF

President, Rev. Leith Anderson
Vice President of Governmental Affairs, Galen Carey

National Bible Association

The National Bible Association is an autonomous, interfaith organization of lay people who advocate regular Bible reading and sponsors National Bible Week (Thanksgiving week) each November. Program activities include public service advertising, distribution of nonsectarian literature and thousands of local Bible Week observances by secular and religious organizations. The Association also urges constitutionally acceptable use of the Bible in public school classrooms, i.e., the study of the Bible in literature. All support comes from individuals, corporations and foundations.

Founded in 1940 by a group of business and professional people, the Association offers daily Bible readings in several English and Spanish translations on its website and has the IRS nonprofit status of a 501(c)(3) educational association.

Headquarters

1865 Broadway, New York, NY 10023 Tel. (212)408-1390 Fax (212)408-1448
Media Contact, Pres., Thomas R. May

Officers

Cpsn., Philip J. Clements
Vice-Cpsns.; Robert Cavalero; John W. Pugsley; John M. Templeton,Jr., M.D.
Pres., Thomas R. May
Treas., Paul Werner
Sec., J. Marshall Gage

The National Conference for Community and Justice

The National Conference for Community and Justice, founded in 1927 as the National Conference of Christians and Jews, is a human relations organization dedicated to fighting bias, bigotry and racism in America. The NCCJ promotes understanding and respect among all races, religions and cultures through advocacy, conflict resolution and education.

Programmatic strategies include interfaith and interracial dialogue, youth leadership workshops, workplace training, human relations research, and the building of community coalitions. NCCJ has 65 regional offices staffed by approximately 350 people. Nearly 200 members comprise the National Board of Advisors and members from that group form the 27-member National Board of Directors. Each regional office has its own Regional Board of Directors with a total of about 2,800. The National Board of Advisors meets once annually, the National Board of Directors at least three times annually.

Headquarters
328 Flatbush Ave., Brooklyn, NY 11217 Tel.
(718)783-0044 Fax (718)783-4143
Media Contact, Dir. of Communications, Diane
Powers

Officers
Pres. & CEO, Sanford Cloud, Jr.

National Conference on Ministry to the Armed Forces

The Conference is an incorporated civilian agency. Representation in the Conference with all privileges of the same is open to all endorsing or certifying agencies or groups authorized to provide chaplains for any branch of the Armed Forces.

The purpose of this organization is to provide a means of dialogue to discuss concerns and objectives and, when agreed upon, to take action with the appropriate authority to support the spiritual ministry to and the moral welfare of Armed Forces personnel.

Headquarters
4141 N. Henderson Rd., Ste. 13, Arlington, VA
22203 Tel. (703)276-7905 Fax (703)276-7906
Media Contact, Jack Williamson

STAFF
Coord., Jack Williamson
Admn. Asst., Maureen Francis

OFFICERS
Chpsn., David Peterson
Chpsn.-elect, Robert Jemerson
Sec., Lemuel Boyles
Treas., John Murdoch

National Council of the Churches of Christ in the U.S.A.

The National Council of the Churches of Christ in the U.S.A. is the preeminent expression in the United States of the movement toward Christian unity. The NCC's 35 member communions, including Protestant, Orthodox and Anglican church bodies, work together on a wide range of activities that further Christian unity, that witness to the faith, that promote peace and justice and that serve people throughout the world. Over 45 million U.S. Christians belong to churches that hold Council membership. The Council was formed in 1950 in Cleveland, Ohio, by the action of representatives of the member churches and by the merger of 12 previously existing ecumenical agencies, each of which had a different program focus. The roots of some of these agencies go back to the 19th century.

Headquarters
475 Riverside Dr., New York, NY 10115. Tel.
(212)870-2141

Media Contact, Media Relations Specialist, Mr.
Philip E. Jenks, Tel. (212)870-2228 Fax
(212)870-2030

GENERAL OFFICERS
Pres., The Rev. Peg Chemberlin
Gen. Sec., The Rev. Dr. Michael Kinnamon
Pres.Elect, Kathryn Lohre
Immediate Past Pres., Archbishop Vicken Aykazian
Sec., The Rev. Jose Luis Casal
Vice Pres., The Rev. Dr. Cheryl Wade
Vice Pres., The Right Rev. Johncy Itty
Vice Pres. at Large, Mr. Stan Noffsinger
Vice Pres. at Large, The Rev. Dr. Raymon E. Hunt

THE GENERAL SECRETARIAT
General Secretary, The Rev. Dr. Michael
Kinnamon Tel. (212)870-2141 Fax
(212)870-2817
Chief Operating Officer, Ms. Clare J. Chapman
Media Relations Specialist, Mr. Philip E. Jenks,
Tel. (212)870-2228

ADMINISTRATION AND FINANCE
Controller, Ms. Karen Wang, Tel. (212)870-3351
Assistant Dir. of Administration and Human
Resources, Ms. Joan Gardner, Tel. (212)
870-2258
Dir. of Information Technology, Mr. Julian
DeVia, Tel. (212)870-2541

DEVELOPMENT
Dir. of Development, Mr. Kurt Kaboth, Tel.
(212)870-2333
Dir. of Donor Relations, The Rev. Deborah C.
DeWinter, Tel. (212)870-2513

YEARBOOK OF AMERICAN & CANADIAN CHURCHES
Editor, The Rev. Dr. Eileen W. Lindner, Tel.
(201)417-1969
Assoc. Ed. and Technical Coord., The Rev.
Marcel A. Welty, Tel. (212)870-2379

WASHINGTON OFFICE
110 Maryland Ave. NE Washington, D.C. 20002
Tel. (202)544-2350 Fax (202)543-1297
Dir. of Washington Office, Ms. Cassandra
Carmichael, Tel. (202)481-6298
Office Manager, Mr. Kevin Williams, Tel.
(202)544-2350

COMMUNICATION COMMISSION AND JUSTICE AND ADVOCACY COMMISSION
Senior Program Director for Communication, and for Justice and Advocacy, Mr. Wesley M. Pattillo, Tel. (212)870-2048, Fax (212) 870-2030
Coord. of Television Programming, Ms. Shirley W. Struchen, Tel. (212)870-2227
Eco-Justice Programs, Dir., Ms. Cassandra Carmichael, Tel. (202)481-6298

Eco-Justice Programs, Asst. Dir., Mr. Jordan Blevins, Tel. (202)-481-6943
Eco-Justice Programs, Climate Change and Energy, Ms. Tyler Edgar, Tel. (202)544-2375
Eco-Justice Programs, Advocacy and Outreach Specialist, Carl Magruder, Tel. (202)481-6683
Eco-Justice Programs, Advocacy and Outreach Specialist, Elizabeth McGurk, Tel. (202) 481-6931
Eco-Justice Programs, Environmental Health, Chloe Schwabe, Tel. (202)481-6932
Program for Women's Ministries, Dir., The Rev. Ann Tiemeyer, Tel. (202)870-3407
Washington Advocacy Officer, Racial Justice, The Rev. Nakeisha S. Blount, Tel. (202) 544-2352

EDUCATION AND LEADERSHIP MINISTRIES COMMISSION

Senior Program Director for Education and Leadership Ministries, The Rev. Garland F. Pierce. Tel. (212)870-2267

FAITH AND ORDER COMMISSION AND INTERFAITH RELATIONS COMMISSION

Senior Program Director for Faith and Order, and for Interfaith Relations, Dr. Antonios Kireopoulos, Tel. (212)870-3422

RELATED ORGANIZATIONS

Agricultural Missions – The Rev. Joseph D. Keesecker, Exec. Dir., (212)870-2553, Fax (212)870-2959
Interfaith Center for Corporate Responsibility, Ms. Laura Berry, Exec. Dir., (212)870-2294

National Institute of Business and Industrial Chaplains

NIBIC is the professional organization for workplace chaplains, that includes members from a wide variety of faith groups and work settings, including corporations, manufacturing plants, air and sea ports, labor unions and pastoral counseling centers. NIBIC has six membership categories, including Certified, Clinical, Professional, Affiliates and Organizational.

NIBIC works to establish professional standards for education and practice; promotes and conducts training programs; provides mentoring, networking and chaplaincy information; encourages research and public information dissemination; communicates with business leaders and conducts professional meetings. NIBIC publishes a quarterly newsletter and co-sponsors The Journal of Pastoral Care and Counseling. A public membership meeting and training conference is held annually. NIBIC provides certification for qualified clinical members.

Headquarters

1900 St. James Place, Suite 880, Houston, TX 77056 Tel. (713)266-2456 Fax (713)266-0845
Media Contact, Rev. Diana C. Dale, D.Min., 1900 St. James Place, Suite 880 Houston, TX 77056 Tel. (713)266-2456 Fax (713)266-0845

Officers

Executive Dir., Rev. Diana C. Dale, D.Min.
Vice Pres., Rev. Dr. Juliette Jones
President, Rev. Robert L. Lewis, Jr., STM
Treas., Rev. Gregory Edwards Board Member, Timothy Bancroft, D.Min.

National Interfaith Cable Coalition, Inc. (NICC)

The National Interfaith Cable Coalition, Inc. (NICC) was formed as a not-for-profit 501(c)3 corporation, in December 1987, and is currently comprised of more than 40 faith groups and organizations from the Jewish and Christian traditions. In September 1988, NICC launched a religious cable network called VISN (Vision Interfaith Satellite Network), later known as the Odyssey Network. Now known as the Hallmark Channel, it is owned and operated by Crown Media Holdings, Inc., in which NICC is a strategic investor. NICC provides regular and prime-time special programming on the network. In 2000, NICC adopted Faith & Values Media as its service mark and expanded its mission to include a significant Web presence, www.FaithStreams.com, which features streaming video and video-on-demand service.

Headquarters

74 Trinity Place, Ste. 1550, New York, NY 10006 Tel. (212)406-4121 Fax (212)406-4105
Media Contact, Christine Luzano

Officers

Chair, Dr. Daniel Paul Matthews
Vice Chair, Elder Ralph Hardy Jr., Esq.
Secretary, Rabbi Daniel Freelander
Treasurer, Betty Elam

STAFF

President and CEO, Edward J. Murray
Exec. Vice President, Beverly Judge

National Interfaith Coalition on Aging

National Interfaith Coalition on Aging (NICA), a constituent unit of the National Council on Aging, is composed of Protestant, Roman Catholic, Jewish and Orthodox national and regional organizations and individuals concerned about the needs of older people and the religious community's response to problems facing the aging population in the United States. NICA was organized in 1972 to address spiritual concerns of older adults through religious sector action.

Mission Statement—The National Interfaith Coalition on Aging (NICA), affiliated with the National Council on the Aging (NCOA), is a

37

diverse network of religious and other related organizations and individual members which promotes the spiritual well being of older adults and the preparation of persons of all ages for the spiritual tasks of aging. NICA serves as a catalyst for new and effective research, networking opportunities, resource development, service provision, and dissemination of information.

Headquarters
c/o NCOA, 1910 L Street, NW, 4th Floor, Washington, DC 20036 Tel. (202)479-6655 Fax (202)479-0735
Media Contact, Rita Chow, Ed.D.

Officers
Chpsn., Rev. Ronald Field
Chpsn.-Elect, Beth Schwartz
Past Chpsn., Jane Stenson
Sec., Donald R. Koepke
Dir., Dr. Rita K. Chow

National Religious Broadcasters

National Religious Broadcasters is an association of Christian communicators, 1,500 organizations which produce religious programs for radio and television and other forms of electronic mass media or operate stations carrying predominately religious programs. NRB member organizations are responsible for more than 75 percent of all religious radio and television in the United States, reaching an average weekly audience of millions by radio, television, and other broadcast media.

Dedicated to the communication of the Gospel, NRB was founded in 1944 to safeguard free and complete access to the broadcast media. By encouraging the development of Christian programs and stations, NRB helps make it possible for millions to hear the good news of Jesus Christ through the electronic media.

Headquarters
9510 Technology Drive, Manassas, VA 20110. Tel. (703)330-7000 Fax (703)330-7100
Media Contact, Pres., Dr. Frank Wright

Officers
Chmn., Ron. L. Harris
1st Vice Chmn., Janet Parshall
2nd Vice Chair: John Fuller
Sec.: Richard Bott
Treas.: Roger Kemp

National Woman's Christian Temperance Union

The National WCTU is a not-for-profit, nonpartisan, interdenominational organization dedicated to the education of our nation's citizens, especially children and teens, on the harmful effects of alcoholic beverages, other drugs and tobacco on the human body and the society in which we live. The WCTU believes in a strong family unit and, through legislation, education and prayer, works to strengthen the home and family.

WCTU, which began in 1874 with the motto, "For God and Home and Every Land," is organized in 58 countries.

Headquarters
1730 Chicago Ave., Evanston, IL 60201 Tel. (708)864-1396
Media Contact, Sarah F. Ward, Tel. 765-345-7600

Officers
Pres., Sarah F. Ward, 33 N. Franklin, Knightstown, IN 46148
Email: sarah@wctu.org
Vice Pres., Rita Wert, 2250 Creek Hill Rd., Lancaster, PA 17601
Promotion Dir., Nancy Zabel, 1730 Chicago Ave., Evanston, IL 60201-4585
Treas., Faye Pohl, P.O. Box 739, Meade, KS 67864
Rec. Sec., Dorothy Russell, 18900 Nestueca Dr., Cloverdale, OR 97112

MEMBER ORGANIZATIONS
Loyal Temperance Legion (LTL), for boys and girls ages 6-12
Youth Temperance Council (YTC), for teens through college age

North American Baptist Fellowship

Organized in 1964, the North American Baptist Fellowship is a voluntary organization of Baptist Conventions in Canada and the United States, functioning as a regional body within the Baptist World Alliance. Its objectives are, (a) to promote fellowship and cooperation among Baptists in North America and (b) to further the aims and objectives of the Baptist World Alliance so far as these affect the life of the Baptist churches in North America. Its membership, however, is not identical with the North American membership of the Baptist World Alliance.

Church membership of the Fellowship bodies is more than 28 million.

The NABF assembles representatives of the member bodies once a year for exchange of information and views in such fields as evangelism and education, missions, stewardship promotion, lay activities and theological education. It conducts occasional consultations for denominational leaders on such subjects as church extension. It encourages cooperation at the city and county level where churches of more than one member group are located.

Headquarters
P.O. Box 6412, Falls Church, VA 22040
Media Contact, Gen. Sec., Rev. Alan Stanford, Ph.D. Tel. 703-655-9696

Pres., Dr. David Emmanuel Goatley, 300 I Street, NE, Suite 104, Washington D.C. 20002
Vice-Pres., Dr. Derrick Harkins, 4606 16th St. NW, Washington, DC 20011
Vice-Pres., Mrs. Bertha Williams, 13520 Corby Rd., Cleveland, OH 44120
Vice-Pres., Dr. Ken Belous, 414-195, The West Mall, Etobicoke, ON M9C5K1, Canada
Vice-Pres., Dr. Don Sewell, 333 N. Washington St., Dallas, TX 75246-1798

Oikocredit- Ecumenical Development Cooperative Society

Based in the Netherlands, EDCS is often called "the churches' bank for the poor." EDCS borrows funds from churches, religious communities and concerned individuals and re-lends the funds to enterprises operated by low-income communities. Launched in 1975 through an initiative of the World Council of Churches, EDCS is organized as a cooperative of religious institutions and is governed by annual membership meetings and an elected board of religious leaders and development and financial professionals.

An international network of 15 EDCS Regional Managers is responsible for lending funds to cooperative enterprises and microcredit institutions. At the present time over $530 million is at work in micro loans. This includes coffee shops, fishing enterprises, handicraft production, truck farming, and many other commercial ventures owned and operated by poor people.

Oikocredit is represented in the United States by Oikocredit USA, a 501(c)3 non-profit corporation. American individuals and congregations can invest in Oikocredit by purchasing one, three, and five year notes paying 0-2% interest that are issued by Oikocredit -USA.

U.S. HEADQUARTERS

P.O. Box 11000, Washington, D.C. 20008, Tel. (202)728-4140, Fax (202)728-4143, Email: office.usa@oikocredit.org, Website: www.oikocredit.org
Media Contact, Regional Manager for North America, Rev. Terry Provance

OFFICERS, EDCS-USA

Exec. Dir., Rev. Terry Provance
Chair, John Paarlberg
Treas., Lura Mack

Parish Resource Center, Inc.

Parish Resource Center, Inc. promotes, establishes, nurtures and accredits local Affiliate Parish Resource Centers whose mission is to equip, coach, and train church leaders. Affiliate centers support and strengthen subscribing congregations of all faiths by providing professional consultants, resource materials and workshops. The Parish Resource Center was founded in 1976 and is located in Lancaster PA. In addition to the Lancaster PA Center, there are three additional free-standing affiliates located in Long Island, NY; Denver, CO.; and New York City. These centers serve congregations from 49 faith traditions.

Headquarters

633 Community Way, Lancaster, PA 17603 Tel. (717)299-9932 Fax (717)299-7229
Media Contact, Pres., Dr. H. David Loughery

Officers

Chairperson, Carolyn Pyfer
Vice-Chair, Dr. Robert Webber
Sec./Treas., David P. Harrison
Pres., Dr. H. David Loughery
Founder: Dr. D. Douglas Whiting

Pentecostal-Charismatic Churches of North America

The Pentecostal-Charismatic Churches of North America (PCCNA) was organized October 19, 1994, in Memphis TN. This organizational meeting came the day after the Pentecostal Fellowship of North America (PFNA) voted itself out of existence in order to make way for the new fellowship.

The PFNA had been formed in October 1948 in Des Moines, IA. It was composed of white-led Pentecostal denominations. The move to develop a multiracial fellowship began when the PFNA Board of Administration initiated a series of discussions with African-American Pentecostal leaders. The first meeting was held July 10-11, 1992, in Dallas, TX. A second meeting convened in Phoenix, AZ, January 4-5, 1993. On January 10-11, 1994, 20 representatives from each of the two groups met in Memphis to make final plans for a Dialogue which was held in Memphis, October 1994.

This racial reconciliation meeting has been called "The Memphis Miracle." During this meeting the PFNA was disbanded, and the PCCNA was organized. The new organization quickly adopted the "Racial Reconciliation Manifesto." Subsequent meetings were held in Memphis, TN (1996), Washington, DC (1997), Tulsa, OK (1998), and Hampton, VA (1999)

In an effort to further increase the spirit of reconciliation, the PCCNA meeting of 2000 was held during the North American Renewal Service committee (NARSC) Conference in St. Louis, Missouri. Furthermore, the PCCNA acted as host for the 19th Pentecostal World Conference held in Los Angeles, California, May 2001.

Headquarters

1445 N. Boonville Ave., Springfield, MO 65802 Tel. (417)862-2781 Ext. 3010 Fax (417)683-6614 E-mail: PCCNA@ag.org

Media Contact, Dr. Charles Crabtree

PCCNA EXECUTIVE BOARD

Chairperson, Dr. Charles T. Crabtree, General Council of the Assemblies of God, 1445 N. Boonville Ave., Springfield, MO 65802 Tel. (417)862-2781 Ext. 3010 Fax (417)683-6614 E-mail: PCCNA@ag.org
Co-Chairperson, Bishop Jerry Macklin, Church of God in Christ, 1027 W. Tennyson Rd, Hayward, CA 94544 Tel. (510)783-9377 Fax (510)783-8673 E-mail: PastorJWM@aol.com
Secretary, Dr. R. Lamar Vest, Church of God, P.O. Box 2430, Cleveland, TN 37320-2430, Tel. (423)478-7308 Fax (423)478-7334
Treasurer, Bishop Randy Howard, Church of God of Prophecy, P.O. Box 2910, Cleveland, TN 37320-2910 Tel. (423)559-5203 Fax (423)472-5037 E-mail: wmcogop@aol.com

EXECUTIVE COMMITTEE MEMBERS-AT-LARGE

Dr. Ron Carpenter, International Pentecostal Holiness Church, P.O. Box 12690, Oklahoma City, OK 73157
Rev. Daniel de Leon, Templo Calvario, 261 W. 5th St, Santa Ana, CA 92703
Rev. Jeff Farmer, Open Bible Churches, 2020 Bell Ave, Des Moines, IA 50315
Rev. Art Gray, International Church of the Foursquare Gospel, 1910 W. Sunset Blvd; Ste 200, Los Angeles, CA 90026
Bishop Clyde Hughes, International Pentecostal Church of Christ, P.O. Box 439, London, OH 43130
Dr. William Morrow, Pentecostal Assemblies of Canada, 2459 Milltower Ct., Mississauga, ON L5N 5Z6 CANADA
Bishop Elijah Williams, The United Holy Church of America, 901 Briarwood St., Reidsville, NC 27320

Project Equality, Inc.

Project Equality is a national, non-profit, interfaith program for affirmative action and equal employment opportunity. Through a Buyer's Guide that is provided to sponsoring organizations and individuals, Project Equality serves as a registry for suppliers of goods and services who commit to equal employment practices. This allows members and friends to economically support those who practice equality and justice with their employees. Project Equality also provides consultation and training for workplace diversity, does EEO audits, and is a resource for Human Resource practices. Project Equality is a leader in creating inclusive and just communities.

Headquarters

7132 Main St., Kansas City, MO 64114-1406 Tel. (816)361-9222 Fax (816)361-8997

Officers

Board Chair, Salvador Mendoza
Interim Executive Director, Cathleen D. Cackler-Veazey, Ph.D.

Religion In American Life, Inc.

Religion In American Life (RIAL) is a unique cooperative program of some 50 major national religious groups (Catholic, Eastern Orthodox, Jewish, Protestant, Muslim, etc.). It provides services for denominationally-supported, congregation-based outreach and growth projects such as the current Invite a Friend program. These projects are promoted through national advertising campaigns reaching the American public by the use of all media. The ad campaigns are produced by a volunteer agency with production-distribution and administration costs funded by denominations and business groups, as well as by individuals.

Since 1949, RIAL ad campaign projects have been among the much coveted major campaigns of The Advertising Council. This results in as much as $35 million worth of time and space in a single year, contributed by media as a public service. Through RIAL, religious groups demonstrate respect for other traditions and the value of religious freedom. The RIAL program also includes seminars and symposia, research and leadership awards and produces a weekly syndicated radio broadcast, "SpiriTalk".

Headquarters

250 E 87th St., Suite 12F, New York, NY 10128-3116 Tel. (203)355-1220 Fax (203)355-1221
Media Contact, Exec. Admin., Martha Mesiti Tel. (203)355-1220

EXECUTIVE COMMITTEE

Natl. Chpsn., Thomas S. Johnson, Chairman & CEO, Greenpoint Bank, NY
Chpsn. of Bd., Rev. Dr. Gordon Sommers
Vice-Chpsns., Bishop Khajag Barsamian, Primate (Armenian Church of America); Most Rev. William Cardinal Keeler, (Archbishop of Baltimore); Rabbi Ronald B. Sobel, (Cong. Emanu-El of the City of N.Y.)
Sec.,Timothy A. Hultquist (Morgan Stanley Dean Witter)
Treas., Robertson H. Bennett (Smith Barney)

STAFF

Pres. & CEO, Robert B. Lennick, Rabbi, D.Min.
Exec. Admin., Martha Mesiti

The Religion Communicators Council, Inc.

RCC is an interfaith, interdisciplinary association of professional communicators who work for religious groups and causes. It was founded in 1929 and is the oldest non-profit professional public relations/communications organization in the world. RCC's more than 600 members include those who work in communications and related fields for church-related institutions, denominational agencies, non-and interdenominational organizations and communications firms who primarily serve religious organizations.

Members represent a wide range of faiths, including Presbyterian, Baptist, United Methodist, Lutheran, Episcopalian, Mennonite, Roman Catholic, Seventh-day Adventist, Jewish, Salvation Army, Brethren, Bahá'í, Disciples, Muslim, Latter-Day Saints and others.

On the national level, RCC sponsors an annual three-day convention, and has published seven editions of a Religious Public Relations Handbook for churches and church organizations, and a videostrip, The Church at Jackrabbit Junction. Members receive a quarterly newsletter (Counselor). There are 13 regional chapters.

RCC administers the annual Wilbur Awards competition to recognize high quality coverage of religious values and issues in the public media. Wilbur winners include producers, reporters, editors and broadcasters nationwide. To recognize communications excellence within church communities, RCC also sponsors the annual DeRose-Hinkhouse Awards for its own members.

In 1970, 1980, 1990, 2000, and in planning form April 7 - 10, 2010 (www.rccongress 2010.org). RCC initiated a global Religious Communications Congress bringing together thousands of persons from western, eastern and third-world nations who are involved in communicating religious faith.

Headquarters
475 Riverside Dr., Rm. 1355, New York, NY 10115 Tel. (212)870-2985 Fax (212)870-2171 Exec. Dir., Shirley Whipple Struchen, Tel. (212)870-2402, Email: SStruchen@rcn.com Web: www.religiouncommunicators.org

2009-2010 Officers
President., Douglas Cannon, Adjunct Professor, Concordia University Texas, Email: dcannon @cannonapr.com

Vice- Pres., Anuttama Dasa, Director of Communication, ISKCON, 10310 Oaklyn Dr., Potomac, MD, 20854, Tel. (301)299-9707, Fax. (301)299-5025, Email: ic@pamho.net

Sec., Deb Christian, Director of Customer Relations, UMR Communications, 1221 Profit Dr., Dallas, TX, 75247, Tel. (800)947-0207 (x147), Fax. (214)631-6610, Email: dchristian @umr.org

Treas., Brian Gray, Editor, Momentum National Catholic Educational Association, 1077 30th St. NW, Ste. 100, Washington, DC 20007, Tel. (202)337-6232, Fax. (202)333-6706, Email: momentum@ncea.org

Religion News Service

Religion News Service (RNS) has provided news and information to the media for 75 years. Owned by Advance Publications, it is staffed by veteran jounalists who cover stories on all of the world religions as well as trends in ethics, morality and spirituality.

RNS provides a daily news service, a weekly news service, and a web service and photo and service. The daily service is also available via the AP Data Features wire, or e-mail. The weekly report is available by wire or e-mail. RNS's Photos Service features stock images and news photography. RNS also offers Religion Press Release Services, which distributes press releases and advisories to religion editors. RNS is syndicated in the United States by Universal Press Syndicate and in Canada by the Canadian Press.

Headquarters
1930 18th Street, NW, Suite B2, Washington, DC 20009, Tel. (202)463-8777 Fax (202)463-0033, Email: info@religionnews.com, Web: www.religionnews.com

Officers
Editor, Kevin Eckstrom

Religion Newswriters Association and Foundation

Founded in 1949, the RNA is a professional association of journalist who write and edit about religion in the general circulating news media. It sponsors annual contests, conferences, online tools and Religion links. It also offers the Lilly Scholarships in Religion to journalists in the US and Canada to take religion courses of their choice. Annual meetings are held in the fall.

Our Mission: To promote excellence in religion reporting in the news media.

Our Vision: RNA will achieve its mission by providing education and other resources for its members by raising awareness of the importance of religion coverage in the secular media.

Headquarters
School of Journalism, 131 Neff Annex, University of Missouri, Columbia, MO 65211, Tel. (573)882-925, Email: Mason@RNA.com, Websit: www.ReligionLink.com
Media Contact, Exec. Dir., Debra Mason

Religions for Peace-USA, Inc.

Religions for Peace-USA, formerly the United States Conference of Religions for Peace, began in the 1970's as a program area and chapter of the World Conference of Religions for Peace (now known simply as Religions for Peace), the world's largest representative interreligious organization. Today, the organization is separately incorporated and registered as an independent 501(c)(3) and focuses its mandate on U.S.-based issues, while retaining a strong link to the international work of the Religions for Peace. As the largest and most broadly based representative multi-religious forum in the United States, RFP-USA engages the religious leaders and experts in interreligious affairs and peace and justice of more than 50 religious traditions. By building on the spiritual, human, and institutional resources of these communities, RFP-USA establishes cooperative efforts among them to address shared challenges. Primary areas of concern for the organization include building interreligious relationships, creating mutual understanding amidst the country's increasing diversity, and examining the role of the U.S. as a citizen of the global community, with particular regard to peace, human rights, and development.

Headquarters
RFP-USA, 777 United Nations Plaza, 9th Floor, New York, NY 10017 Tel. (212)338-9140 Fax (212)983-0098

Officers
Interim Executive Director, Dr. Lucinda Mosher, Email: lmosher@rfpusa.org
Moderator, Dr. Tarnujit Singh Butalia

Religious Conference Management Association, Inc.
The Religious Conference Management Association, Inc. (RCMA) is a faith-based, non-profit, professional organization of men and women who have responsibility for planning and-or managing meetings, seminars, conferences, conventions, assemblies or other gatherings for religious organizations.

Founded in 1972, RCMA is dedicated to promoting the highest professional performance by its members and associate members through the mutual exchange of ideas, techniques and methods.

Today RCMA has 3,000 members who plan 14,000 conventions and meetings that annually attract over 11 million attendees.

The association conducts an annual world conference and exposition that provides a forum for its membership to gain increased knowledge in the arts and sciences of religious meeting planning and management.

RCMA publishes a bi-monthly magazine, Religious Conference Manager; a conference daily, RCMA Highlights; plus a semi-monthly e-newsletter.

Headquarters
7702 Woodland Drive, Suite 120, Indianapolis, IN 46278 Tel. (317)632-1888 Fax (317)632-7909, Website: www.RCMAWEB.ORG
Media Contact, Exec. Dir., Dr. DeWayne S. Woodring, CMP

Officers
Pres., Dr. Melvin L. Worthington, CMP, National Association of Free Will Baptists, 4878 Ayden Golf Club Road, Ayden, NC 28513-7423
Vice-Pres., The Rev. Harry Schmidt, Christian Life College, 400 E. Gregory, Mt. Prospect, IL 60056
Sec.-Treas., The Rev. George O. Stewart, Baptist Pastor's Council, 4234 Lee Road, Cleveland, OH 44128
Exec. Dir., Dr. DeWayne S. Woodring, CMP

The Seminary Consortium for Urban Pastoral Education (SCUPE)
Founded in 1976, SCUPE is an interdenominational agency committed to the development of individuals, congregations and organizations for leadership in urban ministry. For individuals, we offer four accredited graduate-level academic programs, the semester- and-or summer-term Graduate Theological Urban Studies program for seminary students; an M.A. in Community Development degree developed in partnership with North Park University; Nurturing the Call, a year-long sequence of graduate courses in theology and ministry for urban pastors who have not previously attended seminary; and Center for African American Theological Studies, an Africentric 3-year M.Div program.

SCUPE also consults to other ministries and urban institutions, providing specially-designed training programs around issues including diversity, strategic planning, leadership development , and human resource mobilization. We operate an urban ministry resource center and publish the Resource Review, as well as other occasional materials, as a service to the urban church. Every two years, SCUPE also organizes the Congress on Urban Ministry as a training and networking event for those in urban ministry.

Headquarters
200 N. Michigan Ave., Suite 502, Chicago, IL 60601 Tel. (312)726-1200 Fax (312)726-0425
Media Contact, President, Dr. David Frenchak; Director of Development, Nancy Renick

Officers
Chair, Rev. Donald Sharp
Vice Chair, Ms. Cheryl Hammock
Treasurer, Mr. Lamont Change
Secretary, Dr. Bill VanWyngaarden
Lead Program Staff
President, Dr. David Frenchak
Co-Directors, M.A. in Community Development, Rev. Carol Ann McGibbon & Dr. Arthur Lyons
Director, Graduate Theological Urban Studies (GTUS), Glenn Martin Klaassen

Director, Center for African American Theological Studies (CAATS), Sean McMillan Director, Nurturing the Call (NtC), Cynthia Milsap Registrar, Dody Finch

The Alliance for Christian Media

The Alliance for Christian Media is an ecumenical organization dedicated to producing media resources from a mainline Protestant point of view. The flagship production is the weekly radio show, "Day 1," formerly "The Protestant Hour." The Day 1 Web site (http://day1.org) provides sermon transcripts and audio and video resources. Day 1 features preachers from the Cooperative Baptist Fellowship, Episcopal Church, Evangelical Lutheran Church in America, Presbyterian Church (U.S.A.), United Church of Christ, and the United Methodist Church.

Headquarters
644 West Peachtree St, Suite 300, Atlanta, GA 30308-1925 Tel. (404)815-0640 Fax (404)815-0495
Media Contact, Peter Wallace

Officers
Bd. Chpsn., Laurin M. McSwain
Vice-Chpsn., Frank Troutman, Jr.
Pres., The Rev. Canon Louis C. Schueddig
V.P., The Rev. Peter M. Wallace
Treas., Michael Starr
Sec., Frank Troutman, Jr.

Transnational Association of Christian Colleges and Schools

Transnational Association of Christian Colleges and Schools (TRACS). TRACS was established in 1979 to promote the welfare, interests, and development of postsecondary institutions, whose mission is characterized by a distinctly Christian purpose, as defined in our Foundational Standards. TRACS is a voluntary, non-profit, self-governing organization that provides accreditation to Christian postsecondary institutions offering certificates, diplomas, and/or degrees. TRACS is recognized by the United States Department of Education, the Council for Higher Education Accreditation, and the International Network for Quality Assurance Agencies in Higher Education as a national accrediting body for Christian institutions, colleges, universities, and seminaries. The geographic territory of TRACS currently consists of the United States and its territories.

Headquarters
P.O. Box 328, Forest, Virginia 24551 Tel. (434)525-9539 Fax (434)525-9538, Email: info@tracs.org, Web: www.tracs.org
Media Contact: Exec. Dir., Dr. Russell G. Fitzgerald

Officers
Accredition Commission Chairman, Dr. Charles T. Shoemaker
Exec. Dir., Dr. Russell G. Fitzgerald
Assoc. Exec. Dir., Dr. Paul Boatner

United Religions Initiative

The purpose of the United Religions Initiative is to promote enduring, daily interfaith cooperation, to end religiously motivated violence and to create cultures of peace, justice, and healing for the Earth and all living beings.

The United Religions initiative is a growing, global community of over 130 Cooperation Circles, involving thousands of people around the world. The URI is inspired by the leadership potential inherent in every individual, leadership that is discovered and deepened through dialogue with others when dreams are shared and cooperative destinies are realized. The individuals who make up the URI network are committed to interfaith peacebuilding, recognizing that for peace to prevail on earth, "peace must begin with me." They believe that by talking with others who come from different faiths, cultures or spiritual traditions all involved can begin to better understand their own beliefs and recognize their common bonds.

The URI seeks to create safe spaces throughout the world where these interfaith partnerships can be seeded, and the ideas and initiatives that they spark can be practically applied. With the mandate in the URI Charter that each Cooperation Circle represents at least three different faith traditions, the very act of coming together builds peace by creating interfaith cooperation among neighbors and within communities where it may never before have been possible. The Charter "Guidelines for Action" affirms the "essentially self-organizing nature" of the Cooperation Circles and empowers CC participants to "choose what they want to do" while providing guidance for community building. The Guidelines assure that all URI activities and actions demonstrate the following heartfelt considerations, (a) sharing the wisdom and cultures of different faith traditions; (b) nurturing cultures of healing and peace; (c) upholding human rights; (d) supporting the health of the entire Earth; (e) integrating spirituality in issues of economic justice; and (f) providing grassroot support for all URI activities.

The initial vision for the United Religions Initiative began in 1993 with a dream by its founder, Bishop William Swing. He writes that it came with "a sudden realization that religions, together, have a vocation to be a force for good in the world." In just seven years, tens of thousands of people in more than sixty countries around the world have responded to this

43

vision with a resounding, "Yes!" Their affirmations have taken on a myriad of forms. For example, during the 72 Hours Project at the turn of the Millennium, over a million people in 40 countries participated in 200 projects for peace. Highlights included a 12-day interfaith pilgrimage across Pakistan and the celebration of 1 million signature on a petition to ban handguns in Rio de Janeiro.

Headquarters
P.O. Box 29242, San Francisco, CA 94129-0242
Tel. (415)561-2300 Fax (415)562-2313
Media Contact, Kristin Swenson

STAFF
Executive Director, Rev. Cn Charles P. Gibbs
Peacebuilding, Barbara H. Hartford & Sarah Talcott
Global Fundraising, Philanthropy, Jennifer Kirk & LaTonya Trotter
Membership and Organizational Development, Sally Mahe & Cory Robertson
Visions for Peace Among Religions Project, Nancy Nielsen
Annual Giving and Knowledge Management, Sarah Talcott
Financial Manager, Ray Signer

GLOBAL COUNCIL
President and Founding Trustee, Bishop William Swing

AFRICA
Malawi, Joyce N'goma
Uganda, Despina Namwembe
Mozambique, Sabapath Alagiah

ASIA
Pakistan, James Channan
Korea, Jinwol Lee
India, Mohinder Singh

EUROPE
Netherlands, Annie Imbens
United Kingdom, Deepak Naik
Germany, Karimah Stauch

LATIN AMERICA AND THE CARIBBEAN
Argentina, Rosalia Guiterrez
Mexico, Jonathan Rose
Chile, Gerado Gonzalez

MIDDLE EAST
Isreal, George Khory
Isreal, Yehuda Stolov
Egypt, Mohamed Mosaad

MULTI-REGIONAL/NON-GEOGRAPHIC
Yoland Trevino
Jack Lundin
Munirah Shahidi

NORTH AMERICA
United States of America, Don Frew
United States of America, Kay Lindhal
United States of America, Heng Sure

THE PACIFIC
New Zealand, George Armstrong
Philippines, Bonifacio Quirog
Philippines, Shakuntala Moorjani-Vaswani

TRANSITION ADVISORY COMMITTEE
Iftekhar Hai
Rita Semel
Bob Walter

United States Conference for the World Council of Churches
The United States Conference of the World Council of Churches was formed in 1938 when the WCC itself was still in the "Process of Formation." Henry Smith Leiper, an American with many national and international connections, was given the title of "Associate General Secretary" of the WCC and asked to carry out WCC work in the U.S. After the World Council of Churches was officially born in 1948 in Amsterdam, Netherlands, Leiper raised millions of dollars for WCC programs.

Today the U.S. Conference of the WCC is composed of representatives of U.S. member churches of the worldwide body. The U.S. Office of the WCC works to develop relationships among the churches, advance the work of WCC and interpret the council in the United States.

Headquarters
475 Riverside Dr., Rm. 1370, New York, NY 10115 Tel. (212)870-3260 Fax (212)870-2528

Officers
Moderator: The Rev. Dr. Bernice Powell Jackson
Vice-Moderator: Rev. Tyrone Pitts
Vice-Moderator and Secretary/Treasurer: Ms. Anne Glynn Mackoul

Vellore Christian Medical College Foundation
The Vellore Christian Medical College Foundation supports the wide range of programs at Christian Medical College (CMC), Vellore, Tamil Nadu, India, by securing contributions for its major capital equipment and construction goals; grants for program educational, research and health care programs; and funds to support scholarships for medical nursing and allied health students at Vellore and senior faculty study outside of India. The Board also facilitates opportunities for North Americans to volunteer at CMC and fosters working relationships between CMC and institutions in the U.S. Print, DVD and electronic materials about MC's 100+ years as a leading medical college and hospital are available as part of the Board's public education program. A capital campaign to raise one million dollars toward a new campus is now underway.

Headquarters
475 Riverside Dr., Rm. 725, New York, NY 10115 Tel. (212)870-2640 Fax (212)870-2173 Media Contact, President, Dr. Louis L. Knowles E-mail, usaboard@vellorecmc.org

Officers
Pres., Dr. Louis L. Knowles
Chair, Mrs. Edwina Scudder-Youth, 211 Blue Ridge Dr., Levittown, PA 19057
Vice-Chair, Mr. Anish Mathai, 475 Riverside Dr., Rm. 243, New York, NY 10115
Sec., Dr. Alexander Kuruvila, 2063 Gainsborough Dr., Riverside, CA 92606
Treas., Mr. Richard L. Vreeland, 182 Ameren Way, Ballwin, MO 63021

World Day of Prayer International Committee

World Day of Prayer is an ecumenical movement initiated and carried out by Christian women in 170 countries who conduct a common day of prayer on the first Friday of March to which all people are welcome. There is an annual theme for the worship service that has been prepared by women in a different country each year. For March 5, 2010 the WDP Committee of Cameroon has prepared a worship service on the theme, "Let Everything That Has Breath Praise God". The offering at the WDP is gathered by each WDP National/Regional Committee and given to support projects for women and children and to help people who are in need.

Headquarters
World Day of Prayer International Comm., 475 Riverside Dr., Rm. 729, New York, NY 10115 Tel. (212)870-3049, Fax (212)864-8648, Email: wdpic@worlddayofprayer.net
Media Contact, Exec. Dir., Eileen King
World Day of Prayer USA, 475 Riverside Dr., Suite 300, New York, NY 10115 Tel. (212)870-2466, Fax (212)870-2456, Toll-free 866 WDP USA, (866)937-8720, Email: ecalvin@wdpusa.org, Website: wdpusa.org
Media Contact, Executive Director, Elizabeth Calvin

Officers
Chairperson, S. Annette Poitier
Treasurer, Marcia L. Florkey
Africa, Véronique Lusieboko Lutatabio, Assah E. Mgonja
Asia, Zenaida Maturan, Sheree, Suk-Ling Wong
Caribbean and North America, Alison Carter, Marilyn Fortin
Europe, Jean Hackett, Corinna Harbig
Latin America, Elisabeth Delmonte,Ormara Nolla
Middle East, Laila Carmi, Lucy Ishak Guirguis
Pacific, Vaieli Fuiono Piita, Pauline Smit

World Methodist Council-North American Section

The World Methodist Council, one of the 30 or so "Christian World Communions," shares a general tradition which is common to all Christians.

The world organization of Methodists and related United Churches is comprised of 76 churches with roots in the Methodist tradition. These churches found in 132 countries have a membership of more than 40 million.

The Council's North American Section, comprised of ten Methodist and United Church denominations, provides a regional focus for the Council in Canada, the United States and Mexico. The North American Section meets at the time of the quinquennial World Conference and Council, and separately as Section between world meetings. North American Churches related to the World Methodist Council have a membership of approximately 16 million and a church community of more than 30 million.

Headquarters
P.O. Box 518, Lake Junaluska, NC 28745 Tel. (828)456-9432 Fax (828)456-9433
Media Contact, Gen. Sec., George H. Freeman

Officers
General Sec., Dr. George H. Freeman

World Vision

World Vision is a Christian relief and development organization dedicated to helping children and their communities worldwide reach their full potential by tackling the causes of poverty. Motivated by our faith in Jesus, we serve the poor as a demonstration of God's unconditional love for all people. World Vision works with communities in nearly 100 countries to develop long-term solutions that alleviate poverty, provides emergency assistance to children and families affected by natural disasters and civil conflict, and advocates for justice on behalf of the poor. World Vision U.S.—one of 52 national offices in the World Vision Partnership—serves in key United States metropolitan areas, providing intervention for challenged youth, tools that equip strong community leaders, and storehouses that provide essentials for living.

World Vision's Church Relations department facilitates chuch partnerships, connecting U.S. congregations with critical ministry among people in need locally and internationally. Church opportunities include partnerships with international projects, volunteer options through U.S. programs, and educational programs, including youth-oriented 30 Hour Famine and One Life Revolution, and child sponsorship.

Headquarters
P.O. Box 9716, Federal Way, WA 98063-9716 Tel. (253)815-1000

45

Church Relations Vice President, Steve Haas, Tel. (253)815-2698
Media Contact, Dean Owen, Tel. (253)815-2158

Officers
President, Richard Stearns
Senior Vice Presidents, Joan Mussa, Lawrence Probus, Julie Regnier, Atul Tandon, George Ward, Michael Veitenhans

YMCA of the USA

The YMCA is one of the largest private voluntary organizations in the world, serving about 30 million people in more than 100 countries. In the United States, more than 2,000 local branches, units, camps and centers annually serve more than 14 million people of all ages, races and abilities. About half of those served are female. No one is turned away because of an inability to pay.

The Y teaches youngsters to swim, organizes youth basketball games and offers adult aerobics. But the Y represents more than fitness— it works to strengthen families and help people develop values and behavior that are consistent with Christian principles.

The Y offers hundreds of programs including day camp for children, child care, exercise for people with disabilities, teen clubs, environmental programs, substance abuse prevention, family nights, job training and many more programs from infant mortality prevention to overnight camping for seniors.

The kind of programs offered at a YMCA will vary; each is controlled by volunteer board members who make their own program, policy, and financial decisions based on the special needs of their community. In its own way, every Y works to build strong kids, strong families, and strong communities.

The YMCA was founded in London, England, in 1844 by George Williams and friends who lived and worked together as clerks. Their goal was to save other live-in clerks from the wicked life of the London streets. The first members were evangelical Protestants who prayed and studied the Bible as an alternative to vice. The Y has always been nonsectarian and today accepts those of all faiths at all levels of the organization.

Headquarters
101 N. Wacker Dr., Chicago, IL 60606 Tel. (312)977-0031 Fax (312)977-9063
Media Contact, Media Relations Manager, Arnie Collins

Officers
Board Chairman., Daniel E. Casey
Exec. Dir., Niel Nicoll
(Int.) Public Relations Assoc., Arnold Collins

YWCA of the U.S.A.

The YWCA of the U.S.A. is comprised of 313 affiliates in communities and on college campuses across the United States. It serves one million members and program participants. It seeks to empower women and girls to enable them, coming together across lines of age, race, religious belief, economic and occupational status to make a significant contribution to the elimination of racism and the achievement of peace, justice, freedom and dignity for all people.

Headquarters
1015 18th St. Suite 1100, Washington, DC 20036. Tel.: (202)467-0801; Fax: (202)467-0802
Media Contact, Khristina Lew Email: info@ywca.org

Officers
National Pres., Leticia Paez
Sec., Carol O. Markus
Chief Exec. Officer, Margaret Tyndall

Youth for Christ-USA

Founded in 1944, our mission is: YFC reaches young people everywhere, working together with the local church and other like-minded partners to raise up lifelong followers of Jesus who lead by their godliness in lifestyle, devotion to the Word of God and prayer, passion for sharing the love of Christ and commitment to social involvement.

Youth for Christ is active in 180 areas across the U.S., representing over 2,000 different locations where young people are being reached. There are over 70,000 teens involved each week in U.S. programs. Over 1,500 staff, 15,800 volunteers, and 6,300 student leaders are involved in the U.S. YFC/USA is part of an international movement involving over 100 countries, with each country having their own indigenous leadership. Worldwide, over 125,000 young people began a personal relationship with Jesus Christ last year as part of various YFC ministries.

Youth for Christ's core ministries are:
Campus Life (high school) and Campus life (M) Middle School
City Life reaching inner-city teens
Teen Parents - ministry to expectant teens and their children
Juvenile Justice Ministries - ministry to teens in correctional facilities, group homes, emergency shelters, etc.
Friend2Friend - Christian teens reaching their peers

Headquarters
U.S. Headquarters, P.O. Box 4478, Englewood, CO 80155 Tel. (303)843-9000 Fax (303) 843-9002

Canadian Organization, c/o Tecsys, 87 Prince Street, 5th Floor, Montreal, QC H3C 2M7 Tel. (514)866-0001 x 4118 Fax (514)866-3033
Media Contact, VP of Communication, Mark Jevert

Officers
United States, President, Daniel S. Wolgemuth
Canada, National Dir., David Brereton
Youth for Christ Intl. Pres., David Wraight

2. Canadian Cooperative Organizations, National

In most cases, the organizations listed here work on a national level and cooperate across denominational lines. Regional cooperative organizations in Canada are listed in Directory 7, "Canadian Regional and Local Ecumenical Bodies."

Alcohol and Drug Concerns Inc.

Alcohol and Drug Concerns is a registered, non-profit, charitable organization that has a long association with the Christian Church. The organization's mission is to empower youth to make positive lifestyle choices relating to alcohol, tobacco, and other drugs.

The organization was granted a national charter in 1987, moving from an Ontario charter dating back to 1934. Among its services are, Choices F.I.T. (Fostering Independent Thinking)- a substance abuse prevention resource for grade 4 to 8 teachers; an Institute on Addiction Studies; Making the Leap- a substance abuse prevention resource for grade 7 to 8 teachers created by high school students; Drug and Alcohol Game Show for grades 6 to 9- a classroom activity; education and awareness courses for clients of the Ontario Ministry of Corrections.

Headquarters

4500 Sheppard Ave. E, Ste. 112, Toronto, ON M1S 3R6 Tel. (416)293-3400 Fax (416) 293-1142
Media Contact, Robert Walsh, CEO

Officers

Pres., Jean Desgagne, Toronto
Treas., Peter Varley, Toronto
Vice-Pres., Nanci Harris, Toronto
Vice-Pres., Valerie Petroff, Oak Ridges
Vice-Pres., Heidi Stanley, Orillia
Past Pres., Larry Gillians, Napanee
CEO, Robert Walsh

Canadian Bible Society

The Canadian Bible Society is a non-denominational and inter-confessional organization that exists to translate, publish, distribute and encourage the use of the Scriptures, without doctrinal note or comment. Bible Society work was begun in Canada in 1804 by the British and Foreign Bible Society. In 1906, the various auxiliaries of the British and Foreign Bible Society joined together to form the Canadian Bible Society. Today, the Canadian Bible Society has 16 district offices across Canada, a Scripture Translation Office in Kitchener, a French Services Office in Montreal, and a National Support Office in Toronto. Additionally, the Bermuda Bible Society is constituted as an Associate District of the Canadian Bible Society. The Society holds quarterly Board meetings involving one elected representative from each of the districts and from the francophone sector. About 90% of the Society's revenue comes through the generosity of Canadian supporters in the form of donations, bequests and annuity income. Through the Canadian Bible Society's membership in the United States Societies' fellowship, over 67.5 million Bibles, Testaments and Portions were distributed globally in 2004. The complete Bible has been published in over 420 languages, with at least one book of the Bible available in 2377 languages.

Headquarters

C.B.S. National Support Office, 10 Carnforth Rd., Toronto, ON M4A 2S4 Tel. (416)757-4171 Fax (416)757-3376

Officers

National Director, Ted Seres, 10 Carnforth Rd., Toronto, ON M4A 2S4, Tel. (416)757-4171, Fax (416)757-1292, Email: tseres@bible society.ca
Director of Finance, Mr. Nesa Gulasekharam, 10 Carnforth Rd., Toronto, ON M4A 2S4, (416)757-4171, Fax: (416)757-3376, Email: ngulasekharam@biblesociety.ca
Director of Scripture Translation, Mr. Hart Wiens, Frederick Mall, 385 Frederick Street, Kitchener, ON N2H 2P2, Tel. (519)741-8285, Fax (519)741-8357, Email: hwiens@bible society.ca
Directeur du Secteur francophone, Liliane Gordon, 4050 avenue du Parc-Lafontaine, Montreal, QC H2L 3M8, Tel. (514)524-7873, Fax (514)524-6116, Email: lgordon@societe-biblique.ca
Director of Fund Development, Lisa Keizer, 10 Carnforth Rd., Toronto, ON M4A 2S4, Tel. (416)757-4171, Fax (416)757-3376, Email: lkeizer@biblesociety.ca
Director of Scripture Resources, Joel Coppieters, 10 Carnforth Rd., Toronto, ON M4A 2S4, Tel. (416)757-4171, Fax (416)757-3376, Email: lcoppieters@biblesociety.ca
Director of Communications, Marta LoFranco, 10 Carnforth Rd., Toronto, ON M4A 2S4, Tel. (416)757-4171, Fax (416)757-3376, Email: mlofranco@biblesociety.ca
Human Resources Manager/Volunteer Program Coordinator, Ms. Meggy Kwok, 10 Carnforth Rd., Toronto, ON M4A 2S4, Tel. (416)757-4171, Fax (416)757-3376, Email: mkwok@ biblesociety.ca

Canadian Centre for Ecumenism

The Centre has facilitated understanding and cooperation among believers of various Christian traditions and world religions since 1963. An active interdenominational Board of Directors meets annually.

Outreach, ECUMENISM, a quarterly publication, develops central themes such as Rites of Passage, Sacred Space, Interfaith Marriages, Care of the Earth, etc. through contributions from writers of various churches and religions in addition to its regular ecumenical news summaries, book reviews and resources.

A specialized library is open to the public for consultation in the areas of religion, dialogue, evangelism, ethics, spirituality, etc.

Conferences and sessions are offered on themes such as Ecumenism and Pastoral Work, Pluralism, World Religions, Prayer and Unity.

Headquarters

2065 Sherbrooke St. W. Montreal, QC H3H 1G6 Tel. (514)937-9176 Fax (514)937-4986
Email: ccocce@oecumenisme.ca
Website: www.oecumenisme.ca

Officers

Media Contact, Bernice Baranowski
Exec. Dir., Dr. Stuart Brown
Assistant Director, Adèle Brodeur

The Canadian Council of Churches

The Canadian Council of Churches was organized in 1944. Its basic purpose is to provide the churches with an agency for conference and consultation and for such common planning and common action as they desire to undertake. It encourages ecumenical understanding and action throughout Canada through local councils of churches. It also relates to the World Council of Churches and other agencies serving the worldwide ecumenical movement.

The Council has a Governing Board which meets semiannually and an Executive Committee. Program is administered through two commissions—Faith and Witness, Justice and Peace.

Headquarters

47 Queen's Park Crescent East, Toronto, ON M5S 2C3 Tel. (416)972-9494 ext. 22 Fax (416)927-0405
Media Contact, Rev. Dr. Karen Hamilton
Email: Hamilton@ccc-cce.ca
Website: www.ccc-cce.ca

Officers

President: Professor Richard Schneider, 47 Queen's Park Crescent East, Toronto ON M5S 2C3, Tel: (416)972-9494, E-mail: rschneid@yorku.ca
Vice Presidents: The Rev. Dr. James Taylor Christie, 47 Queen's Park Crescent East, Toronto ON M5S 2C3, Tel: (416)972-9494, E-mail: sperocontraspem@rogers.com; Ms. Sandra Demson, 47 Queen's Park Crescent East, Toronto ON M5S 2C3, Tel: (416)972-9494 Fax: (416)922-9328, E-mail: srd@idirect.com; The Rev. Dr. J. Daniel Gibson, 47 Queen's Park Crescent East, Toronto ON M5S 2C3, Tel: (416)972-9494, E-mail: gibsond@execulink.com
Treasurer: Mr. Don Taylor, 47 Queen's Park Crescent East, Toronto ON M5S 2C3 Tel: (416)972-9494, E-mail: maryanddontaylor@sympatico.ca
General Secretary: The Rev. Dr. Karen Hamilton, 47 Queen's Park Crescent East, Toronto ON M5S 2C3, Tel: (416)972-9494 ext.22, E-mail: hamilton@ccc-cce.ca

MEMBER CHURCHES

Anglican Church Canada
Archdiocese of Canada of the Orthodox Church in America
Armenian Orthodox Church-Diocese of Canada
Baptist Convention of Ontario and Quebec
British Methodist Episcopal Church of Canada*
Canadian Conference of Catholic Bishops
Canadian Yearly Meeting of the Religious Society of Friends, Quakers
Christian Church (Disciples of Christ)
Christian Reformed Church in North America-Canadian Ministries
Coptic Orthodox Church of Canada
Ethiopian Orthodox Church in Canada
Evangelical Lutheran Church in Canada
Greek Orthodox Metropolis of Toronto(Canada)
Mennonite Church Canada
Old Catholic Church Union of Utrecht
Presbyterian Church in Canada
Regional Synod of Canada–Reformed Church in America
The Salvation Army - Canada and Bermuda
The United Church of Canada
Ukrainian Orthodox Church of Canada
*Associate Member

Canadian Evangelical Theological Association

In May 1990, about 60 scholars, pastors and other interested persons met together in Toronto to form a new theological society. Arising out of the Canadian chapter of the Evangelical Theological Society, the new association established itself as a distinctly Canadian group with a new name. It sponsored its first conference as CETA in Kingston, Ontario, in May 1991.

CETA provides a forum for scholarly contributions to the renewal of theology and church in Canada. CETA seeks to promote theological work which is loyal to Christ and his Gospel, faithful to the primacy and authority of Scripture and responsive to the guiding force of the historic creeds and Protestant confessions of the Christian Church. In its newsletters and conferences, CETA seeks presentations that will speak to a general theologically-educated audience, rather than to specialists.

CETA has special interest in evangelical points of view upon and contributions to the wider conversations regarding religious studies and church life. Members therefore include pastors, students and other interested persons as well as professional academicians. CETA currently includes about 100 members, many of whom attend its annual conference in the early summer. It publishes the Canadian Evangelical Review and supports an active internet discussion group, which may be accessed by emailing ceta-l@egroups.com.

Headquarters
Peter Robinson, 6121 Heritage Park Cres., Orleans, ON K1C 7G6
Email: p.s.robinson@rogers.com
Media Contact, Peter Robinson

Officers
President: Dr. Jeffrey A. McPherson
Secretary-Treasurer: Peter Robinson
Editor, Canadian Evangelical Review: Dr. Archie Spencer
Executive Members-at-large: Chris Holmes, Dustin Resch

Canadian Tract Society
The Canadian Tract Society was organized in 1970 as an independent distributor of Gospel leaflets to provide Canadian churches and individual Christians with quality materials proclaiming the Gospel through the printed page. It is affiliated with the American Tract Society, which encouraged its formation and assisted in its founding, and for whom it serves as an exclusive Canadian distributor. The CTS is a nonprofit international service ministry.

Headquarters
P.O. Box 2156, LCD 1, Brampton, ON L6T 3S4
Tel. (905)457-4559 Fax (905)457-0529
Media Contact, Mgr., Donna Croft

Officers
Director-Sec., Robert J. Burns
Director, John Neufeld
Director, Patricia Burns

Canadian Society of Biblical Studies-Société Canadienne des Études Bibliques
The object of the Society shall be to stimulate the critical investigation of the classical biblical literatures, together with other related literature, by the exchange of scholarly research both in published form and in public forum.

Headquarters
Media Contact, Exec. Sec., Michele Murray, Dept. of Religion, Bishop's University, Lennoxville,

PQ J1M 1Z7, Email: mmurray@ ubishops.ca, Website www.ccsr.ca/csbs

Officers
Pres., Mary Rose D'Angelo, Dept. of Theology, University of Notre Dame, Notre Dame, IN 46556, Tel.: (219)631-7040, Fax: (219)631-6842,
Vice-Pres., J. Glen Taylor, Wycliffe College, 5 Hoskin Ave., Toronto, ON M57 1H7, Tel.: (416)946-3541, Fax: (416)946-3541; Email: glen.Taylor@utoronto.ca
Exec. Sec., Michele Murray, Dept. of Religion, Bishop's University, Lennoxville, QC J1M 1Z7, Tel.: (819)822-9600, Fax: (819)822-9661, Email: mmurray@ubishops.ca
Treas., Robert A. Derrenbacker, Jr., Regent College, 5800 University Blvd, Vancouver, BC, V6T 2E4, Tel.: (604)221-3349, Fax: (604)224-3097; Email: rderrenbacker@regent-college.edu
Prog. Coord., Christine Mitchell, St. Andrews College, 1121 College Dr., Saskatoon, SK S7N 0W3, Email: ckm365@duke.usask.ca
Comm. Officer, Richard Ascough, Queens' Theological College, Kingston, ON K7L 3N6, Tel. (613)533-6000, Fax: (613)533-6879, Email: rsa@post.queensu.ca
Student Liason Officer, Derek Suderman, Emmanuel College, 11739 McCowan Rd., Stouffville, ON L4A 7X5, Email: derek.suderman@utoronto.ca

The Church Army in Canada
The Church Army in Canada has been involved in evangelism and Christian social service since 1929. Church Army is a Society of Evangelists dedicated to helping bring people from all walks of life into a living relationship with Jesus Christ and His people. We are pressing on toward 80 years in Canada with these endeavours, and many more worldwide.

Headquarters
105 Mountain View Dr., Saint John, NB E2J 5B5
Tel. (888)316-8169 Fax (506)657-8217
Email: hello@churcharmy.com
Media Contact, National Director., Capt. R. Bruce Smith

Officers
National Dir., Capt. R. Bruce Smith
Bd. Chmn., Mr. Peter Bloom

The Churches' Council on Theological Education in Canada, An Ecumenical Foundation
The Churches' Council (CCTE,EF) maintains an overview of theological education in Canada on behalf of its constituent churches and functions as a bridge between the schools of theology and the churches which they serve.

Founded in 1970 with a national and ecumenical mandate, the CCTE,EF provides resources for research into matters pertaining to theological education, opportunities for consultation and cooperation and a limited amount of funding in the form of grants for the furtherance of ecumenical iniatives in theological education.

Headquarters
47 Queen's Park Cres., E., Toronto, ON M5S 2C3 Tel. (416)928-3223 Fax (416)928-3563
Media Contact, Exec. Dir., Robert Faris
Website: www.ccte.ca E-mail: director@ccte.ca

Officers
Bd. of Dir., Chpsn., Dr. Richard C. Crossman, Waterloo Lutheran Seminary, 75 University Ave. W., Waterloo, ON N2L 3C5
Bd. of Dir., Vice-Chpsn., Dr. Dorcas Gordon, Knox College
Treas., Mr. Brian Cox
Exec. Dir., Robert Faris

MEMBER ORGANIZATIONS
The General Synod of the Anglican Church of Canada
Canadian Baptist Ministries
The Evangelical Lutheran Church in Canada
The Presbyterian Church in Canada
The Canadian Conference of Catholic Bishops
The United Church of Canada

Evangelical Fellowship of Canada

The Fellowship was formed in 1964. There are 31 denominations, 124 organizations, 1,200 local churches and 11,000 individual members.

Its purposes are, "Fellowship in the gospel" (Phil. Ch.1 vs.5), "the defence and confirmation of the gospel" (Phil. Ch.1 vs.7) and "the furtherance of the gospel" (Phil. Ch.1 vs.12). The Fellowship believes the Holy Scriptures, as originally given, are infallible and that salvation through the Lord Jesus Christ is by faith apart from works. In national and regional conventions the Fellowship urges Christians to live exemplary lives and to openly challenge the evils and injustices of society. It encourages cooperation with various agencies in Canada and overseas that are sensitive to social and spiritual needs. The Evangelical Fellowship of Canada (EFC) is the national association of evangelical Christians in Canada. It gathers Evangelicals together for impact, influence and identity in ministry and public witness. Since 1964 the EFC has provided a national forum for Evangelicals and a constructive voice for biblical principles in life and society. The EFC affiliates include denominations, ministry organizations, educational institutions and individual congregations, who uphold a common statement of faith. The EFC also has more than 15,000 supporting individuals.

Headquarters
Office, 600 Alden Rd. Ste. 300, Markham, ON L3R 0E7 Tel. (905)479-5885 Fax (905)479-4742

Mailing Address, M.I.P. Box 3745, Markham, ON L3R 0Y4
Media Contact, Pres., Dr. Gary Walsh, 600 Alden Rd., Ste. 300, Markham, ON L3R 0E7 Tel. (905)479-5885 Fax (905)479-4742

Officers
Pres., Bruce J. Clemenger
Chair, Dr. Paul Magnus
Vice-Chair, Dr. Rick Penner
Treas., Lt. Col. David Luginbuhl
Past Pres., Dr. Brian Stiller

EXECUTIVE COMMITTEE
Rev. Scott Campbell; Rev. Carson Pue; Ms. Ruth Andrews; Rev. Stewart Hunter; Ms. Jacqueline Dugas; Dr. Rick Penner; Lt. Col. David Luginbuhl; Dr. Ralph Richardson; Rev. Abe Funk; Rev. Gillis Killam; Dr. Paul Magnus; Rev. Winston Thurton
Task Force on Evangelism-(Vision Canada), Interim Chair, Gary Walsh
Social Action Commission, Chpsn., Dr. James Read
Education Commission, Chpsn., Dr. Glenn Smith
Women in Ministry Task Force, Chpsn., Rev. Eileen Stewart-Rhude
Aboriginal Task Force, Co-Chairs, Ray Aldred; Wendy Peterson
Religious Liberties Commission, Chpsn., Dr. Paul Marshall
Task Force on Global Mission, Chpsn., Dr. Geoff Tunnicliffe

Inter-Varsity Christian Fellowship of Canada

Inter-Varsity Christian Fellowship is a non-profit, interdenominational student movement centering on the witness to Jesus Christ in campus communities, universities, colleges and high schools and through a Canada-wide Pioneer Camping program.

IVCF was officially formed in 1928-29 by the late Dr. Howard Guinness, whose arrival from Britain challenged students to follow the example of the British Inter-Varsity Fellowship by organizing themselves into prayer and Bible study fellowship groups. Inter-Varsity has always been a student-initiated movement emphasizing and developing leadership in the campus to call Christians to outreach, challenging other students to a personal faith in Jesus Christ and studying the Bible as God's revealed truth within a fellowship of believers. A strong stress has been placed on missionary activity, and the triennial conference held at Urbana, IL. (jointly sponsored by U.S. and Canadian IVCF) has been a means of challenging many young people to service in Christian vocations. Inter-Varsity works closely with and is a strong believer in the work of local and national churches.

51

Headquarters
64 Prince Andrew Place, Toronto, ON M3C 2H4
Tel. (416)443-1170 Fax (416)443-1499
Media Contact, Pres., Geri Rodman

Officers
President and CEO, Geri Rodman, 64 Prince
Andrew Place, Toronto, ON M3C 2H4 Tel.
(416)443-1170 ext. 117, Fax (416)443-1499,
Email: grodman@ivcf.ca

Interchurch Communications

Interchurch Communications is made up of
the communication units of the Anglican
Church of Canada, the Evangelical Lutheran
Church in Canada, the Presbyterian Church in
Canada, the Canadian Conference of Catholic
Bishops (English Sector), and the United
Church of Canada. ICC members collaborate on
occasional video or print coproductions and on
addressing public policy issues affecting reli-
gious communications.

Headquarters
3250 Bloor St. W., Etobicoke, ON M8X 2Y4

MEMBERS
Mr. William Kokesch, Canadian Conference of
Catholic Bishops, 90 Parent Ave., Ottawa, ON
K1N 7B1 Tel. (613)241-9461 Fax (613)241-
8117, Email: kokesch@cccb.ca
Religious Television Associates, 3250 Bloor St.
W., Etobicoke, ON M8X 2Y4 Tel. (416)231-
7680 Fax (416)232-6004

John Howard Society of Ontario

The John Howard Society of Ontario is a registered non-profit charitable organization providing services to individuals, families and groups at
all stages in the youth and criminal justice system. The Society also provides community education on critical issues in the justice system and
advocacy for reform of the justice system. The
mandate of the Society is the prevention of crime
through service, community education, advocacy
and reform.

Founded in 1929, the Society has grown from
a one-office service in Toronto to 17 local
branches providing direct services in the major
cities of Ontario and a provincial office providing justice policy analysis, advocacy for reform
and support to branches.

Headquarters
6 Jackson Pl., Toronto, ON M6P 1T6 Tel.
(416)604-8412 Fax (416)604-8948
Media Contact, Exec. Dir., William Sparks

Officers
Pres., Susan Reid-MacNevin, Dept. of Sociology,
Univ. Of Guelph, Guelph, ON N1G 2W1
Vice-Pres., Richard Beaupe, 4165 Fernand St.,
Hamner, ON B3A 1X4
Treas., Jack Battler, Waterloo, ON

Sec., Peter Angeline, OISE, 252 Bloor St. W.,
Toronto, ON
Exec. Dir., William Sparks

LOCAL SOCIETIES
Collins Bay; Hamilton; Kingston; Lindsay;
London; Niagara; Oshawa; Ottawa; Peel;
Peterborough; Sarnia; Sault Ste. Marie;
Sudbury; Thunder Bay; Toronto; Waterloo;
Windsor

Lutheran Council in Canada

The Lutheran Council in Canada was orga-
nized in 1967 and is a cooperative agency of the
Evangelical Lutheran Church in Canada and
Lutheran Church-Canada.

The Council's activities include communications, coordinative service and national liaison in
social ministry, chaplaincy and scout activity.

Headquarters
302-393 Portage Ave., Winnipeg, MB R3B 3H6
Tel. (204)984-9150 Fax (204)984-9185
Media Contact, Pres., Rev. Ralph Mayan, 3074
Portage Ave., Winnipeg, MB R3K 0Y2 Tel.
(204)895-3433 Fax (204)897-4319

Officers
Pres., Bishop Raymond Schultz
Sec., Rev. Leon C. Gilbertson
Vice Pres., Rev. Ralph Mayan

Mennonite Central Committee Canada (MCCC)

Mennonite Central Committee Canada was
organized in 1964 to continue the work which
several regional Canadian inter-Mennonite agencies had been doing in relief, service, immigration and peace. All but a few of the smaller
Mennonite groups in Canada belong to MCC
Canada.

MCCC is part of the Mennonite Central
Committee (MCC) International which has its
headquarters in Akron, Pa. from where most of
the overseas development and relief projects are
administered. In 2000-2001 MCCC's income
was $25 million, about 47 percent of the total
MCC income. There were 408 Canadians out of
a total of 867 MCC workers serving in North
America and abroad during the same time period.

The MCC office in Winnipeg administers projects located in Canada. Domestic programs of
Voluntary Service, Native Concerns, Peace and
Social Concerns, Food Program, Employment
Concerns, Ottawa Office, Victim-Offender
Ministries, Mental Health and Immigration are
all part of MCC's Canadian ministry. Whenever
it undertakes a project, MCCC attempts to relate
to the church or churches in the area.

Headquarters
134 Plaza Dr., Winnipeg, MB R3T 5K9 Tel.
(204)261-6381 Fax (204)269-9875

52

Communications, Rick Fast, 134 Plaza Dr., Winnipeg, MT R3T 5K9 Tel. (204)261-6381 Fax (204)269-9875

Officers
Exec. Dir., Donald Peters

Project Ploughshares

Project Ploughshares is an ecumenical peace centre of the Canadian Council of Churches, established in 1976 to implement the churches' imperative to seek and pursue peace. Project Ploughshares works with churches, governments, and non-governmental organizations, in Canada and internationally, to identify, develop, and advance approaches that build peace and prevent war, and promote the peaceful resolution of political conflict. Project Ploughshares is sponsored by eight national Canadian churches and is affiliated with the Institute of Peace and Conflict Studies, Conrad Grebel University College, University of Waterloo. Publications include The Ploughshares Monitor (quarterly), The Armed Conflicts Report (annually), Briefings and Working Papers (occasional).

Headquarters
Project Ploughshares, 57 Erb Street West, Waterloo, ON, Canada N2L 6C2 Tel. (519)888-6541 Fax (519)888-0188, E-mail: plough@ plough shares.ca, Website: www.ploughshares.ca
Media Contact: Director, John Siebert, (519)888 6541 X 702, jsiebert@ploughshares.ca

Officers
Executive Director, John Siebert
Associate Director, Nancy Regehr
Chair, Moira Hutchinson
Treasurer, Philip Creighton
Secretary, Rev. Dr. Martin Rumscheidt

SPONSORING ORGANIZATIONS
Anglican Church of Canada
Canadian Catholic Organization for Development & Peace
Canadian Unitarian Council
Canadian Voice of Women for Peace
Canadian Yearly Meeting, Religious Society of Friends
Evangelical Lutheran Church in Canada
Mennonite Central Committee Canada
Presbyterian Church in Canada
United Church of Canada

Religious Television Associates

Religious Television Associates was formed in the early 1960s for the production units of the Anglican, Baptist, Presbyterian, Roman Catholic Churches and the United Church of Canada. In the intervening years, the Baptists have withdrawn and the Lutherans have come in. RTA provides an ecumenical umbrella for joint productions in broadcasting and develop-

ment education. The directors are the heads of the Communications Departments participating in Interchurch Communications.

Headquarters
c/o The United Church of Canada, 3250 Bloor St. W., Etobicoke, ON M8X 2Y4 Tel. (416)231-7680 ext. 4076 Fax (416)231-3103
Media Contact, Shane Chadden

Participants
The Anglican Church of Canada
Canadian Conference of Catholic Bishops
The Canadian Council of Churches
The Evangelical Lutheran Church in Canada
The Presbyterian Church in Canada
The United Church of Canada

Scripture Union

Scripture Union is an international interdenominational missionary movement working in 130 countries.

Scripture Union aims to work with the churches to make God's Good News known to children, young people and families and to encourage people of all ages to meet God daily through the Bible and prayer.

In Canada, a range of daily Bible guides are offered to individuals, churches, and bookstores from age four through adult. Sunday School curriculum and various evangelism and discipling materials are also offered for sale.

Children's ministry is offered to churches through summer sports camps and training for sports outreach programs.

Headquarters
1885 Clements Rd., Unit 226, Pickering, ON L1W 3V4 Tel. (905)427-4947 Fax (905) 427-0334
Media Contact, President, John Irwin, Email: jirwinc617@rogers.com

Officers
Chair of the Board, Harold Murray, 216 McKinnon Pl. NE, Calgary, AB T2E 7B9, Tel. (403)276-4716, Email: hjmurray@home.com
President, Robert Szo, 1885 Clements Rd., Unit 226, Pickering, ON L1W 3V4, Email: robert@scriptureunion.ca

Student Christian Movement of Canada

The Student Christian Movement of Canada was formed in 1921 from the student arm of the YMCA. It has its roots in the Social Gospel movements of the late 19th and early 20th centuries. Throughout its intellectual history, the SCM in Canada has sought to relate the Christian faith to the living realities of the social and political context of each student generation.

The present priorities are built around the need to form more and stronger critical Christian communities on Canadian campuses within which individuals may develop their social and political analyses, experience spiritual growth and fellowship and bring Christian ecumenical witness to the university.

The Student Christian Movement of Canada is affiliated with the World Student Christian Federation.

Headquarters
310 Danforth Ave., Toronto, ON M4K 1N6 Tel. (416)463-4312 Fax (416)466-6854
Media Contact, Natl. Coord., Sheilagh McGlynn

Officers
Natl. Coord., Sheilagh McGlynn, Email: info@scmcanada.org

Women's Inter-Church Council of Canada

Women's Inter-Church Council of Canada is a national Christian women's council that encourages women to grow in ecumenism, to strengthen ecumenical community, to share their spirituality and prayer, to engage in dialogue about women's concerns and to stand in solidarity with one another. The Council calls women to respond to national and international issues affecting women and to take action together for justice. WICC sponsors the World Day of Prayer and Fellowship of the Least Coin in Canada. Human rights projects for women are supported and a quarterly magazine "Making Waves" distributed.

Headquarters
47 Queen's Park Cres. E, Toronto, ON M5S 2C3 Tel. (416)929-5184 Fax (416)929-4064
Media Contact, Communications Coordinator, Gillian Barfoot

Officers
Pres., Claire Heron
Exec. Dir., Pat Allinson

CHURCH MEMBER BODIES
African Methodist Episcopal, Anglican Church of Canada, Canadian Baptist Ministries, Christian Church (Disciples of Christ), Evangelical Lutheran Church in Canada, Mennonite Central Committee, Presbyterian Church in Canada, Religious Society of Friends, Roman Catholic Church, The Salvation Army in Canada, United Church of Canada

World Vision Canada

World Vision Canada is a Christian humanitarian relief and development organization. Although its main international commitment is to translate child sponsorship into holistic, sustainable community development, World Vision also allocates resources to help Canada's poor and complement the mission of the church.

World Vision's Reception Centre assists government-sponsored refugees entering Canada. The NeighbourLink program mobilizes church volunteers to respond locally to people's needs. A quarterly publication, Context, provides data on the Canadian family to help churches effectively reach their communities. The development education program provides resources on development issues. During the annual 30-Hour Famine, people fast for 30 hours while discussing poverty and raising funds to support aid programs.

Headquarters
1 World Dr., Mississauga, ON L5T 2Y4 Tel. (905)821-3030 Fax (905)821-1356
Media Contact, Philip Maher, Tel. (905) 567-2726

Officers
Pres., Dave Toycen
Vice-Pres., Intl. & Govt. Relations, Linda Tripp; Natl. Programs, Don Posterski; Fin. & Admin., Charlie Fluit; Donor Development Group, Brian Tizzard

Young Men's Christian Association in Canada

The YMCA began as a Christian association to help young men find healthy recreation and meditation, as well as opportunities for education, in the industrial slums of 19th century England. It came to Canada in 1851 with the same mission in mind for young men working in camps and on the railways.

Today, the YMCA maintains its original mission, helping individuals to grow and develop in spirit, mind and body, but attends to those needs for men and women of all ages and religious beliefs. The YMCA registers 1.5 million participants in 250 communities that are served by 64 autonomous associations across Canada.

The program of each association differs according to the needs of the community, but most offer one or more programs in each of the following categories, health and fitness, child care, employment councelling and training, recreation, camping, community support and outreach, international development and short-term accommodation.

The YMCA encourages people of all ages, races, abilities, income and beliefs to come together in an environment which promotes balance in life, breaking down barriers and helping to create healthier communities.

Headquarters
42 Charles St. E., 6th Floor., Toronto, ON M4Y 1T4 Tel. (416)967-9622 Fax (416)967-9618
Media Contact, Sol Kasimer

Officers
Chpsn., Ray Mantha
CEO, Sol Kasimer

Young Women's Christian Association of-du Canada

The YWCA of-du Canada is a national voluntary organization serving 44 YWCAs and YM-YWCAs across Canada. Dedicated to the development and improved status of women and their families, the YWCA is committed to service delivery and to being a source of public education on women's issues and an advocate of social change. Services provided by YWCAs and YM-YWCAs include adult education programs, residences and shelters, child care, fitness activities, wellness programs and international development education. As a member of the World YWCA, the YWCA of-du Canada is part of the largest women's organization in the world.

Headquarters
80 Gerrard St. E., Toronto, ON M5B 1G6 Tel. (416)593-9886 Fax (416)971-8084
Media Contact, Int. CEO, Margaret MacKenzie

Officers
Pres., Ann Mowatt

Youth for Christ-Canada

Youth For Christ is an interdenominational organization founded in 1944 by Torrey Johnson. Under the leadership of YFC's 11 national board of directors, Youth For Christ-Canada cooperates with churches and serves as a mission agency reaching out to young people and their families through a variety of ministries.

YFC seeks to have maximum influence in a world of youth through high-interest activities and personal involvement. Individual attention is given to each teenager through small group involvement and counselling. These activities and relationships become vehicles for communicating the message of the Gospel.

Headquarters
822-167 Lombard Ave., Winnipeg, MB R3B 0V3 Tel. (204)989-0056 Fax (204)989-0067

Officers
Natl. Dir., Randy L. Steinwand

3. Religious Bodies in the United States

The United States, with its staunch constitutional stance on religious freedom and successive waves of immigrants over the last three centuries, has proved to be a fertile soil for the development of varied Christian traditions. In the directory that follows, some 227 distinct church traditions are represented. Many of these groups represent the processes of dividing and re-uniting that are a hallmark of American religious life. Many churches listed here represent those with a long tradition in Europe, Africa, or Asia predating their American tenure. Others are American-born churches. The researcher may be helped by consulting the churches grouped by tradition at the end of this directory in the section entitled, "Religious Bodies in the United States Arranged by Families." In this section, all the Baptists bodies are listed together, all the Lutheran bodies, Methodists, etc.

The following directory information is supplied by the national headquarters of each church. Each listing contains a brief description of the church, followed by the national headquarters contact information, which includes a mailing address, telephone and fax numbers, email and website addresses (when available), and the name of the media contact. After the headquarters, there are data regarding the church officers or leaders, including names, titles, and contact information (when contact information differs from the headquarters). There is a staggering array of churches, each with its own form of organization; not all of them refer to their leaders as "officers." In some places, the reader will find the term "Bishops," "Board Members," or "Executives" in place of "Officers." Finally, when applicable, each entry contains a list of the names of church publications.

The churches are printed in alphabetical order by the official name of the organization. There are a few instances in which certain churches are more commonly known by another name. In such cases, the reader is referred incidentally within the text to the appropriate official name. Churches that are member communions of the National Council of the Churches of Christ in the U.S.A. are marked with an asterisk (*).

Other useful information about the churches listed here can be found in other chapters or directories within the book: Statistical information for these churches can be found in the tables toward the end of this book in Section III. Further, more extensive information about the publications listed in this directory can be found in Directory 10, "Religious Periodicals in the United States."

The organizations listed here represent the denominations to which the vast majority of church members in the United States belong. It does not include all religious bodies functioning in the United States. The Encyclopedia of American Religions (Gale Research Inc., P.O. Box 33477, Detroit MI 48232-5477) contains names and addresses of additional religious bodies.

Advent Christian Church

The Advent Christian Church is a conservative, evangelical denomination which grew out of the Millerite movement of the 1830s and 1840s. The members stress the authority of Scripture, justification by faith in Jesus Christ alone, the importance of evangelism, disciple-making, and world missions and the soon visible return of Jesus Christ.

Organized in 1860, the Advent Christian Church maintains headquarters in Charlotte, N.C., with regional offices in Rochester, N. H., Princeton, N.C., Ellisville, MO., Sumas, WA, and Lenoir, N.C. Missions are maintained in India, Nigeria, Ghana, Japan, Liberia, Croatia, New Zealand, Malaysia, the Philippines, Mexico, South Africa, Namibia, Honduras, China, Kenya, Malawi, Mozambique, Congo, Romania, and Memphis, Tenn.

The Advent Christian Church maintains doctrinal distinctives in three areas- conditional immortality, the sleep of the dead until the return of Christ and belief that the kingdom of God will be established on earth made new by Jesus Christ.

Headquarters
P.O. Box 690848, Charlotte, NC 28227, Tel. (704)545-6161 x202 Fax (704)573-0712
Media Contact, Exec. Director, Ronald P. Thomas, Jr.

Email: execdirect@adventchristian.org
Website: www.adventchristian.org

Periodicals
Advent Christian News, Maranatha, Advent Christian Witness, Prayer & Praise, Weekly E-newsletter; www.ACGC.us

African Methodist Episcopal Church*

This church began in 1787 in Philadelphia when persons in St. George's Methodist Episcopal Church withdrew as a protest against color segregation. In 1816 the denomination was started, led by Rev. Richard Allen who had been ordained deacon by Bishop Francis Asbury and was subsequently ordained elder and elected and consecrated bishop.

Headquarters
3801 Market St., Suite 300, Philadelphia, PA 29204, Tel. (215)662-0506
Email: cio@ame-church.com
Website: www.AME-Church.com

Officers
Senior Bishop, Bishop John Richard Bryant, Presiding Bishop, Fourth Episcopal District, African Methodist Episcopal Church, 5627 South Michigan Avenue, 3rd Floor, Chicago, IL 60637, Tel. (773)955-9825 Fax (773)955-9840.

Chief Ecumenical & Urban Affairs Officer, Bishop John F. White, African Methodist Episcopal Church, 4601 Sheridan Street, Suite 318, Hollywood, FL 33021., Tel. (954)438-6378; Fax (954)438-9243.

Pres., Gen. Bd., Bishop William Phillips DeVeaux Sr., 2900 Chamblee-Tucker Road, Bldg 3, Atlanta, GA 30341, Tel. (770)220-1770 Fax (770)220-9996.

Pres. Council of Bishops 2009 – 2010, Bishop Carolyn Tyler Guidry, 5450 Executive Place, Jackson, MS 39206, Tel. (601)366-8240; Fax (601)366-8175

GENERAL OFFICERS

Dr. Clement W. Fugh; Dr. Richard Allen Lewis; Dr. Daryl B. Ingram; Dr. Johnny Barbour; Jr., Dr. George F. Flowers; Dr. Dennis C. Dickerson; Dr. Jerome V. Harris; Dr. James Wade; Dr. Calvin H. Sydnor, III

Bishop John F. White, Ecumenical Officer/ Chaplains; Bishop Richard Franklin Norris (First Episcopal Dist.); Bishop Adam Jefferson Richardson, Jr. (Second Episcopal Dist.); Bishop Cornal Garnett Henning Sr. (Third Episcopal Dist.); Bishop John R. Bryant (Fourth Episcopal Dist.); Bishop T. Larry Kirkland (Fifth Episcopal Dist.); Bishop William Phillips DeVeaux (Sixth Episcopal Dist.); Bishop Preston Warren Williams, II (Seventh Episcopal Dist.); Bishop Carolyn Tyler Guidry (Eighth Episcopal Dist.); Bishop James L. Davis (Ninth Episcopal Dist.); Bishop Gregory Gerald McKinley Ingram (Tenth Episcopal Dist.); Bishop McKinley Young (Eleventh Episcopal Dist.); Bishop Samuel L. Green Sr. (Twelfth Episcopal Dist.); Bishop Vashti Murphy McKenzie (Thirteenth Episcopal Dist.); Bishop David Rwhynica Daniels, Jr. (Fourteenth Episcopal Dist.); Bishop Wilfred J. Messiah (Fifteenth Episcopal Dist.); Bishop Sarah F. Davis (Sixteenth Episcopal Dist.); Bishop Paul Jones Mulenga Kawimbe (Seventeenth Episcopal Dist.); Bishop E. Earl McCloud Jr. (Eighteenth Episcopal Dist.); Bishop Jeffrey N. Leath (Nineteenth Episcopal Dist.); Bishop Julius McAllister Sr. (Twentieth Episcopal District)

Periodicals

The A.M.E. Review, The Christian Recorder, Journal of Christian Education, Women's Missionary Magazine, Secret Chamber, Voice of Mission

The African Methodist Episcopal Zion Church*

The A.M.E. Zion Church is an independent body, having withdrawn from the John Street Methodist Church of New York City in 1796. The first bishop was James Varick.

Headquarters

Dept. of Records & Research, 3225 West Sugar Creek Rd., Charlotte, NC 28269 Tel.(704)599-4630 Fax (704)688-2549, Email: jlgsa@aol.com

Media Contact, Gen. Sec.-Aud., Dr. W. Robert Johnson, III

Email: gensec17@yahoo.com; eljohnson@amez hqtr.org

Website: www.amez.org

Officers

Sr. Bishop, Bishop George W.C. Walker, Sr.

BOARD OF BISHOPS OFFICERS
Sr. Bishop, Bishop George W.C. Walker, Sr.

BOARD OF BISHOPS OFFICERS

*Pres., Warren M. Brown, 12904 Canoe Court, Fort Washington, MD 20744, Tel. (301)203-1677; Office: 9500 Arena Drive, Suite 102, Largo, MD 20774, Tel. (301)322-3866; Fax: (301)322-3862, Email: amezmidatlantic2@aol.com

Sec., Kenneth Monroe, 4633 Old Lowery Road, Shannon, NC 28386; Tel. (910)843-8274; Fax (910)843-8702, Office Phone (910)987-1991, Episcopal Address: 1408 Jack White Drive, Rock Hill, SC 29732 Tel. (803)328-1068, Email: Zion95@embarqmail.com

Asst. Sec., Louis Hunter, Sr., P.O. Box 2987, Suwanee, GA 30024, OR, 1314 Churchill Downs Dr., Waxhaw, NC 28173, Office Tel. (678)482-5937 Fax (678)714-1686, Email: Bishoplhunter@aol.com

Treas., George W.C. Walker, Sr., 1314 Churchill Downs Dr., Waxhaw, NC 28173; Tel. (704)243-3880, Fax (704)243-3882; Mailing Address: P.O. Box 26770, Charlotte, NC 28221-6770, Office: 3225 W. Sugar Creek Rd., Charlotte, NC 28269 Tel. (704)599-4630, Fax (704)688-2540, Email: gwalker046@aol.com

*Note: Presidency rotates every six (6) Months according to seniority.

ACTIVE MEMBERS

George Edward Battle Jr., 18403 Dembridge Lane, Davidson, NC 28036 Tel. (704)895-2236, Office: Two Wachovia Center, 301 South Tryon St., Suite 1755, Charlotte, NC 28202 Tel. (704)332-7600 Fax (704)343-3745 Email: gebjneed@bellsouth.net

Warren Matthew Brown, 12904 Canoe Court, Ft. Washington, MD 20744 Tel. (301)203-1677, Office: 9500 Arena Drive, Suite 102, Largo, MD 20774; Tel. (301)322-3866 Fax (301)322-3862, Email: amezmidatlantic2@aol.com

Samuel Chuka Ekemam, Sr., Office-Mail: A.M.E. Zion Church Area Headquarters, 1 Zion Hill Plaza, (Ugwu Orji), Okigwe Road, P.O. Box 8000, Owerri, Imo State, Nigeria. Home Phone from US: (1pm-5pm EST) 011-234-808-680-3447; Direct Line: 011-234-803-213-3767; Office from US: 011-234-803-301-8280, Email: bishopamezng@yahoo.com

Mildred B. Hines, 2011 Stearns Drive, Los Angeles, CA 90034 Tel. (323)559-0098, Email: mildred.hines@att.net

Roy A. Holmes, 22071 Sunset Dr., Richton Park, IL 60471 Tel. (708)679-1552 Fax (708)679-1562, Email: bishopraholmes92@sbcglobal.net

Louis Hunter, Sr., P.O. Box 2987, Suwanee, GA 30024 Office Tel. (678)482-5937 Fax (678)714-1686, Email: bishoplhunter@aol.com

James E. McCoy, 808 South Lawrence St., Montgomery, AL 36104-5055 Tel. (334)269-6365 Fax (334)269-6369, Email: aflamez@bellsouth.net
Kenneth Monroe, 4633 Old Lowery Road, Shannon, NC 28386 Tel. (910)843-8274 Fax (910)843-8702; Office Phone (910)987-1991, Episcopal Address: 1408 Jack White Drive, Rock Hill, SC 29732 Tel. (803)328-1068, Email: Zion95@embarqmail.com
Dennis V. Proctor, 8369 Governor Grayson Way, Ellicott City, MD 21043 Tel. (410)418-4364 Fax (410)418-5834, Email: Bishopproctor@aol.com
Darryl B. Starnes, Sr., 3220 Brownes Creek Road, Charlotte, NC 28269 Tel. (704)599-8718 Fax (704)599-5407, Email: BishopDBStarnes@aol.com
Richard Keith Thompson, Office: 3050 Berks Way, Raleigh, NC 27614 Tel. (919)554-8994; Fax (919)556-6049. Email: enced@ncrrbiz.com
George W.C. Walker, Sr., 1314 Churchill Downs Drive, Waxhaw, NC 28173; Tel. (704)243-3880, Fax (704)243-3882; Mailing Address: P.O. Box 26770, Charlotte, NC 28221-6770, Office: 3225 W. Sugar Creek Road, Charlotte, NC 28269 Tel. (704)599-4630 Fax (704)688-2540, Email: gwalker046@aol.com

RETIRED MEMBERS
Cecil Bishop, P.O. Box 78535, Charlotte, NC 28271 Tel. (704)996-7669 Fax (704)770-0348
Clarence Carr, 965 Charlton Trace, Marietta, GA 30064 Tel. (770)420-9332
Nathaniel Jarrett, Jr., 18031 South Pheasant Lake Dr., Tinley Park, IL 60477 Tel. (708)802-9873 Fax (708)429-3911
Joseph Johnson, 320 Walnut Point Dr., Matthews, NC 28105 Tel. (704)849-0521; Email: djjj85@windstream.net
Marshall H. Strickland, 2000 Cedar Circle Drive, Baltimore, MD 21228 Tel. (410)744-7330 Fax (410)788-5510

EPISCOPAL ASSIGNMENTS
Piedmont Episcopal District: Blue Ridge, West Central North Carolina, Western North Carolina, Jamaica (all divisions) Conferences: Bishop George W. C. Walker, Sr.
Eastern West Africa Episcopal District: Central Nigeria, Lagos - West Nigeria, Nigeria, Northern Nigeria, Rivers, Mainland, Cross River, South Eastern, and Southern Conferences: Bishop Samuel Chuka Ekemam, Sr.
North Eastern Episcopal District: New England, New York, Western New York, and Bahamas Islands Conferences: Bishop George Edward Battle, Jr.
Eastern North Carolina Episcopal District: Albemarle, Cape Fear, Central North Carolina, North Carolina, Virgin Islands, and South Africa (Zimbabwe) Conferences: Bishop Richard Keith Thompson
Mid-Atlantic II Episcopal District: East Tennessee-Virginia, India, London-Midlands,

Philadelphia-Baltimore, Virginia, East Angola, West Angola Conferences: Bishop Warren M. Brown
Mid-West Episcopal District: Indiana, Kentucky, Michigan, Missouri, Tennessee, and Central Africa: Bishop Roy A. Holmes
Mid-Atlantic I Episcopal District: Allegheny, New Jersey, Ohio, Guyana/Suriname, Trinidad-Tobago, and Barbados Conferences: Bishop Louis Hunter, Sr.
Alabama/Florida Episcopal District: Alabama, Cahaba, Central Alabama, North Alabama, South Alabama, West Montgomery Alabama, Florida, and South Florida Conferences: Bishop James E. McCoy
South Atlantic Episcopal District: Georgia, Palmetto, Pee Dee, and South Carolina Conferences: Bishop Kenneth Monroe
Southwestern Delta: Arkansas, Louisiana, Oklahoma, South Mississippi, West Tennessee-Mississippi and Texas Conferences: Bishop Darryl B. Starnes, Sr.
Western Episcopal District: Alaska, Arizona, California, Oregon-Washington, Southwest Rocky Mountains, and Colorado Conferences: Bishop Dennis V. Proctor
Western West Africa: Cote D'Ivoire, East Ghana, Liberia, Mid-Ghana, North Ghana, Togo, and West Ghana Conferences: Bishop Mildred B. Hines

GENERAL OFFICERS AND DEPARTMENTS
Address and telephone number for all Departments (except where indicated) is 3225 West Sugar Creek Rd., Charlotte, NC 28269 Tel. (704)599-4630 and Mailing Address for all Departments (except where indicated) is P.O. Box 26770, Charlotte, NC 28221
Department of Records and Research: W. Robert Johnson, III, Gen. Sec.-Aud., Fax (704)688-2549, Email: j1gsa@aol.com or rojohnson@amezhqtr.org
Department of Finance: Mrs. Shirley Welch, Chief Financial Officer, Fax (704)688-2553, Email: shwelch@amezhqtr.org
Star of Zion: Mike Lisby, Editor, Fax (704)688-2556, Email: sozbusiness@yahoo.com
A.M.E. Zion Quarterly Review and Secretary A.M.E. Zion Historical Society: James D. Armstrong, Sec.-Editor, P.O. Box 33247, Charlotte, NC 28233, Fax (704)688-2544, Email: jaarmstrong@amezhqtr.org
Heritage Hall, Livingstone College, 701 W. Monroe Street, Salisbury, NC 28144 Tel. (704)216-6094
Department of Overseas Missions and Missionary Seer: Kermit DeGraffenreidt, Sec.-Editor, 475 Riverside Drive, Room 1935, New York, NY 10115 Tel. (212)870-2952 Fax (212)870-2808
Department of Brotherhood Pensions and Ministerial Relief: David Miller, Sec.-Treas., Fax (704)599-4580; Mailing Address: P.O.

Box 217114, Charlotte, NC 28221, Email: damiller@amezhqtr.org

Christian Education Department: Raymon Hunt, Sec., Fax (704)688-2550, Email: rehunt@amezhqtr.org, Website: www.cedamezion.org.

Department of Church School Literature: Mary A. Love, Editor, Fax (704)688-2548, Email: malove@amezhqtr.org

Department of Church Extension and Home Missions: Terrence J. Jones, Sec.-Treas., Fax (704)688-2552, Email: tejones@amezhqtr.org

Bureau of Evangelism: Otis T. McMillan, Dir., P.O. Box 217258, Charlotte, NC 28221, Fax (704)688-2547, Email: otmcmillan@embarqmail.com

Public Affairs and Convention Manager: George E. McKain, II, Dir., P.O. Box 1417, Summerville, SC 29484 Tel. (843)276-3411 Fax (843)821-1735, Email: zionpagem2@aol.com; Hqtrs. Tel. (704)599-4630

Department of Health and Social Concerns: Bernard Sullivan, Dir., Email: bernardsullivan2@yahoo.com

A.M.E. Zion Publishing House: David Baker, General Manager, Fax (704)688-2541, Email: dabaker@amezhqtr.org

JUDICIAL COUNCIL

Pres., Rev. Dr. E. Alex Brower, Esq. 235B State Street, Hudson, NY 12534

Vice Pres., Rev. Dr. Richard Chapple, 1449 W. Adams Boulevard, Los Angeles, CA 90007

Clerk, Ms. Monica S. Reed, 1641 Rosedale Avenue, Knoxville, TN 37915-1929

Juraldine Battle-Hodge, Esq., 1017 North Burbank Drive, Montgomery, AL 26117. Email: battle@bellsouth.net

Rev. Dr. Charlotte Brown-Williams, Esq., 1131 Lynbrook Drive, Charlotte, NC 28221

Rachel R. Dawson, Esq. 4106 South Ellis, Chicago, IL

Elmira J. Jackson, Esq., 194 Wood Hollow Lane, New Rochelle, NY 10804

Rev. Dr. William McKenith, 247 Glove Avenue, Union, NJ 07083

Rev. Dr. John L. Walker, Sr., Esq., 6510 Adak Street, Seat Pleasant, MD 20743

Pres. Emeritus of Counsel, Hon. Adle M. Riley

CONNECTIONAL LAY COUNCIL

General President, Yvonne A. Tracey, 502 Ferndale Drive, Salisbury, NC 28144; (704)637-8687; Fax: (704)636-4562; Email: ytracey@bellsouth.net

First Vice Pres., Yvonne Baskerville, 1812 Allison St. NW, Washington, DC 20011; (202)726-5547; Email: eyb1022@yahoo.com

Second Vice-Pres., Effie B. Woodard, P.O. Box 662, Broadway, NC 27505; (919)258-6868; Cell: (919)356-6608; Email: ebw108@windstream.net

Secretary, Delores Lancaster, 674 Azalea Drive, Rockville, MD 20850; (301)340-2590; Email: dlancaster674@aol.com

Treasurer, Trubbie R. Leeper, 2310 Yorktown Avenue, Gastonia, NC 28054; (704)866-0742; Email: jessipoppy@yahoo.com

Financial Sec., Ira Rudolph Golden, 188 Hillside Avenue, White Plains, NY 10603; Home: (914)285-9796; Cell; (914)960-7755; Email; IRBAGO@aol.com

Chaplain, Charles Montgomery, 11436 Studebaker Road, Norwalk, CA 90650; (562)864-6180, Email: cpmonty@aol.com

Editor, "The Laity Speaks/The Connection", Rhandi M. Stith, Carrington Arms, 33 Lincoln Ave., Apt. 10L, New Rochelle, NY 10801. (914)235-3596; Fax (914)637-2518; Email: Rhandim@aol.com

GENERAL OFFICERS OF THE WOMEN'S HOME AND OVERSEAS MISSIONARY SOCIETY

General President, Dr. Barbara L. Shaw, 5630 Bradford Lake Lane, Charlotte, NC 28269. Office: (704)599-4630. Email: bshawmax@comcast.net

First Vice-President, Dr. Gloria G. Williams, 804 Prospect Avenue, Raeford, NC 28376 Tel. (910)875-2205 Fax (910)875-8214. Email: gwilli5103@alol.com

Second Vice-President, Mrs. Joyce A. Reid, 5309 Dayan Dr., Charlotte, NC 28216 Tel (704)596-3842 Fax (704)921-8323, Email: ejr5309@aol.com

Exec. Secretary, Mrs. Rosetta J. Dunham, P.O. Box 26846, Charlotte, NC 28221-6846 Tel. (704)599-4630 Fax (704)688-2554, Email: rodunham@amezhqtr.org

Recording Secretary, Ms. Dorothy McFarlane, 88 Fawcett Close, Wye Street, Battersea London, England SW 112LU. Tel. +44207-228-8114/+447946292755. Email: dorothymc2@yahoo-co-uk-

General Treasurer, Mrs. Pamela R. Valentine, 692 N. Hawkins Ave., Akron, OH 44313 Tel. (330)864-4890 Fax (330)499-4475, Email: puvalentine@neo.rr.com

General Coordinator of YAMS, Mrs. Dawn L. Walker, 823 South Indiana Ave., Griffith, Indiana 46319 Tel. (219)922-1361, Email: dlwsweetspirit@aol.com

Secretary, Youth Missionary Society, Mrs. Charlrean B. Mapson, P.O. Box 1267, Wilmington, NC 28402 Tel. (910)251-0682 Fax (910)362-9202, Email: ysec@chuckmapson.net

Superintendent of Buds of Promise, Ms. Barbara Epps, 3204 Reid Avenue, Charlotte, NC 28208. Tel. (704)372-7580. Fax (704)-372-7580. Email: bepps1@carolina.rr.com

Secretary, Bureau of Supply, Mrs. Henrietta Daniel, 7535 Apache Plume Drive, Houston, TX 77071. Tel.(713)729-3436. Fax (713)729-9486. Email: henriettadaniel@sbcglobal.net

Chairman, Life Members Council, Mrs. Loveleen "Dee" Perkins, 5303 Brewer Road, Beltsville, MD 20705. Tel.(301)937-0244. Fax (301)937-4041. Email: dperkins02@yahoo.com

Editor, Women's Section, Missionary Seer, Mrs. Christina Penrose, 506 Fairdale Street, Friendswood, TX 77546. Tel. (281)996-1304. Fax (832)201-8137. Fax (718)604-2094

Periodicals

Star of Zion, Quarterly Review, Church School Herald, Missionary Seer, Vision Focus, Evangel

Albanian Orthodox Archdiocese in America

The Albanian Orthodox Church in America traces its origins to the groups of Albanian immigrants which first arrived in the United States in 1886, seeking religious, cultural and economic freedoms denied them in the homeland.

In 1908 in Boston, the Rev. Fan Stylian Noli (later Archbishop) served the first liturgy in the Albanian language in 500 years, to which Orthodox Albanians rallied, forming their own diocese in 1919. Parishes began to spring up throughout New England and the Mid-Atlantic and Great Lakes states. In 1922, clergy from the United States traveled to Albania to proclaim the self-governance of the Orthodox Church in the homeland at the Congress of Berat.

In 1971 the Albanian Archdiocese sought and gained union with the Orthodox Church in America, expressing the desire to expand the Orthodox witness to America at large, giving it an indigenous character. The Albanian Archdiocese remains vigilant for its brothers and sisters in the homeland and serves as an important resource for human rights issues and Albanian affairs, in addition to its programs for youth, theological education, vocational interest programs and retreats for young adults and women.

Headquarters

523 E. Broadway, S. Boston, MA 02127
Media Contact, Sec., Dorothy Adams, Tel. (617)268-1275 Fax (617)268-3184Website: www.oca.org

Officers

Metropolitan Herman, Tel. (617)268-1275
Chancellor, V. Rev. Arthur E. Liolin, 60 Antwerp St., East Milton, MA 02186, Tel. (617)698-3366
Lay Chpsn., William Poist, 40 Forge Village Rd., Westford, MA 01885, Tel. (978)392-0759
Treas., Cynthia Vasil Brown, 471 Capt. Eames Circle, Ashland, MA 01721 (508)881-0072

Albanian Orthodox Diocese of America

This Diocese was organized in 1950 as a canonical body administering to the Albanian faithful. It is under the ecclesiastical jurisdiction of the Ecumenical Patriarchate of Constantinople (Istanbul).

Headquarters

6455 Silver Dawn Lane, Las Vegas, NV 89118, Tel. (702)365-1989 Fax (702)365-1989
Media Contact, His Grace Bishop Ilia Katra

Officers

His Grace Bishop Ilia Katra, 6455 Silver Dawn Lane, Las Vegas, NV 89118, Tel. (702)365-1989 Fax (702)365-1989

The Allegheny Wesleyan Methodist Connection (Original Allegheny Conference)

This body was formed in 1968 by members of the Allegheny Conference (located in eastern Ohio and western Pennsylvania) of the Wesleyan Methodist Church, which merged in 1966 with the Pilgrim Holiness Church to form The Wesleyan Church.

The Allegheny Wesleyan Methodist Connection is composed of persons "having the form and seeking the power of godliness, united in order to pray together, to receive the word of exhortation, and to watch over one another in love, that they may help each other to work out their salvation." There is a strong commitment to congregational government and to holiness of heart and life. There is a strong thrust in church extension within the United States and in missions worldwide.

Headquarters

P.O. Box 357, Salem, OH 44460, Tel. (330)337-9376 Fax (330)337-9700
Media Contact, Pres., Rev. William Cope
Email: awmc@juno.com

Officers

Pres., Rev. William Cope, P.O. Box 357, Salem, OH 44460
Vice Pres., Rev. David Blowers, 1856 Marion-Williamsport Road, E, Marion, OH 43302
Sec., Rev. Jonathan Troyer, 2700 17th Street, NW, Canton, OH 44708-2954
Treas., James Kunselman, 1022 Newgarden Ave., Salem, OH 44460

Periodicals

The Allegheny Wesleyan Methodist

Alliance of Baptists*

The Alliance of Baptists is an association of individuals and churches dedicated to the preservation of historic Baptist principles, freedoms, and traditions, and to the expression of our ministry and mission through cooperative relationships with other Baptist bodies and the larger Christian community.

From its inception in early 1987, the Alliance has stood for those values that have distinguished the Baptist movement from its beginnings nearly four centuries ago—the freedom and accountability of every individual in matters of faith; the freedom of each congregation under the authority of Jesus Christ to determine its own ministry and mission; and religious freedom for all in relationship to the state.

Headquarters

1328 16th St. N.W., Washington, DC 20036, Tel. (202)745-7609 Fax (202)745-0023

Media Contact, Exec. Dir., Rev. Dr. Stan Hastey
Email: shastey@allianceofbaptists.org
Website: www.allianceofbaptists.org

Officers

Exec. Dir., Rev. Dr. Stan Hastey
Assoc. Dir., Jeanette Holt
Pres., Rev. Jim Hopkins, Oakland, CA
Vice Pres., Kristy Arneson Pullen, Ashburn, VA
Sec., Amy Jacks Dean, Charlotte, NC

Periodicals

Connections

The American Association of Lutheran Churches

This church body was constituted on November 7, 1987. The AALC was formed by laity and pastors of the former American Lutheran Church in America who held to a high view of Scripture (inerrancy and infallibility). This church body also emphasizes the primacy of evangelism and world missions and the authority and autonomy of the local congregation.

Congregations of the AALC are distributed throughout the continental United States from Long Island, N.Y., to Los Angeles. The primary decision-making body is the General Convention, to which each congregation has proportionate representation.

Headquarters

The AALC National Office, 6600 N. Clinton Street, Augustine Hall, #13, Fort Wayne, Indiana 46825, Tel. (260)452-3213 Fax (260)452-3215 Mailing Address: The AALC, 921 East Dupont Rd., #920, Fort Wayne, IN 46825-1551

Media Contact, Admn. Asst. to the AALC, Rev. Fred Balke, Email: fbalke@taalc.org
Email: theaalc@taalc.org
Website: www.taalc.org

Officers

Rev. Franklin E. Hays, Presiding Pastor, The American Association of Lutheran Churches, Tel. (260)452-3213, Email: presidingpastor@taalc.org Rev. Richard Eddy, Assistant Presiding Pastor Rev. Mark Homp, Secretary Mr. Jim Daman, Treasurer Rev. Richard Shields, ALTS President; Director of Pastoral Formation and Congregational Development; Administrative Ass't. to the Presiding Pastor, Tel. (260)452-3213, Email: rpshields@ taalc.org Rev. Fred Balke, Director of Communications, The AALC; Evangel Editor & Admn. Asst. to the AALC, Email: fbalke@taalc.org

American Lutheran Theological Seminary (ALTS), Pres., Rev. Richard Shields, 6600 N. Clinton Street, Fort Wayne, IN 46825, Tel. (260)452-3213, Email: rpshields@taalc.org
Rev. Fred Balke, Registrar

Periodicals

The Evangel

The American Baptist Association

The American Baptist Association (ABA) is an international fellowship of independent Baptist churches voluntarily cooperating in missionary, evangelistic, benevolent and Christian education activities throughout the world. Its beginnings can be traced to the landmark movement of the 1850s. Led by James R. Graves and J.M. Pendleton, a significant number of Baptist churches in the South, claiming a New Testament heritage, rejected as extrascriptural the policies of the newly formed Southern Baptist Convention (SBC). Because they strongly advocated church equality, many of these churches continued doing mission and benevolent work apart from the SBC, electing to work through local associations. Meeting in Texarkana, TX, in 1924, messengers from the various churches effectively merged two of these major associations, the Baptist Missionary Association of Texas and the General Association, forming the American Baptist Association.

Since 1924, mission efforts have been supported in Australia, Africa, Asia, Canada, Central America, Europe, India, Israel, Japan, Korea, Mexico, New Zealand, South America and the South Pacific. An even more successful domestic mission effort has changed the ABA from a predominantly rural southern organization to one with churches in 48 states.

Through its publishing arm in Texarkana, the ABA publishes literature and books numbering into the thousands. Major seminaries include the Missionary Baptist Seminary, founded by Dr. Ben M. Bogard in Little Rock, AR; Texas Baptist Seminary, Henderson, TX; Oxford Baptist Institute, Oxford, MS; and Florida Baptist Schools in Lakeland, FL.

While no person may speak for the churches of the ABA, all accept the Bible as the inerrant Word of God. They believe Christ was the virgin-born Son of God, that God is a triune God, that the only church is the local congregation of scripturally baptized believers and that the work of the church is to spread the gospel.

Headquarters

4605 N State Line Ave. Texarkana, TX 75503, Tel. (903)792-2783
Media Contact, Steve Reeves, Public Relations Director
Email: bssc@abaptist.org
Website: www.abaptist.org

Officers

President, Roger Copeland, 5902 Trinity Heights, Texarkana, AR 71854
Vice Presidents, James Calhoun, 2105 Shadow Ridge Court, Arkadelphia, AR 71923; Darrel Owens, 3048 CR 3201 W, Mt. Enterprise, TX 75681, James A. Crain, 1520 Fincher Creek, Minden, LA 71055
Recording Clerks, Terry Parrish, 19 Eastwood, Bryant AR 72022

61

Publications, Editor in Chief, Larry Clements; Bus. Mgr., Wayne Sewell, 4605 N. State Line Ave., Texarkana, TX 75503

Meeting Arrangements Director, Edgar N. Sutton, P.O. Box 240, Alexander, AR 72002

Sec.-Treas. of Missions, Randy Cloud, P.O. Box 1050 Texarkana, TX 75504

American Baptist Churches in the U.S.A.*

Originally known as the Northern Baptist Convention, this body of Baptist churches changed the name to American Baptist Convention in 1950 with a commitment to hold the name in trust for all Christians of like faith and mind who desire to bear witness to the historical Baptist convictions in a framework of cooperative Protestantism.

In 1972 American Baptist Churches in the U.S.A. was adopted as the new name. Although national missionary organizational developments began in 1814 with the establishment of the American Baptist Foreign Mission Society and continued with the organization of the American Baptist Publication Society in 1824 and the American Baptist Home Mission Society in 1832, the general denominational body was not formed until 1907. American Baptist work at the local level dates back to the organization by Roger Williams of the First Baptist Church in Providence, R. I. in 1638.

Headquarters

American Baptist Churches Mission Center
P.O. Box 851, Valley Forge, PA 19482-0851, Tel. (610)768-2000 Fax (610)768-2320

Media Contact, Assoc. Gen'l. Secretary for Mission Resource Development, the Rev. Dr. Leo S. Thorne, Tel. (610)768-2318 Fax (610)768-2320, Email: leo.thorne@abc-usa.org

Email: richard.schramm@abc-usa.org
Website: www.abc-usa.org

Officers

Pres., Mary Hulst, Email: MaryH@abc-usa.org
Vice Pres., Frank Christine, Jr., Email: frankchristinejr@abc-usa.org
Budget Review Officer, James Ratliff, Email: jamesratliff@abc-usa.org
Gen. Sec., A. Roy Medley, Tel. (610)768-2273, Email: roy.medley@abc-usa.org
Assoc. Gen. Sec.-Treas., Lloyd Hamblin;, Tel. (610)768-2280; Email: lloyd.hamblin@abc-usa.org

REGIONAL ORGANIZATIONS

Central Region, ABC of, John S. Williams, 5833 SW 29th St. Ste. A, Topeka, KS 66614-5500

Chicago, ABC of Metro, Larry L. Greenfield, 7035 W. Grand Ave # 102, Chicago, IL 60707

Cleveland Baptist Assoc., Leonard Thompson, 6060 Rockside Woods Blvd., Ste. 317, Cleveland, OH 44131

Connecticut, ABC of, Judy G. Allbee, 90 A North Main St., West Hartford, CT 06107-1924

Dakotas, ABC of, Riley H. Walker, 1101 W. 22nd St., Sioux Falls, SD 57105-1699

District of Columbia Bapt. Conv., Jeffrey Haggray, 1628 16th St., NW, Washington, DC 20009-3099

Evergreen Baptist Association, Marcia Patton, 409 Third Ave., South Ste. A, Kent, WA 98032

ABC of the Great Rivers Region, J. Dwight Stinnett, P.O. Box 3786, Springfield, IL 62708-3786

Indiana, ABC of, Larry D. Mason, 1350 N. Delaware St., Indianapolis, IN 46202-2493

Indianapolis, ABC of Greater, Jean Friesen, Interim, P.O. Box 421487., Indianapolis, IN 46242-1487

Los Angeles, ABC of, Samuel S. Chetti, 3325 Wilshire Blvd., # 800, Los Angeles, CA 90010-1746

Maine, ABC of, Alfred Fletcher, P.O. Box 6149, China Village, ME 04926-6149

Massachusetts, ABC of, Anthony Pappas, 20 Milton St., Dedham, MA 02026-2967

Metropolitan New York, ABC of, James O. Stallings, 475 Riverside Dr., Rm. 432, New York, NY 10115-0432

Michigan, ABC of, Michael A. Williams, 4578 S. Hagadorn Rd., East Lansing, MI 48823-5396

Mid-American Baptist Churches, Marshall Peters, 2400 86th St. Ste. !5., Des Moines, IA 50322-4380

Nebraska, ABC of, Susan E. Gillies, 6404 Maple St., Omaha, NE 68104-4079

New Jersey, ABC of, Lee Spitzer, 3752 Nottingham Way, Ste. 101, Trenton, NJ 08690-3802

New York State, ABC of, William A. Carlsen, 5865 E. Seneca Turnpike, Jamesville, NY 13078

Northwest, ABC of, Charles Revis, 601 S. Ross Point Road, Post Falls, ID 83854-7726

Ohio, ABC of, Lawrence Swain, 136 N. Galway Dr., Granville, OH 43023-9579

Oregon, ABC of, Stephen Bils, 0245 SW Bancroft St., Ste. G, Portland, OR 97239-4270

Pennsylvania & Delaware, ABC of, Frank Frisch Korn, 106 Revere Lane, Coatesville, PA 19320

Philadelphia Baptist Assoc., James E. McJunkin, Jr., 8711 Ridge Ave., Philadelphia, PA 19128-2023

Puerto Rico, Baptist Churches of, Roberto Dieppa-Baez, PMB 477, P.O. Box 6022, Carolina, PR 00984-6022

Rhode Island, ABC of, Liliana Da Valle, P.O. Box 330, Exeter, RI 02822

Rochester-Genesee Region, ABC of, Alan Newton, 1100 S. Goodman, # 320 Rochester, NY 14620

Rocky Mountains, ABC of, Steven Van Ostran, 6855 S. Havava St. # 220, Centennial, CO 80112

South, ABC of the, Walter L. Parrish, II, 5124 Greenwich Ave., Baltimore, MD 21229-2393

Vermont-New Hampshire, ABC of, Rohn Peterson, One Oak Ridge Rd., Bldg. B 3, Suite 4A, West Lebanon, NH 03784

West, Growing Healthy Churches, ABC of the, Paul D. Borden, 2420 Camino Ramon, Ste. 140, San Ramon, CA 94583-4207

West Virginia Baptist Convention, David L. Carrico, P.O. Box 1019, Parkersburg, WV 26102-1019

Wisconsin, ABC of, Arlo R. Reichter, 15330 Watertown Plank Rd., Elm Grove, WI 53122-2391

BOARDS

American Baptist Assembly, Green Lake, WI 54941; Pres., Kenneth P. Giacoletto

American Baptist Historical Society, W 2511 State Road 23 or 3001 Mercer University Dr. Atlanta, GA 30341-4155 Admn. Archivist, Deborah B. VanBroekhoven; Pres., Trinette V. McCray

American Baptist Men, Pres., David Edwards

American Baptist Women's Ministries, Exec. Dir., Virginia Holmstrom; Pres., Barbara Anderson

Bd. of Intl. Ministries, Exec. Dir., Reid Trulson; Pres., Thomas Lacy

Bd. of Natl. Ministries, Exec. Dir., Aidsand F. Wright-Riggins; Pres., Annie Marie LeBarbour

Ministers & Missionaries Benefit Bd., Exec. Dir., Sumner M. Grant; Pres., George Tooze, 475 Riverside Dr., New York, NY 10115

Minister Council, Dir., Joseph Kutter; Pres., Alice B. Greene

Periodicals

Tomorrow Magazine, The Secret Place, American Baptist Quarterly, The Christian Citizen, On Location, Mission in America

The American Carpatho-Russian Orthodox Greek Catholic Church

The American Carpatho-Russian Orthodox Greek Catholic Church is a self-governing diocese that is in communion with the Ecumenical Patriarchate of Constantinople. The late Patriarch Benjamin I, in an official Patriarchal Document dated Sept. 19, 1938, canonized the Diocese in the name of the Orthodox Church of Christ.

Headquarters

312 Garfield St., Johnstown, PA 15906, Tel. (814)539-4207 Fax (814)536-4699

Media Contact, Chancellor, V. Rev. Protopresbyter Frank P. Miloro, Tel. (814)539-8086 Fax (814)536-4699

Email: archdiocese@goarch.org

Website: www.goarch.org

Officers

Bishop, Metropolitan Nicholas Smisko, 312 Garfield St., Johnstown, PA 15906, Tel. (814)539-4207, Fax (814)536-4699

Chancellor, V. Rev. Protopresbyter Frank P. Miloro, 249 Butler Ave., Johnstown, PA 15906, Tel. (814)539-9143, Fax (814)536-4699, Email: acrod@helicon.net

Treas., V. Rev. Protopresbyter Ronald A. Hazuda, 1115 East Ave., Erie, PA 16503, Tel. (814)453-4902

Periodicals

The Church Messenger

American Evangelical Christian Churches

Founded in 1944, the A.E.C.C is composed of individual ministers and churches who are united in accepting "Seven Articles of Faith." These seven articles are-the Bible as the written word of God; the Virgin birth; the deity of Jesus Christ; Salvation through the atonement; guidance of our life through prayer; the return of the Saviour; the establishment of the Millennial Kingdom.

The American Evangelical Christian Churches offers the following credentials-Certified Christian Worker, Commission to Preach, Licensed Minister and Ordained Minister to those who accept the Seven Articles of Faith, who put unity in Christ first and are approved by A.E.C.C.

A.E.C.C seeks to promote the gospel through its ministers, churches and missionary activities.

Churches operate independently with all decisions concerning local government left to the individual churches.

The organization also has ministers in Canada, England, Bolivia, Philippines Thailand, Brazil and South America.

Headquarters

P.O. Box 47312, Indianapolis, IN 46227, Tel. (317)788-9280 Fax (317)788-1410

Media Contact, Dr. Charles Wasielewski, Sr., 51 Wells Rd, Barton, NY 13734-1818

Email: aeccoffice@infoblvd.net

Website: www.aeccministries.com

Officers

INTERNATIONAL OFFICERS

Mod., Dr. Charles Wasielewski, Box 51, Wells Rd., Barton, NY 13734, Tel. (607)565-4074

Sec., Dr. Gene McClain, 520 Blooming Pike, Morgantown, IN 46160, Tel. (812)597-5021

Treas., Dr. Michael Ward, Sr., 4802 Chervil Ct., Indianapolis, IN 46237, Tel. (317)888-2095

Bd. Member, Dr. Allen Kent, 550 E. Shoeline Drive, Long Beach, CA 90802, Tel. (562) 590-7294

Missions Coordinator, Dr. Douglas Schlemmer, P.O. Box 409, Twin Peaks, CA 92391, Tel. (909)338-6495

REGIONAL MODERATORS

Northwest Region, Rev. Alvin House, P.O. Box 393, Darby MT 59829 Tel.(406)821-3141

Central-West Region, Rev. Charles Clark, Box 314, Rockport, IL 62370 Tel.(217)437-2507

Far West Region, Pastor Richard Cuthbert, 1195 Via Serville, Cathedral City, CA 92234, Tel. (706)321-6682

Lowell Ford, 397 Shamrock Lane, Newark, OH, 43055, Tel. (614)309-3419

Northeast Region, Rev. John Merrill, P.O. Box 183, East Smithfield, PA 18817 Tel.(717) 596-4598

East Region, James R. Brown, 17404 W. Washington, Hagerstown, MD 21740, Tel. (301)797812f1

Southeast Region, Rev. James Fullwood, 207 5th Avenue, N.E., Lutz, FL 33549

STATE MODERATORS

Rev. James Brown, Maryland
Rev. John W. Coats, Delaware
Brenda Osborne, New York
Dr. Berton G. Heleine, Illinois
Rev. R. Eugene Hill, New Jersey
Rev. Kenneth Pope, Washington
Rev. Art Mirek, Michigan
Rev. Charles Jennings, Pennsylvania
Rev. Jerry Myers, Indiana

FOREIGN OUTREACH MINISTRIES

American Evangelical Christian Churches-Canada

Regional Moderator, Dr. Stephen K. Massey, 730 Ontario street, Suite 709, Toronto, Ontario M4X 1N3, Canada (416)323-9076

Philippine Evangelical Christian Churches

Director, Rev. Alan A. Olubalang, P.O. Box 540, Cotabato City, Philippines 9600

American Evangelical Christian Churches-Philippines

Regional Moderator, Rev. Oseas Andres, P.O. Box 2695, Central Post Office, 1166 Q.C. Metro Manila, Philippines

Periodicals

The American Evangelical Christian Churches Newsletter "AECC Communique"

American Rescue Workers

Major Thomas E. Moore was National Commander of Booth's Salvation Army when a dispute flared between Booth and Moore. Moore resigned from Booth's Army and due to the fact that Booth's Army was not incorporated at the time, Moore was able to incorporate under said name. The name was changed in 1890 to American Salvation Army. In 1913 the current name American Rescue Workers was adopted.

It is a national religious social service agency which operates on a quasimilitary basis. Membership includes officers (clergy), soldiers-adherents (laity), members of various activity groups and volunteers who serve as advisors, associates and committed participants in ARW service functions.

The motivation of the organization is the love of God. Its message is based on the Bible. This is expressed by its spiritual Ministry, the purposes of which are to preach the gospel of Jesus Christ and to meet human needs in his name without discrimination. It is a branch of the Christian Church . . . A Church with a Mission.

Headquarters

Operational Headquarters, 25 Ross Street, Williamsport, PA 17701, Tel. (570)323-8693 Fax (570)323-8694

National Field Office, 11116 Gehr Road, Waynesboro, PA 17268-9101, Tel. (717)762-2965

Media Contact, Natl. Communication Sec./Natl Special Services Dir., Col. Robert N. Coles, Rev., Natl. Field Ofc., Fax (717)762-8109 Email: amerscwk@pcspower.net Website: www.arwus.com

Officers

Commander-In-Chief & Pres. Of Corp., General Claude S. Astin, Jr. Rev

Natl. Bd. Pres., Col. Sam Astin (Claude S. Astin, III)

Ordination Committee, Chpsn., Gen. Paul E. Martin, (Emeritus) Rev.

Natl. Chief Sec., Col. Dawn R. Astin, NQ-643 Elmira St., Williamsport, PA 17701

Periodicals

The Rescue Herald

Amish—please see Old Order Amish Church.

Anglican Orthodox Church, see Orthodox Anglican Church.

Anglo-Lutheran Catholic Church

The Anglo-Lutheran Catholic Church (ALCC) was founded in November, 1997 as the Evangelical Community Church-Lutheran (ECCL) by former members of the Lutheran Church-Missouri Synod. It began as a single independent congregation, St. Michael's Lutheran Church, Kansas City Missouri. The first pastor of St. Michael's Lutheran Church was the Rev. Irl A. Gladfelter. The Constitution and Canon Law of the ECCL require all clergy to be ordained (or re-ordained) into the historic apostolic succession upon their entry into the ECCL. Those already ordained in the historic apostolic succession in lineages considered technically valid by the Catholic Church are not re-ordained.

The ECCL officially changed its name to "Anglo-Lutheran Catholic Church" in October, 2007. The term, "Anglo" in the name reflects the fact that from its founding, this Church has been considerably influenced by the Anglo- Catholic ("high church") faction within Anglicanism.

Consistent with its ecumenical goal of eventual incorporation into the Catholic Church in whichever form is felt to be the most appropriate by the Vatican, through the years, the Anglo-Lutheran Catholic Church (ALCC) modified its theology, polity, worship, and spirituality to the point where it has rejected all aspects of Lutheran and Anglican faith, polity, worship, and spirituality which are not in full agreement with the faith, polity, worship, and spirituality of the Catholic Church and the teachings of the Catholic Magesterium. The ecclesiastical government of the Anglo-Lutheran Catholic is hierarchal and episcopal (governed by bishops.) The structure of this Church at the international, national, diocesan, and parish levels, and the role of the laity is the same as that of the Catholic Church. The code of doctrine and discipline are contained in the ALCC's Constitution, Canon Law Code, Church Regulations, and in areas not covered by those documents, by the Code of Canon Law of the

Catholic Church (Vatican Library Edition, 1989.) In July of 2008 it began requiring all clergy to sign the Mandatum, which is a vow in the form of a signed contract to not teach, preach, write, or publish anything contrary to the Catholic Magisterium.

At this time, the ALCC has six (6) archdioceses, one (1) diocese, and two (2) ethnic non-geographic dioceses in the United States. It has a vicar general in Kenya, a priest in Germany, and also has a presence in Canada, Southern Sudan, Northwest Uganda, and Northeast Congo. The ALCC has appointed Archbishops with jurisdiction as Minor Metropolitans for Europe, Sub-Saharan Africa, North America, and Southeast Asia (though it has no Asian presence at this time.) The ALCC is in Full Communion with the Evangelical Marian Catholic Church in the U. S. In Great Britain, the ALCC is in Full Communion with the following "Continuing Anglican Churches: Traditional Anglo-Catholic Com-munion, Traditional Church of England, Anglican Church-Traditional Rite, Traditional Episcopal Church in Scotland, Traditional Church in Wales, and the Traditional English Church.

International Headquarters

Office of the Metropolitan Archbishop, Office of the Director of Temporal Administration and Finance, St. Michael's House, 1200 N. E. 81st Terrace, Kansas City, Missouri 64118-1361 Chancery: (816)468-9691, Email: ALCC lutherans@kc.rr.com
Email: ALCClutherans@kc.rr.com
Website: www.anglolutherancatholic.org/

Officers

Office of the Metropolitan Archbishop, The Most Rev. Irl A. Gladfelter, M.Div., S.T.M., D.D., Tel. (816) 468-9691, Email: ALCClutherans@kc.rr.com

Vicar General of the Anglo-Lutheran Catholic Church, Office of the Metropolitan Archbishop, The Most Rev. Robert W. Edmondson, D.Min., D.D., P. O. Box 6172, Pittsburgh, PA 15212, Tel. (412)741-9009, Email: DeoEtEcclesia@yahoo.com

Office for the Promotion of Christian Unity, Office of the Metropolitan Archbishop, The Most Rev. Robert W. Edmondson, D.Min., D.D., P. O. Box 6172, Pittsburgh, PA 15212, Tel. (412)741-9009, Email: DeoEtEcclesia@yahoo.com

Office of the Director of Temporal Administration and Finance, Office of the Metropolitan Archbishop, St. Michael's House, 1200 N.E. 81st Terrace, Kansas City, Missouri 64118-1361, Tel. 816-468-9691, EMail: ALCC lutherans@kc.rr.com

Director of Evangelism and Church Growth, Office of the Metropolitan Archbishop, The Rev. Msgr. Thomas Stover O.S.A., M.Div., D. Min., 1115 East 19th Street, Minneapolis, MN 55404, Tel. (612) 554-5368, Website: www.holytrinityalcc.org, Email: toms@holy trinityalcc.org

Office of the Dean of the Holy Synod, The Most Rev. Tan Binh Phan Nguyen, 2389 Alden Woods Drive, Jonesboro, GA 30236, Tel. (770)210-9346, Email: lavanglutheran@yahoo.com

Office for Specialized Ministries, The Most Rev. Raymond W. Copp, Psy.D., 564 Spring Oaks Drive, West Chester, PA 19382, Tel. (610)639-1082, Email: rwcopp@gp4u.us

Director for Hospital and Hospice Chaplaincies (O.S.M.), The Most Rev. Raymond W. Copp, Psy.D., 564 Spring Oaks Drive, West Chester, PA 19382, Tel. (610) 639-1082 Email: rwcopp@gp4u.us

Director for Police, Fire and Correctional Institution Chaplaincies (O.S.M.), The Most Rev. Raymond W. Copp, Psy.D., 564 Spring Oaks Drive, West Chester, PA 19382, Tel. (610) 639-1082, Email: rwcopp@gp4u.us

Office for Pastoral Assistance to Health Care Workers, The Most Rev. Chaplen Luyimba Kweri, B.A.Th., M.Div., D.D., 4606 N. W. Kenwood, Kansas City, MO 64116, Tel. (816) 454-3172, Email: bishopkweri@sbcglobal.net

Office of the Vicar General for Vietnamese Churches, The Most Rev. Tan Binh Phan Nguyen, 2389 Alden Woods Drive Jonesboro, GA 30236, Tel. (770)210-9346, Email: lavanglutheran@yahoo.com

The Antiochian Orthodox Christian Archdiocese of North America

The spiritual needs of Antiochian faithful in North America were first served through the Syro-Arabian Mission of the Russian Orthodox Church in 1895. In 1895, the Syrian Orthodox Benevolent Society was organized by Antiochian immigrants in New York City. Raphael Hawaweeny, a young Damascene clergyman serving as professor of Arabic language at the Orthodox theological academy in Kazan, Russia, came to New York to organize the first Arabic- language parish in North America in 1895, after being canonically received under the omophorion of the head of the Russian Church in North America. Saint Nicholas Cathedral, now located at 355 State St. in Brooklyn, is considered the "mother parish" of the Archdiocese.

On March 12, 1904, Hawaweeny became the first Orthodox bishop to be consecrated in North America. He traveled throughout the continent and established new parishes. The unity of Orthodoxy in the New World, including the Syrian Greek Orthodox community, was ruptured after the death of Bishop Raphael in 1915 and by the Bolshevik revolution in Russia and the First World War. Unity returned in 1975 when Metropolitan Philip Saliba, of the Antiochian Archdiocese of New York, and Metropolitan Michael Shaheen of the Antiochian Archdiocese of Toledo, Ohio, signed the Articles of Reunification, ratified by the Holy Synod of the Patriarchate. Saliba was recognized as the Metropolitan Primate and Shaheen as Auxiliary Archbishop. A second auxiliary to the Metropolitan, Bishop Antoun Khouri, was consecrated at

Brooklyn's Saint Nicholas Cathedral, in 1983. A third auxiliary, Bishop Basil Essey was consecrated at Wichita's St. George Cathedral in 1992. Two additional bishops were added in 1994, Bishop Joseph Zehlaoui and Bishop Demetri Khoury.

The Archdiocesan Board of Trustees (consisting of 60 elected and appointed clergy and lay members) and the Metropolitan's Advisory Council (consisting of clergy and lay representatives from each parish and mission) meet regularly to assist the Primate in the administration of the Archdiocese. Currently, there are 256 parishes and missions in the Archdiocese.

Headquarters
358 Mountain Rd., Englewood, NJ 07631, Tel. (201)871-1355 Fax (201)871-7954
Media Contact, Very Rev. Fr Thomas Zain, 52 78th St., Brooklyn, NY 11209, Tel. (718)748-7940 Fax (718)855-3608
Email: FrJoseph@antiochian.org
Website: www.antiochian.org

Officers
Primate, Archbishop Philip Saliba, 358 Mountain Road, Englewood, NJ 07631 - Metropolitan of New York and all North America, Tel. (210)871-1355
Bishop Antoun Khouri, 358 Mountain Road, Englewood, NJ 07631- Bishop of Miami and the Southeast, Tel. (201)871-1355
Bishop Joseph Zehlaoui, 454 S. Lorraine Blvd., Los Angeles, CA 90020 - Bishop of Los Angeles and the West, Tel. (323)934-3131
Bishop Basil Essey, 1559 N. Woodlawn, Wichita, KS 67208 - Bishop of Wichita and Mid-America, Tel. (316) 687-3169 Bishop Thomas Joseph, 4407 Kanawa, Charleston WV 25304 - Bishop of Oakland, PA, Charleston, WV and the Mid Atlantic, Tel. (304)926-0009 Bishop Alexander Mufarrij, 10820 Rue La Verdue, Montreal, QC H3L2L9 - Bishop of Ottawa, Eastern Canada and Upstate New York, Tel. (514)388-4344

Periodicals
The Word, Again Magazine

Apostolic Catholic Assyrian Church of the East, North American Dioceses

The Holy Apostolic Catholic Assyrian Church of the East is the ancient Christian church that developed within the Persian Empire from the day of Pentecost. The Apostolic traditions testify that the Church of the East was established by Sts. Peter, Thomas, Thaddaeus and Bartholomew from among the Twelve and by the labors of Mar Mari and Aggai of the Seventy. The Church grew and developed carrying the Christian gospel into the whole of Asia and islands of the Pacific. Prior to the Great Persecution at the hands of Tamer'leng the Mongol, it is said to have been the largest Christian church in the world.

The doctrinal identity of the church is that of the Apostles. The church stresses two natures and

two Qnume in the One person, Perfect God-Perfect man. The church gives witness to the original Nicene Creed, the Ecumenical Councils of Nicea and Constantinople and the church fathers of that era. Since God is revealed as Trinity, the appellation "Mother of God" is rejected for the "Ever Virgin Blessed Mary Mother of Christ," we declare that she is Mother of Emmanuel, God with us!

The church has maintained a line of Catholicos Patriarchs from the time of the Holy Apostles until this present time. Today the present occupant of the Apostolic Throne is His Holiness Mar Dinkha IV, 120th successor to the See of Selucia Ctestiphon.

Headquarters
Catholicos Patriarch, His Holiness Mar Dinkha, IV, Metropolitanate Residence, The Assyrian Church of the East, Baghdad, Iraq
Media Contact, Father Sleiman Shequel, 7201 N. Ashland, Chicago, IL 60626, Tel. (773)465-4777 Fax (773)465-0776
Email: ABSoro@aol.com
Website: www.cired.org/ace

Bishops-North America
Diocese Eastern USA, His Grace Bishop Mar Aprim Khamis, 8908 Birch Ave., Morton Grove, IL 60053, Tel. (847)966-0617 Fax (847)966-0012; Chancellor to the Bishop, Rev. Chancellor C. H. Klutz, 7201 N. Ashland, Chicago, IL 60626, Tel. (773)465-4777 Fax (773)465-0776
Diocese Western USA,——, St. Joseph Cathedral, 680 Minnesota Ave., San Jose, CA 95125, Tel. (408)286-7377 Fax (408)286-1236
Diocese of Canada, His Grace Bishop Mar Emmanuel Joseph, St. Mary Cathedral, 57 Apted Ave., Weston, ON M9L 2P2, Tel. (416)744-9311
Comm. on Inter-Church & Religious Ed., His Grace Bishop Mar Bawai, Diocese of Seattle in WA, 165 NW 65th, Seattle, WA 98117, Tel. (206)789-1843

Apostolic Catholic Church

The Apostolic Catholic Church, rooted in the New Testament, affirms the empowerment and the dignity of the poor, the needy and the oppressed by adopting a preferential option for those who are disenfranchised and marginalized in this society. Apostolic Catholicism is radically committed to the unconditional acceptance of all who are in need.

The special mission of the Apostolic Catholic Church is to be Christ's arms and legs, reaching out to those who suffer and are ignored by the world. We choose to serve others, ever mindful of the example of Christ, who "did not cling to his equality with God, but emptied himself to assume the condition of a slave." (Philippians 2: 6-7)

Member: The Council of North American Old Catholic Bishops, the Florida Council of Churches, and International Council of Community Churches.

Headquarters

Apostolic Catholic Church
7813 N. Nebraska Avenue, Tampa, FL 33604
Media Contact: Bishop Charles Leigh 813-238-6060, Email: Bishop-Chuck@apostolic catholicchurch.com
Email: Bishop-Chuck@apostoliccatholic church.com
Website: www.apostoliccatholicchurch.com

Officers

Family Counseling Center, Kids in Bible, St James Catholic Worker House.

Periodicals

The Shofar

Apostolic Catholic Orthodox Church

The Apostolic Catholic Orthodox Church (ACOC) is a communion of persons gathered for worship and public ministry outreach within the Christian Apostolic tradition. The ACOC is creedal, renewal-oriented, and is a part of the autocephalous (self-ruling) Old Catholic Movement, which has its origins in the ancient Catholic Church of the Netherlands. The immediate history of the Old Catholic churches comes out of the reform movement that took place after the First Vatican Council (1869-70). The ACOC maintains a friendly relationship with the Old Catholic Church in the Netherlands.

The bishops of the newly forming churches received episcopal consecration in valid Apostolic lines from the church of the Netherlands, based in Utrecht, which had been a fully autonomous Catholic church. These churches became known as "Old Catholic" in reference to their insistence upon return to the basic tenets of Apostolic Christianity, and as defined by the seven Ecumenical Councils of the undivided Eastern and Western Christian churches.

The Old Catholic independent church movement came to the United States as early as the 1880's. Bishop DeLandes Berghes, an Austrian nobleman, ordained and consecrated a bishop with valid Old Catholic Apostolic lines, was sent to North America in 1914. Two of the bishops he consecrated in 1916, Carmel Henry Carfora and William Francis Brothers, are from whom the ACOC derives its lines of Apostolic Succession.

The Apostolic Catholic Orthodox Church's governance is collegial and synodal, with clergy and lay persons sharing in its spiritual leadership and pastoral outreach, in the Spirit of Christ. Clerical celibacy (which is a matter of discipline) is optional among Old Catholics. In the ACOC, Holy Orders are open to both women and men, single or married. Graduate, Seminary and Clinical Pastoral education are required for candidates for ordination. Decisions pertaining to family planning are left to the conscience of married couples, through prayer and counseling.

Matters of faith in the Apostolic Catholic Orthodox Church are the same as in other liturgical churches as formulated in the apostles and Nicene Creeds. The Offices of bishop, priest, and deacon exist for the service of spiritual leadership in facilitating expressions of life with God - in the celebration of the sacraments, counseling and pastoral care, teaching, and public advocacy of Gospel values. The sacraments are never denied to any person on grounds of gender, race, or marital status. The Holy Eucharist is the center of worship for the ACOC and all who are baptized are welcomed at the Lord's Table.

The Apostolic Catholic Orthodox Church emphasizes the importance of the life of the church as community, that all may be one in Christ (John 17), through mutual helpfulness, ministering to one another and all creation in love, through the diversity of personal giftedness and sensitivity to the particular needs of those being served. The church values and promotes spiritually based, courageous, and compassionate ministry to both personal and global needs. Ongoing spiritual growth is to be nourished through sacred study and contemplative prayer. The ACOC values ecumenical dialogue as an expression of the life of the church.

Headquarters

1900 St. James Place, Suite 880, Houston, TX 77056-4129, Tel (713)266-2456 or (713)977-2855 Fax (713)266-0845
www.apostoliccatholic.org
Email: dcdale@apostoliccatholic.org
Website: www.apostoliccatholic.org

Officers

Presiding Bishop, Most Rev. Diana C. Dale, 1900 St. James Place, Suite 880, Houston, TX 77056-4125, Tel (713)266-2456
Email: dcdale@apostoliccatholic.org
Tresurer, Elizabeth F. Burleigh, J.D., 1900 St. James Place, Suite 880, Houston, TX 77056-41291, Tel (713)334-0499
Ecumenical Officer, Very Rev. Robert L. Lewis Jr., P.O. Box 10483, Rockville, MD 20849 (240)401-0178
Register Agent, Biz Filings (for CA incorporation), 8040 Excelsior Dr., Ste. 200, Madison, WI 53717

BOARD REGIONAL REPRESENTATIVES
West: The Rev. Art Jacobson, 307 S. Dickinson, Rock Rapids, IA 51246
Mid-Continent: The Rev. Marty Shanahan, 1927 Worsworth Ave., St. Paul, MN 55116-2641
East: The Rev. Alexandra Honigsberg, 680 Ft. Washington Ave., Apt. 1B, New York, NY 10040-3917

OTHER ORGANIZATIONS:
Institute of Worklife Ministry, 1900 St. James Place, Suite 880, Houston, TX 77056-4129, Tel (713)266-2456 Fax (713)266-0855
Email: www.apostoliccatholic.org

Periodicals

ACOC Quarterly Bulletin; Worklife Quarterly Newsletter

Apostolic Christian Church (Nazarene)

This body was formed in America by an immigration from various European nations, from a movement begun by Rev. S. H. Froehlich, a Swiss pastor, whose followers are still found in Switzerland and Central Europe.

Headquarters

Apostolic Christian Church Foundation, 1135 Sholey Rd., Richmond, VA 23231, Tel. (804)222-1943 Fax (804)236-0642
Media Contact, Exec. Dir., James Hodges
Email: accf@sprynet.com

Officers

Exec. Dir., James Hodges

Apostolic Christian Churches of America

The Apostolic Christian Churches of America was founded in the early 1830s in Switzerland by Samuel Froehlich, a young divinity student who had experienced a religious conversion based on the pattern found in the New Testament. The church, known then as Evangelical Baptist, spread to surrounding countries. A Froehlich associate, Elder Benedict Weyeneth, established the church's first American congregation in 1847 in upstate New York. In America, where the highest concentration today is in the Midwest farm belt, the church became known as Apostolic Christian.

Church doctrine is based on a literal interpretation of the Bible, the infallible Word of God. The church believes that a true faith in Christ's redemptive work at Calvary is manifested by a sincere repentance and conversion. Members strive for sanctification and separation from worldliness as a consequence of salvation, not as a means to obtain it. Security in Christ is believed to be conditional based on faithfulness. Uniform observance of scriptural standards of holiness are stressed. Holy Communion is confined to members of the church. Male members are willing to serve in the military, but do not bear arms. The holy kiss is practiced and women wear head coverings during prayer and worship.

Doctrinal authority rests with a council of elders, each of whom serves as a local elder (bishop). Both elders and ministers are chosen from local congregations, do not attend seminary and serve without compensation. Sermons are delivered extemporaneously as led by the Holy Spirit, using the Bible as a text.

Headquarters

3420 N. Sheridan Rd., Peoria, IL 61604
Media Contact, Secretary., William R. Schlatter, 14834 Campbell Rd., Defiance, OH 43512, Tel. (419)393-2621 Fax (419)393-2144 Email: wrschlatter@juno.com
Email: Questions@ApostolicChristian.org; wrschlatter@juno
Website: www.apostolicchristian.org

Officers

Sec., Elder William R. Schlatter, 14834 Campbell Rd., Defiance, OH 43512, Tel. (419)393-2621, Fax (419)393-2144
Apostolic Christian World Relief - Humanitarian Aid to the World - www.acworldrelief.org

Periodicals

The Silver Lining

Apostolic Episcopal Church

The Apostolic Episcopal Church on Sept. 23-24, 2000 in New York City signed Concordats of Intercommunion with the following Christian Churches-The Anglican Independent Communion, The Ethiopian Orthodox Coptic Archdiocese of North and South America, The Uniate Western Orthodox Catholic Church, and the Byelorussian Orthodox National Church in Exile under the administration of His Beatitude Yury I.

In effect, the Apostolic Episcopal Church thus became a Uniate Western Rite of the Orthodox Church of the East, using the 1928 Book of Common Prayer. In 1905, under the guidance of Archbishop Tikhon Bellavin (later Patriarch of Moscow), the Holy Synod in St. Petersburg approved the use of the Anglican Liturgy for Western Rite Orthodox Christians. Today this usage is called the Rite of St. Tikhon and is in use among many Orthodox Western Rite Jurisdictions.

This Pilgrimage to Orthodoxy among Anglicans began in 1712 with the Non-Jurors Anglican Hierarchy and faithful. These Non-Jurors were Anglican Clergy who in 1689 refused allegiance to King William III and Queen Mary, the usurpers who had overthrown King James II. In 1712 Metropolitan-Bishop Arsenios of the Alexandrine Patriarchate visited England and received many of these "British Katholicks" into the Orthodox Church.

Headquarters

World Mission HQS: 80-46 234 St. Jamaica, NY 11427-2116, Attn.: The Rt. Rev. Francis C. Spataro DD, Tel. (917)579-0585
Ohio Vicariate: The V. Rev. Michael B. Reed, St. Peter the Aleut Mission, 3423 Hunter Dr., N. Olmstead, OH 44070, Tel. (216)779-0272
Pennsylvania Vicariate: Rev. Dr. Sam Guido DD, OCR, St. Paul's Chapel, 620 Main St. Slatington, PA 18080
NY, Brooklyn Vicariate: Rt. Rev. Louis Milazzo, OCR, St. Lucy's, 802 Kent Ave., Clinton Hill, NY 11205. (718)246-4848
Shenouda Seminary Dir.: Rev. Dr. Paget Mack, OCR, OSBM, P.O. Box 673, New York, NY 10035
Belarus Home Mission, AWP, 19 Aqueduct St, Ossining, NY 10562, Tel. (914)762-7093
Media Contact, Rt. Rev. F. C. Spataro, 80-46 234 St., Queens, NY 11427
Email: Vil11427@att.blackberry.net/amworldpat @Verizon.net
Website: http://aec.johnkersey.org

Officers

President, The Rt. Rev. Francis C. Spataro, DD, OCR Tel: (718)740 4134 (24 hour number) Email: vill1427@att.blackberry.net
Archbishop of the Central & Western Province, USA, Dr. Wayne Ellis, PhD, OCR Email: wayneellis@charter.net
OCR Primate: The Rt. Rev. Peter P. Brennan, OCR, DD, Email: ddamdg@aol.com
Vicar for Ohio: The V. Rev. Michael B. Reed, OCR
Emeritus Primate for the AEC, The M. Rev. Bertil Persson, ThD, OCR, Archbishop of Scandinavia & Baltic Republics, Illerstigen 22, S-170 71, Solna, Sweden
Pennsylvania Vicariate: Rev. Dr. Sam Guido, DD LOC Email: samsamtheman@aol.com
Shenouda Seminary Dir.: Rev. Dr. Paget Mack, OSBM
Vicar for Belarus: M. Rev. Emigidiusz J. Ryzy, OCR, DD Email: amworldpat@Verizon.net
The Order of Corporate Reunion; The Vilatte Guild/Society of St. Cassian;

Periodicals

http://aec.johnkersey.org

Apostolic Faith Mission Church of God

The Apostolic Faith Mission Church of God was founded and organized July 10, 1906, by Bishop F. W. Williams in Mobile, Alabama.

Bishop Williams was saved and filled with the Holy Ghost at a revival in Los Angeles under Elder W. J. Seymour of The Divine Apostolic Faith Movement. After being called into the ministry, Bishop Williams went out to preach the gospel in Mississippi, then moved on to Mobile.

On Oct. 9, 1915, the Apostolic Faith Mission Church of God was incorporated in Mobile under Bishop Williams, who was also the general overseer of this church.

Headquarters

Ward's Temple, 806 Muscogee Rd., Cantonment, FL 32533
Media Contact, Natl. Sunday School Supt., Bishop Thomas Brooks, 3298 Toney Dr., Decatur, GA 30032, Tel. (404)284-7596

Officers

BOARD OF BISHOPS

Presiding Bishop, Donice Brown, 2265 Welcome Cir., Cantonement, FL 32535, Tel. (904) 968-5225
Bishop John Crum, 4236 Jackson St., Birmingham, AL, 35217; Bishop Samuel Darden, 25 Taunton Ave., Hyde Park, MA 02136; Bishop James Truss, P.O. Box 495, Lincoln, AL, 35096; Bishop T.C. Tolbert, Jr., 768 Grayton Rd., Ohatchee, AL 36271; Bishop Thomas Brooks, 3298 Toney Drive, Decatur, GA. 30032, Tel: (404)284-7596, Fax: (404)284-7173; Bishop Johnny Cunningham, P.O.Box 472 Century, Fla. 32535, Tel:

(850)256-2443; Bishop Wayne Smiley, 228 Seville Circle, Mary Ester, FL 32569

NATIONAL DEPARTMENTS

Missionary Dept., Pres., Rosa Tolbert, 226 Elston Ave., Anniston, AL 36201
Youth Dept., Pres., Erma McClain, 600 Spencer Ave., Pensacola, FL 32514
Sunday School Dept., Supt., Thomas Brooks, 3298 Toney Dr., Decatur, GA 30032
Mother Dept., Pres., Mother Brenda Brooks, 3298 Toney Dr., Decatur, GA 30032

INTERNATIONAL DEPARTMENTS

Monrovia, Liberia, Bishop Beter T. Nelson, Box 3646, Bush Rhode Island, Monrovia, Liberia

Periodicals

The Three-Fold Vision

Apostolic Faith Mission of Portland, Oregon

The Apostolic Faith Mission of Portland, Oregon, was founded in 1907. It had its beginning in the Latter Rain outpouring on Azusa Street in Los Angeles in 1906.

Some of the main doctrines are justification by faith which is a spiritual new birth, as Jesus told Nicodemus and as Martin Luther proclaimed in the Great Reformation; sanctification, a second definite work of grace; the Wesleyan teaching of holiness; the baptism of the Holy Ghost as experienced on the Day of Pentecost and again poured out at the beginning of the Latter Rain revival in Los Angeles

Mrs. Florence L. Crawford, who had received the baptism of the Holy Ghost in Los Angeles, brought this Latter Rain message to Portland on Christmas Day 1906. It has spread to the world by means of literature which is still published and mailed everywhere without a subscription price. Collections are never taken in the meetings and the public is not asked for money.

Camp meetings have been held annually in Portland, Oregon since 1907, with delegations coming from around the world.

Missionaries from the Portland headquarters have established churches in Korea, Japan, the Philippines, Romania and many countries in Africa.

Headquarters

6615 SE 52nd Ave., Portland, OR 97206, Tel. (503)777-1741 Fax (503)777-1743
Media Contact, Superintendent, Darrel D. LeeWebsite: www.apostolicfaith.org

Officers

President, Rev. Darrel D. Lee

Periodicals

Higher Way

Apostolic Lutheran Church of America

Organized in 1872 as the Solomon Korteniemi Lutheran Society, this Finnish body was

69

incorporated in 1929 as the Finnish Apostolic Lutheran Church in America and changed its name to Apostolic Lutheran Church of America in 1962. This body stresses preaching the Word of God. There is an absence of liturgy and formalism in worship. A seminary education is not required of pastors. Being called by God to preach the Word is the chief requirement for clergy and laity. The church stresses personal absolution and forgiveness of sins, as practiced by Martin Luther, and the importance of bringing converts into God's kingdom.

Headquarters

P.O. Box 2948
Battle Ground, WA 98604-2948
Media Contact, Secretary, Gary Bertham
Website: www.apostolic-lutheran.org

Officers

Chairman, Wilfred Sikkila, 57 Ashby Road #2, New Ipswich, N.H. 03071
Treas., Ben Johnson, 98920 Keller Rd., Astoria, OR 97103
Secretary, Gary Bertham, 124 Binney Hill Road, New Ipswich, N.H. 03071

Periodicals

Christian Monthly

Apostolic Orthodox Catholic Church of North America

The Christian Church was established by the Lord Jesus Christ and His Holy Apostles in Jerusalem in 33 A.D. From Jerusalem, the Church spread to other centers of the known world, including Constantinople (founded in 37 A.D.) and Kiev (45 AD.), founded by St. Andrew the First-Called Holy Apostle. In 864, missionary of the Church of Constantinople further extended the Orthodox Christian Faith in present-day Russia. In 988, Rus' Prince Vladimir converted and declared Orthodoxy the State religion, while hundreds of thousands were baptized in the Dnieper River at Kiev. The resulting Russian Orthodox Church became the greatest safe-guard and body of Orthodox Christians in the world.

The history of Holy Synod for the American Diaspora began in 1794 when Russian Orthodox Church missionaries established the first Orthodox mission on North American soil at present-day Kodiak, Alaska. Their missionary efforts continued down the Pacific coast in 1824, then across the whole continent. Being the canonical founder of Orthodox Christianity in North America, the Russian Orthodox Church maintained and presided over all Orthodox missions, churches, and Christians throughout North America without question or challenge for over 100 years. However, the 1917 Bolshevik Revolution which resulted in severe persecution and imprisonment of the Russian Orthodox Mother Church also resulted in the unrestrained rise of old-country nationalism and great ethnic turbulence between Orthodox Catholic Christians

and their churches in North America. They seperated and divided, often violently, along ethnic and nationalist lines with each creating their own old-world ethnic administrations. The once long-held unity and single Orthodox Church canonical administration in North America was destroyed.

The Holy Synod for the American Diaspora is canonically independent and indigenous to North America and comprised of bishops, clergy and faithful possessing unbroken Apostolic Succession since the time of Jesus Christ's appointment of His Twelve Holy Apostles to the present day through American Orthodoxy's Luminary and Defender, Russian Orthodox Prelate-Archbishop Aftimios Ofiesh of Blessed Memory.

The Holy Synod for the American Diaspora maintains unquestionable, canonical Apostolic Succession passed on to its bishops through its Russian Orthodox Mother Church by Archbishop Aftimios Ofiesh, his succeeding Bishops Sophronios Beshara and Christopher Contogeorge, their legal successors and through consecrating support of such memorable Orthodox leaders as Russian Patriarchal Exarch of North America Metropolitan Benjamin Fedchenkov and and Albanian Orthodox Church Metropolitan Theophan Noli. In 1945, the Apostolic Succession and Canonicity of these bishops "and their successors" were declared in binding agreement to be unquestionable, valid, authentic and independent by the Orthodox Church Ecumenical Patriarchate of Constanti-nople, and recognition was furthermore attested to in 1951. English-speaking and non-ethnic restrictive, the Holy Synod for the American Diaspora's further validity is evidenced by its life, mind, discourse and teaching all being governed and practiced in accordance with the Sacred Canons of the Most Ancient Holy Orthodox Catholic Church. The Holy Synod for the American Diaspora embraces the ideals and theology of Orthodoxy and freedom which Archbishop Aftimios Ofiesh stood for, taught and passed on by selfless devotion and love for Christ and His Church, and by his personal example.

Headquarters

Holy Synod for the American Diaspora, P.O. Box 346, Seward, NE 68434, Tel. (503)375-6175
Media Contact, Most Rev. Aftimios (L. Sinclair), Vice-Presiding Archbishop, 4696 Horseshoe Court SE, Salem, OR 97301; Tel (575)375-6175
Email: synod@oldorthodox.org/bastimii@aol.com

Officers

Archbishop, Most Rev. Mar Melchizedek
The Secretary of the Synod, Most. Rev. Bishop Aftimios
Synod of Bishops, Most Rev. Bishop Spyridon, Most Rev. Bishop Valerian, Most Rev. Bishop Maximus

SEMINARY
St Elias School of Orthodox Theology, P.O. Box 346, Seward, NE 68434, Tel. (402)643-9365

Armenian Apostolic Church of America

Widespread movement of the Armenian people over the centuries caused the development of two seats of religious jurisdiction of the Armenian Apostolic Church in the World-the See of Etchmiadzin, in Armenia, and the See of Cilicia, in Lebanon.

In America, the Armenian Church functioned under the jurisdiction of the Etchmiadzin See from 1887 to 1933, when a division occurred within the American diocese over the condition of the church in Soviet Armenia. One group chose to remain independent until 1957, when the Holy See of Cilicia agreed to accept them under its jurisdiction.

Despite the existence of two dioceses in North America, the Armenian Church has always functioned as one church in dogma and liturgy.

Headquarters

Eastern Prelacy, 138 E. 39th St., New York, NY 10016, Tel. (212)689-7810 Fax (212)689-7168 Email: email@armenianprelacy.org
Western Prelacy, 6252 Honolulu Ave., La Crecsenta, CA 91214, Tel. (818)248-7737; Fax (818)248-7745 Email: prelacy@aol.com
Media Contact, Vazken Ghougassian Email: prelacy@gis.net
Website: www.armprelacy.org

Officers

Eastern Prelacy, Prelate, Archbishop Oshagan Choloyan
Eastern Prelacy, Chpsn., Hagop Khatchadouzian
Western Prelacy, Prelate, Archbishop Moushegh Mardirossian
Western Prelacy, Chpsn., Dr. Garo Hagopian

DEPARTMENTS
Eastern Prelacy Offices, Executive Director, Vazken Ghougassian
AREC, Armenian Religious Educ. Council, Exec. Coord., Deacon Shant Kazanjian
ANEC, Armenian Natl. Educ. Council

Periodicals

Outreach

Armenian Apostolic Church, Dioceses of America*

The Armenian Apostolic Church was established at the foot of the biblical mountain of Ararat in the ancient land of Armenia, where two of Christ's Holy Apostles, Saints Thaddeus and Bartholomew, preached Christianity in the 1st century. In A.D. 303, the kingdom of Armenia became history's first Christian nation, when king Tiridates III was baptized by Saint Gregory the Illuminator. Gregory became the patron saint of Armenian, the first in a line of 132 Catholic of all Armenians, and founder, in A.D. 303, of the historic Mother See of Holy Etchmiadzin, which still serves as the central, preeminent shrine of the worldwide Armenian Church. The present-day Catholics of All Aremians is His Holiness Karekin II. Khrimian. Armenian immigrants built the first Armenian church in the new world in Worcester, MA, under the jurisdiction of Holy Etchmiadzin.

In 1891, in fulfillment of a petition to Holy Etchmiadzin, Armenian immigrants to America built and witnessed the consecration of the New World's first Armenian church in Worcester, Massachusetts. In 1898, the 125th Catholicos of All Armenians, Mgrdich Khrimian, established a diocesan jurisdiction for the burgeoning communities in North and South America; today, the Diocese of the Armenian Church of America (Eastern) administers parishes in the eastern half of the U.S., with separate dioceses governing parishes in California (Western Diocese, established 1927), Canada (the Canadian Diocese, established 1984), and South America (various jurisdictions and dates). Other centers of major significance for the Armenian Apostolic Church are the Catholicate of Cilicia (located in Lebanon), the Armenian Patriarchate of Jerusalem, and the Armenian Patrichate of Constantinopole.

Headquarters

Eastern Diocese, 630 Second Ave., New York, NY 10016-4885, Tel. (212)686-0710 Fax (212)779-3558, Website: www.armenianchurch.net
Western Diocese, 3325 North Glenoaks Blvd., Burbank, CA 91504, Tel. (818)558-7474 Fax (818)558-6333, Website: www.armenian churchwd.com
Canadian Diocese, 615 Stuart Ave., Outremont, QC H2V 3H2, Tel. (514)276-9479 Fax (514)276-9960, Website: www.armenianchurch.ca
Media Contact, Karine Abalayn, Public Relations Coordinator, Eastern Diocese, Tel. (212)686-0710, Email: publicrelations@armenianchurch.org
Email: mgizlechyan@armenianchurchwd.com
Website: www.armenianchurch.org

Officers

EASTERN DIOCESE
Primate, Archbishop Khajag Barsamian
Diocesan Council, Chpsn., Ara Boyajian

WESTERN DIOCESE
Primate, Archbishop Hovnan Derderian
Diocesan Council, Chpsn., Joseph Kanimian, Esq., Tel. (818)558-7474

CANADIAN DIOCESE
Primate, Bishop Bagrat Galstanian, Tel. (514)276-9479

Periodicals

The Armenian Church Magazine (Eastern Diocese), The Mother Church Magazine (Western Diocese)

Assemblies of God

From a few hundred delegates at its founding convention in 1914 at Hot Springs, Ark., the

71

Assemblies of God has become one of the largest church groups in the modern Pentecostal movement with over 61 million adherents worldwide. Throughout its existence it has emphasized the power of the Holy Spirit to change lives and the participation of all members in the work of the church.

The revival that led to the formation of the Assemblies of God and numerous other church groups early in the 20th century began during times of intense prayer and Bible study. Believers in the United States and around the world received spiritual experiences like those described in the Book of Acts. Accompanied by baptism in the Holy Spirit and its initial physical evidence of "speaking in tongues," or a language unknown to the person, their experiences were associated with the coming of the Holy Spirit at Pentecost (Acts 2), so participants were called Pentecostals.

The church also believes that the Bible is God's inspired infallible Word to man, that salvation is available only through Jesus Christ, that divine healing is made possible through Christ's suffering and that Christ will return again for those who love Him. In recent years, this Pentecostal revival has spilled over into almost every denomination in a wave of revival sometimes called the charismatic renewal.

Assemblies of God leaders credit their church's rapid and continuing growth to its acceptance of the New Testament as a model for the present-day church. Aggressive evangelism and missionary zeal at home and abroad characterize the denomination.

Assemblies of God believers observe two ordinances-water baptism by immersion and the Lord's Supper, or Holy Communion. The church is Trinitarian, holding that God exists in three persons-Father, Son and Holy Spirit.

Headquarters

Media Contact: Juleen Turnage, Dir. of Public Relations, Assemblies of God 1445 N. Boonville Ave., Springfield, MO 65802-1894, Tel. (417)862-2781 Fax (417)862-5554 Email: info@ag.org
Email: Statistics@ag.org
Website: www.ag.org/top

Officers

Gen. Supt., George O. Wood
Asst. Supt., L. Alton Garrison
Gen. Sec., James T. Bradford
Gen. Treas., Doug Clay
World Missions, Exec. Dir., L. John Bueno
AG U.S. Missions, Exec. Dir., Zollie L. Smith, Jr.
Great Lakes: Larry H. Griswold, P.O. Box 620, Carlinville IL, Tel. (217)854-4600 Fax (614)396-0701
Gulf: Douglas Fulenwider, P.O. Box 7388, Alexandria, LA 71306, Tel. (318)445-6238, Fax (318)473-9344
North Central: Clarence W. St John, 1315 Portland Ave. S., Minneapolis, MN 55404, Tel. (612)332-2409, Fax (612)332-2510
Northeast: H. Robert Rhoden, 3525 Corrotoman Rd., Glen Allen, VA 23060, Tel. (804)755-6181

Northwest: Warren Bullock, 3535 Auburn Way S, Auburn, WA 98092, Tel. (253)833-8252, Fax (253)351-2943
South Central: J. Don George, 4401 N. Highway 161, Irving, TX 75038, Tel. (972)261-1919 Fax (972)261-1895
Southeast: Dan Betzer, 6901 Harbor Ln., Ft. Myers, FL 33919, Tel. (239)936-6277, Fax (239)936-9365
Southwest, Richard Dresselhaus, 6126 Bernadette Ln., San Diego, CA 92120 Tel. (619)286-9361
Language Area—West Spanish, Jesse Miranda Jr., 55 Fair Drive, Costa Mesa, CA 92626, Tel. (714)556-3610, Fax (714)966-5471
Language Area Other, Nam Soo Kim, 13030 31st Ave Flushing NY 11354, Tel. (718)321-7800, Fax (718)321-9394
Ethnic Fellowship, John E. Maracle, P.O. Box 83387, Phoenix, AZ 85071, Tel. (602)216-6001, Fax (602)216-6004
Language Area – East Spanish, Saturnino Gonzalez, 830 California Woods Cir, Orlando FL 32824, Tel. (407)850-9861, Fax (407)852-9887
Ordained Female – A. Elizabeth Grant, P.O. Box 990, Springfield MO 65801, Tel. (417)833-5562, Fax (417)833-5568
Ordained Pastor under 40 – R Bryan Jarrett, P.O. Box 99, Wylie, TX 75098, Tel. (417)495-1116, Fax (972)495-4913
Division of the Treasury, Gen. Treas., Doug Clay
Division of Church Ministries and Discipleship, Executive Director, L. Alton Garrison
Division of World Missions, Exec Dir., L. John Bueno
Division of U.S. Missions, Exec. Dir., Zollie L. Smith, Jr.
Division of Publication, Gospel Publishing House, Natl. Dir., J. T. Wray
Division of Communications, Natl. Dir., Juleen Turnage

Periodicals

Enrichment - A Journal for Pentecostal Ministry High Adventure, Today's Pentecostal Evangel, Heritage, On Course

Assemblies of God International Fellowship (Independent/Not affiliated)

April 9, 1906 is the date commonly accepted by Pentecostals as the 20th-century outpouring of God's spirit in America, which began in a humble gospel mission at 312 Azusa Street in Los Angeles. This spirit movement spread across the United States and gave birth to the Independent Assemblies of God (Scandinavian). Early pioneers instrumental in guiding and shaping the fellowship of ministers and churches into a nucleus of independent churches included Pastor B. M. Johnson, founder of Lakeview Gospel Church in 1911; Rev. A. A. Holmgren, a Baptist minister who received his baptism of the Holy Spirit in the early Chicago outpourings, was publisher of Sanningens Vittne, a voice of the Scandinavian Independent Assemblies of God and also served as secretary of the fellowship for many years; Gunnar Wingren, missionary pioneer in Brazil; and Arthur F. Johnson, who served for many years as chairman of the Scandinavian Assemblies.

In 1935, the Scandinavian group dissolved its incorporation and united with the Independent Assemblies of God of the U.S. and Canada which by majority vote of members formed a new corporation in 1986, Assemblies of God International Fellowship (Independent/Not Affiliated).

Headquarters
6325 Marindustry Dr., San Diego, CA 92121, Tel. (858)677-9701 Fax (858)677-0038
Media Contact, Exec. Dir. & Ed., Rev. T. A. Lanes
Email: admin@agifellowship.org
Website: www.agifellowship.org

Officers
Exec. Dir., Rev. T. A. Lanes
Sec., Rev. George E. Ekeroth
Treas., M. J. Ekeroth
Canada, Sec., Harry Nunn, Sr., 15 White Crest Ct., St. Catherines, ON 62N 6Y1

Periodicals
Fellowship

Associate Reformed Presbyterian Church (General Synod)

The Associate Reformed Presbyterian Church (APR) developed from two groups that formed in Scotland in 17th and 18th Centuries—the Covenanters and Seceders. These two movements developed into the Reformed Presbyterian Church of Scotland and the Associate Church of Scotland respectively, and their members migrated to America because of religious and political upheaval in Britain. The two merged in 1782 and eventually became known as the Associate Reformed Presbyterian Church. The church continues its commitment to the fundamental truths on which it was founded: the Lordship of Jesus Christ and the free offer of the Gospel of grace.

We are a Presbyterian and Reformed Chuch rooted in the historic Reformed tradition as expressed in the Westminster Confession of Faith and Catechisms. Each local congregation elects ruling elders to the session, and deacons to the diaconate. In this representative form of government, the session oversees the total ministry of the congregation and is concerned primiarily with the spiritual life of the church. The diaconate is concerned primarily with material needs.

The governing body above the local session is the presbytery, which oversees a group of congregations in a specific geographical area. The hightest governing body is the General Synod, composed of all ARP ministers and at least one elder from each congregation. The Synod meets annually to worship together and conduct business.

Headquarters
Associate Reformed Presbyterian Center, 1 Cleveland St., Greenville, SC 29601-3696, Tel. (864)232-8297

Email: modquery@arpsynod.org
Website: www.arpsynod.org

Officers
Moderator: The Rev. John R. de Witt, Th. D., D. D., 6 Quinine Hill, Columbia, SC 29204, 803-787-8586, JohnCandidus@aol.com
Moderator-Elect: Mr. Steven Maye, 6517 Buggy Whip Lane, Waxhaw, NC 28173, 704-843-9650, smaye@drakecap.net
Principal Clerk: The Rev. C. Ronald Beard, D.D., 3132 Grace Hill Rd., Columbia, SC 29204, 803-782-3896, rbcard1@sc.rr.com
Treasurer: Guy H. Smith, III, 1 Cleveland St., Greenville, SC 29601-3696, Tel. (864)232-8297
Agencies at ARP Center in Greenville, SC:
Central Services: Paul Bell, Executive Director, pbell@arpsynod.org
Christian Education Ministries: Rev. Brent Turner, D. Min., Exec. Director
Outreach North America: Rev. Alan Avera, D. Min., Executive Director
The Associate Reformed Presbyterian: Mrs. Delores McDonald, Editor, onadir@arpsynod.org
Word Witness, Board of Foreign Missions: Rev. Frank van Dalen, Executive Director, fvandalen@worldwitness.org

OTHER INSTITUTIONS
Bonclarken Conference Center, Pres., Joseph "Chip" Sherer, 500 Pine Drive., Flat Rock, NC 28731, Tel. (828)692-2223, chserer@bonclarken.com
Erskine College and Theological Seminary: Rev. Randall Ruble, Ph.D., President, 2 Washington Street, Due West, SC 29639, 864-379-8833, ruble@erskine.edu
ARP Women's Ministries: Mrs. Kathy Barron, President, 146 Grinders Circle, Greer, SC 29650, 864-292-5821, jkbarron@erskine.edu

Periodicals
The Associate Reformed Presbyterian, The Adult Quarterly

The Association of Free Lutheran Congregations

The Association of Free Lutheran Congregations, rooted in the northern European revival movements, was organized in 1962 by a Lutheran Free Church remnant which rejected merger with The American Lutheran Church. The original 42 congregations were joined by other like-minded conservative Lutherans, and there has been more than a sixfold increase in the number of congregations. Members subscribe to the Apostles', Nicene and Athanasian creeds; Luther's Small Catechism; and the Unaltered Augsburg Confession. The Fundamental Principles and Rules for Work (1897) declare that the local congregation is the right form of the kingdom of God on earth, subject to no authority but the Word and the Spirit of God.

Distinctive emphases are, (1) the infallibility and inerrancy of Holy Scriptures as the Word of God; (2) congregational polity; (3) the spiritual

73

unity of all believers, resulting in fellowship and cooperation transcending denominational lines; (4) evangelical outreach, calling all to enter a personal relationship with Jesus Christ; (5) a wholesome Lutheran pietism that proclaims the Lordship of Jesus Christ in all areas of life and results in believers becoming the salt and light in their communities; (6) a conservative stance on current social issues.

A two-year Bible school and a theological seminary are in suburban Minneapolis. The AFLC is in fellowship with sister churches in Canada, Brazil, Mexico, and India.

Headquarters
3110 E. Medicine Lake Blvd., Minneapolis, MN 55441, Tel. (763)545-5631 Fax (763)545-0079
Media Contact, Pres., Rev. Elden K. Nelson
Email: webmaster@aflc.org
Website: www.aflc.org

Officers
Pres., Rev. Elden K. Nelson, 3110 E. Medicine Lake Blvd., Minneapolis, MN 55441, Tel. (763)545-5631, Fax. (763)545-0079, Email: president@aflc.org
Vice Pres., Rev. Michael Brandt, 3110 E. Medicine Lake Blvd., Minneapolis, MN 55441, Tel(763)545-5631, Email: vpres@aflc.org
Sec., Rev. Brian Davidson, 3110 E. Medicine Lake Blvd., Minneapolis, MN 55441, Tel(763)545-5631 Fax(763)545-0079 Email:briand@aflc.org

Periodicals
The Lutheran Ambassador

Association of Independent Evangelical Lutheran Churches

The AIELC was established, as a response to the affiliation need of independent missions and churches originally of the Latino community in the USA and worldwide, which are commited to the learning and teaching of Lutheran Doctrine and Theology. We are a Lutheran denomination that provide support and guidance to independent missions and churches to be better prepared for the work in the Kingdom of God at the light of Lutheran understanding of Confessing Christ. As part of our affiliation process we don't ask independent missions and churches to surrender their buildings or administrative independency; nor do we require them to provide financial support to the main denomination itself.

Our current worlwide membership is estimated as approximately 35,000 members with Churches in Scotland, Channel Islands, India, South Africa, Argentina, Ecuador, Colombia, Puerto Rico, Haiti, Chile and the USA. We have active Concordat with religious bodies in the USA and abroad, among them the Evangelical Community Church-Lutheran, the Athanasian Catholic Church of the Augsburg Confession, and the Lutheran Orthodox Church. We hold active membership at the Queens Federation of Churches in New York.

Headquarters
14020 27th Avenue; Astoria, NY 11102, Tel. (718)278-3894
Email: mainoffice@aielc.org
Web:www.associationofindependentevangelicallutheranchurches.org

Officers
The Rev. Dr. Pedro Bravo-Guzmán, Presiding Bishop, 14-22 27th Ave, Astoria, NY 11102, Tel. (718) 278-3894, Email: pbravoguzman@aielc.org
The Rev. Dr. Francis C. Spataro, Bishop Emeritus, 14-22 27th Ave, Astoria, NY 11102, Tel. (718)278-3894, Email: vil11427@mycingular.blackberry.net
The Rev. Dr. Peter P. Brennan, Bishop Visitor, 14-22 27th Ave, Astoria, NY 11102, Tel. (718)278-3894, Email: Ddamdg@aol.com
The Rev. Dr. Bishop Louis Marcel Pierre, Bishop for the Caribbean, 14-22 27th Ave, Astoria, NY 11102, Tel. (718)278-3894, Email: louispierre_73@hotmail.com
The Rev. Dr. Bishop Louis Mphahlele, Bishop for Africa, 14-22 27th Ave, Astoria, NY 11102, Tel. (718)278-3894, Email: lutheranunited@webmail.co.za
The Rev. Dr. Bishop Adolfo Acuña, Bishop for South America, 14-22 27th Ave, Astoria, NY 11102, Tel. (718)278-3894, Email: icli_comunicaciones@yahoo.com.ar
The Rev. Paul Lorentzen, Assistant to the Presiding Bishop, 14-22 27th Ave, Astoria, NY 11102, Tel. (718)278-3894, Email: pal10314@aol.com
Miss Christine Dobush, Public Relations Director, 14-22 27th Ave, Astoria, NY 11102, Tel. (718)-278-3894, Email: cdobush@inch.com
Dr. Jeannette Cano-Landivar, Secretary, 14-22 27th Ave, Astoria, NY 11102, Tel. (718)278-3894, Email: aielcsecretariat@aielc.org
Ivan Egas Alprecht., Treasurer, 14-22 27th Ave, Astoria, NY 11102, Tel. (718)278-3894, Email: aielcsecretariat@aielc.org The Rev. Dr. Juan Verdugo Martinez, Lutheran Biblical Institute in Chile, Dean, 14-22 27th Ave, Astoria, NY 11102, Tel. (718)278-3894, Email: pentateuco754@hotmail.com
Global Aid Foundation

Association of Vineyard Churches

Vineyard USA is a community of 600 churches committed to building the church and living under the reign of God. It officially started in Southern California in 1982 under the leadership of John Wimber. The Board of Directors is the governing Board for Vineyard USA. The form of government is Free Church and thus the local Vineyards are free to govern as they desire as long as they do not violate the faith or practices of the Vineyard community. Vineyard USA consists of eight regions under the direction of a Regional Overseer. Each region also has Area Pastoral Care Leaders who give oversight to a small group of pastors in a geographic area. The

National Director is the CEO of the National Office and works with the National Board to see that Vineyard USA achieves its purpose.

Headquarters
5115 Grove West Blvd., Stafford, TX 77477, Tel. (281)313-8463 Fax (281)313-8464
Email: info@vineyardusa.org
Website: vineyardusa.org

Officers
National Dir., Berten A. Waggoner, Email: lucierosser@vineyardusa.org
Secretary, Doug Anderson, Email: doug@vineyardusa.org
Treasurer, Brian Anderson
Vineyard Music USA, Vineyard Resources USA, Mercy Response

Periodicals
Cutting Edge

Baptist Bible Fellowship International
Organized on May 24, 1950 in Fort Worth, Tx., the Baptist Bible Fellowship was founded by about 100 pastors and lay people who had grown disenchanted with the policies and leadership of the World Fundamental Baptist Missionary Fellowship, an outgrowth of the Baptist Bible Union formed in Kansas City in 1923 by fundamentalist leaders from the Southern Baptist, Northern Baptist and Canadian Baptist Conventions. The BBF elected W. E. Dowell as its first president and established offices and a three-year (now four-year with a graduate school) Baptist Bible College.

The BBF statement of faith was essentially that of the Baptist Bible Union, adopted in 1923, a variation of the New Hampshire Confession of Faith. It presents an infallible Bible, belief in the substitutionary death of Christ, his physical resurrection and his premillennial return to earth. It advocates local church autonomy and strong pastoral leadership and maintains that the fundamental basis of fellowship is a missionary outreach. The BBF vigorously stresses evangelism and the international missions office reports 901 adult missionaries working on 110 fields throughout the world.

There are BBF-related churches in every state of the United States, with special strength in the upper South, the Great Lakes region, southern states west of the Mississippi, Kansas and California. There are seven related colleges and one graduate school or seminary.

A Committee of Forty-Five, elected by pastors and churches within the states, sits as a representative body, meeting in three subcommittees, each chaired by one of the principal officers-an administration committee chaired by the president, a missions committee chaired by a vice-president and an education committee chaired by a vice-president.

World Mission Service Center
Baptist Bible Fellowship Missions Bldg., 720 E. Kearney St., Springfield, MO 65803, Tel. (417)862-5001 Fax (417)865-0794

Mailing Address, P.O. Box 191, Springfield, MO 65801
Media Contact, Mission Dir., Dr. Bob Baird, P.O. Box 191, Springfield, MO 65801
Email: csbc@cherrystreet.org
Website: www.bbfi.org

Officers
Pres., Rev. Bill Monroe, P.O. Box 12809, Florence, SC 29504, Tel. (843)662-0453, WK (417)-862-5001
First Vice Pres., Rev. Mike Peper, 4150 Market St., Aston, PA 19014, Tel. (610)497-0700, WK (417)862-5001
Second Vice Pres., Keith Gillming, 3025 N Lindbergh Blvd., St. Louis, MO 63074, Tel. (314)291-6919
Sec., Rev. Don Elmore, P.O. Box 7150, Springdale, AR 72766, Tel. (479)751-4255
Treas., Rev. Ken Armstrong, 2200 Prairin St., Emporia, KS, Tel. (316)342-4142

Periodicals
The Baptist Bible Tribune, The Preacher

Baptist General Conference
The Baptist General Conference, rooted in the pietistic movement of Sweden during the 19th century, traces its history to Aug. 13, 1852. On that day a small group of believers at Rock Island, Illinois, under the leadership of Gustaf Palmquist, organized the first Swedish Baptist Church in America. Swedish Baptist churches flourished in the upper Midwest and Northeast, and by 1879, when the first annual meeting was held in Village Creek, Iowa, 65 churches had been organized, stretching from Maine to the Dakotas and south to Kansas and Missouri.

By 1871, John Alexis Edgren, an immigrant sea captain and pastor in Chicago, had begun the first publication and a theological seminary. The Conference grew to 324 churches and nearly 26,000 members by 1902. There were 40,000 members in 1945 and 135,000 in 1993.

Many churches began as Sunday schools. The seminary evolved into Bethel, a four-year liberal arts college with 1,800 students, and theological seminaries in Arden Hills, Minnesota. and San Diego, California. Missions and the planting of churches have been main objectives both in America and overseas. Today churches have been established in the United States, Canada and Mexico, as well as twenty countries overseas. In 1985 the churches of Canada founded an autonomous denomination, The Baptist General Conference of Canada.

The Baptist General Conference is a member of the Baptist World Alliance, the Baptist Joint Committee on Public Affairs and the National Association of Evangelicals. It is characterized by the balancing of a conservative doctrine with an irenic and cooperative spirit. Its basic objective is to seek the fulfillment of the Great Commission and the Great Commandment.

75

Headquarters

2002 S. Arlington Heights Rd., Arlington Heights, IL 60005, Tel. (847)228-0200 Fax (847)228-5376
Email: gmarsh@baptistgeneral.org
Website: www.bgcworld.org

Officers

Pres. & Chief Exec. Officer, Dr. Gerald Sheveland, 2002 S. Arlington Hts. Rd., Arlington Heights, IL 60005, Tel. (847)228-0200 Fax (847)228-5376; Email: jsheveland@baptistgeneral.org

Exec, Vice Pres., Ray Swatkowski, (address/ph/fax same as above), Email: rswatkowski@baptistgeneral.org

Director of Mission Advance, Dr. Lou Petrie, (address/ph/fax same as above), Email: lpetrie@baptistgeneral.org

Director of Finance, Stephen R. Schultz, (address/ph/fax same as above), Email: sschultz@baptistgeneral.org

Director of National Ministries, Rev. Paul Johnson, (address/ph/fax same as above), Email: pauljchp@aol.com

Director of International Ministries: Dr. Ronald Larson, (address/ph/fax same as above), Email: rlarson@aol.com

OTHER ORGANIZATIONS
Bd. of Trustees, Bethel College & Seminary, Pres., Dr. George K. Brushaber, 3900 Bethel Dr., St. Paul, MN 55112

Periodicals

BGC World

Baptist Missionary Association of America

A group of regular Baptist churches organized in associational capacity in May, 1950, in Little Rock, Ark., as the North American Baptist Association. The name changed in 1969 to Baptist Missionary Association of America. There are several state and numerous local associations of cooperating churches. In theology, these churches are evangelical, missionary, fundamental and for the most part premillennial.

Headquarters

9219 Sibly Hole Rd., Little Rock, AR, Tel. (501)455-4977 Fax (501)455-3636
Mailing Address, P.O. Box 193920, Little Rock, AR 72219-3920
Media Contact, Dir. of Disciple Guide Information Services, Texarkana, TX 75505, Tel. (870)772-4550 Fax (903)586-0378
Email: bmaam@bmaam.com
Website: www.bmaam.com

Presiding Officers

President: Dr. Philip Attebery, 3030 Meadowlark Ln., Tyler, TX 75701-6042, (903)586-2501, FAX (903)586-0378, attebery@bmats.edu

First Vice President: Paul Bullock, 6710 Countryside Dr., Texarkana, AR 71854-2410, (870)330-9528 or (903)832-2063, pastor.rrbc@yahoo.com

Second Vice President: Ed Stephenson, 93 Elliott Rd., Greenbrier, AR 72058-9265, (501)679-5848, ed@springhillbaptistchurch.info

Recording Secretaries: Jerome Cooper, 4613 Loop 245, Texarkana, Arkansas 71854-1263, (870)772-4550 or (903)278-9249, jerome@disciple guide.org; Greg Medenwald, 310 Quail Hollow Pl., Hattiesburg, MS 39402-8974, (601) 264-8087 or (601)264-8987, magnoliabcms@aol.com; James Ray Raines, 5609 N. Locust St., North Little Rock, AR 72116-6229, (501)945-2640 or (501)758-4093, jam@aristotle.net

BMA Theological Seminary, Department of Christian Education
Dr. Charley Holmes, President
1530 East Pine Street
Mailing address: P.O. Box 670
Jacksonville, TX 75766-0670
(903)586-2501, FAX (903)586-0378

Other Organizations

LIFEWORD MEDIA MINISTRIES
Department of Radio/Television: Executive Director: George L. Reddin, 611 Locust Ave., (Mailing Address: P.O. Box 6), Conway, AR 72033-0006, (501)329-6891, Fax (501)329-7951, george@lifeword.org
Web: www.lifeword.org

DISCIPLEGUIDE CHURCH RESOURCES
Department of Church Resources: Executive Director: Kevin W. Clayton, D.Min. 4613 Loop 245, Texarkana, AR 71854-1263, (870)772-4550, Fax (870)772-5451, kevin@discipleguide.org
Web: www. DiscipleGuide.org
Publishing Ministry: Jerome Cooper, publishing ministry director, jerome@discipleguide.org, 4613 Loop 245, Texarkana, AR 71854-1263, (870)772-4550; Orders (800)333-1442; Fax (870)772-5451
Conference Ministry: Donny Parrish, conference ministry director, donny@discipleguide.org P.O. Box 10356, Conway, AR 72034-0005, (501)513-3726; Fax (501)513-2159
Camp Ministry: Daniel Springs Baptist Encampment; James Speer, camp ministry director, jspeer9064@discipleguide.org P.O. Box 310, Gary, TX 75643-0310, (903)685-2433; (800)332-2309; Fax (903)685-2422
Bobby Hudgens, research and development officer, bhudgens@discipleguide.org, 4613 Loop 245, Texarkana, AR 71854-1263, (870)772-4550, Fax (870)772-5451

BMAA DEPARTMENT OF MISSIONS
Executive Director: Grady L. Higgs, 9219 Sibley Hole Rd., Little Rock, AR, (Mailing Address: P.O. Box 30910, Little Rock, AR 72260-0016),

(501)455-4977, Fax (501)455-3636, ghiggs@ bmaam.com or bmaam@bmaam.com
Web: www.bmaam.net
Director of Operations-North America: Larry Barker, 9219 Sibley Hole Rd., Little Rock, AR 72209, (Mailing address: P.O. Box 30910, Little Rock, AR 72260), (501)455-4977, Fax (501)455-3636, larry@bmaam.com.
Director of Operations-Missions Support Ministries: Dr. Ralph Izard, 9219 Sibley Hole Rd., Little Rock, AR 72209, (Mailing address: P.O. Box 30910, Little Rock, AR 72260), (501)455-4977, Fax (501)455-3636, bmmi@ bmaam.com
Director of Operations-Europe/Asia/Africa/ Australia: Jerry D. Kidd, 9219 Sibley Hole Rd., Little Rock, AR 72209, (Mailing address: P.O. Box 30910, Little Rock, AR 72260), (501)455-4977, Fax (501)455-3636, jkidd@ bmaam.com
Director of Operations-Latin America: Felix Knott, 9219 Sibley Hole Rd., Little Rock, AR 72209, (Mailing address: P.O. Box 30910, Little Rock, AR 72260), (501)455-4977, Fax (501)455-3636, knott@bmaam.com
Director of Operations-Armed Forces & Institutional Chaplaincy: (LTC) David Norvell, 4328 Loma de Brisas, El Paso, TX 79934-3702, (915)307-6978, dnorvell@ elp.rr.com
Director of Student Ministries: Donny Parrish, P.O. Box 126, Forney, TX 75126-0126, (972)564-9553, donny@fellowshipforney.org
Assistant to Executive Director: Dr. John D. Smith, 9219 Sibley Hole Rd., Little Rock, AR 72209, (Mailing address: P.O. Box 30910, Little Rock, AR 72260), (501)455-4977, Fax (501)455-3636, jdsmith@aol.com

NATIONAL BROTHERHOOD
President: Matt Hudson, 1530 Loden Road, Fulton, MS 38843-8819, (662)862-2510, mlhudson85@yahoo.com

NATIONAL WOMEN'S MISSIONARY AUXILIARY
President: Lisa Hudson, 1530 Loden Road, Fulton, MS 38843-8819, (662)862-2510, lisawmapres@yahoo.com

Beachy Amish Mennonite Churches

The Beachy Amish Mennonite Church was established in 1927 in Somerset County, Pa. following a division in the Amish Mennonite Church in that area. As congregations in other locations joined the movement, they were identified by the same name. There are currently 97 churches in the United States, 9 in Canada and 34 in other countries. Membership in the United States is 7,059, according to the 1996 Mennonite Yearbook.

Beachy Churches believe in one God eternally existent in three persons (Father, Son and Holy Spirit); that Jesus Christ is the one and only way

to salvation; that the Bible is God's infallible Word to us, by which all will be judged; that heaven is the eternal abode of the redeemed in Christ; and that the wicked and unbelieving will endure hell eternally.

Evangelical mission boards sponsor missions in Central and South America, Belgium, Ireland, and in Kenya, Africa.

The Mission Interests Committee, founded in 1953 for evangelism and other Christian services, sponsors homes for handicapped youth and elderly people, mission outreaches among the North American Indians in Canada and a mission outreach in Europe.

Headquarters
Media Contact, Paul L. Miller, 7809 S. Herren Rd. Partridge, KS 67566, Tel. (620)567-2286
Email: ivanbeachy@emypeople.net

Officers
Amish Mennonite Aid, Sec.-Treas., Ivan Beachy, 8916 Mission Home Rd., Free Union, VA 22940, Tel. (434)985-4954
Mission Interests Committee, Sec.-Treas., Melvin Gingerich, 42555 900W, Topeka, IN 46571, Tel. (219)593-9090
Choice Books of Northern Virginia, Supervisor, Simon Schrock, 4614 Holly Ave., FairFax, VA 22030, Tel. (703)830-2800
Calvary Bible School, Sec., Treas., Timothy J. Stoltzfus, 5815 Sulfur Mt. Rd., Harrison, AR 72601, Tel. (870)741-1614
Penn Valley Christian Retreat, Bd. Chmn., Wayne Schrock, RR 2, Box 165, McVeytown, PA 17015, Tel. (717)529-2935

Periodicals
The Calvary Messenger

Berean Fellowship of Churches

Founded 1932 in North Platte, Nebraska, this body emphasizes conservative Protestant doctrines.

Headquarters
5 Camelot Way, Box 1264, Kearney, NE 68845
Tel (308)234-5373 Fax (308)234-5373
Media Contact, Pres., Pastor Doug Shada
Email: BereanChurches@aol.com
Website: www.bereanfellowship.org

Officers
Pres., Doug Shada
Vice Pres., Richard Crocker, 419 Lafayette Blvd., Cheyenne, WY 82009, Tel. (307)635-5914
Sec., Frank Van Campen, 513 Education Dr., Malcolm, NE 68402
Treas., Virgil Wiebe, 125 Split Rock Cir., Hollister, MO 65672

The Bible Church of Christ, Inc.

The Bible Church of Christ was founded on March 1, 1961 by Bishop Roy Bryant, Sr. Since that time, the Church has grown to include congregations in the United States, Africa and India.

The church is Trinitarian and accepts the Bible as the divinely inspired Word of God. Its doctrine includes miracles of healing, deliverance and the baptism of the Holy Ghost.

Headquarters
1358 Morris Ave., Bronx, NY 10456, Tel. (718) 588-2284 Fax (718) 992-5597
Media Contact, Pres., Bishop Roy Bryant, Sr
Email: bccbookstore@earthlink.net
Website: www.thebiblechurchofchrist.org

Officers
Pres., Bishop Roy Bryant, Sr. Vice Pres., Bishop Darue Bryant
Sec., Mother Sissieretta Bryant
Treas., Elder Artie Burney

EXECUTIVE TRUSTEE BOARD
Chpsn., Bishop Christopher Powell, 1069 Morris Ave., Bronx, NY 10456, Tel. (718)992-4653

OTHER ORGANIZATIONS
Christian Bookstore, Mgr., Deacon Kenneth Anderson, Tel. (718)293-1928
Foreign Missions, Pres., Sr. Autholene Smith, Tel. (914)664-4602
Home Missions: Pres., Evangelist Mary Jackson, Tel. (718)992-4653
Minister of Education: Minister Abraham Jones, Tel. (718)588-2284
Ministers of Music, Ray Crenshaw, Tyrone Sumter, Ann Dunston
Prison Ministry Team, Evangelist Marvin Smith
Public Relations, Minister Abraham Jones
Sunday Schools, Gen. Supt., Elder A. M. Jones
Alan Bryant Memorial Institute, Principal, Moses Tolborh, Chocolate City, Monrobia, Liberia
Theological Institute, Pres., Dr. Roy Bryant, Sr.; Dean, Elder A. M. Jones
Vessels Unto Honor Deliverance Ministries, Pres., Elder Antoinette Cannaday
Youth, Pres., Deacon Tommy Robinson
Bishops: Bishop Roy Bryant, Sr., Bishop Eddie Citronnelli, Bishop Christopher Powell
Presiding Elders: Delaware: Elder Edward Cannon, R R Box 70-B5, Daimond Acre, Dagsboro, DE 19939, Tel. (302)732-3351; Mount Vernon: Elder Artie Burney, 100 W. 2nd St., Mount Vernon, NY 10550, Tel. (914)664-4602; Bronx, Elder Anita Robinson, 1358 Morris Ave., Bronx, NY 10456, Tel. (718)588-2284; Annex, Elder Reginald Gullette, 1069 Morris Ave., Bronx, NY 10456, Tel. (718)992-4653; Schenectady, New York: Elder Monica Hope, 1132 Congress St., Schenectady, New York 12303, Tel. (518)382-5625; North Carolina: Elder Darue Bryant, 512 W. Vernon Ave., Kingston, N.C. 28502, Tel. (252)527-7739; India, Dr. B. Veeraswamy, 46-7-34, Danavaya Peta, Rajahmunry, India, 533103

Periodicals
The Gospel Light, The Challenge, The Voice

Bible Fellowship Church
The Bible Fellowship Church grew out of divisions in the Mennonite community in Pennsylvania in the 1850s. Traditional church leadership resisted the freedom of expression and prayer meetings initiated by several preachers and church leaders. These evangelical Mennonites formed the Evangelical Mennonite Society. Over the next two decades various like minded groups in Canada, Ohio and Pennsylvania joined the Society.

In 1959 the Conference became the Bible Fellowship Church and new articles of faith were ratified. They now hold a unique combination of Reformed doctrines with insistence on "Believer Baptism" and Premillennialism.

Headquarters
Bible Fellowship Church, 3000 Fellowship Drive, Whitehall, PA 18052
Media Contact, David T. Allen, 1640 Ashley Court, Kutztown, PA 19530, Tel. (610)285-2964
Email: DTA10@aol.com
Website: www.bfc.org

Officers
Chmn., William A. Schloneckev, 23 Anglin Drive, Newark, DE 19713
Vice-Chmn., Randall A. Grossman, 1400 Oak Lane, Reading, PA 19604
Sec., David A. Thomann, 745 Village Rd., Lancaster, PA 17602
Asst. Sec., David T. Allen, 1640 Ashley Court, Kutztown, PA 19530

BOARDS AND COMMITTEES
Executive Board, Bible Fellowship Church
Bd. of Christian Education
Board of Extension
Bible Fellowship Church Homes, Inc.
Board of Pensions
Board of Pinebrook Bible Conference
Board of Missions Committee On Credentials
Board of Publication and Printing
Bd. of Victory Valley Camp
Bd. Of Church Health
Board of Higher Education Board Of Youth & Adults Committee On Ministerial Candidates Strategic Planning Committee Ministerial Relations Committee Conference Judicatory
Committee on Credentials
Committee on Nominations

Periodicals
Fellowship News

Bible Holiness Church
This church came into being about 1890 as the result of definite preaching on the doctrine of holiness in some Methodist churches in southeastern Kansas. It became known as The Southeast Kansas Fire Baptized Holiness Association. The name was changed in 1945 to The Fire Baptized Holiness Church and in 1995 to Bible Holiness Church. It is entirely Wesleyan in doctrine, episcopal in church organization and intensive in evangelistic zeal.

Headquarters
304 Camp Dr., Independence, KS 67301, Tel.
(620)331-3049
Media Contact, Gen. Supt., Leroy Newport

Officers
Gen. Supt., Leroy Newport
Gen. Sec., Michael Schaper, 944 Linns Mill Rd.,
Troy, MO 63379
Gen. Treas., Philip Davolt, 10624 Bluestem,
Wichita, KS 67207

Periodicals
The Flaming Sword, John Three Sixteen

Bible Way Church of Our Lord Jesus Christ World Wide, Inc.

This body was organized in 1957 in the Pentecostal tradition for the purpose of accelerating evangelistic and foreign missionary commitment and to effect a greater degree of collective leadership than leaders found in the body in which they had previously participated.

The doctrine is the same as that of the Church of Our Lord Jesus Christ of the Apostolic Faith, Inc., of which some of the churches and clergy were formerly members.

This organization has churches and missions in Africa, England, Guyana, Trinidad and Jamaica, and churches in 25 states in America. The Bible Way Church is involved in humanitarian as well as evangelical outreach with concerns for urban housing, education and economic development.

Headquarters
4949 Two-Notch Rd., Columbia, SC 29204, Tel.
(800)432-5612 Fax (803)691-0583
Media Contact, Chief Apostle, Presiding Bishop
Huie Rogers
Email: mr.ed5strings@worldnet.att.net
Website: www.biblewaychurch.org

Officers
Presiding Bishop, Bishop Huie Rogers, 4949
Two Notch Rd., Columbia, SC 29204, Tel.
(800)432-5612 Fax (803)691-0583

Brethren in Christ Church

The Brethren in Christ Church was founded in Lancaster County, Pa. in about the year 1778 and was an outgrowth of the religious awakening which occurred in that area during the latter part of the 18th century. This group became known as "River Brethren" because of their original location near the Susquehanna River. The name "Brethren in Christ" was officially adopted in 1863. In theology they have accents of the Pietist, Anabaptist, Wesleyan and Evangelical movements.

Headquarters
General Church Office, P.O. Box A, Grantham, PA
17027, Tel. (717)697-2634 Fax (717)697-7714
Media Contact, Dr. Warren L. Hoffman, Mod.,
Tel. (717)697-2634 Fax (717)697-7714
Email: dwinger@messiah.edu
Website: www.bic-church.org

Officers
Dr. Warren L. Hoffman, Mod. & Gen. Church
Office Contact info.
Darrell S. Winger, Gen. Sec. & Gen. Church
Office Contact info.
Elizabeth Brown, Treas. & Gen. Church Office
Contact info.

OTHER ORGANIZATIONS
General Conference Board, Chpsn., Dr. Mark
Garis, 504 Swartley Rd., Hatfield, PA 19440
Bd. for World Missions, Dr. Grace Holland,
Chair, 21A Junction Rd., Dillsburg, PA.
17019-9469; Exec. Dir., Rev. John Brubaker,
P.O. Box 390, Grantham, PA 17027-0390
Bd. for Stewardship Services, Terry Hoke; Chair;
Box A, Grantham, PA 17027; Pension Fund
Trustees, Eric Mann, Chair
Brethren in Christ Foundation, Elvin H. Peifer,
CEO, P.O.Box 290, Grantham, PA, 17027-0290

Brethren Church (Ashland, Ohio)

The Brethren Church (Ashland, Ohio) was organized by progressive-minded German Baptist Brethren in 1883. They reaffirmed the teaching of the original founder of the Brethren movement, Alexander Mack, and returned to limited congregational government.

Headquarters
524 College Ave., Ashland, OH 44805, Tel.
(419)289-1708 Fax (419)281-0450
Media Contact, Rev. Ken Hunn Official Position:
Executive Director Tel; (419)289-1708 Fax
(419)281-0450 Email: Ken@brethrenchurch.org
Email: brethren@brethrenchurch.org
Website: www.brethrenchurch.org

Officers
Executive Dir., Rev. Ken Hunn
Dir. of Administrative Services, Mr. Stanley
Gentle

Periodicals
The Brethren Evangelist

Calvary Chapel

Calvary Chapel is a non-denominational Christian church which began in 1965 in Costa Mesa, California. Calvary Chapel's pastor, Chuck Smith became a leading figure in what has become known as the "Jesus Movement."

It has been estimated that in a two-year period in the mid '70s, Calvary Chapel of Costa Mesa had performed well over eight thousand baptisms. During that same period, we were instrumental in 20,000 conversions to the Christian faith. Our decadal growth rate had been calculated by church growth experts to be near the ten thousand percent level. Calvary Chapel also ministers over the airwaves, and this must account for many of those who travel long distances to fellowship here. A Nielsen survey indicated that our Sunday morning Calvary Chapel service is the most listened-to program in the area during the entire week. As of 1987, Calvary's outreach has included numerous radio programs, television broadcasts, and the production and distribution of tapes and records. The missions outreach is considerable. Calvary Chapel not only supports Wycliffe Bible Translators, Campus Crusade, Missionary Aviation Fellowship, and other groups, but we donate to Third World needs. We then built a radio station in San Salvador and gave it to the local pastors there. We also gave money to Open Doors to purchase the ship that, in tandem with a barge, delivered one million Bibles to mainland China. Our financial commitment to missions exceeds the local expense budget by over 50%.

Today, Calvary Chapel of Costa Mesa, the church which only had twenty-five members has established more than five hundred affiliate Calvary Chapels across the world and is among the world's largest churches with more than thirty-five thousand calling it their home church. It is one of the ten largest Protestant churches in the United States.

Headquarters

Calvary Chapel of Costa Mesa (Main Office), 3800 S. Fairway Street, Santa Ana, CA 92704-7014, Tel. (714)979-4422
Email: costamesa@calvarychapel.com
Website: www.calvarychapel.com

Officers

The Catholic Church

The largest single body of Christians in the United States, The Catholic Church is under the spiritual leadership of His Holiness the Pope. Its establishment in America dates back to the priests who accompanied Columbus on his second voyage to the New World. A settlement, later discontinued, was made in 1565 at St. Augustine, Florida. The continuous history of this Church in the Colonies began at St. Mary's in Maryland, in 1634.

Headquarters

INTERNATIONAL ORGANIZATION
His Holiness the Pope, Bishop of Rome, Vicar of Jesus Christ, Supreme Pontiff of the Catholic Church.
Pope Benedict XVI, Joseph Ratzinger (born April 16, 1927; installed April 24, 2005)

APOSTOLIC NUNCIO TO THE UNITED STATES
Archbishop Pietro Sambi, 3339 Massachusetts Ave., N.W., Washington, DC 20008, Tel. (202)333-7121 Fax (202)337-4036
U.S. ORGANIZATION
United States Conference of Catholic Bishops, 3211 Fourth St NE, Washington, DC 20017-1194., Tel. (202)541-3000
The United States Conference of Catholic Bishops (USCCB) is an assembly of the hierarchy of the United States and the U.S. Virgin Islands who jointly exercise certain pastoral functions on behalf of the Christian faithful of the United States. The purpose of the Conference is to promote the greater good which the Church offers humankind, especially through forms and programs of the apostolate fittingly adapted to the circumstances of time and place. This purpose is drawn from the universal law of the Church and applies to the episcopal conferences which are established all over the world for the same purpose.

The bishops themselves constitute the membership of the Conference and are served by a staff of over 350 people, priests and religious located at the Conference headquarters in Washington, DC. There is also a small Office of Film and Broadcasting in New York City and a branch office of Migration and Refugee Services in Miami. The bishops themselves form approximately 50 committees, each with its own particular responsibility.

The Conference is organized as a corporation in the District of Columbia. Its purposes under civil law are, "To unify, coordinate, encourage, promote and carry on Catholic activities in the United States; to organize and conduct religious, charitable and social welfare work at home and abroad; to aid in education; to care for immigrants; and generally to enter into and promote by education, publication and direction the objects of its being."
Email: commdept@usccb.org
Website: www.usccb.org

Officers

UNITED STATES CONFERENCE OF CATHOLIC BISHOPS (USCCB)
GENERAL SECRETARIAT
General Sec., Msgr. David Malloy, 3211 4th St. NE, Washington DC 20017-1194, Tel. (202)541-3000, Email: CommDept@usccb.org
Assoc. Gen. Sec., Mr. Bruce E. Egnew, Assoc. Gen. Sec., Nancy Wisdo, Assoc. Gen. Sec. Msgr. Ronny Genkins, 3211 4th St. NE, Washington DC 20017-1194, Tel. (202)541-3000, Email: CommDept@usccb.org

OFFICERS
President: Cardinal Francis George, OMI, Chicago
Vice President: Bishop Gerald F. Kicanas, Tucson
Treasurer: Archbishop Joseph E. Kurtz, Louisville
Secretary: Bishop George V. Murry, SJ, Youngstown

COMMITTEES AND CHAIRS:
Administrative: Cardinal Francis George, OMI
Budget and Finance: Archbishop Joseph E. Kurtz
Canonical Affairs and Church Governance: Bishop Thomas Paprocki
Catholic Education: Bishop Thomas Curry
Clergy, Consecrated Life, and Vocations: Cardinal Sean O'Malley, OFM Cap
Communications: Bishop Gabino Zavala
Cultural Diversity in the Church: Bishop Jaime Soto
Divine Worship: Bishop Arthur Serratelli
Doctrine: Archbishop Donald Wuerl
Domestic Justice and Human Development: Bishop William Murphy

Ecumenical and Interreligious Affairs: Archbishop Wilton Gregory
Evangelization and Catechesis: Bishop Richard Malone
Executive Committee: Cardinal Frances George, OMI
International Justice and Peace: Bishop Howard Hubbard
Laity, Marriage, Family Life, and Youth: Archbishop Roger L. Schwietz, OMI
Migration: Bishop John Wester
National Collections: Bishop Kevin Farrell
Priorities and Plans: Bishop George Murry, SJ
Pro-Life Activities: Cardinal Daniel DiNardo
Protection of Children and Young People: Bishop Blasé Cupich
For information on related organizations and individual dioceses, consult the Official Catholic Directory (published annually by P.J. Kenedy and Sons) and the USCCB website (www.usccb.org).

Periodicals
Catholic News Service, Origins, Bishops Committee on the Liturgy Newsletter

Christ Catholic Church

The church is a catholic communion established in 1968 to minister to the growing number of people who seek an experiential relationship with God and who desire to make a total commitment of their lives to God. The church is catholic in faith and tradition. Participating cathedrals, churches and missions are located in several states.

Headquarters
405 Kentling Rd., Highlandville, MO 65669, Tel. (417)443-3951
Media Contact, Archbishop, Most Rev. Karl Pruter
Email: bishopkarl@juno.com
Website: www.christcatholicchurch.com

Officers
Archbishop, Most Rev. Karl Pruter, P.O. Box 63, Highlandville, MO 65669

Periodicals
St. Willibrord Journal

Christ Community Church (Evangelical-Protestant)

This church was founded by the Rev. John Alexander Dowie on Feb. 22, 1896 at Chicago, Ill. In 1901 the church founded the city of Zion, IL and moved their headquarters there. Theologically, the church is rooted in evangelical orthodoxy. The Scriptures are accepted as the rule of faith and practice. Other doctrines call for belief in the necessity of repentance for sin and personal trust in Christ for salvation.

The Christ Community Church is a denominational member of The National Association of Evangelicals. It has work in six other nations in addition to the United States. Branch ministries are found in Tonalea, Arizona.

Headquarters
2500 Dowie Memorial Dr., Zion, IL 60099, Tel. (847)746-1411 Fax (847)746-1452
Email: frontoffice@ccczion.org
Website: www.ccczion.org

Officers
Senior Pastor, Ken Langley

Christadelphians

The Christadelphians are a body of people who believe the Bible to be the divinely inspired word of God, written by "Holy men who spoke as they were moved by the Holy Spirit" (2 Pet. 1:21). They believe that the Old Testament presents God's plan to establish His Kingdom on earth in accord with the promises He made to Abraham and David; and that the New Testament declares how that plan works out in Jesus Christ, who died a sacrificial death to redeem sinners. They believe in the personal return of Jesus Christ as King, to establish "all that God spoke by the mouth of his holy prophets from of old" (Acts 3:21). They believe that at Christ's return many of the dead will be raised by the power of God to be judged. Those whom God deems worthy will be welcomed into eternal life in the Kingdom on earth. Christadelphians believe in the mortality of man; in spiritual rebirth requiring belief and immersion in the name of Jesus; and in a godly walk in this life. They have no ordained clergy, and are organized in a loose worldwide confederation of autonomous congregations (ecclesias) in approximately 100 countries. They are conscientiously opposed to participation in war. They endeavor to be enthusiastic in work, loyal in marriage, generous in giving, dedicated in preaching, and cheerful in living.

The denomination was organized in 1844 by Dr. John Thomas, who came to the United States from England, and who devoted his life to a search for the truth of God from the Bible. Dr. Thomas claimed no special revelation or position. Although his Bible scholarship is highly respected, he is not revered as a prophet in any way. The name Christadelphian ("Brethren in Christ") was adopted in 1864. Initially limited mostly to English-speaking countries, the denomination now exists worldwide.

Primary activities in North America include Sunday worship and Sunday Schools, midweek Bible classes, Bible Schools, and inter-ecclesial gatherings. In addition, the Williamsburg Christadelphian Foundation (WCF) sponsors and assists charitable and preaching activities in many parts of the world, both by itself and in conjunction with the outreach work of the Christadelphian Bible Missions.

(In North America, there are two Christadelphian groups, Central and Unamended.)

Headquarters
Media Contact, Trustee, Norman D. Zilmer, Christadelphian Action Society, 904 Woodview Court, Mahomet, IL 61853-3623, Tel. (217)590-4108 Fax (847)888-3334
Email: nzilmer@aol.com
Website: www.christadelphia.org

81

Officers

(Co-Ministers) Norman Fadelle, 815 Chippewa Dr., Elgin, IL 60120; Norman D. Zilmer, 904 Woodview Ct, Mahomet, IL 61853-3623, Email:nzilmer@aol.com/nfadelle@juno.com

Related Organizations

Williamsburg Christadelphian Foundation (WCF) www.wcfoundation.org

Periodicals

Christadelphian Tidings (www.Tidings.org), Christadelphian Advocate (www.Christa-delphia.org)

Christian Brethren (also known as Plymouth Brethren)

Christian Brethren churches are bound together by common beliefs and practices but not by central organization. They are committed to the inerrancy of Scripture, to Trinitarian doctrine, and to the evangelical message of salvation by faith apart from works or sacrament. Their most recognizable feature is the weekly observance of the Lord's Supper as the focus of a full length service of worship, not prearranged and not clergy-led.

Originating in England and Ireland in the late 1820s, the Brethren were influenced by the counsel of Anthony Norris Groves, an English dentist, and the teaching of John Nelson Darby, an Irish clergyman. They recovered aspects of church practice and simplicity that had been obscured in the course of the centuries, such as an unwillingness to establish denominational governing structures and a reluctance to accept sectarian names. The nickname Plymouth Brethren arose spontaneously when a large Plymouth congregation was evangelizing throughout the English countryside. In recent years the term Christian Brethren has replaced Plymouth Brethren for the open branch of the movement in Canada and the British Commonwealth and to some extent in the United States. Neither name has legal status, except where required by national governments. There are no central offices and no corporate property in the USA or Canada.

In the late 1840s the movement divided. The so-called open assemblies, led initially by George Mueller of orphanage fame, stressed evangelism and foreign missions. It has grown to be the larger of the two branches. The autonomy of local congregations permits variations in practice and generally avoids wide-ranging division.

The other branch focused more on doctrinal and ecclesiastical issues. From it came notable Bible teachers like Darby, William Kelly, C.H. Mackintosh (CHM), and F. W. Grant. Their books have had a wide influence, especially among premillennialists. These assemblies stress the interdependency of congregations. Local church decisions on doctrine and discipline are generally held to be binding on all assemblies. At times, when actions were debatable, division spread throughout the group. By 1900, there were seven or eight main groups. Since 1925, some divisions have been healed, reducing that number to three or four.

Headquarters

CORRESPONDENT
John H. Rush, 2872 Illinois Avenue, Dubuque, IA 52001 Tel.(563)557-8535
Email: jrush@emmaus.edu

Related Organizations

Believers' Bookshelf, P.O. Box 261 Sunbury, PA 17801

Believers' Stewardship Services, 2250 Chaney Rd., Dubuque, IA 50201, Tel. (563)582-4818

ECS Ministries, 2250 Chaney Rd., Dubuque, IA 50201, Tel. (563)585-2070

Emmaus Bible College, 2570 Asbury Rd., Dubuque, IA 52001-3044, Tel. (563)588-8000

Christian Missions in Many Lands, P.O. Box 13, Spring Lake, NJ 07762-0013, Tel. (732) 449-8880

Interest Ministries, 2060 Stonington Ave., Suite 101, Hoffman Estates, IL 60195, Tel. (847)519-1495

Stewards Foundation, 14285 Midway Rd., Ste. 330, Addison, TX 75001-3622, Tel. (972) 726-6550

Stewards Ministries, 18-3 E. Dundee Rd., Ste. 100, Barrington, IL 60010, Tel. (847)842-0227

Christian Church (Disciples of Christ) in the United States and Canada*

Born on the American frontier in the early 1800s as a movement to unify Christians, this body drew its major inspiration from Thomas and Alexander Campbell in western Pennsylvania and Barton W. Stone in Kentucky. Developing separately, the "Disciples, under Alexander Campbell, and the "Christians," led by Stone, united in 1832 in Lexington, Ky.

The Christian Church (Disciples of Christ) is marked by informality, openness, individualism, and diversity. The Disciples claim no official doctrine or dogma. Membership is granted after a simple statement of belief in Jesus Christ and baptism by immersion—although most congregations accept transfers baptized by other forms in other denominations. The Lord's Supper—generally called Communion—is open to Christians of all persuasions. The practice is weekly Communion, although no church law insists upon it.

Thoroughly ecumenical, the Disciples helped organize the National and World Councils of Churches. The church is a member of the Churches Uniting in Christ. The Disciples and the United Church of Christ have declared themselves to be in "full communion" through the General Assembly and General Synod of the two churches. Official theological conversations have been going on since 1967 directly with the Roman Catholic Church.

Disciples have vigorously supported world and national programs of education, agricultural assistance, urban reconciliation, care of persons with retardation, family planning, and aid to victims of war and calamity. Operating ecumenically, Disciples' personnel or funds work in more than 100 countries outside North America.

Three manifestations or expressions of the church (general, regional and congregational) operate as equals, with strong but voluntary covenantal ties to one another. Entities in each manifestation manage their own finances, own their own property, and conduct their own programs. A General Assembly meets every two years and has voting representation from each congregation.

Headquarters

Disciples Center, 130 E. Washington St., P.O. Box 1986, Indianapolis, IN 46206-1986, Tel. (317)635-3100 Fax (317)635-3700

Media Contact, Communication Ministries, Executive Director, Wanda Bryant Wills Email: cmiller@cm.disciples.org

Officers

Gen. Minister & Pres., Rev. Dr. Sharon E. Watkins, Tel. (317)635-3100 Fax (317)713-2417, Email: swatkins@ogmp.disciples.org

Mod., D. Newell Williams, Brite Divinity School, Texas Christian University, P.O. Box 298130, Fort Worth, Texas 76129, Tel. (817)257-7575 Email: n.williams@tcu.edu.

1st Vice Mod., Ayanna Johnson, 2324 Orchard St, Blue Island, Illinois, Tel. (773)483-2115

2nd Vice Mod., Robert (Bob) Alvarez, Forest Park, Georgia, Tel. (770)614-0314, Email: bobalvarez@npointgroup.com.

GENERAL OFFICERS

Gen. Minister & Pres., Rev. Dr. Sharon E. Watkins, Tel. (317)635-3100 Fax (317)713-2417, Email: swatkins@ogmp.disciples.org

Assoc. Gen. Minister & Vice Pres., Todd A Adams, Tel. (317)635-3100 FAX (317)713-2417, Email: tadams@ogmp.disciples.org

Assoc. Gen Min. & Admin. Sec. Of the National Convocation, Timothy M. James, Email: tjames@ogmp.disciples.org

GENERAL MINISTRIES

Board of Church Extension, dba Church Extension, Pres., James L. Powell, 130 E. Washington St., P.O. Box 7030, Indianapolis, IN 46207-7030, Tel. (317)635-6500 Fax (317)635-6534, Email: bce@churchextension.org

Christian Board of Publication (Chalice Press), Pres., Cyrus N. White, 1221 Locust St., Suite 1200, St. Louis, MO 63166-0179, Tel. (314)231-8500 or (800)366-3383 Fax (314)231-8524, Email: customerservice@cbp21.com

Christian Church Foundation, Inc., Pres., Gary W. Kidwell, Tel. (317)635-3100 or (800)366-8016 Fax (317)635-1991, Email: jcullumb@ccf.disciples.org

Council on Christian Unity, Inc., Pres., Robert K. Welsh, Tel (317)713-2586 Fax (317)713-2588, Email: rwelsh@ccu.disciples.org

Disciples of Christ Historical Society, Pres., Glen T. Carson, 1101 19th Ave. S., Nashville, TN 37212-2196, Tel. (615)327-1444 Fax (615)327-1445, Email: mail@dishistsoc.org

Higher Education and Leadership Ministries (HELM), Pres., Dennis L. Landon, 11477 Olde Cabin Rd., Ste. 310, St. Louis, MO 63141-7130, Tel. (314)991-3000 Fax (314)991-2957, Email: dhe@dhedisciples.org

Division of Homeland Ministries, dba Disciples Home Missions, Pres., Ron Degges, Tel. (317)635-3100 or (888)346-2631, Fax (317)635-4426, Email: homelandministries@dhm.disciples.org

Division of Overseas Ministries, Pres., David A. Vargas, Fax (317)635-4323, Email: dom@disciples.org

Disciples Benevolent Services, Pres., Dennis Hagemann, 149 Weldon Parkway, Suite 115, Maryland Heights, MO 63043-3103, Tel. (314)993-9000 Fax (314)993-9018, Email: nba@nbacares.org

Pension Fund, Pres., James P. Hamlett, 130 E. Washington St., Indianapolis, IN 46204-3645, Tel. (317)634-4504 Fax (317)634-4071, Email: pfcc1@pension.disciples.org

REGIONAL UNITS OF THE CHURCH

Alabama-Northwest Florida, Regional Minister, John P. Mobley, 861 Highway 52, Helena, AL 35080-7743, Tel. (205)425-5245 Fax (205)425-5246, Email: alnwfl@aol.com

Arizona, Regional Minister, Dennis L. Williams, 4423 N. 24th St., Ste 700, Phoenix, AZ 85016-5544, Tel. (602)468-3815 Fax (602)468-3816, Email: region@arizonadisciples.com

California, Northern-Nevada, Regional Min. and Pres., Ben Bohren, 9260 Alcosta Blvd., C-18, San Ramon, CA 94583-4143, Tel. (925)556-9900 Fax (925)556-9904, Email: info@ccncn.org

Canada, Regional Minister, Catherine Hubbard, P.O. Box 25087, London, ON N6C 6A8, Tel. (519)472-9083 Fax (519)637-6407 Email: ccic1@sympatico.ca

Capital Area, Regional Minister, Lari R. Grubbs, 11501 Georgia Ave., Ste. 400, Wheaton, MD 20902-1955 Tel (301)942-8266 Fax (301)942-8366, Email: lgrubbs@cccadisciples.org

Central Rocky Mountain Region, Interim Exec. Regional Minister, Ralph S. Detema, 2950 Tennyson #300, Denver, CO 80212-3029, Tel. (303)561-1790 Fax (303)561-1795, Email: jrowe@crmrdoc.org

Florida, Regional Minister, William C. Morrison, Jr., 924 N. Magnolia Ave., Ste. 200, Orlando, FL 32803-3845, Tel. (407)843-4652, Fax (407)843-0272, Email: RegionalOffice@floridadisciples.org

Georgia, Regional Minister, Ray Miles, 2370 Vineville Ave., Macon, GA 31204-3163, Tel. (478)743-8649 or (800)755-0485 Fax (478)741-1508, Email: ccinga@bellsouth.net

Great River Region, Executive Regional Minister, Barbara E. Jones, 9302 Geyer Springs Rd, P.O.Box 192058, Little Rock, AR 72219-2058, Tel. (501)562-6053 & (888)241-5531, Fax (501)562-7089

83

Idaho, South, Regional Minister, Larry Crist, 6465 Sunrise Ave., Nampa, ID 83686-9461, Tel. (208)468-8976, Fax (208)468-8973, Email: ccsi1@mindspring.com

Illinois and Wisconsin, Interim Regional Minister and Pres., Beth Dobyns, 1011 N. Main St., Bloomington, IL 61701-1753, Tel. (309)828-6293 Fax (309)829-4612, Email: herb@cciwdiciples.org

Indiana, Regional Minister, Richard L. Spleth, 1100 W. 42nd St., Indianapolis, IN 46208-3375, Tel. (317)926-6051 Fax (317)931-2034, Email: cci@ccindiana.org

Kansas, Regional Minister/Pres., Paxton Jones, 2914 S.W. MacVicar Ave., Topeka, KS 66611-1787, Tel. (785)266-2914 Fax (785)266-0174, Email: ccks@ksmessenger.org

Kansas City, Greater, Regional Min./Pres., Paul J. Diehl, Jr., 5700 Broadmoor, Ste. 907, Mission, KS 66202-2404, Tel. (913)432-1414, Fax (913)432-3598, Email: KCDisciple@aol.com

Kentucky, General Minister, J. Gregory Alexander, 1125 Red Mile Rd., Lexington, KY 40504-2660, Tel. (859)233-1391 Fax (859)233-2079, Email: cck@ccinky.net

Michigan, Regional Minister, Jon Lacey, 2820 Covington Ct., Lansing, MI 48912-4830, Tel. (517)372-3220 Fax (517)372-2705, Email: ccmr@michigandisciples.org

Mid-America Region, Regional Minister, Danny Stewart, 3328 Bennett Ln., P.O. Box 104298, Jefferson City, MO 65110-4298, Tel. (573)636-8149 Fax (573)636-2889, Email: ccma@socket.net

Montana, Regional Minister, Ruth A, Fletcher, 1019 Central Ave., Great Falls, MT 59401-3784, Tel. (406)452-7404 Fax (406)452-7404, Email: ccmt@bresnan.net

Nebraska, Regional Ministers, Kenneth W. Moore, 1268 S. 20th St., Lincoln, NE 68502-1612, Tel. (402)476-0359 or (800)580-8851 Fax (402)476-0350, Email: ccnebraska@alltel

North Carolina, Regional Minister, John M. Richardson, 509 N.E. Lee St., P.O. Box 1568, Wilson, NC 27894-1568, Tel. (252)291-4047 Fax (252)291-3338, Email: ccnc@ncdisciples.org

Northeastern Region, Regional Minister, Mary Anne Glover, 765 Lafayette Ave., Brooklyn, NY - 11411-1414 Tel (718)443-9120 Fax (718)949-5460, Email: nedisciples@verizon.net

Northwest Region, Regional Minister and Pres., Sandra Messick, 18000 72nd Ave, S, Suite 171, Kent, WA, 98032-2506, Tel. (253)893-7202 Fax (425)251-4967, Email: nwrcc@disciplesnw.org

Ohio, Regional Pastor and Pres., William H. Edwards, 355 E. Campus View Blvd, Suite 110, Columbus, OH 43235-5616, Tel. (614)433-0343 Fax (614)433-7285, Email: ccio@ccinoh.org

Oklahoma, Regional Pastor, Thomas R. Jewell, 301 N.W. 36th St., Oklahoma City, OK 73118-8661, Tel. (405)528-3577 Fax (405)528-3584, Email: tjewell@okdisciples.org

Oregon, Co-Regional Ministers, Douglas Wirt & Cathy Myers-Wirt, 0245 S.W. Bancroft St., Ste. F, Portland, OR 97239-4267, Tel. (503)226-7648 Fax (503)226-0598, Email: odmail@oregondisciples.org

Pacific Southwest Region, Co-Regional Minister-Pres., Don & Susan Gonzales Dewey, 2401 N. Lake Ave., Altadena, CA 91001-2418, Tel. (626)296-0385, Fax (626)296-1280, Email: pswr@discipleswr

Pennsylvania, Regional Minister, William Allen, 105 Water St., Suite #7, New Stanton, PA 15672-0900, Tel. (724)925-1350 Fax (724)925-1358, Email: cjohns@padisciples.org

South Carolina, Regional Minister, Sotello V. Long, 1293 Orange Grove Rd., Charleston, SC 29407-3947, Tel. (843)852-4537 Fax (843)744-5787, Email: rcccsc@aol.com

Southwest Region, Regional Minister Dani Loving Cartwright, P.O. Box 1689, Fort Worth, TX 76101-1689, Tel. (817)926-4687 Fax (817)926-5121, Email: ccsw@ccsw.org

Tennessee, Regional Minister and Pres., Glen J. Stewart, 7980 Coley Davis Rd, Nashville, TN 37221- 2397, Tel. (615)646-3705 Fax (615)646-3707, Email: ccdctn@bellsouth.net

Upper Midwest Region, Regional Minister and Pres., Don Hiscox & Bill Spangler-Dunning, 3300 University Ave., P.O. Box 41217, Des Moines, IA 50311-0504, Tel. (515)255-3168 Fax (515)255-2625, Email: dh@uppermidwestcc.org

Virginia, Regional Minister, George Lee Parker, 1290 Enterprise Dr., Lynchburg, VA 24502-5744, Tel. (434)846-3400 Fax (434)528-4919, Email: regoffice.ccinva@verizon.net

West Virginia, Regional Minister, Thaddaeus B. Allen, 1402 Washington Ave. Parkersburg, WV 26101-3427, Tel. (304)428-1681 Fax (304)428-1684, Email: linda@ccwv.org

Periodicals

DiscipleWorld, Call To Unity

Christian Church of North America, General Council

Originally known as the Italian Christian Church, its first General Council was held in 1927 at Niagara Falls, N.Y. This body was incorporated in 1948 at Pittsburgh, Pa., and is described as Pentecostal but does not engage in the "the excesses tolerated or practiced among some churches using the same name."

The movement recognizes two ordinances-baptism and the Lord's Supper. Its moral code is conservative and its teaching is orthodox. Members are exhorted to pursue a life of personal holiness, setting an example to others. A conservative position is held in regard to marriage and divorce. The governmental form is, by and large, congregational. District and National officiaries, however, are referred to as Presbyteries led by Overseers.

The group functions in cooperative fellowship with the Italian Pentecostal Church of Canada and the Evangelical Christian Churches-Assemblies of God in Italy. It is an affiliate member of the Pentecostal Fellowship of North America and of the National Association of Evangelicals.

Headquarters
1294 Rutledge Rd., Transfer, PA 16154-2299, Tel. (724)962-3501 Fax (724)962-1766
Exec. Sec., Christine Marini; Asst., Candace Tarr
Email: ifcahq@neohio.twcbc.com
Website: www.ifcaministry.com

Officers
Executive Bd., Gen. Overseer, Rev. Dennis G. Karaman, 1294 Rutledge Road, Transfer, PA. 16154
Exec. Vice Pres., Rev. Joseph Shipley, 44-19 Francis Lewis Blvd., Bayside, NY 11361
Asst. Gen. Overseers, Rev. Joseph Shipley 44-19 Francis Lewis Blvd., Bayside, NY 11361; Rev. Trevor Cobarn,
3325 Dry Brook Rd., Falconer, NY 14733; Rev. Patrick Bossio, Sr., 667 Capitol, Lincoln Park, MI 48146;
Rev Thomas Geyser, 2 Cynthia Circle, Medway, MA 02062, Rev. Douglas Bedgood, Sr., 442 Trinidad Ln.,
Teadkwood Village, Largo, FL 33770

DEPARTMENTS
Benevolence, Rev. Eugene De Marco, 136 Dana Dr., New Brighton PA 15066
Home Missions, Rev. Richard George, 3395 Waterside Dr., Akron, OH 44319
Faith, Order & Credentials, Rev. Rev. Joseph Shipley, 44-19 Francis Lewis Blvd, Bayside, NY 11361
Missions, Rev. Mark Charles, 703 Somcenter Rd., Mayfield Hts., OH 44143
Publications Relations, Rev. John Tedesco, 1188 Heron Rd., Cherry Hill, NJ 08003
Lay Ministries, Rev. Carmine Zottoli, 27D Shear Hill Rd., Mahopac, NY 10541
Education, Rev. Lucian Gandolfo, 3141 Highland Dr. Easton, PA. 18045

Periodicals
Vista

Christian Churches and Churches of Christ

The fellowship, whose churches were always strictly congregational in polity, has its origin in the American movement to "restore the New Testament church in doctrine, ordinances and life" initiated by Thomas and Alexander Campbell, Walter Scott and Barton W. Stone in the early 19th century.

Headquarters
Media Contact, No. American Christian Convention Dir., Rod Huron, 4210 Bridgetown Rd., Box 11326, Cincinnati, OH 45211, Tel. (513)598-6222 Fax (513)598-6471
Email: Jowston@cwv.edu
Website: www.cctoday.com; www.nacctheconnectingplace.org

Officers

CONVENTIONS
North American Christian Convention, Dir., Rod Huron, 4210 Bridgetown Rd., Box 11326, Cincinnati, OH 45211, Tel. (513)598-6222; NACC Mailing Address, Box 39456, Cincinnati, OH 45239
National Missionary Convention, Coord., Walter Birney, Box 11, Copeland, KS 67837, Tel. (316)668-5250
Eastern Christian Convention, Kenneth Meade, 5300 Norbeck Rd., Rockville, MD 20853, Tel. (301)460-3550

Periodicals
Christian Standard, Restoration Herald, Horizons, The Lookout

The Christian Congregation, Inc.

The Christian Congregation is a denominational evangelistic association that originated in 1787 and was active on the frontier in areas adjacent to the Ohio River. The church was an unincorporated organization until 1887. At that time a group of ministers who desired closer cooperation formally constituted the church. The charter was revised in 1898 and again in 1970.

Governmental polity basically is congregational. Local units are semi-autonomous. Doctrinal positions, strongly biblical, are essentially universalist in the sense that ethical principles, which motivate us to creative activism, transcend national boundaries and racial barriers. A central tenet, John 13 vs.34-35, translates to such respect for sanctity of life that abortions on demand, capital punishment and all warfare are vigorously opposed. All wars are considered unjust and obsolete as a means of resolving disputes.

Early leaders were John Chapman, John L. Puckett and Isaac V. Smith. Bishop O. J. Read was chief administrative and ecclesiastic officer for 40 years until 1961. Rev. Dr. Ora Wilbert Eads has been general Superintendent since 1961. Ministerial affiliation for independent clergymen is provided.

Headquarters
812 W. Hemlock St., LaFollette, TN 37766
Media Contact, Gen. Supt., Rev. Ora W. Eads, D.D., Tel. (423)562-5809
Email: Revalnas@aol.com
Website: netministries.org/see/churches.exe/ch10619

Officers
Gen. Supt., Rev. Ora W. Eads, D.D., 812 W. Hemlock St. LaFollette, TN 37766

Christian Methodist Episcopal Church*

The Christian Methodist Episcopal Church (CME) is a historically African-American denomination that was established in Jackson, Tennessee in 1870 when a group of former slaves, representing eight annual conferences of the Methodist

85

Episcopal Church South organized the Colored Methodist Episcopal Church in America. In 1954 at its General Conference in Memphis, Tennessee it was overwhelmingly voted to change the term "Colored" to "Christian". On January 3, 1956 the official name became Christian Methodist Episcopal Church. Its boundaries reach from the continental United States, Alaska, Haiti, Jamaica, and the West African countries of Nigeria, Ghana, and Liberia. One of its most significant witnessing arenas has been the education of African Americans. Today the CME Church supports Paine College, August, GA; Lane College, Jackson, TN; Miles College, Birmingham, AL; Texas College, Tyler, TX; and the Phillips School of Theology in Atlanta, GA.

Headquarters
First Memphis Plaza, 4466 Elvis Presley Blvd., Memphis, TN 38116
Media Contact, Exec. Sec., Attorney Juanita Bryant, 3675 Runnymede Blvd., Cleveland Hts., OH 44121, Tel. (216)382-3559 Fax (216)382-3516, Email: juanbr4law@aol.com
Email: juanbr4law@aol.com
Website: www.c-m-e.org

Officers
Exec. Sec., Attorney Juanita Bryant, 3675 Runnymede Blvd., Cleveland Hts., OH 44121, Tel. (216)382-3559 Fax (216)382-3516, Email: juanbr4law@aol.com

OTHER ORGANIZATIONS
Christian Education, Gen. Sec., Dr. Carmichael Crutchfield, 4466 Elvis Presley Blvd., Ste. 214, Box 193, Memphis, TN 38116-7100, Tel. (901)345-0580 Fax (901)345-4118
Lay Ministry, Gen. Sec., Dr. Victor Taylor, 9560 Drake Ave., Evenston, IL 60203, Tel. (800)782-4335 x. 6029, Fax (312)345-6056, Email: taylor617@comcast.net
Evangelism & Missions, Gen. Sec., Dr. Willie C. Champion, 102 Pearly Top Dr., Glen Heights, TX 75154, Tel. (214)372-9505, Email: champ_dr@sbcglobal.net
Finance, Sec., Dr. Joseph C. Neal, Jr., P.O. Box 75085, Los Angeles, CA 90075, Tel. (323)233-5050
Editor, The Christian Index, Dr. Kenneth E. Jones, P.O. Box 431, Fairfield, AL 35064, Tel. (205929-1640 Fax (205)791-1910, Email: Goodoc@aol.com
Publication Services, Gen. Sec., Rev. William George, 4466 Elvis Presley Blvd., Memphis, TN 38116, Tel. (901)345-0580 Fax (901)767-8514, Email: WEG38@aol.com
Personnel Services, Gen. Sec., Rev. Tyrone T. Davis, P.O. Box 74, Memphis, TN 38101-0074, Tel. (901)261-3228, Email: tyrone.t.davis@concast.net
Women's Missionary Council, Pres., Dr. Elnora P. Hamb, 11321 S. Aberdeen St., Chicago, IL 60643, Tel. (773)264-2273, Email: hamb@sbcglobal.net Ministry to Men, Gen. Sec., Mr.

Leo Pinkett, 2850 Shoreland De. S.W., Atlanta, GA 30331, Email: lpinkettace@yahoo.com
BISHOPS
First District, Bishop William H. Graves, Sr., 4466 Elvis Presley Blvd., Ste. 222, Memphis, TN 38116, Tel. (901)345-0580
Second District, Bishop E. Lynn Brown, 7030 Reading Rd., Suite 244, Cincinnati, OH 45237, Tel. (513)772-8622, Email: bishopelynn brown84@yahoo.com
Third District, Bishop Paul A. G. Stewart, Sr., 5925 W. Florissant Ave., St. Louis, MO 63136, Tel. (314)381-3111, Email: BishopPStewart@aol.com
Fourth District, Bishop Thomas L. Brown Sr., P.O. Box 2793, Jackson, MS 39207, Tel. (601)398-3926, Email: thomasl30087@bellsooth.net
Fifth District, Bishop Lawerence L. Reddick III, 310 18th St., N, Ste. 400D, Birmingham, AL 35203, Tel. (205)655-0346 Fax (205)251-4371, Email: reddick3@bellsouth.net
Sixth District, Bishop Othal H. Lakey, 1776 Peachtree Rd. NW, Suite 210, South Tower, Atlanta, GA 30309, Tel. (404)745-9689, Fax (404)745-0691
Seventh District, Bishop Thomas L. Hoyt, Jr., 6524 16th St. N.W., Washington, DC, Tel. (318)820-9512 & (318)780-8467, Email: thoytjr@aol.com
Eighth District, Bishop Ronald M. Cunningham., 1616 E. Illinois, Dallas, TX 75216, Tel. (214) 372-9073, Email: bishoprc7302@aol.com
Ninth District, Bishop Henry M. Williamson, 3844 W. Slauson Ave., Ste. 1, Los Angeles, CA 90043, Tel. (213)294-3830, Email: hwillia531@aol.com
Tenth District, Bishop Kenneth Wayne Carter, 2202 Emerald Oaks Ct., Arlington, TX 76017, Tel: (817)468-1397, Email: KWCarter@hotmail.com
Retired, Bishop Nathaniel L. Linsey, Canterbury Subdivision, 190 Squire Lane, Fayettsville, GA 30214, Tel. (770)460-6897, Email: linseyn@bellsouth.net; Bishop Dotcy I. Isom, 4326 Richwood Place, Memphis, TN 36125, Tel. (901)753-8123; Bishop Marshall Gilmore, 683 Beacontree Court, Concord, NC 28027, Tel. (704)786-3226

Periodicals
The Christian Index, The Missionary Messenger

The Christian and Missionary Alliance

The Christian and Missionary Alliance was formed in 1897 by the merger of two organizations begun in 1887 by Dr. Albert B. Simpson, The Christian Alliance and the Evangelical Missionary Alliance. The Christian and Missionary Alliance is an evangelical church that stresses the sufficiency of Jesus as Savior, Sanctifier, Healer, and Coming King and has earned a worldwide reputation for its missionary accomplishments. The Canadian districts became autonomous in 1981 and formed The Christian and Missionary Alliance in Canada.

Natonal Office

P.O. Box 35000, Colorado Springs, CO 80935-3500, Tel. (719)599-5999 Fax (719)593-8234
Media Contact, Rick Memphill, Director of Communications
Email: info@cmalliance.org
Website: www.cmalliance.org

Officers

Pres., Rev. Gary M. Benedict D.D.
Corp. Vice Pres., Rev. Jonathan G. Schaeffer
Corp. Sec., Mr. Timothy D. Savoloja
Vice Pres., for Development Dennis K. Whalen
Vice Pres. for International Ministries, Rev. Robert L. Fetherlin, D. Min.
Vice Pres. for Church Ministries, John F. Soper
Vice Pres. for Operations/Treasurer, Mr. Kenneth E. Baldes, MBA BOARD OF DIRECTORS
Chpsn., Rev. Ronald J. Morrison
Vice Chpsn., Rev. Douglas L. Grogan

DISTRICTS

Cambodian, Rev. Nareth May, 1616 S. Palmetto Ave., Ontario, CA 91762, Tel. (909)988-9434
Central, Rev. Jeffrey A Miller, 1218 High St., Wadsworth, OH 44281, Tel. (330)336-2911
Central Pacific, Rev. R. Douglas Swinburne, J. R., 715 Lincoln Ave., Woodland, CA 95695 Tel. (530)662-2500
E. Pennsylvania, Rev. J. Wayne Spriggs, 1200 Spring Garden Dr., Middletown, PA 17057, Tel. (717)985-9240
Great Lakes, Rev. Jeffrey P. Brown, 2250 Huron Parkway, Ann Arbor, MI 48104 Tel. (734) 677-8555
Hmong, Rev. Naolue T Kure, 12287 Pennsylvania St., Thornton, CO 80241, Tel. (303)252-1793
Korean, Rev. Hyung J. Moon, 550 Durie Avenue, #201, Closter, NJ 07640 201-750-6750
Metropolitan, Rev. Bruce K. Terpstra, P.O.Box 7060, 275 Sussex Ave., Ste. B, Newark, NJ 07107, Tel. (973)412-7025
MidAmerica, Rev. Randall S. Burg, 1301 S. 119th St., Omaha, NE 68144, Tel. (402)330-1888
Mid-Atlantic, Rev. Randall B. Corbin, D.Min., Jr., 292 Montevue Lane, Frederick, MD 21702, Tel. (301)620-9934
Midwest, Rev. Jonathan W. Rich, 260 Glen Ellyn Road, Bloomingdale, IL 60108, Tel. (630) 893-1355
Native American, Rev. Craig S. Smith, 19019 N. 74th Dr., Glendale, AZ 85308, Tel. (623) 561-8134
New England, Rev. Richard E. Bush, D.Min., P.O. Box 288, South Easton, MA 02375 Tel. (508)238-3820
Northeastern, Rev. Daniel P. Miller, 6275 Pillmore Dr., Rome, NY 13440 Tel (315)336-4720
Northwestern, Rev. Donald A. Wiggins, 6425 CTYRD 30 #, 740 St. Bonifacius, MN 55375 Tel. (952)446-9318
Ohio Valley, Rev . P. David Klinsing, D.Min., 4050 Executive Park Dr., Ste.402, Cincinnati, OH 45241, Tel. (513)733-4833

Pacific NW, Rev. Matthew C. Boda, P.O. Box 1030, Canby, OR 97013 Tel. (503)266-2238
Puerto Rico, Rev. Luis F. Felipa, P.O. Box 191794, San Juan, PR 00919, Tel. (787)281-0101
Rocky Mountain, Rev. Timothy P. Owen, D.Min., 2545 St. Johns Ave., Billings, MT 59102 Tel. (406)656-4233
South Atlantic, Rev. L. Ferrell Towns, 10801 Johnston Rd., Ste. 125, Charlotte, NC 28226, Tel. (704)543-0470
South Pacific, Rev. William W. Malick, 4130 Adams St., Ste. A, Riverside, CA 92504 Tel. (909)351-0111
Southeastern, Rev. Charles R. Hughes Jr, D.D., P.O. Box 720430, Orlando, FL 32872-0430 Tel. (407)823-9662
Southern, Rev. Fred G. King, 5998 Deerfoot Parkway, Trussville, AL 35173 Tel. (205)661-9585
Southwestern, Rev. Mark R Searing, 5600 E. Loop 820 South, Ste. 100, Fort Worth, TX 76119 Tel. (817)561-0879
Spanish Central, Rev. Angel M. Garcia, P.O.Box 5477 McAllen, TX 78504, Tel (956)565-1600
Spanish Eastern, Rev. Jorge Cuevas, P.O.Box 865, Union City, NJ 07087, Tel. (201)866-7202
Vietnamese, Dr. Tai Anh Nguyen, Th.D., 2275 W. Lincoln Ave., Anaheim, CA 92801 Tel. (714)491-8007
W. Great Lakes, Rev. Gary E. Russell, W6107 Aerotech Dr., Appleton, WI 54914, Tel. (920)734-1123
W. Pennsylvania, Rev. Jeffrey A. Norris, P.O.Box 600, Punxsutawney, PA 15767, Tel. (814)938-6920

NATIONAL ETHNIC ASSOCIATIONS
African-American
President, Rev. Terrence L. Nichols, 120 Lancaster Way, Vallejo, CA 94591, Tel. (707)310-3926
Exec. Sec., Rev. Gus H. Brown, 688 Diagonal Rd., Akron, OH 44320 Tel. (330)376-4654
Chinese, President, Rev. Abraham H. Poon., DMin., 2360 McLaughlin Ave., San Jose, CA 95122-3560, Tel. (408)280-1021
Dega, President, Rev. Ha Giao Cilpam, 3119 Westerwood Dr., Charlotte, NC 28214 Tel. (704)393-7159
Filipino, President, Exec. Dir., Rev. Abednego Ferrer, 20143 Royal Ave., Hayward, CA 94541 Tel. (510)887-6261
Haitian, President, Rev. Emmanuel Seide, 14 Glen Rd., West Hempstead, NY. 11552, Tel. (516)594-1046

ETHNIC/CULTURAL MINISTRIES
Arab & South Asian, Rev. Joseph S. Kong, P.O. Box 35000, Colorado Springs, CO 80935 Tel. (719)599-5999 x2052
Alliance Jewish Ministries, Rev. Abraham Sandler, 9820 Woodfern Rd., Philadelphia, PA 19115, Tel. (215)676-5122

Periodicals
Alliance Life

87

Christian Reformed Church in North America

The Christian Reformed Church represents the historic faith of Protestantism. Founded in the United States in 1857 and active in Canada since 1905, it asserts its belief in the Bible as the inspired Word of God, and is creedally united in the Belgic Confession (1561), the Heidelberg Catechism (1563), and the Canons of Dort (1618-19).

Headquarters
2850 Kalamazoo Ave., SE, Grand Rapids, MI 49560, Tel. (616)224-0832 Fax (616)224-5895
Media Contact, Exec. Dir., Rev. Gerard Dykstra
Email: executive-director@crcna.org
Website: www.crcna.org

Officers
Exec. Dir. of Ministries, Rev. Gerard Dykstra
Dir. of Canadian Ministries, Rev. Bruce Adema
Director of Finance and Administration, Mr. John Bolt

OTHER ORGANIZATIONS
Back to God Ministries International, Dir. Dr. Robert C. Heerspink
Christian Reformed Home Missions, Dir., Vacant
Christian Reformed World Missions, US, Dir., Dr. Gary Bekker
Christian Ref. World Missions, Canada, Dir., Albert Karsten
Christian Reformed World Relief, US, Dir., Andrew Ryskamp
Christian Reformed World Relief, Canada, Dir., Ms. Ida Kaastra Mutoigo
Faith Alive Christian Resources, Dir., Mark Rice
Ministers' Pension Fund, Admn., Marjorie Csomor

Periodicals
The Banner

Christian Union

Organized in 1864 in Columbus, Ohio, the Christian Union stresses the oneness of the Church with Christ as its only head. The Bible is the only rule of faith and practice and good fruits the only condition of fellowship. Each local church governs itself.

Headquarters
455 Mill Street, Greenfield, OH 45123, Tel. (937)981-2760
Media Contact, Rev. Jim Eschenbrenner, 308 North Waugh Road, Hendrick, IA 52563, Tel. (641)653-4785, Email: jimesch@gmail.com or Rev. Marion Hunerdosse, Pres., 10619 N. Marsh Ave., Kansas City, MO 64157-7756, Tel. (816)781-5044, Email: mlh922@sbcglobal.net
Email: mlh922@sbcglobal.net
Website: www.christianunion.com

Officers
Rev. Marion Hunerdosse, Pres., 10619 N. Marsh Ave., Kansas City, MO 64157-7756, Tel. (816)781-5044, Email: mlh922@sbcglobal.net

Sec., Joseph Cunningham, 1005 N. 5th St., Greenfield, OH 45123, Tel. (937)981-3476, Email: joecuw@gmail.com
Asst. Sec., Jim Eschenbrenner, 308 North Waugh Road., Hedrick, IA 52563, Tel. (641)653-4785, Email: jimesch@gmail.com
Treas., Rev. Neal Skiles, 80 Licking View Dr., Heath, OH 43056-1530, Tel.740-522-4845 Fax (740)522-6076, Email: skiles@roadrunner.com

Periodicals
The Christian Union Witness; Christian Union Witness Express (bulletin)

Church of the Brethren*

Eight German Pietists/Anabaptists, including their leader, Alexander Mack, founded the Brethren movement in 1708 in Schwarzenau, Germany. Begun in reaction to spiritual stagnation in state churches, the Brethren formed their own movement, modeled on the first-century church. They practice believer baptism, anointing, and the love feast. They have no other creed than the New Testament, hold to principles of nonviolence, no force in religion, Christian service, and simplicity. They migrated to the colonies beginning in 1710 and settled at Germantown, Pennsylvania, moving westward and southward over the next 200 years. Emphasis on religion in daily life led to the formation of Brethren Volunteer Service in 1948, which continues today.

Headquarters
Church of the Brethren General Offices, 1451 Dundee Ave., Elgin, IL 60120, Tel. (847)742-5100x206 Fax (847)753-6103, Email: cobweb@brethren.org
Brethren Service Center, 500 Main Street, P.O. Box 188, New Windsor, MD 21776-0188, Tel. (410)635-8710 Fax (410)635-8789, bsc_gb@brethren.org
Media Contact, Cheryl Brumbaugh-Cayford, Director of News Services, 1451 Dundee Ave., Elgin, IL 60120 (847)742-5100 x260, Fax (847)742-1407, cbrumbaugh-cayford_gb@brethren.org
Email: cobweb@brethren.org; jclements@brethren.org
Website: www.brethren.org

Officers
Moderator: Shawn Flory Replogle, 200 N. Carrie St., McPherson, KS 67460; Email: shawn.replogle@sbcglobal.net
Moderator-elect: Robert E. Alley, 1570 Bluewater Rd., Harrisonburg, VA 22801; Email: realley@comcast.net
Secretary: Fred W. Swartz, 102 W. Rainbow Dr., Bridgewater, VA 22812; Email: acsecretary@brethren.org
Annual Conference Director: Chris Douglas, 1451 Dundee Ave., Elgin, IL 60120; Tel: (847) 742-5100; Email: cdouglas@brethren.org

EXECUTIVE LEADERSHIP FORUM:
General Secretary: Stanley J. Noffsinger, 1451 Dundee Ave., Elgin, IL 60120; Tel: 847-742-5100; Email: snoffsinger@brethren.org
Executive Director, Centralized Resources and Chief Financial Officer/Treasurer: Judy E. Keyser, 1451 Dundee Ave., Elgin, IL 60120; Tel: 847-742-5100; Email: jkeyser@brethren.org
Executive Director and Publisher, Brethren Press: Wendy McFadden, 1451 Dundee Ave., Elgin, IL 60120; Tel: 847-742-5100; Email: wmcfadden@brethren.org
Executive Director, Congregational Life Ministries: Jonathan A. Shively, 1451 Dundee Ave., Elgin, IL 60120; Tel: 847-742-5100; Email: jshively@brethren.org
Executive Director, Global Mission Partnerships: Jay A. Wittmeyer, 1451 Dundee Ave., Elgin, IL 60120; Tel: 847-742-5100; Email: mission@brethren.org
Executive Director, Brethren Service Center: Roy E. Winter, P.O. Box 188, New Windsor, MD 21776; Tel: 410-635-8748; Email: rwinter@brethren.org
Executive Director, Ministry: Mary Jo Flory-Steury, 1451 Dundee Ave., Elgin, IL 60120; Tel: 847-742-5100; Email: mjflorysteury@brethren.org
Executive Director, Systems and Services and Assistant Treasurer: LeAnn Wine, 1451 Dundee Ave., Elgin, IL 60120; Tel: 847-742-5100; Email: lwine@brethren.org
Manager, Office Operations: Nancy B. Miner, 1451 Dundee Ave., Elgin, IL 60120; Tel: 847-742-5100; Email: nminer@brethren.org
Director, Human Resources: Karin Krog, 1451 Dundee Ave., Elgin, IL 60120; Tel: 847-742-5100; Email: kkrog@brethren.org

Periodicals
Messenger

Church of Christ
Joseph Smith and five others organized the Church of Christ on April 6, 1830 at Fayette, New York. In 1864 this body was directed by revelation through Granville Hedrick to return in 1867 to Independence, Missouri to the "consecrated land" dedicated by Joseph Smith. They did so and purchased the temple lot dedicated in 1831.

Headquarters
Temple Lot, 200 S. River St., P.O. Box 472, Independence, MO 64051, Tel. (816)833-3995
Media Contact, Gen. Church Rep., William A. Sheldon, P.O. Box 472, Independence, MO 64051, Tel. (816)833-3995 Website: church-of-christ.com

Officers
Council of Apostles, Secy., Apostle Smith N. Brickhouse, P.O. Box 472, Independence, MO 64051

Gen. Bus. Mgr., Bishop Alvin Harris, P.O. Box 472, Independence, MO 64051

Periodicals
Zion's Advocate

The Church of Christ (Holiness) U.S.A.
The Church of Christ (Holiness) U.S.A. has a Divine commission to propagate the gospel throughout the world, to seek the conversion of sinners, to reclaim backsliders, to encourage the sanctification of believers, to support divine healing, and to advance the truth for the return of our Lord and Savior Jesus Christ. This must be done through proper organization.

The fundamental principles of Christ's Church have remained the same. The laws founded upon these principles are to remain unchanged. The Church of Christ (Holiness) U.S.A. is representative in form of government; therefore, the final authority in defining the organizational responsibilities rests with the national convention. The bishops of the church are delegated special powers to act in behalf of or speak for the church. The pastors are ordained ministers, who under the call of God and His people, have divine oversight of local churches. However, the representative form of government gives ministry and laity equal authority in all deliberate bodies. With the leadership of the Holy Spirit, Respect, Loyalty and Love will greatly increase.

Headquarters
329 East Monument Street, P.O. Box 3622, Jackson, MS 39207, Tel. (601)353-0222 Fax (601)353-4002
Media Contact, Maurice D. Bingham, Ed. D., Senior Bishop Emeritus
Email: Everything@cochusa.com
Website: www.cochusa.com

Officers
BOARD OF BISHOPS
Senior Bishop Emeritus, Maurice D. Bingham, Ed. D., P.O. Box 6182, Jackson, MS 39308, Tel. (601)353-0222, Email: Pminis3659@aol.com
Eastern Diocese, Bishop Lindsay E. Jones, 4053 Portland Ridge Drive, Florissant, MO 63034, Tel. (314)355-1775, Email: Ljones5@aol.com
North Central Diocese, Bishop Bennett Wolfe, 14315 River Oak Court, Florissant, MO 63034, Tel. (314)741-4590, Email: Ned6@Hotmail.com
Senior Bishop, Northern Diocese, Bishop Emery Lindsay, 62 West 111th Place, Chicago, IL 60628, Tel. (773)821-0088, Email: Bpelind@aol.com
Pacific Northwest Diocese, Bishop Robert Winn, 1376 Oakwood Ave, Vallejo, CA 94591, Tel. (707)554-2493, Email: Awinner323@aol.com
South Central Diocese, Bishop Joseph Campbell, Jr., P.O. Box 3663, Jackson, MS 39207, Tel. (601)373-6223, Email: Bisjcsd@Bellsouth.net

Southeastern Diocese, Bishop Victor P. Smith, 3783 Treebark Trail, Decatur, GA 30034, Tel. (404)288-4885, Email: Victor@hotmail.com
Southwestern Diocese, President Bishop Vernon Kennebrew, 13900 Edgemond Drive, Little Rock, AR 72212, Tel. (501)954-7676
Western Diocese, Bishop Robert Winn, 1376 Oakwood Ave, Vallejo, CA 94591, Tel. (707)554-2493, Email: Awinner323@aol.com
Board Member, Bishop James K. Mitchell, 1580 Waite St., Gary, IN 46404, Tel. (219)944-0051, Email: Jasmitch9@aol.com

Periodicals
Truth

Church of Christ, Scientist

The Church of Christ, Scientist, was founded in 1879 by Mary Baker Eddy "to commemorate the word and works of our Master [Christ Jesus], which should reinstate primitive Christianity and its lost element of healing" (Church Manual, p. 17). Central to the Church's mission is making available worldwide Mrs. Eddy's definitive work on health and Bible-based Christian healing, Science and Health With Key to the Scriptures, as well as its publications, Internet sites, and broadcast programs, all of which respond to humanity's search for spiritual answers to today's pressing needs.

The Church also maintains an international speakers' bureau to introduce the public to Christian Science and Mrs. Eddy. Christian Science practitioners, living in hundreds of communities worldwide are available full-time to pray with anyone seeking comfort and healing. And Christian Science teachers hold yearly classes for those interested in a more specific understanding of how to practice the Christian Science system of healing.

The worldwide activities and business of the Church are transacted by a five-member Board of Directors in Boston. About 2000 congregations, each democratically organized and governed, are located in approximately 80 countries. The church has no clergy. Worship services are conducted by lay persons elected to serve as Readers. Each church maintains a Reading Room—a bookstore open to the community for spiritual inquiry and research; and a Sunday School where young people discuss the contemporary relevance of ideas from the Bible and Science and Health.

Headquarters
The First Church of Christ, Scientist, 210 Massachusetts Avenue, Boston, MA 02115
Media Contact, Mgr., Committees on Publication, Phil Davis, Tel. (617)450-3300 Fax (617)450-3992 Website: www.spirituality.com and www.churchofchristscientist.org

Officers
Bd. of Directors: J. Thomas Black; Michael Pabst; Margaret Rogers; Mary Metzner Trammell; Nathan Talbot
President, Allison Phinney

Treas., Edward Odegaard
Clk., Nathan Talbot
First Reader, Curtis Wahlberg
Second Reader, Elizabeth Schaefer
Christian Science College Organizations, Website tmcyouth.com/cso

Periodicals
The Christian Science Monitor (www.csmonitor.com), The Christian Science Journal, Christian Science Sentinel, The Herald of Christian Science (13 languages), Christian Science Quarterly Bible Lessons in 16 languages and English Braille

Church Communities International

Church Communities International is a movement of Christian Church Communities originating in Germany in 1920. Driven to England by Nazi persecution in 1937, Church Community members migrated to Paraguay in 1942 with the help of the Mennonite Church. In 1954 the first Church Community in the United States was founded in Rifton New York, where it continues to flourish. Today, a dozen Church Communities are located in New York and Pennsylvania as well as others in Australia, England, Germany and Thailand. Within each Church Community, residents practice their faith in the manner and spirit of the first-century Christians and the Reformation of the early 1500's, sharing everything in common and caring for each other and their neighbors. Members are baptized as adults on confession of the Apostolic Creed, making a voluntary lifetime commitment to living out the teachings of Jesus.

Headquarters
2032 Route 213, Rifton, NY 12471, Tel. (845)658-8351
Media Contact: Johann Huleatt, Tel. (845)658-7766 Email: johannh@rifton.com

Officers
Pedo Cavanna - Secretary Treasurer, 10 Hellbrook Lane, Ulster Park, NY 12487
Church Communities Foundation

The Church of God

The Church of God was established in about 28 A.D. by Jesus Christ on Mt. Kurn Hattin (Mark 3:13-15). It was endued with power on the Day of Pentecost, but was in operation prior to this point in time.

The true Church plunged into the Dark Ages on June 14th, 325 A.D. with the signing of the "Nicene Creed" and remained in darkness for 1578 years. From 325 A.D. to 1903, God was not asleep! He began revealing the truth to men once again: Martin Luther—justification by faith; John Wesley—sanctification; Dr. Albert Simpson—divine healing; (though some received the Holy Ghost prior to 1903, it is generally regarded the Pentecostal Movement began with a Holy Ghost revival in California in 1906—Dr. Seymour).

On June 13,1903 The Church arose from darkness (as prophesied by Isaiah 60:1-5) in North Carolina. In 1923 a disruption caused a split in the Church, resulting in two groups both calling themselves the Church of God. In 1933 God gave the banner (Psalms 60:3, 4), the Church flag, to His Church; to those who feared Him too much to be led astray from the truth. (August 31, 2001 the Holy Ghost gave a new design for the banner of truth.) On May 2nd, 1952 "of Prophecy" was added to the name Church of God. In 1990, the Church of God of Prophecy departed from theocratic government. Through the Holy Ghost, God called for a Solemn Assembly to be held July 23-25, 1993. On July 24th, the Holy Ghost gave direction to separate ourselves from the apostasy of the past three years, and to continue truly as The Church of God, clearly designating Robert J. Pruitt as the General Overseer. The Church of God thus returned to the true theocracy.

This constituted not a new organization, but the reorganization of The Church of God as the true theocracy of God, the exclusive Body of Christ:

1. Which was set in order by Christ and functioned in theocratic order until A.D. 325;
2. Which arose from the Dark Ages on June 13, 1903;
3. Which continued true to God in "faith and practice, government and discipline" following the 1923 disruption;
4. Which is doing likewise since the similar disruption in 1993.

Details of the future are, of course, unknown; but the prophecies of God are clear concerning His Church. The hour is late, but the brightness of the "Arise, Shine" lies just ahead. Without a doubt, perfection will be attained, for it has already been declared of the Church that Christ will "present it unto himself a glorious church, not having spot, or wrinkle, or any such thing; but that it should be holy and without blemish." (Ephesians 5:27; see also Revelations 19:6-9).

Headquarters
P.O. Box 450, Charleston, TN 37310, U.S.A., Tel. (423)339-8264

Officers
General Overseer, Stephen Smith, 197 Tillie Road, Cleveland, TN Field Secretary, Ray D. Dupre
Field Secretary, Robert F. Strong
Field Secretary, Donaldo Acosta
General Treasurer/ Assistant Editor of The Evening Light, Kevin D. Werkheiser
World Mission Coordinator/ Bible Training Institute Director, Herman D. Ard
Mission Representative (Africa, Asia & Europe), Robert J. Hawkins, Jr.
Assembly Band Movement Coordinator, Donald W. Branscum
Evangelism Coordinator, Lanny W. Carter
Church of Prophecy Marker Association Coordinator, Melvin Byers, Jr.

Sunday School Coordinator, Maudie E. Wood
Victory Leaders Band Coordinator, Sharon Griffin
Women's Missionary Band Coordinator, Betty Bishop

STATES
Alabama, James C. Anders
Alaska, Michael A. Grant
Arizona/Colorado/New Mexico/Texas (W), James R. Horne
Arkansas/Kansas/Missouri/Oklahoma/Texas (E), Dewayne Smith
Idaho (S)/California/Nevada/Utah, Serafin Pimentel
Idaho (N)/Montana (W)/Oregon/Washington, Ray D. Adams
Florida/Georgia, Melvin F. Kramer
Indiana/Illinois (S)/Kentucky/Ohio, Paul S. Jernigan
Louisiana/Mississippi, A. T. Dewberry
North Carolina, Melvin Byers, Jr.
South Carolina, Carl J. Neal
Pennsylvania/Delaware/Maryland/Massachusets, James T. Smith
Virginia/ West Virginia, Clive Jared
N. Dakota/S. Dakota/Minnesota/Montana (E)/ Nebraska/Wyoming, Delbert G. Bock
Tennessee, Ray D. Dupre
Wisconsin/Illinois (N)/Iowa/Michigan, E. Roger Ammons

COUNTRIES
Argentina/Brazil/Paraguay/ Uruguay, David Coronel
Bahamas/Cayman/Turks & Caicos Islands, George C. Forbes
Belize/Honduras/El Salvador/Spain, Donaldo Acosta
Bolivia/Ecuador, Benito Ramos Quispe
Canada East, E. Roger Ammons
Canada West, Ray Adams
Cameroon/Democratic Republic of Congo/ Republic of Congo, Patrice T. Kalamba
Chile, Javier Diaz
England, Robert J. Hawkins Jr.
Guatemala, Manuel S. Castro
Haiti, Louis E. Gaddis
India (South), Isaac Thomas Adimavunkal
India (North), Ch. Paul Sudhaker
Indonesia, Kalmen E. Nainggolan
Kenya/Ethiopia/Tanzania/Zimbabwe, Renison Mbogo Ngurukiri
Mexico, José G. Bañuelos
Nepal, Herman D. Ard
Nicaragua/Costa Rica/Panama, Caleb Hernández Ramírez
Nigeria, Matthew Ogunmola
Peru, Leonardo Luna
Philippines, Danilo M. Orcino
Puerto Rico/Dominican Republic/St. Vincent/ Netherlands Antilles, Juan Pimentel
Uganda/Burundi/Rwanda, Makohá F. Agati
Zambia, Alfred Nsofwa

Periodicals
The Evening Light

Church of God (Anderson, Indiana)

The Church of God (Anderson, Indiana) began in 1881 when Daniel S. Warner and several associates felt constrained to forsake all denominational hierarchies as formal creeds, trusting solely in the Holy Spirit as their overseer and the Bible as their statement of belief.

These people saw themselves at the forefront of a movement to restore unity and holiness to the church, not to establish another denomination, but to promote primary allegiance to Jesus Christ so as to transcend denominational loyalties.

Deeply influenced by Wesleyan theology and Pietism, the Church of God has emphasized conversion, holiness and attention to the Bible. Worship services tend to be informal, accentuating expository preaching and robust singing. There is no formal membership. Persons are assumed to be members on the basis of witness to a conversion experience and evidence that supports such witness. The absence of formal membership is also consistent with the church's understanding of how Christian unity is to be achieved- that is, by preferring the label Christian before all others. The Church of God is congregational in its government. Each local congregation may call any recognized Church of God minister to be its pastor and may retain him or her as long as is mutually pleasing. Ministers are ordained and disciplined by state or provincial assemblies made up predominantly of ministers. National program agencies serve the church through coordinated ministries and resource materials. There are Church of God congregations in 89 foreign countries, most of which are resourced by one or more missionaries. There are slightly more Church of God adherents overseas than in North America.

Headquarters

General Director (President): Dr. Ronald V. Duncan, P.O. Box 2420,Anderson, IN 46018-2420, Tel. (765)642-0256 Fax (765)648-2191
Media Contact: David Farlow, Chief of Strategic Communications, Email: dfarlow@chog.org
Email: rduncan@chog.org
Website: www.chog.org

Officers

General Director (President): Dr. Ronald V. Duncan, D. Min., D.D.
Vice President, Douglas A. Shearer Treasurer, Allan J. Smith Secretary, Joni A. Burnett, CPS 1201 E 54th Street, P.O. Box 2420, Anderson, IN 46018-2420, Tel. (765)642-0256 Fax (765)648-2191 Media Contact: David Farlow, Chief of Strategic Communications, Email: dfarlow@chog.org

OTHER CHURCH OF GOD ORGANIZATIONS:
Board of Pensions, President: Jeffery A. Jenness, Box 2299, Anderson IN 46018
Warner Press, Inc., President: Eric King, Box 2499, Anderson IN 46018
Anderson University, President: James L. Edwards, 1100 E 5th St., Anderson IN 46012

Mid-America Christian University, President: John Fozard, 3500 SW 119th St., Oklahoma City OK 73170
Warner Pacific College, Interim President: Andrea Cook, 2219 SE 68th Ave, Portland OR 97215
Warner University, President: Gregory V. Hall, 13895 Hwy 27, Lake Wales, FL 33859
Women of the Church of God, Executive Director: Arnetta Bailey, Box 2328, Anderson, IN 46018

Periodicals

Missions Magazine, Pathways to God, Communion, People to People, YMI Update, CHOG News, Multiplication Moments, Advance, Global Uplink

The Church of God in Christ

The Church of God in Christ was founded in 1897 in Lexington, Mississippi by Bishop Charles Harrison Mason, a former Baptist minister, and organized as a Pentecostal Church during the early stages of the holiness movement and, more specifically, as an outgrowth of the Azusa Street Revival of Los Angeles, California, in 1906-9.

Initial growth of the church was attributable to the organization of four departments between 1910-1916, the Women's Department, the Sunday School, Young People's Willing Workers and Home and Foreign Missions.

The Church is Trinitarian and teaches the infallibility of Holy Scripture, the need for regeneration and baptism of the Holy Ghost evidenced by speaking in tongues. It emphasizes holiness as God's standard for Christian conduct and recognizes as ordinances Holy Communion, Water Baptism and Feet Washing.

Its governmental structure is basically episcopal and consists of three branches. The General Board represents the Executive Branch, the General Assembly is the Legislative Branch, and the Judiciary Board represents the Judicial Branch

Headquarters

Mason Temple Church of God in Christ, 938 Mason St., Memphis, TN 38126, Tel. (901)947-9300
Elder J.H. Lyles, Jr., General Secretary, Mailing Address, P.O. Box 320, Memphis, TN 38101
Email: EJOHNCOGIC@aol.com
Website: www.cogic.org

Officers

THE PRESIDIUM:
Presiding Bishop, Bishop C.E. Blake, 938 Mason St., Memphis, TN 38126 (901)947-9340
1st Assistant, Bishop N. Haynes, 1267 Whispering Oaks Dr., Desoto, TX 75115, (214) 375-4105
2nd Assistant, Bishop P.A. Brooks, 30945 Wendbrook Ln., Beverly Hills, MI 48025, (313) 835-5329
Secretary, Bishop W.W. Hamilton, 14570 Mountain Quail Rd., Salinas, CA 93908, (831) 395-2774

Asst. Secretary, Bishop R.L.H. Winbush, 235 Diamond Dr., Lafayette, LA 70501, (318) 232-6958
Member, Bishop C.D. Owens, 406 Roswell St., Marietta, GA 30060, (770) 590-8510
Member, Bishop L.R. Anderson, 1023 E. Brook Hollow Dr., Phoenix, AZ 85022, (602) 993-4906
Member, Bishop G.D. McKinney, 5825 Imperial Ave., San Diego, CA 92114, (619) 262-2671
Member, Bishop S.L. Green, Jr., 41 St. Johns Dr., Hampton, VA 23666, (757) 380-6118
Member, Bishop N.W. Wells, 717 Bridgeview Bay, Muskegon, MI 49441, (231) 722-3219
Member, Bishop J.W. Macklin, 1027 W. Tennyson Road, Haywood, CA 94544, (510) 783-9377

GENERAL OFFICERS:
General Secretary, Elder A.Z. Hall, Jr., P.O. Box 320, Memphis, TN 38101, (901) 947-9356
General Treasurer, Bishop S.L. Lowe, 938 Mason St., Memphis, TN 38126, (901) 947-9319
Financial Secretary, Bishop F.O. White, 312 Grand Ave., Freeport, NY 11520, (516) 623-7513

ELECTED OFFICERS, DEPARTMENTAL HEADS AND AUXILLIARY LEADERS
Chairman–General Assembly: Bishop J.O. Patterson, Jr., 229 Danny Thomas, Memphis, TN 38126
Chairman–Judiciary Board: Bishop T.L. Westbrook, 1623 S. 11th St., Tacoma, WA 98405
Chairman–Board of Bishops: Bishop J. Sheard, 19511 Afton Rd., Detroit, MI 48203
Chairman–Board of Trustees: Bishop C.M Ford, 4525 S. Wabash, Chicago, IL 60653, (773) 538-4526
Chief of Staff: Bishop J.L. Maynard, 930 Mason St., Memphis, TN 38126, (901) 947-9338
Chief Accountant: Minister A. Perpener, P.O. Box 320, Memphis, TN 38126, (901) 947-9361
National Properties: Elder D.L.S. Wells, 938 Mason St., Memphis, TN 38126, (901) 947-9332
Chairman–Pastors/Elders: Elder D. Hutchins
Adjutant General: Bishop Matthew Williams, 1516 Dumont Dr., Valrico, FL 33594
President–Women's Dept.: Mother W.M. Rivers, P.O. Box 1052, Memphis, TN 38101, (901)
President–Missions Dept.: Bishop C.L. Moody, P.O. Box 320, Memphis, TN 38101, (901) 947-9316
President–Evangelism: Bishop R. White, 4121 Thurman Dr., Conley, GA 30288, (404) 361-7020
President–Youth Dept.: Elder Michael Hill, 23746 Riverside Dr., Lathrup, MI 48076
President–Sunday School: Elder Alton Gatlin, 229 Diamond Dr., Lafayette, LA 70501
President–Music Dept.: Professor I. Stevenson
President–Men's Conference: Bishop D. Hines, 8605 W. Goodhope Rd., Milwaukee, WI 53224
President–Sunshine Band: Dr. R.L. Howard
President–Purity: Missionary T. Cotton
Executive Director–Fine Arts: Mrs. S.J. Powell
CEO–Publishing House: Dr. D.A. Hall, Sr., 930 Mason St., Memphis, TN 38126

Chairman–Board of Pub.: Bishop R.L.H. Winbush, 235 Diamond Dr., Lafayette, LA 70501
Manager–COGIC Bookstore: Mrs. G. Miller, 285 S. Main, Memphis, TN 38101, (901) 947-9304
EDUCATIONAL INSTITUTIONS:
Charles Harrison Mason Theological Seminary, 671 Beckwith St. SW, Atlanta, GA 30314 Attn: Dean O.L. Haney
C.H. Mason System of Bible Colleges, 930 Mason St., Memphis, TN 38126 Attn: Dr. M.L. Johnson
All Saints Bible College, 930 Mason St., Memphis, TN 38126 Attn: Dr. P. Little
Saints Academy, C.H. Mason Highway, Lexington, MS Attn: Elder L. Weems

Periodicals
The Whole Truth Magazine, The Voice of Missions, The McBrayer Report

Church of God in Christ, International

The Church of God in Christ, International was organized in 1969 in Kansas City, Mo., by 14 bishops of the Church of God in Christ of Memphis, Tenn. The doctrine is the same, but the separation came because of disagreement over polity and governmental authority. The Church is Wesleyan in theology (two works of grace) but stresses the experience of full baptism of the Holy Ghost with the initial evidence of speaking with other tongues as the Spirit gives utterance.

Headquarters
170 Adelphi St., Brooklyn, NY 11205, Tel. (718)625-9175
Media Contact, Natl. Sec., Rev. Sis. Sharon R. Dunn
Email: laity@cogic.org
Website: www.cogic.org/main

Officers
Presiding Bishop, Most Rev. Carl Williams, Jr.
Vice Presiding Bishop, Rt. Rev. J. C. White
Exec. Admn., Horace K. Williams, Word of God Center, Newark, NJ
Women's Dept., Natl. Supervisor, Evangelist Elvonia Williams
Youth Dept., Pres., Dr. Joyce Taylor, 137-17 135th Ave., S., Ozone Park, NY 11420
Music Dept., Pres., Isaiah Heyward
Bd. of Bishops, Chpsn., Bishop J. C. White, 360 Colorado Ave., Bridgeport, CT 06605

Church of God in Christ, Mennonite

The Church of God in Christ, Mennonite was organized by the evangelist-reformer John Holdeman in Ohio. The church unites with the faith of the Waldensians, Anabaptists and other such groups throughout history. Emphasis is placed on obedience to the teachings of the

93

Bible, including the doctrine of the new birth and spiritual life, noninvolvement in government or the military, head-coverings for the women, beards for the men and separation from the world shown by simplicity in clothing, homes, possessions and lifestyle. The church has a worldwide membership of about 22,225, largely concentrated in the United States and Canada.

Headquarters

P.O. Box 313, 420 N. Wedel Ave., Moundridge, KS 67107, Tel. (620)345-2532 Fax (620) 345-2582

Media Contact, Dale Koehn, P.O. Box 230, Moundridge, KS 67107, Tel. (620)345-2532 Fax (620)345-2582, Email: dalekoehn.gp@ cogicm.org

Email: dalekoehn.gp@cogicm.org

Periodicals

Messenger of Truth

Church of God (Cleveland, Tennessee)

It is one of America's oldest Pentecostal churches founded in 1886 as an outgrowth of the holiness revival under the name Christian Union. In 1907 the church adopted the organizational name Church of God. It has its foundation upon the principles of Christ as revealed in the Bible. The Church of God is Christian, Protestant, foundational in its doctrine, evangelical in practice and distinctively Pentecostal. It maintains a centralized form of government and a commitment to world evangelization. The first church of Canada was established in 1919 in Scotland Farm, Manitoba. Paul H. Walker became the first overseer of Canada in 1931.

Headquarters

Intl. Offices, 2490 Keith St., NW, Cleveland, TN 37320, Tel. (423)472-3361 Fax (423)478-7066

Media Contact, Dir. of Communications, T. Scot Carter, P.O.Box 2430, Cleveland, TN 37320-2430, Tel. (423)478-7112 Fax (423)478-7066

Email: jrobinson@churchofgod.org

Website: www.churchofgod.org

Officers

General Overseer, Dr. Raymond F. Culpepper, P.O. Box 2430, Cleveland, TN 37320-2430, Tel. (423)478-7137, Fax (423)478-7275, gocog@ churchofgod.org.

First Assistant General Overseer, Dr. Timothy M. Hill, P.O. Box 2430, Cleveland, TN 37320-2430, Tel. (423)478-7136, Fax (423)478-7379, cog1a@churchofgod.org

Second Assistant General Overseer, Dr. Mark L. Williams, P.O. Box 2430, Cleveland, TN 37320-2430, Tel. (423)478-7126, Fax (423) 478-7263, cog2a@churchofgod.org

Third Assistant General Overseer, Dr. David M. Griffis, P.O. Box 2430, Cleveland, TN 37320-2430, Tel. (423)478-7133, Fax (423)478-7247, cog3a@churchof god.org

Secretary General, Dr. Wallace J. Sibley, P.O. Box 2430, Cleveland, TN 37320-2430, Tel. (423)478-7127, Fax (423)478-7052, cogsecgeneral@churchofgod.org

Canada-Eastern, Rev. Daniel J. Vassell, P.O. Box 2036, Brampton, ON L6T 3TO, Tel. (905)270-8083, Fax (905)270-6720

Canada-Western, Rev. Vaughn D. Mathews, P,O. Box 54055, 2640 52 St. NE, Calgary, AB T1Y 6S6, Tel. (403)293-8817 Fax (403)293-3466

Canada-Quebec-Maritimes, Rev. Jacques Houle, 19 Orly, Granby, QC J2H 1Y4, Tel. (450)378-4442 Fax (450)378-8646

Canada-National, Dr. Ken Bell, P.O. Box 2430, Cleveland, TN 37320-2430, Tel. (423)478-7138 Fax (423)478-7443

DEPARTMENTS

Benefits Board—CEO, Arthur D. Rhodes

Business & Records—Exec. Dir., Julian B. Robinson

Care Ministries—Dir., Donnie W. Smith

Chaplains Commission—Dir., Robert D. Crick

Communications, Media Ministries—Dir., T. Scot Carter

Division of Education—Chancellor, Donald S. Aultman

Education—European Theological Bible Seminary, Dir., Paul Schmidgall

Education—USA Hispanic Educational Ministries Dir., Rigoberto Ramos

Education—International Bible College, Pres., Philip Siggelkow

Education—Lee University, Pres., Charles Paul Conn

Education—Patten University, Pres., Gary Moncher

Education—Puerto Rico Bible College, Pres., Ildefonso Caraballo

Education—Pentecostal Theological Seminary, President, Steven J. Land

Evangelism & Home Missions—Dir., Jimmy D. Smith

Evangelism—Hispanic Ministries, Dir., Fidencio Burgueno

Evangelism—Native American Ministries, Dir., Douglas M. Cline

Lay Ministries—Dir., Leonard C. Albert

Legal Services—Dir., Dennis W. Watkins

Men/Women of Action—Dir., L. Hugh Carver

Military/Multi-Cultural/Romanian —Dir., G. Dennis McGuire

Ministerial Care—Dir., Bill Leonard

Ministerial Development/School of Ministry— Dir., Donald S. Aultman

Ministry to Israel—Dir., J. Michael Utterback

Ministry to the Military—Dir., Robert A. Moore

Music Ministries—Dir., Delton L. Alford

Pentecostal Resource Center—Director, Barbara McCullough

Pentecostal Research Center—Dir., David G. Roebuck

Publications—Dir., Joseph A. Mirkovich

SpiritCare—Dir., Gene D. Rice

Stewardship—Dir., Kenneth R. Davis

94

Women's Ministries—Coordinator, Jan Timmerman
World Missions—Dir., Douglas LeRoy
Youth & Christian Education—Dir., Thomas A. Madden

Periodicals
Church of God Evangel, Church of God Editorial Evangelica, Save Our World, Ministry Now Profiles

Church of God by Faith, Inc.

Founded 1914, in Jacksonville Heights, Florida., by Elder John Bright, this church believes the word of God as interpreted by Jesus Christ to be the only hope of salvation and Jesus Christ the only mediator for people.

Headquarters
1315 Lane Ave. S., Suite 6, Jacksonville, FL 32205, Tel. (904)783-8500 Fax (904)783-9911
Media Contact, Ofc. Mgr., Sarah E. Lundy
Email: natl-hq@cogbf.org
Website: www.cogbf.org

Officers
Presiding Bishop, James E. McKnight, P.O. Box 121, Gainesville, FL 32601
Treas., Elder John Robinson, 300 Essex Dr., Ft. Pierce, FL 34946
Exec. Sec., David C. Rourk, 207 Chestnut Hill Drive, Rochester, NY. 14617
Ruling Elder, James E. McKnight, Jr., P.O. Box 101, Starke, FL 32091

The Church of God of the Firstborn

The Church of God of the Firstborn was founded by Pentecostal evangelist Adolph Gustav Etterman in 1936. Headquarters are located in Newton, KS, where annual summer conferences are held. In 2002, the denomination consisted of 26 congregations, located primarily in the south central United States and in Mexico. In recent years, the number of Caucasian churches has declined and Hispanic membership has surged. James Etterman, the son of the founder, became president of the denomination in 1986.

Headquarters
P.O. Box 1041
720 S. Kansas Ave.
Newton, KS 671114-1041
Media Contact, Pres., Rev. James Etterman

Officers
Pres., Rev. James Etterman

Periodicals
The True Messenger

Church of God General Conference (Oregon, IL and Morrow, GA)

This church is the outgrowth of several independent local groups of similar faith. Some were in existence as early as 1800, and others date their beginnings to the arrival of British immigrants around 1847. Many local churches carried the name Church of God of the Abrahamic Faith.

State and district conferences of these groups were formed as an expression of mutual cooperation. A national organization was instituted at Philadel-phia in 1888. Because of strong convictions on the questions of congregational rights and authority, however, it ceased to function until 1921, when the present General Conference was formed at Waterloo, Iowa.

The Bible is accepted as the supreme standard of faith. Adventist in viewpoint, the second (pre-millenial) coming of Christ is strongly emphasized. The church teaches that the kingdom of God will be literal, beginning in Jerusalem at the time of the return of Christ and extending to all nations. Emphasis is placed on the oneness of God and the Sonship of Christ, that Jesus did not pre-exist prior to his birth in Bethlehem and that the Holy Spirit is the power and influence of God. Membership is dependent on faith, repentance and baptism by immersion.

The work of the General Conference is carried on under the direction of the board of directors. With a congregational church government, the General Conference exists primarily as a means of mutual cooperation and for the development of yearly projects and enterprises.

The headquarters and Bible College were moved to Morrow, Ga. in 1991.

Headquarters
P.O. Box 100,000, Morrow, GA 30260, Tel. (404)362-0052 Fax (404)362-9307
Media Contact, Tim Jones
Email: info@abc-coggc.org
Website: www.abc-coggc.org

Officers
Chief Administrative Officer, Mr. Tim Jones, Box 100,000, Morrow, GA 30260, Tel. (404)362-9307, Email: tjones@abc-coggc.org
Chpsn., Pastor Jeff Fletcher, 653 Highway 17, Piedmont, SC 29673, Tel. (864)947-9555, Email: revjeff@carter.net
Vice Chpsn., Rob Helenburg, 12811 Madeley Ct., Fairfax, VA 22033, Tel. (703)378-0190, Email: wrobinh@verizon.net
Sec., Robert See, 19201 Strawberry Hill Rd, South Bend, IN 46614, Tel. (574)299-1521, Email: bobsarasee@sbcglobal.net
Treas., Larry Bolhous, 213 N. Church St., Winnebago, IL 61088, Tel. (815)335-2906, Email: winsvalu@mchsi.com

OTHER ORGANIZATIONS
Bus. Admn., Operations Manager, Mr. Gary Burnham, Box 100,000, Morrow, GA 30260, Tel. (404)362-0052 Fax (404)362-9307, Email: gburnham@abc-coggc.org
Atlanta Bible College, President, Mr. Tim Jones, Box 100,000, Morrow, GA 30260, Tel. (404)362-9307, Email: tjones@abc-coggc.org

Periodicals
The Restitution Herald and Progress Journal, A Journal From the Radical Reformation, Church of God

Church of God, Mountain Assembly, Inc.

The church was formed in 1895 and organized in 1906 by J. H. Parks, S. N. Bryant, Tom D. Moses and William Douglas.

Headquarters

256 N. Florence Ave., P.O. Box 157, Jellico, TN 37762, Tel. (423)784-8260 Fax (423)784-3258
Media Contact, Gen. Sec.-Treas., Rev. James Kilgore
Email: cgmahdq@jellico.com
Website: www.cgmahdq.org

Officers

Gen. Overseer, Rev. Donnie Hill
Asst. Gen. Overseer, World Missions Dir., Rev. Jay Walden
Gen. Sec.-Treas., Rev. James Kilgore
Youth Ministries & Camp Dir., Rev. Jon Walden

Periodicals

The Gospel Herald

Church of God of Prophecy

The Church of God of Prophecy is one of the churches that grew out of the work of A. J. Tomlinson in the first half of the twentieth century. Historically it shares a common heritage with the Church of God (Cleveland Tennessee) and is in the mainstream of the classical Pentecostal-Holiness tradition.

At the death of A.J. Tomlinson in 1943, M.A. Tomlinson was named General Overseer and served until his retirement in 1990. He emphasized unity and fellowship unlimited by racial, social, or political differences. The next General Overseer, Billy D. Murray, Sr., who served from 1990 until his retirement in 2000, emphasized a commitment to the promotion of Christian unity and world evangelization. In July 2000, Fred S. Fisher, Sr. was duly selected to serve as the fourth General Overseer of the Church of God of Prophecy until his retirement in September 2006. In August 2006, Bishop Randall E. Howard, then Global Outreach Ministries Director, was selected as the fifth General Overseer of the Church.

From its beginnings, the Church has based its beliefs on "the whole Bible, rightly divided," and has accepted the Bible as God's Holy Word, inspired, inerrant and infallible. The church is firm in its commitment to orthodox Christian belief. The Church affirms that there is one God, eternally existing in three persons, Father, Son and Holy Spirit. It believes in the deity of Christ, His virgin birth, His sinless life, the physical miracles He performed, His atoning death on the cross, His bodily resurrection, His ascension to the right hand of the Father and His Second coming. The church professes that salvation results from grace alone through faith in Christ, that regeneration by the Holy Spirit is essential for the salvation of sinful men, and that sanctification by the blood of Christ makes possible personal holiness. It affirms the present ministry of the Holy Spirit by Whose

indwelling believers are able to live godly lives and have power for service. The church believes in, and promotes, the ultimate unity of believers as prayed for by Christ in John 17. The church stresses the sanctity of human life and is committed to the sanctity of the marriage bond and the importance of strong, loving Christian families. Other official teachings include Holy Spirit baptism with tongues as initial evidence; manifestation of the spiritual gifts; divine healing; premillenial second-coming of Christ; total abstinence from the use of tobacco, alcohol and narcotics; water baptism by immersion; the Lord's supper and washing of the saints' feet; and a concern for moderation and holiness in all dimensions of lifestyle.

The Church is racially integrated on all levels, including top leadership. Women play a prominent role in church affairs, serving in pastoral roles and other leadership positions. The church presbytery has recently adopted plurality of leadership in the selection of a General Oversight Group. This group consists of eight bishops located around the world who, along with the General Overseer, are responsible for inspirational leadership and vision casting for the church body.

The Church has local congregations in all 50 states and more than 120 nations worldwide. Organizationally there is a strong emphasis on international missions, evangelism, youth and children's ministries, women's and men's ministries, stewardship, communications, publishing, leadership development and discipleship.

Headquarters

CHURCH OF GOD OF PROPHECY INTERNATIONAL OFFICES
P.O. Box 2910, Cleveland, TN 37320-2910
Email: betty@cogop.org
Website: www.cogop.org

Officers

Gen. Overseer, Bishop Randall E. Howard General Presbyters, Sherman Allen, Sam Clements, David Browder, Clayton Endecott, Felix Santiago, Brice Thompson
International Offices Ministries Directors Finance, Communications, and Publishing, Benjamin Feliz Global Outreach Ministries, David Bryan

Periodicals

White Wing Messenger (ENG), White Wing Messenger (Spanish).

The Church of God (Seventh Day), Denver, Colorado

The Church of God (Seventh Day) began in southwestern Michigan in 1858, when a group of Sabbath-keepers led by Gilbert Cranmer refused to give endorsement to the visions and writings of Ellen G. White, a principal in the formation of the Seventh-Day Adventist Church. Another branch of Sabbath-keepers, which developed near Cedar Rapids, Iowa, in 1860, joined the Michigan church in 1863 to publish a paper called The Hope of Israel, the predecessor to the Bible Advocate, the church's present publication. As membership grew and spread into Missouri and Nebraska, it organized the General Conference of the Church of God in 1884. The words "Seventh Day" were added to its name in 1923. The headquarters of the church was in Stanberry, Missouri, from 1888 until 1950, when it moved to Denver.

The Church teaches salvation is a gift of God's grace, and is available solely by faith in Jesus Christ, the Savior; that saving faith is more than mental assent, it involves active trust and repentance from sin. Out of gratitude, Christians will give evidence of saving faith by a lifestyle that conforms to God's commandments, including the seventh-day Sabbath, which members observe as a tangible expression of their faith and rest in God as their Creator and Redeemer. The church believes in the imminent, personal, and visible return of Christ; that the dead are in an unconscious state awaiting to be resurrected, the wicked to be destroyed, and the righteous to be rewarded to eternal life in the presence of God on a restored earth. The church observes two ordinances, baptism by immersion and an annual Communion service accompanied by foot washing.

Headquarters
330 W. 152nd Ave., P.O. Box 33677, Denver, CO 80233, Tel. (303)452-7973 Fax (303)452-0657
Media Contact, Pres., Whaid Rose
Email: whaidrose@cog7.org
Website: www.cog7.org

Officers
MINISTRIES
Missions Ministrics, Dir., William Hicks,
Publications/Bible Advocate Press, Dir., Keith Michalak
Ministries Training, Dir., Larry Marrs
Young Adult Ministry, Dir., Christy Lang
Youth Ministry, Dirs., Kurt & Kristi Lang
Women's Ministry, Dir., Grace Sanchez

Periodicals
The Bible Advocate (English & Spanish), Churchright (English & Spanish)

The Church of Illumination
The Church of Illumination was organized in 1908 for the express purpose of establishing congregations at large, offering a spiritual, esoteric, philosophic interpretation of the vital biblical teachings, thereby satisfying the inner spiritual needs of those seeking spiritual truth, yet permitting them to remain in, or return to, their former church membership.

Headquarters
Beverly Hall, 5966 Clymer Rd., Quakertown, PA 18951, Tel. (800)779-3796
Media Contact, Dir. General, Gerald E. Poesnecker, P.O. Box 220, Quakertown, PA 18951, Tel. (215)536-7048 Fax (215)536-7058
Email: bevhall@comcat.com
Website: www.soul.org

Officers
Dir.-General, Gerald E. Poesnecker, P.O. Box 220, Quakertown, PA 18951

The Church of Jesus Christ (Bickertonites)
This church was organized in 1862 at Green Oak, PA, by William Bickerton, who obeyed the Restored Gospel under Sidney Rigdon's following in 1845.

Headquarters
Sixth St., Monongahela, PA 15063, Tel. (412)258-3066
Exec. Sec., Carl Frammolino

Officers
Pres., Paul Palmieri, 319 Pine Dr., Aliquippa, PA 15001 Tel.
First Counselor, Thomas M. Liberto, 6154 Stream View Dr., San Diego, CA 92115-6915
Second Counselor, Peter A. Scolaro, Ridge Way Dr., Rochester, MI 48307-1771
Exec. Sec., Carl J. Frammolino
Missionary Benevolent Association

Periodicals
The Gospel News

The Church of Jesus Christ of Latter-day Saints
This church was organized April 6, 1830, at Fayette, N.Y., by Joseph Smith. Members believe Joseph Smith was divinely directed to restore the gospel to the earth, and that through him the keys to the Aaronic and Melchizedek priesthoods and temple work also were restored. Members believe that both the Bible and the Book of Mormon (a record of the Lord's dealings with His people on the American continent 600 B.C. - 421 A.D.) are scripture. Membership is over thirteen million.

In addition to the First Presidency, the governing bodies of the church include the Quorum of the Twelve Apostles, the Presidency of the Seventy, the Quorums of the Seventy and the Presiding Bishopric.

Headquarters
47 East South Temple St., Salt Lake City, UT 84150, Tel. (801)240-1000 Fax (801)240-1167
Media Contact, Dir., Media Relations, Michael Purdy, Tel. (801)240-2363 Fax (801)240-1167
Email: PorterDS@ldschurch.org
Website: www.lds.org

Officers
Pres., Thomas S. Monson
1st Counselor, Henry B. Eyring
2nd Counselor, Dieter F. Uchtdorf
Quorum of the Twelve Apostles, Pres., Boyd K. Packer; L. Tom Perry; Russell M. Nelson; Dallin H. Oaks; M. Russell Ballard; Richard G. Scott; Robert D. Hales; Jeffrey R. Holland; David A. Bednar; Quentin L. Cook; D. Todd Christofferson; Neil L. Andersen

AUXILIARY ORGANIZATIONS
Sunday Schools, Gen. Pres., Russell T. Osguthorpe
Relief Society, Gen. Pres., Julie Beck
Young Women, Gen. Pres., Elaine Dalton
Young Men, Gen. Pres., David L. Beck
Primary, Gen. Pres., Cheryl C. Lant

Periodicals
The Ensign, Liahona, New Era, Friend Magazine

Church of the Living God (Motto, Christian Workers for Fellowship)

The Church of the Living God was founded by William Christian in April 1889 at Caine Creek, Arkansas. It was the first black church in America without Anglo-Saxon roots and not founded by white missionaries.

Chief Christian, as he is now referred, was born a slave in Mississippi on Nov. 10, 1856 and grew up uneducated. In 1875, he united with the Missionary Baptist Church and began to preach. In 1888, he left the Baptist Church and began what was known as Christian Friendship Work. Believing himself to have been inspired by the Spirit of God through divine revelation and close study of the Scriptures, he was led to the truth that the Bible refers to the church as The Church of the Living God (I Timothy. Ch.3 vs.15). In 1889, he established the Church of the Living God organization.

The organization is nondenominational, nonsectarian and Trinitarian and believers in the infallibility of the Scriptures. It emphasizes believer's baptism by immersion, the use of water and unleavened bread element in the Lord's Supper and the washing of feet that is required only when one unites with the church.

The local organizations are know as "Temple" rather than as "Churches" and are subject to the authority of the general assembly. The presiding officer is styled as "chief bishop." The ministry includes bishops, overseers, evangelists, pastors, missionaries and local preachers. The Executive Board is in charge of the operation of the entire organization, in the absence of the Annual Assembly. Synod, Annual, General Assembly meets quadrennial.

The Church of the Living God, now headquartered in Cincinnati, Ohio, has been in existence for more than 114 years. It is represented by approximately 10,000 members throughout 25 states within the U.S. The presiding officer, Chief Bishop W. E. Crumes, has led the organization for more than 30 years.

Headquarters
430 Forest Ave., Cincinnati, OH 45229, Tel. (513)569-5660 Fax (513)569-5661; Media Contact: Chief Bishop, W. E. Crumes

EXECUTIVE BOARD
Chief Bishop, W. E. Crumes, 430 Forest Ave., Cincinnati, OH 45229
Vice Chief Bishop, Robert D. Tyler, 3802 Bedford, Omaha, NE 68110

Exec. Sec., Bishop C. A. Lewis, 1360 N. Boston, Tulsa, OK 73111
Gen. Sec., Elder Raymond Powell, Sr., 2159 E. 95th St., Chicago, IL 60617
Gen. Treas., Elder Harry Hendricks, 11935 Cimarron Ave., Hawthorne, CA 90250
Bishop E. L. Bowie, 2037 N.E. 18th St., Oklahoma City, OK 73111
Bishop Leroy Smith, Jr., 1418 Faraday, Peoria, IL 61605
Bishop Jeff Ruffin, 302 E. Monte Way, Phoenix, AZ 85040
Bishop S. E. Shannon, 1034 S. King Hwy., St. Louis, MO 63110
Bishop, Elbert Jones, 4522 Melwood, Memphis, TN 38109
Bishop, Harold Edwards, P.O.Box 411489, Dallas, TX 75249

NATIONAL DEPARTMENTS
Convention Planning Committee
Young People's Progressive Union
Christian Education Dept.
Sunday School Dept.
Natl. Evangelist Bd.
Natl. Nurses Guild
Natl. Women's Work Dept.
Natl. Music Dept.
Natl. Usher Board
Natl. Sec. Office

Periodicals
The Gospel Truth

Church of the Lutheran Brethren of America

The Church of the Lutheran Brethren of America was organized in December 1900. Five independent Lutheran congregations met together in Milwaukee, Wisconsin, and adopted a constitution patterned very closely on that of the Lutheran Free Church of Norway.

The spiritual awakening in the Midwest during the 1890s crystallized into convictions that led to the formation of a new church body. Chief among the concerns were church membership practices, observance of Holy Communion, confirmation practices and local church government.

The Church of the Lutheran Brethren practices a simple order of worship with the sermon as the primary part of the worship service. It believes that personal profession of faith is the primary criterion for membership in the congregation. The Communion service is reserved for those who profess faith in Christ as savior. Each congregation is autonomous and the synod serves the congregations in advisory and cooperative capacities.

The synod supports a world mission program in Cameroon, Chad, Japan and Taiwan. Approximately 40 percent of the synodical budget is earmarked for world missions. A growing home mission ministry is planting new congregations in the United States and Canada. Affiliate organizations operate several retirement, nursing homes, conference and retreat centers.

Headquarters

1020 Alcott Ave., W., Box 655, Fergus Falls, MN 56538, Tel. (218)739-3336 Fax (218)739-5514
Media Contact, Pres., Rev. Joel Egge
Email: clba@clba.org, sdolsen@clba.org
Website: www.clba.org

Officers

Pres., Rev. Joel Egge
Vice Pres., Rev. Matthew Rogness
Sec., Rev. Paul Larson, 1020 Alcott Ave. W, Fergus Falls, MN 56537
Exec. Dir. of Finance, Bradley Martinson
Lutheran Brethren Seminay President, Dr. David Veum
International Missions, Exec. Dir., Rev. Matthew Rogness

Periodicals

Faith & Fellowship

Church of the Lutheran Confession

The Church of the Lutheran Confession held its constituting convention in Watertown, S.D., in August of 1960. The Church of the Lutheran Confession was begun by people and congregations who withdrew from church bodies that made up what was then known as the Synodical Conference over the issue of unionism. Following such passages as I Corinthians 1 vs.10 and Romans 16 vs.17-18, the Church of the Lutheran Confession holds the conviction that mutual agreement with the doctrines of Scripture is essential and necessary before exercise of church fellowship is appropriate.

Members of the Church of the Lutheran Confession uncompromisingly believe the Holy Scriptures to be divinely inspired and therefore incrant. They subscribe to the historic Lutheran Confessions as found in the Book of Concord of 1580 because they are a correct exposition of Scripture.

The Church of the Lutheran Confession exists to proclaim, preserve and spread the saving truth of the gospel of Jesus Christ, so that the redeemed of God may learn to know Jesus Christ as their Lord and Savior and follow him through this life to the life to come.

Headquarters

501 Grover Rd., Eau Claire, WI 54701, Tel. (715)836-6622
Media Contact, Pres., Daniel Fleischer Tel.(361)241-5147
Email: JohnHLau@juno.com
Website: www.clclutheran.org

Officers

Pres., Rev. John Schierenbeck, 3015 Ave. K NW, Winter Haven, FL 33881
Mod., Rev. Paul Nolting, 208 Gall Path, Mankato, MN 56001
Vice Pres., Rev. Mark Bernthal, 3232 West Point Rd., Middleton, WI 53562, Tel. (608)233-2244
Sec., Rev. Wayne Eichstadt, 417 Woodhaven Lane, Mankato MN 56001
Treas., Dr. James Sydow, 500 Grover Rd., Eau Claire, WI 54701
Archivist, Prof. David Lau, 507 Ingram Dr., Eau Claire, WI 54701
Statistician, Dr. James Sydow, 500 Grover Rd., Eau Claire, WI 54701

Periodicals

The Lutheran Spokesman, Journal of Theology

Church of the Nazarene

The Church of the Nazarene resulted from the merger of three independent holiness groups. The Association of Pentecostal Churches in America, located principally in New York and New England, joined at Chicago in 1907 with a largely West Coast body called the Church of the Nazarene and formed the Pentecostal Church of the Nazarene. A southern group, the Holiness Church of Christ, united with the Pentecostal Church of the Nazarene at Pilot Point, Texas, in 1908. In 1919 the word "Pentecostal" was dropped from the name. Principal leaders in the organization were Phineas Bresee, William Howard Hoople, H. F. Reynolds and C. B. Jernigan. Dr. H. F. Reynolds organized the first Canadian congregation in 1902 at Oxford, Nova Scotia. The Church of the Nazarene emphasizes entire sanctification or Christian Holiness. It stresses the importance of a devout and holy life and a positive witness through Christ-like character shaped by the Holy Spirit. Nazarenes express their faith through evangelism, compassionate ministries, and education. The church is connectional. Its polity combines episcopal, presbyterian, and congregational elements. Churches call pastors. Districts conduct annual assemblies and elect leaders. The quadrennial General Assembly, a delegated body, is international in scope and establishes doctrine and order, elects the general superintendents (currently six), and elects members to various church boards and agencies. Internationally the church has 13 liberal arts colleges and universities, five graduate seminaries, 34 Bible colleges, three schools of nursing, an education college, and a junior college. The church maintains 794 missionaries in 151 world areas. World services include medical, educational and religious ministries. Books, periodicals and other Christian literature are published at the Nazarene Publishing House. The church is a member of the Christian Holiness Partnership, National Association of Evangelicals, the World Methodist Council, and the European Methodist Council.

Headquarters

Global Ministry Center, 17001 Prairie Star Parkway, Lenexa, KS 66220, Tel. (913)577-0600 Fax (913)577-0848
Media Contact, Gen. Sec./Operations Officer (OO), Dr. David P. Wilson, Tel. (913)577-0600; Fax: (913)577-0848 Email: dwilson@nazarene.org
Email: ssm@nazarene.org
Website: www.nazarene.org

Officers

Gen. Supts., Dr. Eugénio R. Duarte; Dr. David W. Graves; Dr.Jerry D. Porter; Dr. Stan A. Toler; Dr. J.K. Warrick; Dr. Jesse C. Middendorf; 17001 Prairie Star Parkway, Lenexa, KS 66220, Tel. (913)577-0500

Gen. Sec./Operation Officer (OO), Dr. David P. Wilson, Tel. (913)577-0500 Fax (816)822-9071 Email: dwilson@nazarene.org

Gen. Treas./Financial Officer (FO), Dr. Marilyn McCool (913)577-0500 Fax: (913)577-0843 Email: mmccool@nazarene.org

Sunday School and Discipleship Ministries International Director, Dr. Woodie Stevens, 17001 Prairie Star Parkway, Lenexa, KS 66220, Tel: (913)577-0500 Fax: (913)577-0891, Email: stevens@nazarene.org

USA/Canada Mission/Evangelism Director, Dr. Tom Nees, 17001 Prairie Star Parkway, Lenexa, KS 66220, Tel. (913)577-0500 Fax (913)577-0891, Email: tnees@nazarene.org

Education Commissioner, Dr. LeBron Fairbanks, 17001 Prairie Star Parkway, Lenexa, KS 66220, Tel. (913)577-0500 Fax (913)577-0858, Email: lfairbanks@nazarene.org

Nazarene Youth International Director., Rev. Gary Hartke, 17001 Prairie Star Parkway, Lenexa, KS 66220, Tel. (913)577-0500 Fax (913)577-0858, Email: ghartke@nazarene.org

World Mission Director., Dr. Louie Bustle, 17001 Prairie Star Parkway, Lenexa, KS 66220, Tel. (913)577-0500 Fax (913)577-0886, Email: lbustle@nazarene.org

Periodicals

Holiness Today, Preacher's Magazine, Grow Magazine

Church of Our Lord Jesus Christ of the Apostolic Faith, Inc.

This church body was founded by Bishop R.C. Lawson in Columbus, Ohio, and moved to New York City in 1919. It is founded upon the teachings of the apostles and prophets, Jesus Christ being its chief cornerstone.

Headquarters

2081 Adam Clayton Powell Jr. Blvd., New York, NY 10027, Tel. (212)866-1700

Media Contact, Exec. Sec., Bishop Thomas. E. Woolfolk, P.O. Box 119, Oxford, NC 27565, Tel. (919)693-9449 Fax (919)693-6115

Email: tewmsw@embarqmail.com

Website: www.apostolic-faith.org

Officers

Board of Apostles

Bishop William L. Bonner; Chief Apostle

Bishop Matthew A Norwood., Presiding Apostle

Bishop Robert L Sanders Sr., Vice Pres

Bishop Gentle L. Groover

Bishop Fred Rubin

Bishop James A. Maye

Bishop Henry A. Moultrie, II

Bishop Wesley M. Taylor

Bishop Samuel R. Peters, Sr.

Bishop Walter L. Jackson

Bishop Bradford Berry

Bishop Herbert Edwards

Bd. of Bishops, Chmn., Bishop James Darby

Bd. of Presbyters, Chairman, Elder Marcus McCoy

Exec. Sec., Bishop Thomas E. Woolfolk

Natl. Rec. Sec., Bishop Raymond J. Keith, Jr.

Natl. Fin. Sec., Bishop Clarence Groover

Natl. Corr. Sec., Bishop Darryl Forhand

Natl Treas., Deacon Winston Knox

Periodicals

Contender For The Faith, Minute Book, and The Beacon

Church of the United Brethren in Christ, USA

The Church of the United Brethren in Christ had its beginning with Philip William Otterbein and Martin Boehm, who were leaders in the revival movement in Pennsylvania and Maryland from the late 1760s into the early 1800s.

On Sept. 25, 1800, they and others associated with them formed a society under the name of United Brethren in Christ. Subsequent conferences adopted a Confession of Faith in 1815 and a constitution in 1841. The Church of the United Brethren in Christ adheres to the original constitution as amended in 1957, 1961 and 1977.

Headquarters

302 Lake St., Huntington, IN 46750, Tel. (260)356-2312 Fax (260)356-4730 x 210

Media Contact, Communications Dir., Steve Dennie

Email: steve@ub.org

Website: www.ub.org

Officers

Bishop, Rev. Phil Whipple

Finance Director, Marci Hammel

Director of Higher Education, Dr. G. Blair Dowden

Global Ministries Director, Rev. Jeff Bleijerveld

Communications Director, Mr. Steve Dennie

Churches of Christ

Churches of Christ are autonomous congregations whose members appeal to the Bible alone to determine matters of faith and practice. There are no central offices or officers. Publications and institutions related to the churches are either under local congregational control or are independent of any congregation. Churches of Christ shared a common fellowship in the 19th century with the Christian Churches/Churches of Christ and the Christian Church (Disciples of Christ). This fellowship ended in the decades following the American Civil War due to erosion of confidence in Scripture among many of those who formed denominational ties. This shift in belief embraced theistic evolution, doubted the complete truth of Scripture, and permitted unscriptural practices into the work and worship of the church. Chief among the changes in practice were using instrumental music in worship, permitting women to officiate in worship services, and conducting the work of the church through centralized agencies. Churches of Christ, following this division, remained strongly united in their belief in the inerrancy and sufficiency of Scripture. From this standpoint, they affirm faith in one God who subsists in three persons: Father, Son, and Holy Spirit; they teach that salvation is through the sacrificial death of Christ and is available to all who come to God through repentance and faith, initially expressed through confession of faith and baptism by immersion. Churches of Christ follow the New Testament pattern to direct every facet of the teaching and work of the church.

Headquarters

Media Contact, Ed., Gospel Advocate, Mr. Neil Anderson, 1006 Elm Hill Pike, Nashville, TN 37102, Tel. (800)251-8446 Fax (615)254-7411Website:

Periodicals

Action, Christian Woman, Christian Bible Teacher, The Christian Chronicle, Firm Foundation, Gospel Advocate, Guardian of Truth, Restoration Quarterly, Think, 21st Century Christian, Rocky Mountain Christian, The Spiritual Sword, Word and Work

Churches of Christ in Christian Union

Organized in 1909 at Washington Court House, Ohio, as the Churches of Christ in Christian Union, this body believes in the new birth and the baptism of the Holy Spirit for believers. It is Wesleyan, with an evangelistic and missionary emphasis.

The Reformed Methodist Church merged with the Churches of Christ in Christian Union in 1952.

Headquarters

Box 10, 1553 Lancaster Pike, Circleville, OH 43113, Tel. (740)474-8856 Fax (740)477-7766
Media Contact, General Secreatry, Rev. Ralph Hux

Officers

Gen. Supt., Dr. Tom Hermiz
Asst. Gen. Supt., Rev. Dan Harrison General Secreatry, Rev. Ralph Hux
Gen. Treas., Rev. Bruce Crabtree
Gen. Bd. of Trustees, Chpsn., Dr. Tom Hermiz; Vice-Chpsn., Rev. Dan Harrison
District Superintendents, West Central District, Rev. Joe Duvall; South Central District, Rev. Mike Holbrook; Northeast District, Rev. Brad Dixon; West Indies District, Joseph Atherly

Periodicals

The Evangelical Advocate

Churches of God, General Conference

The Churches of God, General Conference (CGGC) had its beginnings in Harrisburg, Pa., in 1825.

John Winebrenner, recognized founder of the Church of God movement, was an ordained minister of the German Reformed Church. His experience-centered form of Christianity, particularly the "new measures" he used to promote it, his close connection with the local Methodists, his "experience and conference meetings" in the church and his "social prayer meetings" in parishioners' homes resulted in differences of opinion and the establishment of new congregations. Extensive revivals, camp meetings and mission endeavors led to the organization of additional congregations across central Pennsylvania and westward through Ohio, Indiana, Illinois and Iowa.

In 1830 the first system of cooperation between local churches was initiated as an "eldership" in eastern Pennsylvania. The organization of other elderships followed. General Eldership was organized in 1845, and in 1974 the official name of the denomination was changed from General Eldership of the Churches of God in North America to its present name.

The Churches of God, General Conference, is composed of 5 Regions in the United States and 1 conference in Haiti. The polity of the church is presbyterial in form. The church has mission ministries in the southwest among native Americans and is extensively involved in church planting and whole life ministries in Bangladesh, Brazil, Haiti and India.

The General Conference convenes in business session triennially. An Administrative Council composed of 16 regional representatives is responsible for the administration and ministries of the church between sessions of the General Conference.

Headquarters

Legal Headquarters, United Church Center, Rm. 213, 900 S. Arlington Ave., Harrisburg, PA 17109, Tel. (717)652-0255
Administrative Offices, General Conf. Exec. Dir., Pastor Edward L. Rosenberry, P.O. Box 926, 700 E. Melrose Ave., P.O. Box 926, Findlay, OH 45839, Tel. (419)424-1961 Fax (419)424-3343, Email: director@cggc.org
Media Contact, Editor, Mrs. Rachel L. Foreman, P.O. Box 926, Findlay, OH 45839, Tel. (419) 424-1961 Fax (419)424-3343, communications@cggc.org
Email: director@cggc.org
Website: www.cggc.org

Officers

Pres., Pastor Dennis Hamsher, Email: dmasher@comcast.net
Sec., Pastor E. David Green, 700 E. Melrose Ave., P.O. Box 1132, Findlay, OH 45839, Tel. (419)423-7694 Fax (419)423-9092, Email: GLCdirector@cggc.org
Treas., Robert E. Stephenson, 700 E. Melrose Ave., P.O. Box 926, Findlay, OH 45839, Tel. (419)424-1961 Fax (419)424-3433, Email: treasurer@cggc.org

DEPARTMENTS
Cross-Cultural Ministries, Pastor Don Dennison
Pensions, Mr. James P. Thomas
Denominational Communications, Mrs. Rachel L. Foreman
Youth & Family Ministries, Pastor J. Lance Finley Publications, Kris Cupp
CGWM - Churches of God Women's Ministries

Periodicals
The Church Advocate, The Gem, The Missionary Signal

Community of Christ

Community of Christ's mission is to proclaim Jesus Christ and promote communities of joy, hope, love, and peace. Founded on April 6, 1830, this Christian denomination is present in nearly 50 nations with approximately 250,000 members worldwide. The church's Temple, located in the international headquarters complex, is dedicated to peace, reconciliation, and healing of the Spirit. Priesthood includes both men and women.

Headquarters
International Headquarters, 1001 W. Walnut, Independence, MO 64050-3562, Tel. (816)833-1000 Fax (816)521-3096
Media Contact; Kendra Friend, Email: kfriend@cofchrist.org; or Jennifer Killpack, Email: jkillpack@cofchrist.org
Email: blindgren@CofChrist.org
Website: www.CofChrist.org

Officers
(Mailing address for all officers is 1001 W. Walnut, Independence, MO 64050, Tel. (816)833-1000)
First Presidency:
President, Stephen M. Veazey, Email: sveazey@cofchrist.org
Counselor, David D. Schaal, Email: dschaal@cofchrist.org
Counselor, Becky Savage, Email: bsavage@cofchrist.org
Council of Twelve Apostles
President, James E. Slauter, Email: jslauter@cofchrist.org
Presiding Bishopric:
Presiding Bishop, Stephen M. Jones, Email: sjones@cofchrist.org
Counselor, R. Paul Davis, Email: pdavis@cofchrist.org
Counselor, David J. Brown, Email: dbrown@cofchrist.org
Presiding Evangelist:
David R. Brock, Email: dbrock@cofchrist.org
World Church Secretary:
Andrew Shields, Email: ashields@cofchrist.org
Public Relations, Fax (816)521-3043
Kendra Friend, Email: kfriend@cofchrist.org
Jennifer Killpack, Email: jkillpack@cofchrist.org

Periodicals
Herald

Congregational Holiness Church

This body was organized in 1921 and embraces the doctrine of Holiness and Pentecost. It carries on mission work in Mexico, Honduras, Costa Rica, Cuba, Brazil, Guatemala, India, Nicaragua, El Salvador, Venezula, Panama, Chile, Argentina, Belize, Zimbabwe, Haiti, and Peru.

Headquarters
3888 Fayetteville Hwy., Griffin, GA 30223, Tel. (404)228-4833 Fax (404)228-1177
Media Contact, Gen. Supt., Bishop Ronald Wilson
Email: chchurch@bellsouth.net
Website: www.chchurch.com

Executive Board
Gen. Supt., Bishop Ronald Smith
1st Asst. Gen. Supt., Rev. William L. Lewis
2nd Asst. Gen. Supt., Rev. Wayne Hicks
Gen. Sec., Rev. Leslee Bailey
Gen. Treas., Rev. Stephen Phillips
World Missions Supt., Rev. Billy Anderson

Periodicals
The Gospel Messenger

Conservative Baptist Association of America (CBAmerica)

The Conservative Baptist Association of America (now known as CBAmerica) was organized May 17, 1947 at Atlantic City, N.J. The Old and New Testaments are regarded as the divinely inspired Word of God and are therefore infallible and of supreme authority. Each local church is independent, autonomous and free from ecclesiastical or political authority.

CBAmerica provides wide-ranging support to its affiliate churches and individuals through nine regional associations. CBA offers personnel to assist churches in areas such as growth and health conflict resolution and financial analysis. The association supports its clergy with retirement planning, referrals for new places of ministry and spiritual counseling. The Conservative Baptist Women's Ministries assists women in the church to be effective in their personal growth and leadership.

Each June or July there is a National Conference giving members an opportunity for fellowship, inspiration and motivation.

Headquarters
1501 W. Mineral Ave., Suite B, Littleton, CO 80120-5612, Tel. (888)627-1995 or (720)283-3030 Fax (720)283-3333
Media Contact, Executive Director, Dr. Dennis L. Gorton
Email: cba@cbamerica.org
Website: www.cbamerica.org

Other Organizations
CBInternational, Exec. Dir., Dr. Hans Finzel, 1501 W. Mineral Ave., Littleton, CO 80120-5612

Mission to the Americas, Exec. Dir., Rev. Rick Miller, Box 828, Wheaton, IL 60189
Conservative Baptist Higher Ed. Council, Dr. Bert Downs, Western Seminary, 5511 S. E. Hawthorne Blvd., Portland, OR 97215

Periodicals

Front Line Turnings

Conservative Congregational Christian Conference

In the 1930s, evangelicals within the Congregational Christian Churches felt a definite need for fellowship and service. By 1945, this loose association crystallized into the Conservative Congregational Christian Fellow-ship, committed to maintaining a faithful, biblical witness.

In 1948 in Chicago, the Conservative Congregational Christian Conference was established to provide a continuing fellowship for evangelical churches and ministers on the national level. In recent years, many churches have joined the Conference from backgrounds other than Congregational. These churches include Community or Bible Churches and churches from the Evangelical and Reformed background that are truly congregational in polity and thoroughly evangelical in conviction. The CCCC welcomes all evangelical churches that are, in fact, congregational. The CCCC believes in the necessity of a regenerate membership, the authority of the Holy Scriptures, the Lordship of Jesus Christ, the autonomy of the local church and the universal fellowship of all Christians.

The Conservative Congregational Christian Conference is a member of the World Evangelical Congregational Fellowship (formed in 1986 in London, England) and the National Association of Evangelicals.

Headquarters

8941 Highway 5, Lake Elmo, MN 55042, Tel. (651)739-1474 Fax (651)739-0750
Media Contact, Conf. Min., Mrs. Diane Johnson
Email: ccc4@juno.com
Website: www.ccccusa.com

Officers

Pres., Rev. Larry Wood, 1852 Catalpa, Berkley MI 48072
Vice Pres., Rev. Peter W. Murdy, 4 Plympton St, Middleboro MA 02346
Conf. Min., Rev. Dr. Stephen A. Gammon, 8941 Highway 5, Lake Elmo MN 55042
Controller, Rev. Tay E. Kersey, 8450 Eastwood Rd., Moundsview, MN 55112
Treas., Mrs. Karen Sloat, 45505 Meadow Lake Dr, Indio CA 92201
Sec., Rev. Dr. D. Phil Corr, 106 Park Lane Dr, Charles City IA 50616
Editor, Rev. Ken McGarvey, 121 Chatuga Dr, Loudon TN 37774
Historian, Rev. Alwyn York, 709 N. Cheyenne Ave., Hardin MT 59034

Periodicals

Foresee

Conservative Lutheran Association

The Conservative Lutheran Association (CLA) was originally named Lutheran's Alert National (LAN) when it was founded in 1965 by 10 conservative Lutheran pastors and layman meeting in Cedar Rapids, Iowa. Its purpose was to help preserve from erosion the basic doctrines of Christian theology, including the inerrancy of Holy Scripture. The group grew to a worldwide constituency, similarly concerned with maintaining the doctrinal integrity of the Bible and the Lutheran Confessions.

Headquarters

Trinity Lutheran Church, 4101 E. Nohl Ranch Rd., Anaheim, CA 92807, Tel. (714)637-8370
Media Contact, Pres., Rev. P. J. Moore
Email: PastorPJ@ix.netcom.com
Website: www.tlcanaheim.com/CLA

Officers

Pres., Rev. P. J. Moore, 4101 E. Nohl Ranch Rd., Anaheim, CA 92807, Tel. (714)637-8370
Vice Pres., Rev. Dr. R. H. Redal, 409 Tacoma Ave. N., Tacoma, WA 98403, Tel. (206)383-5528
Faith Seminary, Dean, Rev. Dr. Michael J. Adams, 3504 N. Pearl St., P.O. Box 7186, Tacoma, WA 98407, Tel. (888)777-7675 Fax (206)759-1790

Coptic Orthodox Church*

This body is part of the ancient Coptic orthodox Church of Alexandria, Egypt which is currently headed by His Holiness Pope Shenouda III, 116th Successor to St. Mark the Apostle. Egyptian immigrants have organized many parishes in the United States. Copts exist outside Egypt in Africa, Europe, Asia, Australia, Canada and the United States. The total world Coptic community is estimated at 27 million. The church is in full communion with the other members of The Oriental Orthodox Church Family, The Syrian Orthodox Church, Armenian Orthodox Church, Ethiopian Orthodox Church, the Indian Orthodox Church and the Eritrean Orthodox Church.

Headquarters

427 West Side Ave., Jersey City, NJ 07304
Email: Webmaster@coptic.org
Website: www.coptic.org

Officers

Bishop of Los Angeles, Bishop Serapion, 3803 3803 W. Mission Blvd., Pomona, CA 91766, Tel. (909)865-8378 Fax (909)865-8348; Email: bishopserapion@lacopts.org

Periodicals

Agape Magazine, El Keraza

Cumberland Presbyterian Church

The Cumberland Presbyterian Church was organized in Dickson County, Tennessee, on Feb. 4, 1810. It was an outgrowth of the Great Revival of 1800 on the Kentucky and Tennessee frontier. The founders were Finis Ewing, Samuel King and

Samuel McAdow, ministers in the Presbyterian Church who rejected the doctrine of election and reprobation as taught in the Westminster Confession of Faith.

By 1813, the Cumberland Presbytery had grown to encompass three presbyteries, which constituted a synod. This synod met at the Beech Church in Sumner County, Tenn., and formulated a "Brief Statement" which set forth the points in which Cumberland Presbyterians dissented from the Westminster Confession. These points are-

1. That there are no eternal reprobates;
2. That Christ died not for some, but for all people;
3. That all those dying in infancy are saved through Christ and the sanctification of the Spirit;
4. That the Spirit of God operates on the world, or as coextensively as Christ has made atonement, in such a manner as to leave everyone inexcusable.

From its birth in 1810, the Cumberland Presbyterian Church grew to a membership of 200,000 at the turn of the century. In 1906 the church voted to merge with the then-Presbyterian Church. Those who dissented from the merger became the nucleus of the continuing Cumberland Presbyterian Church.

Headquarters

8207 Traditional Place, Cordova, TN, 38016, Tel. (901)276-4572 Fax (901)272-3913
Media Contact, Stated Clk., Rev. Robert D. Rush, Fax (901)272-3913
Email: assembly@cumberland.org
Website: www.cumberland.org

Officers

Mod., Mr. Sam Suddarth, Jr., P.O. Box 518, Nolensville, TN 37135, Email: jenkinsoffice@united.net
Stated Clk., The Rev. Robert D. Rush, Tel.(901)276-4572 x 225 Fax (901)276-4578, Email: rdr@cumberland.org

INSTITUTIONS

Cumberland Presbyterian Children's Home, Exec. Dir., Rev. Kevin Henson, Drawer G, Denton, TX 76202, Tel. (940)382-5112 Fax (940)387-0821; Email: cpch@cpch.org
Cumberland Presbyterian Center, Tel.(901)276-4572 Fax (901)272-3913 or (901)276-4578
Memphis Theological Seminary, 168 E. Parkway S., Memphis, TN 38104, Tel. (901)458-8232 Fax (901)452-4051, Website: www.memphis seminary.edu, Pres., Dr. Jay Earheart -Brown
Bethel University, Pres., Dr. Robert Prosser, 325 Cherry St., McKenzie, TN 38201, Tel. (901)352-4004 Fax (901)352-4069; Email: prosserb@bethel-college.edu
Historical Foundation, Archivist, Susan K. Gore, 8207 Traditional Place, Cordova, TN, 38016, Tel. (901)276-8602 Fax (901)272-3913, Email: skg@cumberland.org

BOARDS

Ministry Council, Exec. Dir. Ms. Edith Gholson, 8207 Traditional Place, Cordova, TN, 38016,

Email: emg@cumberland.org., Tel (901)276-4572, Fax (901)276-4578
Communications Team: Team Leader: Mr. Mark Davis, 8207 Traditional Place, Cordova, TN, 38016, Email: MDavis@cumberland.org, Tel. (901)276-4572, Fax (901)276-4758
Discipleship Team: Team Leader: Rev. Frank Ward, 8207 Traditional Place, Cordova, TN, 38016, Email: Fdw@cumberland.org, Tel. (901)276-4572, Fax (901)276-4758
Missions Ministry Team: Team Leader: Rev. Michael G. Sharpe, 8207 Traditional Place, Cordova, TN, 38016, Email: mgs@cumberland.org, Tel. (901)276-4572, Fax (901)276-4758
Pastoral Development Team: Team Leader: Rev. Milton Ortiz, 8207 Traditional Place, Cordova, TN, 38016, Email: Fdw@cumberland.org, Tel. (901)276-4572, Fax (901)276-4758

Periodicals

The Cumberland Presbyterian, The Missionary Messenger

Cumberland Presbyterian Church in America

This church, originally known as the Colored Cumberland Presbyterian Church, was formed in May 1874. In May 1869, at the General Assembly meeting in Murfreesboro, Tennessee, Moses Weir of the Black delegation sucessfully appealed for help in organizing a separate African church so that- Blacks could learn self-reliance and independence; they could have more financial assistance; they could minister more effectively among Blacks; and they could worship close to the altar, not in the balconies. He requested that the Cumberland Presbyterian Church organize Blacks into presbyteries and synods, develop schools to train black clergy, grant loans to assist Blacks to secure hymnbooks, Bibles and church buildings and establish a separate General Assembly.

In 1874 the first General Assembly of the Colored Cumberland Presbyterian Church met in Nashville. The moderator was Rev. P. Price and the stated clerk was Elder John Humphrey.

The denomination's General Assembly, the national governing body, is organized around three program boards and agencies: Finance, Publication and Christian Education, and Missions and Evangelism. Other agencies of the General Assembly are under these three program boards.

The church has four synods (Alabama, Kentucky, Tennessee and Texas), 15 presbyteries and 153 congregations. The CPC extends as far north as Cleveland, Ohio, and Chicago, as far west as Marshalltown, Iowa, and Dallas, Texas, and as far south as Selma, Alabama.

Headquarters

Media Contact, Stated Clk., Rev. Dr. Robert. Stanley Wood, 226 Church St., Huntsville, AL 35801, Tel. (205)536-7481 Fax (205)536-7482
Email: mleslie598@aol.com
Website: www.cumberland.org/cpca

Officers

Mod., Rev. Endia Scruggs, 1627 Carroll Rd., Harvest, AL 35749

Stated Clk., Rev. Dr. Rorbert. Stanley Wood, 226 Church St., Huntsville, AL 35801, Tel. (205)536-7481

SYNODS

Alabama, Stated Clk., Arthur Hinton, 511 10th Ave. N.W., Aliceville, AL 35442

Kentucky, Stated Clk., Mary Martha Daniels, 8548 Rhodes Ave., Chicago, IL 60619

Tennessee, Stated Clk., Elder Clarence Norman, 145 Jones St., Huntington, TN 38334

Texas, Stated Clk., Arthur King, 2435 Kristen, Dallas, TX 75216

Disciples of Christ—please see Christian Church (Disciples of Christ) in the United States and Canada.

Elim Fellowship

The Elim Fellowship, a Pentecostal Body established in 1947, is an outgrowth of the Elim Missionary Assemblies formed in 1933.

It is an association of churches, ministers and missionaries seeking to serve the whole Body of Christ. It is of Pentecostal conviction and charismatic orientation, providing ministerial credentials and counsel and encouraging fellowship among local churches. Elim Fellowship sponsors leadership seminars at home and abroad and serves as a transdenominational agency sending long-term, short-term and tent-making missionaries to work with national movements.

Headquarters

1703 Dalton Rd., Lima, NY 14485, Tel. (585)582-2790 Fax (585)624-1229

Media Contact, Gen. Sec., Rev. Chris Ball

Email: executive@elimfellowship.org

Website: www.ElimFellowship.org

Officers

Pres., Rev. Dr. Ronald V. Burgio

Gen. Treas., Stephanie Zeller

Periodicals

Elim Herald

The Episcopal Church*

The Episcopal Church entered the colonies with the earliest settlers at Jamestown, Va., in 1607 as the Church of England. After the American Revolution, it became autonomous in 1789 as The Protestant Episcopal Church in the United States of America. (The Episcopal Church became the official alternate name in 1967.) Samuel Seabury of Connecticut was elected the first bishop and consecrated in Aberdeen by bishops of the Scottish Episcopal Church in 1784.

In organizing as an independent body, the Episcopal Church created a bicameral legislature, the General Convention, modeled after the new U.S. Congress. It comprises a House of Bishops and a House of Deputies and meets every three years. A 38-member Executive Council, which meets three times a year, is the interim governing body. An elected presiding bishop serves as Primate and Chief Pastor.

After severe setbacks in the years immediately following the Revolution because of its association with the British Crown and the fact that a number of its clergy and members were Loyalists, the church soon established its own identity and sense of mission. It sent missionaries into the newly settled territories of the United States, establishing dioceses from coast to coast, and also undertook substantial missionary work in Africa, Latin America and the Far East. Today, the overseas dioceses are developing into independent provinces of the Anglican Communion, the worldwide fellowship of 38 churches in communion with the Church of England and the Archbishop of Canterbury.

The beliefs and practices of The Episcopal Church, like those of other Anglican churches, are both Catholic and Reformed, with bishops in the apostolic succession and the historic creeds of Christendom regarded as essential elements of faith and order, along with the primary authority of Holy Scripture and the two chief sacraments of Baptism and Eucharist.

Headquarters

EPISCOPAL CHURCH CENTER

815 Second Ave., New York, NY 10017, Tel. (212)716-6240 or (800)334-7626 Fax (212)867-0395 or (212)490-3298

Media Contact, Dir. of News Service., Robert Williams, Tel. (212)922-5385

Email: cepting@episcopalchurch.org

Website: www.ecusa.anglican.org

Officers

Presiding Bishop & Primate, Most Rev. Katharine Jefferts-Schori

Chief Operating Officer, Linda Watt

Treas., Kurt Barnes

Canon to the Primate and Presiding Bishop, The Rev. Canon Charles Robertson

House of Deputies, Pres., Bonnie Anderson

Exec. Officer and Sec. of the General Convention, Sec. Of the House of Deputies, Sec. Of the Domestic and Foreign Missionary Society, and Sec. Of the Executive Council, The Rev. Gregory Straub

OFFICE OF THE PRESIDING BISHOP

Presiding Bishop, Most Rev. Katharine Jefferts Schori, Tel. (212)716-6276

Chief Operating Officer, Linda Watts, Tel. (212)922-5313

Canon to the Presiding Bishop, Rev. Canon Charles Robertson, Tel. (212)922-5282

Exec. Dir., Church Deployment Office, Rev. Vacant, Tel. (212)-922-5251 Asst. Dir., Church Deployment Office, Pamela Ramsden, Tel. (212)716-6063

Coordinator for Ministry Development, The Rev. Dr. Melford E. Holland, Jr., Tel. (212)922-5246

105

Exec. Dir., Office of Pastoral Dev., Rt. Rev. Clayton Matthews, Tel. (212)716-6163

Exec. Sec., General Board of Examining Chaplains, The Rev. Dr. Richard F. Tombaugh, Tel. (860)233-2271

Chaplaincies, Suffragan Bishop, Rt. Rev., George Packard, Tel. (212)716-6202

Convocation of American Churches in Europe, Bishop-in-Charge, Rt. Rev. Pierre Whalon, Tel. 011-33-1-472-01792

Deputy, Ecumenical and Interfaith Relations, The Rt. Rev. C. Christopher Epting, Tel. (212)716-6220

ADMINISTRATION AND FINANCE

Treasurer of the Domestic and Foreign Missionary Society and Chief Financial Officer, Kurt Barnes, Tel. (212)922-5296

Controller, Alpha Conteh, Tel. (212)922-5366

Archivist, Mark Duffy, Tel. (512)472-6816

Director, Human Resources Management, John Colon, Tel. (212)716-6331

SERVICE, EDUCATION AND WITNESS

Director of Mission, The Rev. Canon Brian Grieves, Tel. (212)922-5207

Dir., Advocacy Center, Canon Margaret S. Larom, Tel. (212)716-6224

Dir., of Evangelism and Congrgational Life, The Rev. Suzanne E. Watson, Tel. (212)716-6185

Dir., of Partnership Center, Ms. Antoinette (Toni) Daniels, Tel. (212)716-6332

Dir., Mission Leadership Center, The Rev. Margaret Rose, Tel. (212)716-6332

President, Episcopal Relief and Development, Robert Radtke, Tel. (212)716-6020

BISHOPS IN THE U.S.A.

Presiding Bishop & Primate, Most Rev. Katharine Jefferts-Schori, 815 Second Ave, New York, NY 10017, Tel. (212)716-6276

Pastoral Dev., The Rt. Rev. F. Clayton Matthews, 815 Second Ave, New York, NY 10017, Tel. (212)716-6163

The Rt. Rev. Gladstone Bailey Adams III, Bishop of Central New York, 310 Montgomery Street, Suite 200, Syracuse, NY 13202-2093

The Rt. Rev. James Marshall Adams, Bishop of Western Kansas, P.O. Box 2507, Salina, KS 67402-2507

The Rt. Rev. J. Neil Alexander, Bishop of Atlanta, 2744 Peachtree Road NW, Atlanta, GA 30305

The Rt. Rev. Lloyd Emmanuel Allen, Bishop of Honduras, IMC-SAP; Dept. 215, P.O. Box 52-3900, Miami, FL 33152-3900

The Rt. Rev. David Alvarez, Bishop of Puerto Rico, P.O. Box 902, St Just, PR 00978-0902

The Rt. Rev. Marc Handley Andrus, Bishop of California, 1055 Taylor Street, San Francisco, CA 94108

The Rt. Rev. John C. Bauerschmidt, Bishop of Tennessee, 50 Vantage Way, Suite 107, Nashville, TN 37228

The Rt. Rev. Nathan D. Baxter, Bishop of Central Pennsylvania, PO Box 11937, Harrisburg, PA 17108

The Rt. Rev. Mark M. Beckwith, Bishop of Newark, 31 Mulberry Street, Newark, NJ 07102

The Rt. Rev. Peter H. Beckwith, Bishop of Springfield, 821 South 2nd Street, Springfield, IL 62704-2694

The Rt. Rev. Barry L. Beisner, Bishop of Northern California, 1318 27th Street, Sacramento, CA 95816

The Rt. Rev. Larry R. Benfield, Bishop of Arkansas, PO Box 164668, Little Rock, AR 72216

The Rt. Rev. Thomas E. Breidenthal, Bishop of Southern Ohio, 412 Sycamore Street, Cincinnati, OH 45202

The Rt. Rev. C. Franklin Brookhart Jr., Bishop of Montana, 515 North Park Avenue, Helena, MT 59601

The Rt. Rev. J. Jon Bruno, Bishop of Los Angeles, PO Box 512164, Los Angeles, CA 90026

The Rt. Rev. John C. Buchanan, Provisional Bishop of Quincy, 3601 North North, Peoria, IL 61604

The Rt. Rev. Dr. Joe G. Burnett, Bishop of Nebraska, 109 North 18th Street, Omaha, NE 68102

The Rt. Rev. Bruce Caldwell, Bishop of Wyoming, 123 South Durbin, Casper, WY 82601

The Rt. Rev. John Bryson Chane, Bishop of Washington, Episcopal Ch. House, Mt. St. Alban, Washington, DC 20016-5094

The Rt. Rev. George E. Councell, Bishop of New Jersey, 808 West State Street, Trenton, NJ 08618-5326

The Rt. Rev. Michael Bruce Curry, Bishop of North Carolina, 200 West Morgan Street, Suite 300, Raleigh, NC 27601-1338

The Rt. Rev. Clifton Daniel III, Bishop of East Carolina, PO Box 1336, Kinston, NC 28503

The Rt. Rev. C. Andrew Doyle, Bishop of Texas, 1225 Texas Avenue, Houston, TX 77002

The Rt. Rev. Philip M. Duncan II, Bishop of Central Gulf Coast, 102 N. Baylen St., PO Box 13330, Pensacola, FL 32591-3330

The Rt. Rev. Francisco Duque, Bishop of Colombia, Cra. 6 No. 49-85, Bogota Colombia

The Rt. Rev. Jean Zache Duracin, Bishop of Haiti, c/o Lynx Air, P.O. Box 407139, Fort Lauderdale, FL 33340

The Rt. Rev. Dan T. Edwards, Bishop of Nevada, 6135 South Harrison Drive, Suite 1, Las Vegas, NV 89120-4076

The Rt. Rev. Thomas Clark Ely, Bishop of Vermont, 5 Rock Point Road, Burlington, VT 05408

The Rt. Rev. Robert L. Fitzpatrick, Bishop of Hawaii, 229 Queen Emma Square, Honolulu, HI 96813-2304

The Rt. Rev. Leopold Frade, Bishop of Southeast Florida, 525 NE 15th Street, Miami, FL 33132

The Rt. Rev. J. Michael Garrison, Bishop of Western New York, 1114 Delaware Avenue, Buffalo, NY 14209

The Rt. Rev. Robert R. Gepert, Bishop of Western Michigan, 535 S. Burdick St., Suite 1 Kalamazoo, MI 49007

The Rt. Rev. Wendell N. Gibbs Jr., Bishop of Michigan, 4800 Woodward Avenue, Detroit, MI 48201-1399

The Rt. Rev. Duncan Montgomery Gray III, Bishop of Mississippi, PO Box 23107, Jackson, MS 39225-3107

The Rt. Rev. Mary Gray-Reeves, Bishop of El Camino Real, 1092 Noche Buena Street, Seaside, CA 93955

The Rt. Rev. Orlando J. Guerrero, Bishop of Venezuela, Centro Diocesano, Ave. Caroni No. 100, Colinas de Bello Monte, Caracas Venezuela

The Rt. Rev. Edwin F. Gulick Jr., Bishop of Kentucky, 425 S. Second St., Louisville, KY 40202

The Rt. Rev. E. Ambrose Gumbs, Bishop of Virgin Islands, PO Box 7488, Charlotte Amalie, St. Thomas, VI 00801

The Rt. Rev. Dorsey F. Henderson Jr., Bishop of Upper South Carolina, 1115 Marion Street, Columbia, SC 29201

The Rt. Rev. Julio Cesar Holguín, Bishop of Dominican Republic, DMG 13602, 100 Airport Avenue, Venice, FL 34285

The Rt. Rev. Herman Hollerith IV, Bishop of Southern Virginia, 600 Talbot Hall Road, Norfolk, VA 23505

The Rt. Rev. Mark Hollingsworth Jr., Bishop of Ohio, 2230 Euclid Avenue, Cleveland, OH 44115-2499

The Rt. Rev. S. Johnson Howard, Bishop of Florida, 325 Market Street, Jacksonville, FL 32202

The Rt. Rev. Barry R. Howe, Bishop of West Missouri, PO Box 413227, 420 West 14th Street, Kansas City, MO 64141-3227

The Rt. Rev. John W. Howe, Bishop of Central Florida, 1017 East Robinson Street, Orlando, FL 32801

The Rt. Rev. Carolyn T. Irish, Bishop of Utah, PO Box 3090, 75 South 200 East, Salt Lake City, UT 84110-3090

The Rt. Rev. Russell E. Jacobus, Bishop of Fond du Lac, 1051 N. Lynndale Drive Suite 1B, Appleton, WI 54914-3094

The Rt. Rev. James L. Jelinek, Bishop of Minnesota, 1730 Clifton Place, Suite 201, Minneapolis, MN 55403-3242

The Rt. Rev. Charles E. Jenkins III, Bishop of Louisiana, 1623 7th Street, New Orleans, LA 70115-4411

The Rt. Rev. Don E. Johnson, Bishop of West Tennessee, 692 Poplar Avenue, Memphis, TN 38105

The Rt. Rev. William Michie Klusmeyer, Bishop of West Virginia, PO Box 5400, 1608 Virginia Street East, Charleston, WV 25361-0400

The Rt. Rev. Edward J. Konieczny, Bishop of Oklahoma, 924 North Robinson, Oklahoma City, OK 73102

The Rt. Rev. David J.H. Lai, Bishop of Taiwan, 7, Lane 105. Hangchow South Road Sec.1, Taipei 10060 Taiwan

The Rt. Rev. Jerry A. Lamb, Provisional Bishop of San Joaquin, 1528 Oakdale Road, Modesto, CA 95355

The Rt. Rev. Stephen T. Lane, Bishop of Maine, 143 State Street, Portland, ME 04101

The Rt. Rev. Mark J. Lawrence, Bishop of South Carolina, 126 Coming Street, Charleston, SC 29413

The Rt. Rev. Jeffrey D. Lee, Bishop of Chicago, 65 East Huron Street, Chicago, IL 60611

The Rt. Rev. Peter James Lee, Bishop of Virginia, 110 West Franklin Street, Richmond, VA 23220

The Rt. Rev. Gary R. Lillibridge, Bishop of West Texas, PO Box 6885, San Antonio, TX 78209

The Rt. Rev. Edward S. Little II, Bishop of Northern Indiana, 117 North Lafayette Boulevard, South Bend, IN 46601

The Rt. Rev. Henry I. Louttit Jr., Bishop of Georgia, 611 East Bay Street, Savannah, GA 31401

The Rt. Rev. William H. Love, Bishop of Albany, 68 South Swan Street, Albany, NY 12210

The Rt. Rev. D. Bruce MacPherson, Bishop of Western Louisiana, Box 2031, Alexandria, LA 71309

The Rt. Rev. Paul V. Marshall, Bishop of Bethlehem, 333 Wyandotte Street, Bethlehem, PA 18015

The Rt. Rev. James R. Mathes, Bishop of San Diego, 2728 Sixth Avenue, San Diego, CA 92103

The Rt. Rev. J. Scott Mayer, Bishop of Northwest Texas, 1802 Broadway, Lubbock, TX 79401

The Rt. Rev. Steven A. Miller, Bishop of Milwaukee, 804 East Juneau Avenue, Milwaukee, WI 53202

The Rt. Rev. Alfredo Morante, Bishop of Litoral, Apartado Aereo 0901-5250, Guayaquil Ecuador

The Rt. Rev. Robert J. O'Neill, Bishop of Colorado, 1300 Washington Street, Denver, CO 80203

The Rt. Rev. S. Todd Ousley, Bishop of Eastern Michigan, 924 North Niagara Street, Saginaw, MI 48602

The Rt. Rev. Henry Nutt Parsley Jr., Bishop of Alabama, 521 North 20th Street, Birmingham, AL 35203

The Rt. Rev. F. Neff Powell, Bishop of Southwestern Virginia, PO Box 2279, 1000 First Street SW, Roanoke, VA 24009-2279

The Rt. Rev. Kenneth L. Price Jr., Provisional Bishop of Pittsburgh, 4099 William Penn Highway, Suite 502, Monroeville, PA 15146

The Rt. Rev. Gregory H. Rickel, Bishop of Olympia, 1551 10th Avenue E, Seattle, WA 98102

The Rt. Rev. Bavi E. Rivera, Provisional Bishop of Eastern Oregon, 601 Union Street, Box 1548, The Dalles, OR 97058

The Rt. Rev. Creighton L. Robertson, Bishop of South Dakota, 500 South Main Avenue, Sioux Falls, SD 57104-6814

The Rt. Rev. V. Gene Robinson, Bishop of New Hampshire, 63 Green Street, Concord, NH 03301

The Rt. Rev. Sean W. Rowe, Bishop of Northwestern Pennsylvania, 145 West 6th Street, Erie, PA 16501

The Rt. Rev. Luis Ruiz, Bishop of Ecuador Central, Calle El Tiempo No. 37-189 y El Comercio, Sector El Batan, Quito, Ecuador,

The Rt. Rev. Stacy F. Sauls, Bishop of Lexington, PO Box 610, 203 East Fourth St., Lexington, KY 40588-0610

The Rt. Rev. Alan Scarfe, Bishop of Iowa, 225 37th Street, Des Moines, IA 50312-4399

The Rt. Rev. Gordon Paul Scruton, Bishop of Western Massachusetts, 37 Chestnut Street, Springfield, MA 01103

The Rt. Rev. James J. Shand, Bishop of Easton, 314 North Street, Easton, MD 21601

The Rt. Rev. M. Thomas Shaw III, SSJE, Bishop of Massachusetts, 138 Tremont Street, Boston, MA 02111

The Rt. Rev. Prince G. Singh, Bishop of Rochester, 935 East Avenue, Rochester, NY 14607

The Rt. Rev. Mark S. Sisk, Bishop of New York, 1047 Amsterdam Avenue, New York, NY 10025

The Rt. Rev. Andrew D. Smith, Bishop of Connecticut, 1335 Asylum Avenue, Hartford, CT 06105-2295

The Rt. Rev. Dabney T. Smith, Bishop of Southwest Florida, 7313 Merchant Court, Sarasota, FL 34240

The Rt. Rev. George Wayne Smith, Bishop of Missouri, 1210 Locust Street, St. Louis, MO 63103

The Rt. Rev. Kirk Stevan Smith, Bishop of Arizona, 114 West Roosevelt Street, Phoenix, AZ 85003-1406

The Rt. Rev. Michael Gene Smith, Bishop of North Dakota, 3600 South 25th Street, Fargo, ND 58104-6861

The Rt. Rev. James M. Stanton, Bishop of Dallas, 1630 North Garrett Avenue, Dallas, TX 75206

The Rt. Rev. Eugene T. Sutton, Bishop of Maryland, 4 East University Parkway, Baltimore, MD 21218

The Rt. Rev. G. Porter Taylor, Bishop of Western North Carolina, 900-B Centre Park Drive, Asheville, NC 28805

The Rt. Rev. Brian James Thom, Bishop of Idaho, 1858 West Judith Lane, Boise, ID 83705

The Rt. Rev. Charles G. vonRosenberg, Bishop of East Tennessee, 814 Episcopal School Way, Knoxville, TN 37932

The Rt. Rev. James Edward Waggoner Jr., Bishop of Spokane, 245 East 13th Avenue, Spokane, WA 99202-1114

The Rt. Rev. Orris G. Walker Jr., Bishop of Long Island, 36 Cathedral Avenue, P.O. Box 510, Garden City, NY 11530

The Rt. Rev. Catherine M. Waynick, Bishop of Indianapolis, 1100 West 42nd Street, Indianapolis, IN 46208

The Rt. Rev. Dean E. Wolfe, Bishop of Kansas, Bethany Place, 835 SW Polk, Topeka, KS 66612-1688

The Rt. Rev. Geralyn Wolf, Bishop of Rhode Island, 275 North Main Street, Providence, RI 02903

The Rt. Rev. Wayne P. Wright, Bishop of Delaware, 2020 N. Tatnall Street, Wilmington, DE 19802

Periodicals

Episcopal Life

Episcopal Orthodox Church, see Orthodox Anglican Church.

The Estonian Evangelical Lutheran Church

For information on the Estonian Evangelical Lutheran Church (EELC), please see the listing in Chapter 4, "Religious Bodies in Canada."

Headquarters

383 Jarvis St., Toronto, ON M5B 2C7
Email: konsistoorium@eelk.ee
Website: www.eelk.ee

The Evangelical Church

The Evangelical Church was born June 4, 1968 in Portland, Oregon, when 46 congregations and about 80 ministers, under the leadership of V. A. Ballantyne and George Millen, met in an organizing session. Within two weeks a group of about 20 churches and 30 ministers from the Evangelical United Brethren and Methodist churches in Montana and North Dakota became a part of the new church. Richard Kienitz and Robert Strutz were the superintendents.

Under the leadership of Superintendent Robert Trosen, the former Holiness Methodist Church became a part of the Evangelical Church in 1969, bringing its membership and a flourishing mission field in Bolivia. The Wesleyan Covenant Church joined in 1977, with its missionary work in Mexico, in Brownsville, Texas and among the Navajos in New Mexico.

The Evangelical Church in Canada, where T. J. Jesske was superintendent, became an autonomous organization on June 5, 1970. In 1982, after years of discussions with the Evangelical Church of North America, a founding General Convention was held at Billings, Montana, where the two churches united. In 1993 the Canadian conference merged with the Canadian portion of the Missionary Church to form the Evangelical Missionary Church. The new group maintains close ties with their American counterparts. Currently there are nearly 150 U.S. congregations of the Evangelical Church. The headquarters is located in Minneapolis, Minnesota.

The following guide the life, program and devotion of this church- faithful, biblical and sensible preaching and teaching of those truths proclaimed by scholars of the Wesleyan-Arminian viewpoint; an itinerant system which reckons with the rights of individuals and the desires of the congregation; local ownership of all church properties and assets.

The church is officially affiliated with the Christian Holiness Partnership, the National Association of Evangelicals, Wycliffe Bible Translators, World Gospel Mission and OMS International. The denomination has nearly 150 missionaries.

Headquarters
Denominational Office, 9421 West River Rd., Minneapolis, MN 55444, Tel. (763)421-2589 Fax (763)424-9230
Media Contact, Gen. Supt., Brian Eckhardt
Email: ecdenom@usfamily.net
Website: www.TheEvangelicalChurch.org

Officers
Gen. Supt., Brian Eckhardt, 9421 West River Rd., Minneapolis, MN 55444
Denominational Secretary, Dr. Bruce Moyer, P.O. Box 29, University Park, IA 52595, Tel. (641)673-8391
Exectuive Director, Evangelical Church Mission, Rev. Duane Erickson, 9421 West River Rd., Minneapolis, MN 55444

Periodicals
HeartBeat, The Evangelical Challenge

The Evangelical Church Alliance
What is known today as the Evangelical Church Alliance began in 1887 under the name World's Faith Missionary Association. Years later, on March 28, 1928, a nonprofit organization was incorporated in the state of Missouri under the same name. In October, 1931, the name Fundamental Ministerial Association was chosen to reflect the organization's basis of unity.

On July 21, 1958, during the annual convention at Trinity Seminary and Bible College in Chicago, Illinois, a more comprehensive constitution was created and the name was changed to The Evangelical Church Alliance.

The ECA licenses and ordains ministers who are qualified providing them with credentials from a recognized ecclesiastical body; provides training courses through the Bible Extension Institute for those who have not had the opportunity to attend Seminary or Bible School; provides Associate Membership for churches and Christian organizations giving opportunity for fellowship and networking with other evangelical ministers and organizations who share the same goals and mission, while remaining autonomous; provides endorsement for military, prison, hospital & other institutional chaplains; provides Regional Conferences and an Annual International Conference where members can find fellowship, encouragement and training; cooperates with churches in finding new pastors when they have openings.

ECA is an international, nonsectarian, Evangelical organization.

Headquarters
205 W. Broadway St., P.O. Box 9, Bradley, IL 60915, Tel. (815)937-0720 Fax (815)937-0001
Media Contact, Pres./CEO, Dr. Samuel Goebel
Email: info@ecainternational.org
Website: www.ecainternational.org

Officers
Pres./CEO, Dr. Samuel Goebel Chairman, Dr. George L. Miller First Vice Chairman, Dr. Rene Moreno Vice Pres. Dr. Henry A. Roso

Periodicals
The Evangel

The Evangelical Congregational Church
This denomination had its beginning in the movement known as the Evangelical Association, organized by Jacob Albright in 1796. A division which occurred in 1891 in the Evangelical Association resulted in the organization of the United Evangelical Church in 1894. An attempt to heal this division was made in 1922, but a portion of the United Evangelical Church was not satisfied with the plan of merger and remained apart, taking the above name in 1928. This denomination is Wesleyan-Arminian in doctrine, evangelistic in spirit and Methodist in church government, with congregational ownership of local church property.

Congregations are located from New Jersey to Illinois. A denominational center, two retirement villages and a seminary are located in Myerstown, Pennsylvania. Three summer youth camps and three camp meetings continue evangelistic outreach. A worldwide missions movement includes conferences in North East India, Liberia, Mexico, Costa Rica, and Japan. The denomination is a member of National Association of Evangelicals.

Headquarters
Evangelical Congregational Church Center, 100 W. Park Ave., Myerstown, PA 17067, Tel. (800)866-7581 Fax (717)866-7383
Media Contact, Bishop, Rev. Kevin S. Leibensperger, Tel. (717)866-7581
Email: eccenter@eccenter.com
Website: www.eccenter.com/church

Officers
Presiding Bishop, Rev. Kevin S. Leibensperge
1st Vice Chpsn., Rev. Frederick Marry, Jr.,
Sec., Rev. Kirk Marks
Conference Attorney, David Roland, Esquire
Treas., Deborah Patterson, Millersville, PA
E.C.C. Retirement Village, Pres., Steven J. Reiter, Fax (717)866-6448
Evangelical Theological Seminary, Pres., Michael W Sigman, Fax (717)866-4667

OTHER ORGANIZATIONS
Global Ministries Commission, Director., Rev. Randall L Sizemore
Controller, Kevin Henry, Myerstown, PA ECC Benefits Coop, Pres., Becky Reigle

Window on the World (Global Ministries Commission)

The Evangelical Covenant Church

The Evangelical Covenant Church has its roots in historic Christianity as it emerged during the Protestant Reformation, in the biblical instruction of the Lutheran State Church of Sweden and in the great spiritual awakenings of the 19th century.

The Covenant Church adheres to the affirmations of the Protestant Reformation regarding the Holy Scriptures, believing that the Old and the New Testament are the Word of God and the only perfect rule for faith, doctrine and conduct. It has traditionally valued the historic confessions of the Christian church, particularly the Apostles' Ethe Nicene Creed, while at the same time emphasizing the sovereignty of the Word over all creedal interpretations. It has especially cherished the pietistic restatement of the doctrine of justification by faith as basic to its dual task of evangelism and Christian nurture. It recognizes the New Testament emphasis upon personal faith in Jesus Christ as Savior and Lord, the reality of a fellowship of believers which acknowledges but transcends theological differences, and the belief in baptism and the Lord's Supper as divinely ordained sacraments of the church.

While the denomination has traditionally practiced the baptism of infants, in conformity with its principle of freedom it has also recognized the practice of believer baptism. The principle of personal freedom, so highly esteemed by the Covenant, is to be distinguished from the individualism that disregards the centrality of the Word of God and the mutual responsibilities and disciplines of the spiritual community.

Headquarters

5101 N. Francisco Ave., Chicago, IL 60625, Tel. (773)784-3000 Fax (773)784-4366
Media Contact, Donald L. Meyer, Email: don.meyer@covchurch.org
Email: Elliott.johnson@covchurch.org
Website: www.covchurch.org

Officers

Pres., Dr. Glenn R. Palmberg
Exec. Vice Pres., Rev. Donn Engebretson
Vice Pres. Finance, Dr. Dean A. Lundgren

ADMINISTRATIVE BOARDS
Executive Board, Rev. D. Darrell Griffes, Chair
Bd. of Women Ministries, Exec.. Minister, Rev. Ruth Y. Hill
Bd. Of Nominations, Advisory Member, (vacant)
Bd. of the Ordered Ministry, Exec. Minister, Rev. Dr. David Kersten
Bd. of Pensions & Benefits, Dir. of Pensions, Dean A. Lundgren
Bd. of Benevolence, Pres. of Covenant Ministries of Benevolence, David A. Dwight, 5145 N. California Ave., Chicago, IL 60625

North Park University, Pres., Dr. David l. Parkyn, 3225 W. Foster Ave., Chicago, IL 60625; North Park Theological Seminary, Pres. And Dean, Dr. John E. Phelan Jr.

SERVICE ORGANIZATIONS
National Covenant Properties, Pres., David W. Johnson, 5101 N. Francisco, Chicago, IL 60625, Tel. (773)784-3000
Covenant Trust Company, Pres., Charles A. Walles, 5215 Old Orchard Rd., Ste 725, Skokie, IL 60077 Tel.: (847) 583-3200, (800) 483-2177

REGIONAL CONFERENCES OF THE E.C.C.
Central Conference, Supt., Rev. Jerome O. Nelson, 3319 W. Foster Ave., Chicago, IL 60625, Tel. (773)267-3060
East Coast Conference, Supt., Rev. Howard K. Burgoyne, 52 Missionary Rd., Cromwell, CT 06416, Tel. (860)635-2691
Great Lakes Conference, Supt., Rev. Richard Lucco, 42219 Ann Arbor Road. E., Plymouth, MI 48170, Tel. (734)451-4670
Midwest Conference, Supt., Rev. Kenneth P. Carlson, 13304 W. Center Rd. #223, Omaha, NE 68144, Tel. (402)334-3060
North Pacific Conference, Supt., Rev. Mark A. Novak, 9311 SE 36th t., Ste 120, Mercer Island, WA 98040, Tel. (206)275-3903
Northwest Conference, Supt., Rev. James A. Fretheim, 3106 47th Avenue S., Minneapolis, MN 55406, Tel. (612) 721-4893
Pacific Southwest Conference, Supt., Rev. Evelyn M. R. Johnson, 1333 Willow Pass Rd., Ste 212, Concord, CA 94502, Tel. (925)677-2140
Southeast Conference, Supt., Rev. Kurt A. Miericke, 1759 W. Broadway St., #7, Oviedo, FL 32765, Tel. (407)977-8009
Canada Conference, Supt., Rev. Jeffrey Anderson, P.O. Box 34025 RPO, Fort Richmond, Winnipeg, MB R3T, Tel. (204)269-3437
Midsouth Conference, Supt., Rev. Garth T Bolinder, 6119 E. 91st Street, Ste. 2000, Tulsa, OK 74137, Tel. (918)481-9097
E.C.C. of Alaska, Field Dir., Rev. Rodney J. Sawyer, P.O. Box 770749, Eagle River, AK 99577, Tel. (907)694-6348
The Paul Carlson Partnership (affiliated)
Pres., Rev. Cartis D. Peterson Exec. Dir., Rev. James V. Sundholm, 5101 N. Francisco Ave., Chicago, IL, 60625 Tel: (773)907-3302

Periodicals

Covenant Companion, Covenant Quarterly, Covenant Home Altar

The Evangelical Free Church of America

In October 1884, 27 representatives from Swedish churches met in Boone, Iowa, to establish the Swedish

Evangelical Free Church. In the fall of that same year, two Norwegian-Danish groups began worship and fellowship (in Boston and in Tacoma) and by 1912 had established the Norwegian-Danish

Evangelical Free Church Association. These two denominations, representing 275 congregations, came together at a merger conference in 1950.

The Evangelical Free Church of America is an association of local, autonomous churches across the United States and Canada, blended together by common principles, policies and practices. A 12-point statement addresses the major doctrines but also provides for differences of understanding on minor issues of faith and practice.

Overseas outreach includes 500 missionaries serving in 31 countries.

Headquarters
901 East 78th St., Minneapolis, MN 55420-1300, Tel. (952)854-1300 Fax (952)853-8488
Media Contact, Exec. Dir. of International Mission, Timothy Addington
Email: president@efca.org
Website: www.efca.org

Officers
Pres., Dr. William J. Hamel, Minneapolis, MN
Senior Vice President, ReachGlobal: Timothy Addington, Minneapolis, MN
Senior Vice President, Finance and Operations: Jay O. Turner, Minneapolis, MN
Executive Director, ReachNational: Rev. Fritz Dale, Minneapolis, MN
Chairman: Rev. Robert Harrell, Austin, TX
Sececretary: Rev. David Rodquist, Minneapolis, MN
Moderator: Rev. Quintin Stieff, Des Moines, IA
Vice Moderator: Steven Hawn, St. Paul, MN

Periodicals
EFCA Today

Evangelical Friends International – North American Region

The organization adjusted its name from Evangelical Friends International in 2008 to better reflect that this ministry is assuredly a church movement. The North American Region ministers alongside other regions around the world under the banner of the Evangelical Friends Church International. The Strategic vision - as formulated by the North American Director, Dr. John P. Williams Jr. - reads "In joyful obedience to Jesus' Great Commission - and in the spirit of His Great Commandment - our movement purposes to serve the church and the world in love, multiplying disciples and churches in the power of the Holy Spirit so that our children's grandchildren and generations of the un-reached will be compelled to join.

Headquarters
5350 Broadmoor Cir. NW, Canton, OH 44709, Tel. (330)493-1660 Fax (330)493-0852
Media Contact, Gen. Supt., Dr. John P. Williams, Jr.
Email: efcer@aol.com
Website: www.evangelical-friends.org

Yearly Meetings
Evangelical Friends Church, Eastern Region, Ron Johnson, 5350 Broadmoor Cir., N.W.,

Canton, OH 44709, Tel. (330)493-1660 Fax (330)493-0852
Rocky Mountain YM, John Brawner, 3350 Reed St., Wheatridge, CO 80033, Tel. (303)238-5200 Fax (303)238-5200
Mid-America YM, Duane Hansen, 2018 Maple, Wichita, KS 67213, Tel. (316)267-0391 Fax (316)267-0681
Northwest YM, Mark Ankeny, 200 N. Meridian St., Newberg, OR 97132, Tel. (503)538-9419 Fax (503)538-9410
Alaska YM, Sam Williams, P.O. Box 687, Kotzebue, AK 99752, Tel. (907)442-3906
Evangelical Friends Church Southwest, YM, Linda Coop, P.O. Box 1607, Whittier, CA 90609-1607, Tel. (562)947-2883 Fax (562)947-9385

Periodicals
The Friends Voice

Evangelical Lutheran Church in America*

The Evangelical Lutheran Church in America (ELCA) was organized April 30-May 3, 1987, in Columbus, Ohio, bringing together the 2.25 million-member American Lutheran Church, the 2.85 million-member Lutheran Church in America, and the 100,000-member Association of Evangelical Lutheran Churches.

The ELCA is, through its predecessors, the oldest of the major U.S. Lutheran churches. In the mid-17th century, a Dutch Lutheran congregation was formed in New Amsterdam (now New York). Other early congregations were begun by German and Scandinavian immigrants to Delaware, Pennsylvania, New York and the Carolinas.

The first Lutheran association of congregations, the Pennsylvania Ministerium, was organized in 1748 under Henry Melchior Muhlenberg. Numerous Lutheran organizations were formed as immigration continued and the United States grew.

In 1960, The American Lutheran Church (ALC) was created through a merger of an earlier American Lutheran Church, formed in 1930, the Evangelical Lutheran Church, begun in 1917, and the United Evangelical Lutheran Church started in 1896. In 1963 the Lutheran Free Church, formed in 1897, merged with the ALC.

In 1962, the Lutheran Church in America (LCA) was formed by a merger of the United Lutheran Church in America, formed in 1918, with the Augustana Evangelical Lutheran Church, begun in 1860, the American Evangelical Lutheran Church, founded in 1872, and the Finnish Evangelical Lutheran Church or Suomi Synod, founded in 1891.

The Association of Evangelical Lutheran Churches arose in 1976 from a doctrinal split within the Lutheran Church-Missouri Synod.

The ELCA, through its predecessor church bodies, was a founding member of the Lutheran World Federation, the World Council of Churches, and the National Council of the Churches of Christ in the USA.

The church is divided into 65 geographical areas called synods. These 65 synods are grouped into nine regions for mission, joint programs and service.

Headquarters
8765 W. Higgins Rd., Chicago, IL 60631, Tel. (773)380-2700 Fax (773)380-1465
Media Contact, Dir. for News, John Brooks, Tel. (773)380-2958 Fax (773)380-2406
Email: info@elca.org
Website: www.elca.org

Officers
Presiding Bishop, Rev. Mark S. Hanson
Sec., Rev. Dr. Lowell G. Almen
Treas., Ms. Christina L. Jackson-Skelton
Vice Pres., Mr. Carlos E. Pena
Exec. for Admn., Rev. Charles S. Miller
Office of the Presiding Bishop, Exec. Asst to the Presiding Bishop for Federal Chaplaincies, Rev. Darrell D. Morton; Exec. Asst. to the Presiding Bishop, Ms. Myrna J. Sheie

PROGRAM UNITS
Vocation and Education, Exec. Dir., Rev. Stanley Nolson, Chpsn., Dr. Kathryn L. Johnson
Global Mission, Exec. Dir., Rev. Rafael Malpica Padilla, Bd. Chpsn., Rev. Virginia Anderson-Larson
Evangelical Outreach and Congregational Mission, Exec. Dir., Rev. Dr. Richard A. Magnus, Jr.; Chpsn., Mr. Francis R Ramos-Scharron
Church in Society, Exec. Dir., Rev. Rebecca S. Larson; Chpsn., Ms. Kristin Anderson-Ostrom
ELCA Publishing House, Exec. Dir., Ms. Beth A. Lewis; Bd. Chpsn., Ms. Annette Citzler; Women of the ELCA, Exec. Dir., Ms. Linda Post Bushkofsky; President., Ms. Carmen K. Richards

COMMISSIONS
Multicultural Ministries, Exec. Dir., Rev. Sherman Hicks; Chpsn., Mr. Aureo F. Andino

OTHER CHURCHWIDE UNITS
Conference of Bishops, Church Periodical, Editor, Mr. Daniel J. Lehmann; Shpsn. Rev. Karen Bockelman; Rev. E. Roy Riley
Development Services, Exec. Dir., Rev. Donald M. Hallberg, Stat. Ms. Tonia I. Lindquist
ELCA Bd. of Pensions, Exec. Dir., Mr. John G. Kapanke; Bd. Chpsn, Ms. Mary S. Ranum

SECTIONS
Communication Services, Dir., Ms. Kristi Bangert
Ecumenical and Inter-Religious Relations, Dir., Rev. Randall R. Lee
Human Resources, Dir., Ms. Else B Thompson
Research & Evaluation, Dir., Dr. Kenneth W. Inskeep
Synodical Relations, Executive for Synodical Relations, Rev. Kathie Bender Schwich
Worship and Liturgical Resources, Dir., Rev. Michael L. Burk

SYNODICAL BISHOPS

REGION 1
Alaska, Rev. Michael F. Keys, 1847 W. Northern Lights Blvd., #2, Anchorage, AK 99517-3343, Tel. (907)272-8899 Fax(907)274-3141

Northwest Washington, Rev. Wm Chris Boerger, 5519 Pinney Ave. N, Seattle, WA 98103-5899, Tel. (206)783-9292 Fax(206)783-9833
Southwestern Washington, Rev. Robert D. Hofstad, 420 121st St., S., Tacoma, WA 98444-5218, Tel. (253)535-8300 Fax(253)535-8315
Eastern Washington-Idaho, Rev. Martin D. Wells, 314 South Spruce St., Ste. A, Spokane, WA 99204-1098, Tel. (509)838-9871 Fax(509)838-0941
Oregon, Rev. Paul R. Swanson, 2800 N. Vancouver Ave., Ste. 101, Portland, OR 97227-1643, Tel. (503) 413-4191 Fax (503)413-2407
Montana, Rev. Dr. Richard R. Omland, 2415 13th Ave. S., Great Falls, MT 59405-5199, Tel. (406)453-1461 Fax (406)761-4632
Regional Coord., Mr. Steven H. Lansing, Region 1, 766-B John St., Seattle, WA 98109-5186, Tel. (206)624-0093 Fax (206)626-0987

REGION 2
Sierra Pacific, Rev. David G. Mullen, 401 Roland Way, #215, Oakland, CA 94621-2011, Tel. (510)430-0500 Fax(510)430-8730
Southwest California, Rev. Dean W. Nelson, 1300 E. Colorado St., Glendale, CA 91205-1406, Tel. (818)507-9591 Fax (818)507-9627
Pacifica, Rev. Murray D. Finck, 23655 Via Del Rio, Ste. B, Yorba Linda, CA 92887-2738, Tel. (714)692-2791 Fax (714)692-9317
Grand Canyon, Rev. Stephen S. Talmage, Interchurch Center 4423 N. 24th St., Ste. 400, Phoenix, AZ 85016-5544, Tel. (602)957-3223 Fax (602)956-8104
Rocky Mountain, Rev. Allan C. Bjornberg, 455 Sherman St., Ste. 160, Denver, CO 80203, Tel. (303)777-6700 Fax (303)733-0750
Region 2, Ms. Margaret Schmitt Ajer, Region 2, 3755 Avocado Blvd., PMB 411, La Mesa, CA 91941 Tel (619)460-9312 Fax (619)460-9314

REGION 3
Western North Dakota, Rev. Duane C. Danielson, 1614 Capitol Way, P.O. Box 370, Bismarck, ND 58502-0370, Tel. (701)223-5312 Fax (701)223-1435
Eastern North Dakota, Rev. Richard J. Foss, 1703 32nd Ave., S., Fargo, ND 58103-5936, Tel. (701)232-3381 Fax (701)232-3180
South Dakota, Rev. Andrea F. DeGroot-Nesdahl, Augustana College, 29th & S. Summit, Sioux Falls, SD 57197-0001, Tel. (605)247-4011 Fax (605)274-4028
Northwestern Minnesota, Rev. Rolf P. Wangberg, Concordia College, 901 8th St. S., Moorhead, MN 56562-0001, Tel. (218)299-3019 Fax (218)299-3363
Northeastern Minnesota, Rev. E. Peter Strommen, 1105 E. Superior St., Upper Suite, Duluth, MN 55802-2085, Tel. (218)724-4424 Fax (218)724-4393
Southwestern Minnesota, Rev. Jon V. Anderson 175 E. Bridge St., P.O. Box 499, Redwood Falls, MN 56283-0499, Tel. (507)637-3904 Fax (507)637-2809

112

Minneapolis Area, Rev. Craig E. Johnson, 122 W. Franklin Ave., Ste. 600, Minneapolis, MN 55404-2474, Tel. (612)870-3610 Fax (612)870-0170

Saint Paul Area, Rev. Peter Rogness, 105 W. University Ave., St. Paul, MN 55103-2094, Tel. (651)224-4313 Fax (651)224-5646

Southeastern Minnesota, Rev. Harold L. Usgaard, Assisi Heights, 1001 14th St. NW, Ste. 300, Rochester, MN 55901-2511, Tel. (507)280-9457 Fax (507)280-8824

Regional Coord., Rev. Craig A. Boehlke, Region 3, Luther Seminary, 2481 Como Ave., St. Paul, MN 55108-1445, Tel. (651)649-0454 x 232, Fax (651)649-0468

REGION 4

Nebraska, Rev. David L. deFreese, 4980 S. 118th St., Ste. D, Omaha, NE 68137-2220, Tel. (402)896-5311 Fax (402)896-5354

Central States, Rev. Dr. Gerald L. Mansholt, 3210 Michigan Ave., 4th Fl., Kansas City, MO 64109, Tel. (816)861-6584, Fax (816)861-4753

Arkansas-Oklahoma, Rev. Floyd M. Schoenhals, 693 S. 66th E. Ave., Ste. 310, Tulsa, OK 74133-1760, Tel. (918)492-4288 Fax (918)491-6275

Northern Texas-Northern Louisiana, Rev. Kevin S. Kanouse, 1230 Riverbend Dr., Ste. 105, P.O. Box 560587, Dallas, TX 75356-0587, Tel. (214)637-6865 Fax (214)637-4805

Southwestern Texas, Rev. Ray Tiemann, 1090 Oestreich Dr., Seguin, TX 78155, Tel. (830)379-9900 Fax (830)379-9990

Texas-Louisiana Gulf Coast, Rev. Paul J. Blom, 12707 North Fwy, #580, Houston, TX 77060-1239, Tel. (281)873-5665 Fax (281)875-4716

Acting Regional Coord., Rev. Donald R. Just, 7016 Ameranth Ln, Austin, TX, 78723, Tel.(512)585-4809 Fax (512)272-9699

REGION 5

Metropolitan Chicago, Rev. Paul R. Landahl, 1420 West Dickens Ave., Chicago, IL 60614-3004, Tel. (773)248-0021 Fax (773)248-8455

Northern Illinois, Rev. Gary M. Wollersheim, 103 W. State St., Rockford, IL 61101-1105, Tel. (815)964-9934 Fax (815)964-2295

Central-Southern Illinois, Rev. Warren D. Freiheit, 524 S. Fifth St., Springfield, IL 62701-1822, Tel. (217)753-7915 Fax (217)753-7976

Southeastern Iowa, Rev. Philip L. Hougen, 2635 Northgate Dr., P.O. Box 3167, Iowa City, IA 52244-3167, Tel. (319)338-1273 Fax (319)351-8677

Western Iowa, Rev. Michael A. Last, 318 E. Fifth St., P.O. Box 577, Storm Lake, IA 50588-0577, Tel. (712)732-4968 Fax (712)732-6540

Northeastern Iowa, Rev. Steven L. Ullestad, 201-20th St. SW, P.O. Box 804, Waverly, IA 50677-0804, Tel. (319)352-1414 Fax (319)352-1416

Northern Great Lakes, Rev. Thomas A. Skrenes, 1029 N. Third St., Marquette, MI 49855-3588, Tel. (906)228-2300 Fax (906)228-2527

Northwest Synod of Wisconsin, Rev. Robert D. Berg, 12 W. Marshall St., P.O. Box 730, Rice Lake, WI 54868-0730, Tel. (715)234-3373 Fax (715)234-4183

East-Central Synod of Wisconsin, Rev. James A. Justman, 16 Tri-Park Way, Appleton, WI 54914-1658, Tel. (920)734-5381 Fax (920)734-5074

Greater Milwaukee, Rev. Paul W. Stumme-Diers, 1212 S. Layton Blvd., Milwaukee, WI 53215-1653, Tel. (414)671-1212 Fax (414)671-1756

South-Central Synod of Wisconsin, Rev. George G. Carlson, 2909 Landmark Pl., Ste. 202, Madison, WI 53713-4237, Tel. (608)270-0201 Fax (608)270-0202

La Crosse Area, Rev. April Culring Larson, 3462 Losey Blvd. S., La Crosse, WI 54601-7217, Tel. (608)788-5000 Fax (608)788-4916

Regional Coord., Rev. Carl R. Evenson, Region 5, 675 Deerwood Dr., Ste. 4., Neenah, WI 54956-1629, Tel. (920)720-9880 Fax (920)720-9881

REGION 6

Southeast Michigan, Rev. John H. Schreiber, 218 Fisher Bldg., 3011 W. Grand Ave., Detroit, MI 48202-3011, Tel. (313)875-1881 Fax (313)875-1889

Northwest Lower Michigan, Rev. Gary L. Hansen, 801 S. Waverly Rd., Ste. 201, Lansing, MI 48917-4254, Tel. (517)321-5066 Fax (517)321-2612

Indiana-Kentucky, Rev. James R. Stuck, 911 E. 86th St., Ste. 200, Indianapolis, IN 46240-1840, Tel. (317)253-3522 Fax (317)254-5666

Northwestern Ohio, Rev. Marcus C. Lohrmann, 621 Bright Rd., Findlay, OH 45840-6987, Tel. (419)423 3664 Fax (419)423-8801

Northeastern Ohio, Rev. Lee M. Miller, Interim Bishop, 1890 Bailey Rd., Cuyahoga Falls, OH 44221-5259, Tel. (330)929-9022 Fax (330)929-9018

Southern Ohio, Rev. Dr. Callon W. Holloway, Jr., 300 S. 2nd St., Columbus, OH 43215-5001, Tel. (614)464-3532 Fax (614)464-3422

Regional Coord., Marilyn McCann Smith, Region 6, P.O. Box 91, 119 1/2 N. Main St. Bluffton, OH 45817, Tel. (419)369-4006 Fax (419)369-4007

REGION 7

New Jersey, Rev. E. Roy Riley, Jr., 1930 State Highway. 33, Hamilton Square, Trenton, NJ 08690-1799, Tel. (609)586-6800 Fax (609)586-1597

New England, Rev. Margaret G. Payne, 20 Upland St., Worcester, MA 01607-1624, Tel. (508)791-1530 Fax (508)797-9295

Metropolitan New York, Rev. Stephen P. Bouman, Interchurch Center, 475 Riverside Dr., Ste.1620, New York, NY 10115, Tel. (212)665-0732 Fax (212)665-8640

Upstate New York, Rev. Marie C. Jerge, 890 E. Brighton Ave., Syracuse, NY 13205, Tel. (315)446-2502 Fax (315)446-4642

Northeastern Pennsylvania, Rev. Dr. David R. Strobel, 4865 Hamilton Blvd., Wescosville, PA 18106-9705, Tel. (610)395-6891 Fax (610)398-7083

Southeastern Pennsylvania, Rev. Claire S. Burkat, 506 Haws Ave., Norristown, PA 19401-4543, Tel. (610)278-7342 Fax (610)696-2782

Slovak Zion, Rev. Wilma S. Kucharek, 124 Barbero Dr., Torrington, CT 06790, P.O.Box 1003 (06790-1003), Tel. (860)482-6100 Fax (860)482-7463

Regional Coord., Rev. Peggy M. Wvertele, Tel. (215)248-6319 Fax (215)248-7377

REGION 8

Northwestern Pennsylvania, Rev. Ralph E. Jones, 308 Seneca St., 5th Fl., Oil City, PA 16301, Tel. (814)677-5706 Fax (814)676-8591

Southwestern Pennsylvania, Rev. Donald J. McCoid, 9625 Perry Hwy., Pittsburgh, PA 15237-5590, Tel. (412)367-8222 Fax (412)369-8840

Allegheny, Rev. Gregory R. Pile, 701 Quail Ave., Altoona, PA 16602-3010, Tel. (814)942-1042 Fax (814)941-9259

Lower Susquehanna, Rev. Carol S. Hendrix, 900 S. Arlington Ave., Ste. 208, Harrisburg, PA 17109-5031, Tel. (717)652-1852 Fax (717)652-2504

Upper Susquehanna, Rev. Dr. A. Donald Main, Rt. 192 & Reitz Blvd., P.O. Box 36, Lewisburg, PA 17837-0036, Tel. (570)524-9778 Fax (570)524-9757

Delaware-Maryland, Rev. Dr. H. Gerard Knoche, 700 Light St., Baltimore, MD 21230-3850, Tel. (410)230-2860 Fax (410)230-2871

Metropolitan Washington, D.C., Rev. Theodore F. Schneider, 1030-15th St., NW, Ste 1010, Washington, DC 20005-1503, Tel. (202)408-8110 Fax (202)408-8114

West Virginia-Western Maryland, Rev. Ralph W. Dunkin, The Atrium, 503 Morgantown Avenue, Ste. 100, Fairmont, WV 26554-4374, Tel. (304)363-4030 Fax (304)366-9846

Regional Coord., Rev. Judith Cobb, Lutheran Theological Sem. at Gettysburg, 61 Seminary Ridge, Gettysburg, PA 17325-1795, Tel. (717)338-3033 x 2133 Fax (717)334-3469

REGION 9

Virginia, Rev. James F. Mauney, Roanoke College, 221 College Ln., Bittle Hall, P.O. Drawer 70, Salem, VA 24153-0070, Tel. (540)389-1000 Fax (540)389-5962

North Carolina, Rev. Leonard H. Bolick, 1988 Lutheran Synod Dr., Salisbury, NC 28144-4480, Tel. (704)633-4861 Fax (704)638-0508

South Carolina, Rev. David A. Donges, 1003 Richland St., P.O. Box 43, Columbia, SC 29202-0043, Tel. (803)765-0590 Fax (803)252-5558

Southeastern, Rev. Ronald B. Warren, 100 Edgewood Ave., NE, Ste. 1600, Atlanta, GA 30303, Tel. (404)589-1977 Fax (404)521-1980

Florida-Bahamas, Rev. Edward R. Benoway, 3838 W. Cypress St., Tampa, FL 33607-4897, Tel. (813)876-7660 Fax (813)870-0826

Caribbean, Rev. Margarita Martinez, PMB Num 359 Ste. 1, 425 CARR 693, Ste. 1, Dorado, PR 00646-4802, Tel. (787)273-8311 Fax (787)796-3365

Regional Coord., Rev. Harvey L. Huntley Jr., Region 9, Lutheran Theological Southern Seminary, 4201 N. Main St., Columbia, SC 29203, Tel. (803)461-3263 Fax (803)461-3380

Periodicals

The Lutheran, Lutheran Partners, Lutheran Woman Today, Seeds for the Parish

Evangelical Lutheran Synod

The Evangelical Lutheran Synod had its beginning among the Norwegian settlers who brought with them their Lutheran heritage. The synod was organized in 1853. It was reorganized in 1918 by those who desired to adhere to the synod's principles not only in word but also in deed.

The synod owns and operates Bethany Lutheran College and Bethany Lutheran Theological Seminary. It has congregations in 20 states and maintains foreign missions in Peru, Chile, India, Korea, the Czech Republic, Latvia, and Ukraine. It operates a seminary in Lima, Peru and in Ternopil, Ukraine.

Headquarters

6 Browns Court, Mankato, MN 56001, Tel. (507)344-7356 Fax (507)344-7426

Media Contact, Pres., John A. Moldstad

Email: jamjr@blc.edu

Website: www.EvLuthSyn.org

Officers

Pres., Rev. John A. Moldstad, 6 Browns Ct., Mankato, MN 56001

Sec., Rev. Craig Ferkenstad, 37777 State Hwy 22, St. Peter, MN 56082

Vice Pres., Rev. Glenn Obengerger, 12309 Pacific Ave., Tacoma, WA 98444

OTHER ORGANIZATIONS

Lutheran Synod Book Co., Bethany Lutheran College, 700 Luther Dr., Mankato, MN 56001

Bethany Lutheran Theological Seminary, 6 Browns Court, Mankato, MN 56001

Periodicals

Lutheran Sentinel, Lutheran Synod Quarterly, Young Branches, Oak Leaves, Mission News

Evangelical Mennonite Church—please see Fellowship of Evangelical Churches.

Evangelical Methodist Church

The Evangelical Methodist Church was organized in 1946 at Memphis, Tenn., largely as a movement of people who opposed modern liberalism and wished for a return to the historic Wesleyan position. In 1960, it merged with the Evangel Church (formerly Evangelistic Tabernacles) and with the People's Methodist Church in 1962.

Headquarters

P.O. Box 17070, Indianapolis, IN 46217, Tel. (317)780-8017 Fax (317)780-8078

Media Contact, Gen. Conf. Sec.-Treas., Rev. James A. Coulston

Email: headquarters@emchurch.org
Website: www.emchurch.org

Officers
Gen. Supt., Dr. Edward W. Williamson
Gen. Conf. Sec.-Treas., Rev. James A. Coulston

Periodicals
The Connection

Evangelical Presbyterian Church

The Evangelical Presbyterian Church (EPC), established in March 1981, is a conservative denomination of 8 geographic presbyteries. From its inception with 12 churches, the EPC has grown to 250 churches with a membership of over 90,000.

Planted firmly within the historic Reformed tradition, evangelical in spirit, the EPC places high priority on church planting and development along with world missions. Over Eighty missionaries serve the church's mission.

Based on the truth of Scripture and adhering to the Westminster Confession of Faith plus its Book of Order, the denomination is committed to the "Essentials of the faith." The historic motto "In essentials, unity; in nonessentials, liberty; in all things charity" catches the irenic spirit of the EPC, along with the Ephesians theme, "truth in love."

The Evangelical Presbyterian Church is a member of the World Reformed Fellowship, World Alliance of Reformed Churches, National Association of Evangelicals, World Evangelical Fellowship and the Evangelical Council for Financial Accountability.

Headquarters
Office of the General Assembly, 17197 N. Laurel Park Dr., Suite 567, Livonia, MI 48152, Tel. (734)742-2020 Fax (734)742-2033
Media Contact, Stated Clerk, Dr. Jeffrey Jeremiah
Email: EPCHURCH@epc.org
Website: www.epc.org

Officers
Administration Committee, Chmn., Bill Vogles, 1314 Stonecreek Drive, Lawrence, KS 66049
Board of Benefits, Chmn., Rev. Ron Horgan, c/o EPC, 17197 N. Laurel Park Dr. Suite 567, Livonia, MI 48152
Comm. on Christian Educ. & Publ., Chmn., Rev. Tommy Overton, First Presbyterain Church of Rome, 101 E. Third Avenue 77459 College Ministries Committee, Chmn., Rev. Pedro Govantes, Grace Presbyterain, 133 Shrewsbury Court, Pennington, NJ 08534
Committee on Fraternal Relations, Chmn., Dr. Don Fortson, 400 Leighton Court, Matthews, NC 28105-6586
Committee on National Outreach, Chmn., Dr. Shawn Robinson, Clayton Community Church, 6055 Main Street, Clayton, CA 94517
Committee on World Outreach, Chmn., Mr. Jim Thomason, 3470 Wrights Valley Road, Bluefield VA 24605

Committee on Ministerial Vocation, Chmn., Mr. Bill Meeks, 712 E. Monroe, St. Louis MO 63122
Committee on Women's Ministries, Chmn., Libby Cooper, 2030 Ralston Ct., Florence, SC 29505
Committee on Theology, Chmn., Rev. Paul Husband, Tunica Presbyterain Church, Tunica, MS 38676-1095
Committee on Student Ministries, Chmn., Rev. Brandor Bates, Lakeside Presbyterain Church, 2070 Sillway Road, Brandon MS 39047

PRESBYTERIES
Central South, Stated Clk., Rev. Ken Van Kampen, Atoka Presbyterain Church, 1041 Atoka Idaville Rd., Atoka, TN 38004
East, Stated Clk., Rev. Ron Meyer, Fourth Presbyterian Church, 5500 River Road, Bethesda, MD 20816
Florida, Stated Clk., Rev. Robert Garment, Hope EPC, 4680 Thomasville Rd., Tallahassee, FL 32309
Mid-America, Stated Clk., Mr. Dexter Kuhlman, 1926 Prospector Ridge, Ballwin, MO 63011
Mid-Atlantic, Stated Clk., Dr. Howard Shockley, P.O. Box 10, Moore, SC 29369
Midwest, Stated Clk., Mr. John C. Manon, P.O. Box 6047, Auburn, IN 46706-6047
Southeast, Stated Clk., Mr. Walter "Jerry" Clothier, 1605 Verdi Lane, Knoxville, TN 37922
West, Stated Clk., Rev. Marc Huebl, 1250 S. Buckely Rd., Suite # 146, Aurora, CO 80017

Fellowship of Evangelical Bible Churches

This Fellowship grew out of the immigration of Mennonites from Russia/Ukraine into the praire states and provinces between 1874-1880. Established with an emphasis on true repentance, conversion, and a life committed to Jesus as Savior and Lord, the Fellowship was founded in 1889 under the leadership of Isaac Peters and Aaron Wall. The founding churches were located in Mountain Lake, Minnesota, and in Henderson and Jansen, Nebraska. The Fellowship has since grown to 43 churches with approximately 5000 members in Canada, Paraguay and the United States.

World evangelization has been an integral part of the Fellowship since its beginning. Today, for every 50 members in the home churches, one missionary is serving. The Fellowship does not direct its own mission efforts, but participates with existing evangelical "faith" mission agencies. Personnel from Fellowship churches serve under in 22 countries under almost 40 agencies.

Doctrinally, the Fellowship has its roots in historic Anabaptism but was strongly influenced by the Bible School Movement. Believer's baptism is by immersion. The Fellowship is holding fast to the inerrancy of Scripture; the deity of Christ; and the need for spiritual regeneration by faith in the death, burial and resurrection of Jesus Christ as payment for sin. Members look forward to the imminent return of Jesus Christ and retain a sense of urgency to share the gospel with those who have never heard of God's redeeming love.

Headquarters
3339 N 109th Plz., Omaha, NE 68164, Tel. (402)965-3860 Fax (402)965-3871
Admn., Paul Boeker, 3339 N 109th Plz., Omaha, NE 68164, Tel. (402)965-3860 Fax (402)965-3871, Email: info@febcministries.org
Email: info@febcministries.org
Website: www.febcministries.org

Officers
Interim President, Mr.Don Krehbiel, 1514 Park Wild Ave., Omaha, NE 68108, Email: pres@febcministries.org
Admn., Paul Boeker, 3339 N 109th Plz., Omaha, NE 68164, Tel. (402)965-3860 Fax (402)965-3871,Email: info@febcministries.org
Ministries Coordinator, Harvey Schultz, 3011 3rd Ave. East, P.O. Box 8, Waldheim, SK S0K 4R0, Tel. (306)945-2220 Fax (306)945-2088, Email: ministries@febcministries.org

Periodicals
Fellowship Focus

Fellowship of Evangelical Churches

The Evangelical Mennonite Church is an American denomination in the European free church tradition, tracing its heritage to the Reformation period of the 16th century. The Swiss Brethren of that time believed that salvation could come only by repentance for sins and faith in Jesus Christ; that baptism was only for believers; and that the church should be separate from controls of the state. Their enemies called them Anabaptists, since they insisted on rebaptizing believers who had been baptized as infants. As the Anabaptist movement spread to other countries, Menno Simons became its principal leader. In time his followers were called Mennonites.

In 1693 a Mennonite minister, Jacob Amman, insisted that the church should adopt a more conservative position on dress and style of living and should more rigidly enforce the "ban" - the church's method of disciplining disobedient members. Amman's insistence finally resulted in a division within the South German Mennonite groups; his followers became known as the Amish.

Migrations to America, involving both Mennonites and Amish, took place in the 1700s and 1800s, for both religious and economic reasons.

The Evangelical Mennonite Church was formed in 1866 out of a spiritual awakening among the Amish in Indiana. It was first known as the Egly Amish, after its founder Bishop Henry Egly. Bishop Egly emphasized regeneration, separation and nonconformity to the world. His willingness to rebaptize anyone who had been baptized without repentance created a split in his church, prompting him to gather a new congregation in 1866. The conference, which has met annually since 1895, united a number of other congregations of like mind. This group became The Defenseless Mennonite Church in 1898 and has been known as the Evangelical Mennonite Church since 1948. At the 2003 convention the delegates voted to change the name to Fellowship of Evangelical Churches.

Headquarters
Resource Center
1420 Kerrway Ct., Fort Wayne, IN 46805, Tel. (260)423-3649 Fax (260)420-1905
Media Contact, Admn. Asst., Lynette Augsburger
Email: FECministries@aol.com
Website: www.fecministries.org

Officers
Pres., Mr. Ronald J. Habegger, 1535 Holliston Tr., Fort Wayne, IN 46825
Chpsn., Rev. Matt Boyers, 22130 Co Rd. A, Archbold, OH 43502
Vice-Chpsn., Rev. Steve Shaffer, 3115 W. Forsythe Rd., Peoria, IL 61614
Sec., Mark Wyse, 7183 SR 66, Archbold, OH 43502
Treas., David Hopper, 16806 US 20 A # 18, West Unity, OH 43570

Periodicals
FEConnections

Fellowship of Fundamental Bible Churches

The churches in this body represent the 1939 separation from the Methodist Protestant Church, when some 50 delegates and pastors (approximately one-third of the Eastern Conference) withdrew to protest the union of the Methodist Protestant Church with the Methodist Episcopal Church and the Methodist Episcopal Church South, and what they considered the liberal tendencies of those churches. These churches subsequently changed their name to the Bible Protestant Church. In 1985, this group again changed its name to the Fellowship of Fundamental Bible Churches to more accurately define their position.

As fundamentalists, this group strongly adheres to the historic fundamentals of the faith, including the doctrine of separation. This group accepts a literal view of the Bible and, consequently, accepts premillennial theology and a pre-tribulational rapture.

The churches are currently located in New Jersey, New York, Pennsylvania, Virginia, Michigan, and California. It is a fellowship of independent Bible and Baptist churches. Baptism, by immersion, and the Lord's Supper, as a memorial, are recognized as ordinances. There are currently 22 churches representing 1200 members. This constituent body is a member of the American Council of Christian Churches.

The Fellowship of Fundamental Bible Churches owns and operates Tri-State Bible Camp and Conference Center in Montague, New Jersey, oversees a mission board called Fundamental Bible Missions, and conducts a Bible Institute called Fundamental Bible Institute.

Headquarters
P.O. Box 206, Penns Grove, NJ 08069
Media Contact, Sec., Rev. Edmund G. Cotton, 80 Hudson St., Port Jervis, NY 12771, Tel. (845)856-7695
Email: ecotton@citlink.net
Website: www.churches-ffbc.org

Officers
Pres., Rev. Daniel Boyle, 16 Little Brooklyn Road, Warwick, NY 10990, Tel. (845)258-2111, Email: boyce@cleaninter.net
Vice-Pres., Rev. Mr. Frank D'Agostino, 104 Memorial Lane, Mount Laurel, NJ 08054, Tel. (856)802-9542, Email: Frankthecarguy@verizon.net
Sec., Rev. Edmund G. Cotton, 80 Hudson Street, Port Jervis, NY 12771, Tel. (845)856-6795, Email: ecotton@citlink.net
Treas., Rev. Stepehn Racite, 6 Tamara Lane, Cornwall, NY 12518, Tel. (845)534 3335, Email: sracite@verizon.net

Fellowship of Grace Brethren Churches
A division occurred in the Church of the Brethren in 1882 on the question of the legislative authority of the annual meeting. It resulted in the establishment of the Brethren Church under a legal charter requiring congregational government. This body divided in 1939 with the Grace Brethren establishing headquarters at Winona Lake, Ind., and the Brethren Church at Ashland, Ohio.

Headquarters
Media Contact, Fellowship Coord., Rev. Thomas Avey, P.O. Box 386, Winona Lake, IN 46590, Tel. (219)269-1269 Fax (219)269-4066
Email: fgbc@fgbc.org
Website: www.fgbc.org

Officers
Mod., Dr. Galen Wiley, 22713 Ellsworth Ave., Minerva, OH 44657
1st Mod.-Elect, Dr. James Custer, 2515 Carriage Rd., Powell, OH 43065
2nd Mod.-Elect, Dr. Ron Manahan, 2316 E. Kemo Ave., Warsaw, IN 46580
Fellowship Coord., Rev. Thomas Avey, P.O. Box 386, Winona Lake, IN 46590, Tel. (219)269-1269 Fax (219)269-4066
Sec., Fellowship Coord., Rev. Thomas Avey, P.O. Box 386, Winona Lake, IN 46590
Treas., Thomas Staller, 2311 S. Cost-a-Plenty Drive, Warsaw, IN 46580

OTHER BOARDS
Grace Brethren International Missions, Exec. Dir., Rev. Tom Julien, P.O. Box 588, Winona Lake, IN 46590

Grace Brethren Home Missions, Exec. Dir., Larry Chamberlain, P.O. Box 587, Winona Lake, IN 46590
Grace College & Seminary, Pres., Ronald E. Manahan, 200 Seminary Dr., Winona Lake, IN 46590, Tel. (210)372-5100
Brethren Missionary Herald Co., Pub. & Gen. Mgr., James Bustram, P.O. Box 544, Winona Lake, IN 46590
CE National, Exec. Dir., Rev. Ed Lewis, P.O. Box 365, Winona Lake, IN 46590
Grace Brethren Navajo Ministries, Dir., Steve Galegor, Counselor, NM 87018
Grace Village Retirement Community, Admn., Jeff Carroll, P.O. Box 337, Winona Lake, IN 46590
Natl. Fellowship of Grace Brethren Ministries, Pres., Dr. Steve Taylor, 132 Summerall Ct., Aiken, SC 29801 Women's Missionary Council, Pres., Janet Minnix, 3314 Kenwick Tr., S.W., Roanoke, VA, 24015
Grace Brethren Men International, Pres., Morgan Burgess, 163 N. Franklin St., Delaware, OH 43015

Free Christian Zion Church of Christ
This church was organized in 1905 at Redemption, Ark., by a company of African-American ministers associated with various denominations. Its polity is in general accord with that of Methodist bodies.

Headquarters
1315 S. Hutchinson St., Nashville, AR 71852
Media Contact, Gen. Sec., Shirlie Cheatham

Officers
Chief Pastor, Willie Benson, Jr.

Free Methodist Church of North America
The Free Methodist Church was organized in 1860 in Western New York by ministers and laymen who had called the Methodist Episcopal Church to return to what they considered the original doctrines and lifestyle of Methodism. The issues included human freedom (anti-slavery), freedom and simplicity in worship, free seats so that the poor would not be discriminated against and freedom from secret oaths (societies) so the truth might be spoken freely at all times. The founders emphasized the teaching of the entire sanctification of life by means of grace through faith.

The denomination continues to be true to its founding principles. It communicates the gospel and its power to all people without discrimination through strong missionary, evangelistic and educational programs. Six colleges, a Bible college and numerous overseas schools train the youth of the church to serve in lay and ministerial roles.

Its members covenant to maintain simplicity in life, worship, daily devotion to Christ, responsible stewardship of time, talent and finance.

117

Headquarters

World Ministries Center, 770 N. High School Rd., Indianapolis, IN 46214, Tel. (317)244-3660 Fax (317)244-1247
Mailing Address, P.O. Box 535002, Indianapolis, IN 46253, Tel. (800)342-5531
Media Contact, Yearbook Ed., P.O. Box 535002, Indianapolis, IN 46253
Email: info@fmcna.org
Website: www.freemethodistchurch.org

Officers

Bishop David W. Kendall; Bishop David T. Roler; Bishop Mathew A. Thomas
General Conference Secretary, Mr Byron Forbes
Dir. of Administraion and Finance, Mr. Dale Hill
Free Methodist Communications, Gerald Coates
Free Methodist World Missions, Dr. Arthur Brown
Men's Ministries International, Director, Rev. Jeffrey Johnson
Women's Ministries International, President, LaWanda Bullock

Periodicals

Light and Life Magazine; Free Methodist World Mission People

Friends General Conference

Friends General Conference (FGC) is an association of fourteen yearly meetings open to all Friends meetings which wish to be actively associated with FGC's programs and services. Friends General Conference includes Baltimore, Canadian, Illinois, Lake Erie, New England, New York, Northern, Ohio Valley, Philadelphia, South Central and Southeastern Yearly Meetings; Alaska Friends Conference, Southern Appalachian Yearly Meeting and Association, and Piedmont Friends Fellowship; plus seven independently affiliated monthly meetings. Friends General Conference is primarily a service organization with the stated purpose of nurturing the spiritual life within its constituency of predominantly unprogrammed Friends. FGC offers services to all Friends, but has no authority over constituent meetings. A Central Committee, to which constituent Yearly Meetings name appointees (in proportion to membership), and its Executive Committee, are responsible for the direction of FGC's programs and services which include a bookstore, conferences, and traveling ministries program. The 1995 Central Committee approved the following Minute of Purpose,

Friends General Conference is a Quaker organization in the unprogrammed tradition of the Religious Society of Friends which primarily serves affiliated yearly and monthly meetings. It is our experience that,

**Faith is based on direct experience of God.

**Our lives witness this experience individually and corporately.

**By answering that of God in everyone, we build and sustain inclusive community.

Friends General Conference provides resources and opportunities that educate and invite members and attenders to experience, individually and corporately, God's living presence, and to discern and follow God's leadings. Friends General Conference reaches out to seekers and to other religious bodies inside and outside the Religious Society of Friends.

Headquarters

1216 Arch St., 2B, Philadelphia, PA 19107, Tel. (215)561-1700 Fax (215)561-0759 Email: Friends@fgcquaker.org
Media Contact, Gen. Sec., Bruce Birchard
Email: friends@fgcquaker.org
Website: www.fgcquaker.org

Officers

Gen. Sec., Bruce Birchard, 1216 Arch St., 2B Philadelphia, PA 19107
Presiding Clerk, Marian Beane, 7125 Cardigan Ave, Charlotte, NC 28215
Treas., Byron Sandford, 515 E Capitol St. SE, Washington DC 20003-1142

YEARLY MEETINGS

Alaska Friends Conference, Clerk, Bill Schoder-Ehri, 480 Grubstake Ave., Homer, AK, 99603-7639, Tel. (907)479-5257, Email: lovenest@ptialaska.net
*Baltimore, Clerk, Lauri Perman; Staff, Robert H. Robinson, 17100 Quaker Ln., Sandy Spring, MD 20860, Tel. (301)774-7663, Email: rileyrobinson@bym-rsf.org
*Canadian, Clerk, Beverley Shepard; Staff, Kerry McAdam, 91A Fourth Ave., Ottawa, ON K1S 2L1, Tel. (613)235-8553, Email: cym-office@quaker.ca
Illinois, Clerk, Susanna Davison; Staff, Sharon Haworth, 608 W. Illinois St. Urbana, Il. 61801, Tel. (217)384-9591 Email: shaworth@sbcglobal.net
Lake Erie, Clerk, Shirley Bechil, 185 Pineviews Dr. Alma, MI 48801-2156, Tel. (989)463-4539 Email: bechill@alma.edu
*New England, Clerk, Christopher McCandless; Staff, Katharine Clark, 901 Pleasant St., Worcester, MA 01602-1908, Tel. (508) 754-6760, Email: adminsec@neym.org
*New York, Clerk, Linda Chidsey; Staff, Helen Garay Toppins, 15 Rutherford Pl., New York, NY 10003, Tel. (212)673-5750, Email: office@nyym.org
Northern, Clerk, Doug Kirk, 1602 Wicklowway Madison, WI 53711, Tel: (608)442-1642, Email: quirks@tds.net
Ohio Valley, Clerk, Virginia Wood; Staff, Krystin Schmidt, P.O. Box 1333, Richmond, IN 47374, Email: vwovym@donet.com
Philadelphia, Clerk, Thomas Swain, 1515 Cherry St., Philadelphia, PA 19102, Tel. (215)241-7210, Email: tswain@ccil.org
Piedmont Friends Fellowship, Clerk, Virginia Driscoll, 504 Willowbrookt Dr., Greensboro, NC 27403, Tel. (336)855-5233, Email: dachelmama@yahoo.com
South Central, Clerk, John Coffin, 7106

Shamrock, Little Rock, AR 72205, Tel. (501)663-1439, Email: joticof@aol.com
*Southeastern, Clerk, Susan Taylor; Staff, Lyn Cope-Robinson P.O. Box 510975, Melbourne Beach, FL 32951, Tel. (321)724-1162, Email: admin@seym.org
Southern Appalachian, Clerk, Kristi Estes; Email: adminasst@sayma.org
*also affiliated with Friends United Meeting

Periodicals
Newsletter, FGConnections, Friends Journal

Evangelical Friends International—North American Region is listed under "E."
Friends Evangel is listed under Religious Society of Friends, Central Yearly Meeting.
Philadelphia Yearly Meeting of the Religious Society of Friends is listed under "P."
Religious Society of Friends (Conservative) is listed uner "R."
Religious Society of Friends (Unaffiliated Meetings) is listed under "R."

Friends United Meeting*

Friends United Meeting was organized in 1902 (the name was changed in 1963 from the Five Years Meeting of Friends) as an association of North American yearly meetings to facilitate a united Quaker witness in missions, peace work, Christian education and outreach.

Today Friends United Meeting is comprised of 30 full-member and 3 association member yearly meetings representing about half the Friends in the world. FUM's current work includes programs of mission and service, leadership development and outreach. FUM publishes Christian education curriculum, books of Quaker history and religious thought and a magazine, Quaker Life.

Headquarters
101 Quaker Hill Dr., Richmond, IN 47374-1980, Tel. (765)962-7573 Fax (765)966-1293, Website: www.fum.org
Media Contact, Interim General Secretary, Sylvia Graves
Email: info@fum.org
Website: www.fum.org

Officers
Presiding Clk., Kelly Kellum
Treas., John Norris
Gen. Sec., Sylvia Graves

DEPARTMENTS
Global Ministries, Sylvia Graves
Quaker Life, Ed., Katie Terrell
Friends United Press, Ed., Katie Terrell

YEARLY MEETINGS
Baltimore Yearly Meeting, 17100 Quaker Ln., Sandy Spring, MD 20860-1296, Tel. (301)774-7663, (800)962-4766 Fax (301)774-7087 www.bym-rsf.org, Howard Fullerton, clerk; Riley Robinson, Gen. Sec.
Bware Yearly Meeting, P.O. Box 179, Suna-Migori 40400, Kenya East Africa; Samuel

Kaguli Omondi, Gen. Sect., Epainitus Adego Ominde, Gen Supt., Daniel Ole Siakati, Presiding Clerk
Canadian Yearly Meeting, 91-A Fourth Ave., Ottawa ON K1S 2L1, Canada, Tel. & Fax (888)296-3222 Fax (613)235-1753; Ann Mitchell, clerk; Email: cym@web.net
Central Yearly Meeting, P.O.Box 1510, Kakamega 50100, Kenya, E. Africa, Seth Shikunzi Okang'a, Gen Sect., Evans Nyenzo, Gen. Supt., Joseph Mmbwavi, Presiding Clerk
Chavakali Yearly Meeting, P.O. Box 102, Chavakali 50317, Kenya, East Africa; Elijah Mwavalie Vieliza, Gen. Sect., Hezekiah Ngadi Buliva, Gen. Supt., Gerishom Mwavali, Presiding Clerk
Cuba Yearly Meeting, Calle 20 #118 Esquina Paz, Reparto Vista, Alegre 80300, Hoguin, Cuba; Ramon Gonzalez-Longoria, Presiding Clerk
Chwele Yearly Meeting, P.O. Box 428 Chwele 50202, Kenya, East Africa, Stephen Sikulu Kisiangani, Gen. Sect., Alex Waliaula, Gen. Supt., Joseph Mamai Makokha, Presiding Clerk
East Africa Yearly Meeting of Friends, (Kaimosi) P.O. Box 35, Tiriki 50309, Kenya, East Africa; Ephraim Konzolo Muhadi, Gen. Sec., Erastus Kesohole, Gen Supt., Lucas Mudoga, Presiding Clerk
East Africa Yearly Meeting of Friends (North), P.O. Box 544, Kitale, Kenya, East Africa; James Mugalavai, Gen. Sec., Billy Wekesa, Gen. Supt., John Walukhu, Presiding Clerk
Elgon East Yearly Meeting, P.O. Box 2322, Kitale 30200, Kenya, East Africa; Philip Wasike Musungu, Gen. Sec., Isaac Wangila, Gen. Supt, Humphrey Mutende, Presiding Clerk. Elgon Religious Society of Friends, (West) P.O. Box 4, Lugulu Via Webuye, Kenya, East Africa, Peter Kiliswa Keya, Gen. Sec., John W. Ngoya, Gen. Supt., Amos A. Dodo, Presiding Clerk
Great Plains Yearly Meeting, 2611 Bader Dr, Central City, NE 68826, (316)262-0471; Email: greatplainsyearlymeeting.org, Laura Dugan, Clerk
Indiana Yearly Meeting, 4715 N. Wheeling Ave., Muncie, IN 47304-1222, Tel. (765)284-6900 Fax (765)284-8925, Email: iyminfo@iym.org; Greg Hinshaw, Clerk; Doug Shoemaker, Gen. Supt.
Iowa Yearly Meeting, Box 657, Oskaloosa, IA 52577-0657, Tel. (641)673-6830 Fax (641) 673-9718; Email: iaym@mahaska.org; John Rainocs, Clerk, Ron Bryan, Gen. Superintendent
Jamaica Yearly Meeting, 4 Worthington Ave., Kingston 5, Jamaica West Indies, Tel. (876)926-7371, Horace Hall, Presiding Clerk
Kakamega Yearly Meeting, P.O. Box 465, Kakamega 50100, Kenya, East Africa; Harun Wesley Sasita, Gen. Sec., Patrick L Muganda, Gen. Supt., Jared Waudo Wangila, Presiding Clerk

Lugari Yearly Meeting, P.O. Box 483, Turbo 30106, Kenya, East Africa; Enock Were, Gen. Sec., Jotham Nyongesa Situma, Gen. Supt., Alex Kimiya, Presiding Clerk

Malava Yearly Meeting, P.O. Box 26, Malava 50103, Kenya, East Africa; Simon Belengu, Gen. Sec., Stephen Koikoi, Gen. Supt., Andrew Mulupi Khayisie, Presiding Clerk

Nairobi Yearly Meeting, P.O. Box 8321, Nairobi 00300, Kenya, East Africa; Churchill Malimo, Gen. Sec., Henry Apencha, Gen. Supt., Midikira Churchil Kibisu, Presiding Clerk

New England Yearly Meeting, 901 Pleasant St., Worcester, MA 01602-1908, Tel. (508)754-6760, Email: neym@neym.org; Linda Jenkins, Clerk; Jonathan Vogel-Borne, Field Secretary

New York Yearly Meeting, 15 Rutherford Pl., New York, NY 10003, Tel. (212)673-5750, Email: office@nyym.org; Heather Cook, Clerk; Christopher Sammond, General Secretary

North Carolina Yearly Meeting, 4811 Hilltop Rd, Greensboro, NC 27407, Tel. (336)292-6957 Fax (336)292-1905, Email: ncfriends@ncymfum.org; Judy Ritter, Clerk; John Porter, Gen. Superintendent

Southeastern Yearly Meeting, P.O. Box 510795, Melbourne Beach, FL 32951-0795, Tel. (321)724-1162; Susan Taylor, Clerk; Lyn Cope-Robinson, Adm. Sec., Sec: admin@seym.org

Tuloi Yearly Meeting, P.O. Box 128, Kapsabet 50305, Kenya, East Africa; Moses S. Khayumbi, Gen. Sec., John Musanga Kidziiri, Gen. Supt., Simon Vuhasio, Presiding Clerk

Uganda Yearly Meeting, P.O. Box 2384, Mbale, Uganda, East Africa; Nambafu Julius, Gen. Sec., Wopicho Apollo, Clerk, Francis Wamalia, Gen. Supt.

VIHIGA Yearly Meeting of Friends, P.O. Box 160, Vihiga 50310, Kenya, East Africa, Lam Kisanya Osodo, Gen. Sec., Zebedee Musudia, Gen. Supt., Hezekiah Atsiaya, Presiding Clerk

Vokoli Yearly Meetings, P.O. Box 266, Wodanga 50311, Kenya, East Africa; Ephraim Mudoga Ludeki, Gen. Sec., Timothy Kisago, Gen Supt., Gerishom Lumasia, Presiding Clerk

Western Association of the Religious Society of Friends, 13205 E Philadelphia St, Whittier, CA 90601 Tel (562)698-9805, Email: warsf@inreach.com

Western Yearly Meeting, P.O. Box 70, Plainfield, IN 46168; Tel (800)909-3452 & (317)839-2789 Fax (317)839-2616, Email: westernym@sbcglobal.net; Steve and Marlene Pediso, Co-Superintendents, Jim Crew, Clerk

Wilmington Yearly Meeting, Pyle Center Box 1194, Wilmington, OH 45177; Tel (937)382-2491 Fax (937)382-7077, Email: patwym@aol.com; Lois Hackney, Clerk; Marvin Hall, Ex. Sec.

Periodicals

Quaker Life, Katie Terrell Wonsik, editor

Full Gospel Assemblies International

The Full Gospel Assemblies International was founded in 1962 under the leadership of Dr. Charles Elwood Strauser. The roots of Full Gospel Assemblies may be traced to 1947 with the beginning of the Full Gospel Church of Coatesville, Pennsylvania. As an Assemblies of God Pentecostal church, the Full Gospel Church of Coatesville was active in evangelization and educational ministries to the community. In service to the ministers and students of the Full Gospel Church ministries, the Full Gospel Trinity Ministerial Fellowship was formed in 1962, later changing its name to Full Gospel Assemblies International.

Retaining its original doctrine and faith, Full Gospel Assemblies is Trinitarian, believing that the Bible is God's infallible Word to mankind, baptism in the Holy Spirit according to Acts 2, divine healing is made possible by the sufferings of our Lord Jesus Christ, and in the imminent return of Christ for those who love him.

The body of Full Gospel Assemblies is an evangelical missionary fellowship sponsoring ministry at home and abroad, composed of self governing ministries and churches. Congregations, affiliate ministries and clerical body are located throughout the United States and over 15 countries of the world.

Headquarters

International Headquarters: 3018 E Lincoln Hwy, Parkesburg, PA

Mailing Address, P.O. Box 1230, Coatesville, PA 19320, Tel. (610)857-2357, Fax (610)857-3109

Media Contact, Simeon Strauser

Officers

Chairman, Simeon J. Strauser
Exec. Dir. of Ministry, Edward Popovich
Exec. Sec., Carol Strauser
Exec. Trustee, J. Victor Fisk
Chpsn., Simeon Strauser, Sadsburyville, PA
J. Victor Fisk, Apollo, PA
Bette Elgin, Zenia, CA
Reginald Licht, Prairie du Sac, WI Raymond Favicha, Spring Hill, FL
Edward Popovich, Burgesttstown, PA

Periodicals

Full Gospel Ministries Outreach Report, Denominational Code

Full Gospel Fellowship of Churches and Ministers International

In the early 1960s a conviction grew in the hearts of many ministers that there should be closer fellowship between the people of God who believed in the apostolic ministry. At the same time, many independent churches were experiencing serious difficulties in receiving authority from the IRS to give governmentally accepted tax-exempt receipts for donations.

In September 1962 a group of ministers met in Dallas, Texas, to form a Fellowship to give expression to the essential unity of the Body of Christ under the leadership of the Holy Spirit—a unity that goes beyond individuals, churches or organizations. This was not a movement to build another denomination, but rather an effort to join ministers, churches and ministry organizations of like mind across denominational lines.

To provide opportunities for fellowship and to support the objectives and goals of local and national ministries- regional conventions and an annual international convention are held.

Headquarters

1000 N. Belt Line Rd., Irving, TX 75061, Tel. (214)492-1254

Media Contact & Convention Planner, Sec., Dr. Harry Schmidt, 400 E. Gregory, Mt. Prospect, IL 60056

Email: TheFellowship@fgfcmi.org

Website: www.fgfcmi.org

Officers

Pres., Rev. Gene Evans, P.O. Box 813, Douglasville, GA 30133

1st Vice Pres, Dr. Harry Schmidt, 400 E. Gregory, Mt. Prospect, IL 60056

Sec., Rev. Phillip Vance, 1035 S. Grand, Pullamn, WA 99163-2161

Treas., Rev. Steve Biffle, 3833 Westerville Road, Columbus, OH 43224

Business Admin., Bryan Crowson, 1000 N. Belt Line Rd., Irving, TX 75061 Assist. Bus. Admin., S.K. Biffle, 1000 N. Belt Line Rd., Irving, TX 75061

Office Manager, Mrs. Anita Sullivan, 1000 N. Belt Line Rd., Irving, TX 75061

Vice-Pres. at Large, Rev. Don Westbrook, 3518 Rose of Sharon Rd., Durham, NC 27712

Chmn. of Evangelism, Rev. Billy Gibson, 4249 Winding Brook Dr., Plano, TX 75093

Chmn of Mission, Rev. David Robinson, 1121 Shuler St., Elgin. IL 60123

Chmn of Youth, Rev. Steven K. Biffle, 3833 Westerville Rd., Columbus, OH 43224

Past Pres., Rev. Don Arnold, 1001 Lake Carolyn Parkway # 403, Irving TX 75039

REGIONAL VICE PRESIDENTS

Southeast, Rev. Steve Holder, 103 Hawkins Dr., Pikeville, NC 27863

South Central, Rev. Billy Gibson, 4249 Winding Brook Dr., Plano, TX 75093

Southwest, Dr. George Stover, 4870 Janell Dr., Las Vegas, NV 89149

Northeast, Rev. Derwin Lowe, 6099 Ocean Gateway, Trappe, MD 21673

North Central, Rev. David Robinson, 1121 Shuler Street, Elgin, IL 60123

Northwest, Rev. Jon R. Engstrom, 19605 12th Ave. W, Lynnwood, WA 98036

Periodicals

Fellowship Tidings

Fundamental Methodist Church, Inc.

This group traces its origin through the Methodist Protestant Church. It withdrew from The Methodist Church and organized on August 27, 1942.

Headquarters

1034 N. Broadway, Springfield, MO 65802

Media Contact, Betty Nicholson, Rt. 2, Box 397, Ash Grove, MO 65604, Tel. (417)672-2268

Officers

Treas., and Sec., Betty Nicholson, Rt. 2, Box 397, Ash Grove, MO 65604, Tel. (417)672-2268

General Association of General Baptists

Similar in doctrine to those General Baptists organized in England in the 17th century, the first General Baptist churches were organized on the Midwest frontier following the Second Great Awakening. The first church was established by the Rev. Benoni Stinson in 1823 at Evansville, Ind.

Stinson's major theological emphasis was general atonement - Christ tasted death for every man. The group also allows for the possibility of apostasy. It practices open Communion and believer's baptism by immersion.

Called 'liberal' Baptists because of their emphasis on the freedom of man, General Baptists organized a General Association in 1870 and invited other 'liberal' Baptists (e.g., 'Free Will' and Separate Baptists) to participate.

The policy-setting body is composed of delegates from local General Baptist churches and associations. Each local church is autonomous but belongs to an association. The group currently consists of more than 60 associations in 16 states, as well as associations in the Philippines, Guam, Saipan, Jamaica, Honduras, and India. Ministers and deacons are ordained by a presbytery.

The denomination operates Oakland City University in Oakland City, Indiana, and Nursing Homes in Illinois and Missouri. General Baptists belong to the Baptist World Alliance, the North American Baptist Fellowship and the National Association of Evangelicals.

Headquarters

100 Stinson Dr., Poplar Bluff, MO 63901, Tel. (573)785-7746 Fax (573)785-0564

Media Contact, Exec. Dir., Dr. Ron Black

Email: ron.black@generalbaptist.com

Website: www.generalbaptist.com

Officers

Mod., Dr. Chris Vaught

Clk., Rev. Dennis Powell

Exec. Dir., Dr. Ron Black

OTHER ORGANIZATIONS

International Missions, Dir., Dr. Jack Eberhardt

National Missions, Dir., Dr. Stephen Gray

Women's Ministries, Dir., Patti Thornton

Oakland City University, Dr. Ray Barber, President, 138 North Lucretia St., Oakland City, IN 47660

Congregational Ministries, Dir., Dr. Franklin Dumond, 100 Stinson Dr., Poplar Bluff, MO 63901

Pastoral Ministries, Dir., Dr. John Sloan, 100 Stinson Dr., Poplar Bluff, MO 63901

Admin., Financial Services, Financial Officer, Linda McDonough, 100 Stinson Dr., Poplar Bluff, MO 63901

Stinson Press, Inc., Pres., Rev. Dale Bates, 400 Stinson Dr., Poplar Bluff, MO 63901

Nursing Home Board, CEO Rev. Jack Cole, Rt. #3, Box 650, Campbell, MO 63933

Compassionate Care Adoption Agency, Dir., Rev. Darrell Hillouse, 26 Jones Road, Sebree, KY 42455 Stewardship/General Baptist Investment Fund Dir., Rev. Stephen Naff, 100 Stinson Dr., Poplar Bluff, MO 63901

Periodicals
The General Baptist Messenger, Capsule, Voice, Woman to Woman

General Association of Regular Baptist Churches

This association was founded in May, 1932, in Chicago by a group of churches which had withdrawn from the Northern Baptist Convention (now the American Baptist Churches in the U.S.A.) because of doctrinal differences. Its Confession of Faith, which it requires all churches to subscribe to, is essentially the old, historic New Hampshire Confession of Faith with a premillennial ending applied to the last article.

The churches of the General Association of Regular Baptist Churches voluntarily join together to accomplish four goals. (1) Champion Biblical truth—committed to communicating the whole counsel of God in its timeless relevance. (2) Impact the world for Christ—obeying the Lord's Great Commission to take the life-changing gospel to the entire world. (3) Perpetuate Its Baptist heritage—faithfully promoting its Scriptural legacy and identity. (4) Advancing GARBC churches—strengthening existing churches and planting new churches for the purposes of evangelism and edification.

Headquarters
1300 N. Meacham Rd., Schaumburg, IL 60173, Tel. (847)843-1600 Fax (847)843-3757
Media Contact, Natl. Rep., Dr. John Greening
Email: garbc@garbc.org
Website: www.garbc.org

Officers
Chpsn., Rev. Richard Van Heukelum, Waterloo IA
Vice Chpsn., Rev. Bradley Quick, Elyria OH
Treas., Michael Nolan, Schaumburg IL
Sec., Dr. John Hartag, III, Cambridge IA
Natl. Rep., Dr. John Greening, Schaumburg IL

Periodicals
Baptist Bulletin, Synergy Newsletter, E-Info Newsletter

General Church of the New Jerusalem

The General Church of the New Jerusalem, also called the New Church, was founded in 1897. It is based on the teachings of the 18th Century scientist Emanuel Swedenborg, and stresses the oneness of God, who is the Lord Jesus Christ, a life of faith and love in service to others, in true married love, and in life after death.

Headquarters
1100 Cathedral Rd, P.O. Box 743, Bryn Athyn, PA 19009, Tel. (267)502-2682
Media Contact, Ed., Church Journal, Rev. Kurt H. Asplundh, Box 26, Bryn Athyn, PA 19009, Tel. (267)502-2682 Fax (267)502-4929
Email: svsimpso@newchurch.edu
Website: www.newchurch.org

Officers
Presiding Bishop, Rt. Rev. Thomas L. Kline
Sec., Susan V. Simpson
Treas., Dvid Frazier

Periodicals
New Church Life

General Conference of Mennonite Brethren Churches

A small group, requesting that closer attention be given to prayer, Bible study and a consistent lifestyle, withdrew from the larger Mennonite Church in the Ukraine in 1860. Anabaptist in origin, the group was influenced by Lutheran pietists and Baptist teachings and adopted a quasi-congregational form of church government. In 1874 and years following, small groups of these German-speaking Mennonites left Russia, settled in Kansas and then spread to the Midwest west of the Mississippi and into Canada. Some years later the movement spread to California and the West Coast. In 1960, the Krimmer Mennonite Brethren Conference merged with this body.

Today the General Conference of Mennonite Brethren Churches conducts services in many European languages as well as in Vietnamese, Mandarin and Hindi. It works with other denominations in missionary and development projects in 25 countries outside North America.

Headquarters
4812 E. Butler Ave., Fresno, CA 93727, Tel. (209)452-1713 Fax (209)452-1752
Media Contact, Exec. Sec., Marvin Hein

Officers
Mod., Ed Boschman, 12630 N. 103rd Ave., Suite 215, Sun City, AZ 85351
Asst. Mod., Herb Kopp, 200 McIvor Ave., Winnipeg, NB R20 028
Sec., Valerie Rempel
Exec. Sec., Marvin Hein

Periodicals
Christian Leader

Grace Gospel Fellowship

The Grace Gospel Fellowship was organized in 1944 by a group of pastors who held to a dispensational interpretation of Scripture. Most had ministries in the Midwest. Two prominent leaders were J. C. O'Hair of Chicago and Charles Baker of Milwaukee. Subsequent to 1945, a Bible Institute was founded (now Grace Bible College of Grand Rapids, Mich.), and a previously organized foreign mission (now Grace Ministries International of Grand Rapids) was affiliated with the group. Churches have now been established in most sections of the country.

The body has remained a fellowship, each church being autonomous in polity. All support for its college, mission and headquarters is on a contributory basis.

The binding force of the Fellowship has been the members' doctrinal position. They believe in the Deity and Saviorship of Jesus Christ and subscribe to the inerrant authority of Scripture. Their method of biblical interpretation is dispensational, with emphasis on the distinctive revelation to and the ministry of the apostle Paul.

Headquarters

Media Contact, Pres., Frosty Hansen, 2125 Martindale SW, P.O. Box 9432, Grand Rapids, MI 49509, Tel. (616)245-0100 Fax (616)241-2542

Email: ggfinc@aol.com

Website: www.ggfusa.org

Officers

Pres., Traynor ("Frosty") Hansen, Jr.

OTHER ORGANIZATIONS

Grace Bible College, Pres., Rev. Ken Kemper, 1011 Aldon St. SW, Grand Rapids, MI 49509

Grace Ministries Intl., Exec. Dir., Dr. Samuel Vinton, 2125 Martindale Ave. SW, Grand Rapids, MI 49509

Prison Mission Association, Gen. Dir., Donald Sommer, P.O. Box 1587, Port Orchard, WA 98366-0140

Grace Publications Inc., Exec. Dir., Wayne Schoonover, 2125 Martindale Ave. SW, Grand Rapids, MI 49509

Bible Doctrines to Live By, Exec. Dir., Lee Homoki, P.O. Box 2351, Grand Rapids, MI 49501

Periodicals

Truth

Greek Orthodox Archdiocese of America*

The Orthodox Church today, numbering over 250 million worldwide, is a communion of self-governing Churches, each administratively independent of the other, but united by a common faith and spirituality. Their underlying unity is based on identity of doctrines, sacramental life and worship, which distinguishes Orthodox Christianity. All recognize the spiritual preeminence of the Ecumenical Patriarch of Constantinople who is acknowledged as primus inter pares, first among

equals. All share full communion with one another. The living tradition of the Church and the principles of concord and harmony are expressed through the common mind of the universal episcopate as the need arises. In all other matters, the internal life of each independent Church is administered by the bishops of that particular Church. Following the ancient principle of the one people of God in each place and the universal priesthood of all believers, the laity share equally in the responsibility for the preservation and propagation of the Christian faith and Church.

THE GREEK ORTHODOX ARCHDIOCESE OF AMERICA

Before the establishment of an Archdiocese in the Western Hemisphere there were numerous communities of Greek Orthodox Christians. The first Greek Orthodox community in the Americas was founded in New Orleans, LA by a small colony of Greek merchants. History also records that on June 26, 1768 the first Greek colonists landed at St. Augustine,FL, the oldest city in America. The first permanent community was founded in New York City in 1892, today's Archdiocesan Cathedral of the Holy Trinity and the See of the Archbishop of America. The Greek Orthodox Archdiocese of North and South America was incorporated in 1921 and officially recognized by the State of New York in 1922.

The Greek Orthodox Archdiocese of America is composed of the Direct Archdiocesan District—New York and eight Metropolises: Chicago, Pittsburgh, Boston, Denver, Atlanta, Detroit, San Francisco and New Jersey. It is governed by the Archbishop and the Synod of Bishops. The Synod of Bishops is headed by the Archbishop and comprised of the Metropolitans who are in charge of a metropolis.It has all the authority and responsibility which the Church canons provide for a provincial synod.

Headquarters

8-10 E. 79th St., New York, NY 10021, Tel. (212)570-3500 Fax (212)570-3569

Media Contact, Nikki Stephanopoulos, Director, News and Information/Public Affairs, Tel. (212)570-3530 Fax. (212)774-0215 Email: nikki@goarch.org

Email: archdiocese@goarch.org

Website: www.goarch.org

Officers

HOLY EPARCHIAL SYNOD OF BISHOPS

His Eminence Archbishop Demetrios, Primate of the Greek Orthodox Archdiocese of America, Exarch of the Atlantic and Pacific Oceans, Chairman of the Holy Synod of Bishops, Greek Orthodox Church in America, 8-10 East 79th Street, New York, NY 10021, Tel. (212)570-3500, Fax (212)570-3592

METROPOLIS'

His Eminence Metropolitan Iakovos of Chicago, Metropolis of Chicago, 40 East Burton Place, Chicago, IL 60610, Tel. (312)337-4130 Fax (312)337-9391

His Eminence Metropolitan Maximos of Pittsburgh, Metropolis of Pittsburgh, 5201 Ellsworth Avenue, Pittsburgh, PA 15232, Tel. (412)621-5529 Fax (412)621-1522

His Eminence Metropolitan Methodios of Boston, Metropolis of Boston, 162 Goddard Avenue, Brookline, MA 02146, Tel. (617)277-4742, Fax (617)739-9229

His Eminence Metropolitan Isaiah of Denver, Metropolis of Denver, 4610 East Alameda Avenue, Suite D1, Denver, CO 80222, Tel. (303)333-7794 Fax (303)333-7796

His Eminence Metropolitan Alexios of Atlanta, Metropolis of Atlanta, 2480 Clairmont Road NE, Atlanta, GA 30329, Tel. (404)634-9345 Fax (404)634-2471

His Eminence Metroplitan Nicholas of Detroit, Metropolis of Detroit, 19405 Renfrew Road, Detroit, MI 48221, Tel. (313)664-5433 Fax (313)864-5543

His Eminence Metropolitan Gerasimos of San Francisco, Metropolis of San Francisco, 372 Santa Clara Avenue, San Francisco, CA 94127, Tel. (415)753-3075 Fax (415)753-1165

His Eminence Metropolitan Evangelos of New Jersey, Metropolis of New Jersey 629 Springfield Road, Kenilworth, NJ 07033, Tel. (908)686-0003 Fax (908)686-0046

Auxiliary Bishops: His Grace Bishop Dimitrios of Xanthos, His Grace Bishop Savas of Troas,His Grace Bishop Andonios of Phasiane, His Grace Bishop Demetrios of Mokissos.

CLERGY-LAITY CONGRESS

The Clergy-Laity Congress, the highest legislative body of the Archdiocese, is convened biennially and presided over by the Archbishop. It is concerned with all matters, other than doctrinal or canonical, affecting the life, growth and unity of the Church, the institutions, finances, administration, educational and philanthropic concerns and its increasing growing role in the life of the nations of the Western Hemisphere. The delegates are the pastors and elected lay representatives.

There are 560 parishes, 840 priests and approximately 1.5 million faithful in the Greek Orthodox Archdiocese of America

THE ARCHDIOCESAN COUNCIL

The Archdiocesan Council is the deliberative body of the Greek Orthodox Archdiocese which meets in the interim period between Clergy-Laity Congresses, held every two years.

Executive Committee, His Eminence Archbishop Demetrios Chairman

The Holy Synod of Bishops

Vice Chairman, Michael Jaharis; Nicholas Bouras, Treasurer; Catherine Bouffides-Walsh, Secretary; George Behrakis, Elini Huszagh, Peter Kikis, George Mathews, Anthony Stefanis, George Vourvoulias; Emanuel G. Demos, General Counsel to the Archdiocese.

INSTITUTIONS

Archdiocesan Cathedral of the Holy Trinity

The Rev. Frank Marangos, Dean, 319-337 East 74th Street, New York, NY 10021, Tel. (212)288-3215 Fax (212)288-5876 Website: www.thecathedral.goarch.org

Hellenic College/Holy Cross School of Theology, The Rev. Nicholas Triantafilou, President, 50 Goddard Avenue, Brookline, MA 02445, Tel. (617)731-3500 Fax (617)850-1460, Email: admission@hchc.edu

Saint Basil Academy, The Rev. Constantine L. Sitaras, Director, 79 Saint Basil Road Garrison, NY 10524, Tel. (845)424-3500 Fax (845)424-4172, Email: stbasil@bestweb.net, Website: www.stbasil.goarch.org

St. Michael's Home, His Grace Bishop Andonios of Phasiane,Director, 3 Lehman Terrace, Yonkers, NY 10705, Tel. (914)476-3374 Fax (914)476-1744, Email: Stmichaelshome@msn.com, Website: stmichael.goarch.org

ARCHDIOCESE OF NEW YORK

Office of the Archbishop, Alice Keurian; Director; Office of the Chancellor,His Grace Bishop Savas of Troas, Chancellor; Office of Administration, Jerry Dimitriou, Executive Director.

ARCHDIOCESAN DEPARTMENTS

Registry, Finance, Stewardship & LOGOS, Religious Education, Greek Education, Communications, Internet Ministries, Information Technologies, Youth and Young Adults, Camping Ministry, Ionian Village Ecumenical, Interfaith/Interchurch Marriages, Archives, Benefits

Related Organizations, auxiliaries

Ladies Philoptochos Society, Presbyters Council, Sisterhood of Presvyteres, Retired Clergy of America, National Forum of Greek Orthodox Musicians, Hellenic Cultural Center, Archons of the Ecumenical Patriarchate, Archbishop Iakovos Leadership 100 Endowment Fund, St. Photios National Shrine, International Orthodox Christian Charities(IOCC), Orthodox Christian Mission Center, Trinity Children & Family Services.

OTHER JURISDICTIONS OF THE ECUMENICAL PATRIARCHATE IN THE USA

Albanian Orthodox Diocese in America; Belarusian Council of Orthodox Churches in North America; American Carpatho-Russian Orthodox Greek Catholic Diocese of the USA; Ukrainian Orthodox Church of the USA

Periodicals

THE ORTHODOX OBSERVER

The Holy Eastern Orthodox Catholic and Apostolic Church in North America, Inc.

Canonically established by the Russian Orthodox Synod of Bishops in North America on Feb. 2, 1927 this church was incorporated on Feb. 1, 1928 by Archbishop Aftimios Ofiesh, the first Archbishop-president. Archbishop Aftimios continued as head of this church until he reposed in July 1966. The name and logo are registered service marks of this church. We are a western rite Church but some of our clergy do celebrate the Eastern Liturgy.

The first Synod included Archbishop Aftimios and Bishops Sophronios and Zuk. Over the years many have claimed to be this Church, its successor, this Church under a different name or having our lines. These are members of the independent movement who claim to have lines of apostolic succession that are traced back to us but not recognized by this or nay canonical Church since they were not administered in accordance to the Rudder (Canons) of the Orthodox Church.

Headquarters
Monastery: St. Pachomius Monastery, P.O.Box 8122, Columbus, OH 43201
Primate, Metropolitan Victor
Email: tmetropolitan@theocacna.org
Website: www.theocacna.org

Officers
Archbishop Peter Mar Kepa - Archdiocese of the East
Metropolitan Victor - Archdiocese of the West
Bishop Christopher - Diocese of Houston, Tx.
Bishop Cassian - Diocese of Columbus, Oh.
Bishop Arthur - Diocese of Michigan

SYNOD ADVISORS
Archbishop James
Bishop Donald
Society: The Society of Clerks Secular of St. Basil, est. 1931

Holy Ukrainian Autocephalic Orthodox Church in Exile
This church was organized in a parish in New York in 1951 by Ukrainian laymen and clergy who settled in the Western Hemisphere after World War II. In 1954 two bishops, immigrants from Europe, met with clergy and laymen and formally organized the religious body.

Headquarters
103 Evergreen St., W. Babylon, NY 11704

Officers
Admn., Rt. Rev. Serhij K. Pastukhiv

House of God, Which is the Church of the Living God, the Pillar and Ground of the Truth, Inc.
This body, founded by Mary L. Tate in 1919, is episcopally organized.

Headquarters
1301 N. 58th St., Philadelphia, PA 19131
Media Contact, Sec., Rose Canon, 515 S. 57th St., Philadelphia, PA 19143, Tel. (215)474-8913

Officers
Bishop, Raymond W. White, 6107 Cobbs Creek Pkwy., Philadelphia, PA 19143, Tel. (215) 748-6338

Hungarian Reformed Church in America*
A Hungarian Reformed Church was organized in New York in 1904 in connection with the Reformed Church of Hungary. In 1922, the Church in Hungary transferred most of its congregations in the United States to the Reformed Church in the U.S. Some, however, preferred to continue as an autonomous, self-supporting American denomination, and these formed the Free Magyar Reformed Church in America. This group changed its name in 1958 to Hungarian Reformed Church in America.

This church is a member of the World Alliance of Reformed Churches, Presbyterian and Congregational, the World Council of Churches and the National Council of Churches of Christ.

Headquarters
Bishop's Office, 13 Grove St., Poughkeepsie, NY 12601, Tel. (914)454-5735

Officers
Bishop, Rt. Rev. Alexander Forro
Chief Lay-Curator, Prof. Stephen Szabo, 464 Forest Ave., Paramus, NJ 07652
Gen. Sec. (Clergy), Rt. Rev. Stefan M. Torok, 331 Kirkland Pl., Perth Amboy, NJ 08861, Tel. (908)442-7799
Gen Sec. (Lay), Zoltan Ambrus, 3358 Maple Dr., Melvindale, MI 48122
Eastern Classes, Dean (Senior of the Deans, Chair in Bishop's absence), Very Rev. Imre Bertalan, 10401 Grosvenor Pl., #1521, Rockville, MD 20852, Tel. (301)493-5036 Fax (301)571-5111; Lay-Curator, Balint Dalugh, 519 N. Muhlenberg St., Allentown, PA 18104
New York Classes, Supervisor, Rt. Rev. Alexander Forro; Lay-Curator, Laszlo B. Vanyi, 229 E 82nd St., New York, NY 10028
Western Classes, Dean, V. Rev. Andor Demeter, 3921 W. Christy Dr., Phoenix, AZ 85029; Lay-Curator, Zolton Kun, 2604 Saybrook Dr., Pittsburgh, PA 15235

Periodicals
Magyar Egyhaz

Hutterian Brethren
Small groups of Hutterites derive their names from Jacob Hutter, a 16th-century Anabaptist who taught true discipleship after accepting Jesus as Saviour, advocated communal ownership of property and was burned as a heretic in Austria in 1536.

Many believers are of German descent and still use their native tongue at home and in church. Much of the denominational literature is produced in German and English. "Colonies" share property, practice non-resistance, dress plainly, do not participate in politics and operate their own schools. There are 428 colonies with 42,000 members in North America. Each congregation conducts its own youth work through Sunday school. Until age 15, children attend German and English school which is operated by each colony. All youth ages 15 to 20 attend Sunday school. They are baptized as adults upon confession of faith, around age 20.

Headquarters

Media Contact, Philip J. Gross, 3610 N. Wood Rd., Reardon, WA 99029, Tel. (509)299-5400 Fax (509)299-3099

Email: philsjg@juno.com

Officers

Smiedleut Chmn., No. 1, Jacob Waldner— Blumengard Colony, Box 13 Plum Coulee, MB R0G 1R0, Tel. (204)829-3527

Smiedleut Chmn., No. 2, Jacob Wipf, Spring Creek Colony, 36562 102 Street, Forbes, ND 58439, Tel. (701)358-8621

Dariusleut, Chmn., No. 1, Martin Walter, Springpoint Colony, Box 249, Pincher Creek, AB T0K 1W0 Phone (403)553-4368

Lehrerleut, Chmn., Rev. John Wipf, Rosetown Colony, Box 1509, Rosetown, SK S0L 2V0, Tel. (306)882-3344

IFCA International, Inc.

This group of churches was organized in 1930 at Cicero, Illinois, by representatives of the American Council of Undenominational Churches and representatives of various independent churches. The founding churches and members had separated themselves from various denominational affiliations. Founders included J. Oliver Buswell of Wheaton College, Billy McCarrell of Cicero Bible Church and Moody Bible Institute, and M. R. DeHaan of Grand Rapids, MI and Radio Bible Class. Members have included J. Vernon McGee, Charles Ryrie, John Walvoord, and John MacArthur.

The IFCA provides a way for independent churches and ministers to unite in close fellowship and cooperation, in defense of the fundamental teachings of Scripture and in the proclamation of the gospel of God's grace.

Today it consists of 1000 associated churches and 1200 individual members (pastors, professors, missionaries, chaplains, and other Christian workers.)

Headquarters

3520 Fairlanes, Grandville, MI 49418, Tel. (616)531-1840 Fax (616)531-1814

Mailing Address, P.O. Box 810, Grandville, MI 49468-0810

Media Contact, Exec. Dir., Dr. Les Lofquist

Email: office@ifca.org

Website: www.ifca.org

Officers

Exec. Dir., Dr. Les Lofquist

Pres. of Board, Rev. Earl Brubaker

Periodicals

The Voice

International Church of the Foursquare Gospel

Founded by Aimee Semple McPherson in 1927, the International Church of the Foursquare Gospel proclaims the message of Jesus Christ the Savior, Healer, Baptizer with the Holy Spirit and Soon-coming King. Headquartered in Los Angeles, this evangelistic missionary body of believers consists of nearly 1,900 churches in the United States and Canada. The International Church of the Foursquare Gospel is incorporated in the state of California and governed by a Board of Directors who direct its corporate affairs. A Foursquare Cabinet, consisting of the Corporate Officers, Board of Directors and District Supervisors of the various districts of the Foursquare Church in the United States and other elected or appointed members, serves in an advisory capacity to the President and the Board of Directors. Each local Foursquare Church is a subordinate unit of the International Church of the Foursquare Gospel. The pastor of the church is appointed by the Board of Directors and is responsible for the spiritual and physical welfare of the church. To assist and advise the pastor, a church council is elected by the local church members. Foursquare churches seek to build strong believers through Christian education, Christian day schools, youth camping and ministry, Foursquare Women International who support and encourage Foursquare missionaries abroad, local radio and television ministries, the Foursquare World ADVANCE Magazine and over 550 Bible colleges worldwide. Worldwide missions remains the focus of the Foursquare Gospel Church with 38,217 churches and meeting places, 49,287 national pastors, leaders and 4,113,981 members with a combined constituency nearing 5 million in over 140 countries of the world. The Church is affiliated with the Pentecostal/Charismatic Churches of North America, the National Association of Evangelicals and the Pentecostal World Conference.

Headquarters

1910 W. Sunset Blvd., Ste. 200, P.O. Box 26902, Los Angeles, CA 90026-0176, Tel. (213)989-4234 Fax (213)989-4590

Media Contact, Editor, Dr. Ron Williams

Email: comm@foursquare.org

Website: www.foursquare.org

Officers

President: Dr. Jack W. Hayford

Vice President/General Supervisor: Rev. Glenn C. Burris Jr.

Vice President/Director of Global Operations and Missions: Rev. Michael Larkin

Vice President/Church Operations: Rev. James C. Scott Jr.

Vice President/Director of Urban and Multicultural Ministries: Rev. Arthur J. Gray II

Vice President/Corporate Secretary-Treasurer: Dr. Sterling Brackett

Chief Financial Officer: Rev. Jeffrey L. Bird

Vice President/Chief Information Technologies Officer: Rev. Dan Ussery

All of the above can be reached through the corporate address: International Church of the Foursquare Gospel, P.O. Box 26902, Los Angeles, CA 90026, Tel. (888)635-4234; Fax: 213-989-4590; Email: comm@foursquare.org; Website: www.foursquare.org

Periodicals

Foursquare World ADVANCE

126

International Council of Community Churches*

This body is a fellowship of locally autonomous, ecumenically minded, congregationally governed, non-creedal Churches. The Council came into being in 1950 as the union of two former councils of community churches, one formed of black churches known as the Biennial Council of Community Churches in the United States and Elsewhere and the other of white churches known as the National Council of Community Churches.

Headquarters

21116 Washington Pky., Frankfort, IL 60423-3112, Tel. (815)464-5690 Fax (815)464-5692
Media Contact, Exec. Dir., Rev. Michael E. Livingston
Email: icccml@sbcglobal.net

Officers

Pres., Mrs. Saundra Nelson
Vice Pres., Rev. Paul Drake
Vice Pres., Rev.William Grossman
Sec., Rev. Dick Griffith
Treas., Nick Brame

OTHER ORGANIZATIONS
Commission on Laity and Church Relations, Emma Smith
Commission on Ecumenical and Inter-faith Relations, Rev. Herman Harmelink, III
Commission on Clergy Relations, Rev. Glenn Clay
Commission on Faith, Justice & Mission, Rev. Dr. Richard Griffith
Women's Christian Fellowship, Pres., Rev. Cay Randall-May
Samaritans (Men's Fellowship), Pres., Abraham Wright
Youth Fellowship, Pres., Victoria Wells

Periodicals

The Christian Community, The Inclusive Pulpit, Key Lay Notes, Clergy comminique

International Fellowship of Bible Churches, Inc

Founded August, 1988 from three groups of ministers and churches of conservative Wesleyan holiness tradition. Sponsor mission works in six countries on four continents. Locally autonomous congregations cooperate for missions, education, youth camps, religious gatherings, etc. Congregational goverment at Assembly level. International Assembly held biannually on even numbered years. Officers include General Superintendent and a 20-member Board comprised of 10 clergy and 10 non-clergy, elected by the International Assembly. The International Fellowship of Bible Churches, Incorporated is an association of autonomous congregations and parachurch ministries joined together by common persuasions, purposes and principles. International refers to our commitment to maintaining a consciousness of the global and universal nature of the Church of Jesus Christ, as well as our firm commitment to active service as part of that uni-

versal and international church. The Fellowship currently operates an international ministry in several locations across the globe. Fellowship refers to our commitment to the autonomy of the local congregation while maintaining the belief that we really do need each other. Bible refers to our commitment to the authority of Scripture as the final guide for all matters of faith and practice, both public and private. Churches refers to our belief that ministry occurs most efficiently and effectively at the local church level, not at the denominational or organizational level.

Headquarters

3511 N. Geraldine Avenue, Oklahoma City, OK 73008, Tel. & Fax (405)948-9388
Media Contact, Gen. Superintendent, William Harrison Sillings
Email: williamsillins@ibfc.org
Website: www.ifbc.org

Officers

Gen. Superintendent, William Harrison Sillings, 3511 N. Geraldine Avenue, Oklahoma City, OK 73008, Tel. & Fax (405)948-9388, Email: williamsillins@ibfc.org
Secretary, Rev. Howard Russell, 16163 Galehouse Rd., Doylesville, OH 44230, Tel. (330)798-5248 Fax (330)658-1431, Email: hrussell@cbnews.org
Treasurer, Rev. Ronald Ruyle, 7512 S. Villa, Oklahoma City, OK 73159, Tel. (405)681-7475
Director of Missions, Rev. Robert Gilbert, 5334 Old Mission Rd., Chattanooga, TN 3741, Tel. (423)296-8612 Fax (423)499 0357, Email: rgilbert@precept.org
Director of Chaplains, Rev. Gary Hedges, P.O. Box 5555, Ft. Oglethorpe, GA 30742, Tel. (706)861-7733 Fax (706)861-7777, Email: gary@chswebsite.com
Pastoral Consultant, Rev. Don Hicks, 116 Rosewood Way, Parachute, CO 81635, Tel. (970)285-9609

The International Pentecostal Church of Christ

At a General Conference held at London, Ohio, Aug. 10, 1976, the International Pentecostal Assemblies and the Pentecostal Church of Christ consolidated into one body, taking the name International Pentecostal Church of Christ.

The International Pentecostal Assemblies was the successor of the Association of Pentecostal Assemblies and the International Pentecostal Missionary Union. The Pentecostal Church of Christ was founded by John Stroup of Flatwoods, Ketucky, on May 10, 1917 and was incorporated at Portsmouth, Ohio, in 1927. The International Pentecostal Church of Christ is an active member of the Pentecostal/Charismatic Churches of North America, as well as a member of the National Association of Evangelicals.

The priorities of the International Pentecostal Church of Christ are to be an agency of God for

127

evangelizing the world, to be a corporate body in which people may worship God and to be a channel of God's purpose to build a body of saints being perfected in the image of His Son.

The Annual Conference is held each year during the first full week of August in London, Ohio.

Headquarters

2245 St. Rt. 42 SW, P.O. Box 439, London, OH 43140, Tel. (740)852-4722 Fax (740)852-0348
Media Contact, Gen. Overseer, Clyde M. Hughes
Email: hqipcc@aol.com
Website: members.aol.com/hqipcc

Officers

EXECUTIVE COMMITTEE

Gen. Overseer, Clyde M. Hughes, P.O. Box 439, London, OH 43140, Tel. (740)852-4722 Fax (740)852-0348

Asst. Gen. Overseer, B.G. Turner, RR5, Box 1286, Harpers Ferry, WV 25425, Tel. (304)535-221 Fax (304)535-1357

Gen. Sec., Asa Lowe, 513 Johnstown Rd., Chesapeake, VA 23322, Tel. (757)547-4329

Gen. Treas., Ervin Hargrave, P.O. Box 439, London, OH 43140, Tel. (740)852-4722 Fax (740)852-0348

Dir. of Global Missions, Dr. James B. Keiller, P.O. Box 18145, Atlanta, GA 30316, Tel. (404) 627-2681 Fax (404)627-0702

DISTRICT OVERSEERS

Central District, Lindsey Hayes, 609 Lansing Rd., Akron, OH 44312, Tel. (330)784-3453

Mid-Eastern District, H. Gene Boyce, 705 W. Grubb St., Hertford, NC 27944, Tel. (252)426-5403

Mountain District, Terry Lykins, P.O. Box 131, Staffordsville, KY 41256, Tel. (606)297-3282

New River District, Calvin Weikel, RR. 2, Box 300, Ronceverte, WV 24970, Tel. (304)647-4301

North Central District, Edgar Kent, P.O. Box 275, Hartford, MI 49057, Tel. (616)621-3326

North Eastern District, Wayne Taylor, 806 8th St., Shenandoah, VA 22849, Tel. (540) 652-8090

South Eastern District, Frank Angie, 2507 Old Peachtree Rd., Duluth, GA 30097, Tel. (770) 476-5196

Tri-State District, Cline McCallister, 5210 Wilson St., Portsmouth, OH 45662, Tel. and Fax (740)776-6357

Portugese District, Pedro Messias, 34 Woodside Ave., Danbury, CT 06810, Tel. (203)790-9628

OTHER ORGANIZATIONS

Beulah Heights Bible College, Pres., Samuel R. Chand, P.O. Box 18145, Atlanta, GA 30316, Tel. (404)627-2681 Fax (404)627-0702

Women's Ministries, Gen. Pres., Janice Boyce, 121 W. Hunters Tr., Elizabeth City, NC 27909, Tel. and Fax (252)338-3003

Pentecostal Ambassadors, Dustin Hughes, National Youth Dir., P.O Box 439, London, OH 43140, Tel. (740)852-0448 Fax (740)852-0348

National Christian Education Dept., Dir., Dustin Hughes, P.O. Box 439, London, OH 43140, Tel. (740)852-0448 Fax (740)852-0348

Periodicals

The Bridegroom's Messenger, The Pentecostal Leader

International Pentecostal Holiness Church

This body grew out of the National Holiness Association movement of the nineteenth century, with roots in Methodism. Beginning in the South and Midwest, the church represents the merger of the Fire-Baptized Holiness Church founded by B. H. Irwin in Iowa in 1895; the Pentecostal Holiness Church founded by A. B. Crumpler in Goldsboro, North Carolina, in 1898; and the Tabernacle Pentecostal Church founded by N. J. Holmes in 1898.

All three bodies joined the ranks of the pentecostal movement as a result of the Azusa Street revival in Los Angeles in 1906 and a 1907 pentecostal revival in Dunn, N.C., conducted by G. B. Cashwell, who had visited Azusa Street. In 1911, the Fire-Baptized and Pentecostal Holiness bodies merged in Falcon, N.C., to form the present church; the Tabernacle Pentecostal Church was added in 1915 in Canon, Georgia.

The church stresses the new birth, the Wesleyan experience of sanctification, the pentecostal baptism in the Holy Spirit, evidenced by speaking in tongues, divine healing and the premillennial second coming of Christ.

Headquarters

P.O. Box 12609, Oklahoma City, OK 73157-2609, Tel. (405)787-7110 Fax (405)789-3957
Media Contact, Joe Iaguinta.
Email: RCarpenter@iphc.org
Website: www.iphc.org

Officers

Gen. Supt., Bishop Ronald W. Carpenter, Sr.

Vice Chpsn. Executive Director of Evangelism USA, Dr. Ronald Carpenter, Sr.

Exec. Dir. Of World Missions Ministries, Dr. A.D.Beacham Jr. Executive Director of Church Education Ministries, Rev. Talmadge Gardner

Executive Director of Stewardship Ministries/ General Secretary-Treasurer, Rev. Edward W. Wood

OTHER ORGANIZATIONS

The Publishing House (LifeSprings Resources), CEO, Greg Hearn, Franklin Springs, GA 30639

Women's Ministries, Exec. Dir., Mrs. Jewelle Stewart

Men's Ministries, Exec. Dir., Rev. Bill Terry, P.O. Box 12609, Oklahoma City, OK 73157

Periodicals

IPHC Experience

Jehovah's Witnesses

Modern-day Jehovah's Witnesses began in the early 1870s when Charles Taze Russell was the leader of a Bible study group in Allegheny City, Pennsylvania. In July 1879, the first issue of Zion's Watch Tower and Herald of Christ's Presence (now called The Watchtower which is published in 175 languages with a circulation of 37,252,000 appeared. In 1884 Zion's Watch Tower Tract Society was incorporated, later changed to Watch Tower Bible and Tract Society. Congregations spread into other states and countries, and followers witnessed from house to house.

By 1913, printed sermons were in four languages in 3,000 newspapers in the United States, Canada and Europe. Hundreds of millions of books, booklets and tracts were distributed. Publication of the magazine now known as Awake! Began in 1919. Today, it is published in more than 80 languages and has a circulation of upwards of 36,725,000). In 1931 the name Jehovah's Witnesses, based on Isaiah 43 vs.10-12, was adopted.

During the 1930s and 1940s, and as recently as 2002, Jehovah's Witnesses fought many court cases in the interest of preserving freedom of speech, press, assembly and worship. They have won a total of 50 cases before the United States Supreme Court. A missionary training school was established in 1943, and it has been a major factor in the international expansion of the Witnesses. There are now 7.1 million Witnesses in 236 lands.

Jehovah's Witnesses believe in one almighty God, Jehovah, who is the Creator of all things. They believe in Jesus Christ as God's Son, the first of His creations. While Jesus is now an immortal spirit in heaven, ruling as King of God's Kingdom, he is still subject to his heavenly Father, Jehovah God. Christ's human life was sacrificed as a ransom to open up for obedient mankind the opportunity of eternal life. With Christ in heaven, 144,000 individuals chosen from among mankind will rule in righteousness over an unnumbered great crowd who will survive the destruction of wickedness and receive salvation into an earth cleansed of evil. (Rev. Ch.7 vs.9, 10; Ch.14 vs.1-5). These, along with the resurrected dead, will transform the earth into a global earthly paradise and will have the prospect of living forever on it.

Headquarters
25 Columbia Heights, Brooklyn, NY 11201-2483, Tel. (718)560-5000x25263
Media Contact, Office of Public Information, J. R. Brown
Editorial Contact, Writing Department, James N. PellechiaWebsite: www.watchtower.org

Officers
Pres. Watch Tower Bible and Tract Society of Pennsylvania, Don Adams

Periodicals
Awake!, The Watchtower

The Korean Presbyterian Church Abroad*

This body came into official existence in the United States in 1976 and is currently an ethnic church, using the Korean and English language.

Headquarters
General Assembly of the Korean Presbyterian Church in America
17200 Clark Ave., Bellflower, CA 90706, Tel. (714)816-1100 Fax (714)816-1120 Officers
General Secretary, Rev. Jacob Se Jang, 5848 Pimlico Road, Baltimore, MD 21209, Tel. (410)236-8939 Moderator, Rev. Dr. Young Chin Huh, 12601 Leda Lane, Garden Grove, CA 92840, Tel. (714)537-2687

The Latvian Evangelical Lutheran Church in America

This body was organized into a denomination on Aug. 22, 1975 after having existed as the Federation of Latvian Evangelical Lutheran Churches in America since 1955. This church is a regional constituent part of the Lutheran Church of Latvia Abroad, a member of the Lutheran World Federation and the World Council of Churches.

The Latvian Evangelical Lutheran Church in America works to foster religious life, traditions and customs in its congregations in harmony with the Holy Scriptures, the Apostles', Nicean and Athanasian Creeds, the unaltered Augsburg Confession, Martin Luther's Small and Large Catechisms and other documents of the Book of Concord.

The LELCA is ordered by its Synod (General Assembly), executive board, auditing committee and district conferences.

Headquarters
7225 Oak Highlands Dr., Kalamazoo, MI 49009, Tel. (269) 375-0389 Email. kaugars@earthlink.net
Media Contact, Juris Pulins, 9531 Knoll Top Rd., Union, IL 60180, Tel. (815)923-5919
Email: pulins@earthlink.net

Officers
Pres., Dean Lauma Zusevics, Tel. (414) 421-3934 Email: izunpz@wi.rr.com
Vice Pres., Rev. Anita Varsberga-Paza Email: macavp@yahoo.com
Sec.,Girts Kaugars, 7225 Oak Highlands Dr., Kalamazoo, MI 49009, Tel. (269) 375-0389 Email: kaugars@charter.net
Treas., Vilmars Beinikis, 17 John Dr., Old Bethpage, NY 11804, Tel. (516)293-8432

Periodicals
Cela Biedrs, Lelba Zinas

The Liberal Catholic Church—Province of the United States of America

The Liberal Catholic Church was founded Feb. 13, 1916 as a reorganization of the Old Catholic Church in Great Britain with the Rt. Rev. James I. Wedgwood as the first Presiding Bishop. The first ordination of a priest in the United States was Fr. Charles Hampton, later a Bishop. The first Regionary Bishop for the American Province was the Rt. Rev. Irving S. Cooper (1919-1935).

Headquarters

Pres., The Rt. Rev. William S.H. Downey, 1206 Ayers Ave., Ojai, CA 93023, Tel. (805)646-2573 Fax (805)646-2575

Media Contact, Regionary Bishop, The Rt. Rev. William S.H. Downey

Email: W.Downey@sbcglobal.net

Website: www.thelcc.org

Officers

Pres. & Regionary Bishop, The Rt. Rev. William S.H. Downey

Vice Pres., Rev. L. Marshall Heminway, P.O. Box 19957 Hampden Sta., Baltimore, MD 21211-0957

Sec. (Provincial), Rev. Lloyd Worley, 1232 24th Ave. Ct., Greeley, CO 80631, Tel. (303)356-3002

Provost, Rev. Lloyd Worley

Treas., Rev. Milton Shaw

BISHOPS

Regionary Bishop for the American Province, The Rt. Rev. William S.H. Downey

Aux. Bishops of the American Province, Rt. Rev. Dr. Robert S. McGinnis, Jr., 3612 N. Labarre Rd., Metaire, LA 70002; Rt. Rev. Joseph L. Tisch, P.O. Box 1117, Melbourne, FL 32901; Rt. Rev. Dr. Hein VanBeusekom, 12 Krotona Hill, Ojai, CA 93023; Rt. Rev. Ruben Cabigting, P.O. Box 270, Wheaton, IL 60189; The Rt. Rev. Lawrence Smith 9740 S. Avers Ave., Evergreen Park, IL.

Periodicals

Ubique

The Lutheran Church—Missouri Synod (LCMS)

The Lutheran Church - Missouri Synod (LCMS), which was founded in 1847, has nearly 6,200 congregations in the United States and has active work or mission relationships in 88 countries. It has 2.4 million members and is the second-largest Lutheran denomination in North America.

The LCMS is a mission-oriented, Bible-based, confessional Christian denomination. It accepts the teachings of Martin Luther that inspired the Protestant Reformation of the Christian church in the 16th century. The Synod's beliefs can be summed up in three phrases: Grace alone, Scripture alone, Faith alone.

The church has more than 9,000 rostered pastors and some 11,500 additional rostered (called) church workers. Women are active in church work, although they do not occupy clergy positions. Serving in positions such as teachers, deaconesses, and social workers, women comprise approximately half of total rostered workers.

The members' responsibility for congregational leadership is a distinctive characteristic of the LCMS. Power is vested in voters' assemblies, generally comprised of adults of voting age. Synod decision making is given to the delegates at triennial national and district conventions, where the franchise is equally divided between lay and pastoral representatives.

LCMS educational institutions serve all ages from pre-school to college. LCMS congregations operates one of the largest Protestant elementary and secondary school system in the nation and some 26,500 students are enrolled in the LCMS' 10 colleges and universities and two seminaries.

The LCMS is known for mass-media outreach through "The Lutheran Hour," broadcast around the world by Lutheran Hour Ministries; syndicated and streaming programming on KFUO radio; "This Is The Life" dramas on television; and the products of Concordia Publishing House, the third-largest Protestant, church-owned publisher, whose Arch Books children's series alone has sold more than 60 million copies.

The LCMS works with 300 Recognized Service Organizations (RSOs) to extend its social ministry. The LCMS is also a founding partner of Lutheran Services in America, a social service organization that serves one in every 50 Americans.

Headquarters

The Lutheran Church—Missouri Synod, International Center, 1333 S. Kirkwood Road, St. Louis, MO 63122-7295

Media Contact, Director, Public Affairs & Media Relations, Ms. Vicki Biggs, Tel. (314)996-1236 Managing Editor, Reporter, Mr. Joe Isenhower, Tel. (314)996-1231 Fax (314)996-1126

Managing Editor, The Lutheran Witness, Mr. James Heine, Tel. (314) 996-1212 Fax (314) 996-1126

Email: infocenter@lcms.org

Website: www.lcms.org

Officers

Pres., Dr. Gerald B. Kieschnick, St. Louis, MO, Tel. (314)965-9000

1st Vice Pres., Dr. William R. Diekelman, St. Louis, MO, Tel. (314)965-9000

2nd Vice Pres., Dr. Paul L. Maier, Kalamazoo, MI Tel. (314)965-9000

3rd Vice Pres., Dr. John C. Wohlrabe, Virginia Beach, VA Tel. (314)965-9000

4th Vice Pres., Dr. Dean W. Nadasdy, Woodbury, MN Tel. (314)965-9000

5th Vice Pres., Dr. David D. Buegler, Avon, OH Tel. (314)965-9000

Sec., Dr. Raymond L. Hartwig, St. Louis, MO, Tel. (314)965-9000

Treas., Dr. Thomas W. Kuchta, St. Louis, MO, Tel. (314)965-9000

Chief Admn. Officer, Mr. Ronald Schultz, St. Louis, MO, Tel. (314)965-9000

Legal Counselor, Mrs. Sherri Strand, Thompson Coburn, LLP, 1 US Bank Plaza, St. Louis, MO 63101, Tel. (314)552-6000

BOARD OF DIRECTORS

Dr. Victor T. Belton, Decatur, GA; Mr. Walter Brantz, Cody, WY; Mr. Kermit Brashear, Omaha, NE; Dr. William Diekelman, St. Louis, MO; Dr. Betty Duda, Cocoa Beach, FL; Dr. Gloria Edwards, Portola Vally, CA; Dr. Raymond L. Hartwig, St. Louis, MO; Dr.

Gerald B. Kieschnick, St. Louis, MO; Dr. Tom Kuchta, St. Louis, MO; Dr. Robert Kuhn, Oviedo, FL; Chaplain Donald Muchow, Buda, TX; Mr. David Piehler, Wausau, WI; Mr. Curtis Pohl, St. Michail, MN; Mr. Roy Schmidt, Bay City, MI; Dr. Kurt Senske, Austin, TX; Mr. Walter Tesch, Wauwatosa, WI

BOARDS AND COMMISSIONS
Black Ministry, Exec. Dir., Dr. Frazier Odom
Communication Services, Exec. Dir., Mr. David Strand
District & Congregational Services, Interim Exec. Dir., Mr. William R. Cochran
Ministerial Growth and Support, Exec. Dir., Rev. David Meunch Mission Services, Exec. Dir., Dr. Thomas Zehnder Pastoral Education, Exec. Dir., Rev. Glen Thomas
Theology & Church Relations, Exec. Dir., Dr. Joel D. Lehenbauer
University Education, Exec. Dir., Dr. Kurt Krueger
World Relief and Human Care, Exec. Dir., Rev. Matthew C. Harrison
Worship, Exec. Dir., Rev. David Johnson

RELATED ORGANIZATIONS
Concordia Plan Services, Pres., Mr. Jim Sanft, St. Louis, MO, Tel. (314)965-9000
LCMS Foundation, Pres., Rev. Thomas Ries, St. Louis, MO, Tel. (314)965-9000
Lutheran Church Extension Fund, Pres., Mr. Merle Freitag, St. Louis, MO, Tel. (314)965-9000
Concordia Publishing House, Pres., Mr. Bruce Kintz, 3558 S. Jefferson Ave., St. Louis, MO 63118-3968, Tel. (314)268-1000
Concordia Historical Institute, Interim Dir., Rev. Marvin Huggins, 804 Seminary Place, St. Louis, MO 63105, Tel. (314)505-7900
Lutheran Hour Ministries, Exec. Dir., Mr. Bruce Wurdeman, 660 Mason Ridge Ctr. Dr., St. Louis, MO, 63141-8557, Tel. (314)317-4100
Lutheran Women's Missionary League, Pres., Ms. Jan Wendorf, 3558 S. Jefferson Ave., St. Louis, MO 63118, Tel. (314)268-1530
KFUO Radio, Dir. of Broadcast Operations, Mr. Dennis Stortz, 85 Founders Lane, St. Louis, MO 63105, Tel. (314)725-3030

Periodicals
The Lutheran Witness (www.lcms.org/witness),
Reporter (www.reporter.lcms.org)

Lutheran Evangelical Protestant Church (GCEPC)

General Conference
Concordia Theologica Institute International, P.O. Box 5184, West Columbia SC 29171 USA, Telephone: (803)739-6960, Fax: 803/739-0847
Email: generalconference@lutheranepc.com
Website: http://lutheranepc.com

Officers
Executive Officer: Rev. Jessica L. Johnston
Regional Bishops: Rev. R. Dale Carpenter,North Carolina
Council Rev. Dr. David A. Church, California
Rev. Dr. Harvey Allan Menden,Georgia

Rev. Dennis Overlien, Wisconsin
Rev. Dr. Bob E. Tutrone, Pennsylvania (Interim)
Ecumenical Liaison Caribbean and All Regions
Ambassador: Rev. Ralf Muller
Trinidad-Tabago, West Indies
LEPC Chaplaincy
Bishop of Chaplaincy: Rev. Dr. Robert E. Tutrone
Cresco, Pennsylvania USA
LEPC Canada
National Bishop: Rev. Dr. P. John McMahon
Concordia Theologica Canada
Ottawa Ontario Canada
LEPC Kenya
National Bishop: Rev. Dr. Fred M. Macharia
Concordia Theologica Kenya
Nairobi, Kenya
LEPC Nigeria
National Bishop: Rev. Israel Ilpeka
CTI Affiliate Freedom School
Lagos, Nigeria
LEPC Espana
National Bishop: Rev. Dr. Francesco Reale
Concordia Theologica Espana
Pego (Alicante) Spain

Apostolic Lutheran Church of America is listed under "A."
Conservative Lutheran Association is listed under "C."
Evangelical Lutheran Church in America is listed under "E."
Evangelical Lutheran Synod is listed under "E."
The American Association of Lutheran Churches is listed under "A."

Malankara Orthodox Syrian Church, Diocese of America*

Malankara (Indian) Orthodox Church is an ancient Church of India and it traces its origin to as far back as A. D. 52 when St. Thomas one of the Disciples of Jesus Christ came to India and established Christanity in the South Western parts of the sub-continent.

The St. Thomas Christians or the Syrian Christians exist at present in different churches and denominations. But a major section of the parent body of St. Thomas Christians which has maintained its independent nature constitute the Orthodox Church under the Catholicos of the East and Malankara Metropolitan, whose seat is at Devalokam, Kottayam, Kerala, India. The Church has dioceses and churches in most parts of India as well as in the United States, Canada, United Kingdom, Western Europe, Persian Gulf nations, South Africa, Malaysia, Singapore, Australia and New Zealand. The official title of the head of the Church is the "Catholicos of the East, Catholicos of the Apostolic throne of St. Thomas and the Malankara Metropolitan". The present Catholicos of the East and Malankara Metropolitan is H.H. Mar Baselios Mar Thoma Didymos I.

The Church, though modern in its vision and outlook, keeps the traditional Orthodox faith and liturgy. It accepts the first three Ecumenical

131

Synods. The liturgy now in use is the translation of the liturgy adopted from the Antiochian Church in the 17th century. However, the liturgical rites are uniquely Indian. Today the Church uses liturgy in Malayalam,Syriac, Hindi, and English.

The Indian Orthodox community inherited many aspects of Indian civilization and they are as any other member of any other community in India, in their customs, manners, and life style. The Church has a Theological Seminary at Kottayam, Kerala, which was established in AD 1815. Another seminary is situated in Nagpur, Maharashtra. The latter was established fairly recently in the later part of the 20th century.

Headquarters

Indian Orthodox Church Center, 80-34 Commonwealth Boulevard, Bellerose, NY 11426, Tel. (718)470-9844 Fax (718)470-9219

Media Contact, His Grace Mathews Mar Barnabas, Diocesan Metropolitan

Email: Malankara@malankara.org

Website: www.malankara.org/american

Officers

Diocesan Metropolitan: His Grace Mathews Mar Barnabas

Assistant Metropolitan: His Grace Zachariah Mar Nicholovos

Diocesan Sec., The Rev. Fr. John Thomas

Secretary to the Metropolitan: The Rev. Dn. Ciby Mathew

Public Relations Director: The Very Rev. Dr. P. S. Samuel Cor Episcopos

Periodicals

Diocesan Voice, Family and Youth Conference Souvenir

Mar Thoma Syrian Church of India*

According to tradition, the Mar Thoma Church was established as a result of the apostolic mission of St. Thomas, the apostle in 52 AD. Church history attests to the continuity of the community of faithful, throughout the long centuries in India. The liturgy and faith practices of the Church were based on the relationship between the Church in Kerala, India, which St. Thomas founded, with the East-Syrian and Persian Churches. This started in the 3rd century and continued up to the 16th century. In the 17th century, the Malabar Church of St. Thomas (as the Church in Kerala was known) renewed her relationship with the Orthodox Patriarchate of Antioch as part of the resistance to forced Latinization by the Portuguese. This process also led to the development of the Kerala Episcopacy, whereby the first Indian Bishop Mar Thoma I was consecrated in Kerala.

The Mar Thoma Church retains her Eastern Orthodoxy. She follows an Orthodox worship form and liturgy, believes in the catholicity of grace, is missionary and evangelistic in approach. She derives Episcopal succession from the Syrian Orthodox Church of Antioch and follows Eastern Reformed Theology. She is independent, autonomous, and indigenous, constitutionally combining democratic values and Episcopal authority. She has been in full communion with the Anglican Church since 1954.

The Mar Thoma Church has been dynamically involved in the socio-cultural settings of North America and Europe for the past 30 years. Fundamentally an immigrant Church, she has contextualized her ministry in her new life situation without compromising the rich ethos and tradition received from her motherland of Kerala, India. Currently, under the rubric of the Diocese, there are 51 parishes and 20 congregations. In order to cater to the ministerial needs of the Diocese, there are 48 clergy as well as functioning organizations for children, youth, women, and evangelistic work. The Diocese is presided over by the Diocesan Bishop, The Rt. Rev. Dr. Euyakim Mar Coorilos, Episcopa.

The history of the Mar Thoma Church in the North American and European continent represents the dreams and aspirations of the faithful members of the Church. Commencing as a small prayer group in Queens, New York, in 1972, the first approved parish was recognized in New York in 1976. The churches in North America and United Kingdom have become constituents of the newly formed "Diocese of North America and United Kingdom." The Headquarters has subsequently moved to its current location at 2320 South Merrick Avenue, Merrick, N.Y.

Headquarters

Sinai Mar Thoma Center, 2320 S. Merrick Avenue, Merrick, New York 11566, Tel. (516) 377-3311 Fax (516)377-3322

Email: webmaster@marthomachurch.org

Website: www.marthomanae.org

Officers

Diocesan Bishop, Rt. Rev. Dr. Geevarghese Mar Theodosiusk, 2320 Merrick Ave, Merrick NY 11566, Tel. (516)377-3311, Cell (516)655-1852, Fax (516)377-3322, Email: mtcmartheo@yahoo.com.ph, or marthoma diocese@gmail.com

Diocesan Bishop's Sec., Rev. Vinoy Daniel, 2320 Merrick Ave, Merrick NY 11566, Tel. (516) 377-3311 Cell (516)754-6110 Fax (516) 377-3322, Email: vinoydanielachen@yahoo.com.in or marthomadiocese@gmail.com

Diocesan Treasurer, Mr. Chacko Mathew, 18 Park Drive East, Syosset NY 11791, Tel. (516)364-1854 Cell (917)578-4679 Fax (516)377-3322, Email: sunnysusan2@gmail.com.ph, or martho madiocese@gmail.com

Periodicals

Mar Thoma Messenger

Church of God in Christ, Mennonite is listed under "C."

General Conference of Mennonite Brethren Churches is listed under "G."

Mennonite Church USA

Mennonite Church USA, with 109,000 members, is one of several denominations that traces their beginnings to the Protestant Reformation in the early 1500s. Mennonites hold common core beliefs with other Christian denominations, but they live out God's call in some ways that make them distinct. Mennonites believe in giving ultimate loyalty to God rather than to the nations in which they live. They believe that Jesus revealed a way for people to live peacefully and nonviolently, and they seek to be peacemakers in everyday life.

Mennonite church USA is committed to sharing its faith and passion for Jesus with others and is open to anyone who confesses Jesus Christ as Lord and Savior and wants to live as Jesus taught.

The vision statement of Mennonite Church USA reads, "God calls us to be followers of Jesus Christ and, by the power of the Holy Spirit, to grow as communities of grace, joy, and peace, so that God's healing and hope flow through us to the world."

Mennonite Church USA—its congregations, area conferences, Executive Board, ministry offices and churchwide agencies—focus on four priorities as it seeks to nurture missional congregations that join in God's activity in the world:

1. In our holistic witness we practice and proclaim the Gospel of Jesus Christ through a seamless web of evangelism, justice and peacebuilding.

2. We create a culture of call by calling, training anf nurturing new leaders.

3. We honor the dignity and value of all people, regardless of their race or ethnicity and denounce racist behavior.

4. We build global connections by fostering and developing partnerships with the broader body of Christ around the world. Mennonite Church USA lists as its strengths a high level of integrity recognized in both society and the religious community; high church attendance (90% of members attend church regularly); expanded global awareness through exposure to other world cultures; strong commitment to nonviolence and use of conflict resolution skills; above average giving to the work of the church; a natural communitarian impulse demonstrated by an emphasis on congregational relationships and mutual accountability; strong support of volunteer efforts, relief and service activities; and a holistic theology that holds word and deed together.

Headquarters

Newton office: 722 Main St., Newton KS 67114, Tel. (316)283-5100, Fax (316)283-0454, Email: info@mennoniteusa.org, Website: www.mennoniteusa.org, toll free number for all churchwide agencies (866)866-2872

Elkhart office: P.O. Box 1245, 1601 W. Beardsley Ave., Elkhart IN 46515-1245, Tel. (574)523-3040, Fax (574)293-1892, Email: info@mennoniteusa.org, Website: www.mennoniteusa.org, toll free number for all churchwide agencies (866)866-2872

Email: info@MennoniteUSA.org
Website: www.MennoniteChurchUSA.org

Officers

Moderator, Edward Diller, 30 Thomas Point Dr., Ft. Thomas KY 41075, Tel. (859)781-2796, edd@mennoniteusa.org

Moderator-elect, Dick Thomas, 2176 Lincoln Hwy. East, Lancaster PA 17602, Tel. (717)299-0436, ext. 306, richardt@mennoniteusa.org

Acting Executive Director, J. Ron Byler, P.O. Box 1245, 1601 W. Beardsley Ave., Elkhart IN 46515-1245, Tel. (574)523-3040, Fax (574)293-1892, ronb@mennoniteusa.org

Mennonite Education Agency, Executive Director, Carlos Romero, 63867 County Rd. 35, Suite 1, Goshen IN 46528-9621, Tel. (574)642-3164, Fax (574)642-4863, info@mennoniteeducation.org

Mennonite Mission Network, Executive Director, Stanley Green, P.O. Box 370, 1601 W. Beardsley Ave., Elkhart IN 46515-0370, Tel. (574)294-7523, Fax (574)294-8669, info@mennonitemission.net

Mennonite Mission Network, President, Larry Miller, P. O. Box 486, Goshen IN 46527, Tel. (574)533-9511, Fax (574)533-5264, mma@mma-online.org

Mennonite Publishing Network, Executive Director, Ron Rempel, 616 W. Walnut Ave., Scottdale PA 15683-1999, Tel. (800)245-7894, Fax (724)887-3111, info@mpn.net

Periodicals

The Mennonite, Leader, Rejoice!, Mennonite Historical Bulletin, Mennonite Quarterly Review, Purpose

Evangelical Methodist Church is listed under "E."

Fundamental Methodist Church, Inc. is listed under "F."

Methodist Church—please see The United Methodist Church.

The Missionary Church

The Missionary Church was formed in 1969 through a merger of the United Missionary Church (organized in 1883) and the Missionary Church Association (founded in 1898). It is evangelical and conservative with a strong emphasis on missionary work and church multiplication.

There are three levels of church government with local, district and general conferences. There are 13 church districts and 7 mission districts in the United States. The general conference meets every two years. The denomination operates one college [Bethel College, Mishawaka, IN] in the United States.

Headquarters

3811 Vanguard Dr., P.O. Box 9127, Ft. Wayne, IN 46899-9127, Tel. (260)747-2027 Fax (260) 747-5331

Media Contact, Pres., Rev. William Hossler
Email: ronphipps@mcusa.org
Website: www.mcusa.org

Officers

Pres., Rev. William Hossler
Sec., Rev. Dave Engbrecht
Treas., Darrel Schlabach
Director of U.S. Ministries, Rev. Robert Ransom
Director of World PartnersUSA, Rev. David Mann
Healthy Church Initiatives Coordinator, Dr. Dan Riemenschneider
Servant Leadership Coordinator, Rev. Greg Getz
Support Ministries Coordinator, Rev. Ron Phipps
Pastoral Leadership Institute Director, Rev. Greg Getz
Director of Development/Communications, Dr. Tom Murphy
Dir. of Ad. Services, Eric Smith
Director of Financial Services, Neil Rinehart
Coordinator of Church Multiplication, Rev. Jeff Getz
Coordinator of Ethnic Ministries, Rev. Jose Manuel Mendez
Missionary Men Liaison, Rev. Ron Phipps
Missionary Women Intl., Pres., Sharon Moore
Missionary Church Investment Foundation, Mr. Eric Smith

Periodicals

Missionary Church Today

Moravian Church in America (Northern Province, Southern Province)*

In 1735 German Moravian missionaries of the pre-Reformation faith of Jan Hus came to Georgia, in 1740 to Pennsylvania, and in 1753 to North Carolina. They established the American Moravian Church, which is broadly evangelical, ecumenical, liturgical, "conferential" in form of government and has an episcopacy as a spiritual office. The Northern and Southern Provinces of the church operate on a semi-autonomous basis.

Headquarters

Denominational offices or headquarters are called the Provincial Elders' Conference.
See addresses for Northern and Southern Provinces,

NORTHERN PROVINCE HEADQUARTERS
1021 Center St., P.O. Box 1245, Bethlehem, PA 18016-1245, Tel. (610)867-7566 Fax (610) 866-9223
Media Contact, Ms. Deanna Hollenbach

PROVINCIAL ELDERS' CONFERENCE, NORTHERN PROVINCE
Pres., Rev. David L. Wickmann, Email: dave@mcnp.org
Other Members: Glenn Hertzog, Stephen Gohdes, James Hicks, David Bennett, William Kiessling, JoEllen LaPrade, Jill Westbrook
Comptroller, Christina Giesler, 1021 Center St., P.O. Box 1245, Bethlehem, PA 18016-1245

NORTHERN PROVINCE
1021 Center St., P.O. Box 1245, Bethlehem, PA 18016-1245, Tel. (610)867-7566 Fax (610) 866-9223

Northern Province Pres., Rev. David L. Wickmann, P.O. Box 1245, Bethlehem, PA 18016-1245, Email: dave@mcnp.org
Eastern District Pres., Rev. David Bennett P.O. Box 1245, Bethlehem, PA 18016-1245
Western District
Pres., Rev. James T. Hicks, P.O. Box 386, Sun Prairie, WI 53590
Canadian District Pres., Rev. Stephen Gohdes, 600 Arcadia Dr. SE, Calgary, AB T2J 0B8, Email: sgohdes@shaw.ca

SOUTHERN PROVINCE HEADQUARTERS
459 S. Church St., Winston-Salem, NC 27101 Winston-Salem, NC 27108, Tel. (336)725-5811 Fax (336)723-1029
Website, www.moravian.org (for Moravian Church, Northern and Southern Provinces)

PROVINCIAL ELDERS' CONFERENCE, SOUTHERN PROVINCE
Pres., Rt. Rev.Wayne Burkette
Other Members, Ms. Donna Hurt; Rev. Richard Sides, Rt. Rev. Lane Sapp, Ms. Kathy Sparks
Asst. to Pres., Robert Hunter, Email: rhunter@mcsp.org

ALASKA PROVINCE
P.O. Box 545, 361 3rd Ave., Bethel, AK 99559

PROVINCIAL ELDERS' CONFERENCE, ALASKA PROVINCE
Pres., Rev.Peter Green
Vice-Pres., Frank Matthew, Sr.
Sec., Moses Owen
Treas., Arthur Sharp
Dir. of Theological Education, - Ray Caldwell
Email: gloria@mcnp.org, wburkette@mcsp.org
Website: www.moravian.org

Periodicals

The Moravian

Mormons—please see The Church of Jesus Christ of Latter-day Saints. See also Community of Christ.

National Association of Congregational Christian Churches

This association was organized in 1955 in Detroit, Michigan, by delegates from Congregational Christian Churches committed to continuing the Congregational way of faith and order in church life. Participation by member churches is voluntary.

Headquarters

P.O. Box 288, Oak Creek, WI 53154, Tel. (414)764-1620 Fax (414)764-0319
Media Contact, Assoc. Exec. Sec., Rev. Dr. Donald P. Olsen, 8473 So. Howell Ave., Oak Creek, WI 53154, Tel. (414)764-1620 Fax (414)764-0319
Email: naccc@naccc.org
Website: www.naccc.org

Officers

Exec. Sec., Rev. Dr. Thomas M. Richard, 8473 South Howell Ave., Oak Creek, WI 53154

Assoc. Exec. Secs., Rev. Phil Jackson and Rev. Dr. Donald P. Olsen

Periodicals
The Congregationalist

National Association of Free Will Baptists

This evangelical group of Armenian Baptists was organized by Paul Palmer in 1727 at Chowan, North Carolina. Another movement (teaching the same doctrines of free grace, free salvation and free will) was organized June 30, 1780, in New Durham, N.H., but there was no connection with the southern organization except for a fraternal relationship.

The northern line expanded more rapidly and extended into the West and Southwest. This body merged with the Northern Baptist Convention Oct. 5, 1911, but a remnant of churches reorganized into the Cooperative General Association of Free Will Baptists Dec. 28, 1916, at Pattonsburg, Mo.

Churches in the southern line were organized into various conferences from the beginning and finally united in one General Conference in 1921.

Representatives of the Cooperative General Association and the General Conference joined Nov. 5, 1935 to form the National Association of Free Will Baptists.

Headquarters
5233 Mt. View Rd., Antioch, TN 37013-2306, Tel. (615)731-6812 Fax (615)731-0771
Mailing Address, P.O. Box 5002, Antioch, TN 37011-5002
Media Contact, Exec. Sec., Keith Burden CMP
Email: webmaster@nafwb.org
Website: www.nafwb.org

Officers
Exec. Sec., Keith Burden CMP
Mod., Tim York, 623 Knollwood Drive, LaVergne, TN 37086

DENOMINATIONAL AGENCIES
Free Will Baptist Foundation, Dir., David Brown
Free Will Baptist Bible College, Pres., Mathew Pinson
International Missions Dept., Dir., Rev. James Forlines
Home Missions Dept., Dir., Rev. Larry Powell
Bd. of Retirement, Dir., Rev. D. Ray Lewis
Historical Commission, Chpsn., Dr. Darrell Holley, 3606 West End Avenue, Nashville, TN 37205
Comm. for Theological Integrity, Chpsn., Rev. Leroy Forlines, 3606 West End Avenue, Nashville, TN 37205
Music Commission, Chpsn., Chris Truett, 1936 Banks School Road, Kinston, NC 28504
Media Comm., Chpsn., Keith Fletcher, P.O. Box 17306, Nashville, TN 37217
Randall House Publications, Dir., Rev. Ron Hunter
Women Nationally Active for Christ, Exec. Sec., Danita High
Master's Men Dept., Dir., Kenneth Akers

Periodicals
ONE Magazine, Co-Laborer

National Baptist Convention of America, Inc.*

The National Baptist Convention of America, Inc., was organized in 1880. Its mission is articulated through its history, constitution, articles of incorporation and by-laws. The Convention (corporate churches) has a mission statement with fourteen (14) objectives including fostering unity throughout its membership and the world Christian community by proclaiming the gospel of Jesus Christ; validating and propagating the Baptist doctrine of faith and practice, and its distinctive principles throughout the world; and harnessing and encouraging the scholarly and Christian creative skills of its membership for Christian writing and publications.

Headquarters
777 S. R.L. Thornton Fwy., Ste. 205, Dallas, TX 75203, Tel. (214)946-8913 Fax (214)946-9619
Email: president@nbcamerica.net; djones@nbcamerica.net
Website: www.nbcamerica.net

Officers
Pres., Rev. Stephen J. Thurston, President, 1327 Pierre Ave., Shreveport, LA 71103, Tel. (773)224-5570 Fax (773)224-8200 Gen. Rec. Sec., Rev. Tolbert
Historian, Dr. Clarence C. Pennywell, 2016 Russell Rd., Shreveport, LA 71107
Corres. Sec., 6614 South Western Ave., Los Angeles, CA 90047
Administrative Assistant, Ms. LaJuanda Jones, Tel. (800)543-4019 x 10 / (214)942-3311 Fax (318)222-7512; Email: LaJuanda.jones@tx.twcbc.com

Periodicals
The Lantern

National Baptist Convention, U.S.A., Inc.*

The National Baptist Convention, one of the oldest African American organization in the nation, traces it history back to 1895. It was formed as a cosolidation of the Baptist Foreign Mission Convention (1880), Consolidated American Baptist Convention (1896), and the National Baptist Educational Convention (1882). Rev. W. H. Alpine of Alabama was the first president of the Baptist Foreign Mission Board which later became the Baptist Foreign Mission Convention, USA.

The constitution of the convention 1895 states:
Whereas, It is the sense of the Colored Baptists of the United States of America, convened in the city of Atlanta, Georgia, September 28, 1895 in the several organizations as 'The Baptist Foreign Mission Convention of the United States of America' hithero engaged in Mission work on the West Coast of Africa: and the 'National Baptist Convention' which

has been engaged in mission work in the United States of America; and the 'National Baptist Educational Convention,' which has sought to look after the educational interest that the interest of the way of the Kingdom of God requires that the several bodies above named should, and do now, unite in one body. Therefore, we do now agree to and adopt the following constitution:

This body shall become known and styled, The National Baptist Convention of the United States of America.

The object of this convention shall be "to do mission work in the United States of America, in Africa, and elsewhere and to foster the cause of education." Dr. L.M. Luke was elected the first Corresponding Secretary of the Foreign Board. In October, 1896 Rev. L.G. Jordan, pastor of the Union Baptist Church of Philadelphia was selected successor of Luke (The Epoch of Negro Baptists and The Foreign Mission Board, NBC, USA, Inc. Dr. Edward A. Freeman, The Central Seminary Press 1953.)

In September 1915 at the annual meeting of the convention the constitution was revised with the following changes:

The particular business and object of this Convention shall be to promote a growth and propagamation of religion, morality, and intelligence among the races of mankind, by engaging in missionary work in the United States of America, and elsewhere, by fostering the cause of education and publishing and circulating literature, and in providing the necessary ways and means for carrying on such work.

Headquarters
1700 Baptist World Center Dr., Nashville, TN 37207, Tel. (615)228-6292 Fax (615)226-5935Officers
Pres., Dr. William J. Shaw, 1700 Baptist World Center Dr., Nashville, TN 37207, Tel. (615)228-6292 Fax (615)226-5935
Gen. Sec., Dr. Harry Blake, Mt. Canaan Baptist Church, 1666 Alston St., Shreveport, LA 71101, Tel. (318)227-9993

Periodicals
Mission Herald

National Missionary Baptist Convention of America*
The National Missionary Baptist Convention of America was organized in 1988 as a separate entity from the National Baptist Convention of America, Inc., after a dispute over control of the convention's publishing efforts. The new organization intended to remain committed to the National Baptist Sunday Church School and Baptist Training Union Congress and the National Baptist Publishing Board.

The purpose of the National Missionary Baptist Convention of America is to serve as an agency of Christian education, church extension and missionary efforts. It seeks to maintain and safeguard full religious liberty and engage in social and economic development.

Headquarters
4269 S. Figueroa St., Los Angeles, CA 90037, Tel. (323)846-1950 Fax (323)846-1964
Media Contact, Dr. Melvin Von Wade, Sr.
Email: gensec@jiacom.net
Website: www.nmbca.com

Officers
Pres., Dr. C.C. Robertson, President, Dallas, Texas
Vice President-at-Large, Dr. Nehemiah Davis, Fort Worth, Texas
Vice Pres., Ecumenical Affairs, Dr. L.C. Firle Collins, MS
Vice Pres., Auxiliaries, Dr. Bernard Black, Phoenix, AZ
Vice Pres., Boards, Dr. A. Charles Bowie, Cleveland, OH
Vice Pres., Financial Affairs, Dr. Ray W. Williams, Oakland, CA
Pres., National Baptist Publishing Bd., Dr. T. B. Boyd, III, 6717 Centennial Blvd., Nashville, TN 37209
Gen. Sec., Dr. A. Wayne Johnson, 106 NE Ivy St., Portland, OR 97212, Tel. (503)281-4925 Fax (503)281-6520, Email: gensec@jiacom.net
Corres. Sec., Dr. Walter Houston, Houston, TX
Treas., Dr. William R. Lott, Chicago, IL
Rec. Sec., Dr. T.L. Brown, Dallas, TX

National Organization of the New Apostolic Church of North America
The New Apostolic Church of North America claims common origin with the Catholic Apostolic movement in England, which began with the calling of an apostle in 1832. The New Apostolic Church distinguished itself from the parent body in 1863 by recognizing a succession of Apostles.

Headquarters
3753 N. Troy St., Chicago, IL 60618
Media Contact: Winfred Jacob, Tel. (814)833-6063 Fax (814)833-6308
Email: info@nak.org
Website: www.nak.org

Officers
Pres., Rev. Leonard R. Kolb, 1703 Peninsula Drive, Erie, PA 16505-4242
Vice Pres., Rev. John W. Fendt, Jr., 2 Willets Ln., Plandome, NY 11030-1023
Treas. & Sec., Ellen E. Eckhardt, 6380 N. Indian Rd., Chicago, IL 60646
Asst. Treas.: Mr. K. Stefan Heinzelmann, 3753 N. Troy St. Chicago, IL 60618

Periodicals
Our Family; Vision

National Primitive Baptist Convention, Inc.
Throughout the years of slavery and the Civil War, the Negro population of the South worshipped with the white population in their various churches. At the time of emancipation, their white brethren helped them establish their own churches, granting

them letters of fellowship, ordaining their deacons and ministers and helping them in other ways.

The doctrine and polity of this body are quite similar to that of white Primitive Baptists, yet there are local associations and a national convention, organized in 1907.

Each church is independent and receives and controls its own membership. This body was formerly known as Colored Primitive Baptists.

Headquarters
6433 Hidden Forest Dr., Charlotte, NC 28213, Tel. (704)596-1508
Media Contact, Elder T. W. SamuelsOfficers

Officers
Natl. Convention, Pres., President – Elder Ernest Ferrell, Tallahassee, FL
Natl. Convention, Vice Pres., Elder Bernard Yates, Pensacola, FL
Natl. Convention, Secretary, Elder W. J. Williams, Tampa, Florida
Natl. Church School Training Union, Pres., Dr. Jonathan Yates, Mobile, AL
Natl. Ushers Congress, Pres., Dea.. Carl Batts, 21213 Garden View Dr., Maple Heights, OH 44137
Publishing Bd., Chpsn., Elder John R. Cox, Birmingham, AL
Women's Congress, Pres., Mother Ann Cartes, Dallas, TX
Natl. Laymen's Council, Pres., Dea. Densimore Robinson, Huntsville, AL
Natl. Youth Congress, Pres., Minister Jacques Mood, Concord, NC

National Spiritualist Association of Churches

This organization is made up of believers that Spiritualism is a science, philosophy and religion based upon the demonstrated facts of communication between this world and the next.

Headquarters
NSAC General Offices, Rev. Sharon L. Snowman, Secretary, P.O. Box 217, Lily Dale, NY 14752-0217
Media Contact, Rev. Lelia Cutler, 7310 Midfield St. #1, Norfolk, VA 23505-4126
Email: nsac@nsac.org
Website: www.nsac.org

Officers
Pres., Rev. Lelia Cutler, 7310 Midfield St. #1, Norfolk, VA 23505-4126
Vice Pres., Rev. Catherine Snell 23 Pleasant St. Windham, NH 03087
Sec., Rev. Sharon L. Snowman, P.O. Box 217, Lily Dale, NY 14752, Tel. (716)595-2000 Fax (716)595-2020
Treas., Peter Berg, 20916 Bellerive Dr., Pflugerville, TX 78660

OTHER ORGANIZATIONS
Department of Education, Rev. Barbara Starr, Director, 4245 Woodmont Road, Great Cacapon, WV 25422

Department of Lyceums, Rev. Arsenia Williams, Director, 10913 S. Parnell, Chicago, IL 60628
Department of Missionaries, Rev. E. Ann Otzelberger, Director, 4332 Woodlynne Lane, Orlando, FL 32812-7562
Department of Phenomenal Evidence, Revs. Brian and Lynn Kent, Directors 28-3rd Street 4308, Warren, RI 02885
Department of Public Relations, Mary Montgomery Clifford, Director, 2426 North Kimball Street, Chicago, IL 60647
Department of Publications, Joe Owen, Director, 5 Third St. Suite 724, San Francisco, CA 94103
NSAC Healing Center, Rev. Kathleen Rottino, President, 74 Scenic Dr., Lebanon, CT 06249
NSAC Minsterial Association, Rev. Barbara Star, NST, Pres., 4245 Woodmont Road, Great Cacapon, WV 25422
National Spiritualist Teachers Club, Rev. E. Ann Otzelberger, NST, Pres., 4332 Woodlynne Lane, Orlando, FL 32812
Spiritualist Healers League, Rev. E. Annotzelberger, NST President
Licentiate Ministers & Certified Mediums Society, Rev. Janet Tisdale, NST, Pres., 1616 N. Alta Mesa Drive #51, Mesa, AZ 85205
The Stow Memorial Foundation, Sec., Rev. Sharon L. Snowman, P.O. Box 217, Lily Dale, NY 14752, Tel. (716)595-2000 Fax (716)595-2020
Spiritualist Benevolent Society, Inc., P.O. Box 217, Lily Dale, NY 14752

Periodicals
The National Spiritualist, Spotlight

Netherlands Reformed Congregations

The Netherlands Reformed Congregations trace their denominational origin to several U.S. congreagtions in the latter half of the nineteenth century. In the early 1900s several more congregations were organized. After the Second Wolrd War, iimigration from the Netherlands gave rise to still more congregations, especially in Canada. Currently a little over half the mebership resides in Canada. Their sister denomination in the Netherlands is the Gereformeerde Gemeenten, which were organized in 1907.

Doctrinal standards are the confession of Faith (1561), the Heidelberg Catechism (1563), and the Canons of Dordt (1618-1619). This indicates the denomination is rooted in the Reformation of 1517. The congregation are divided into three Classes, which meet at least one a year. Every two years a Synod is held.

Headquarters
Media Contact, Rev. A.H. Verhoef, 1142 Lakeshore Rd. W, RR#3, St. Catharines, ON L2R 6P9 CANADA, Tel. (905)935-4934

OTHER ORGANIZATIONS
Netherlands Reformed Book and Publishing, 1233 Leffingwell NE, Grand Rapids, MI 49505

Periodicals

The Banner of Truth, Paul (mission magazine), Insight Into, Learning and Living

The New Church—please see General Church of the New Jerusalem.

North American Baptist Conference

Churches belonging to this conference emanated from Germany Baptist immigrants of more than a century ago. Although scattered across Canada and the U.S., they are bound together by a common heritage, a strong spiritual unity, a Bible-centered faith and a deep interest in missions. Their two main priorities are Leadership Development and Church Multiplication. Note, The details of general organization, officers, and periodicals of this body will be found in the North American Baptist Conference directory in the "Religious Bodies in the United States" section of this Yearbook.

Headquarters

1 S. 210 Summit Ave., Oakbrook Terrace, IL 60181, Tel. (630)495-2000 Fax (630)495-3301

Media Contact, Marlene Minor, Senior Leader/Stewardship and Communications

Email: serve@nabconf.org

Website: www.nabconference.org

Officers

Exec. Dir., Rev. Ron Berg, 1 So 210 Summit Ave., Oakbrook Terrace, IL 60181, Tel. (630)495-2000 Fax (630)475-3301, Email: RBerg@nabconf.org

OTHER ORGANIZATIONS

Church Extension Investors Fund, Dir., Les D. Collins

Periodicals

NABtoday

North American Old Roman Catholic Church (Archdiocese of New York)

This body is identical with the Roman Catholic Church in faith but differs from it in discipline and worship. The Mass is offered with the appropriate rite either in Latin or in the vernacular. All other sacraments are taken from the Roman Pontifical. This jurisdiction allows for married clergy.

PRIMATIAL HEADQUARTERS

60 ST. Felix St., Brooklyn, NY 11217-1206, Tel. (718)855-0600

Media Contact, Primate, Most Rev. Albert J. Berube

Email: info@orccna.org

Website: www.orccna.org

Officers

Primate, The Most Rev. Albert J. Berube

Diocese of New York, Ordinary, Most Rev. Albert J. Berube

Diocese of Montreal & French Canada, Ordinary, Most Rev. Gerard Marcoux

The Old Catholic Orthodox Church

The Old Catholic Orthodox Church (formerly, the Apostolic Orthodox Old Catholic Church) was founded in Illinois in the year 1985, originally as a Spanish speaking community of faith. It has now grown to include English speaking and other international provinces. We subscribe to the Apostles', Nicene and Athanasian Creeds as matters of faith. Along with upholding all sacraments of the One, Holy, Catholic and Apostolic Church.

Headquarters

The Most Reverend Jorge Rodriguez-Villa, Apostolic Primate (Presiding Bishop)

P.O. Box 80193, Rancho Santa Margarita, CA 92688, Tel. (323) 806-4045

Website: www.oldcatholicorthodoxchurch.org

Officers

The Most Reverend Jorge Rodriguez-Villa, Apostolic Primate (Presiding Bishop)

The Most Rev. William Anthony Harrison, Apostolic Vicar General

Old German Baptist Brethren Church

This group separated from the Church of the Brethren (formerly German Baptist Brethren) in 1881 in order to preserve and maintain historic Brethren Doctrine.

Headquarters

Vindicator Ofc. Ed., Steven L. Bayer, 6952 N. Montgomery County Line Rd., Englewood, OH 45322-9748, Tel. (937)884-7531

Periodicals

The Vindicator

Old Order Amish Church

The congregations of this Old Order Amish group have no annual conference. They worship in private homes. They adhere to the older forms of worship and attire. This body has bishops, ministers and deacons.

Der Neue Amerikanische Calendar

c/o Raber's Book Store, 2467 C R 600, Baltic, OH 43804, LeRoy Beachy, Beachy Amish Mennonite Church, 4324 SR 39, Millerburg, OH 44654, Tel./Fax (330)893-2883Officers

Old Order (Wisler) Mennonite Church

This body arose from a separation of Mennonites dated 1872, under Jacob Wisler, in opposition to what were thought to be innovations.

The group is in the Eastern United States and Canada. Each state, or district, has its own organization and holds semi-annual conferences.

Headquarters

Media Contact, Amos B. Hoover, 376 N. Muddy Creek Rd., Denver, PA 17517, Tel. (717)484-4849 Fax (717)484-104

Periodicals

Home Messenger, Exchange Messenger

Open Bible Churches

Open Bible Churches (formerly, Open Bible Standard Churches) originated from two revival movements, Bible Standard Conference, founded in Eugene, Oregon, under the leadership of Fred L. Hornshuh in 1919, and Open Bible Evangelistic Association, founded in Des Moines, Iowa, under the leadership of John R. Richey in 1932.

Similar in doctrine and government, the two groups amalgamated on July 26, 1935 as "Open Bible Standard Churches, Inc." with headquarters in Des Moines, Iowa.

The original group of 210 ministers has enlarged to incorporate over 2,500 ministers and 1,509 churches in 40 countries. The first missionary left for India in 1926. The church now ministers in Asia, Africa, South America, Europe, Canada, Mexico, Central America, and the Caribbean Islands.

Historical roots of the parent groups reach back to the outpouring of the Holy Spirit in 1906 at Azusa Street Mission in Los Angeles and to the full gospel movement in the Midwest. Both groups were organized under the impetus of pentecostal revival. Simple faith, freedom from fanaticism, emphasis on evangelism and missions and free fellowship with other groups were characteristics of the growing organizations.

The highest governing body of Open Bible Churches meets biennially and is composed of all ministers and one voting delegate per 100 members from each church. A National Board of Directors, elected by the national and regional conferences, conducts the business of the organization. Official Bible College is Eugene Bible College in Oregon.

Open Bible Standard Churches is a charter member of the National Association of Evangelicals and of the Pentecostal/Charismatic Churches of North America. It is a member of the Pentecostal World Conference.

NATIONAL OFFICE
2020 Bell Ave., Des Moines, IA 50315, Tel. (515)288-6761 Fax (515)288-2510
Media Contact, Exec. Dir., Communications & Resources, Jeff Farmer, Tel. (515)288-6761 Fax (515)288-2510
Email: info@openbible.org
Website: www.openbible.org

Officers
Pres., Jeffrey E. Farmer, 2020 Bell Ave., Des Moines, Iowa 50315, Tel. (515)288-6761 Fax. (515)288-2510, Email: jeff@openbible.org
Esq., Sec.-Treas., Teresa A. Beyer, 2020 Bell Ave., Des Moines, Iowa 50315, Tel. (515)288-6761 Fax (515)288-2510, Email: tbeyer@openbible.org
Dir., of Intl. Min., Vince S. McCarty, 2020 Bell Ave., Des Moines, Iowa 50315, Tel. (515)288-6761 Fax (515)288-2510, Email: missions@openbible.org

Periodicals
Message of the Open Bible

The (Original) Church of God, Inc.

This body was organized in 1886 as the first church in the United States to take the name "The Church of God." In 1917 a difference of opinion led this particular group to include the word (Original) in its name. It is a holiness body and believes in the whole Bible, rightly divided, using the New Testament as its rule and government.

Headquarters
P.O. Box 592, Wytheville, VA 24382
Media Contact, Gen. Overseer, Rev. William Dale, Tel. (800)827-9234

Officers
Gen. Overseer, Rev. William Dale
Asst. Gen. Overseer, Rev. Alton Evans

The Orthodox Anglican Church

This body was incorporated in 1964 as a self-governing Orthodox Anglican church. The Church is committed to the Biblical world view contained in the Holy Scriptures, confessed in the three ancient creeds of the Catholic Church (the Apostles', Nicene, and Athanasian Creeds), experienced in the Sacraments, and practiced through the use of orthodox editions of the Book of Common Prayer. The Church is the United States member of the Orthodox Anglican Communion, the creation of which it authorized in 1967. The Orthodox Anglican Communion is a fellowship of churches around the world that adhere to orthodox theology. In 1971 the Church opened its own theological educational institution: clergy in the United States are trained at the denomination's school, St. Andrew's Theological college and Seminary.

Headquarters
464 County Home Road, Lexington, NC 27292, Tel. (336)236-9565 Fax (336)236-4822, Website: www.orthodoxanglican.net
Email: eoc@orthodoxanglican.net
Website: www.orthodoxanglican.net

Officers
Presiding Bishop, The Most Rev. Scott McLaughlin, The Chancery Of The Archdiocese, 464 County Home Road, Lexington, NC 27292, Tel. (336) 236-9565 Fax (336)236-4822; Email: abpmclaughlin@orthodoxanglican.net

Periodicals
The Episcopal Orthodox Encounter

The Orthodox Church in America*

The Orthodox Church of America entered Alaska in 1794 before its purchase by the United States in 1867. Its canonical status of independence (autocephaly) was granted by its Mother Church, the Russian Orthodox Church, on April 10, 1970, and it is now known as The Orthodox Church in America.

139

Headquarters

P.O. Box 675, Syosset, NY 11791-0675, Tel. (516)922-0550 Fax (516)922-0954

Media Contact, Dir. of Ministries and Communications, V. Rev. Andrew Jarmus, PO. Box 675, Syosset, NY 11791, Tel. (516)922-0550 Fax (516)922-0954, Email: ajarmus@oca.org

Email: ajarmus@oca.org

Website: www.oca.org

Officers

HOLY SYNOD OF BISHOPS

RULING BISHOPS

Primate, Archbishop of Washington & New York, Metropolitan of All America & Canada, His Beatitude, Most Blessed Jonah, P.O. Box 675, Syosset, NY 11791

Archbishop of Pittsburgh & Western PA, Most Rev. Kyrill, P.O. Box R, Wexford, PA 15090

Archbishop of Dallas, Archbishop Dmitri, 4112 Throckmorton, Dallas, TX 75219

Archbishop of Detroit, Rt. Rev. Nathaniel, P.O. Box 309, Grass Lake, MI 49240-0309

Archbishop of Chicago, Rt. Rev. Job, 927 N. LaSalle, Chicago, IL 60610

Bishop of San Francisco and Los Angeles, Rt. Rev. Benjamin, 1520 Green Street, San Fransisco, CA 94123

Bishop of Ottawa and Canada, Rt. Rev. Seraphim, P.O. Box 179, Spencerville, ON K0E 1X0, Tel. (613)925-5226

Bishop of Boston, Rt. Rev. Nikon, P.O.Box 149, Southbridge, MA 01550, Tel. (508)764-3222

Bishop of Philadelphia and Eastern PA, Rt. Rev. Tikhon, P.O.Box 130, South Canaan, PA 18459

AUXILIARY BISHOPS

Bishop of Dearborn Heights, Rt. Rev. Irineu, 23300 Davison Ave. West, Detriot, MI 48223

Bishop of Mexico City, Rt. Rev. Alejo, Rio Consulado e Irapuato, Col. Penon de los banos, 15520 Mexico D.F.

RETIRED BISHOPS

Retired Metropolitan, Most Blessed Theodosius, 156 Rifgon Drive, Canonsburg, PA 15317

Retired Archbishop, Most Rev. Gregory, P.O.Box 94, Jackson, NJ 08527-0094

Retired Archbishop, Most Rev. Lazar, 37323 Hawkins Pickle Rd., Dewdney, BC, Canada V0M 1H0

Retired Bishop, Rt. Rev. Mark, 9511 Sun Pointe Dr., Boynton Beach, FL 33437

Retired Bishop, Rt. Rev. Varlaam, 37323 Hawkins Pickle Rd., Dewdney, BC, Canada V0M 1H0 6.Retired Bishop, Rt. Rev. Nikolai

Alumni Association of St. Herman Seminary, 414 Mission Rd., Kodiak, AK 99615-9985

Alumni Association of St. Tikhon Seminary, South Canaan, PA 18459

Alumni Association of St. Vladimir Seminary, 575 Scarsdale Rd., Crestwood, NY 10707

Orthodox Peace Fellowship, P.O. Box 390838, Cambridge, MA 02139

Orthodox Theological Society of America, 50 Goddard Ave., Brookline, MA 02445

Association of Romanian Orthodox Ladies' Auxiliaries of America, P.O. Box 309, Grass Lake, MI 49240

Association of Romanian Canadian Orthodox Ladies' Auxiliaries, Box 4023, Regina, SK, Canada S4P 3R9

Fellowship of Orthodox Christians in America, 10 Downs Drive, Wilkes-Barre, PA 18705

Orthodox Brotherhood USA, P.O. Box 309, Grass Lake, MI 49240

Orthodox Brotherhood of Canada, Box 4023, Regina, SK, Canada S4P 3R9

American Romanian Orthodox Youth, P.O. Box 309, Grass Lake, MI 49240

Project Mexico, P.O. Box 120028, Chula Vista, CA 91912

Orthodox Christian Adoption Referral Service, P.O. Box 675, Syosset, NY 11791

Fellowship of Orthodox Stewards, P.O. Box 675, Syosset, NY 11791

Orthodox Christian Publications Center, 4653 Memphis Villas South, Brooklyn, OH 44144

The Orthodox Presbyterian Church

On June 11, 1936, certain ministers, elders and lay members of the Presbyterian Church in the U.S.A. withdrew from that body to form a new denomination. Under the leadership of the late Rev. J. Gresham Machen, noted conservative New Testament scholar, the new church determined to continue to uphold the Westminster Confession of Faith as traditionally understood by Presbyterians and to engage in proclamation of the gospel at home and abroad.

The church has grown modestly over the years and suffered early defections, most notably one in 1937 that resulted in the formation of the Bible Presbyterian Church under the leadership of Dr. Carl McIntire. It now has congregations throughout the states of the continental United States.

The denomination is a member of the North American Presbyterian and Reformed Council and the International Council of Reformed Churches.

Headquarters

607 N. Easton Rd., Bldg. E, Box P, Willlow Grove, PA 19090-0920, Tel. (215)830-0900 Fax (215)830-0350

Media Contact, Stated Clerk, Rev. Donald J. Duff

Email: duff.1@opc.org

Website: www.opc.org

Officers

Moderator of General Assembly, The Rev. William Shishko, 65 Weber Ave., Malvene, NY 11565-1739., Tel. (516)437-3210 Email: strange.1@opc.org

Stated Clk., Rev. Donald J. Duff

Periodicals

New Horizons in the Orthodox Presbyterian Church

Patriarchal Parishes of the Russian Orthodox Church in the U.S.A.*

This group of parishes is under the direct jurisdiction of the Patriarch of Moscow and All Russia, His Holiness Aleksy II, in the person of a Vicar Bishop, His Grace Mercurius, Bishop of Zaraisk.

Headquarters

St. Nicholas Cathedral, 15 E. 97th St., New York, NY 10029, Tel. (212)996-6638 Fax (212) 427-5003
Media Contact, Sec. to the Bishop, Igumen Joseph, Tel. (212)996-6638
Email: bmercurius@ruscon.com
Website: www.russianchurchusa.org

Officers

Secretary to the Bishop, Igumen Joseph
Secretary of the Representation, Very Rev. Alexander Abramov

Pentecostal Assemblies of the World, Inc.

This organization is an interracial Pentecostal holiness of the Apostolic Faith, believing in repentance, baptism in Jesus's name and being filled with the Holy Ghost, with the evidence of speaking in tongues. It originated in the early part of the century in the Middle West and has spread throughout the country.

Headquarters

3939 Meadows Dr., Indianapolis, IN 46205, Tel. (317)547-9541 Fax (317)543-0513
Media Contact, Admin., John E. Hampton, Fax (317)543-0512
Website: www.pawinc.org

Officers

Presiding Bishop, Horace E. Smith
Suff. Bishop, A. Glenn Brady, General Secretary, Youngstown, OH
Bishops, Arthus Brazier; George Brooks; Ramsey Butler; Morris Golder; Francis L. Smith, Francis L.; Brooker T. Jones; C. R. Lee; Robert McMurray; Philip L. Scott; William L. Smith; Samuel A. Layne; Freeman M. Thomas; James E. Tyson; Charles Davis; Willie Burrell; Harry Herman; Jeremiah Reed; Jeron Johnson; Clifton Jones; Robert Wauls; Ronald L. Young; Henry L. Johnson; Leodis Warren; Thomas J. Weeks; Eugene Redd; Thomas W. Weeks, Sr.; Willard Saunders; Davis L. Ellis; Earl Parchia; Vanuel C. Little; Norman Wagner; George Austin; Benjamin A. Pitt; Markose Thopil; John K. Cole; Peter Warkie; Norman Walters; Alphonso Scott; David Dawkins
Gen. Sec, Suffragan Bishop Edward Roberts
Assist. Gen Sec., Suffragan Bishop A. Glenn Brady
Gen. Treas., Suffragan Bishop Mark C. Tolbert
Asst. Treas., Suffragan Bishop Carl A. Turner

Pentecostal Church of God

Growing out of the pentecostal revival at the turn of the 20th century, the Pentecostal Church of God was organized in Chicago on Dec. 30, 1919,

as the Pentecostal Assemblies of the U.S.A. The name was changed to Pentecostal Church of God in 1922; in 1934 it was changed again to The Pentecostal Church of God of America, Inc.; and finally the name became the Pentecostal Church of God (Incorporated.) in 1979.

The International Headquarters was moved from Chicago, Illinois to Ottumwa, Iowa, in 1927, then to Kansas City, Missouri, in 1933 and finally to Joplin, Missouri, in 1951.

The denomination is evangelical and pentecostal in doctrine and practice. Active membership in the National Association of Evangelicals and the Pentecostal/Charismatic Churches North America is maintained.

The church is Trinitarian in doctrine and teaches the absolute inerrancy of the Scripture from Genesis to Revelation. Among its cardinal beliefs are the doctrines of salvation, which includes regeneration; divine healing, as provided for in the atonement; the baptism in the Holy Ghost, with the initial physical evidence of speaking in tongues; and the premillennial second coming of Christ.

Headquarters

4901 Pennsylvania, P.O. Box 850, Joplin, MO 64802, Tel. (417)624-7050 Fax (417)624-7102
Media Contact, Gen. Sec., Wayman C. Ming Jr.
Email: generalsecretary@pcg.org
Website: www.pcg.org

Officers

Gen. Bishop., Dr. Charles G. Scott
Gen. Sec., Wayman C. Ming Jr.

OTHER GENERAL EXECUTIVES
Dir. of World Missions, Rev. Loyd L. Naten
Dir. of Indian Missions, Dr. C. Don Burke
Dir. of Youth Ministries, Rev. Joe Skiles, Jr.
Dir. of Home Missions, Rev. Harry O. "Pat" Wilson

ASSISTANT GENERAL SUPERINTENDENTS/ BISHOPS
Northwestern Division, Rev. Donald Manning
Southwestern Division, Rev. Jan Lake
North Central Division, Rev. Joseph Skiles, Sr.
South Central Division, Rev. John Norvell
Northeastern Division, Rev. Thomas E. Branham
Southeastern Division, Rev. C.W. Goforth

OTHER DEPARTMENTAL OFFICERS
Bus. Mgr., Gabriel Espinoza
Director of Women's Ministry, Mrs. Janice Scott

Periodicals

The Pentecostal Messenger

Pentecostal Fire-Baptized Holiness Church

Organized in 1918, this group consolidated with the Pentecostal Free Will Baptists in 1919. It maintains rigid discipline over members.

Headquarters

P.O. Box 261, La Grange, GA 30241-0261, Tel. (706)884-7742
Media Contact, Gen. Mod., Wallace B. Pittman, Jr.

Officers

Gen. Treas., Alan Sparkman, 1961 Norjon circle, Clio, SC 29525, Tel. (843)586-9095
Gen. Sec., Joel Powell, 16841 Springs Mill Rd. Lauringbury, NC 28352, Tel. (901)462-3379
Gen. Mod., Wallace B. Pittman, Jr.
Gen. Supt. Mission Bd., Jerry Powell, Rt. 1, Box 384, Chadourn, NC 28431

The Pentecostal Free Will Baptist Church, Inc.

The Cape Fear Conference of Free Will Baptists, organized in 1855, merged in 1959 with The Wilmington Conference and The New River Conference of Free Will Baptists and was renamed the Pentecostal Free Will Baptist Church, Inc. The doctrines include regeneration, sanctification, the Pentecostal baptism of the Holy Ghost, the Second Coming of Christ and divine healing.

Headquarters

P.O. Box 1568, Dunn, NC 28335, Tel. (910)892-4161 Fax (910)892-6876
Media Contact, Gen. Supt., Preston Heath
Email: pheath@intrstar.net
Website: www.pfwb.org

Officers

Gen. Supt., Rev. Preston Heath
Asst. Gen. Supt., Jim Wall
Gen. Sec., Mr. Stephen Garriss
Gen. Treas., Mr. Dewayne Weeks
Christian Ed. Dir., Rev. Randy Barker
World Witness Dir., Rev. Hobbs
Gen. Services Dir., Ms. Cathy Muzingo
Ministerial Council Dir., Rev. Ed Taturn
Ladies' Auxiliary Dir., Dollie Davis
Heritage Bible College, Pres., Dr. Dwarka Ramphal
Crusader Youth Camp, Dir., Rev. Randy Barker

OTHER ORGANIZATIONS
Heritage Bible College
Crusader Youth Camp
Blessings Bookstore, 1006 W. Cumberland St., Dunn, NC 28334, Tel. (910)892-2401

Periodicals

The Messenger

Philadelphia Yearly Meeting of the Religious Society of Friends*

PYM traces its roots to the yearly meeting of 1681 in Burlington, New Jersey. For more than three centuries, PYM has served Monthly Meetings and Quarterly Meetings throughout eastern Pennsylvania, southern New Jersey, eastern Maryland and Delaware.

Headquarters

Philadelphia Yearly Meeting, 1515 Cherry Street, Philadelphia, PA 19102-1479, Tel. (215)241-7000 Fax (215)241-7045 Website: www.pym.orgWebsite: www.pym.org

Officers

Presiding Clerk, Thomas Swain, 1515 Cherry Street, Philadelphia, PA 19102-1479
General Secretary, Arthur M. Larrabee

Periodicals

PYM News

Pillar of Fire

The Pillar of Fire was founded by Alma Bridwell White in Denver on Dec. 29, 1901 as the Pentecostal Union. In 1917, the name was changed to Pillar of Fire. Alma White was born in Kentucky in 1862 and taught school in Montana where she met her husband, Kent White, a Methodist minister, who was a University student in Denver.

Because of Alma White's evangelistic endeavors, she was frowned upon by her superiors, which eventually necessitated her withdrawing from Methodist Church supervision. She was ordained as Bishop and her work spread to many states, to England, and since her death to Liberia, West Africa, Malawi, East Africa, Yugoslavia, Spain, India and the Philippines.

The Pillar of Fire organization has a college and two seminaries stressing Biblical studies. It operates eight separate schools for young people. The church continues to keep in mind the founder's goals and purposes.

Headquarters

P.O. Box 9159, Zarephath, NJ 08890, Tel. (732)356-0102
Western Headquarters, 1302 Sherman St., Denver, CO 80203, Tel. (303)427-5462
Media Contact, 1st Vice Pres., Robert B. Dallenbach, 3455 W. 83 Ave., Westminster, CO 80031, Tel. (303)427-5462 Fax (303)429-0910
Email: info@zarephath.edu
Website: www.gospelcom.net/pof

Officers

Pres. & Gen. Supt., Dr. Robert B. Dallenbach
1st Vice Pres. & Asst. Supt., Rev. Joseph Gross
2nd Vice Pres./Sec.-Treas., Lois R. Stewart
Trustees, Kenneth Cope; S. Rea Crawford; Lois Stewart; Dr. Donald J. Wolfram; Robert B. Dallenbach; Rob W. Cruver; Joseph Gross

Plymouth Brethren—please see Christian Brethren.

Polish National Catholic Church of America*

After a number of attempts to resolve differences regarding the role of the laity in parish administration in the Roman Catholic Church in Scranton, Pennsylvania, this Church was organized in 1897. With the consecration to the episcopacy of the Most Rev. Francis Hodur, this Church became a member of the Old Catholic Union of Utrecht in 1907.

Headquarters

Office of the Prime Bishop, 1006 Pittston Ave., Scranton, PA 18505, Tel. (570)346-9131

Media Contact, Prime Bishop, Most Rev. Robert M. Nemkovich, 1006 Pittston Ave., Scranton, PA 18505, Tel. (570)346-9131 Fax (570)346-2188
Email: PNCCCenter@adelphia.net
Website: www.PNCC.org

Officers

Prime Bishop, Most Rev. Robert M. Nemkovich, 115 Lake Scranton Rd., Scranton, PA 18505
Central Diocese, Bishop, Rt. Rev. Anthony Mikovsky, 529 E Locust St. Scranton, PA 18505
Eastern Diocese, Bishop, Rt. Rev. Thomas J. Gnat, 166 Pearl St., Manchester, NH 03104
Buffalo-Pittsburgh Diocese, Bishop, Rt. Rev. Thaddeus S. Peplowski, 5776 Broadway, Lancaster, NY 14086
Western Diocese, Rt. Rev. Anthony D. Kopka, 920 N. Northwest Hwy., Park Ridge, IL 60068
Canadian Diocese, Bishop, Rt. Rev. Sylvester Bigaj, 880 Barton Steet East, Hamilton, ON L8L3B7, Canada
Ecumenical Officer, Rev. Robert M. Nemkovich, Jr.
Savonarola Theological Seminary, 1031 Cedar Avenue, Scranton, PA 18505 Rector: Most Rev. Robert M. Nemkovich Vice Rector: Rev. Dr. Czeslaw Kuliczkowski

Periodicals

God's Field, Polka

Evangelical Presbyterian Church is listed under "E."

General Assembly of the Korean Presbyterian Church in America is listed under "K"

Presbyterian Church in America

The Presbyterian Church in America is an Evangelical, Reformed covenant community of churches in the United States and Canada committed to a common doctrinal standard (The Westminster Standards), mutual accountability (representative church government), and cooperative ministry. The PCA traces its historical roots to the First General Assembly of the Church of Scotland of 1560, the establishment of the Presbytery of Philadelphia, 1789, and the General Assembly of the Southern Presbyterian Church, Augusta in 1861. Organized in 1973 by conservative churches formerly associated with the Presbyterian Church in the United States, the Church was first known as the National Presbyterian Church but changed its name in 1974 to the Presbyterian Church in America. The PCA seeks to be "Faithful to the Scriptures, True to the Reformed Faith, and Obedient to the Great Commission." In 1982 the Reformed Presbyterian Church, Evangelical Synod joined the PCA bringing with it a rich tradition that had antecedents in colonial America.

The PCA holds to the ancient creeds of the Church such as the Apostles' Creed and the Nicene Creed and has a firm commitment to its doctrinal standards, The Westminster Confession of Faith, Larger and Shorter Catechisms, that have been significant in Presbyterianism since 1645, These doctrinal standards reflect the distinctives of the Reformed tradition, Calvinism, and Covenant Theology. Ministers, ruling elders, and deacons are required to subscribe to the Westminster Standards in good faith. Individuals are received by a Session as communing members of the Church upon their profession of faith in Jesus Christ as Lord and Saviour, their promise to live a Christian lifestyle, and their commitment to worship and service in the Church.

The PCA is a connectional Church, led by ruling elders (lay leaders) and teaching elders (ministers). The Session governs a local congregation; the Diaconate carries out mercy ministries. The Presbytery is responsible for regional matters and the General Assembly is responsible for national matters in the USA and Canada. Cooperative ministry is carried out through over sixty Presbyteries and ten General Assembly Ministries.

The educational institutions of the Church are Covenant College of Lookout Mountain,GA and Covenant Theological Seminary of St. Louis, MO. The PCA and the Orthodox Presbyterian Church participate in a joint publication venture, Great Commission Publications, for the publication of Christian Education materials.

In its ecumenical relations the PCA is a member of the North American Presbyterian and Reformed Council, the National Association of Evangelicals, and the World Reformed Fellowship.

The General Assembly approved a statement of purpose, "It is the purpose of the PCA to bring glory to God as a worshiping and serving community until the nations in which we live are filled with churches that make Jesus Christ and His word their chief joy, and the nations of the world, hearing the Word, are discipled in obedience to the Great Commission."

The Church has grown beyond its origin in the southeastern states to have congregations in forty-nine states in the USA and in several provinces of Canada. Growth is due to the PCA's ministry in evangelism, discipleship, church planting, church renewal, and campus ministry. Indicative of her concern for cross-cultural ministry, the PCA has the largest international missionary force in Presbyterian Church history.

Headquarters

1700 N. Brown Rd., Lawrenceville, GA 30043-8122, Tel. (678)825-1000
Email: ac@pcanet.org
Website: www.pcanet.org

Officers

Moderator: Mr. Bradley Bradford, 4124 Oak Lawn Avenue, Dallas, TX 75219-3152 Phone: 214-528-9422. Email: brad@plantchurch.org
Stated Clerk/Coordinator of Administration – Dr. L. Roy Taylor, 1700 N. Brown Rd., Suite 105, Lawrenceville, GA 30043-8122, Tel. (678) 825-1100, Email: ac@pcanet.org

Christian Education & Publications Coordinator–Dr. Charles Dunahoo, 1700 N. Brown Rd., Suite 102, Lawrenceville, GA 30043-8122, Tel. (678)825-1100, Email: cep@pacnet.org
Mission to the World Coordinator–Dr. Paul D. Kooistra, 1600 N. Brown Rd., Lawrenceville, GA 30043-8141, Tel. (678)-823-0004, Email: mtw@mtw.org
Mission to North America Coordinator–Dr. James C. Bland, 1700 N. Brown Rd., Suite 101, Lawrenceville, GA 30043-8122, Tel. (678)825-1200, Email: mna@pcanet.org
Reformed University Ministries Coordinator–Dr. Rod Mays, 1700 N. Brown Rd., Suite 104, Lawrenceville, GA 30043-8122, Tel. (678) 825-1070, Email: rum@pcanet.org
PCA Foundation President–Mr. Randel Stair, 1700 N. Brown Rd., Suite 103, Lawrenceville, GA 30043-8122, Tel. (678)825-1040, Email: pcaf@pcanet.org
PCA Retirement and Benefits Inc., Pres.–Mr. Gary D. Campbell, 1700 North Brown Road, Suite 106, Lawrenceville, GA 30043-8143, Tel. (678)825-1260, Email: gcampbell@pcanet.org
Ridge Haven Conference Director–
Covenant College President–Dr. Niel Nielson, 14049 Scenic Highway, Lookout Mountain, GA 30750, Tel. (706)820-1560, Fax (706)820-2165, Email: webmaster@covenant.edu
Covenant Theological Seminary President–Dr. Bryan Chapell, 12330 Conway Rd., St. Louis, MO 63141, Tel. (314)434-4044, Fax (314)434-4819, Email: president@covenantseminary.edu

Periodicals
ByFaith, Equip, Covenant, Mission Report, The View

Presbyterian Church (U.S.A.)*

The Presbyterian Church (U.S.A.) was organized June 10, 1983, when the Presbyterian Church in the United States and the United Presbyterian Church in the United States of America united in Atlanta. The union healed a major division which began with the Civil War when Presbyterians in the South withdrew from the Presbyterian Church in the United States of America to form the Presbyterian Church in the Confederate States.

The United Presbyterian Church in the United States of America had been created by the 1958 union of the Presbyterian Church in the United States of America and the United Presbyterian Church of North America. Of those two uniting bodies, the Presbyterian Church in the U.S.A. dated from the first Presbytery organized in Philadelphia, about 1706. The United Presbyterian Church of North America was formed in 1858, when the Associate Reformed Presbyterian Church and the Associate Presbyterian Church united.

Strongly ecumenical in outlook, the Presbyterian Church (U.S.A.) is the result of at least 10 different denominational mergers over the last 250 years. A restructure, adopted by the General Assembly meeting in June 1993, has been implemented. The Presbyterian Church (U.S.A.) dedicated its new national offices in Louisville, Kentucky in 1988.

Headquarters
100 Witherspoon St., Louisville, KY 40202, Tel. (888)728-7228 Fax (502)569-5018
Media Contact, Assoc. Dir. for Communications, Barry Creech, Tel. (502)569-5515 Fax (502)569-8073
Email: presytel@pcusa.org
Website: www.pcusa.org

Officers
Mod., Rev Bruce Reyes-Chow, 100 Witherspoon St, Louisville KY 40202, Tel. (888)728-7228
Vice Mod., Rev. Bryon Wade, 100 Witherspoon St, Louisville KY 40202, Tel. (888)728-7228
Stated Clk., Rev. Gradye Parsons, 100 Witherspoon St, Louisville KY 40202, Tel. (888)728-7228

THE OFFICE OF THE GENERAL ASSEMBLY
100 Witherspoon St, Louisville KY 40202-1396, Tel. (888)728-7228 x. 5424 Fax (502)569-8005
Stated Clk., Rev. Gradye Parsons
Strategic Operations, Dir., Rev. Thomas Hay
Middle Governing Body Relations, Coord., Rev. Jill Hudson
Dept. of the Stated Clerk, Dir., Loyda Aja
Dept. of Constitutional Services, Dir., Rev. Mark Tammen
Ecumenical & Agency Relations, Dir., Rev. Robina Winbush
Dept. of Communication, Development & Technology, Dir., Rev. Kerry Clements
Dept. of Hist., Philadelphia, 425 Lombard St., Philadelphia, PA 19147, Tel. (215)627-1852 Fax (215)627-0509; Dir., Frederick J. Heuser, Jr.; Deputy Dir., Margery Sly

GENERAL ASSEMBLY MISSION COUNCIL
Exec. Dir., Linda Valentine
Deputy Exec. Dir. for Mission, Rev. Tom Taylor
Deputy Exec. Dir. for Communication & Funds Development, Eld Karen Schmidt
Deputy Exec. Dir. for Shared Services & Chief Financial Officer, Eld Joey Bailey
Theology, Worship & Education, Dir., Rev. Joseph Small
Evangelism & Church Growth, Dir., Rev. Eric Hoey
Peace & Justice, Dir, Eld Sara Lisherness
Relief & Development, Int Dir., Eld Sara Lisherness
World Mission, Dir., Rev. Hunter Farrell
Racial Ethnic & Women's Ministries/ Presbyterian Women, Dir., Rev. Rhashell Hunter

BOARD OF PENSIONS
200 Market St., Philadelphia, PA 19103-3298, Tel. (800)773-7752 Fax (215)587-6215
Pres., & CEO, Robert W. Maggs, Jr.

PRESBYTERIAN CHURCH (U.S.A.) FOUNDATION
200 E. Twelfth St., Jeffersonville, IN 47130, Tel. (812)288-8841 Fax (502)569-5980
Pres. & CEO, Robert E. Leech

PRESBYTERIAN CHURCH (U.S.A.) INVESTMENT & LOAN PROGRAM, INC.
Tel. (800)903-7457 Fax (502)569-8868
Pres. & CEO, James L. Hudson

144

PRESBYTERIAN PUBLISHING CORPORATION
Pres. & CEO, Marc Lewis

SYNOD EXECUTIVES
Alaska-Northwest, Rev. Joyce Emery Martin, Int., 217 6th Ave. N., Seattle, WA 98109, Tel. (206)448-6403

Boriquen in Puerto Rico, Rev. Edwin Quiles Rodriquez Int., Ave. Hostos Edificio 740, Cond. Medical Center Plaza, Ste. 216, Mayaguez, PR 00680, Tel. (787)832-8375

Covenant, Eld. Margaret Haney, 1911 Indian Wood Cir #B, Tel. (419)754-4050

Lakes & Prairies, Rev. Philip Brown, 8012 Cedar Ave. S., Bloomington, MN 55425-1210, Tel. (612)854-0144

Lincoln Trails, Rev. Carol McDonald and Rev. David Crittenden, 1100 W. 42nd St., Indianapolis, IN 46208-3381, Tel. (317)923-3681

Living Waters, Rev. Terry Newland, 318 Seaboard Ln, Ste. 205, Franklin, TN 37067, Tel. (615)261-4008

Mid-America, Vacant, 6400 Glenwood, Ste. 111, Overland Park, KS 66202-4072, Tel. (913)384-3020

Mid-Atlantic, Rev. David McKee, P.O. Box 27026, Richmond, VA 23261 7026, Tel. (804)342-0016

Northeast, Rev. Clinton McCoy and Eld Mary Lynne Flowers, 5811 Heritage Landing Dr., East Syracuse, NY 13057-9360, Tel. (315)446-5990

Pacific, Rev. Robert Brinks, 8 Fourth St., Petaluma, CA 94952-3004, Tel. (707)765-1772

Rocky Mountains, Rev. Zane Buxton, 7061 S University Blvd #206., Centennial, CO 80211, Tel. (303)477-9070

South Atlantic, Rev. Reginald Parsons, 118 E. Monroe St., Ste. 3, Jacksonville, FL 32202, Tel. (904)356-6070

Southern California & Hawaii, Eld Margy Wentz, Temp, 1501 Wilshire Blvd., Los Angeles, CA 90017-2293, Tel. (213)483-3840

Southwest, Rev. Janet DeVries, 401 E. 4th St. #A, Tucson, AZ 85705, Tel. (520)791-9600

The Sun, Rev. Judy R. Fletcher, 6100 Colwell Blvd #200, Irving, TX 75039, Tel. (214)390-1894

The Trinity, Rev. Bruce G. Stevens, 3040 Market St., Camp Hill, PA 17011-4599, Tel. (717)737-0421

Periodicals

American Presbyterians, Journal of Presbyterian History, Presbyterian News Service, Church & Society Magazine, Horizons, Presbyterians Today, Interpretation, Presbyterian Outlook

Primitive Advent Christian Church

This body split from the Advent Christian Church. All its churches are in West Virginia. The Primitive Advent Christian Church believes that the Bible is the only rule of faith and practice and that Christian character is the only test of fellowship and communion. The church agrees with Christian fidelity and meekness; exercises mutual watch and care; counsels, admonishes, or reproves as duty may require and receives the same from each other

as becomes the household of faith. Primitive Advent Christians do not believe in taking up arms.

The church believes that three ordinances are set forth by the Bible to be observed by the Christian church, (1) baptism by immersion; (2) the Lord's Supper, by partaking of unleavened bread and wine; (3) feet washing, to be observed by the saints' washing of one another's feet.

Headquarters

Media Contact, Sec.-Treas., Roger Wines, 1971 Grapevine Rd., Sissonville, WV 25320, Tel. (304)988-2668

Officers

Pres., Herbert Newhouse, 7632 Hughart Dr., Sissonville, WV 25320, Tel. (304)984-9277

Vice Pres., Roger Hammons, 273 Frame Rd., Elkview, WV 25071, Tel. (304)965-6247

Sec. & Treas., Roger Wines, 1971 Grapevine Rd., Sissonville, WV 25320, Tel. (304)988-2668

Primitive Baptists

This group of Baptists has churches in the United States, the Philippines, India and Africa. While they oppose centralization and modern mission boards, they believe in the circulation of the gospel. They preach salvation by grace alone.

Headquarters

P.O. Box 38, Thornton, AR 71766, Tel. (501) 352-3694

Media Contact, Elder W. Hartsel Cayce

Officers

Elder W. Hartsel Cayce

Elder Lasserre Bradley, Jr., Box 17037, Cincinnati, OH 45217, Tel. (513)821-7289

Elder S. T. Tolley, P.O. Box 68, Atwood, TN 38220, Tel. (901)662-7417

Periodicals

Baptist Witness

Primitive Methodist Church in the U.S.A.

Hugh Bourne and William Clowes, local preachers in the Wesleyan Church in England, organized a daylong meeting at Mow Cop in Staffordshire on May 31, 1807, after Lorenzo Dow, an evangelist from America, told them of American camp meetings. Thousands attended and many were converted but the Methodist church, founded by the open-air preacher John Wesley, refused to accept the converts and reprimanded the preachers.

After waiting for two years for a favorable action by the Wesleyan Society, Bourne and Clowes established The Society of the Primitive Methodists. This was not a schism, Bourne said, for "we did not take one from them ... it now appeared to be the will of God that we ... should form classes and take upon us the care of churches in the fear of God." Primitive Methodist missionaries were sent to New York in 1829. An American conference was established in 1840.

Missionary efforts reach into Guatemala, Spain and other countries. The denomination joins in federation with the Evangelical Congregational Church, the United Brethren in Christ Church and the Southern Methodist Church and is a member of the National Association of Evangelicals.

The church believes the Bible is the only true rule of faith and practice, the inspired Word of God. It believes in one Triune God, the Deity of Jesus Christ, the Deity and personality of the Holy Spirit, the innocence of Adam and Eve, the Fall of the human race, the necessity of repentance, justification by faith of all who believe, regeneration witnessed by the Holy Spirit, sanctification by the Holy Spirit, the second coming of the Lord Jesus Christ, the resurrection of the dead and conscious future existence of all people and future judgments with eternal rewards and punishments.

Headquarters
Media Contact, Pres., Rev. Kerry Ritts, 723 Preston Ln., Hatboro, PA 19040, Tel. (215)672-1576
Email: pmconf@juno.com
Website: www.primitivemethodistchurch.org

Officers
Pres., Rev. Kerry R. Ritts, 730 Preston Ln., Hatboro, PA 19040-2321, Tel.(215)672-1576
Vice Pres., Rev. Frank Hrabak, 1122 Frosty Hollow Rd., Langhorne, PA 19047-5719, Tel. (215)757-3049
Recording Secretary, Rev. David Sargent, 5021 Willow Ave., Bowling Green, FL 33834-2880, Tel. (863)375-9913
General. Secretary., Rev. David Allen, Jr., 1199 Lawrence St., Lowell, MA 01852-5526, Tel. (978)453-2052
Email: pahson@earthlink.net
Treas., Mr. Raymond C. Baldwin, 18409 Mill Run Ct., Leesburg, VA 20176-4583, Email: Rbaldwin32@aol.com

Progressive National Baptist Convention, Inc.*
This body held its organizational meeting in Cincinnati in November, 1961. Subsequent regional sessions were followed by the first annual session in Philadelphia in 1962.

Headquarters
601 50th Street, N.E., Washington, DC 20019, Tel. (202)396-0558 Fax (202)398-4998
Media Contact, Gen. Sec., Dr. Tyrone S. Pitts
Email: fmccraw@pnbc.org
Website: www.pnbc.org

Officers
CONVENTION OFFICERS
Dr. T. DeWitt Smith Jr., President
Dr. Carroll A. Baltimore Sr., 1st Vice President
Dr. James C. Perkins, 2nd Vice President
Dr. Tyrone S. Pitts, General Secretary

REGIONAL VICE PRESIDENTS
Dr. Frank Blackshear, Eastern Region
Rev David Peoples, Midwest Region
Dr. Wilbur Lewis, Southwest Region

Dr. Michael N. Harris, Southern Region
Dr. Francis Sarpong, International Region
Dr. Terry Streeter, Congress of Christian Education
Mrs. Brenda Tribett, Executive Director, Christian Education
Rev. James H. Hunter, Chairman, Mission Ministry
Dr. Earl Trent, Executive Director, Mission Ministry
Mrs. Arlene Tyler, Women's Department, 8220 Cheyenne St., Detroit, MI 48228
Mr. Wilmer Jones, Laymen's Department
The Rev. Samuel Nixon, Seminarian Development
Mr. Clifton Caldwell, Young Adult Men
Ms. Denise Carter-McCormick, Young Adult Women
Mrs. Rita Johnson, Principal, Nannie Helen Burroughs School, Tel. (202)398-5266

Protestant Reformed Churches in America
The Protestant Reformed Churches (PRC) have their roots in the sixteenth century Reformation of Martin Luther and John Calvin, as it developed in the Dutch Reformed churches. The denomination originated as a result of a controversy in the Christian Reformed Church in 1924 involving the adoption of the "Three Points of Common Grace." Three ministers in the Christian Reformed Church, the Reverends Herman Hoeksema, George Ophoff, and Henry Danhof, and their consistories (Eastern Avenue, Hope, and Kalamazoo, respectively) rejected the doctrine. Eventually these men were deposed, and their consistories were either deposed or set outside the Christian Reformed Church. The denomination was formed in 1926 with three congregations. Today the denomination is comprised of some twenty-eight churches (more than 7,000 members) in the USA and Canada. The presbyterian form of church government as determined by the Church Order of Dordt is followed by the PRC. The doctrinal standards of the PRC are the Reformed confessions - the Heidelberg Catechism, Belgic Confession of Faith, and Canons of Dordrecht. The doctrine of the covenant is a cornerstone of their teaching. They maintain an unconditional, particular covenant of grace that God establishes with His elect.

Headquarters
16511 South Park Ave., South Holland, IL 60473, Tel. (708)333-1314
Media Contact, Stated Clerk, Don Doezema, 4949 Ivanrest Ave., Grandville, MI 49418, Tel. (616)531-1490
Email: doezema@prca.org
Website: www.prca.org

Officers
Stat. Clk., Don Doezema, 4949 Ivanrest Ave., Grandville, MI 49418, Tel. (616)531-1490, Fax (616)531-3033, Email: doezema@prca.org

Periodicals
The Standard Bearer

Quakers—please see Friends.

Reformed Catholic Church

The Reformed Catholic Church was founded in 1988, and incorporated in 1989, as an alternative to the structures and strictures of the Roman Catholic Church, yet without denying basic catholic beliefs of faith and love, spirituality and community, prayer and sacramentality. The Reformed Catholic Church is a federation of independent churches offering a progressive alternative in the Catholic tradition. It is a newly formed rite, as in the tradition of the Orthodox churches of the Catholic tradition and the Old Catholic Church of Utrecht. It remains a Catholic Church, and its priests are considered Catholic priests.

Headquarters
P.O. Box 2, Worthington, OH 43085-9998
Email: PresidingBishop@reformedcatholic-church.org
Website: www.reformedcatholicchurch.org

Officers
Metropolitan Archbishop, Archbishop Phillip Zimmerman, DD RSJ, P.O. Box 2, Worthington, OH 43085-9998 Bishop David Frazee, DD RSJ, 1529 Runaway Bay, Suite 1 D Columbus, OH 43204 Bishop Patrick Batuyong, DD, 1712 Connally Drive, Atlanta, GA 30316 Bishop Peter Posthumus, DD OPJB, 255 Plymouth SE East Grand Rapids, MI 49506 Bishop Shane Price, DD, 825 N. 26th St. Bismark, ND 58501 Bishop Raelyn Scott, DD RCF, 2202 Greenwood, Weatherford, TX 76088

Reformed Church in America*

The Reformed Church in America was established in 1628 by the earliest settlers of New York. It is the oldest Protestant denomination with a continuous ministry in North America. Until 1867 it was known as the Reformed Protestant Dutch Church.

The first ordained minister, Domine Jonas Michaelius, arrived in New Amsterdam from The Netherlands in 1628. Throughout the colonial period, the Reformed Church lived under the authority of the Classis of Amsterdam. Its churches were clustered in New York and New Jersey. Under the leadership of Rev. John Livingston, it became a denomination independent of the authority of the Classis of Amsterdam in 1776. Its geographical base was broadened in the 19th century by the immigration of Reformed Dutch and German settlers in the midwestern United States. The Reformed Church now spans the United States and Canada.

The Reformed Church in America accepts as its standards of faith the Heidelberg Catechism, Belgic Confession and Canons of Dort. It has a rich heritage of world mission activity. It claims to be loyal to reformed tradition which emphasizes obedience to God in all aspects of life.

Although the Reformed Church in America has worked in close cooperation with other churches, it has never entered into merger with any other denomination. It is a member of the World Alliance of Reformed Churches, the World Council of Churches and the National Council of the Churches of Christ in the United States of America. In 1998 it also entered into a relationship of full communion with the Evangelical Lutheran Church in America, Presbyterian Church (U.S.A.), and the United Church of Christ by way of the Formula of Agreement. In 2007 it also entered into full communion with the Christian Reformed Church in North America.

Headquarters
475 Riverside Dr., New York, NY 10115, Tel. (212)870-3243 Fax (212)870-2499
Media Contact, Communication Officer, Paul Boice, 4500 60th St. SE, Grand Rapids, MI 49512, Tel. (616)698-7071 Fax (616)698-6606
Email: dmorris@rca.org
Website: www.rca.org

Officers
President, The Rev. James Seawood, 475 Riverside Dr., 18th Floor, New York, NY 10115
General Synod Council, Moderator, Rev. Dr. Carol Bechtel, 475 Riverside Dr., 18th Floor, New York, NY 10115
General Secretary, The Rev. Wesley Granberg-Michaelson, 475 Riverside Dr., 18th Floor, New York, NY 10115; 4500 60th St. S.E., Grand Rapids, MI 49512
Operations and Support, Director & Assistant Secretary, The Rev. Kenneth Bradsell
Global Mission, Director, The Rev. Jhonny Alicea-Baez
Leadership/Revitalization, Director, The Rev. Kenneth Eriks
Church Multiplication/Discipleship, Director, The Rev. Kenneth Eriks
Finance Services, Treasurer, Ms. Barbara Boers

Periodicals
Perspectives, RCA Today

Reformed Church in the United States

Lacking pastors, early German Reformed immigrants to the American colonies were led in worship by "readers." One reader, schoolmaster John Philip Boehm, organized the first congregations near Philadelphia in 1725. A Swiss pastor, Michael Schlatter, was sent by the Dutch Reformed Church in 1746. Strong ties with the Netherlands existed until the formation of the Synod of the German Reformed Church in 1793.

The Eureka Classis, organized in North and South Dakota in 1910 and strongly influenced by the writings of H. Kohlbruegge, P. Geyser and J. Stark, refused to become part of the 1934 merger of the Reformed Church with the Evangelical Synod of North America, holding that it sacrificed the Reformed heritage. (The merged Evangelical and Reformed Church became part of the United Church of Christ in 1957.) Under the leadership of pastors W. Grossmann and W. J. Krieger, the Eureka Classis in 1942 incorporated as the continuing Reformed Church in the United States.

The growing Eureka Classis dissolved in 1986 to form a Synod with four regional classes. An heir to the Reformation theology of Zwingli and Calvin, the Heidelberg Catechism, the Belgic Confession and the Canons of Dort are used as the confessional standards of the church. The Bible is strictly held to be the inerrant, infallible Word of God.

The RCUS supports Dordt College, Mid-America Reformed Seminary, New Geneva Theological Seminary, West Minster Theological Seminary in California, and Hope Haven. The RCUS is the official sponsor to the Reformed Confessing Church of Zaire.

Headquarters
Media Contact, Rev. Frank Walker Th.M., 6121 Pine Vista Way, Elk Grove City, CA 95758-4205, Tel. (661)827-9885
Email: TriWheeler@aol.com
Website: www.rcus.org

Officers
Pres., Rev. Vernon Pollema, 235 James Street, Shafter, CA 93263, Tel. (661)746-6907
Vice Pres., Rev. Robert Grossmann, Th.M., 1905 200th St., Garner, IA 50438, Tel. (515)923-3060
Stated Clk., Rev. Frank Walker Th.M., 5601 Spring Blossom St., Bakersfield, CA 93313-6025, Tel. (661)827-9885
Treas., Clayton Greiman, 2115 Hwy. 69, Garner, IA 50438, Tel. (515)923-2950

Reformed Episcopal Church

The Reformed Episcopal Church was founded December 2, 1873 in New York City by Bishop George David Cummins, an assistant bishop in the Protestant Episcopal Church from 1866 until his departure to found the new jurisdiction. Cummins and other evangelical Episcopalians were concerned about the exclusiveness propagated by what they perceived to be an excessive ritualism sweeping the church. Throughout the late 1860's evangelicals and ritualists clashed over ceremonies, vestments, open or closed communion, the Articles of Religion, interpretation of the meaning of the sacraments, and the understanding of Apostolic Succession.

In October, 1873, other bishops of the Protestant Episcopal Church publically attacked Cummins in major newspapers for his participation in an ecumenical communion service sponsored by the Evangelical Alliance. Cummins resigned from the Episcopal Church and drafted a call to organize a new Episcopal Church for the "purpose of restoring the old paths of their fathers". On December 2, 1873, a Declaration of Principle which expressed the evangelical understanding of the Articles of Religion was adopted. Dr. Charles Edward Cheney of Chicago was elected bishop to serve with Bishop Cummins. The Second General Council, meeting in May, 1874 in New York City, approved a Constitution and Canons and adopted the 1785 Proposed Book of Common Prayer for use in the New Church. Other notable early bishops (1876) included Rufus Nicholson, Edward Cridge, of Victoria, B.C., and Samuel Fallows through whom the episcopate of the church was perpetuated.

In recent years the Reformed Episcopal Church has revised the Book of Common Prayer to conform to the 1662 and 1928 Prayer Books. The Church continues to embrace the Thirty-Nine Articles of Religion, and has affirmed the Chicago-Lambeth Quadrilateral of 1886-1888.

From 1993 until 2003 the Reformed Episcopal Church was in dialogue with the Episcopal Church U.S.A. at which time it was discontinued.

The Reformed Episcopal Church subsequently became a member of the Common Cause Partnership, an association of traditional Anglicans, becoming a founding sub-jurisdiction of the Anglican Church in North America officially formed from that body in Ft. Worth, Texas in June, 2009.

The Reformed Episcopal Church presently consists of six geographic dioceses and one domestic missionary diocese in the United States and Canada. Active missionary work continues in several countries including Germany and Cuba. Previous missionary jurisdictions in India and Liberia have been granted autonomy.

Seminaries operated by the church are located in Philadelphia, PA, Houston, TX, and Summerville, SC.

The Reformed Episcopal Church is a member of the National Association of Evangelicals and the Anglican Church in North America.

Headquarters
826 2nd Ave, Blue Bell, PA 19422-1257, Tel. (215)483-1196 Fax (215)483-5235
Media Contact, Rt. Rev. Leonard Riches
Media Contact, Rt. Rev. Royal U. Grote, Jr., Church Growth Office, 211 Byrne Ave., Houston, TX 77009, Tel. (713)862-4929
Email: wycliffe@jps.net
Website: recus.org

Officers
President and Presiding Bishop, The Right Reverend Leonard W. Riches, M. Div., D.D., 85 Smithtown Road, Pipersville, PA 18947, Tel. (610)294-8001, Fax (610)294-8009
Vice President & Media Officer, Committee on Doctrine & Worship, Diocese of Mid-America (DMA), Diocese of the Northeast & Mid-Atlantic (DNE-MA), The Right Reverend Royal U. Grote, Jr., 4142 Dayflower, Katy, Texas 77449, Tel. (281)463-9454, or (800)732-3433, Fax (281)463-2304, Email: Royalrec1@aol.com

Secretary, Mrs. Tonya M. Forsberg, 826 Second Avenue Blue Bell, PA 19422, Tel. (610)292-9581, Fax (610)292-9853

Assistant Secretary, Mrs. Bonnie C. Abboud, 826 Second Avenue Blue Bell, PA 19422, Tel. (610)292-9581, Fax (610)292-9853

Treasurer and Commission on Theological Education, Board of Foreign Missions, The Venerable Dr. Jon W. Abboud, 826 Second Avenue Blue Bell, PA 19422, Tel. (610)292-9581, Fax (610)292-9853

Ecumenical Officer and Diocese of Mid-America (DMA), Suffragan, The Rt. Reverend Ray R. Sutton, 4327 Hollow Oak Dr., Dallas, TX 75287, Email: psalmwhosoever@aol.com

Committee on Constitution & Canons, The Venerable Dr. James T. Payne, P.O. Box 973, Missouri City, TX 77459, Tel. (713)434-1117

BISHOPS

DOW: Bishop (Organizing), St. Paul Church, The Rt. Rev. Richard Boyce, 2340 N. 155th St., Seattle, WA 98133, Email: bpboyce1@msn.com

Diocese of Western Canada & Alaska (DWC-A), The Rt Rev. Charles W. Dorrington, 70-7570 Tetayut, Saanichton, BC, Canada V8M 2H4, Tel. (250)727-3722, Email: recwcan@island.net

Diocese of Central & Eastern Canada (DC-EC), Rt. Rev. Michael Fedechko, 320 Armstrong St., New Liskeard, ON POJ 1PO, Tel. (705)645-4565, Email: trinityfed@hotmail.com

Diocese of Mid-America (DMA), The Rev. George B. Fincke, 1902 Centre Square, Moorhead, MN 56560, Email: KOGvicar@yahoo.com

DSE: Bishop Ordinary, Liberty RE Church, The Rt. Rev. Alphonza Gadsden, Sr., P.O. Box 657, St. Stephen, SC 29479-0657, Email: bishop gadsden@att..net

Diocese of the Northeast & Mid-Atlantic (DNE-MA), The Rt. Rev. David L. Hicks, 117 Redford Rd., Oreland, PA 19075, Email: bishophicks@comcast.net

The Rt. Rev. Gerhard Meyer, Richberg Str. #11, 34639 Schwarzenborn, Germany, Email: bischof.Meyer@rekd.de

Missionary Diocese of the Dentral States (MDCS), The Rt. Rev. Daniel R. Morse, 4011 Farmingham Woods Dr., Hermitage, TN 37076, Email: dmorse3738@aol.com

DOW: Bishop, St. Augustine Church The Rt. Rev. Winfield Mott, P.O. Box 2325, Deming, NM 88031, Email: staugustine@zianet.com,

Diocese of the Northeast & Mid-Atlantic (DNE-MA), Rt. Rev. David Hicks, Coadjutor, Rt. Rev. Daniel G. Cox, (semi-Retired), 826 Second Ave, Blue Bell, PA 19422, Tel. (610)292-9581, Fax (61)292-9853, Email: nicaea@aol.com

Diocese of the West (DOW), Organizing Bishop, The Rt. Rev. Richard Boyce, 2340 N. 155th St., Seattle, WA 98133, Phone: (206)525-1618, Fax: (206) 526-90 Email: bpboyce1@msn.com; Rt. Rev. Winfield Mott

Ordinary, Diocese of the Southeast (DSE), The Rt. Rev. Al Gadsden, 705 S. Main St., Summerville, SC 2948, Tel. (843)873-3451, Fax: (843)873-345, Email: bishopgadsden@att.net

Royal U. Grote, Jr., 211 Byrne Ave., Houston, TX 77009

James C. West, Sr., 408 Red Fox Run, Summerville, SC 29485

Robert H. Booth, 1611 Park Ave., #212, Quakertown, PA 18951

Gregory K. Hotchkiss, 318 E. Main St., Somerville, NJ 08876

George B. Fincke, 155 Woodstock Circle, Vacaville, CA 95687-3381

Daniel R. Morse, 11259 Wexford Dr., Eads, TN 38025

Michael Fedechko, Box 2532, New Liskeard, ON P0J 1P0

Charles W. Dorrington, 626 Blanshard St., Victoria, BC V8W 3G6

Ray R. Sutton, 17405 Muirfield Dr., Dallas TX 75287, Tel. (972)248 6505

OTHER ORGANIZATIONS

Bd. of Foreign Missions, Pres., Dr. Barbara J. West, 316 Hunters Rd., Swedesboro, NJ 08085, Tel. (609) 467-1641

Bd. of Natl. Church Extension, Pres., Rt. Rev. Royal U. Grote, Jr., 211 Byrne Ave., Houston, TX 77009, Tel. (713)862-4929

Publication Society, Pres., Rt. Rev. Royal U. Grote; 211 Byrne Ave., Houston, TX 77009, Tel. (713)862-4929, 7372 Henry Ave., Philadelphia, PA 19128 25-956-0655

The Reapers, Pres., Susan Higham, 472 Leedom St., Jenkintown, PA 19046

Committee on Women's Work, Pres., Joan Workowski, 1162 Beverly Rd., Rydal, PA 19046

Periodicals

Reformed Episcopalians

Reformed Mennonite Church

This is a small group of believers in Pennsylvania, Ohio, Michigan, Illinois, and Ontario, Canada who believe in non-resistance of evil, and non-conformity to the world and who practice separation from unfaithful worship. They believe that Christian unity is the effect of brotherly love and are of one mind and spirit. Their church was established in 1812 by John Herr who agreed with the teachings of Menno Simon as well as those of Jesus Christ.

Headquarters

Lancaster County only, Reformed Mennonite Church, 602 Strasburg Pike, Lancaster, PA 17602

Media Contact, Bishop, Glenn M. Gross. Tel. (717)697-4623

Email: beehlerg@quadro.net

Website: www.reformedmennonitechurch.org

Officers

Bishop Glenn M. Gross, 906 W. Grantham Rd., Mechanicsburg, PA 17055

Reformed Methodist Union Episcopal Church

The Reformed Methodist Union Episcopal church was formed after a group of ministers withdrew from the African Methodist Episcopal Church following a dispute over the election of ministerial delegates to the General Conference.

These ministers organized the Reformed Methodist Union church during a four-day meeting beginning on January 22, 1885 at Hills Chapel (now known as Mt. Hermon RMUE church), in Charleston, South Carolina. The Rev. William E. Johnson was elected president of the new church. Following the death of Rev. Johnson in 1896, it was decided that the church would conform to regular American Methodism (the Episcopacy). The first Bishop, Edward Russell Middleton, was elected, and "Episcopal" was added to the name of the church. Bishop Middleton was consecrated on Dec. 5, 1896, by Bishop P. F. Stephens of the Reformed Episcopal Church.

Headquarters

1136 Brody Ave., Charleston, SC 29407

Media Contact, Gen. Secretary, Brother Willie B. Oliver, P.O. Box 1995, Orangeburg, SC 29116, Tel. (803)536-3293

Officers

Bishop, Rt. Rev. Leroy Gethers, Tel. (803)766-3534

Asst. Bishop, Rt. Rev. Jerry M. DeVoe, Jr.

Gen. Sec., Brother Willie B. Oliver

Treas., Rev. Daniel Green

Sec. of Education, Rev. William Polite

Sec. of Books Concerns, Sister Ann Blanding

Sec. of Pension Fund, Rev. Joseph Powell

Sec. of Church Extension, Brother William Parker

Sec. of Sunday School Union, Sister Wine

Sec. of Mission, Rev. Warren Hatcher

Reformed Presbyterian Church of North America

Also known as the Church of the Covenanters, this church's origin dates back to the Reformation days of Scotland when the Covenanters signed their Covenants in resistance to the king and the Roman Church in the enforcement of state church practices. The Church in America has signed two Covenants in particular, those of 1871 and 1954. The Westminster Confession of Faith and the Larger and Shorter Catechism are among the subordinant standards of the denomination.

Headquarters

Media Contact, Stated Clk., James K. McFarland, 7408 Penn Ave., Pittsburgh, PA 15208, Tel. (412)731-1177 Fax (412)731-8861

Email: RPTrustees@aol.com

Website: www.reformedpresbyterian.org

Officers

Mod., The Rev. Dr. Jonathan Watt, 2907 Fifth Ave., Beaver Falls, PA, 15010, Tel. (724)846-5430

Clk., J. Bruce Martin, 310 Main St., Ridgefield Park, NJ 07660, Tel. (201)440-5993

Asst. Clk., Raymond E. Morton, 411 N. Vine St., Sparta, IL 62286, Tel. (618)443-3419

Stated Clk., James K. McFarland, 7408 Penn Ave., Pittsburgh, PA 15208, Tel. (412)731-1177

Geneva College, 3200 College Ave, Beaver Falls, PA 15010, Tel. (724)846-5100 Pres., Kenneth A. Smith, Ph.D.

Reformed Presbyterian Theological Seminary, 7418 Penn Ave., Pittsburgh, 15208, Tel. (412) 731-8690, Pres., The Rev. Jerry F. O' Neill, D.D.

Reformed Presbyterian Home, 2344 Perrysville Ave., Pittsburgh, PA 15214, Tel. (412)321-4139 Director, Margaret Hemphill

Crown and Covenant Publications, 7408 Penn Ave., Pittsburgh, PA 15208, Tel. (412)241-0436 Drew and Lynne Gordon Managing Editors.

Periodicals

The Witness, The Reformed Presbyterian Witness

Reformed Zion Union Apostolic Church

This group was organized in 1869 at Boydton, VA., by Elder James R. Howell of New York, a minister of the A.M.E. Zion Church, with doctrines of the Methodist Episcopal Church.

Headquarters

Rt. 1, Box 64D, Dundas, VA 23938, Tel. (804) 676-8509

Media Contact, Bishop G. W. Studivant

Officers

Exec. Brd., Chair, Rev. Hilman Wright, Tel. (804)447-3988

Sec., Joseph Russell, Tel. (804)634-4520

Religious Society of Friends (Conservative)

These Friends mark their present identity from separations occurring by regions at different times from 1845 to 1904. They hold to a minimum of organizational structure. Their meetings for worship, which are unprogrammed and based on silent, expectant waiting upon the Lord, demonstrate the belief that all individuals may commune directly with God and may share equally in vocal ministry.

They continue to stress the importance of the Living Christ and the experience of the Holy Spirit working with power in the lives of individuals who obey it.

YEARLY MEETINGS

North Carolina YM, Sidney Lee Kitchens, P.O.Box 4591, Greensboro, NC 27404, Tel. (252)587-2571

Iowa YM, Deborah Frisch, Clerk, 3400 King Dian Blvd, Des Moines, Iowa 50311

Ohio YM, Seth Hinshaw, Clerk, 61830 Sandy Ridge Road, Barnesville, OH 43713

Religious Society of Friends (Unaffiliated Meetings)

Though all groups of Friends acknowledge the same historical roots, 19th-century divisions in theology and experience led to some of the current organizational groupings. Many newer yearly meetings, have chosen not to identify with past divisions by affiliating in traditional ways with the larger organizations within the Society.

Headquarters

Central Yearly Meeting [Friends Evangel] (I), Supt., Michael Williams, P.O. Box 122, Westfield, IN 46074, Tel. (765)857-2347 Fax (765)857-2347, Website: www.centralyearly meetingoffriends.org

Intermountain Yearly Meeting (I), Clerk and Contact: Claire Leonard, Email: imymclerk@hotmail.com, Website: www.imym.org

North Pacific Yearly Meeting (I), Clerk, Helen Dart, Contact Person: Turtle Robb, P.O. Box 5023, Bellingham, WA 98227, Tel. (360)312-8234, Email: secretary@npym.org

Pacific Yearly Meeting (I), Clerk & Contact, Marilee Eusebio, Website: www.pacificyearly meeting.org

Email: margaretf@fwccamericas.org

Website: www.centralyearlymeetingof friends.org

Meetings

Central Yearly Meeting: 150 Members
Intermountain Yearly Meeting: 1,083 Members
North Pacific Yearly Meeting: 850 Members
Pacific Yearly Meeting: 1,453 Members

Periodicals

Western Friend, Friends Evangel

The Roman Catholic Church—please see The Catholic Church.

The Romanian Orthodox Church in America

The Romanian Orthodox Church in America is an autonomous Archdiocese chartered under the name of "Romanian Orthodox Archdiocese in America." The diocese was founded in 1929 and approved by the Holy Synod of the Romanian Orthodox Church in Romania in 1934. The Holy Synod of the Romanian Orthodox Church granted ecclesiastical autonomy in American Diocese on July 12, 1950. The Diocese continues to hold dogmatic and canonical ties with the Holy Synod and the Romanian Orthodox Patriarchate of Romania.

In 1951, approximately 40 parishes with their clergy from the United States and Canada separated from this church. In 1960, they joined the Russian Orthodox Greek Catholic Metropolia, now called the Orthodox Church in America, which reordained for these parishes a bishop with the title "Bishop of Detroit and Michigan."

On June 11, 1973 the Holy Synod of the Romanian Orthodox church elevated the Bishop of Romanian Orthodox Missionary Episcopate in America to the rank of Archbishop.

Headquarters

5410 N. Newland Ave. Chicago IL 60656, Tel. (773) 774-1677 Fax (773)774-1805

Media Contact, Archdiocesan Secretary, V. Rev. Fr. Daniel Adrian Ene, 56 Andrews Street, Victor, NY 14564-1262

Tel/Fax: 585-924-8737, Email: frdaniel@romanianholytrinity.org

Email: ArchNicolae@aol.com, romarch67@aol.com

Website: www.romarch.org

Officers

Archbishop: His Eminence Dr. Nicolae Condrea, 5410 N. Newland Ave. Chicago IL 60656, Tel. (773)774-1677 Fax (773)774-1805; Email: romarch67@aol.com

Vicar: V. Rev. Fr. Nicholas Apostola, 44 Midland St., Worcester, MA 01602-4217, Tel. (508)845-0088 Fax (508)845-8850, Email: frnick@stnicholaschurch.org

Inter-Church Relations, Dir., V. Rev. Fr. Nicholas Apostola, 44 Midland St., Worcester, MA 01602-4217, Tel. (508)845-0088; Fax (508)845-8850

Email: frnick@stnicholaschurch.org

Periodicals

Credinta-The Faith

The Romanian Orthodox Episcopate of America

This body of Eastern Orthodox Christians of Romanian descent is part of the Autocephalous Orthodox Church in America.

Headquarters

2535 Grey Tower Rd., Jackson, MI 49201, Tel. (517)522-4800, Website: www.roea.org

Mailing Address, P.O. Box 309, Grass Lake, MI 49240-0309

Media Contact, Ed. -Sec., Rev. Archdeacon David Oancea, P.O.Box 185, Grass Lake, MI 49240-0185, Tel. (517)522-3656

Email: chancery@roea.org

Website: www.roea.org

Officers

Ruling Hierarch, Most Rev. Archbishop Nathaniel Popp

P.O. Box 309, Grass Lake, MI 49240-0309

Periodicals

Solia-The Herald, Good News- Buna Vestire (in Canada only)

The Russian Orthodox Church Outside of Russia

This group was organized in 1920 to unite in one body of dioceses the missions and parishes of the Russian Orthodox Church outside of Russia. The governing body, set up in Constantinople, was sponsored by the Ecumenical Patriarchate. In November 1950, it came to the United States. The Russian Orthodox Church Outside of Russia emphasizes being true to the old traditions of the Russian Church. In May 2007, it re-established communion with the Moscow Patriarchate.

Headquarters
75 E. 93rd St., New York, NY 10128, Tel. (212)534-1601 Fax (212)426-1086
Media Contact, Dep. Sec., Nicholas A. Ohotin, Tel: (212)534-1610 x 37
Email: nohotin@synod.com

SYNOD OF BISHOPS
Pres., His Eminence Metropolitan Hilarion
Vice Pres., His Eminence Archbishop Kyrill, Tel: (212)534-1601

Periodicals
Living Orthodoxy, Orthodox Family, Orthodox Russia, Pravoslavnaya Rus, Pravoslavnaya Zhisn, Orthodox America

The Salvation Army

The Salvation Army, founded in 1865 by William Booth (1829-1912) in London, England, and introduced into America in 1880, is an international religious and charitable movement organized and operated on a paramilitary pattern and is a branch of the Christian church. To carry out its purposes, The Salvation Army has established a widely diversified program of religious and social welfare services which are designed to meet the needs of children, youth and adults in all age groups.

Headquarters
615 Slaters Ln., Alexandria, VA 22313, Tel. (703)684-5500 Fax (703)684-5538
Media Contact: National Community Rel. & Dev. Secretary, Major George Hood, Tel. (703)684-5526 Fax (703)684-5538 Email: george_hood@usn.salvationarmy.org
Email: george_hood@usn.salvationarmy.org
Website: www.salvationarmyusa.org

Officers
Natl. Commander, Commissioner Israel L. Gaither
Natl. Chief Sec., Colonel David Jeffrey
Natl. Community Relations and Development Secretary, Dir., Major George Hood

TERRITORIAL ORGANIZATIONS
Central Territory, 10 W. Algonquin Rd., Des Plaines, IL 60016, Tel. (847)294-2000 Fax (847)294-2299; Territorial Commander, Commissioner Barry Swanson
Eastern Territory, 440 W. Nyack Rd., P.O. Box C-635, West Nyack, NY 10994, Tel. (914)620-7200 Fax (914)620-7766; Territorial Commander, Commissioner Lawrence Moretz
Southern Territory, 1424 Northeast Expressway, Atlanta, GA 30329, Tel. (404)728-1300 Fax (404)728-1331; Territorial Commander, Commissioner Maxwell Feener
Western Territory, 180 E. Ocean Blvd., Long Beach, CA, Tel. (562)436-7000 Fax (562)491-8792; Territorial Commander, Commissioner Philip Swyers

Periodicals
The War Cry

The Schwenkfelder Church

The Schwenkfelders are the spiritual descendants of the Silesian nobleman Caspar Schwenkfeld von Ossig (1489-1561), a scholar, reformer, preacher and prolific writer who endeavored to aid in the cause of the Protestant Reformation. A contemporary of Martin Luther, John Calvin, Ulrich Zwingli and Phillip Melanchthon, Schwenkfeld sought no following, formulated no creed and did not attempt to organize a church based on his beliefs. He labored for liberty of religious belief, for a fellowship of all believers and for one united Christian church.

He and his cobelievers supported a movement known as the Reformation by the Middle Way. Persecuted by state churches, ultimately 217 Schwenkfelders exiled from Silesia emigrated to Pennsylvania in six migrations, 1731 - 1734. The largest migration, about 180 landed at Philadel-phia Sept. 22, 1734. In 1782, the Society of Schwenk-felders, the forerunner of the present Schwenkfelder Church, was formed. The church was incorporated in 1909.

The Schwenkfelder Church is a voluntary association of six Schwenkfelder Churches at Palm, Worcester, Lansdale, Norristown and two in Philadelphia, Pennsylvania.

They practice adult baptism, dedication and baptism of children, and observe the Lord's Supper regularly with open Communion. In theology, they are Christo-centric; in polity, congregational; in missions, world-minded; in ecclesiastical organization, ecumenical.

The ministry is recruited from graduates of accredited theological seminaries. The churches take leadership in ecumenical concerns through ministerial associations, community service and action groups, councils of Christian education and other agencies.

Headquarters
105 Seminary St., Pennsburg, PA 18073, Tel. (215)679-3103
Media Contact, David W. Luz
Email: info@schwenkfelder.com

Officers
Mod., H. Drake Williams, Jr., Paoli, PA
Vice Mod., Darlene Jones, Green Lane, PA
Sec., Leah Tyson, Norristown, PA
Treas., Pat McGinnis, Central Schwenkfelder Church, Worcester, PA 19490

Periodicals
The Schwenkfeldian

Separate Baptists in Christ

The Separate Baptists in Christ are a group of Baptists found in Indiana, Ohio, Kentucky, Tennessee, Virginia, West Virginia, Florida and

North Carolina dating back to an association formed in 1758 in North Carolina and Virginia.

Today this group consists of approximately 100 churches. They believe in the infallibility of the Bible, the divine ordinances of the Lord's Supper, feetwashing, baptism and that those who endureth to the end shall be saved.

The Separate Baptists are Arminian in doctrine, rejecting both the doctrines of predestination and eternal security of the believer.

At the 1991 General Association, an additional article of doctrine was adopted. "We believe that at Christ's return in the clouds of heaven all Christians will meet the Lord in the air, and time shall be no more," thus leaving no time for a literal one thousand year reign. Seven associations comprise the General Association of Separate Baptists.

Headquarters
Media Contact, Clk., Greg Erdman, 10102 N. Hickory Ln., Columbus, IN 47203, Tel. (812)526-2540
Email: mail@separatebaptist.org
Website: www.separatebaptist.org

Officers
Mod., Rev. Jim Goff, 1020 Gagel Ave., Louisville, KY 40216
Asst. Mod., Rev. Jimmy Polston, 785 Kitchen Rd., Mooresville, IN 46158, Tel. (317)831-6745
Clk., Greg Erdman, 10102 N. Hickory Ln., Columbus, IN 47203, Tel. (812)526-2540
Asst. Clk., Rev. Mattew Cowan, 174 Oak Hill School Rd., Lot 30, Smiths Grove, KY 42171, Tel. (270)678-5599

Serbian Orthodox Church in the U.S.A. and Canada*
The Serbian Orthodox Church is an organic part of the Christian Orthodox Church. As a local church it received its autocephaly from Constantinople in 1219 A.D.

In 1921, a Serbian Orthodox Diocese in the United States of America and Canada was organized. In 1963, it was reorganized into three dioceses, and in 1983 a fourth diocese was created for the Canadian part of the church. The Serbian Orthodox Church in the USA and Canada received its administrative autonomy in 1928. However, it remains canonically an integral part of the Serbian Orthodox Patriarchate with its see in Belgrade. The Serbian Orthodox Church is in absolute doctrinal unity with all other local Orthodox Churches.

Headquarters
St. Sava Monastery, P.O. Box 519, Libertyville, IL 60048, Tel. (847)367-0698
Email: oea@oea.serbian-church.net
Website: oea.serbian-church.net

BISHOPS
Metropolitan of Midwestern America, Most Rev. Metropolitan Christopher

Bishop of Canada, Georgije, 5A Stockbridge Ave., Toronto, ON M8Z 4M6, Tel. (416)231-4009
Bishop of Eastern America, Rt. Rev. Bishop Mitrophan, 138 Carriage Hill Dr., Mars, PA 16046, Tel. (724)772-8866
Diocese of Western America, Bishop Maxim, 2541 Crestline Terr., Alhambra, CA 91803, Tel. (818)264-6825

OTHER ORGANIZATIONS
Brotherhood of Serbian Orth. Clergy in U.S.A. & Canada, Pres., V. Rev. Dennis Pavichevich
Federation of Circles of Serbian Sisters
Serbian Singing Federation

Periodicals
The Path of Orthodoxy

Seventh-day Adventist Church
The Seventh-day Adventist Church grew out of a worldwide religious revival in the mid-19th century. People of many religious persuasions believed Bible prophecies indicated that the second coming or advent of Christ was imminent.

When Christ did not come in the 1840s, a group of these disappointed Adventists in the United States continued their Bible studies and concluded they had misinterpreted prophetic events and that the second coming of Christ was still in the future. This same group of Adventists later accepted the teaching of the seventh-day Sabbath and became known as Seventh-day Adventists. The denomination organized formally in 1863.

The church was largely confined to North America until 1874, when its first missionary was sent to Europe. Today, over 65,961 congregations meet in 203 countries and areas of the world. Membership exceeds 16 million and increases between three and a half to four percent each year.

In addition to a mission program, the church has the largest worldwide Protestant parochial school system with approximately 7,597 schools with more than 1,545,000 students on elementary through college and university levels.

The Adventist Development and Relief Agency (ADRA) helps victims of war and natural disasters, and many local congregations have community service facilities to help those in need close to home.

The church also has a worldwide publishing ministry with 61 printing facilities producing magazines and other publications in over 369 languages and dialects. In the United States and Canada, the church sponsors a variety of radio and television programs, including Christian Lifestyle Magazine, It Is Written, Breath of Life, Ayer, Hoy, y Mañana, Voice of Prophecy, and La Voz de la Esperanza.

The North American Division of Seventh-day Adventist includes 58 Conferences which are grouped together into nine organized Union Conferences. The various Conferences work under the general direction of these Union Conferences.

153

Headquarters

12501 Old Columbia Pike, Silver Spring, MD 20904-6600, Tel. (301)680-6000

Media Contact, Dir., Communication, Rajmund Dabrowski

Email: kjones@gc.adventist.org

Website: www.adventist.org

WORLD-WIDE OFFICERS

Pres., Jan Paulsen

Sec., Matthew A. Bediako

Treas., Robert E. Lemon

WORLD-WIDE DEPARTMENTS

Adventist Chaplaincy Ministries, Dir., Gary R Councell

Children's Ministries, Dir., Linda Mei Lin Koh

Education, Dir.,C. Garland Dulan

Communication, Dir., Rajmund Dabrowski

Family Ministries, Dir., Ronald M. Flowers

Health Ministries, Dir., Allan R. Handysides

Ministerial Assoc., Dir., —

Public Affairs & Religious Liberty, Dir., John Graz

Publishing, Dir., Howard F Faigao

Sabbath School & Personal Ministries, Jonathan Kuntaraf

Stewardship, Dir., Erika Puni

Trust Services, Jeffrey K. Wilson

Women's Ministries, Heather-Dawn Small

Youth, Baraka G. Muganda

NORTH AMERICAN OFFICERS

Pres., Don C. Schneider

Vice Pres., Larry D Blackmer; Debra Brill; Alvin M. Kibble; R. Ernest Castillo

Sec., G. Alexander Bryant

Treas., Thomas Evans

Assoc. Treas., C. Michael Park; Delbert L. Johnson; Kenneth W. Osborn, Marshall L Chase, Patricia L. Horst

NORTH AMERICAN ORGANIZATIONS

Atlantic Union Conf., P.O. Box 1189, South Lancaster, MA 01561-1189; Pres., Donald G. King

Canada, Seventh-day Adventist Church in Canada (see Dir. 4)

Columbia Union Conf., 5427 Twin Knolls Rd., Columbia, MD 21045; Pres., David Weigley

Lake Union Conf., P.O. Box 287, Berrien Springs, MI 49103; Pres., Don Livesayt

Mid-America Union Conf., P.O. Box 6128, Lincoln, NE 68506; Pres., Roscoe J. Howard III

North Pacific Union Conf., Pres., 5709 N 20th Street, Ridgefield, WA 98642-7742; Pres., Max C. Torkelson II

Pacific Union Conf., P.O. Box 5005, Westlake Village, CA 91359; Pres., Ricardo B. Graham

Southern Union Conf., P.O. Box 849, Decatur, GA 30031; Pres., Gordon L. Retzer

Southwestern Union Conf., P.O. Box 4000, Burleson, TX 76097; Pres., Max A. Trevino

Periodicals

ADRA Works, The Adventist Chaplain, Adventist Review, ASI Magazine, Children's Friend, Christian Record, College and University Dialogue, Collegiate Quarterly, Cornerstone Youth Resource Magazine, Cornerstone Connections, Elder's Digest, Encounter, For God and Country, Geoscience Reports, Evangelist, Message, Ministry, Mission, Origins, Our Little Friend, Primary Treasure, Publishing Mirror, Shabbat Shalom, Shepherdess International Journal, Signs of the Times, Transmissions, Vibrant Life, Voice of Prophecy News, Winner, Women of Spirit, Young and Alive, Youth Ministry ACCENT

Seventh Day Baptist General Conference, USA and Canada

Seventh Day Baptists emerged during the English Reformation, organizing their first churches in the mid-1600s. The first Seventh Day Baptists of record in America were Stephen and Ann Mumford, who emigrated from England in 1664. Beginning in 1665 several members of the First Baptist Church at Newport, R.I. began observing the seventh day Sabbath, or Saturday. In 1671, five members, together with the Mumfords, formed the first Seventh Day Baptist Church in America at Newport.

Beginning about 1700, other Seventh Day Baptist churches were established in New Jersey and Pennsylvania. From these three centers, the denomination grew and expanded westward. They founded the Seventh Day Baptist General Conference in 1802.

The organization of the denomination reflects an interest in home and foreign missions, publications and education. Women have been encouraged to participate. From the earliest years religious freedom has been championed for all and the separation of church and state, advocated.

Seventh Day Baptists are members of the Baptist World Alliance and Baptist Joint Committee. The Seventh Day Baptist World Federation has 17 member conferences on six continents.

Headquarters

Seventh Day Baptist Center, 3120 Kennedy Rd., P.O. Box 1678, Janesville, WI 53547-1678, Tel. (608)752-5055 Fax (608)752-7711 Media Contact, Ex. Dir., Robert Appel Financial Dir., Morgan D. Shepard

Email: sdbgen@inwave.com

Website: www.seventhdaybaptist.org

OTHER ORGANIZATIONS

Seventh Day Baptist Missionary Society, Exec. Dir., Kirk Looper, 119 Main St., Westerly, RI 02891

Seventh Day Bapt. Bd. of Christian Ed., Exec. Dir., Rev. Andrew Camenga, Box 115, Alfred Station, NY 14803

Women's Soc. of the Gen. Conference, Pres., Mrs. Marjorie Jacob, P.O. Box 122, Pomona Park, FL 32181-0122

American Sabbath Tract & Comm. Council, Dir. of Communications, Rev. Kevin J. Butler,

3120 Kennedy Rd., P.O. Box 1678, Janesville, WI 53547

Seventh Day Baptist Historical Society, Historian, Nicholas Kersten, 3120 Kennedy Rd., P.O. Box 1678, Janesville, WI 53547

Seventh Day Baptist Center on Ministry, Dir. of Pastoral Services, Rev. Gordon Lawton, 3120 Kennedy Rd., P.O. Box 1678, Janesville, WI 53547

Periodicals

Sabbath Recorder

Southern Baptist Convention

The Southern Baptist Convention was organized on May 10, 1845, in Augusta, Georgia. Cooperating Baptist churches are located in all 50 states, the District of Columbia, Puerto Rico, American Samoa and the Virgin Islands. The members of the churches work together through 1,182 district associations and 42 state conventions or fellowships. The Southern Baptist Convention has an Executive Committee and 12 national agencies - four boards, six seminaries, one commission, and one auxiliary organization.

The purpose of the Southern Baptist Convention is "to provide a general organization for Baptists in the United States and its territories for the promotion of Christian missions at home and abroad and any other objects such as Christian education, benevolent enterprises, and social services which it may deem proper and advisable for the furtherance of the Kingdom of God". (Constitution, Article II)

The Convention exists in order to help the churches lead people to God through Jesus Christ.

From the beginning, there has been a mission desire to share the Gospel with the peoples of the world. The Cooperative Program is the basic channel of mission support. In addition, the Lottie Moon Christmas Offering for Foreign Missions and the Annie Armstrong Easter Offering for Home Missions support Southern Baptists' world mission programs.

In 2008, there were approximately 5,541 foreign missionaries serving in foreign countries and more than 5,611 home missionaries serving in North America.

Headquarters

901 Commerce St., Nashville, TN 37203, Tel. (615)244-2355

Media Contact, Vice Pres. for Convention Relations, Roger S. Oldham, Tel. (615)244-2355 Fax (615)782-8684

Email: bmerrell@sbc.net

Website: www.sbc.net

Officers

Pres., Johnny M. Hunt, 11905 Highway 92, Woodstock, GA 30188

Recording Sec., John Yeats, 1250 MacArthur Dr., Alexandria, LA 71303

Executive Committee, Pres., Morris H. Chapman; Vice Pres., Convention News, Will Hall; Vice Pres., Convention Relations, Roger S. Oldham; Vice Pres., Convention Policy, Augie Boto; Vice Pres., Cooperative Program, Bob Rodgers

GENERAL BOARDS AND COMMISSION

International Mission Board, Pres., Jerry A. Rankin, 3806 Monument Ave, Richmond, VA 23230, Tel. (804)353-6655, ext. 1207

North American Mission Board, Pres., Geff Hammond, 4200 No. Point Pkwy., Alpharetta, GA 30022-4176, Tel. (770) 410-6519

Guidestone Financial Resources, Pres., O. S. Hawkins, 2401 Cedar Springs Rd, Dallas, TX 75201, Tel. (214)720-4700

LifeWay Christian Resources, Pres., Thomas Rainer, One Lifeway Plaza, Nashville, TN 37234, Tel. (615)251-2605

Ethics and Religious Liberty Commission, Pres., Richard D. Land, 901 Commerce St., Suite 550, Nashville, TN 37203, Tel. (615)782-8404

STATE CONVENTIONS

Alabama, Rick Lance, 2001 E. South Blvd., Montgomery, AL 36116, Tel. (334)288-2460

Alaska, David N. Baldwin, 1750 O'Malley Rd., Anchorage, AK 99516, Tel. (907)344-9627

Arizona, Steve Bass, 2240 N. Hayden Rd., Ste. 100 Scottsdale, AZ 85257, Tel. (480)945-0880

Arkansas, Emil Turner, 10 Remington Dr., Little Rock, AR 72204, Tel. (501)376-4791 x 5102

California, Fermin A. Whittaker, 678 E. Shaw Ave., Fresno, CA 93710, Tel. (559)229-9533 x230

Colorado, Mark Edlund, 7393 So. Alton Way, Centennial, CO 80112, Tel. (303)771-2480

Dakota Baptist Convention, Jim Hamilton, P.O.Box 777, Sioux Falls, SD 57101, Tel. (605)271-9224

District of Columbia, Rev. Jeffrey Haggray, 1628 16th St. NW, Washington, DC 20009, Tel. (202)265-1526

Florida, John Sullivan, 1230 Hendricks Ave., Jacksonville, FL 32207, Tel. (904)396-2351 x8101

Georgia, J. Robert White, 6405 Sugarloaf Pkwy., Duluth, GA 30097, Tel. (770)455-0404

Hawaii, Veryl F. Henderson, 2042 Vancouver Dr., Honolulu, HI 96822, Tel. (808)946-9581 x229

Illinois, Nate Adams, 3085 Stevenson Dr, Springfield, IL 62794, Tel. (217)786-2600

Indiana, Stephen P. Davis, 900 N. High School Rd., Indianapolis, IN 46214, Tel. (317)241-9317

Iowa, Jimmy L. Barrentine, Suite #27, 2400 86th St., Des Moines, IA 50322, Tel. (515)278-4369

Kansas-Nebraska, R. Rex Lindsay, 5410 W. Seventh St., Topeka, KS 66606, Tel. (785)228-6800

Kentucky, Bill F. Mackey, 13420 Eastpoint Centre Dr., Louisville, KY 40223, Tel. (502)245-4101

Louisiana, David E. Hankins, 1250 MacArthur Dr., Alexandria, LA 71303, Tel. (318)448-3402

Maryland-Delaware, David H. Lee, 10255 Old Columbia Rd., Columbia, MD 21046, Tel. (410)290-5290

Michigan, Michael R. Collins, 8420 Runyan Lake Rd., Fenton, MI 48430, Tel. (810)714-1907

Minnesota-Wisconsin, Leo Endel, 519 16th St. SE, Rochester, MN 55904, Tel. (507)282-3636

Mississippi, James R. Futral, 515 Mississippi St., Jackson, MS 39201, Tel. (601)968-3800

Missouri, David Tolliver, 400 E. High St., Jefferson City, MO 65101, Tel. (573)635-7931 x200

Montana, Fred Hewett, 1130 Cerise Rd., Billings, MT 59101-7336, Tel. (406)252-7537

Nevada, Thane E. Barnes, 406 California Ave., Reno, NV 89509, Tel. (775)786-0406

New England, James Wideman, 87 Lincoln St., Northborough, MA 01532, Tel. (508)393-6013 x224

New Mexico, Joseph L. Bruce, P.O. Box 94485, Albuquerque, NM 87199, Tel. (505)924-2300 x11

New York, Terry M. Robertson, 6538 Baptist Way, East Syracuse, NY 13057, Tel. (315)433-1001

North Carolina, Milton A. Hollifield Jr., 205 Convention Dr., Cary, NC 27511, Tel. (919)467-5100 x102

Northwest, Bill Crews, 3200 NE 109th Ave., Vancouver, WA 98682, Tel. (360)882-2100

Ohio, Jack P. Kwok, 1680 E. Broad, Columbus, OH 43203, Tel. (614)827-1777

Oklahoma, Anthony L. Jordan, 3800 N. May Ave., Oklahoma City, OK 73112, Tel. (405)942-3800

Pennsylvania-South Jersey, David C. Waltz, 4620 Fritchey St., Harrisburg, PA 17109, Tel. (717)652-5856

Puerto Rico/Virgin Islands, Carlos Rodriguez, MSC 811, 138 W. Churchhill, San Juan, PR 00926-6023

South Carolina, James W. Austin, 190 Stoneridge Dr., Columbia, SC 29210, Tel. (803)765-0030 x1200

Tennessee, James M. Porch, 5001 Maryland Way, Brentwood, TN 37027, Tel. (615)371-2090

Texas, (BGCT) Baptist General Convention of Texas, Randel Everett, 333 N. Washington, Dallas, TX 75246, Tel. (214)828-5301

Texas, (SBTC) Southern Baptists of Texas, James W. Richards, 4500 State Hwy. 360, Grapevine, TX 76051, Tel. (817)552-2500

Utah-Idaho, Rob Lee, 12401 South 450 East #G-1, Draper, UT 84020, Tel. (801)572-5350

Virginia, (BGAV) Baptist General Association of Virginia, John V. Upton Jr., 2828 Emerywood Pkwy. Richmond, VA 23226, Tel. (804)915-2430 x223

Virginia, (SBCV) Southern Baptist Conservatives of Virginia, Jeffrey B. Ginn, 4101 Cox Rd., Suite 100, Glen Allen, VA 23060, Tel. (804)270-1848

West Virginia, Terry L. Harper, Number One Missions Way, Scott Depot, WV 25560, Tel. (304)757-0944

Wyoming, Lynn Nikkel, 3925 Casper Mountain Rd., Casper, WY 82601, Tel. (307)472-4087

Periodicals
The Commission, SBC Life, On Mission

Southern Methodist Church

Organized in 1939, this body is composed of congregations desirous of continuing in true Biblical Methodism and preserving the fundamental doctrines and beliefs of the Methodist Episcopal Church, South. These congregations declined to be a party to the merger of the Methodist Episcopal Church, The Methodist Episcopal Church, South and the Methodist Protestant Church into The Methodist Church.

Headquarters
425 Broughton St., Orangeburg, SC 29115, Tel. (803)536-1378 Fax (803)535-3881
Media Contact, Pres., Rev. John T. Hucks, Jr.
Email: smchq@juno.com; smpresid@bellsouth.net

Officers
Pres., Rev. John T. Hucks, Jr.
Dir. Of Admin. & Finance, Rev. Cecil Clark, 425 Broughton St., Orangeburg, SC 29115
Director of Foreign Missions, Rev. Marvin Clark, 425 Broughton St., Orangeburg, SC 29115
Southern Methodist College Pres., Rev. Gary Briden, P.O. Box 1027, Orangeburg, SC 29116-1027

Periodicals
The Southern Methodist

Sovereign Grace Believers

The Sovereign Grace Believers are a contemporary movement which began its stirrings in the mid-1950s when some pastors in traditional Baptist churches returned to a Calvinist-theological perspective.

The first "Sovereign Grace" conference was held in Ashland, Kentucky, in 1954 and since then, conferences of this sort have been sponsored by various local churches on the West Coast, Southern and Northern states and Canada. This movement is a spontaneous phenomenon concerning reformation at the local church level. Consequently, there is no interest in establishing a Sovereign Grace Baptist "Convention" or "Denomination." Each local church is to administer the keys to the kingdom.

Most Sovereign Grace Believers formally or informally relate to the "First London" (1646), "Second London" (1689) or "Philadelphia" (1742) Confessions.

There is a wide variety of local church government in this movement. Many Calvinist Baptists have a plurality of elders in each assembly. Other Sovereign Grace Believers, however, prefer to function with one pastor and several deacons.

Membership procedures vary from church to church but all require a credible profession of faith in Christ, and proper baptism as a basis for membership.

Calvinistic Baptists financially support gospel efforts (missionaries, pastors of small churches at home and abroad, literature publication and distribution, radio programs, etc.) in various parts of the world.

Headquarters

Media Contact, Corres., Jon Zens, P.O. Box 548, St. Croix Falls, WI 54024, Tel. (651)465-6516
Fax (651)465-5101
Email: jon@searchingtogether.org
Website: www.searchingtogether.org

Periodicals

Searching Together, Sound of Grace

The Swedenborgian Church*

Founded in North America in 1792 as the Church of the New Jerusalem, the Swedenborgian Church was organized as a national body in 1817 and incorporated in Illinois in 1861. Its biblically-based theology is derived from the spiritual, or mystical, experiences and exhaustive biblical studies of the Swedish scientist and philosopher Emanuel Swedenborg (1688-1772).

The church centers its worship and teachings on the historical life and the risen and glorified present reality of the Lord Jesus Christ. It looks with an ecumenical vision toward the establishment of the kingdom of God in the form of a universal Church, active in the lives of all people of good will who desire and strive for freedom, peace and justice for all. It is a member of the NCCC and active in many local councils of churches.

With churches and groups throughout the United States and Canada, the denomination's central administrative offices and its seminary, "Swedenborg House of Studies" are located in Newton, Massachusetts and Berkeley, California. Affiliated churches are found in Africa, Asia, Australia, Canada, Europe, the United Kingdom, Japan, South Korea and South America. Many philosophers and writers have acknowledged their appreciation of Swedenborg's teachings.

Headquarters

11 Highland Ave., Newtonville, MA 02460, Tel. (617)969-4240 Fax (617)964-3258
Media Contact, Central Ofc. Mgr., Martha Bauer
Email: manager@swedenborg.org
Website: www.swedenborg.org

Officers

Pres., Rev. Christine Laitner, 10 Hannah Court, Midland, MI 48642
Vice Pres., James Erickson, 1340 Snelling Ave, N.,St. Paul, MN 55108
Rec. Sec., Susan Wood, 552 Fifth Court, Palm Beach Gardens, FL 33410-5105
Treas., Lawrence Conant, 290 Berlin St., Apt. 89, Clinton, MA 01510, Tel. (978) 368-6269
Ofc. Mgr., Martha Bauer, Tel. (617)969-4240
Email: manager@swedenborg.org

Periodicals

The Messenger, Our Daily Bread

Syriac-Greek Antiochian Orthodox Catholic Church

The Syriac-Greek Antiochian Orthodox Catholic Church was established in May of 1892 as the American Orthodox Catholic Archdiocese of America, and was canonized by His Holiness Ignatius Peter III, Patriarch of Antioch. It was this same Patriarch that issued the Bull for the consecration of its first Archbishop Metropolitan, Timotheos Vilathi, as Patriarch Ignatius later named him. The Syriac-Greek Antiochian Orthodox Catholic Church is an Eastern Rite jurisdiction but also has a Western Rite Vicariate. It is the only true Byzantine Rite jurisdiction coming from Metropolitan Timotheos. The Synod of Bishops is referred to as the "Syriac-Greek Antiochian Synod of Bishops." First parishes of this jurisdiction were established in Wisconsin among Belgians, Italians, Slavs, and other ethnic groups. After Archbishop Timotheos' consecration, parishes were later formed in Ohio, Indiana, Illinois, and New York, and some missionary work begun in Canada. Today parishes exist throughout the United States and several foreign countries.

After much disagreement with the Syriac Patriarchate concerning administration, especially in the appointing of bishops, and the Christology issue, i.e., Christ's two Natures that surfaced at the Council of Chalcedon, Archbishop Timotheos separated from the Patriarchate. A Consistory was convened on January 1, 1910 concerning the future of the Archdiocese of America. The Bishops agreed upon and decided that, "Our reality as a branch, a part of the true Catholic and Orthodox Church of God, is not dependent upon the recognition of any ecclesiastical authority outside the Councils of our own American Ecclesiastical Consistory and National Synod of Bishops and Clergy. "Archbishop Timotheos believed strongly in the truths of the Council of Chalcedon and all the Ecumenical Councils, and the right of the American Church to name its own bishops, and from then on the Church was known as Autocephalous and severed from the Patriarchate of Antioch. However, after this time several schisms occurred that gave way to some heretical and newly established "churches" that caused the Church to eventually be renamed "Syriac-Greek Antiochian Orthodox Catholic." In 1960, the Greek Apostolic Succession of Antioch was added to the Church when Bishop Joseph John Skureth was consecrated an Archbishop. This was done at St Nicholas Russian Orthodox Greek Catholic Cathedral in New York New York. It was presided over by Archbishop Konstantin (Nikolaevich Wendland) and assisted by Bishop Dositheus (Ivanchenko). His Holiness Patriarch Aleksij of the Russian Orthodox Church, consecrated Archbishop Konstantin in 1958. Although this was done through the Russian Orthodox Church, the Apostolic Succession of Archbishop Konstantin is traced back to His Holiness Gregorios (Haddad) IV, Greek Patriarch of Antioch through Patriarch Aleksij."

In 1980, after the retirement for health reasons of Archbishop John, Archbishop Joseph of Blessed

157

Memory became the newly enthroned Metropolitan Primate of the Church. He possessed Apostolic Succession from both the Syrian and Greek Antiochian Orthodox Churches later giving the Synod its the name of Syriac-Greek Antiochian Orthodox Catholic Church. In 1987, before the death of Metropolitan Joseph, a meeting was held at St. Paul's Monastery in LaPorte, Indiana and Very Right Reverend Archimandrite Stephen (Thomas) was duly elected Metropolitan Primate. He was consecrated Bishop on October 18th, 1987, by Metropolian Joseph assisted by Archbishop George of Chicago (IL) and Bishop Norman of Central Indiana at St. Mary's Chapel, LaPorte, Indiana. In the following year Bishop Stephen was enthroned as Metropolitan Primate. Metropolitan Archbishop Stephen has caused the Church to grow throughout the world. In 1994-96, he endured many sufferings in Colorado as the result of some clergy who went astray and who took part in a conspiracy to ruin the name of the Archbishop for their own gain. These clergy were since deposed of their faculties and offices. An Old Catholic group in Canada quickly made some, which were not yet ordained deacons or priests, and without having completed seminary studies, instant priests. Some of these, within days, were made bishops, and most left this Old Catholic group to create their own groups. Since that time, the Church has experienced peace, growth, and new viability.

There is one monastic order, The Monastic Community of Saint Basil, which is open to men and women, is currently headquartered in St Cloud Minnesota, with additional offices at St. Andrew the Apostle Cathedral in Duluth, Minnesota. The Metropolis and Chancery Center is located in Cleveland Ohio. The Church has 1 monastery and 4 convents: Our Lady of Sitka Monastery, Cleveland OH; St Mary Mother of God Convent, Democratic Republic of the Congo in Africa; Holy Archangels Convent, Democratic Republic of the Congo in Africa; St Anne Convent, Lagos Nigeria; and St Barbara Convent, London England.

At the Synod of Bishops meeting in 2008, it was decided to amend the name of the Church from Syro-Russian Orthodox Catholic Church to Syriac-Greek Antiochian Orthodox Catholic Church. This was done to better describe the Church and the sources of its Apostolic Succession, i.e., the Syriac and Greek Patriarchates of Antioch. The Synod of Bishops currently consists of His Beatitude Metropolitan Stephen, His Eminence Archbishop Timothy, His Grace Bishop John (India), His Grace Bishop Joshua (North Carolina), His Grace Bishop Simeon (Ohio), Bishop-elect Samson (Tanzania), Right Reverend Chorbishop Haralambos (Alaska), and Chorbishop-elect Spiridon (Uganda Africa). Missions and parishes exist in Canada, Cuba, Democratic Republic of the (African) Congo, India, Kenya Africa, Nigeria Africa, Pakistan, Tanzania Africa, Uganda Africa, and the United States.

Headquarters

Metropolis and Chancery, 4202 Newark Avenue, Cleveland OH 44109; 216.651.4757
Primate: Metropolitan Stephen
Coadjutor: Archbishop Timothy of Cleveland
Email: rbsocc@juno.com
Website: www.rbsocc.org

Officers

His Beatitude Metropolitan Archbishop Stephen, Primate, 4202 Newark Avenue, Cleveland OH 44109, Tel. (216) 651.4757, Email: rbsocc@juno.com .

His Eminence Archbishop Timothy, Archdiocese of the Americas & Dependencies; 4202 Newark Avenue, Cleveland OH 44109, Tel. (216) 543.6377

V.R. Father Patrick Lemming, Archdiocesan Chaplain, St James the Apostle House & Chapel, 304 Grace Avenue, Sevierville TN 37862, Tel. (865) 429-3641.

His Grace Bishop Joshua, Eastern Vicariate, Salem-Winston North Carolina

His Grace Bishop Simeon, Vicar General and Western Vicariate - Cleveland OH

Father Stephen Lawrence DDS JCD, Metropolis Judicial Vicar - Carlsbad CA

Father Steven M Johnson, Chancery Official and Academic Archives, St Thomas House, 1719 South 7th Avenue, St Cloud MN 56301

Father Demetrios E Wruck DC, Senior Advisor to Metropolitan - Maui Hawaii

Father Padraig Kneafsey, Archdiocesan Advisor - County Mayo Ireland

Synodal Council Advisors:
VR Father Paul Jensen, Honorary - Texas
Dr Peter Smyth, Honorary - Ontario Canada
Father Stephen Lawrence - California
Father Steven M Johnson - Minnesota
Dr Andrew Gill - Texas
Dr Audrey Daniel - South Carolina
Dr Bekki Medsker - South Carolina
Dr Hamptom Bumgarner - New Jersy
Dr Janet Maus - Maryland
Dr Sandra Dobiash - Colorado

Christ the Pantocrator Sovereign Order of Chivalry; Father Demetrios E Wruck DC, Protector of Chivalric Orders of the Metropolia.

Commission on Religious Counseling and Healing; Father Stephen Lawrence, DDS DCh, President, Dr. Peter Smyth (Canadian Liaison).

Monastic Community of St Basil and Sisters of the Community of St Basil; and Sisters of the Community of St Basil, Mother Helena (Abbess, St Mary Mother of God Convent, Democratic Republic of the Congo, Africa).

Periodicals

Orthodox Christian Herald, St Mark (Seminary & College) Newsletter

Syrian (Syriac) Orthodox Church of Antioch*

The Syrian Orthodox Church of Antioch traces its origin to the Patriarchate established in

Antioch by St. Peter the Apostle. It is under the supreme ecclesiastical jurisdiction of His Holiness the Syrian Orthodox Patriarch of Antioch and All the East, now residing in Damascus, Syria. The Syrian Orthodox Church—composed of several archdioceses, numerous parishes, schools and seminaries—professes the faith of the first three Ecumenical Councils of Nicaea, Constantinople and Ephesus, and numbers faithful in the Middle East, India, the Americas, Europe, Australia and New Zealand.

The first Syrian Orthodox faithful came to North America during the late 1800s, and by 1907 the first Syrian Orthodox priest was ordained to tend to the community's spiritual needs. In 1949, His Eminence Archbishop Mor Athanasius Y. Samuel came to America and was appointed Patriarchal Vicar in 1952. The Archdiocese was officially established in 1957. In 1995, the Archdiocese of North America was divided into three separate Patriarchal Vicariates (Eastern United States, Western United States and Canada), each under a hierarch of the Church.

There are 32 official archdiocesan parishes in the United States, located in Arizona, California, District of Columbia, Florida, Georgia, Indiana, Illinois, Massachusetts, Michigan, Nevada, New Jersey, New York, Oregon, Rhode Island, Texas and Virginia. In Canada, there are six official parishes - three in the Province of Ontario and two in the Province of Quebec and one in the Province of Alberta.

Headquarters
Archdiocese for the Eastern U.S., 260 Elm Avenue, Teaneck, NJ 07666, Tel. (201)801-0660 Fax (201)801-0603, Email: hasio@syrianorthodoxchurch.org
Archdiocese of the Western U.S., 417 E. Fairmount Rd., Burbank, CA 91501, Tel. (818)845-5089 Fax (818)953-7203, Email: MorClemis@hotmail.com
Media Contact, Archdiocesan Gen. Sec., Very Rev. Chorepiscopus John Meno, 260 Elm Ave., Teaneck, NJ 07666, Tel. (201)907-0122 Fax (201)907-0551
Email: hasio@syrianorthodoxchurch.org
Website: www.syrianorthodoxchurch.org

Officers
Archdiocese for Eastern U.S., Archbishop, Mor Cyril Aphrem Karim
Archdiocese of the Western U.S., Archbishop, Mor Clemis Eugene Kaplan

The Syro-Russian Orthodox Catholic Church, —please see Syriac-Greek Antiochian Orthodox Catholic Church.

Triumph the Church and Kingdom of God in Christ Inc. (International)
This church was given through the wisdom and knowledge of God to the Late Apostle Elias Dempsey Smith on Oct. 20, 1897, in Issaquena County, Mississippi, while he was pastor of a Methodist church.

The Triumph Church, as this body is more commonly known, was founded in 1902. Its doors opened in 1904 and it was confirmed in Birmingham, Alabama, with 225 members in 1915. It was incorporated in Washington, D.C. in 1918 and currently operates in 31 states and overseas. The General Church is divided into 13 districts, including the Africa District.

Triumphant doctrine and philosophy are based on the principles of life, truth and knowledge; the understanding that God is in man and is expressed through man; the belief in manifested wisdom and the hope for constant new revelations. Its concepts and methods of teaching the second coming of Christ are based on these and all other attributes of goodness.

Triumphians emphasize that God is the God of the living, not the God of the dead.

Headquarters
213 Farrington Ave. S.E., Atlanta, GA 30315
Media Contact, Bishop Zephaniah Swindle, 7114 Idlewild, Pittsburg, PA 15208, Tel. (412) 731-2286

Officers
Chief Bishop, Bishop Zephaniah Swindle, Rt. 1, Box 1927, Shelbyville, TX 75973, Tel. (936) 598-3082
Gen. Bd of Trustees, Chmn., Rev. Oprah Francis
Gen. Rec. Sec., Bishop R.D. Clarke
Gen. Treas., Bishop W.R. Matt Malcolm

True Orthodox Church of Greece (Synod of Metropolitan Cyprian), American Exarchate
The American Exarchate of the True (Old Calendar) Orthodox Church of Greece adheres to the tenets of the Eastern Orthodox Church, which considers itself the legitimate heir of the historical Apostolic Church.

When the Orthodox Church of Greece adopted the New, or Gregorian, Calendar in 1924, many felt that this breach with tradition compromised the Church's festal calendar, based on the Old, or Julian, Calendar, and its unity with world Orthodoxy. In 1935, three State Church Bishops returned to the Old Calendar and established a Synod in Resistance, the True Orthodox Church of Greece. When the last of these Bishops died, the Russian Orthodox Church Abroad consecrated a new Hierarchy for the Greek Old Calendarists and, in 1969, declared them a Sister Church.

In the face of persecution by the State Church, some Old Calendarists denied the validity of the Mother Church of Greece and formed two synods, now under the direction of Archbishop Chrysostomos of Athens and Archbishop Andreas of Athens. A moderate faction under Metropolitan Cyprian of Oropos and Fili does not maintain communion with the Mother Church of Greece, but recognizes its validity and seeks a restoration

159

of unity by a return to the Julian Calendar and traditional ecclesiastical polity by the State Church. About 1.5 million Orthodox Greeks belong to the Old Calendar Church.

The first Old Calendarist communities in the United States were formed in the 1930s. The Exarchate under Metropolitan Cyprian was established in 1986. Placing emphasis on clergy education, youth programs, and recognition of the Old Calendarist minority in American Orthodoxy, the Exarchate has encouraged the establishment of monastic communities and missions. Cordial contacts with the New Calendarist and other Orthodox communities are encouraged. A center for theological training and Patristic studies has been established at the Exarchate headquarters in Etna, California.

In July 1994, the True Orthodox Church of Greece (Synod of Metropolitan Cyprian), the True Orthodox Church of Romania, the True Orthodox Church of Bulgaria, and the Russian Orthodox Church Abroad entered into liturgical union, forming a coalition of traditionalist Orthodox bodies several million strong.

Headquarters

St. Gregory Palamas Monastery, P.O. Box 398, Etna, CA 96027-0398, Tel. (530)467-3228 Fax (530) 467-5828

Media Contact, Exarch in America, His Eminence, Archbishop Chrysostomos

Officers

Acting Synodal Exarch in America, His Grace Bishop Auxentios

Chancellor of the Exarchate, The Very Rev. Raphael Abraham, 3635 Cottage Grove Ave. S.E., Cedar Rapids, IA 52403-1612

Periodicals

Orthodox Tradition

Ukrainian Orthodox Church of the U.S.A.*

The Ukrainian Orthodox Church of the USA has its origin in the ancient lands of Rus-Ukraine (present day Ukraine). It was to the inhabitants of these lands that the Apostle Andrew first preached the Gospel. Christianization began early in the history of Rus-Ukraine by missionaries from the Orthodox Christian See of Constantinople. In 988 AD, the Saintly Prince Volodymyr, crowned a process of Christian Evangelization begun in the 4th century, by personally accepting Orthodox Christianity and inspiring his subjects to do the same. The baptism of Volodymyr, his household and the inhabitants of Kyiv, altered the face of Kyivan Rus-Ukraine and Slavic history for all time. Kyiv became the spiritual heart of Orthodox Christians in Rus-Ukraine. It was from this See that missionaries were sent into every corner of St. Volodymyr's realm. Through their efforts the

Gospel was preached and new communities were established. The Mother Church of Kyiv and its See of Saint Sophia, modeled after Constantinople's See of the same name, gave birth to many Orthodox Christian centers and communities in the west, east and north of the Dnipro river, among them the Orthodox Christian See of Moscow, Russia (Rosia).

The Ukrainian Orthodox Church of USA ministers to the needs of the faithful whose ancestral roots are in Ukraine. The Church found haven in America in the early 1920's. Its first bishop, Metropolitan Ioan (John) Teodorovych, arrived from Ukraine in 1924 and shepherded the Church as Metropolitan until his death in 1971. His successor, Archbishop Mstyslav, arrived in the USA in 1950, and shepherded the Church as Metropolitan from 1971 until his death in 1993. It was Metropolitan Mstyslav who, as a consequence of Ukraine's independence, was named Patriarch of Kyiv and All Ukraine, in 1990. Previous to 1996 there were two Ukrainian Orthodox jurisdictions in the USA. Formal unification of the Ukrainian Orthodox Church of USA, shepherded by His Beatitude Metropolitan Constantine, and the Ukrainian Orthodox Church of America, shepherded by His Grace Bishop Vsevolod, was concluded in November 1996.

Headquarters

Saint Andrew the Firstcalled Apostle Ukrainian Orthodox Church Center, P.O. Box 495, South Bound Brook, NJ 08880, Tel. (732)356-0090 Fax (732)356-5556

Media Contact, His Eminence Antony, Archbishop of New York, Consistory President

Email: consistory@uocofusa.org

Website: www.uocofusa.org

Officers

Metropolitan, His Beatitude Constantine, 1803 Sidney Street, Pittsburgh, PA 15203

CENTRAL EPARCHY
Eparchial Bishop, Metropolitan Constantine
Eparchial See, St. Volodymyr Cathedral, 5913 State Rd., Parma, OH 44134, Tel. (440) 885-1509
Eparchial Territory: Florida, Georgia, Ohio, Western Pennsylvania

EASTERN EPARCHY
Eparchial Bishop, Archbishop Antony.
Eparchial Seat, St. Volodymyr Cathedral, 160 West 82nd St. New York, NY 10024, Tel. (212) 873-8550
Eparchial Territory: Connecticut, Deleware, Massachusetts, Maryland, New Jersey, New York, Pennsylvania and Rhode Island

WESTERN EPARCHY
Eparchial Bishop, Archbishop Vsevolod
Eparchial Seat, St. Volodymyr Cathedral, 2230-50 West Cortez St. Chicago, IL 60622, Tel. (312)278 2827

Eparchial Territory: Arizona, California, Colorado, Illinois, Indiana, Michigan, Minnesota, North Dakota, Nebraska, Oregon, Washington, Wisconsin, Ontario Province

COUNCIL OF BISHOPS OF THE UKRAINIAN ORTHODOX CHURCH OF THE USA
Metropolitan Constantine - Chair
Achbishop Antony - Secretary
Achbishop Vsevolod - Member

METROPOLITAN COUNCIL MEMBERS
Archimandrite Andriy - Vice-chairman
Protopresbyter William Diakiw
Protopresbyter Frank Estocin, JCB
Protopriest John Nakonachny
Protopriest Michael Kochis
Protopriest Eugene Meschisen
Protopriest Bazyl Zawierucha
Dr. Gayle Woloschak - English Language Secretary
Mr. Emil Skocypec
Dr. Paul Micevych
Dr. George Krywolap- Ukrainian Language Secretary
Dr. Anatol Lysyj
Mrs. Helen Greenleaf
Mr. Michael Kapeluck
Daria Pishko, Ukrainian Orthodox League President
Mrs. Nadia Mirchuk, United Ukrainian Orthodox Sisterhoods President
Mr. Michael Heretz, Saint Andrew Society, President

CONSISTORY
Consistory President, His Eminence Antony, Archbishop of New York, P.O. Box 495, South Bound Brook, NJ 08880, Tel. (732)356-0090 Fax (732)356-5556, Email, uocofusa@aol.com
Vice Pres., Protopresbyter Willam Diakiw
Sec., Protopriest Frank Estocin
Treas., Mr. Emil Skocypec
Member, Protopriest John Nakonachny
Member, Protopriest Bazyl Zawierucha
Member, Dr. George Krywolap
Deaneries: New England – Protopriest Roman Tarnavsky, Dean; New York/New York, Protopresbyter Taras Chubenko, Dean; Mid-Atlantic, Protopresbyter Frank Estocin, Dean; Pittsburgh, Protopresbyter George Hnatko, Dean; Penn-Ohio, V. Rev. Dennis Kristof, Dean; Upstate New York, V. Rev. Mykola Krywonos, Dean; Florida, Protopresbyter Michael Petlak, Dean; Chicago, V. Rev. Bohdan Kalyniuk, Dean; Minneapolis, V. Rev. Evhen Kumka, Dean; West Coast, Rev. Vasile Sauciur, Dean
Ecclesiastical Court: Rev. Stephen Masliuk, President, Rev. Vasile Sauciur, Rev. Myroslav Schirta, Mr. Michael Slavich, Mr. Wesley Dunn
Audit Commission: Ms. Hanja Cherniak, Chairman, V. Rev. Yurij Siwko, V. Rev. Timothy Tomson, Mr. Edward Zetick, Mrs. Mary Lee Leszczuk

Office of Youth and Young Adult Ministry: Natalie Kapeluck-Nixon, Director
Office of Missions and Christian Ministry: Rev. Deacon Dr. Ihor Mahlay, Director
Office of Family and Adult Ministry: Rev. Harry Linsinbigler, Director
Office of Religious Education: Rev. Harry Linsinbigler, Temporary Director
Office of Development: Dr. Stephen Sivulich, Director
Office of Financial Affairs: Eng. Emil Skocypec, Director
Office of External Affairs and Interchurch Relations: Protopresbyter Frank Estocin, Director
Office of Publications: Protopresbyter William Diakiw, Director
Office of Archival and Historical Information: Dr. George Krywolap
Office of Public Relations: Hieromonk Daniel, Director
All Saints Camp: Stephen Sheptak, Director
Historical and Educational Museum Complex: Natalia Honcharenko, Director
St. Sophia Seminary: V. Rev. Bazyl Zawierucha, Rector
St. Sophia Seminary – Ukrainian Orthodox Church Library: Larissa Bulya, Librarian
Jr. Ukrainian Orthodox League: Mark Meschisen, President
St. Andrew Cemetery: Anastasia Hrybowych, Director
St. Andrew Bookstore: Shirley Skocypec, Director

Periodicals
Ukrainian Orthodox Word, Vira

Unitarian Universalist Association of Congregations

History: The Unitarian Universalist Association (UUA), created in 1961 through a consolidation of the Universalist Church of America with the American Unitarian Association, combines two liberal religious traditions. The religion traces its roots back to Europe where in 1569, the Transylvanian king, John Sigismund (1540-1571), issued an edict of religious freedom. The religious philosophy led to the organization of the Universalists in this country in 1793, and the Unitarians (organized here in 1825).

Beliefs: Founders of Universalism believed in universal salvation of all humans by God, while founders of Unitrarianism believed in the unity of God (as opposed to the Trinity). Unitarian Universalism is a liberal, creedless religion with Judeo-Christian roots. It draws also from Eastern, humanist, and other religious traditions, and encourages its members to seek religious truth out of their own reflection and experience. The denomination teaches tolerance and respect for other religious viewpoints and affirms the worth and dignity of every person.

Organization and Government: The Unitarian Universalist Association consists of 1,046 congre-

161

gations in the United States and Canada, with over 220,000 members, and is served by more than 1,700 ministers. The Association is the fastest-growing liberal religion in North America, at an average annual rate of between 1 and 2 percent. Each member congregation within the UUA is governed independently. In North America, the Association is made up of 19 Districts (served by a District Executive who is a member of the UUA staff), with each congregation having district affiliation. The Association is governed by an elected Board of Trustees, chaired by an elected Moderator. An elected President, three vice presidents, and directors of five departments form the Executive Staff that administers the daily activities of the Association.

The General Assembly, held each June in a different UUA District, serves as the Association's annual business meeting. The UUA includes Departments of Ministry and Professional Leadership; Lifespan Faith Development; Congregational Services; Identity Based Ministries; District Services; Advocacy and Witness; Financial Development; and Communications. "UU World", published quarterly, is the denominational journal. Beacon Press, an internationally honored trade publishing house, is wholly owned by the Unitarian Universalist Association.

Headquarters
25 Beacon Street, Boston, MA 02108, Tel. (617) 742-2100 Fax (617)367-3237
Media Contact, Janet Hayes, Public Relations Director, Tel. (617)742-2100 x 386
Email: jhurley@uua.org
Website: www.uua.org

Officers
President, The Rev. William Sinkford
Moderator, Gini Courter
Executive Vice President, Kathleen C. Montgomery

Periodicals
UU World, InterConnections

The United Catholic Church, Inc.
History: In 1996, a group of Independent Catholic Bishops, meeting in Synod, asked then Bishop, Robert M. Bowman to draw up guidelines for "inclusivity." Under these guidelines a fellowship of independent Catholic churches and clergy was born under the leadership of now Archbishop Robert M. Bowman. This fellowship was incorporated in the State of Florida as a not-for-profit corporation in August of 1996 for the purposes of educatiing and ordaining clergy, organizing dioceses, parishes and ministries, conducting religious services, entering into various affiliations with other Christian churches, and educating the public on religious, moral and social issues. In June 2006, Bishop Rose Tressel became Presiding Bishop.

Headquarters
Media Contact: Bishop Rose Tressel, Presiding Bishop, 51 Hilltop Rd., Bethany, CT 06524, Tel: (203)393-3260, Email: unitedcatholic@snet.net
Email: catholic@rmbowman.com
Website: www.united-catholic-church.org

Officers
Bishop Rose Tressel, Presiding Bishop, 51 Hilltop Rd., Bethany CT 06524, Tel: (203) 393-3260, Email: unitedcatholic@snet.net
Archbishop Robert M. Bowman, Founding Bishop (Retired), 1494 Patriot Dive, Melbourne, FL 32940, Tel: (321)258-0582, Email: bob@rmbowman.com
Monsignor William Menter, Vicar General, 271 Dickinson St. NE, Palm Bay, FL 32907, Tel: (321)956-6792, Email: menterwm@earthlink.net
Bishop Bernardo Morales, Docesan Bishop, 6315 Bass Highway, P.O.Box 702192, St. Cloud, FL 34771 Tel: (407)498-0333, Email: bmorales3@cfl.rr.com Bishop Hollis Dodge, Diocesan Bishop, 802 Donaghue St., Staunton, VA 24401, Tel: (540)448-4623, Email: hollisdodge@msn.com
Bishop Terry Boyer, Associate Church Bishop, 5960 SE 15th Loop, Gresham, OR 97080, Tel: (971) 322-8032, Email: revboyertm@iccwest.com

Periodicals
The United Catholic Quarterly

United Christian Church
The United Christian Church originated about 1864. There were some ministers and laymen in the United Brethren in Christ Church who disagreed with the position and practice of the church on infant baptism, voluntary bearing of arms and belonging to oath-bound secret combinations. This group developed into United Christian Church, organized at a conference held in Campbelltown, Pennsylvania, on May 9, 1877. The principal founders of the denomination were George Hoffman, John Stamn and Thomas Lesher. Before they were organized, they were called Hoffmanites.

The United Christian Church has district conferences, a yearly general conference, a general board of trustees, a mission board, a board of directors of the United Christian Church Home, a camp meeting board, a young peoples' board and local organized congregations.

It believes in the Holy Trinity and the inspired Holy Scriptures with the doctrines they teach. The church practices the ordinances of Baptism, Holy Communion and Foot Washing.

It welcomes all into its fold who are born again, believe in Jesus Christ as Savior and Lord and have received the Holy Spirit.

Headquarters
Media Contact, Presiding Elder, John W. Graybill, 35 Oakwood Dr. Palmyra, PA. 17078, Tel: (717)838-4798, Email: graybilly@aol.com

162

Officers

Presiding Elder, Elder John W. Graybill

Conf. Sec., Mr. Lee Wenger, 1625 Thompson Ave., Annville, PA 17003

Conf. Moderator, Elder Gerald Brinser, 2360 Horseshoe Pike, Annville, PA 17003

OTHER ORGANIZATIONS

Mission Board, Pres., Elder John Graybill, 35 Oakwood Drive, Palmyra, PA 17078 Email: graybilly@aol.com; Sec., Elder David Heagy, 4129 Oak St., Lebanon, PA 17042; Treas., Mr. Robert Morgan, 1413 Harding Ave., Hershey, PA 17033

United Church of Christ*

The United Church of Christ was constituted on June 25, 1957 by representatives of the Congregational Christian Churches and of the Evangelical and Reformed Church, in Cleveland, Ohio.

The Preamble to the Constitution states, "The United Church of Christ acknowledges as its sole head, Jesus Christ . . . It acknowledges as kindred in Christ all who share in this confession. It looks to the Word of God in the Scriptures, and to the presence and power of the Holy Spirit . . . It claims . . . the faith of the historic Church expressed in the ancient creeds and reclaimed in the basic insights of the Protestant Reformers It affirms the responsibility of the Church in each generation to make this faith its own in . . . worship, in honesty of thought and expression, and in purity of heart before God . . . it recognizes two sacraments, Baptism and the Lord's Supper."

The creation of the United Church of Christ brought together four unique traditions-

(1) Groundwork for the Congregational Way was laid by Calvinist Puritans and Separatists during the late 16th-early 17th centuries, then achieved prominence among English Protestants during the civil war of the 1640s. Opposition to state control prompted followers to emigrate to the United States, where they helped colonize New England in the 17th century. Congregationalists have been self-consciously a denomination from the mid-19th century.

(2) The Christian Churches, an 18th-century American restorationist movement emphasized Christ as the only head of the church, the New Testament as their only rule of faith, and "Christian" as their sole name. This loosely organized denomination found in the Congregational Churches a like disposition. In 1931, the two bodies formally united as the Congregational Christian Churches.

(3) The German Reformed Church comprised an irenic aspect of the Protestant Reformation, as a second generation of Reformers drew on the insights of Zwingli, Luther and Calvin to formulate the Heidelberg Catechism of 1563. People of the German Reformed Church began immigrating to the New World early in the 18th century, the heaviest concentration in Pennsylvania. Formal organization of the American denomination was completed in 1793. The church spread across the country. In the Mercersburg Movement, a strong emphasis on evangelical catholicity and Christian unity was developed.

(4) In 19th-century Germany, Enlightenment criticism and Pietist inwardness decreased longstanding conflicts between religious groups. In Prussia, a royal proclamation merged Lutheran and Reformed people into one United Evangelical Church (1817). Members of this new church way migrated to America. The Evangelicals settled in large numbers in Missouri and Illinois, emphasizing pietistic devotion and unionism; in 1840 they formed the German Evangelical Church Society in the West. After union with other Evangelical church associations, in 1877 it took the name of the German Evangelical Synod of North America.

On June 25, 1934, this Synod and the Reformed Church in the U.S. (formerly the German Reformed Church) united to form the Evangelical and Reformed Church. They blended the Reformed tradition's passion for the unity of the church and the Evangelical tradition's commitment to the liberty of conscience inherent in the gospel.

Headquarters

700 Prospect Avenue, Cleveland, OH 44115, Tel. (216)736-2100 Fax (216)736-2103 Toll-free 866-822-8224 (866-UCC-UCC4)

Media Contact, Rev. J. Bennett Guess, 700 Prospect Ave., Cleveland, OH 44115, Tel. (216)736-2177 Fax (216)736-2223

Email: kellys@ucc.org

Website: www.ucc.org

Officers

Gen. Minister and Pres., Rev. Geoffrey A. Black

Assoc. Gen. Minister, Ms. Edith A. Guffey

Exec. Minister, Wider Church Ministries, Rev. Cally Rogers-Witte

Exec. Minister, Justice and Witness Ministries, Rev. M. Linda Jaramillo

Exec. Minister, Local Church Ministries, Rev. Stephen L. Sterner

ORGANIZATIONS

Office of General Ministries, National Office, 700 Prospect Avenue, Cleveland, Ohio 44115., Tel. (216)736-2100 Fax (216)736-2103, General Minister and President, Rev. John H. Thomas; Associate General Minister, Ms. Edith A. Guffey

Justice and Witness Ministries, National Offices (as above), Tel. (216)736-3700 Fax (216)736-3703, Franklinton Center at Bricks, P.O. Box 220, Whitakers, NC 27891, Tel. (252)437-1723 Fax (252)437-1278, Washington Office, 100 Maryland Avenue North East, Suite 330, Washington, DC. 20002 Tel. (202)543-1517 Fax (202)543-5994, Centro Romero, 173 W. Hall Ave., San Ysidro, CA 92173, Tel. (619)428-8700 Fax (619) 428-8705, Executive Minister, Rev. M. Linda Jaramillo Local Church Ministries, National Offices, Tel. (216)736-3800 Fax (216)736-3803. Executive Minister, Rev. Stephen L. Sterner

Wider Church Ministries, National Offices (as above), Tel. (216)736-3200 Fax (216)736-3203, Global Ministries of the Christian Church and United Church of Christ, P.O. Box 1986, Indianapolis, IN 46206, Tel. (317)713-2575 Fax (317)635-4323, Executive Minister, Rev. Cally Rogers-Witte;

Pension Boards, Main Office, 475 Riverside Drive, New York, NY 10115., Tel. (212)729-2700 Fax (212)729-2701; National Office, 700 Prospect Ave., Cleveland, OH 44115, Tel. (216)736-2271 Fax (216)736-2274, President/Chief Executive Officer, Mr. Michael A. Downs

United Church Foundation, Inc., 475 Riverside Drive, Room 1020, New York, NY 10115., Tel. (212)729-2600 Fax (212)729-2601, President, Mr. Donald G. Hart

Council for Health and Human Services Ministries, National Office (as above)., Tel. (216) 736-2250 Fax (216)736-2251, President and Chief Executive Officer, Rev. Bryan W. Sickbert

CONFERENCES

WESTERN REGION

California, Nevada Northern, Rev. Mary Susan Gast, 21425 Birch Street, Hayward, CA 94541-2131

California, Nevada Southern, Rev. Jane Fisler Hoffman, Interim, 2401 N. Lake Ave., Altadena, CA 91001

Central Pacific, Rev. Walter John Boris, 0245 SW Bancroft St. Ste. E, Portland, OR 97239

Hawaii, Rev. Charles Buck, 1848 Nu'uanu Ave., Honolulu, HI 96817

Montana-Northern Wyoming, Rev. Randall Hyvonen, 2016 Alderson Ave., Billings, MT 59102

Pacific Northwest, Rev. Michael Denton, 325 N. 125th St., Seattle, WA 98133

Rocky Mountain, Rev. Tom Rehling, 1140 W. 5th Ave., Denver, CO 80204

Southwest, Rev. John Dorhauer, 4423 N. 24th St., Ste. 600, Phoenix, AZ 85016

West Central Region

Iowa, Rev. Rich Pleva, 5609 Douglas Ave., Des Moines, IA 50310

Kansas-Oklahoma, Rev. David Hansen, 1245 Fabrique, Wichita, KS 67218

Minnesota, Rev. Karen Smith Sellers, 122 W. Franklin Ave., Rm. 323, Minneapolis, MN 55404

Missouri, Mid-South, Rev. Jeffrey Whitman, 411 E. Lockwood Ave., St. Louis, MO 63119

Nebraska, Rev. Roddy Dunkerson, 3151 Sout St., Ste. B, Lincoln, NE 68502

Northern Plains, Rev. Wade Schemmel, 1200 E. Highland Acres Rd., Bismarck, ND 58501

South Dakota, Rev. Mare Stewart (Acting), 3500 S. Phillips Ave., #100, Sioux Falls, SD 57105-6864

GREAT LAKES REGION

Illinois, Rev. Phil Hart, Interim, 1840 Westchester Blvd. #200, Westchester, IL 60154

Illinois South, Rev. Sheldon Culver, 1312 Broadway, Highland, IL 62249

Indiana-Kentucky, Rev. Stephen C. Gray, 1100 W. 42nd St. #350, Indianapolis, IN 46208

Michigan, Judith Youngman (Interim), P.O. Box 1006, 5945 Park Lake Rd., East Lansing, MI 48826

Ohio, Rev. Robert Molsberry, 6161 Busch Blvd.,#95, Columbus, OH 43229

Wisconsin, Rev. David Moyer, 4459 Gray Rd., P.O. Box 435, De Forest, WI 53532-0495

SOUTHERN REGION

Florida, Rev. Kent Siladi, 924 N Magnolia Ave. #250, Orlando, FL 32803

South Central, Rev. Doug Anders, 9022 Long Point Rd., Houston, TX 77055

Southeast, Rev. Timothy C. Downs, 1330 W Peachtree St., Ste. 350, Atlanta, GA 30309

Southern, Rev. Steve Camp, 252-B. Fifth St., Burlington, NC 27215

MIDDLE ATLANTIC REGION

Central Atlantic, Rev. John R. Deckenback, 916 S. Rolling Rd., Baltimore, MD 21228

New York, Rev. Geoffrey A. Black, 5575 Thompson Rd., DeWitt, NY 13214

Penn Central, Rev. Marja Coons-Torn, 900 S. Arlington Ave. #112, Harrisburg, PA 17109

Penn Northeast, Rev. Alan C. Miller, 431 Delaware Ave., Palmerton, PA 18071

Pennsylvania Southeast, Rev. F. Russell Mittman, 505 S. Second Ave., P.O. Box 26400-0400, Collegeville, PA 19426-0400

Penn West, Rev. Alan McLarty, 320 South Maple Ave., Greensburg, PA 15601

New England Region

Connecticut, Rev. Davida Foy Crabtree, 125 Sherman St., Hartford, CT 06105

Maine, Rev. David R. Gaewski, 28 Yarmouth Crossing Dr., P.O. Box 966, Yarmouth, ME 04096

Massachusetts, Rev. Jim Antal, 1 Badger Rd., Framingham, MA 01702

New Hampshire, Rev. Gary Schulte, 140 Sheep Davis Rd, Pembroke, NH 03275

Rhode Island, Rev. Charles Barnes, 8 Summer St., Pawtucket, RI 02860

Vermont, Rev. Lynn Bujnak, 36 N. Main St., Randolph, VT 05060

Nongeographic

Calvin Synod, Rev. Koloman K. Ludwig, 7319 Tapper Ave., Hammond, IN 46324

Periodicals

United Church News, Common Lot

United Holy Church of America, Inc.

The United Holy Church of America, Inc. is an outgrowth of the great revival that began with the outpouring of the Holy Ghost on the Day of Pentecost. The church is built upon the foundation of the Apostles and Prophets, Jesus Christ being the cornerstone.

During a revival of repentence, regeneration and holiness of heart and life that swept through the South and West, the United Holy Church was born. The founding fathers had no desire to establish a denomination but were pushed out of organized churches because of this experience of holiness and testimony of the Spirit-filled life.

On the first Sunday in May 1886, in Method, North Carolina, what is today known as the United Holy Church of America, Inc. was born. The church was incorporated on Sept. 25, 1918.

Baptism by immersion, the Lord's Supper and feet washing are observed. The premillennial teaching of the Second Coming of Christ, Divine healing, justification by faith, sanctification as a second work of grace and Spirit baptism are accepted.

Headquarters

5104 Dunstan Rd., Greensboro, NC 27405, Tel. (336)621-0669

Media Contact, Gen. Statistician, Ms. Jacquelyn B. McCain, 1210 N. Euclid Ave., Apt. A, St. Louis, MO 63113-2012, Tel. (314)367-8351 Fax (314)367-1835

Email: books@mohistory.org

Officers

GENERAL ADMINISTRATION

Gen. Pres., The Rt. Rev. Odell McCollum, 707 Woodmark Run, Gahanna, OH 43230, Tel. (614)475-4713, Fax (614)475-4713

Gen. Vice Pres., Bishop Elijah Williams, 901 Briarwood St., Reidsville, NC 27320, Tel. (919) 349-7275

Gen. 2nd Vice-Pres., The Rt. Rev. Kenneth O. Robinson, Sr., 33 Springbrook Road, Nanuet, NY 10954-4423, Tel. (914)425-8311, Fax (914)352-2686

Gen. Rec. Sec., Rev. Mrs. Elsie Harris, 2304 Eighth Street, Portsmouth, VA 23704 Tel (757)399-0926

Asst. Rec. Sec., Mrs. Cassandra Jones, 3869 JoAnn Drive, Cleveland, OH 44122, Tel. (216)921-0097

Gen. Fin. Sec., Vera Perkins-Hughes, P.O. Box 6194, Cleveland, OH, Tel. (216)851-7448

Asst. Fin. Sec., Bertha Williams, 4749 Shaw Dr., Wilmington, NC 28405, Tel. (919)395-4462

Gen. Corres. Sec., Ms. Gwendolyn Lane, 3069 Hudson Street, Columbus, OH 43219

Gen. Treas., Louis Bagley, 8779 Wales Dr., Cincinnati, OH 45249, Tel. (513)247-0588

GENERAL OFFICERS

Gen Pres. Missionary Dept., Rev. Ardelia M. Corbett, 519 Madera Dr., Youngstown, OH 44504, Tel. (216)744-3284

Gen. Evangelism & Extension Dept., Pres., Elder Clifford R. Pitts, 3563 North 14th St., Milwaukee, WI 53206, Tel. (414)244-1319

Gen. Bible Church School Dept., Superin-tendent, Robert L. Rollins, 1628 Avondale Ave., Toledo, OH 43607, Tel. (419)246-4046

Gen. Y.P.H.A., Pres., Elder James W. Brooks, Rt. 3 Box 105, Pittsboro, NC 27312, Tel. (919)542-5357

Gen. Ushers Department, Pres., Ms. Sherly M. Hughes, 1491 East 191st Street, #H-604, Euclid, OH 44117, Te. (216)383-0038

Gen. Educ. Dept., Elder Roosevelt Alston, 168 Willow Creek Run, Henderson, NC 27636, Tel. (919)438-5854

Gen. Music Dept., Chair, Rosie Johnson, 2009 Forest Dale Dr., Silver Spring, MD 20932

Gen. Historian, Dr. Chester Gregory, Sr., 1302 Lincoln Woods Dr., Baltimore, MD 21228, Tel. (410)788-5144

Gen. Counsel, Mr. Joe L. Webster, Esquire, Attorney-At-Law, P.O. Box 2301, Chapel Hill, NC 27515-2301, Tel. (919)542-5150

UHCA Academy, Dir., Ms. Stephanie Davis, The United Holy Church of America, Inc., 5104 Dunstan Road, Greensboro, NC 27405, Tel. (336)621-0069

Gen. Statistician, Ms. Jacquelyn B. McCain, 1210 N. Euclid Ave., Apt. A, St. Louis, MO 63113-2012, Tel. (314)367-8351 Fax (314) 367-1835

PRESIDENTS OF CONVOCATIONAL DISTRICTS

Barbados District; The Rt. Rev. Jestina Gentles, 5 West Ridge St., Britton's Hill, St. Michael, BH2 Barbados, West Indies, Tel. (246)427-7185

Bermuda Dist., The Rt. Rev. Calvin Armstrong, P.O. Box 234, Paget, Bermuda, Tel. (441)296-0828 or (441)292-8383

Central Western Dist., Bishop Bose Bradford, 6279 Natural Bridge, Pine Lawn, MO 63121, Tel. (314)355-1598

Ghana, West Africa Dist., The Rt. Rev. Robert Blount, 231 Arlington Av., Jersey City, NJ 07035, Tel. (201)433-5672

New England Dist., The Rt. Rev. Lowell Edney, 85 Woodhaven St., Mattapan, MA 02126, Tel. (617)296-5366

Northern Dist., The Rt. Rev. Kenneth O. Robinson, Sr., 33 Springbrook Rd., Nanuet, NY 10954, Tel. (914)425-8311

Northwestern Dist., The Rt. Rev. M. Daniel Borden, 8655 North Melody Lane, Macedonia, OH 44056, Tel. (330)468-0270

Pacific Coast Dist., The Rt. Rev. Irvin Evans, 235 Harvard Rd., Linden, NJ 07036, Tel. (908) 925-6138

Southeastern Dist., The Rt. Rev. James C. Bellamy, 1825 Rockland Dr., SE, Atlanta, GA 30316, Tel. (404)241-1821

Southern Dist.- Goldsboro, The Rt. Rev. Ralph E. Love, Sr., 200 Barrington Rd., Greenville, NC 27834, Tel. (252)353-0495

Southern Dist.- Henderson, The Rt. Rev. Jesse Jones, 608 Cecil Street, Durham, NC 27707, Tel. (919)682-8249

St. Lucia Dist., The Rt. Rev. Carlisle Collymore, P.O. Box 51, Castries, St. Lucia, West Indies, Tel. (758)452-5835

Virginia Dist., The Rt. Rev. Albert Augson, 1406 Melton Ave., Richmond, VA 23223, Tel. (804) 222-0463

West Virginia Dist., The Rt. Rev. Alvester McConnell, Route 3, Box 263, Bluefield, WV 24701, Tel. (304)248-8046

Western North Carolina Dist., The Rt. Rev. Elijah Williams, 901 Briarwood St., Reidsville, NC 27320-7020, Tel. (336)349-7275

United House of Prayer

The United House of Prayer was founded and organized as a hierarchical church in the 1920s by the late Bishop C. M. Grace, who had built the first House of Prayer in 1919 in West Wareham, MA, with his own hands. The purpose of the organization is to establish, maintain and perpetuate the doctrine of Christianity and the Apostolic Faith throughout the world among all people; to erect and maintain houses of prayer and worship where all people may gather for prayer and to worship the almighty God in spirit and in truth, irrespective of denomination or creed, and to maintain the Apostolic faith of the Lord and Savior, Jesus Christ.

Headquarters

628 M St. NW, Washington, DC 20001, Tel. (202)289-9890 Fax (202)289-3690

Media Contact, Apostle S. Green

Email: apostlegreen@hotmail.com

Officers

CEO, Bishop S. C. Madison, 1665 N. Portal Dr. NW, Washington, DC 20012, Tel. (202)882-3956 Fax (202)829-4717

NATIONAL PROGRAM STAFF

The General Assembly, Presiding Officer, Bishop S. C. Madison, 1665 N. Portal Dr. NW, Washington, DC 20012, Tel. (202)882-3956 Fax (202)829-4717

General Council Ecclesiastical Court, Clerk, Apostle R. Price, 1665 N. Portal Dr. NW, Washington, DC 20012, Tel. (202)882-3956 Fax (202)829-4717

Nationwide Building Program, General Builder, Bishop S. C. Madison, 1665 N. Portal Dr. NW, Washington, DC 20012, Tel. (202)882-3956 Fax (202)829-4717

Special Projects, Dir., Apostle S. Green

Annual Truth & Facts Publication, Exec. Editor, Bishop S. C. Madison, 1665 N. Portal Dr. NW, Washington, DC 20012, Tel. (202)882-3956 Fax (202)829-4717

The United Methodist Church*

The United Methodist Church was formed April 23, 1968, in Dallas by the union of The Methodist Church and The Evangelical United Brethren Church. The two churches shared a common historical and spiritual heritage. The Methodist Church resulted in 1939 from the unification of three branches of Methodism - the Methodist Episcopal Church, the Methodist Episcopal Church, South, and the Methodist Protestant Church.

The Methodist movement began in 18th-century England under the preaching of John Wesley, but the Christmas Conference of 1784 in Baltimore is regarded as the date on which the organized Methodist Church was founded as an ecclesiastical organization. It was there that Francis Asbury was elected the first bishop in this country.

The Evangelical United Brethren Church was formed in 1946 with the merger of the Evangelical Church and the Church of the United Brethren in Christ, both of which had their beginnings in Pennsylvania in the evangelistic movement of the 18th and early 19th centuries. Philip William Otterbein and Jacob Albright were early leaders of this movement among the German-speaking settlers of the Middle Colonies.

Headquarters

Media Contact, Executive Director, Public Information, Diane Degnan, Tel. (615)742-5406, Email: ddegnan@umcomm.org

General Information, Director, InfoServ, Vicki Wallace, 1-800-251-8140, Fax (615)742-5423, Email: infoserv@umcom.org

Email: infoserv@umcom.umc.org

Website: www.umc.org

Officers

General Conference, Sec., Rev. L. 'Gere' Fitzgerald Reist II, 216 State St, Harrisburg, PA 17101-1109, Tel. (570)724-3113, Email: freist@cpcumc.org

Council of Bishops: Pres., Bishop Gregory V. Palmer, 5900 S 2nd St., 62711, P.O. Box 19215, Springfield, IL 62794-9215, Tel. (217)529-3820 Fax (217)529-4190, Email: ILareaoffice@igrc.org

Sec., Robert E. Hayes, Jr. 1501 NW 24th St, 73106, P.O. Box 60467, Oklahoma City, OK 73146-0467, Tel. (405)530-2025 Fax (405) 530-2040, Email: jharris@okumc.org

JURISDICTIONAL BISHOPS

NORTH CENTRAL JURISDICTION:

Chicago Episcopal Area, Bishop Hee-Soo Jung, 77 W. Washington St., Ste. 1820, Chicago, IL 60602-3181, Tel. (312)346-9766 x 102 Fax (312)214-9031, Email: hsjung@umcnic.org

Dakotas Episcopal Area, Bishop Deborah L. Kiesey, 1331 W. University Ave., P.O. Box 460, Mitchell, SD 57301-0460, Tel. (605)996-6552 Fax (605)996-1766, Email: bishop@dakotasumc.org

Illinois Episcopal Area, Bishop Gregory V. Palmer, (5900 S 2nd St., 62711), P.O. Box 19215, Springfield, IL 62794-9215, Tel. (217)529-3820 Fax (217)529-4190, Email: ILareaoffice@igrc.org

Indiana Episcopal Area, Bishop Michael J. Coyner, 1100 W. 42nd St., Ste. 210, Indianapolis, IN 46208-3382, Tel. (317)924-1321 Fax (317)924-4859, Email: Bishopcoyner@inareaumc.org

Iowa Episcopal Area, Bishop Julius C. Trimble, 2301 Rittenhouse St, Des Moines, IA 50321-

3101, Tel. (515)974-8902 Fax (515)974-8952, Email: bishopjc.trimble@iaumc.org

Michigan Episcopal Area, Bishop Jonathan D. Keaton (2164 University Park Dr., Ste. 250, Okemos, MI 48864), P.O. Box 25068, Lansing MI 48909-5068, Tel. (517)347-4030 Fax (517)347-4003, Email: bishopsoffice@miareaumc.org

Minnesota Episcopal Area, Bishop Sally Dyck, 122 W. Franklin Ave., Ste. 200, Minneapolis, MN 55404-2472, Tel. (612)870-4007 Fax (612) 870-3587, Email: sally.dyck@minnesotaumc.org

Ohio East Episcopal Area, Bishop John L. Hopkins (8800 Cleveland Ave. NW 44720-4598), P.O. Box 2800, North Canton, OH 44720-0800, Tel. (330)499-3972 x 112 Fax (330)497-4911, Email: bishop@eocumc.com

Ohio West Episcopal Area, Bishop Bruce R. Ough, 32 Wesley Blvd., Worthington, OH 43085-3585, Tel. (614)844-6200 x 215 Fax (614)781-2625, Email: Bishop@wocumc.org

Wisconsin Episcopal Area, Bishop Linda Lee, 750 Windsor St., Ste. 303, Sun Prairie, WI 53590-2149, Tel. (608)837-8526 Fax (608)837-0281, Email: episcopaloffice@wisconsinumc.org

NORTHEASTERN JURISDICTION:

Albany Episcopal Area, Bishop Susan W. Hassinger, 215 Lancaster St., Albany, NY 12210-1131, Tel. (518)426-0386 Fax (518)426-0347, Email: AlbEpisArea@verizon.net

Boston Episcopal Area, Bishop Peter D. Weaver (276 Essex St. 5th Fl., 01840-1516), P.O. Box 249, Lawrence, MA 01842-0449, Tel. (978)682-7555 x 250 Fax (978)682-9555, Email: bishopsoffice@neumc.org

Harrisburg Episcopal Area, Bishop Jane Allen Middleton, 303 Mulberry Dr., Ste. 100, Mechanicsburg, PA 17050-3141, Tel. (717)766-7871 x 3100 Fax (717)766-3210, Email: bishop@cpcumc.org

New Jersey Episcopal Area, Bishop Sudarshana Devadhar, 1001 Wickapecko Dr., Ocean, NJ 07712-4733, Tel. (732)359-1010 Fax (732) 359-1019, Email: Bishop@gnjumc.org

New York Episcopal Area, Bishop Jeremiah J. Park, 20 Soundview Ave., White Plains, NY 10606-3302, Tel. (914)615-2221 Fax (914) 615-2246, Email: Bishop@nyac.com

New York West Episcopal Area, Bishop Marcus Matthews, 1010 East Ave, Rochester, NY 14607-2220, Tel. (585)271-3400 Fax (585) 271-3404, Email: bishopmatthews@frontiernet.net

Philadelphia Episcopal Area, Bishop Peggy Johnson (980 Madison Ave, Norristown,19403), P.O. Box 820, Valley Forge, PA 19482-0820, Tel. (610)666-9090 x233 Fax (610)666-9181, Email: peggy.johnson@epaumc.org

Pittsburgh Episcopal Area, Bishop Thomas J. Bickerton (1204 Freedom Rd., 16066-4999), P.O. Box 5002, Cranberry Township, PA 16066-1902, Tel. (724)776-1499/1599 Fax (724)776-1683, Email: umbishop@wpaumc.org

Washington Episcopal Area (DC), Bishop John R. Schol, 100 Maryland Ave., NE Ste. 510, Washington, DC 20002-5625, Tel. (202)546-3110 Fax (202)546-3186, Email: bishopschol@bwcumc.org

West Virginia Episcopal Area, Bishop Ernest S. Lyght, United Methodist Center, 900 Washington St. E., Ste. 300, Charleston, WV 25301-1710, Tel. (304)344-8330 Fax (304) 344-8330, Email: WVareaumc@aol.com

SOUTH CENTRAL JURISDICTION:

Arkansas Episcopal Area, Bishop Charles N. Crutchfield, 2 Trudie Kibbe Reed Dr, Little Rock, AR 72202-3770, Tel. (501)324-8007 Fax (501)324-8021, Email: bishopcnc@arumc.org

Dallas Episcopal Area, Bishop Earl W. Bledsoe, P.O. Box 866186, Plano, TX 75086-6188, Tel. (972)526-5015 Fax (972) 526-5014, Email: bishop@ntcumc.org

Fort Worth Episcopal Area,Bishop Michael J. Lowry, 464 Bailey Ave., Fort Worth, TX 76107-2153, Tel. (817)877-5222 Fax (817) 332-4609, Email: bishop@ctcumc.org

Houston Episcopal Area, Bishop Janice Riggle Huie, 5215 Main St., Houston, TX 77002-9792, Tel. (713)528-6881 Fax (713)529-7736, Email: bishop.huie@txcumc.org

Kansas Episcopal Area, Bishop Scott J. Jones 9440 E. Boston St, Ste 160, Wichita, KS 67207-3603, Tel. (316)686-0600 Fax (316)684-0044, Email: kansasbishop@kswestumc.org

Louisiana Episcopal Area, Bishop William W. Hutchinson, 527 North Blvd., Baton Rouge, LA 70802-5700, Tel. (225)346-1646 x 212 Fax (225)387-3662, Email: enixmore@bellsouth.net

Missouri Episcopal Area, Bishop Robert C. Schnase, 3601 Amron Ct, Columbia, MO 65202-1918, Tel. (573)441-1770 Fax (573)441-0765, Email: rschnase@moumethodist.org

Nebraska Episcopal Area, Bishop Ann Brookshire Sherer, 2641 N. 49th St., Lincoln, NE 68504-2802, Tel. (402)466-4955 Fax (402)466-7931, Email: bishopsherer@umcneb.org

Northwest Texas-New Mexico Episcopal Area, Bishop D. Max Whitfield, 11816 Lomas Blvd NE, Albuquerque, NM 87112-5614, Tel. (505)255-8786 Fax (505)255-8738, Email: whitmax@nmconfum.com

Oklahoma Episcopal Area, Bishop Robert E. Hayes, Jr. (1501 NW 24th St, 73106), P.O. Box 60467, Oklahoma City, OK 73146-0467, Tel. (405)530-2025 Fax (405)530-2040, Email: jharris@okumc.org

San Antonio Episcopal Area, Bishop James E. Dorff (16400 Huebner Rd, 78248-1694), P.O. Box 781688, San Antonio, TX 78278-1688, Tel. (210)408-4502 Fax (210)408-4501, Email: bishop@umcswtx.org

SOUTHEASTERN JURISDICTION:

Alabama-West Florida Episcopal Area, Bishop Paul L. Leeland, 100 Interstate Park Dr., Ste 120 A, Montgomery, AL 36109-5488, Tel. (334)277-1787 Fax (334)277-0109, Email: bishop@awfumc.org

Birmingham Episcopal Area, Bishop William H. Willimon, 898 Arkadelphia Rd., Birmingham, AL 35204-5011, Tel. (205)226-7991 Fax (205)226-7998, Email: wwillimon@north alabamaumc.org

Charlotte Episcopal Area, Bishop Larry M. Goodpaster (3400 Shamrock Dr., 28215), P.O. Box 18750, Charlotte, NC 28218-0750, Tel. (704)535-2260 x138 Fax (704)535-9160, Email: bishop@wnccumc.org

Columbia Episcopal Area, Bishop Mary Virginia Taylor, 4908 Colonial Dr., Ste. 121, Columbia, SC 29203-6080, Tel. (803)786-9486 Fax (803)754-9327, Email: bishop@umcsc.org

Florida Episcopal Area, Bishop Timothy W. Whitaker (1122 E. McDonald St., 33801), Lakeland, FL 33801-5641, Tel. (863)688-4427 Fax (863)687-0568, Email: bishop@flumc.org

Holston Episcopal Area, Bishop James E. Swanson, Sr. (217 S Rankin Rd., 37701-2633) P.O. Box 850, Alcoa, TN 37701-0850, Tel. (865)690-4080 Fax (865)690-7112, Email: bishop@holston.org

Louisville Episcopal Area, Bishop Lindsey Davis, 7400 Floydsburg Rd., Crestwood, KY 40014-8202, Tel. (502)425-4240 Fax (502) 425-9232, Email: bishop@kyumc.org

Mississippi Episcopal Area, Bishop Hope Morgan Ward (321 Mississippi St., 39201), P.O. Box 931, Jackson, MS 39205-0931, Tel. (601)948-4561 Fax (601)948-5981, Email: bishop@mississippi-umc.org

Nashville Episcopal Area, Bishop Richard J. Wills, Jr., 520 Commerce St., Ste. 201, Nashville, TN 37203-3714, Tel. (615)742-8834 Fax (615)742-3726, Email: bishop@nasharea.org

North Georgia Episcopal Area, Bishop B. Michael Watson 4511 Jones Bridge Cir. NW, Norcross, GA 30092-1406 Tel.(678)533-1360 Fax (678)533-1361, Email: bishop@ngumc.org

Raleigh Episcopal Area, Bishop Alfred W. Gwinn, Jr. (1307 Glenwood Ave., Rm. 203), P.O. Box 10955, Raleigh, NC 27605-0955, Tel. (919)832-9560 x 242 Fax (919)-832-4721, Email: bishopgwinn@nccumc.org

Richmond Episcopal Area, Bishop Charlene Payne Kammerer (10330 Staples Mill Rd.), P.O. Box 1719, Glen Allen, VA 23060-0659, Tel. (804)521-1102 Fax (804)521-1171, Email: bishopk@vaumc.org

South Georgia Episcopal Area, Bishop James R. King, Jr., 3370 Vineville Ave., Ste. 101, Macon, GA 31204-2331, Tel. (478)475-9286 Fax (478)475-9248, Email: jking@sgaumc.org

WESTERN JURISDICTION:

Denver Episcopal Area, Bishop Elaine J.W. Stanovsky 6110 Greenwood Plaza Blvd, Greenwood Village, CO 80111-4803, Tel. (303)733-0083 Fax (303)733-5047, Email: bishop@rmcumc.com

Los Angeles Episcopal Area, Bishop Mary Ann Swenson (110 S. Euclid Ave., 91101-2421),

P.O. Box 6006, Pasadena, CA 91102-6006, Tel. (626)568-7312 Fax (626)568-7377, Email: bishop@cal-pac.org

Phoenix Episcopal Area, Bishop Minerva G. Carcaño, 1550 E. Meadowbrook Ave., Phoenix, AZ 85014-4040, Tel. (602)266-6956 x209 Fax (602)279-1355, Email: Bishopmc@desertsw.org

Portland Episcopal Area, Bishop Robert T. Hoshibata, 1505 SW 18th Ave., Portland, OR 97201-2599, Tel. (503)226-1530 Fax (503)228-3189, Email: bishop@umoi.org

San Francisco Episcopal Area, Bishop Warner H. Brown, Jr., (1276 Halyard Dr., 95691), P.O. Box 980250, West Sacramento, CA 95798-0250, Tel. (916)374-1510 Fax (916)372-9062, Email: bishop@calnevumc.org

Seattle Episcopal Area, Bishop Grant Hagiya, (816 S 216th St #2, 98198-6331), P.O. Box 13650, Des Moines, WA 98198-1009, Tel. (206)870-6810 Fax (206)870-6811, Email: bishop@pnwumc.org

Periodicals

Mature Years, El Intérprete; New World Outlook; Newscope; Interpreter; Methodist History; Pockets; Response; Social Questions Bulletin; United Methodist Reporter; Quarterly Review; Alive Now; Circuit Rider; El Aposento Alto; Weavings-A Journal of the Christian Spiritual Life; The Upper Room, Faith in Action-online publication.

United Pentecostal Church International

The United Pentecostal Church International came into being through the merger of two oneness Pentecostal organizations - the Pentecostal Church, Inc., and the Pentecostal Assemblies of Jesus Christ. The first of these was known as the Pentecostal Ministerial Alliance from its inception in 1925 until 1932. The second was formed in 1931 by a merger of the Apostolic Church of Jesus Christ with the Pentecostal Assemblies of the World.

The church contends that the Bible teaches that there is one God who manifested himself as the Father in creation, in the Son in redemption, and as the Holy Spirit in regeneration; that Jesus is the name of this absolute deity and that water baptism should be administered in his name, not in the titles Father, Son and Holy Ghost (Acts Ch.2 vs.38, Ch.8 vs.16, and Ch.19 vs.6).

The Fundamental Doctrine of the United Pentecostal Church International, as stated in its Articles of Faith, is "the Bible standard of full salvation, which is repentance, baptism in water by immersion in the name of the Lord Jesus Christ for the remission of sins, and the baptism of the Holy Ghost with the initial sign of speaking with other tongues as the Spirit gives utterance."

Further doctrinal teachings concern a life of holiness and separation, the operation of the gifts of the Spirit within the church, the second coming of the Lord, and the church's obligation to take the gospel to the whole world.

Headquarters
8855 Dunn Rd., Hazelwood, MO 63042, Tel. (314)837-7300 Fax (314)837-4503
Media Contact, Gen. Sec.-Treas., Rev.Jerry Jones
Email: rfuller@upci.org

Officers
Gen. Supt., Rev. Kenneth F. Haney
Asst. Gen. Supts., Rev. Paul. Mooney and Rev. Randy Keyes
Gen. Sec.-Treas., Rev. Jerry Jones
Dir. of Foreign Missions, Rev. Bruce Howell
Gen. Dir. of Home Missions, Rev. Carlton Coon
Editor-in-Chief, Rev. Robert H. Fuller
Gen. Sunday School Dir., Rev. Gary Erickson
Youth Pres., Rev. Todd Gaddy

OTHER ORGANIZATIONS
Pentecostal Publishing House, Mgr., Rev. Robert II. Fuller
Ladies Ministries, Pres., Gwyn Oakes
Stewardship Dept., Dir., Rev., Stephen Drury
Division of Education, Supt., Rev. Don Batchelor
Word Aflame Publications, Editor, Rev. Richard Davis Media Missions Asst. Dir., Rev. Morman R. Paslay II Media Missions Announcer, Rev. J. Hugh Rose
Public Relations, Contact Church Administration
Historical Society & Archives
Urshan Graduate School of Theology

Periodicals
The Pentecostal Herald, World Harvest Today, The North American Challenge, Conqueror, Reflections, Forward, Apostolic Man

The United Pentecostal Churches of Christ

In a time when the Church of Jesus Christ is challenged to send the "Evening Light Message" to the uppermost part of the Earth, a group of men and women came together on May 29, 1992 at the Pentecostal Church of Christ in Cleveland, Ohio to form what is now called The United Pentecostal Churches of Christ.

Organized and established by Bishop Jesse Delano Ellis, II, the United Pentecostal Churches of Christ is about the business of preparing people to see the Lord of Glory. The traditional barriers of yesteryear must not keep saints or like faith apart ever again and this fellowship of Pentecostal, Apostolic Independent Churches have discovered the truth of Our Lord's Prayer in the seventeenth chapter of Saint John, "that they may all be One."

The United Pentecostal Churches of Christ is a fellowship of holiness assemblies which has membership in the universal Body of Christ. As such, we preserve the message of Christ's redeeming love through His atonement and declare holiness of life to be His requirement for all men who would enter into the Kingdom of God. We preach

repentence from sin, baptism in the Name of Jesus Christ, a personal indwelling of the Holy Spirit, a daily walk with the Lord and life after death. Coupled with the cardinal truths of the Church are the age old customs of ceremony and celebration.

Headquarters
10515 Chester Ave., Cleveland, OH 44106, Tel. (216)721-5935 Fax (216)721-6938
Contact Person, Public Relations., Rev. Gwendolyn G. Saunder

REGIONAL OFFICE
493-5 Monroe St., Brooklyn, New York 11221, Tel. (718)574-4100 Fax (718)574-8504
Contact Person, Secretary General., Rev. Rodney McNeil Johnson
Email: community@pcccleveland.com
Website: www.pcccleveland.com

Officers
Presiding Bishop and Prelate, J. Delano Ellis, II, Cleveland, OH
Pastor for Business Administration, Sabrina J. Ellis Senior Assistant Pastor and Bishop Coadjutor, Benjamin T. Douglass
General Secretary, Gwendolyn G. Saunders Assistant Pastor of Worship, Yvonne Tufts Jeans

Periodicals
The Pentecostal Flame

United Zion Church

A branch of the Brethren in Christ which settled in Lancaster County, Pennsylvania, the United Zion Church was organized under the leadership of Matthias Brinser in 1855.

Headquarters
United Zion Retirement Community, 722 Furnace Hills Pk., Lititz, PA 17543
Media Contact, Bishop Charles Brown, 4041 Shanamantown Rd., Annville, PA 17003, Tel. (717)867-1133 Website: www.unitedzion church.org

Officers
Gen. Conf. Mod., Bishop Charles Brown, 4041 Shanamantown Rd., Annville, PA 17003, Tel. (717)867-1133
Asst. Mod., Rev. Paul H. Martin
Gen. Conf. Sec., Rev. Clyde Martin
Gen. Conf. Treas., Kenneth Kleinfelter, 919 Sycamore Lane, Lebanon, PA 17042

Unity of the Brethren

Czech and Moravian immigrants in Texas (beginning about 1855) established congregations which grew into an Evangelical Union in 1903, and with the accession of other Brethren in Texas, into the Evangelical Unity of the Czech-Moravian Brethren in North America. In 1959, it shortened the name to the original name used in 1457, the Unity of the Brethren (Unitas Fratrum, or Jednota Bratrska).

169

Headquarters

4009 Hunter Creek, College Station, TX 77845
Media Contact, Sec. of Exec. Committee, Ginger
McKay, 148 N. Burnett, Baytown, TX 77520
Email: lkoslovsky@teleshare.net
Website: www.unityofthebrethren.org

Officers

President: Claren Kotrla, 1501 Echo Bluff Cove,
Austin Texas 78754, Tel. (512)491-7802,
Email: kotrla@flash.net
1st Vice President: Rev. Linda Chandler, 13108
N. Ridge Circle, Leander, TX 78641, Tel.
(512)267-4826, Email: L77c@aol.com
2nd Vice President: Pastor Joe Emerson, P.O. Box
4615, Temple, TX 76505, Tel. (254)791-0420,
Email: pastorjde@juno.com
3rd Vice President: Rev. James Hejl, 309
Cherrywood Circle, Taylor, TX 76574, Tel.
(512)365-6890, Email: jhejl@austin.rr.com
Secretary: Kathy Harrison, P.O. Box 593, Little
River-Academy, Texas 76554, Tel. (254)721-
1815, Email: kathy@pearson-lawfirm.com
Financial Secretary: Dewyan Weise, 6006 FM
Hwy 765, San Angelo, TX 76905, Email:
DWeise@academicplanet.com Treasurer: James
Marek, 1304 T.H. Johnson Drive, Taylor, Texas
76574, Tel. (512)352-6165, Email: james@
cnbt.com

OTHER ORGANIZATIONS
Bd. of Christian Educ., Dr., Donald Ketcham,
900 N. Harrison, West, TX 76691
Brethren Youth Fellowship, Pres., Jamie Brooke
Bryan, 1231 Four Corners, West, TX 76691
Friends of the Hus Encampment, Jim Baletka,
727 San Benito, College Station, TX 77845
Christian Sisters Union, Pres., Janet Pomykal,
P.O. Box 560, Brenham, TX 77834
Sunday School Union, Pres., Dorothy Kocian,
107 S. Barbara Dr., Waco, TX 76705
Youth Director, Kimberly Stewart, 1500 Lawnmont
Dr., Apt. 208, Round Rock, TX 78664

Periodicals

Brethren Journal

Universal Catholic Church

Founded as a reorganization of the Dutch Old
Catholic Church in 1915-16. In 1941 a controversy broke out in the Church regarding whether
or not certain teachings of Theosophy (reincarnation, etc.) were to become official teachings of
the Church. The Liberal Catholic Church
International split in 2007 into two bodies

Headquarters

741 Cerro Gordo Avenue, San Diego, CA 92102,
USA., Tel. & Fax (619)239-0637

Officers

The Most Rev. Deab Bekken, 741 Cerro Gordo
Ave., San Diego, CA 92102, USA., Tel. & Fax
(619)239-0637, Email: bekken@sbcglobal.net
The Most Rev. Robert Winters, VP and Teasurer,
741 Cerro Gordo Ave., San Diego, CA 92102,

USA., Tel. & Fax (619)239-0637
St. Alban Press, 741 Cerro Gordo Avenue, San
Diego, CA 92102, USA., Tel. & Fax (858)689-
8610, Email: info@stalbanpress.com

Universal Fellowship of Metropolitan Community Churches

The Universal Fellowship of Metropolitan
Community Churches was founded Oct. 6, 1968 by
the Rev. Troy D. Perry in Los Angeles, with a particular but not exclusive outreach to the gay community. Since that time, the Fellowship has grown
to include congregations throughout the world.

The simple declaration of faith of what MCC
believes, as stated in our By-Laws and accepted
by our General Conference is that "Christianity is
the revelation of God in Jesus Christ and is the
religion set forth in the scriptures. Jesus Christ is
foretold in the Old Testament, presented in the
New Testament, and proclaimed by the Christian
Church in every age and in every land."

Founded in the interest of offering a church
home to all who confess and believe, Metropolitan
Community Churches moves in the mainstream of
Christianity. Our faith is based on the principles
outlined in the historic creeds: Apostles and Nicene.

The government of this Fellowship is vested in
its tri-annual General Conference, comprised of
clergy and lay church delegates, who exert the
right of control in all of its affairs, subject to the
provisions of its Articles of Incorporation and By-
Laws. Ongoing leadership is provided by the
Board of Elders and Board of Administration.

Headquarters

Mailing address: P.O. Box 1374, Abilene, TX
79604
Location: 500 Chestnut Street, Suite 1513, Abilene,
TX 79602
Tel. (310)360-8640, Fax (325)675-8977, Email:
info:mccchurch.net
Media Contact, Jim Birkitt, Dir. of Communi-
cations, Email: Communications@MCC
Church.net, Tel. (310)-861-4653
Email: StanKimer@MCCchurch.net
Website: www.mccchurch.org

Officers

Moderator: Rev. Elder Nancy Wilson, 3293
Fruitville Road #105, Sarasota, FL 34237, Tel.
(941)755-5771 Fax (941)847-0867, Email:
RevNancyWilson@MCCchurch.net
Board of Elders: Rev. Elder Ken Martin, Email:
RevKenMartin@MCCchurch.net; Rev. Elder
Diane Fisher, Email: RevDianeFisher@
MCCchurch.net; Rev. Elder Darlene Garner,
Email: RevDarleneGarner@MCCchurch.net;
Rev. Elder Lillie Brock, Email: RevLillie
Brock@MCCchurch.net
Interim Director of Operations: Barbara Crabtree,
P.O. Box 1374, Abilene, TX 79604, Tel.
(310)861-4658 Fax (310)388-1252, Email:
BarbaraCrabtree@MCCchurch.net

Chair, Board of Administration: Rev. Jeff Miner, Email: RevJeffMiner@MCCchurch.net
Chair, Lay Ministry Council: Bryan Parker, Email: LMC@MCCchurch.net
Chair, Global Justice Team: Rev. Pat Bumgardner, Email: Rvpatmccny@aol.com
Chair, Ecumenical and Inter-Religious Team: Stan Kimer, Email: StanKimer@MCCchurch.net
Chair, MCC Theologies Team: Rev. Kharma Amos, Email: KharmaAmos@aol.com
Global HIV / AID Ministry Program: Joshua Love, Email: JoshuaLove@MCCchurch.net
Office of Formation and Leadership Development: Rev. Dr. Mona West, Email: RevMonaWest@MCCchurch.net

Periodicals
MCC Impact

Volunteers of America

Volunteers of America is a Christian Church that answers God's call to transform the world through a ministry of service that feeds, clothes, shelters and demonstrates to all people that they are beloved children of God. As part of that ministry, Volunteers of America provides local human service programs and opportunities for individual and community involvement through local affiliate offices and the National Services Housing and Health Care Division. Volunteers of America has become the largest non profit provider of housing (affordable/senior/homeless shelters) in the US.

Founded in 1896 by Christian social reformers Ballington and Maud Booth, Volunteers of America provides over 100 different types of programs and services in more than 400 communities nationwide. Programs include services for abused and neglected children, youth at risk, the elderly, people with disabilities, homeless individuals and families, and many others. It also provides a national Prison After-Care program that engages local congregations of all denominations as mentors to newly released prisoners. It employs 16,000 individuals whose work is assisted by over 90,000 committed volunteers.

Headquarters
1660 Duke St., Alexandria, VA 22314-3427, Tel. (800)899-0089
Email: voa@voa.org
Website: www.voa.org

Officers
Chpsn., David Kikumoto
Pres., Charles W. Gould, 1660 Duke St., Alexandria, VA. 22314, Tel. (703)341-5000
Vice President, Ministry, Harry V. Quiett, 1660 Duke St., Alexandria, VA. 22314
Tel. (703)341-5084 Fax (703)341-7000
Email: hquiett@voa.org
39 local affiliate offices and one National Services Division. Information accesible through the national website: www.voa.org

Periodicals
Spirit Magazine, Gazette

The Wesleyan Church

The Wesleyan Church was formed on June 26, 1968, through the union of the Wesleyan Methodist Church of America (1843) and the Pilgrim Holiness Church (1897). The headquarters was established at Marion, Ind., and relocated to Indianapolis in 1987,and relocated again in Fishers, Indiana in 2004.

The Wesleyan movement centers around the beliefs, based on Scripture, that the atonement in Christ provides for the regeneration of sinners and the entire sanctification of believers. John Wesley led a revival of these beliefs in the 18th century.

When a group of New England Methodist ministers led by Orange Scott began to crusade for the abolition of slavery, the bishops and others sought to silence them. This led to a series of withdrawals from the Methodist Episcopal Church. In 1843, the Wesleyan Methodist Connection of America was organized and led by Scott, Jotham Horton, LaRoy Sunderland, Luther Lee and Lucius C. Matlack.

During the holiness revival in the last half of the 19th century, holiness replaced social reform as the major tenet of the Connection. In 1947 the name was changed from Connection to Church and a central supervisory authority was set up.

The Pilgrim Holiness Church was one of many independent holiness churches which came into existence as a result of the holiness revival. Led by Martin Wells Knapp and Seth C. Rees, the International Holiness Union and Prayer League was inaugurated in 1897 in Cincinnati. Its purpose was to promote worldwide holiness evangelism and the Union had a strong missionary emphasis from the beginning. It developed into a church by 1913.

The Wesleyan Church is now spread across most of the United States and Canada and in over 90 other countries. The International Conference of The Wesleyan Church, originally named Wesleyan World Fellowship, was organized in 1972 to unite Wesleyan mission bodies developing into mature churches. The Wesleyan Church is a member of the Christian Holiness Partnership, the National Association of Evangelicals and the World Methodist Council.

Headquarters
P.O. Box 50434, Indianapolis, IN 46250, Tel. (317)774-7900
Media Contact, Gen. Sec., Dr. Ronald D. Kelly, Tel. (317)774-7907 Fax (317)744-3924
Email: kellyr@wesleyan.org
Mailing Address: P.O.Box 50434, Indianapolis, IN 46250
Email: generalsecretary@wesleyan.org
Website: www.wesleyan.org

171

Officers

GENERAL SUPERINTENDENTS
Dr. Jo Anne Lyon, Tel. (317)774-3932 Fax (317)774-3931, Email: lyonja@wesleyan.org
Dr. Thomas E. Armiger, Tel. (317)774-3934 Fax (317)774-3931, Email: armigert@wesleyan.org
Dr. Jerry G. Pence, Tel. (317)774-3933 Fax (317)774-3931, Email: pencej@wesleyan.org
General Officers
Gen. Sec., Dr. Ronald D. Kelly, Tel. (317)774-7907 Fax (317)744-3924, Email: kellyr@wesleyan.org
Gen. Treas., Kevin J. Batman, Tel. (317)774-3941 Fax (317)744-3948, Email: batmank@wesleyan.org
Gen. Publisher, Mr. Donald D. Cady, Tel. (317)774-3853 Fax (317)774-3865, Email: cadyd@wesleyan.org
Gen. Director of Communications, Dr. Ronald D. Kelly, Tel. (317)774-7907 Fax (317)774-3924, Email: kellyr@wesleyan.org
Gen. Dir. of Spiritual Formation, Dr. James A. Dunn, Tel. (317)744-3888 Fax (317)774-3880, Email: dunnj@wesleyan.org
Gen. Dir. of Evangelism & Church Growth, Rev. Philip T. Stevenson, Tel. (317)744-3900 Fax (317)774-3899, Email: stevensonp@wesleyan.org
Gen. Dir. of Education & the Ministry, Rev. Kerry D. Kind, Tel. (317)774-3911 Fax (317)774-3915, Email: kindk@wesleyan.org
Gen. Dir. of World Missions, Dr. H. C. Wilson, Tel. (317)774-7950 Fax (317)774-7958, Email: wilsonhc@wesleyan.org

AUXILIARIES/SUBSIDIARY AGENCIES
Stewardship Ministries, Exec. Dir., Rev. Wayne Derr, Tel. (317)774-7339 Fax (317)774-7341, Email: derrw@wesleyan.org
Wesleyan Investment Foundation, Gen. Dir., Dr. Craig A. Dunn, Tel. (317)774-7300 Fax (317)774-7321 Email: wif@wesleyan.org
Wesleyan Pension Fund, Gen. Dir., Dr. Craig A. Dunn, Tel. (317)774-7300 Fax (317)774-7321, Email: dunnc@wesleyan.org
Wesleyan Women, Mrs. Martha Blackburn, Tel. (317)774-7974 Fax (317)774-7975, Email: blackbma@wesleyan.org
Wesleyan Kids for Mission, Mrs. Peggy Ann Camp, Tel. (704)892-3744 Fax (317)570-5254, Email: camppeg@aol.com
Wesleyan Men, Dr. James A. Dunn, Tel. (317)774-3888 Fax (317)774-3880, Email: dunnj@wesleyan.org
Address Service, Tel. (317)744-7900
Archives & Historical Library, Tel. (317)774-7996
Computer Information Services, Tel. (317)774-7922
Wesleyan Publishing House, Tel. (317)774-3853

Periodicals
Wesleyan Life, Wesleyan World

Wesleyan Holiness Association of Churches

This body was founded Aug. 4, 1959 near Muncie, Indiana by a group of ministers and lay-men who were drawn together for the purpose of spreading and conserving sweet, radical, scriptural holiness. These men came from various church bodies. This group is Wesleyan in doctrine and standards.

Headquarters
1141 North US Hwy 27, Fountain City, IN 47341-9757, Tel. (765)584-3199
Media Contact, Gen. Sec.-Treas., Rev. Nathan D. Schockley, 6014 N. US Hwy 31, Columbus, IN 47201

Officers
Gen. Supt., Rev. John Brewer
Asst. Gen. Supt., Rev. Robert W. Wilson, 2346 Neitz Valley Road, Selinsgrove, PA 17870, Tel. (570)539-9821
Gen. Sec.-Treas., Rev. Nathan D. Shockley, 6014 North U.S. Hwy. 31, Columbus, IN 47201, Tel. (812)376-3019
Gen. Youth Pres., Rev. Nathan Shockley, 6014 North U.S. Hwy. 31, Columbus, IN 47201, Tel. (812)376-3019

Periodicals
Eleventh Hour Messenger

Wisconsin Evangelical Lutheran Synod

Organized in 1850 at Milwaukee, Wisconsin, by three pastors sent to America by a German mission society, the Wisconsin Evangelical Lutheran Synod still reflects its origins, although it now has congregations in 50 states and three Canadian provinces. It supports missions in 26 countries.

The Wisconsin Synod federated with the Michigan and Minnesota Synods in 1892 in order to more effectively carry on education and mission enterprises. A merger of these three Synods followed in 1917 to give the Wisconsin Evangelical Lutheran Synod its present form.

Although at its organization in 1850 WELS turned away from conservative Lutheran theology, today it is ranked as one of the most conservative Lutheran bodies in the United States. WELS confesses that the Bible is the verbally inspired, infallible Word of God and subscribes without reservation to the confessional writings of the Lutheran Church. Its interchurch relations are determined by a firm commitment to the principle that unity of doctrine and practice are the prerequisites of pulpit and altar fellowship and ecclesiastical cooperation. It is a founding member of the Confessional Evangelical Lutheran Conference, a federation of 21 like-minded bodies worldwide.

Headquarters
2929 N. Mayfair Rd., Milwaukee, WI 53222, Tel. (414)256-3888 Fax (414)256-3899
MCG Director, Rev. J.D. Liggett
Email: webbin@sab.wels.net
Website: www.wels.net

Officers

Pres., Rev. Mark G. Schroeder, 2929 N Mayfair Rd., Milwaukee, WI 53222, Tel. (414)256-3888 Fax. (414)256-3899
1st Vice Pres., Rev. James R. Huebner, 7318 W. Bluemound Rd., Milwaukee, WI 53213, Tel. (414)271-3006
2nd Vice Pres., Rev. Joel R. Voss, 6700 Crossbrook Drive, Centerville, OH 45459-6963
Sec., Rev. Robert Pasbrig, 876 Fairview Dr., Hartford, WI 53027

OTHER ORGANIZATIONS

Bd. for Ministerial Education, Admn., Rev. Paul T. Prange
Bd. for Parish Services, Admn., Acting Rev. Dave A. Kehl
Bd. for Home Missions, Admn., Rev. Harold J. Hagedorn
Bd. for World Missions, Admn., Rev. Daniel Koelpin

Periodicals

Forward in Christ, Wisconsin Lutheran Quarterly, The Lutheran Educator, Lutheran Leader, Mission Connection

Religious Bodies in the United States Arranged by Families

The following list of religious bodies appearing in the Directory Section of the *Yearbook* shows the "families," or related clusters into which American religious bodies can be grouped. For example, there are many communions that can be grouped under the heading "Baptist" for historical and theological reasons. It should not be assumed, however, that all denominations under one family heading are necessarily consistent in belief or practice. The family clusters tend to represent historical factors more often than theological or practical ones. These family categories provide one of the major pitfalls when compiling church statistics because there is often a tendency to combine the statistics by "families" for analytical and comparative purposes. Such combined totals are deeply flawed, even though they are often used as variables for sociological analysis. The arrangement by families offered here is intended only as a general guide for conceptual organization when viewing the broad sweep of American religious culture.

Religious bodies that cannot be categorized under family headings appear alphabetically and are not indented in the following list.

Adventist Bodies
Advent Christian Church
Church of God General Conference (Oregon,
IL and Morrow, GA)
Primitive Advent Christian Church
Seventh-day Adventist Church

American Evangelical Christian Churches
American Rescue Workers

Anglican Bodies
The Episcopal Church
The Episcopal Orthodox Church
Reformed Episcopal Church

Anglo-Lutheran Catholic Church
Apostolic Catholic Church
Apostolic Christian Church (Nazarene)
Apostolic Christian Churches of America
Apostolic Episcopal Church

Baptist Bodies
Alliance of Baptists
The American Baptist Association
American Baptist Churches in the U.S.A.
Baptist Bible Fellowship International
Baptist General Conference
Baptist Missionary Association of America
Conservative Baptist Association of America
General Association of General Baptists
General Association of Regular Baptist
Churches
National Association of Free Will Baptists
National Baptist Convention of America, Inc.
National Baptist Convention, U.S.A., Inc.
National Missionary Baptist Convention of
America
National Primitive Baptist Convention, Inc.
North American Baptist Conference
Primitive Baptists
Progressive National Baptist Convention, Inc.
Separate Baptists in Christ
Seventh Day Baptist General Conference,
USA and Canada

Southern Baptist Convention
Sovereign Grace Believers
Berean Fellowship of Churches

Brethren (German Baptists)
Brethren Church (Ashland, Ohio)
Church of the Brethren
Fellowship of Grace Brethren Churches
Old German Baptist Brethren Church

Brethren, River
Brethren in Christ Church
United Zion Church

The Catholic Church
Christ Community Church (Evangelical-Protestant)
Christadelphians
Christian Brethren (also known as Plymouth Brethren)
The Christian Congregation, Inc.
The Christian and Missionary Alliance
Christian Union
The Church of Christ (Holiness) U.S.A.
Church of Christ, Scientist
Church Communities International
The Church of Illumination
Church of the Living God
Church of the Nazarene

Churches of Christ - Christian Churches
Christian Church (Disciples of Christ) in the
United States and Canada
Christian Churches and Churches of Christ
Churches of Christ
Churches of Christ in Christian Union

Churches of God
Church of God (Anderson, Indiana)
The Church of God (Seventh Day), Denver,
Colorado
Churches of God, General Conference

Churches of the New Jerusalem
General Church of the New Jerusalem
The Swedenborgian Church
Conservative Congregational Christian
Conference

Eastern Orthodox Churches
Albanian Orthodox Archdiocese in America
Albanian Orthodox Diocese of America
The American Carpatho-Russian Orthodox
Greek Catholic Church
The Antiochian Orthodox Christian
Archdiocese of North America
Apostolic Catholic Assyrian Church of the
East, North American Dioceses
Apostolic Orthodox Catholic Church of North
America
Greek Orthodox Archdiocese of America
The Holy Eastern Orthodox Catholic and
Apostolic Church in North America, Inc.
Holy Ukrainian Autocephalic Orthodox
Church in Exile
The Orthodox Church in America
Patriarchal Parishes of the Russian Orthodox
Church in the U.S.A
The Romanian Orthodox Church in America
The Romanian Orthodox Episcopate of
America
The Russian Orthodox Church Outside of
Russia
Serbian Orthodox Church in the U.S.A. and
Canada
The Syro-Russian Orthodox Catholic Church
True Orthodox Church of Greece (Synod of
Metropolitan Cyprian), American
Exarchate
Ukrainian Orthodox Church of the U.S.A.

The Evangelical Church
The Evangelical Church Alliance
The Evangelical Congregational Church
The Evangelical Covenant Church
The Evangelical Free Church of America
Fellowship of Fundamental Bible Churches
Free Christian Zion Church of Christ

Friends
Evangelical Friends International – North
American Region
Friends General Conference
Friends United Meeting
Philadelphia Yearly Meeting of the Religious
Society of Friends
Religious Society of Friends (Conservative)
Religious Society of Friends (Unaffiliated
Meetings)

Grace Gospel Fellowship
IFCA International, Inc.
International Council of Community
Churches
International Fellowship of Bible Churches,
Inc
Jehovah's Witnesses

Latter-day Saints (Mormons)
Church of Christ
The Church of Jesus Christ (Bickertonites)
The Church of Jesus Christ of Latter-day Saints
Community of Christ

The Liberal Catholic Church— Province of
the United States of America

Lutheran Bodies
The American Association of Lutheran
Churches
Apostolic Lutheran Church of America
The Association of Free Lutheran
Congregations
The Association of Independent Evangelical
Lutheran Churches
Church of the Lutheran Brethren of America
Church of the Lutheran Confession
Conservative Lutheran Association
The Estonian Evangelical Lutheran Church
Evangelical Lutheran Church in America
Evangelical Lutheran Synod
The Latvian Evangelical Lutheran Church in
America
The Lutheran Church— Missouri Synod
Wisconsin Evangelical Lutheran Synod

Mennonite Bodies
Beachy Amish Mennonite Churches
Bible Fellowship Church
Church of God in Christ, Mennonite
Fellowship of Evangelical Bible Churches
Fellowship of Evangelical Churches
General Conference of Mennonite Brethren
Churches
Hutterian Brethren
Mennonite Church, USA
Old Order Amish Church
Old Order (Wisler) Mennonite Church
Reformed Mennonite Church

Methodist Bodies
African Methodist Episcopal Church
The African Methodist Episcopal Zion Church
Allegheny Wesleyan Methodist Connection
(Original Allegheny Conference)
Bible Holiness Church
Christian Methodist Episcopal Church
Evangelical Methodist Church
Free Methodist Church of North America
Fundamental Methodist Church, Inc.
Primitive Methodist Church in the U.S.A
Reformed Methodist Union Episcopal Church
Reformed Zion Union Apostolic Church
Southern Methodist Church
The United Methodist Church
The Wesleyan Church

The Missionary Church

Moravian Bodies
Moravian Church in America (Northern
Province, Southern Province)
Unity of the Brethren

National Association of Congregational Christian Churches
National Organization of the New Apostolic Church of North America
National Spiritualist Association of Churches
North American Old Roman Catholic Church (Archdiocese of New York)

Old Catholic Churches

Apostolic Catholic Orthodox Church
Christ Catholic Church
Liberal Catholic Church (International)
The Old Catholic Orthodox Church (formerly the Apostolic Orthodox Old Catholic Church)
The United Catholic Church, Inc.

Oriental Orthodox Churches

Armenian Apostolic Church of America
Armenian Apostolic Church, Diocese of America
Coptic Orthodox Church
Malankara Orthodox Syrian Church, Diocese of America
Syrian (Syriac) Orthodox Church of Antioch

Pentecostal Bodies

Apostolic Faith Mission Church of God
Apostolic Faith Mission of Portland, Oregon
Assemblies of God
Assemblies of God International Fellowship (Independent/Not affiliated)
Association of Vineyard Churches
The Bible Church of Christ, Inc.
Bible Way Church of Our Lord Jesus Christ World Wide, Inc.
Calvary Chapel
Christian Church of North America, General Council
The Church of God
The Church of God In Christ
Church of God in Christ, International
Church of God (Cleveland, Tennessee)
The Church of God of the Firstborn
Church of God by Faith, Inc.
Church of God, Mountain Assembly, Inc.
Church of God of Prophecy
Church of Our Lord Jesus Christ of the Apostolic Faith, Inc.
Congregational Holiness Church
Elim Fellowship
Full Gospel Assemblies International
Full Gospel Fellowship of Churches and Ministers International
House of God, Which is the Church of the Living God, the Pillar and Ground of the Truth
International Church of the Foursquare Gospel
The International Pentecostal Church of Christ
International Pentecostal Holiness Church
Open Bible Standard Churches
The (Original) Church of God, Inc.

Pentecostal Assemblies of the World, Inc.
Pentecostal Church of God
Pentecostal Fire-Baptized Holiness Church
The Pentecostal Free Will Baptist Church, Inc.
United Holy Church of America, Inc.

United House of Prayer

United Pentecostal Church International
The United Pentecostal Churches of Christ

Pillar of Fire
Polish National Catholic Church of America

Reformed Bodies

Associate Reformed Presbyterian Church (General Synod)
Christian Reformed Church in North America
Cumberland Presbyterian Church
Cumberland Presbyterian Church in America
Evangelical Presbyterian Church
Hungarian Reformed Church in America
Korean Presbyterian Church in America, General Assembly of the
Netherlands Reformed Congregations
The Orthodox Presbyterian Church
Presbyterian Church in America
Presbyterian Church (U.S.A.)
Protestant Reformed Churches in America
Reformed Church in America
Reformed Church in the United States
Reformed Presbyterian Church of North America
United Church of Christ

Reformed Catholic Church
The Salvation Army
The Schwenkfelder Church

Thomist Churches

Mar Thoma Syrian Church of India

Triumph the Church and Kingdom of God in Christ Inc. (International)
Unitarian Universalist Association of Congregations

United Brethren Bodies

Church of the United Brethren in Christ
United Christian Church

Universal Fellowship of Metropolitan Community Churches
Volunteers of America
Wesleyan Holiness Association of Churches

176

4. Religious Bodies in Canada

A large number of Canadian religious bodies were organized by immigrants from Europe and elsewhere, and a smaller number sprang up originally on Canadian soil. In the case of Canada, moreover, many denominations that transcend the U.S.-Canada border have headquarters in the United States. A final section in this directory lists churches according to denominational families. This can be a helpful tool in finding a particular church if you don't know the official name. Complete statistics for Canadian churches are found in the statistical section in Section 3: Table 1 contains memberhsip figures, and Table 4 contains giving figures. Addresses for periodicals are found in the directory entitled, "Religious Periodicals in Canada."

The Anglican Church of Canada

Anglicanism came to Canada with the early explorers such as Martin Frobisher and Henry Hudson. Continuous services began in Newfoundland about 1700 and in Nova Scotia in 1710. The first Bishop, Charles Inglis, was appointed to Nova Scotia in 1787 The Anglican Church of Canada includes a large number of the original inhabitants of Canada (Indians, Inuit and Metis) and has been a strong advocate of their rights.

The Anglican Church of Canada has enjoyed self-government for over a century since 1893 and is an autonomous member of the worldwide Anglican Communion. The Church also has a strong international role in development and disaster relief through the Primate's World Relief and Development Fund (PWRDF). The General Synod, which normally meets triennially (next meeting 2010), consists of the Archbishops, Bishops and elected clerical and lay representatives of the 30 dioceses. Each of the Ecclesiastical Provinces—Canada, Ontario, Rupert's Land and British Columbia—is organized under a Metropolitan and has its own Provincial Synod and Executive Council. Each diocese has its own Diocesan Synod.

Headquarters

Church House, 80 Hayden St., Toronto, ON M4Y 3G2 Tel. (416)924-9192 (Switchboard) 416 924-9199 (Voice mail) Fax (416)968-7983, Web www.anglican.ca
Media Contact, Mr. Vianney (Sam) Carriere
General Email: info@national.anglican.ca

Officers

GENERAL SYNOD OFFICERS
Primate of the Anglican Church of Canada, The Most Rev. Fred J. Hiltz
Prolocutor, Canon Robert Falby
Gen. Sec., The Ven. Michael F. Pollesel
Treas., Gen. Synod, Ms. Michèle George

DEPARTMENTS AND DIVISIONS
Faith, Worship & Ministry, Dir., Rev. Canon Alyson Barnett-Cowan
Financial Management and Dev., Dir., Ms. Michèle George
Inform. Resources Dir., Mr. Vianney (Sam) Carriere
Partnerships, Dir., Ms. Henriette Thompson

Pensions, Dir., Ms. Judith Robinson
Primate's World Relief and Dev. Fund, Dir., Ms. Cheryl Curtis

METROPOLITANS (ARCHBISHOPS)
British Columbia, The Most Rev. Terrence O. Buckle, Metropolitan, Box 31136, Whitehorse YT Y1A 5P7 Tel. (867) 667-7746 Fax (867) 667-6125, E-mail: synodoffice@klondiker.com
Ecclesiastical Province of, Canada, Vacant
Ontario, The Most Rev. Caleb J. Lawrence, Box 841, Schumacher, ON P0N 1G0 Tel. (705) 360-1129 Fax (705) 360-1120 E-mail: dmoose@domaa.ca
Rupert's Land, The Most Rev. David Ashdown, Box 567, Keewatin, ON P0X 1C0, Tel. (807) 547-3353, Fax (807) 547-3356, E-mail: keewatinbishop@shaw.ca

DIOCESAN BISHOPS
Algoma, The Rt. Rev. Stephen Andrews, Box 1168, Sault Ste. Marie, ON P6A 5N7 Tel. (705)256-5061 Fax (705)946-1860, Email: dioceseofalgoma@on.aibn.com
Arctic, The Rt. Rev. Andrew P. Atagotaalnuk, 4910 51st St., Box 190, Yellowknife, NT X1A 2N2, Tel. (867)873-5432 Fax (867)873-8478, Email: diocese@arcticnet.org
Athabasca, Vacant, Box 6868, Peace River, AB T8S 1S6 Tel. (780)624-2767 Fax (780)624-2365, Email: bpath@telusplanet.net
Brandon, The Rt. Rev. James D. Njegovan, Box 21009 WEPO, Brandon, MB R7B 3W8 Tel. (204)727-7550 Fax (204)727-4135, Email: bishopbdn@mts.net
British Columbia, The Rt. Rev. A.J. Cowan, 900 Vancouver St., Victoria, BC V8V 3V7 Tel. (250)386-7781 Fax (250)386-4013, Email: synod@bc.anglican.ca
Caledonia, The Rt. Rev. William J. Anderson, Box 278, Prince Rupert, BC V8J 3P6 Tel. (250)624-6013 Fax (250)624-4299, Email: synodofc@citytel.net
Calgary, Bishop, The Rt. Rev. Derek B.E. Hoskin , #560, 1207 11th Ave., SW, Salgary, AB T3C 0M5, Tel. (403)243-3673 Fax (403)243-2182, Diocesan Email: synod@calgary.anglican.ca
Central Interior, Anglican Parishes (APCI) The Rt. Rev. Barbara Andrews, 360 Nicola St., Kamloops, BC V2C 2P5 Tel. (250) 819-5753 E-mail: apcioffice@shawbiz.ca

Central Newfoundland, The Rt. Rev. F. David Torraville, 34 Fraser Rd., Gander, NF A1V 2E8, Tel. 709-256-2372, Fax 709-256-2396, Email: bishopcentral@nfld.net

Eastern Newfoundland and Labrador, The Rt. Rev. Cyrus C.J. Pitman , 19 King's Bridge Rd., St. John's, NF A1C 3K4 Tel. (709)576-6697 Fax (709)576-7122, Email: cpitman@ anglica-nenl.nf.net

Edmonton, The Rt. Rev. Jane Alexander, 10035 - 103 St., Edmonton, AB T5J 0X5 Tel. (780)439-7344 Fax (780)439-6549, Email: bishop@edmonton.anglican.ca

Fredericton, The Rt. Rev. Claude E.W. Miller, 115 Church St., Fredericton, NB E3B 4C8 Tel. (506)459-1801 Fax (506)459-8475, Email: bishfton@nbnet.nb.ca

Huron, The Rt. Rev. Robert F. Bennett, 190 Queens Ave., London, ON N6A 6H7 Tel. (519)434-6893 Fax (519)673-4151, Email: bishops@huron.anglican.ca

Keewatin, The Most Rev. David N. Ashdown, 915 Ottawa St., Keewatin, ON P0X 1C0 Tel. (807)547-3353 Fax (807)547-3356 Email: dioceseofkeewatin@gokenora.com

Kootenay, The Rt. Rev. John E. Privett, 1876 Richter St., Kelowna, BC V1Y 2M9 Tel. (250)762-3306 Fax (250)762-4150, Email: diocese_of_kootenay@telus.net

Montreal, The Rt. Rev. Barry B. Clarke, 1444 Union Ave., Montreal, QC H3A 2B8 Tel. (514)843-6577 Fax (514)843-3221, Email: bishops.office@montreal.anglican.ca

Moosonee, The Most Rev. Caleb J. Lawrence, Box 841, Schumacher, ON P0N 1G0 Tel. (705)360-1129 Fax (705)360-1120, Email: dmoose@domaa.ca

New Westminster, The Rt. Rev. Michael C. Ingham, 580-401 W. Georgia St., Vancouver, BC V6B 5A1 Tel. (604)684-6306 Fax (604)684-7017, Email: bishop@vancouver.anglican.ca

Niagara, The Rt. Rev. Michael A. Bird, 252 James St. N., Hamilton, ON L8R 2L3 Tel. (905)527-1278 Fax (905)527-1281, Email: bishop@niagara.anglican.ca

Nova Scotia and Prince Edward Is., The Rt. Rev. Susan E. Moxley, 5732 College St., Halifax, NS B3H 1X3 Tel. (902)420-0717 Fax (902)425-0717, Email: office@nspeidiocese.ca

Ontario, The Rt. Rev. George L. R. Bruce, 90 Johnson St., Kingston, ON K7L 1X7 Tel. (613)544-4774 Fax (613)547-3745, Email: synod@ontario.anglican.ca

Ottawa, The Rt. Rev. John H. Chapman, 71 Bronson Ave., Ottawa, ON K1R 6G6 Tel. (613)232-7124 Fax (613)232-7088, Email: dayadmin@ottawa.anglican.ca

Qu'Appelle, The Rt. Rev. Gregory K. Kerr-Wilson, 1501 College Ave., Regina, SK S4P 1B8 Tel. (306)522-1608 Fax (306)352-6808, Email: quappelle@ca sasktel.net

Quebec, The Rt. Rev. Dennis Drainville, 31 rue des Jardins, Quebec, QC G1R 4L6 Tel.

(418)692-3858 Fax (418)692-3876, Email: bishop@quebec.anglican.ca

Rupert's Land, The Rt. Rev. Donald D. Phillips, 935 Nesbitt Bay, Winnipeg, MB R3T 1W6 Tel. (204)922-4200 Fax (204)922-4219, Email: general@rupertsland.ca

Saskatchewan, The Rt. Rev. Michael W. Hawkins, 1308 5th Ave. East, Prince Albert, SK S6V 2H7 Tel. (306)763-2455 Fax (306)764-5172, Email: synod@sasktel.net

Saskatoon, The Rt. Rev. Rodney Andrews, Box 1965, Saskatoon, SK S7K 3S5 Tel. (306)244-5651, Fax (306)933-4606, Email: anglican-bishop@sasktel.net

Toronto, The Rt. Rev. Colin R. Johnson, 135 Adelaide St. East, Toronto, ON M5C 1L8 Tel. (416)363-6021 Fax (416)363-3683, Email: cjohnson@toronto.anglican.ca

Western Newfoundland, The Rt. Rev. Percy D. Coffin, 25 Main St., Corner Brook, NF A2H 1C2 Tel. (709)639-8712 Fax (709)639-1636, Email: dsownc@nf.aibn.com

Yukon, The Most Rev. Terry Buckle, Box 4247, Whitehorse, YT Y1A 3T3 Tel. (867)667-7746 Fax (867)667-6125, Email: synodoffice@ klondiker.com

Periodicals
Anglican Journal (National Newspaper); Ministry Matters

The Antiochian Orthodox Christian Archdiocese of North America

The approximately 130,000 members of the Antiochian Orthodox community in Canada are under the jurisdiction of the Antiochian Orthodox Christian Archdiocese of North America with headquarters in Englewood, N.J. There are churches in Edmonton, Halifax, London, Ottawa, Toronto, Windsor, Montreal, Saskatoon, Charlottestown, PEI, Calgary, and Mississauga.

Headquarters
Metropolitan Philip Saliba, 358 Mountain Rd., Englewood, NJ 07631 Tel. (201)871-1355 Fax (201)871-7954

Website: www.antiochian.org

Media Contact, Rev. Fr. Thomas Zain, 355 State Street, Brooklyn, NY 11217 Tel. (718)855-6225 Fax (718)855-3608 Email: abouna@aol.com

Officers
Bishop Alexander, 10820 Rue Laverdure, Montreal, PQ H3L2L9, Tel. (514)388-4344 Fax (514)388-4051

Periodicals
The Word; Again; Handmaiden

Apostolic Christian Church (Nazarene)

This church was formed in Canada as a result of immigration from various European countries. The body began as a movement originated by the Rev.

S. H. Froehlich, a Swiss pastor, whose followers are still found in Switzerland and Central Europe.

Headquarters
Apostolic Christian Church Foundation, 1135 Sholey Rd., Richmond, VA 23231 Tel. (804) 222-1943
Media Contact, James Hodges

Officers
Exec. Dir., James Hodges

The Apostolic Church in Canada

The Apostolic Church in Canada is affiliated with the worldwide organization of the Apostolic Church with headquarters in Great Britain (www.apostolicworld.net). A product of the Welsh Revival (1904 to 1908), its Canadian beginnings originated in Nova Scotia in 1927. Today its main centers are in Nova Scotia, Ontario and Quebec. This church is evangelical, fundamental and Pentecostal, with special emphasis on the ministry gifts listed in Ephesians 4:11-12.

Headquarters
27 Castlefield Ave., Toronto, ON M4R 1G3
Media Contact, Pres., Rev. D. Karl Thomas, 220 Adelaide St. London, ON N6B-3H4, Tel. (519)438-7036, Email: nlcrevival@goldon.net
Fax (705)742-2948
Website: www.apostolic.ca

Officers
Pres., Rev. D. Karl Thomas, 220 Adelaide St., London, ON N6B 344, Tel. (519)438-7036, Fax (519)438-5800, Email: nlcrevival@goldon.net Natl. Sec., Rev. Phillip Woolridge, 27 Castlefield Ave., Toronto, ON M4R 1G3, Tel. (519)438-7036, Fax (519)438-5800

Periodicals
Canadian News Up-Date

Apostolic Church of Pentecost of Canada Inc.

The Apostolic Church of Pentecost, Incorporated, was founded in 1921 at Winnipeg, Manitoba, by Pastor Frank Small and is a network of ministers and churches providing fellowship, encouragement and accountability in the proclamation of the Gospel of Jesus Christ by the power of the Holy Spirit.

Headquarters
#119-2340 Pegasus Way NE, Calgary, AB T2E 8M5
Email:acop@acop.ca
Website: www.acop.ca
Media Contact, President, Rev. Wes Mills, Tel. (403)273-5777 Fax (403)273-8102

Officers
President., Rev. Wes Mills
Administrator, Mrs. Darla Matchett

Periodicals
Fellowship Focus

Armenian Evangelical Church

Founded in 1960 by immigrant Armenian evangelical families from the Middle East, this body is conservative doctrinally, with an evangelical, biblical emphasis. The polity of churches within the group differ with congregationalism being dominant, but there are presbyterian Armenian Evangelical churches as well. Most of the local churches have joined main-line denominations. All of the remaining Armenian Evangelical (congregational or presbyterian) local churches in the United States and Canada have joined with the Armenian Evangelical Union of North America.

Headquarters
Armenian Evangelical Church of Toronto, 2851 John St., P.O. Box 42015, Markham, ON L3R 5R0 Tel. (905)305-8144
Media Contact, Chief Editor, Rev. Yessayi Sarmazian

A.E.U.N.A. OFFICERS
Min. to the Union, Rev. Karl Avakian, 1789 F. Frederick Ave., Fresno, CA 93720
Mod., Rev. Bernard Geulsgeugian

Officers
Min., Rev. Yessayi Sarmazian

Periodicals
Armenian Evangelical Church

Armenian Holy Apostolic Church - Canadian Diocese

The Canadian branch of the ancient Church of Armenia founded in A.D. 301 by St. Gregory the Illuminator was established in Canada at St. Catharines, Ontario, in 1930. The diocesan organization is under the jurisdiction of the Holy See of Etchmiadzin, Armenia. The Diocese has churches in St. Catharines, Hamilton, Toronto, Ottawa, Vancouver, Mississauga, Montreal, Laval, Windsor, Halifax, Winnipeg, Edmonton and Calgary.

Headquarters
Diocesan Offices, Primate, Canadian Diocese, Archbishop Hovnan Derderian, 615 Stuart Ave., Outremont, QC H2V 3H2 Tel. (514)276-9479 Fax (514)276-9960, Email adiocese@aol.com, Web www.canarmdiocese.org
Media Contact, Exec. Dir. Deacon Hagop Arslanian;Silva Mangassarian, Secretary

Officers
Sec., Silva Mangassarian
Webmaster, Albert Yeglikian

Associated Gospel Churches

The Associated Gospel Churches (AGC) traces its historical roots to the 1890s. To counteract the growth of liberal theology evident in many established denominations at this time, individuals and whole congregations seeking to uphold the final authority of the Scriptures in all

179

matters of faith and conduct withdrew from those denominations and established churches with an evangelical ministry. These churches defended the belief that "all Scripture is given by inspiration of God" and also declared that the Holy Spirit gave the identical word of sacred writings of holy men of old, chosen by Him to be the channel of His revelation to man.

At first this growing group of independent churches was known as the Christian Workers' Churches of Canada, and by 1922 there was desire for forming an association for fellowship, counsel and cooperation. Several churches in southern Ontario banded together under the leadership of Dr. P. W. Philpott of Hamilton and Rev. H. E. Irwin, K. C. of Toronto.

When a new Dominion Charter was obtained on March 18, 1925, the name was changed to Associated Gospel Churches. Since that time the AGC has steadily grown, spreading across Canada by invitation to other independent churches of like faith and by actively beginning new churches.

Headquarters
1500 Kerns Rd., Burlington, ON L7P 3A7
Tel. (905)634-8184 Fax (905)634-6283
Email: admin@agcofcanada.com
Website: www.agcofcanada.com
Administrative Assistant, Donna Leung, 1500 Kerns Rd., Burlington, ON L7P 3A7 Tel. (905)634-8184 Fax (905)634-6283 Email: donna@agcofcanada.com

Officers
Pres., Dr. Bill Fietje, 1500 Kerns Rd., Burlington, ON L7P 3A7 Tel. (905)634-8184 Fax (905)634-6283
Mod., Rev. Randy Jost , 1500 Kerns Rd, Burlington, L7P3A7, el. (905)634-8184 Fax (905)634-6283

Periodicals
Insidedge

Association of Regular Baptist Churches (Canada)
The Association of Regular Baptist Churches was organized in 1957 by a group of churches for the purpose of mutual cooperation in missionary activities. The Association believes the Bible to be God's word, stands for historic Baptist principles, and opposes modern ecumenism.

Headquarters
17 Laverock St., Tottenham, ON L0G 1W0, Tel. 905-936-3786

Officers
Chmn., Rev. S. Kring, 67 Sovereen St., Delhi, ON N4B 1L7

Baptist Convention of Ontario and Quebec
The Baptist Convention of Ontario and Quebec is a family of 365 churches in Ontario and Quebec, united for mutual support and encouragement and united in missions in Canada and the world.

The Convention was formally organized in 1888. Its one educational institution—McMaster Divinity College was founded in 1887. The Convention works through the all-Canada missionary agency, Canadian Baptist Ministries. The churches also support the Sharing Way, the relief and development arm of Canadian Baptist Ministries.

Headquarters
195 The West Mall, Ste. 414, Etobicoke, ON M9C 5K1 Tel. (416)622-8600 Fax (416)622-2308
Media Contact, Exec. Min., Dr. Ken Bellous.
Web Address: www.Baptist.ca

Officers
Past Pres., Rev. John Torrance
President, Mr. Evan Whitehead
1st Vice-Pres., Mrs. Marie Toompuu
2nd Vice Pres., Mr. Don Hallman
Treas.-Bus. Admn., Nancy Bell
Exec. Min., Dr. Ken Bellous

Periodicals
The Canadian Baptist

Baptist General Conference of Canada
The Baptist General Conference was founded in Canada by missionaries from the United States. Originally a Swedish body, BGC Canada now includes people of many nationalities and is conservative and evangelical in doctrine and practice.

Headquarters
#205 15824 131 Avenue Edmonton, AB T5V 1J4 Tel. (780)438-9127 Fax (780)435-2478
Media Contact, Exec. Dir., Jamey S. McDonald

Officers
Exec. Dir., Jamey S. McDonald , #205 15824 131 Avenue Edmonton, AB T5V 1J4 Tel. (780)438-9127 Fax (780)435-2478
Exec. Dir., Gordon H. Sorensen, BGC Stewardship Foundation, #205 15824 131 Avenue Edmonton, AB T5V 1J4 Tel. (780)438-9127 Fax (780)435-2478

DISTRICTS
Baptist Gen. Conf.- Central Canada, Exec. Min., Lorne Meisner, 877 Wilkes Avenue, Winnipeg, MB R3P 1B8 Tel. (204) 772-6742 Fax (204) 269-5505
Baptist General Conference in Alberta, Exec. Min., Cal Netterfield, 11525 23 Ave., Edmonton, AB T6J 4T3 Tel. (780) 438-9126 Fax (780) 438-5258
British Columbia Baptist Conference, Exec. Min., Walter W. Wieser, 7600 Glover Rd., Langley, BC V2Y 1Y1 Tel. (604) 888-2246 Fax (604) 888-0046
Baptist General Conf. in Saskatchewan, Exec. Min., Abe Funk

The Bible Holiness Movement
The Bible Holiness Movement, organized in 1949 as an outgrowth of the city mission work of

the late Pastor William James Elijah Wakefield, an early-day Salvation Army officer, has been headed since its inception by his son, Evangelist Wesley H. Wakefield, its Bishop-General.

It derives its emphasis on the original Methodist faith of salvation and scriptural holiness from the late Bishop R. C. Horner. It adheres to the common evangelical faith in the Bible, the Deity and the atonement of Christ. It stresses a personal experience of salvation for the repentant sinner, of being wholly sanctified for the believer and of the fullness of the Holy Spirit for effective witness. Membership involves a life of Christian love and evangelistic and social activism. Members are required to totally abstain from liquor and tobacco. They may not attend popular amusements or join secret societies. Divorce and remarriage are forbidden. Similar to Wesley's Methodism, members are, under some circumstances, allowed to retain membership in other evangelical church fellowships. Interchurch affiliations are maintained with a number of Wesleyan-Arminian Holiness denominations.

Year-round evangelistic outreach is maintained through open-air meetings, visitation, literature and other media. Noninstitutional welfare work, including addiction counseling, is conducted among minorities. There is direct overseas famine relief, civil rights action, environment protection and antinuclearism. The movement sponsors a permanent committee on religious freedom and an active promotion of Christian racial equality.

The movement has a world outreach with branches in the United States, India, Nigeria, Philippines, Ghana, Liberia, Cameroon, Kenya, Zambia, South Korea, Mulawi, and Tanzania. It also ministers to 89 countries in 42 languages through literature, radio and audiocassettes.

Headquarters
Box 223, Postal Stn. A, Vancouver, BC V6C 2M3 Tel. (250) 492-3376
Media Contact, Bishop-General, Evangelist Wesley H. Wakefield, P.O. Box 223, Postal Station A, Vancouver, BC V6C 2M3 Tel. (250) 492-3376
Website: www.bible-holiness-movement.com

DIRECTORS
Bishop-General, Evangelist Wesley H. Wakefield, (Intl. Leader)
Evangelist M. J. Wakefield, Penticton, BC
Pastor Vincente & Mirasal Hernando, Phillipines
Pastor & Mrs. Daniel Stinnett, 1425 Mountain View W., Phoenix, AZ 85021 Pastor Monday S. Attai, Abak, Akwalbom, Nigeria, West Africa
Pastor Choe Chong Dee, Iksun City, S. Korea
Pastor T. Chandra, Sekhor Rao, India
Pastor and Mrs. Daniel Vandee, Ghana, W. Africa
Pastor Victor Freeman Holmquist, Vancouver, B.C., Canada
Bro. Aaron Louis Birch, Vancouver, B.C., Evangelist, Mrs. Stephen Richards, Uyo, Akwa Ibom State, Nigeria, West Africa

Periodicals
Hallelujah!

Brethren in Christ Church, Canadian Conference
The Brethren in Christ, formerly known as Tunkers in Canada, arose out of a religious awakening in Lancaster County, Pennsylvania late in the 18th century. Representatives of the new denomination reached Ontario in 1788 and established the church in the southern part of the present province. Presently the conference has congregations in Ontario, Alberta, Quebec and Saskatchewan. In theology they have accents of the Pietist, Anabaptist, Wesleyan and Evangelical movements.

Headquarters
Brethren in Christ Church, Gen. Ofc., P.O. Box A, Grantham, PA 17027-0901 Tel. (717)697-2634 Fax (717)697-7714
Canadian Headquarters, Bishop's Ofc., 416 North Service Rd. E., Suite 1, Oakville, ON L6H 5R2, Tel. (905)339-2335
Media Contact, Mod., Dr. Warren L. Hoffman, Brethren in Christ Church Gen. Ofc.

Officers
Mod., Bishop Brian Bell, 416 North Service Road, Suite 1, Oakville, ON L6H 5R2 Tel. (905)339-2335 Fax (905)337-2120
Sec., Betty Albrecht, RR 2, Petersburg, ON N0B 2H0
Sec., Carole Phillips, 416 North Service Rd. E., Suite 1, Oakville, ON L6H 5R2

Periodicals
Evangelical Visitor; "Yes", Shalom

British Methodist Episcopal Church of Canada
The British Methodist Episcopal Church was organized in 1856 in Chatham, Ontario and incorporated in 1913. It has congregations across the Province of Ontario.

Headquarters
430 Grey Street, London, ON N6B 1H3
Media Contact, Gen. Sec., Rev. Jacqueline Collins, 47 Connolly St., Toronto, ON M6N 4Y5 Tel. (416)653-6339

Officers
Gen. Supt., Rt. Rev. Dr. Douglas Birse, R.R. #5, Thamesville, ON N0P 2K0, Tel. (519)692-3628
Asst. Gen. Supt., Maurice M. Hicks, 3 Boxdene Ave., Scarborough, ON M1V 3C9 Tel. (416)298-5715
Gen. Sec., Rev. Jacqueline Collins, 47 Connolly St., Toronto, ON M6N 4Y5 Tel. (416)653-6339
Gen. Treas., Ms. Hazel Small, 7 Wood Fernway, North York, ON M2J 4P6, Tel. (416)491-0313

Periodicals
B.M.E. Church Newsletter

181

Canadian and American Reformed Churches

The Canadian and American Reformed Churches accept the Bible as the infallible Word of God, as summarized in The Belgic Confession of Faith (1561), The Heidelberg Cathechism (1563) and The Canons of Dort (1618-1619). The federation was founded in Canada in 1950 and in the United States in 1955.

Headquarters

Synod, 607 Dynes Rd., Burlington, ON L7N 2V4
Canadian Reformed Churches, Ebenezer Canadian Reformed Church, 607 Dynes Rd., Burlington, ON L7N 2V4
Theological College, Dr. G. H. Visscher, 110 W. 27th St., Hamilton, ON L9C 5A1 Tel. (905)575-3688 Fax (905)575-0799
Media Contact, Rev. Dr. G. Nederveen, 3089 Woodward Ave., Burlington, ON L7N 2M3 Tel. (905)681-7055 Fax (905)681-7055

Periodicals

Reformed Perspective, A Magazine for the Christian Family; Evangel, The Good News of Jesus Christ; Clarion, The Canadian Reformed Magazine; Diakonia-A Magazine of Office-Bearers; Book of Praise; Koinonia, A periodical of the Ministers of the CanRC; Horizon, A quaterly magazine published by the League of CanRC Women Societies; A Gift from Heaven, A Reformed Bible course.

Canadian Baptist Ministries

The Canadian Baptist Ministries has four federated member bodies, (1) Baptist Convention of Ontario and Quebec, (2) Baptist Union of Western Canada, (3) the United Baptist Convention of the Atlantic Provinces, (4) Union d'Églises Baptistes Françaises au Canada (French Baptist Union). Its main purpose is to act as a coordinating agency for the four groups for mission in all five continents.

Headquarters

7185 Millcreek Dr., Mississauga, ON L5N 5R4 Tel. (905)821-3533 Fax (905)826-3441
Website: www.cbmin.org
Media Contact, Communications, David Rogelstad
Email: daver@cbmin.org

Officers

Pres., Doug Coomas
Gen. Sec., Rev. Gart Nelson
Email: NelsonG@cbmin.org

Canadian Baptists of Western Canada

Headquarters

302,902-11 Ave., SW, Calgary, AB T2R 0E7
Media Contact, Exec. Min., Rev. Jeremy Bell

Officers

President: Rev. David Simpson (until April 2009), 8025 Sherwood Dr., Regina, SK S4Y 1G1

Executive Minister; Rev. Jeremy Bell, 5920 Iona Drive, Vancouver BC, V6T 1J6
Alberta Regional Minister: Rev. Sam Breakey, 212, 9333 – 50th St., Edmonton, Alberta T6B 2L5
BCY Regional Minister: Rev. Rob Ogilvie, 201, 20349 88th Ave, Langley, British Columbia V1M 2K5
Heartland Regional Minister: Rev. Ken Thiessen, 3 – 4621 Rae St., Regina, Saskatchewan S4S 6K6
Carey Theological College: President, Dr. Brian Stelck, 5920 Iona Drive, Vancouver BC, V6T 1J6

Canadian Conference of Mennonite Brethren Churches

The conference was incorporated November 22, 1945.

Headquarters

1310 Taylor Ave., Winnipeg, MB R3M 3Z6 Tel. (204)669-6575 Fax (204)654-1865 Toll Free: 888-669-6575 www.mbconf.ca
Media Contact, Exec. Dir., Dave Wiebe

Periodicals

Mennonite Brethren Herald; Le Lien; Chinese Herald; Mennonite Historian

Canadian Convention of Southern Baptists

The Canadian Convention of Southern Baptists was formed at the Annual Meeting, May 7-9, 1985, in Kelowna, British Columbia. It was formerly known as the Canadian Baptist Conference, founded in Kamloops, British Columbia, in 1959 by pastors of existing churches.

Headquarters

100 Convention Way, Cochrane, AB T4C 2G2, Tel. (403)932-5688 Fax (403)932-4937
Email: office@ccsb.ca
Media Contact, Exec. Dir.-Treas., Rev.Gerald Taillon

Officers

Exec. Dir.-Treas., Gerald Taillon, 17 Riverview Close, Cochrane, AB T4C 1K7
Pres., Richard Lamothe, 31 Koho Drive, Ashton, ON K0A 1B0

Periodicals

The Baptist Horizon

Canadian District of the Moravian Church in America, Northern Province

The work in Canada is under the general oversight and rules of the Moravian Church, Northern Province, general offices for which are located in Bethlehem, Pennsylvania. For complete information, see "Religious Bodies in the United States" section of the *Yearbook*.

Headquarters
1021 Center St., P.O. Box 1245, Bethlehem, PA
18016-1245
Media Contact, Ms. Deanna Hollenbach

Officers
Pres.,Rev. Stephen Gohdes, 600 Acadia Dr. SE
Calgary, AB T2J OB8, Email: sgohdes@shaw.ca

Periodicals
The Moravian

Canadian Yearly Meeting of the Religious Society of Friends

Canadian Yearly Meeting of the Religious
Society of Friends was founded in Canada as an
offshoot of the Quaker movement in Great Britain
and colonial America. Genesee Yearly Meeting,
founded 1834, Canada Yearly Meeting
(Orthodox), founded in 1867, and Canada Yearly
Meeting, founded in 1881, united in 1955 to form
the Canadian Yearly Meeting. Canadian Yearly
Meeting is affiliated with Friends United Meeting
and Friends General Conference. It is also a member of Friends World Committee for Consultation.

Headquarters
91A Fourth Ave., Ottawa, ON K1S 2L1 Tel.
(613) 235 - 8553 OR Tel. (888) 296 - 3222 Fax
(613) 235 - 1753
Email: cym-office@quaker.ca
Media Contact, Gen. Sec.-Treas.,

Officers
Gen. Sec.-Treas.,
Clerk, Anne Mitchell
Archivist, Jane Zavitz Bond
Archives, Arthur G. Dorland, Pickering College,
389 Bayview St., Newmarket, ON L3Y 4X2
Tel. (416)895-1700

Periodicals
The Canadian Friend; Quaker Concern

**Catholic Church—please see Roman Catholic
Church**

Christ Catholic Church International

Christ Catholic Church International now has
churches and-or missions in 14 countries spread
over four continents. They are located in the
United States, Canada, Poland, Bahamas,
Ukraine, Trinidad-Tobago, Colombia, Australia,
Slovakia, Belarus, Kenya and the Phillipines.
Some countries have active churches and missions; some just missions and-or prayer groups.

CCCI is an Orthodox-Catholic Communion
tracing Apostolic Succession through the Old
Catholic and Orthodox Catholic Churches.
The church ministers to a growing number of
people seeking an experiential relationship with
their Lord and Savior Jesus Christ in a
Sacramental and Scripture based church.

Headquarters
4695 St. Lawrence Ave., Niagara Falls, ON
L2G 1Y4
Email: dioceseofniagara@cogeco.net
Website: www3.sympatico.ca/dwmullan
Media Contact, The Rt. Rev. John W. Brown, 1504-
75 Queen St., Hamilton, ON L8R 3J3 Tel. (905)
527-9089 Fax (905)522-6240, bishopjohn@
primus.ca

Officers

PRESIDING ARCHBISHOP
The Most Rev. Donald Wm. Mullan, 6190 Barker
St., Niagara Falls, ON L2G 1Y4, Tel.
(905)354-2329, Fax (905)357-9934, dmullan1@
cogeco.net

ARCHBISHOPS
The Most Rev. Jose Ruben Garcia Matiz, Calle
52 Sur #24A-35-Bq. #1, Ap. 301, Santa Fe de
Bogota, D.C., Colombia, South America, Tel.
57-71447 87, jorugama@col1.telecom.com.co

BISHOPS
The Rt. Rev. John Wm. Brown, 1504-75 Queen
St., N. Hamilton, ON L8R 3J3, Tel. 905-522-
6240, bishopjohn@primus.ca
The Rt. Rev. Luis Fernando Hoyos Maldonado,
A. A. 24378 Santa Fe de Bogota, D.C.,
Colombia, South America, Tel. 57-276-68-16,
jourgama@col1.telecom.com.co
The Rt. Rev. Jose Moises Moncada Quevedo,
A.A. 24378 Santa Fe de Bogota, D.C.,
Colombia, South America, Tel. 57-276-68-16,
jourgama@col1.telecom.com.co
The Rt. Rev. Jerome Robben, Vicar General, PO
Box 566, Chesterfield, MO 63006-0566, Tel.
314-205-8422, abbajn17@aol.com
The Rt. Rev. Andrzej J. Sarwa, ul. Krucza 16 27-
600 Sandomierz, Poland, Tel.-Fax 084-(0-15)
833-21-41, andrzej-san@poczta.wp.pl
The Rt. Rev. Robert Smith, 824 Royal Oak Dr.,
Orlando, FL 32809, Tel 407-240-7833,
yshwa@webtv.net The Rt. Rev. Ted Lorah Jr.,
430 Wawassan Drive, PO Box 208, Honey
Brook, PA 19344, Tel 610 273-7209, tlorah@
temple.edu
The Rt. Rev. John Gilbert-Cougar, Box 7305, D. L.
Atkinson Station, Pasadena, TX 77508-7305

Periodicals
St. Luke Magazine

Christian Brethren (also known as Plymouth Brethren)

The Christian Brethren are a loose grouping of
autonomous local churches, often called "assemblies." They are firmly committed to the inerrancy of Scripture and to the evangelical doctrine of
salvation by faith alone apart from works or
sacrament. Characteristics are a weekly Breaking
of Bread and freedom of ministry without a
requirement of ordination. For their history, see
"Religious Bodies in the United States" in the
Directories section of this *Yearbook*.

183

CORRESPONDENT

John Rush, 2872 Illinois Avenue., Debuque, IL 52001, USA, Tel.(563)557-8535

RELATED ORGANIZATIONS

Christian Brethren Churches in Quebec, P.O. Box 1054, Sherbrooke, QC J1H 5L3 Tel. (819) 820-1693 Fax (819)821-9287

Kawartha Lakes Bible College, Box 1101, Peterborough, ON K9J 7H4 Tel. (705)742-2437

Mount Carmel Bible School, 4725 106th Ave., Edmonton, AB T6A 1E7 Tel. (780)465-3015

MSC Canada, 509-3950 14th Ave., Markham, ON L3R 0A9 Tel. (905)947-0468 Fax (905) 947-0352

Vision Ministries Canada, 145 Lincoln Road, Waterloo, ON N2J 2N8 Tel. (519)725-1212 Fax (519)725-9421

Periodicals

News of Quebec (819)820-1693

Christian Church (Disciples of Christ) in Canada

Disciples have been in Canada since 1810, and were organized nationally in 1922. This church served the Canadian context as a region of the whole Christian Church (Disciples of Christ) in the United States and Canada.

Headquarters

Christian Church in Canada, PO Box 23030, 417 Wellington St., St. Thomas, ON N5R 6A3 Tel. (519)633-9083 Fax (519)637-6407, Email ccic@netrover.com

Media Contact, Reg. Min., F. Thomas Rutherford

Officers

Mod., Peter Fountain, PO Box 344, Milton, NS B0T 1P0, Tel. (902)354-5988, pjfountain@ auracom.com

Reg. Min., F. Thomas Rutherford, PO Box 23030, 417 Wellington St., St. Thomas, ON N5R 6A3, Tel. (519)633-9083, Fax (519)637-6407, ccic@netrover.com

Christian Churches / Churches of Christ

First congregation organized: Cross Roads Christian Church, Cross Roads, Prince Edward Island, Canada, 1810, by "Scotch Baptists" influenced by James and Robert Haldane of Edinburgh. Since the 1820s when the writings of Thomas and Alexander Campbell were widely circulated and reprinted in periodicals, these congregations have identified with the 19th-c. "Restoration Movement" (also known as, "Stone-Campbell Movement") which came to be known as "Disciples of Christ." In late 19th-c. Ontario, some congregations separated over the use of musical instruments into a group known as the a capella Churches of Christ. From the 1880s to the 1930s, Disciples of Christ migrating from Ontario and emigrating from the United States organized

congregations in Manitoba, Saskatchewan, Alberta, and British Columbia. From about 1948, when the Disciples of Christ in Canada first moved toward and, then, declared a formal denominational structure in 1968, 65-70 congregations across Canada did not identify with this structure preferring to remain free, congregationally governed fellowships. While especially in western Canada these congregations cooperate and fellowship with congregations identified with the Disciples of Christ in Canada, a capella Churches of Christ, and people and congregations of several other traditions, they generally tend to identify with the interpretation of the Restoration or Stone-Campbell Movement as exemplified by U.S. Christian Churches and Churches of Christ in affinity with the North American Christian Convention, an annual, non-delegated, preaching and teaching convention. (See "The Movement in Canada", Encyclopedia of the Stone-Campbell Movement. Grand Rapids, Mich.: Eerdmans, 2004, pp. 151-163).

Headquarters

Media Contact: Russell E. Kuykendall,25 Grenville Street, 1507, Toronto, ON M4Y 2X5 Tel (416)895-1098, Email kuykendall@ canada.com

Officers

All of the following are free-standing, para-church institutions. Mortgage financing for congregations and para-church institutions: Church of Christ Development Company, Edmonton, Alberta. Church-planting associations: Partners in Atlantic Canada Evangelism, Impact Ontario, and Alberta Church Planting Association. Degree-granting colleges: Maritime Christian College, Charlottetown, PEI, and Alberta Bible College, Calgary, AB. Cross-cultural missions: Church of Christ Mission Jamaica; Church of Christ Mission India; Global Missionary Ministries (Central Europe); Frontier Labourers for Christ Canada (Thailand, Laos, and Myanmar); Graceland Ministries (Poland); Terri Scruggs, Partners with Nationals, Wycliffe Bible Translators; Benevolent Social Services of India; and others. Christian camps: Canoe Cove (PEI), Ontario Christian Assembly, Camp Christian (Pine Lake, AB), Pine Ridge Christian (Grande Prairie, AB), and Double VM (Lumby, BC). Annual fellowship meetings: Maritime Christian Fellowship, Ontario Christian Missionary Conference, Western Canada Christian Convention (with Disciples of Christ and a capella Churches of Christ), and the North American Christian Convention.

Christian and Missionary Alliance in Canada

A Canadian movement, dedicated to the teaching of Jesus Christ the Saviour, Sanctifier, Healer and Coming King, commenced in Toronto in 1887 under the leadership of the Rev. John Salmon. Two years later, the movement united with The Christian Alliance of New York, founded by Rev. A. B. Simpson, becoming the Dominion Auxiliary of the Christian Alliance, Toronto, under the presidency of the Hon. William H. Howland. Its four founding branches were Toronto, Hamilton, Montreal, and Quebec. The movement focused on the deeper life and missions. In 1980, the Christian and Missionary Alliance in Canada became autonomous. Its General Assembly is held every two years.

NATIONAL OFFICE
30 Carrier Dr, Suite 100, Toronto, ON M9W 5T7, Tel. (416)674-7878, Fax (416)674-0808
Email: info@cmacan.org
Media Contact, Director of Communications, Barrie Doyle

Officers
Pres., Dr. Franklin Pyles, pylesf@cmacan.org
Vice-Pres.-Global Ministries, Dr. Ray Downey, downeyr@cmacan.org
Vice-Pres.-Fin., Paul D. Lorimer, lorimerp@cmacan.org
Vice-Pres.-Canadian Ministries, Rev. C. Stuart Lightbody, lightbodys@cmacan.org
Vice-Pres.-Advancement, Rev. David Freeman, freemand@cmacan.org
Chairman of the Board, Dr. T. V. Thomas
Secretary of the Board, Connie Driedger

Periodicals
Alliance Life

Christian Reformed Church in North America
Canadian congregations of the Christian Reformed Church in North America have been formed since 1905. For detailed information about this denomination, please refer to the listing for the Christian Reformed Church in North America in Chapter 3, "Religious Bodies in the United States."

Headquarters
United States Office, 2850 Kalamazoo Ave., S.E., Grand Rapids, MI 49560 Tel. (616)224-0832 Fax (616) 224-5895
Canadian Office, 3475 Mainway, P.O. Box 5070 STN LCR 1, Burlington, ON L7R 3Y8 Tel. (905)336-2920 Fax (905)336-8344
Website: www.crcna.org
Media Contact, Exec. Dir.,Rev. Gerard Dykstra, U.S. Office; Director of Communication, Mr. Henry Hess, Canadian Office

Officers
Executive Director: Rev. Gerard Dykstra
Director of Finance & Administration: Mr. John Bolt, U.S. Office
Director of Denominational Ministries: Mrs. Sandy Johnson

Periodicals
The Banner

Church of God (Anderson, Ind.)
This body is one of the largest of the groups which have taken the name "Church of God." Its headquarters are at Anderson, Indiana. It originated about 1880 and emphasizes Christian unity.

Headquarters
Western Canada Assembly, Chpsn., Egbert Lubek, 4717- 56th St., Camrose, AB T4V 2C4 Tel. (780)672-0772 Fax (780)672-6888
Eastern Canada Assembly, Chpsn., Jim Wiebe, 38 James St., Dundas, ON L9H 2J6
Email: admincoo@telsu.net
Website: www.chog.ca
Media Contact for Western Canada, Executive Dir. Of Ministry Services, Ken Wiedrick, 4717 56th St., Camrose, AB T4V 2C4 Tel. (780)672-0772 Fax (780)672-6888

Periodicals
The Gospel Contact; The Messenger

Church of God in Christ (Mennonite)
The Church of God in Christ, Mennonite was organized by the evangelist-reformer John Holdeman in Ohio. The church unites with the faith of the Waldenses, Anabaptists and other such groups throughout history. Emphasis is placed on obedience to the teachings of the Bible, including the doctrine of the new birth and spiritual life, noninvolvement in government or the military, a head-covering for women, beards for men and separation from the world shown by simplicity in clothing, homes, possessions and lifestyle. The church has a worldwide membership of about 22,225, largely concentrated in the United States and Canada.

Headquarters
P.O. Box 313, 420 N. Wedel Ave., Moundridge, KS 67107 Tel. (620)345-2532 Fax (620) 345-2582
Media Contact, Dale Koehn, P.O.Box 230, Moundridge, KS 67107 Tel. (620)345-2532 Fax (620)345-2582

Periodicals
Messenger of Truth

Church of God (Cleveland, Tenn.)
It is one of America's oldest Pentecostal churches founded in 1886 as an outgrowth of the holiness revival under the name Christian Union. In 1907 the church adopted the organizational name Church of God. It has its foundation upon the principles of Christ as revealed in the Bible. The Church of God is Christian, Protestant, foundational in its doctrine, evangelical in practice and distinctively Pentecostal. It maintains a centralized form of government and a commitment to world evangelization.

The first church in Canada was extablished in 1919 in Scotland Farm, Manitoba. Paul H. Walker became the first overseer of Canada in 1931.

Headquarters

Intl. Offices, 2490 Keith St., NW, Cleveland, TN 37320 Tel. (423)472-3361 Fax (423)478-7066
Media Contact, Dir. of Communications, T. Scot Carter, P.O. Box 2430, Cleveland, TN 37320-2430 Tel. (423)478-7112 Fax (423)478-7066

Officers

EXECUTIVES

General Overseer, Dr. Raymond F. Culpepper, P.O. Box 2430, Cleveland, TN 37320-2430, tel. (423)478-7137, fax (423)478-7275, gocog@churchofgod.org.

First Assistant General Overseer, Dr. Timothy M. Hill, P.O. Box 2430, Cleveland, TN 37320-2430, tel. (423)478-7136, fax (423)478-7379, cog1a@churchofgod.org

Second Assistant General Overseer, Dr. Mark L. Williams, P.O. Box 2430, Cleveland, TN 37320-2430, tel. (423)478-7126, fax (423) 478-7263, cog2a@churchofgod.org

Third Assistant General Overseer, Dr. David M. Griffis, P.O. Box 2430, Cleveland, TN 37320-2430, tel. (423)478-7133, fax (423)478-7247, cog3a@churchofgod.org

Secretary General, Dr. Wallace J. Sibley, P.O. Box 2430, Cleveland, TN 37320-2430, tel. (423) 478-7127, fax (423)478-7052, cogsecgeneral@ churchofgod.org

Canada-Eastern, Reverend Daniel J. Vassell, P.O. Box 2036, Brampton, ON L6T 3TO, Tel. (905)270-8083, Fax (905) 270-6720

Canada-Western, Reverend Vaughn D. Mathews, Box 54055, 2640 52 St. NE, Calgary, AB T1Y 6S6, Tel. (403)293-8817, Fax (403)293-3466

Canada-Quebec-Maritimes, Reverend Jacques Houle, 19 Orly, Granby, QC J2H 1Y4, Tel. (450)378-4442, Fax (450)378-8646

Canada-National, Dr. Ken Bell, P.O. Box 2430, Cleveland, TN 37320-2430 Tel. (423)478-7138 Fax (423)478-7443

DEPARTMENTS

Benefits Board—CEO, Arthur D. Rhodes
Business & Records—Exec. Dir., Julian B. Robinson
Care Ministries—Dir., Donnie W. Smith
Chaplains Commission—Dir., Robert D. Crick
Communications, Media Ministries—Dir., T. Scot Carter
Division of Education—Chancellor, Donald S. Aultman
Education—European Theological Seminary, Dir., Paul Schmidgall
Education—USA Hispanic Educational Ministries Dir., Rigoberto Ramos
Education—International Bible College, Pres., Philip Siggelkow
Education—Lee University, Pres., Charles Paul Conn

Education—Patten University, Pres., Gary Moncher
Education—Puerto Rico Bible College, Pres., Ildefonso Caraballo
Education—Pentecostal Theological Seminary, President, Steven J. Land
Evangelism & Home Missions—Dir., Jimmy D. Smith
Evangelism—Hispanic Ministries, Dir., Fidencio Burgueno
Evangelism—Native American Ministries, Dir., Douglas M. Cline
Lay Ministries—Dir., Leonard C. Albert
Legal Services—Dir., Dennis W. Watkins
Men/Women of Action—Dir., L. Hugh Carver
Military/Multi-Cultural/Romanian—Dir., G. Dennis McGuire
Ministerial Care—Dir., Bill Leonard
Ministerial Development/School of Ministry—Dir., Donald S. Aultman
Ministry to Israel—Dir., J. Michael Utterback
Music Ministries—Dir., Delton L. Alford
Pentecostal Resource Center—Director, Barbara McCullough
Pentecostal Research Center—Dir., David G. Roebuck
Publications—Dir., Joseph A. Mirkovich
SpiritCare—Dir., Gene D. Rice
Stewardship—Dir., Kenneth R. Davis
Women's Ministries—Coordinator, Jan Timmerman
World Missions—Dir., Douglas LeRoy
Youth & Christian Education—Dir., Thomas A. Madden

Periodicals

Church of God Evangel, Editorial Evangelica, Save Our World,; Ministry Now Profiles, Ministries Now Profiles

The Church of God of Prophecy Canada East

The Church of God of Prophecy is one of the churches that grew out of the work of A. J. Tomlinson in the first half of the twentieth century. Historically it shares a common heritage with the Church of God (Cleveland Tennessee) and is in the mainstream of the classical Pentecostal-holiness tradition.

At the death of A.J. Tomlinson in 1943, M.A. Tomlinson was named General Overseer and served until his retirement in 1990. He emphasized unity and fellowship unlimited by racial, social, or political differences. The next General Overseer, Billy D. Murray, Sr., who served from 1990 until his retirement in 2000, emphasized a commitment to the promotion of Christian unity and world evangelization. In July 2000, Fred S. Fisher, Sr. Was duly selected to serve as the fourth General Overseer of the Church of God of Prophecy.

From its beginnings, the Church has based its beliefs on "the whole Bible, rightly divided," and has accepted the Bible as God's Holy Word, inspired, inerrant and infallible. The church is firm in its commitment to orthodox Christian belief. The Church affirms that there is one God, eternally existing in three persons, Father, Son and Holy Spirit. It believes in the deity of Christ, His virgin birth, His sinless life, the physical miracles He performed, His atoning death on the cross, His bodily resurrection, His ascension to the right hand of the Father and his Second coming. The church professes that salvation results from grace alone through faith in Christ, that regeneration by the Holy Spirit is essential for the salvation of sinful men, and that sanctification by the blood of Christ makes possible personal holiness. It affirms the present ministry of the Holy Spirit by Whose indwelling believers are able to live godly lives and have power for service. The church believes in, and promotes, the ultimate unity of believers as prayed for by Christ in John 17. The church stresses the sanctity of human life and is committed to the sanctity of the marriage bond and the importance of strong, loving Christian families. Other official teachings include Holy Spirit baptism with tongues as initial evidence; manifestation of the spiritual gifts; divine healing; premillenial second-coming of Christ; total abstinence from the use of tobacco, alcohol and narcotics; water baptism by immersion; the Lord's supper and washing of the saints' feet; and a concern for moderation and holiness in all dimensions of lifestyle.

The Church is racially integrated on all levels, including top leadership. Women play a prominent role in church affairs, serving in pastoral roles and other leadership positions. The church presbytery has recently adopted plurality of leadership in the selection of a General Oversight Group. This group consists of eight bishops located around the world who, along with the General Overseer, are responsible for inspirational leadership and vision casting for the church body.

The Church has local congregations in all 50 states and more than 100 nations worldwide. Organizationally there is a strong emphasis on international missions, evangelism, youth and children's ministries, women's and men's ministries, stewardship, communications, publishing, leadership development and discipleship.

CHURCH OF GOD OF PROPHECY INTERNATIONAL OFFICES
P.O. Box 2910, Cleveland, TN 37320-2910
Media Contact, National Overseer, Levi Clarke, 5145 Tomken Rd, Mississauga, ON L4 W1P1; Tel. (905) 625-1278; Fax (905)-625-1316. Website: www.cogop.org.

Officers
Gen. Overseer, Bishop Randy E. Howard, Sr.; General Presbyters, Sherman Allen, Sam Clements, Daniel Corbett, Clayton Endecott, Miguel Mojica, José Reyes, Sr., Felix Santiago, Brice Thompson
International Offices Ministries Dirs., Finance, Communications, and Publishing, Perry Gillum; Global Outreach and Administrative Asst. to the General Presbyters, Randy Howard; Leadership Development and Discipleship Ministries, Larry Duncan.

Periodicals
White Wing Messenger (ENG), Victory (Youth Magazine/ Sunday School Curriculum); The Happy Harvester, White Wing Messenger (Spanish).

The Church of Jesus Christ of Latter-Day Saints in Canada
The Church has had a presence in Canada since the early 1830's. Joseph Smith and Brigham Young both came to Eastern Canada as missionaries. There are now 157,000 members in Canada in more than 400 congregations.

Leading the Church in Canada are the presidents of over 40 stakes (equivalent to a diocese). World headquarters is in Salt Lake City, UT (See U.S. Religious Bodies chapter of the Directories section of this *Yearbook*).

Headquarters
50 East North Temple St., Salt Lake City, UT 84150
Media Contact, Public Affairs Dir., Bruce Smith, 1185 Eglinton Ave., Box 116, North York, ON M3C 3C6 Tel. (416)431-7891 Fax (416)438-2723

Church of the Lutheran Brethren
The Church of the Lutheran Brethren of America was organized in December 1900. Five independent Lutheran congregations met together in Milwaukee, Wisconsin, and adopted a constitution patterned very closely to that of the Lutheran Free Church of Norway.

The spiritual awakening in the Midwest during the 1890s crystallized into convictions that led to the formation of a new church body. Chief among the concerns were church membership practices, observance of Holy Communion, confirmation practices and local church government.

The Church of the Lutheran Brethren practices a simple order of worship with the sermon as the primary part of the worship service. It believes that personal profession of faith is the primary criterion for membership in the congregation. The Communion service is reserved for those who profess faith in Christ as savior. Each congregation is autonomous and the synod serves the congregations in advisory and cooperative capacities.

The synod supports a world mission program in Cameroon, Chad, Japan and Taiwan. Approximately 40 percent of the synodical budget is earmarked for world missions. A growing home mission ministry is planting new congregations in the United States and Canada. Affiliate organizations operate several retirement-nursing homes, conference and retreat centers.

Headquarters

1020 Alcott Ave., W., P.O. Box 655, Fergus Falls, MN 56538 Tel. (218)739-3336 Fax (218)739-5514

Email: rmo@clba.org

Website: www.clba.org

Media Contact, Rev. Brent Juliot

Officers

Pres., Rev. Arthur Berge, 72 Midridge Close SE, Calgary, AB T2X 1G1

Vice-Pres., Rev. Luther Stenberg, PO Box 75, Hagen, SK S0J 1B0

Sec., Mr. Alvin Herman, 3105 Taylor Street E., Saskatoon, SK S7H 1H5

Treas., Edwin Rundbraaten, Box 739, Birch Hills, SK S0J 0G0

Youth Coord., Rev. Harold Rust, 2617 Preston Ave. S., Saskatoon, SK S7J 2G3

Periodicals

Faith and Fellowship

Church of the Nazarene in Canada

The Church of the Nazarene in Canada was organized in Nova Scotia in November, 1902 by Rev. H.F. Reynolds. The 160 churches today are organized in five districts, with the Canada National Office located in Brampton, Ontario. The Church of the Nazarene is Methodist in theology, representative in church government and warmly evangelistic. It is a a part of the Church of the Nazarene International.

Headquarters

20 Regan Rd., Unit 9, Brampton, ON L7A 1C3 Tel. (905)846-4220 Fax (905)846-1775

Email: national@nazarene.ca

Website: www.nazarene.ca

Media Contact, Gen. Sec., /Operations Officer, Dr. David Wilson, 17001 Prairie Star Parkway, Lenexa, KS 66220 Tel. (913)577-0600 Fax (913) 577-0548

Officers

Natl. Dir., Dr. Clair MacMillan, 20 Regan Rd. Unit 9, Brampton, ON L7A 1C3 Tel. (905) 846-4220 Fax (905)846-1775, cmacmillan@ nazarene.ca

Exec. Asst., Allan McAlpin, 20 Regan Rd. Unit 9, Brampton, ON L7A 1C3 Tel. (905)846-4220 Fax (905)846-1775, national@nazarene.ca

Churches of Christ in Canada

Churches of Christ are autonomous congregations, whose members appeal to the Bible alone to determine matters of faith and practice. There are no central offices or officers. Publications and institutions related to the churches are either under local congregational control or independent of any one congregation.

Churches of Christ shared a common fellowship in the 19th century with the Christian Churches-Churches of Christ and the Christian Church (Disciples of Christ). Fellowship was broken after the introduction of instrumental music in worship and centralization of church-wide activities through a missionary society. Churches of Christ began in Canada soon after 1800, largely in the middle-eastern provinces. The few pioneer congregations were greatly strengthened in the mid-1800s, growing in size and number.

Members of Churches of Christ believe in the inspiration of the Scriptures, the divinity of Jesus Christ, and immersion into Christ for the remission of sins. The New Testament pattern is followed in worship and church organization.

Headquarters

Media Contact, Man. Ed., Gospel Herald, Max Craddock, 5 Lankin Blvd., ON M4J 4W7 Tel. (416)461-7406 Fax (416)424-1850

Email: maxc@strathmorecofc.ca

Periodicals

Gospel Herald

Community of Christ

Founded April 6, 1830, by Joseph Smith, Jr., the church was reorganized under the leadership of the founder's son, Joseph Smith III, in 1860. The Church is established in nearly 50 countries including the United States and Canada, with nearly a quarter of a million members. A world conference is held every three years in Independence, Missouri. The current president is Stephen M. Veazey.

Headquarters

International Headquarters, 1001 W. Walnut, Independence, MO 64050 Tel. (816)833-1000 Fax (816)521-3043

Ontario Regional Ofc., 390 Speedvale Ave. E., Guelph, ON N1E 1N5

Media Contact, Media Relations, Kendra Friend

Officers

Canada East Mission Centre

Ken Barrows, Mission Centre President, 390 Speedvale Ave E., Guelph, ON N1E 1N5 CANADA, (519)822-4150, Email: kbarrows@ CofChrist.org

Michael Hewitt, Mission Centre Financial Officer, 390 Speedvale Ave. E., Guelph, ON N1E 1N5 CANADA, (519)822-4150, Email: mhewitt@CofChrist.org

Canada West Mission Centre

Darrell Belrose, Mission Centre President, 6415 Ranchview Drive NW, Calgary AB T3G 1B5 CANADA, Tel. (877)411-2632, Email: dbelrose@CofChrist.org

Jim Poirier, Mission Centre Financial Officer, Email: jpoirier@CofChrist.org

Periodicals

Herald

Congregational Christian Churches in Canada

This body originated in the early 18th century when devout Christians within several denominations in the northern and eastern United States, dissatisfied with sectarian controversy, broke away from their own denominations and took the simple title "Christians." First organized in 1821 at Keswick, Ontario, the Congregational Christian Churches in Canada was incorporated on Dec. 4, 1989, as a national organization. In doctrine the body is evangelical, being governed by the Bible as the final authority in faith and practice. It believes that Christian character must be expressed in daily living; it aims at the unity of all true believers in Christ that others may believe in Him and be saved. In church polity, the body is democratic and autonomous. It is also a member of The World Evangelical Congregational Fellowship.

Headquarters
241 Dunsdon St. Ste. 405, Brantford, ON N3R 7C3 Tel. (519)751-0606 Fax (519)751-0852
Media Contact, Rev.David Schrader, 241 Dunsdon St. Ste. 405, Brantford, ON N3R 7C3 Tel. (519)751-0606 Fax (519)751-0852

Officers
Pres., Rev. Jim Potter
Exec. Dir., Rev.David Schrader
Sec., Rev. Ron Holden

Convention of Atlantic Baptist Churches
The Convention of Atlantic Baptist Churches is the largest Baptist Convention in Canada. Through the Canadian Baptist Ministries, it is a member of the Baptist World Alliance.

In 1763 two Baptist churches were organized in Atlantic Canada, one in Sackville, New Brunswick and the other in Wolfville, Nova Scotia. Although both these churches experienced crises and lost continuity, they recovered and stand today as the beginning of organized Baptist work in Canada. Nine Baptist churches met in Lower Granville, Nova Scotia in 1800 and formed the first Baptist Association in Canada. By 1846 the Maritime Baptist Convention was organized, consisting of 169 churches. Two streams of Baptist life merged in 1905 to form the United Baptist Convention. This is how the term "United Baptist" was derived. Today there are 554 churches within 21 associations across the Convention.

The Convention has two educational institutions, Atlantic Baptist University in Moncton, New Brunswick, a Christian Liberal Arts University, and Acadia Divinity College in Wolfville, Nova Scotia, a Graduate School of Theology. The Convention engages in world mission through Canadian Baptist Ministries, the all-Canada mission agency. In addition to an active program of home mission, evangelism, training, social action and stewardship, the Convention operates ten senior citizen complexes and a Christian bookstore.

Headquarters
1655 Manawagonish Rd., Saint John, NB E2M 3Y2 Tel. (506)635-1922 Fax (506)635-0366

Email: cabc@baptist.atlantic.ca
Media Contact, Executive Minister / Director of Communications, Rev. Dr. Bruce Fawcett
website: www.baptist.atlantic.ca

Officers
Pres. (2007 - 2008), Dr. Margaret M. Munro, 32 Holland Drive, Stratford PE C1B 2H4 Tel. (902)569-5477, Email: munro@upei.ca
Vice Pres. (2007 - 2008), Rev. David DuBois, 139 Cowperthwaite Street, Fredericton NB E3A 9W6 Tel. (506)457-1006, Email: pastor.mbc@nb.aibn.com
Exec. Min., Dr. Harry Gardner completed his ministry as Executive Minister on December 31, 2007
Interim Executive Minister: (effective Jan. 1, 2008): Dr. Malcolm W. Beckett, 1655 Manawagonish Road, Saint John NB 3Y2 Tel. (506) 635-1922 Fax: (506) 635-0366, Email: malcolm.beckett@baptist-atlantic.ca
Associate Executive Minister / Director of Communications: Dr. Bruce Fawcett, 1655 Manawagonish Road, Saint John NB E2M 3Y2 Tel. (506) 635-1922 Fax: (506) 635-0366, Email: bruce.fawcett@baptist-atlantic.ca
Dir. of Operations., Mr. Daryl MacKenzie, 1655 Manawagonish Rd., Saint John, NB E2M 3Y2; Tel. (506)635-1922 Fax (506)635-0366, Email: daryl.mackenzie@baptist-atlantic.ca
Dir. of Atlantic Baptist Mission, Dr. Malcolm Beckett, 1655 Manawagonish Rd., Saint John, NB E2M 3Y2 Tel. (506)635-1922 Fax (506)635-0366 Email: malcolm.beckett@baptist-atlantic.ca
Dir. of Youth and Family, (to be voted on at August 2008 Assembly - name being presented): Rev. Dale O. Stairs, 1655 Manawagonish Road, Saint John NB E2M 3Y2 Tel. (506) 635-1922 Fax: (506) 635-0366, Email: dale.stairs@baptist-atlantic.ca
Dir. Of Development, Rev. Greg Jones, 1655 Manawagonish Rd., Saint John, NB E2M 3Y2 Tel. (506)635-1922 Fax (506)635-0366, Email: greg.jones@baptist-atlantic.ca
Part-time Dir. Of Public Witness and Social Concern, Dr. Lois P. Mitchell c/o 1655 Manawagonish Rd., Saint John, NB E2M 3Y2 Tel. (506)635-1922; Fax (506)635-0366; Email: lois.mitchell@baptist-atlantic.ca

The Coptic Orthodox Church in Canada
The Coptic Orthodox Church in North America was begun in Canada in 1964 and was registered in the province of Ontario in 1965. The Coptic Orthodox Church has spread rapidly since then. The total number of local churches in both Canada and the USA exceeded one hundred twenty. Two dioceses, two monasteries with monks and novices, and two theological seminaries were established in the USA.

The Coptic Orthodox Church is the church of Alexandria founded in Egypt by St. Mark the

Apostle in the first century A.D. She is a hierarchical church and the administrative governing body of each local church is an elected Board of Deacons approved by the Bishop. The current patriarch of the church is H. H. Pope Shenouda III, Pope of Alexandria and Patriach of the see of St. Mark. The Coptic Orthodox Church is a member of the Canadian Council of Churches.

Headquarters
St. Mark's Coptic Orthodox Church, 41 Glendinning Ave., Toronto, ON M1W 3E2 Tel. (416)494-4449 Fax (416)494-2631, Email mail@coptorthodox.ca, Web www.stmark. toronto.on.coptorthodox.ca
Media Contact, Fr. Ammonius Guirguis, Tel. (416)494-4449, Fax (416)494-2631, frammonius@coptorthodox.ca

Disciples of Christ—please see Christian Church (Disciples of Christ) in Canada. Doukhobors—please see Union of Spiritual Communities in Christ.

Elim Fellowship Canada
The Elim Fellowship Canada, a Pentecostal body, was established in 1984 as a sister organization of Elim Fellowship in the United States.

This is an association of churches, ministers and missionaries seeking to serve the whole body of Christ. It is Pentecostal and has a charismatic orientation.

Headquarters
379 Golf Road, RR#6, Brantford, ON N3T 5L8 Tel. (519)753-7266 Fax (519)753-5887
Ofc. Mgr., Larry Jones
Email: elim@bfree.on.ca
Website: Bfree.ON.ca/comdir/churchs/elim

Officers
Pres., Howard Ellis, 102 Ripley Crescent., Kitchener, ON N2N 1V4
Vice-Pres., Rev. Errol Alchin, 1694 Autumn Crescent, Pickering, ON L1V 6X5
Sec./Treas., Larry Jones, 107 Hillside Ave., Paris ON K2G 4N1

COUNCIL OF ELDERS
Rev. Bud Crawford, Brampton, ON
Rev. Howard Ellis, Kitchener, ON
Rev. Bernard Evans, Lima, New York
Rev. Claude Favreau, Drummondville, Quebec
Rev. Aubrey Phillips, Blairsville, Georgia

The Estonian Evangelical Lutheran Church Abroad
The Estonian Evangelical Lutheran Church (EELC) was founded in 1917 in Estonia and reorganized in Sweden in 1944. The teachings of the EELC are based on the Old and New Testaments, explained through the Apostolic, Nicean and Athanasian confessions, the unaltered Confession of Augsburg and other teachings found in the Book of Concord.

Headquarters
383 Jarvis St., Toronto, ON M5B 2C7 Tel. (416)925-5465 Fax (416)925-5688
Media Contact, Archbishop, Rev. Udo Petersoo
Email: udo.petersoo@eelk.ee
Website: www.eelk.ee/~e.e.l.k./

Officers
Archbishop, The Rev. Udo Petersoo
Gen. Sec., Mr. Ivar Nippak
Sec./Clerk, Mrs. Eerika Lage

Periodicals
Eesti Kirik

Evangelical Christian Church in Canada
The Evangelical Christian Church in Canada (Christian Disciples) as a religion in Canada can be traced to the formal organization of the Christian Church in 1804, in Bourbon County, Kentucky, under the leadership of Barton Warren Stone (1772-1844). The Stone Movement later merged with the efforts of Thomas Campbell (1774-1854) and his son Alexander Campbell (1788-1844) to become the Restoration Movement that gave birth to the Churches of Christ (Non-Instrumental), the Christian Churches and Churches of Christ, and the Christian Church (Disciples of Christ). The Evangelical Christian Church (Christian Disciples) as a new group within the Restoration tradition was recognized in 2001.

Headquarters
General Superintendent, Rev. David P. Lavigne, 410-125 Lincoln Rd., Waterloo, ON N2J 2N9 Tel. (519)880-9110 Toll free (888)981-8881
Email: cecc@rogers.com
Website: www.cecconline.net

Officers
Gen. Supt., Rev. Dr. David P. Lavigne, (410)125 Lincoln Rd., Waterloo, ON N2J 2N9, Tel. (519)880-9110, Toll free (888)981-8881, Email: cecc@rogers.com
Gen. Sec., Rev. Gordon Horsely, 213 Homestead Drive, Shelburne, On LON1SO, Tel. (519)925-3651

The Evangelical Covenant Church of Canada
A Canadian denomination organized in Canada at Winnipeg in 1904 which is affiliated with the Evangelical Covenant Church of America and with the International Federation of Free Evangelical Churches, which includes 31 federations in 26 countries.

This body believes in the one triune God as confessed in the Apostles' Creed, that salvation is received through faith in Christ as Saviour, that the Bible is the authoritative guide in all matters of faith and practice. Christian Baptism and the Lord's Supper are accepted as divinely ordained sacraments of the church. As descendants of the 19th century northern European pietistic awakening, the group believes in the need of a personal experience of commitment to Christ, the development of a virtuous life and the urgency of spreading the gospel to the "ends of the world."

Four Core Values: To be a Missional Church; To be a Biblical Church; To be a Devotional Church; and to be a Connnectional Church.

Four Ministry Priorities: Leadership Development; Church Planting & Mission; Church Renewal/ Transition; and Christian Services.

Headquarters
PO Box 34025, RPO Fort Richmond, Winnipeg, MB R3T 5T5
Media Contact, Supt., Jeff Anderson

Officers
Pres./Supt., Rev. Jeff Anderson, PO 34025, RPO Fort Richmond, Winnipeg, MB R3T 5T5
Chpsn., Rod Johnson, Box 217, Norquay, SK S0A 2V0
Sec., Judy Nelson, Box 194, Norquay, SK S0A 2V0
Treas., Ingrid Wildman, Box 93, Norquay, SK S0A 2V0

Periodicals
The Covenant Messenger

Evangelical Free Church of Canada

The Evangelical Free Church of Canada traces its beginning back to 1917 when the church in Enchant, Alberta opened its doors. Today the denomination has 140 churches from the West Coast to Quebec. Approximately 80 missionaries are sponsored by the EFCC in 17 countries. The Evangelical Free Church is the founding denomination of Trinity Western University in Langley, British Columbia. Church membership is 8,441, average attendance is 18,455

Headquarters
Mailing Address, P.O. Box 850 LCD1, Langley, BC V3A 8S6 Tel. (604)888-8668 Fax (604) 888-3108
Location, 7600 Glover Rd., Langley, BC
Email: efcc@twu.ca
Website: www.efcc.ca
Media Contact, Executive Assistant Maureen Wilson, P.O. Box 850 LCD1, Langley, BC V3A 8S6 Tel. (604)888-8668 Fax (604)888-3108

Officers
President, Dr. Ron Unruh, P.O.Box 850 LCD 1, Langley, BC, Canada V3A 8S6, Tel (604)888-8668, Fax (604) 888-3108 efcc@twu.ca

Periodicals
The Pulse

Evangelical Lutheran Church in Canada

The Evangelical Lutheran Church in Canada was organized in 1985 through a merger of The Evangelical Lutheran Church of Canada (ELCC) and the Lutheran Church in America—Canada Section.

The merger is a result of an invitation issued in 1972 by the ELCC to the Lutheran Church in America—Canada Section and the Lutheran Church—Canada. Three-way merger discussions took place until 1978 when it was decided that only a two-way merger was possible. The ELCC was the Canada District of the ALC until autonomy in 1967.

The Lutheran Church in Canada traces its history back more than 200 years. Congregations were organized by German Lutherans in Halifax and Lunenburg County in Nova Scotia in 1749. German Lutherans, including many United Empire Loyalists, also settled in large numbers along the St. Lawrence and in Upper Canada. In the late 19th century, immigrants arrived from Scandinavia, Germany and central European countries, many via the United States. The Lutheran synods in the United States have provided the pastoral support and help for the Canadian church.

Headquarters
302-393 Portage Avenue, Winnipeg, MB R3B 3H6 Tel. (204)984-9150 Fax (204)984-9185
Media Contact, Bishop, Rev. Raymond L. Schultz
Evangelical Lutheran Women Inc., ELCIC Group Services Inc.

Periodicals
Canada Lutheran; Esprit

Evangelical Mennonite Conference

The Evangelical Mennonite Conference is a modern church of historic Christian convictions, tracing its indebtedness to the Radical Reformation, which, in turn, is rooted in the Protestant Reformation of the 16th century. The Centre of faith, and of Scripture, is found in Jesus Christ as Saviour and Lord.

The church's name was chosen in 1959. Its original name, Kleine Gemeinde, which means "small church", reflected its origins as a renewal movement among Mennonites in southern Russia. Klaas Reimer, a minister, was concerned about a decline of spiritual life and discipline in the church, and inappropriate involvement in the Napoleanic War. About 1812, Reimer and others began separate worship services, and two years later were organized as a small group.

Facing increasing government pressure, particularly about military service, the group migrated to North America in 1874 to 1875. Fifty families settled in Manitoba and 36 in Nebraska. Ties between the groups weakened and eventually the U.S. group gave up its KG identity. The KG survived several schisms and migrations, dating from its years in Russia through the 1940s.

As an evangelical church, The Evangelical Mennonite Conference holds that Scripture has final authority in faith and practice, a belief in Christ's finished work, and that assurance of salvation is possible. As Mennonite, the denomination has a commitment to discipleship, baptism upon confession of faith, community, social concern, non-violence and the Great Commission. As a conference, it seeks to encourage local churches, to work together on evangelism and matters of social concern, and relates increasingly well to other denominations.

In the year 2006 its membership surpassed 7270, with many more people as treasured adherents and a wider circle of ministry influence. Membership is for people baptized on confession of faith (usually in adolescence or older). Children are considered safe in Christ until they reach an age where they are accountable for their own spiritual decision and opt out; they are considered part of the church, while full inclusion occurs upon personal choice.

The Conference has 60 churches from British Columbia to Ontario (37 in Manitoba) and roughly 149 mission workers in 25 countries. The cultural make-up of the Conference is increasingly diverse, though its Dutch-German background remains dominant nationally. Twelve churches have pastors or leaders who are of non-Dutch-German background.

Some churches have a multiple leadership pattern (ministers and deacons can be selected from within the congregation); others have new patterns. Most churches support their leading minister full time. Its church governance moved from a bishop system to greater local congregational autonomy. It currently functions as a conference of churches with national boards, a conference council, and a moderator.

Women can serve on most national boards, as conference council delegates, as missionaries, and within a wide range of local church activities; while they can be selected locally, they cannot currently serve as nationally recognized or commissioned ministers.

It is a supporting member of Mennonite Central Committee and the Evangelical Fellowship of Canada. About 80 percent of its national budget goes toward mission work in Canada and other countries.

Headquarters
440 Main St., Steinbach, MB R5G 1Z5 Tel. (204)326-6401 Fax (204)326-1613
Email: emconf@mts.net
Media Contact, Conf. Pastor, David Thiessen

Officers
Conf. Mod., Ron Penner
General Sec., Tim Dyck
Conference Pastor, Bd. of Leadership and Outreach, David Thiessen
Bd. of Missions, Exec. Sec., Tim Dyck
Bd. of Missions, Foreign Sec., Ken Zacharias
Bd. of Church Ministries, Exec. Sec.-Editor, Terry M. Smith
Bd. of Trustees, Exec. Sec. Tim Dyck
Canadian Church Planting Coordinator, Exec. Sec. - Ward Parkinson
Conference Youth Minister, Gerald Reimer

Periodicals
The Messenger

Evangelical Mennonite Mission Conference
This group was founded in 1936 as the Rudnerweider Mennonite Church in Southern Manitoba and organized as the Evangelical Mennonite Mission Conference in 1959. It was incorporated in 1962. The Annual Conference meeting is held in July.

Headquarters
Box 52059, Niakwa P.O., Winnipeg, MB R2M 5P9 Tel. (204)253-7929 Fax (204)256-7384
Email: info@emmc.ca
Media Contact, Lil Goertzen
Email: lil@emmc.ca

Officers
Mod.,Jake Thiessen, Box 215, Altona MB R0G 0B0 (204)324-6209, Email: jmcath@mts.net
Vice-Mod., Frank Friesen, Box 1392, Altona MB R0G 0B0 (204)324-8389, Email: frankf@mts.net
Sec., Gin Thiessen, 818-77 University Cres, Winnipeg MB R3T 3N8, (204)475-3107, Email: vjthies@mts.net
Conference Pastor, Allen Kehler, Box 52059, Niakwa PO, Winnipeg MB R2M 5P9, (204) 253-7929, Email: al@emmc.ca
Executive Director, position will be filled as of Sept 15/08
Business Admin., Bob Milks, Box 52059, Niakwa PO, Winnipeg MB R2M 5P9, (204) 253-7929, Email: al@emmc.ca
The Gospel Message, Box 1760, Warman SK S0K 4S0 Tel. (306)242-5001 Fax (306)242-6115;
Radio Pastor, Rev. Ed Martens

Periodicals
EMMC Recorder

The Evangelical Missionary Church of Canada
This denomination was formed in 1993 with the merger of The Evangelical Church of Canada and The Missionary Church of Canada. The Evangelical Missionary Church of Canada maintains fraternal relations with the worldwide body of the Missionary Church, Inc. and with the Evangelical Church of North America. The Evangelical Church of Canada was among those North American Evangelical United Brethern Conferences which did not join the EUB in merging with the Methodist Church in 1968. The Missionary Church of Canada is Anabaptist in heritage. Its practices and theology were shaped by the Holiness Revivals of the late 1800s. The Evangelical Missionary Church consists of 135 churches in two conferences in Canada.

Headquarters
4031 Brentwood Rd., NW, Calgary, AB T2L 1L1 Tel. (403)250-2759 Fax (403)291-4720

192

Media Contact, Exec. Dir., Missions and Administration, G. Keith Elliott
Email: info@emcc.ca

Officers

Pres. and Canada East District, Dist. Supt., Rev. Phil Delsaut, 130 Fergus Ave., Kitchener, ON N2A 2H2 Tel. (519)894-9800 Email: pdelsaut@emcced.ca

Canada West District, Acting Dist. Supt., Rev. Don Adolf, 4031 Brentwood Rd., NW, Calgary, AB T2L 1L1 Tel. (403)291-5525 Fax (403)291-4720 Email: don@emcwest.ca

The Fellowship of Evangelical Baptist Churches in Canada

The Fellowship is a family of 500 Evangelical Baptist Churches across Canada, holding worship services in 13 different languages.

Headquarters

PO Box 457, Guelph ON, Canada, N1H 6K9 Tel. (519)821-4830 Fax (519)821-9829

Periodicals

B.C. Fellowship Baptist; The Evangelical Baptist Magazine; Intercom

Foursquare Gospel Church of Canada

The Western Canada District was formed in 1964 with the Rev. Roy Hicks as supervisor. Prior to 1964 it had been a part of the Northwest District of the International Church of the Foursquare Gospel with headquarters in Los Angeles, California.

A Provincial Society, the Church of the Foursquare Gospel of Western Canada, was formed in 1976; a Federal corporation, the Foursquare Gospel Church of Canada, was incorporated in 1981 and a national church formed. The provincial society was closed in 1994.

Headquarters

B-307 2099 Lougheed Highway, Port CoQuituam, BC V3B1A8, Email: info@foursquare.ca

Media Contact, Pres., Barry J. Buzza, B-307 2099 Lougheed Highway, Port CoQuituam, BC V3B1A8

Officers

Pres., Barry J. Buzza, B-307 2099 Lougheed Highway, Port CoQuituam, BC V3B1A8

Free Methodist Church in Canada

The Free Methodist Church was founded in New York in 1860 and expanded in 1880. It is Methodist in doctrine, evangelical in ministry and emphasizes the teaching of holiness of life through faith in Jesus Christ.

The Free Methodist Church in Canada was incorporated in 1927 after the establishment of a Canadian Executive Board. In 1959 the Holiness Movement Church merged with the Free Methodist Church. Full autonomy for the Canadian church was realized in 1990 with the formation of a Canadian General Conference. Mississauga, Ontario, continues to be the location of the Canadian Headquarters.

The Free Methodist Church ministers in 70 countries through its World Ministries Center in Indianapolis, Indiana.

Headquarters

4315 Village Centre Ct., Mississauga, ON L4Z 1S2 Tel. (905)848-2600 Fax (905)848-2603
Email: ministrycentre@fmc-canada.org
Website: www.fmc-canada.org
Media Contact, Dan Sheffield

Officers

Bishop, Rev. Keith Elford
Dir. of Admn. Ser., Norman Bull
Dir. Of Global and Intercultural Ministries, Rev. Dan Sheffield
Supt., Personnel, Rev. Alan Retzman
Supt., Growth Ministries, in transition

Periodicals

Mosaic

Free Will Baptists

As revival fires burned throughout New England in the mid- and late 1700s, Benjamin Randall proclaimed his doctrine of Free Will to large crowds of seekers. In due time, a number of Randall's converts moved to Nova Scotia. One such believer was Asa McGray, who was to become instrumental in the establishment of several Free Baptist churches. Local congregations were organized in New Brunswick. After several years of numerical and geographic gains, disagreements surfaced over the question of music, Sunday school, church offerings, salaried clergy and other issues. Adherents of the more progressive element decided to form their own fellowship. Led by George Orser, they became known as Free Christian Baptists.

The new group faithfully adhered to the truths and doctrines which embodied the theological basis of Free Will Baptists. Largely through Archibald Hatfield, contact was made with Free Will Baptists in the United States in the 1960s. The association was officially welcomed into the Free Will Baptist family in July 1981, by the National Association.

Headquarters

5233 Mt. View Rd., Antioch, TN 37013-2306 Tel. (615)731-6812 Fax (615)731-0771
Media Contact, Mod., Dwayne Broad, RR 3, Bath, NB E0J 1E0 Tel. (506)278-3771

Officers

Mod., Dwayne Broad
Promotional Officer, Dwayne Broad

193

General Church of the New Jerusalem

The Church of the New Jerusalem, also called The New Church, is a Christian Church founded on the Bible and the Writings of Emanuel Swedenborg (1688-1772). These Writings were first brought to Ontario in 1835 by Christian Enslin.

Headquarters
c/o Olivet Church, 279 Burnhamthorpe Rd., Etobicoke, ON M9B 1Z6 Tel. (416)239-3054 Fax (416)239-4935
E-mail: mgladish@shaw.ca
Website: www.newchurch.org
Media Contact, Exec. Vice-Pres., Rev. Michael D. Gladish

Officers
Pres., Rt. Rev. T. Kline, Bryn Athyn, PA 19009
Exec. Vice-Pres., Rev. Michael D. Gladish
Sec., Carolyn Bellinger, 110 Chapel Hill Dr., Kitchener, ON N2G 3W5

General Conference of the Canadian Assemblies of God

This body had its beginnings in Hamilton, Ontario, in 1912 when a few people of an Italian Presbyterian Church banded themselves together for prayer and received a Pentecostal experience of the baptism in the Holy Spirit. Since 1912, there has been a close association with the teachings and practices of the Pentecostal Assemblies of Canada.

The work spread to Toronto, then to Montreal, where it also flourished. In 1959, the church was incorporated in the province of Quebec. The early leaders of this body were the Rev. Luigi Ippolito and the Rev. Ferdinand Zaffuto. The churches carry on their ministry in both the English and Italian languages.

Headquarters
6724 Fabre St., Montreal, QC H2G 2Z6 Tel. (514)279-1100 Fax (514)279-1131
Media Contact, Gen. Sec., Rev. David DiStaulo, P O Box 1415 Weston B, North York ON M9L 2W9; Tel. (416) 741-3558; Fax (416) 741-9340

Officers
Gen. Supt., Rev. Elio Marrocco, 8111 Weston Rd, Woodbridge ON L4L 9T6; Tel. (905) 265-8828; Fax (905) 264-0546
Gen. Sec., Rev. David DiStaulo, P O Box 1415 Weston B, North York ON M9L 2W9; Tel. (416) 741-3558; Fax (416) 741-9340
Gen. Treas., Rev. David Quackenbush, 686 Ossington, Toronto ON M6G 3T7, Tel. (416)532-3951 Fax (416)532-0267
Overseer, Rev. Mario Catalano, 6550 Maurice-Duplessis, Montreal-North QC H1G 6K9; Tel. (514) 323-3087; Fax (514-323-3074
Overseer, Rev. Raymond Narula, P O Box 28090 North Park Plaza, Brantford ON N3R 7X5; Tel. (519) 759-7990; Fax (519) 759-8379

Greek Orthodox Metropolis of Toronto (Canada)

Greek Orthodox Christians in Canada are under the jurisdiction of the Ecumenical Patriarchate of Constantinople (Istanbul).

Headquarters
86 Overlea Blvd., Toronto, ON M4H 1C6 Tel. (416)429-5757 Fax (416)429-4588
Email: metropolis@gocanada.org

Officers
Metropolitan Archbishop of the Metropolis of Toronto (Canada), His Eminence Metropolitan Archbishop Sotirios

Periodicals
Orthodox Way

Independent Assemblies of God International (Canada)

This fellowship of churches has been operating in Canada for over 60 years. Each church within the fellowship is completely independent.

Headquarters
Media Contact, Gen. Sec., Rev. Paul McPhail, Box 653 Chatham, ON, N7M 5K8, Phone (519)352-1743 Fax (519)3516070, Email: pmcphail@ciaccess.com

Officers
Gen. Sec., Rev. Paul McPhail, Box 653 Chatham, ON, N7M 5K8, Phone (519)352-1743 Fax (519)3516070
Treas., Rev. David Ellyatt, 1795 Parkhurst Ave., London, ON N5V 2C4
Email: david.ellyatt@odyssey.on.ca

Periodicals
The Mantle (published in March, July & October),

Independent Holiness Church

The former Holiness Movement of Canada merged with the Free Methodist Church in 1958. Some churches remained independent of this merger and they formed the Independent Holiness Church in 1960, in Kingston, Ontario. The doctrines are Methodist and Wesleyan. The General Conference is every three years, next meeting in 2004.

Headquarters
Media Contact, Rev. R. E. Votary, 1564 John Quinn Rd., R.R.1, Greely, ON K4P 1J9 Tel. (613)821-2237

Officers
Gen. Supt., Rev. R. E. Votary, 1564 John Quinn Rd., Greeley, ON K4P 1J9
Additional Officers, E. Brown, 104-610 Pesehudoff Cresc., Saskatoon, SK S7N 4H5; Rev. N. Sheets, P. O. Box 1433, Nidawin, SK S0E1E0

Periodicals
Gospel Tidings

Jehovah's Witnesses

For a description of Jehovah's Witnesses see "Religious Bodies in United States" in this edition of the *Yearbook*.

Headquarters

25 Columbia Heights, Brooklyn, NY 11201-2483 Tel. (718)560-5600 Fax (718)560-8850
Canadian Branch Office, Box 4100, Halton Hills, ON L7G 4Y4 Tel. (888)301-4259
Media Contact, Office of Public Information, J. Richard Brown
Media Contact, Office of Public Information in Canada, Mark Ruge Editorial Contact, Writing Department, James N. Pellechia

Latter-Day Saints—please see The Church of Jesus Christ of Latter-Day Saints in Canada.

Lutheran Church—Evangelical Lutheran Church in Canada is listed under "E".

Lutheran Church-Canada

Lutheran Church-Canada was established in 1959 at Edmonton, Alberta, as a federation of Canadian districts of the Lutheran Church - Missouri Synod; it was constituted in 1988 at Winnipeg, Manitoba, as an autonomous church.

The church confesses the Bible as both inspired and infallible, the only source and norm of doctrine and life and subscribes without reservation to the Lutheran Confessions as contained in the Book of Concord of 1580.

Headquarters

3074 Portage Ave., Winnipeg, MB R3K 0Y2 Tel. (204)895-3433 Fax (204)832-3018, Email: info@lutheranchurch.ca
Media Contact, Dir. of Comm., Ian Adnams, communications@lutheranchurch.ca

Officers

Pres.: Rev. Robert Bugbee, 3074 Portage Ave, Winnipeg, MB, R3K 0Y2, Tel. (204)895-3433 ext2212, fax (204)832-3018 president@lutheranchurch.ca,
Pres. Emeritus: Rev. Dr. Ralph Mayan, 6565 Willoughby Way, Langley, BC V2Y 1K3, Tel. (778)278-2094, missions@lutheranchurch.ca
Pres. Emeritus: Rev. Dr. Edwin Lehman, 686 Lee Ridge Road, Edmonton, AB, T6K 0P2, Tel. (780)462-9608, Fax (780)468-2172 edwinlehman@shaw.ca
Vice-Pres.: Rev. Daryl Solie, 935 McCarthy Blvd N, Regina, SK, S4X 3L2, tel. (306)543-9898, poplc@sasktel.net
Vice Pres.: Rev. Robert C. Krestick, 78 John St., W. Waterloo, ON N2L 1B8, Tel. (519)745-5027, Fax (519)745-7165, krestick@redeemerchurch.ca Vice Pres.: Rev. Thomas Kruesel, 201 Birch St, Campbell River, BC, V9W 2S4, tel. (250)287-7771, bethany.lutheran.1@gmail.com
Treas.: Mr. Dwayne Cleave, 3074 Portage Avenue, Winnipeg, MB R3K 0Y2, treasurer@lutheranchurch.ca Tel. (204)-895-3433, Fax (204) 897-4319

DISTRICT OFFICES

Alberta-British Columbia, Pres., Rev. D. Schiemann, 7100 Ada Blvd., Edmonton, AB T5B 4E4 Tel. (780)474-0063 Fax (780)477-9829, info@lccabc.ca
Central, Pres., Rev. T. Prachar, 1927 Grant Dr., Regina, SK S4S 4V6 Tel. (306)586-4434 Fax (306)586-0656, tprachar@accesscomm.ca
East, Pres., Rev. Paul Zabel, 275 Lawrence Ave., Kitchener, ON N2M 1Y3 Tel. (519)578-6500 Fax (519)578-3369, pzabel@lcceastdistrict.ca

Periodicals

The Canadian Lutheran

Mennonite Brethren Churches—please see Canadian Conference of Mennonite Brethren Churches

Mennonite Church Canada

Mennonite Church Canada is a successor denomination of the Conference of Mennonites in Canada, and the bi-national denominations (USA and Canada) of the General Conference Mennonite Church and the Mennonite Church. These groups merged in the late 1990's to become Mennonite Church Canada.

The first Mennonites came to Canada in 1786, moving from Pennsylvania in Conestoga wagons. Over the next 150 years, more arrived by ship from Europe, in at least four successive waves.

Its members hold to traditional Christian beliefs, believer's baptism and congregational polity. They emphasize practical Christianity, opposition to war, service to others and personal ethics.

Some people who have joined the Canadian Mennonite body in recent years have arrived from Asia, from Africa, or from Latin and South America. Native brothers and sisters, whose people were here long before the first conastoga wagons arrived, have added their voices to the mix.

Meanwhile, French-speaking and English-speaking Canadians from the wider community have enriched the Mennonite people. Together we are Christian believers moving into the future under the umbrella of the Mennonite Church Canada. Today we worship in 14 different languages across Canada.

Mennonite Church Canada is affiliated with Mennonite Church USA whose offices are at Newton, Kansas and Elkhart, Indiana. (See, Mennonite Church USA description in the section "Religious Bodies in the United States")

Headquarters

600 Shaftesbury Blvd., Winnipeg, MB R3P 0M4 Tel. (204)888-6781 Fax (204)831-5675
Media Contact, Dan Dyck
Email: ddyck@mennonitechurch.ca
Website: www.mennonitechurch.ca

Officers

Chpsn., Andrew Reesor McDowell
Gen. Sec., Robert J. Suderman

Periodicals

Canadian Mennonite, Intotemak

Mennonite Conference—please see Evangelical Mennonite Conference and Evangelical Mennonite Mission Conference

Mennonite-Reinland—please see Reinland Mennonite Church.

Moravian Church—please see Canadian District of the Moravian Church in America, Northern Province.

Mormons—please see the Church of Jesus Christ of Latter-Day Saints in Canada, and see Community of Christ

North American Baptist Conference

Churches belonging to this conference emanated from German Baptist immigrants of more than a century ago. Although scattered across Canada and the U.S., they are bound together by a common heritage, a strong spiritual unity, a Bible-centered faith and a deep interest in missions. Their two main priorities are Leadership Development and Church Multiplication.

Note, The details of general organization, officers, and periodicals of this body will be found in the North American Baptist Conference directory in the "Religious Bodies in the United States" section of this *Yearbook*.

Headquarters
1 S. 210 Summit Ave., Oakbrook Terrace, IL 60181 Tel. (630)495-2000 Fax (630)495-3301
Media Contact, Ron Norman

Officers
Exec. Dir., Dr. Rob McCleland

Periodicals
N.A.B. Today

The Old Catholic Church of Canada

The church was founded in 1948 in Hamilton, Ontario. The first bishop was the Rt. Rev. George Davis. The Old Catholic Church of Canada accepts all the doctrines of the Eastern Orthodox Churches and, therefore, not Papal Infallibility or the Immaculate Conception. The ritual is Western (Latin Rite) and is in the vernacular language. Celibacy is optional.

Headquarters
2185 Sheridan Park Drive, Apt. 105, Mississauga, ON L5K 1C7 Tel. (905)855-3643
Media Contact, Bishop, The Right Rev. Pat Davies, Vicar General

Officers
Vicar General and Auxiliary Bishop, The Rt. Rev. A.C. Keating, PhD., 5066 Forest Grove Crest, Burlington, ON L7L GG6 Tel. (905)681-9983

Old Order Amish Church

This is the most conservative branch of the Mennonite Church and direct descendants of Swiss Brethren (Anabaptists) who emerged from the Reformation in Switzerland in 1525. The Amish, followers of Bishop Jacob Ammann, became a distinct group in 1693. They began migrating to North America about 1737; all of them still reside in the United States or Canada. They first migrated to Ontario in 1823 directly from Bavaria, Germany and later from Pennsylvania and Alsace-Lorraine. Since 1953 more Amish have migrated to Ontario from Ohio, Indiana and Iowa.

As of 2009 there are 35 congregations in Ontario, each being autonomous. No membership figures are kept by this group, and there is no central headquarters. Each congregation is served by a bishop, two ministers and a deacon, all of whom are chosen from among the male members by lot for life.

Correspondent
Pathway Publishers, David Luthy, Rt. 4, Aylmer, ON N5H 2R3

Periodicals
Blackboard Bulletin; Herold der Wahreit; The Budget; The Diary; Die Botschaft; Family Life; Young Companion, Plain Interests.

Open Bible Faith Fellowship of Canada

This is an Evangelical, Full Gospel Fellowship of Churches and Ministries emphasizing evangelism, missions and the local church for success in the present harvest of souls. OBFF was chartered January 7, 1982.

Headquarters
Niagara Celebration Church, P.O. Box 31020, St. Catharines, ON L2N 7S5 Tel. (905)646-0970

Officers
President, David Youngren
Vice President, Lindsey Burt
Sec./Treasurer, George Woodward
Director, Jim Buslon
Director, Lindsey Burt
Director, Mike Welch
Director, Christer Ihreborg

Orthodox Church in America (Archdiocese of Canada)

The Archdiocese of Canada of the Orthodox Church in America was established in 1916. First organized by St. Tikhon, martyr Patriarch of Moscow, previously Archbishop of North America, it is part of the Russian Metropolia and its successor, the autocephalous Orthodox Church in America.

The Archdiocesan Council meets twice yearly, the General Assembly of the Archdiocese takes place every three years. The Archdiocese is also known as "Orthodox Church in Canada."

Headquarters
P.O. Box 179, Spencerville, ON K0E 1XO Tel. (613)925-5226, Email: zoe@ripnet.com

Bishop of Ottawa & Canada, The Rt. Rev. Seraphim; Chancellor, V. Rev. Dennis Pihach, 15992-107A Ave, Edmonton, AB T5P 0Z2
Treas., Nikita Lopoukhine, PO Box 179, Spencervillt, ON K0E 1X0
Sec., Archpriest Cyprian Hutcheon, P.O. Box 179, Spencerville, ON K0E 1X0

ARCHDIOCESAN COUNCIL
Clergy Members, Rev. Lawrence Farley; Rev. R.S. Kennaugh; Rev. Larry Reinheimer; Igumen Irenee Rochon; Rev. John Jillions, Rev. Ovest Olekshy
Lay Members, David Grier, John Hadjinicolaou, Mother Sophia (Zion), David Rystephanuk, Rod Tkachuk, Sandra Ellis, Alexei Vassiouchkine
Ex Officio, Chancellor; Treas.; Sec.

Periodicals
Canadian Orthodox Messenger

Patriarchal Parishes of the Russian Orthodox Church in Canada

This is the diocese of Canada of the former Exarchate of North and South America of the Russian Orthodox Church. It was originally founded in 1897 by the Russian Orthodox Archdiocese in North America.

Headquarters
St. Barbara's Russian Orthodox Cathedral, 10105 96th St., Edmonton, AB T5H 2G3
Media Contact, Roman Lopushinsky, 11620 134 Ave., Edmonton, AB T5E 1K9, Tel./Fax (780)455-6314

Officers
Admn., Bishop of Kashira, Most Rev. Iov, 10812-108 St., Edmonton, AB T5H 3A6 Tel. (780)420-9945

The Pentecostal Assemblies of Canada

This body is incorporated under the Dominion Charter of 1919 and is also recognized in the Province of Quebec as an ecclesiastical corporation. Its beginnings are to be found in the revivals at the turn of the century, and most of the first Canadian Pentecostal leaders came from a religious background rooted in the Holiness movements.

The original incorporation of 1919 was implemented among churches of eastern Canada only. In the same year, a conference was called in Moose Jaw, Saskatchewan, to which the late Rev. J. M. Welch, general superintendent of the then-organized Assemblies of God in the U.S., was invited. The churches of Manitoba and Saskatchewan were organized as the Western District Council of the Assemblies of God. They were joined later by Alberta and British Columbia. In 1921, a conference was held in Montreal, to which the general chairman of the Assemblies of God was invited. Eastern Canada also became a district of the Assemblies of God, joining Eastern and Western Canada as two districts in a single organizational union.

In 1920, at Kitchener, Ontario, eastern and western churches agreed to dissolve the Canadian District of the Assemblies of God and unite under the name The Pentecostal Assemblies of Canada.

Today the Pentecostal Assemblies of Canada operates throughout the nation and in about 30 countries around the world. Religious services are conducted in more than 25 different languages in the 1,100 local churches in Canada. Members and adherents number about 230,000. The number of local churches includes approximately 100 Native congregations.

Headquarters
2450 Milltower Court, Mississauga, ON L5N 5Z6, Tel. (905)542-7400 Fax (905)542-7313

Officers
Gen. Supt., Rev. William D. Morrow
Asst. Supt., for Ministerial Services, Rev. David E. Hazzard
Asst. Supt. for Financial Resources, Rev. David Ball

DISTRICT SUPERINTENDENTS
British Columbia, Rev. D.R. Wells, 20411 Douglas Crescent, Langley, BC V3S 4B6, Tel. (604)533-2232 Fax (604)533-5405
Alberta, Rev. Lorne D. McAlister, 10585-111 St., #101, Edmonton, AB T5H 3E8 Tel. (403)426-0084 Fax (403)420-1318
Saskatchewan, Rev. J. I. Guskjolen, 3488 Fairlight Dr., Saskatoon, SK S7M 3Z4 Tel. (306)683-4646 Fax (306)683-3699
Manitoba, Rev. R.W. Pierce, 187 Henlow Bay, Winnipeg, MB R3Y 1G4 Tel. (204)940-1000 Fax (204)940-1009
Western Ontario, Rev. D.A Shepherd, 3214 S. Service Rd., Burlington, ON L7N 3J2 Tel. (905)637-5566 Fax (905)637-7558
Eastern Ontario and Quebec, Rev. R. T. Hilsden, Box 337, Cobury, ON K9A 4K8 Tel. (905)373-7374 Fax (905)373-1911
Quebec, Rev. G.C. Connors, 911, Boul Roland-Therrien, Longueuil, QC JAJ 4L3, Tel (4005) 442-2732 Fax (405) 442-3818
Maritime Provinces, Rev. Douglas Moore, Box 1184, Truro, NS B2N 5H1 Tel. (902)895-4212 Fax (902)897-0705

BRANCH CONFERENCES
Eastern Slavic, Rev. A. Muravski, 445 Stevenson Rd., Oshawa, ON L1J 5N8 Tel (905) 576-3584; Western Slavic, Rev. Michael Brandebura, 17-9420 172 St., Edmonton, T5T 6KI Tel (780) 743-2410 Fax (780) 473-2410
Finnish Conference, Rev. P. A. Korpela, 2592 Bayview Ave, North York, ON M2L1B3 Tel (416)733-0854 Fax (416)222-3356

Periodicals
testimony; Enrich; Contact; HonorBound

The Pentecostal Assemblies of Newfoundland

This body began in 1911 and held its first meetings at Bethesda Mission at St. John's. It was incorporated in 1925 as The Bethesda Pentecostal Assemblies of Newfoundland and changed its name in 1930 to The Pentecostal Assemblies of Newfoundland.

Headquarters

57 Thorburn Rd., Box 8895, Stn. "A", St. John's, NF A1B 3T2 Tel. (709)753-6314 Fax (709)753-4945
Email: paon@paon.nf.ca
Media Contact, Gen. Sup't., H. Paul Foster, 57 Thorburn Rd., Box 8895, Stn. "A", St. John's, NF A1B 3T2

Officers

GENERAL EXECUTIVE OFFICERS

Gen. Sup't.: H. Paul Foster, 57 Thorburn Rd., Box 8895, Stn. "A", St. John's, NF A1B 3T2
Gen. Sec.-Treas.: Clarence Buckle, 57 Thorburn Rd., Box 8895, Stn. "A", St. John's, NF A1B 3T2
Ex. Dir. of Home Missions: Andrew R. Anstey, 57 Thorburn Rd., Box 8895, Stn. "A", St. John's, NF A1B 3T2
Ex. Dir. of Ch. Ministries: Robert H. Dewling, 57 Thorburn Rd., Box 8895, Stn. "A", St. John's, NF A1B 3T2

PROVINCIAL DIRECTORS

Sunday School & Children's Ministries: Kelly L. Brenton, 42 Franks Road, Conception Bay South, NL A1X 6W8
Women's Ministries: Catherine J. Snow, 14 Jeddores Lane, Deer Lake, NL A8A 1P4
Men's Ministries: Wilfred S. Buckle, 52 Premier Dr., Corner Brook, NL A2H 1S4
Youth Ministries: B. Dean Brenton, Box 21100, St. John's, NF A1B 3L5
Mature Adult Ministries: Barry D. Pelley, Box 1715, Lewisporte, NL A0G 3A0
Family Ministries: Sharmaine R. Reid, Box 2, Hant's Harbour, NL A0B 1Y0

AUXILIARY SERVICES

Chaplain of Institutions: Robert G. Parsons, 29 Caster's Drive, Mount Pearl, NL A1N 4X3
Pentecostal Senior Citizens Home Administrator: Beverley Bellefleur, Box 130, Clarke's Beach, NF A0A 1W0
Evergreen Manor, Summerford, NF A0G 4E0
Chaplain: Memorial University of Newfoundland, Gregory R. Dewling, Memorial University of Newfoundland, Box 102, St. John's, NF A1C 5S7
Emmanuel Convention Centre Administrator: Sterling E. Warr, P.O. Box 1409, Lewisporte, NL A0G 3A0
Managing Editor, Good Tidings: Burton K. Janes, 57 Thornburn Rd., Box 8895, Stn. "A", St. John's, NF A1B 3T2

Periodicals

Good Tidings

Plymouth Brethren—please see Christian Brethren

Presbyterian Church in America (Canadian Section)

Canadian congregations of the Reformed Presbyterian Church, Evangelical Synod, became a part of the Presbyterian Church in America when the RPCES joined PCA in June 1982. Some of the churches were in predecessor bodies of the RPCES, which was the product of a 1965 merger of the Reformed Presbyterian Church in North America, General Synod and the Evangelical Presbyterian Church. Others came into existence later as a part of the home missions work of RPCES. Congregations are located in seven provinces, and the PCA is continuing church extension work in Canada. The denomination is committed to world evangelization and to a continuation of historic Presbyterianism. Its officers are required to subscribe to the Reformed faith as set forth in the Westminster Confession of Faith and Catechisms.

Headquarters

Media Contact, Dr. Dominic Aquila, Editor Byfaithonline Newletter, New Geneva Seminary, 3622 East Galley Rd., Colorado Springs, CO, 80909 Tel. (719)573-5395 Fax (719)573-5398, Email daquila6@aol.com

Periodicals

Equip for Ministry; Multiply; Network; byFaith

Presbyterian Church in Canada

This is the nonconcurring portion of the Presbyterian Church in Canada that did not become a part of The United Church of Canada in 1925.

Headquarters

50 Wynford Dr., Toronto, ON M3C 1J7 Tel. (416)441-1111 Fax (416)441-2825
Website: www.presbyterian.ca
Media Contact, Principal Clk., Rev. Stephen Kendall or Associate Secretary for Resource Production & Communication, Vacant

Officers

Principal Clk., Rev. Stephen Kendall, 50 Wynford Dr., Toronto, ON M3C 1J7 Tel. (416)441-1111 Fax (416)441-2825, Website: www.presbyterian.ca

Periodicals

Channels; The Presbyterian Message; Presbyterian Record; Glad Tidings; La Vie Chrétienne

Reformed Church in Canada

The Canadian region of the Reformed Church in America was organized under the General

Synod of the Reformed Church in America. The RCA in Canada has 40 churches which includes three classes (lower assemblies). The Reformed churches in Canada are member congregations of the Reformed Church in America and the Regional Synod of Canada (one of eight RCA regional synods established by its General Synod) and three classes, Ontario, Canadian Prairies and British Columbia.

The first ordained minister, Domine Jonas Micahelius, arrive in New Amsterdam from The Netherlands in 1628. Throughout the colonial period, the Reformed Church lived under the authority of the Classis of Amsterdam. Its churches were clustered in New York and New Jersey. Under the leadership of Rev. John Livingston, it became a denomination independent of the authority of the Classis of Amsterdam in 1776. Its geographical base was broadened in the 19th century by the immigration of Reformed Dutch and German settlers in the midwestern United States. The Reformed Church now spans the United States and Canada. The Reformed Church in America accepts as its standards of faith the Heidelberg Catechism, Belgic Confession and Canons of Dort. It has a rich heritage of world mission activity. It claims to be loyal to Reformed tradition which emphasizes obedience to God in all aspects of life.

Although the Reformed Church in America has worked in close cooperation with other churches, it has never entered into merger with any other denomination. It is a member of the World Alliance of Reformed Churches, the World Council of Churches and the National Council of the Churches of Christ in the United States of America. In 1998 it also entered into a relationship of full communion with the Evangelical Lutheran Church in America, Presbyterian Church (U.S.A.), and the United Church of Christ by way of the Formula of Agreement.

Headquarters
475 Riverside Dr., 18th Floor, New York, NY 10115 Tel. (212)870-3243 Fax (212)870-2499 Media Contact, Communications Officer, Paul Boice, 4500 60th St., SE, Grand Rapids, MI 49512 Tel. (616)698-7071 Fax (616)698-6606 Website: www.rca.org

OFFICERS AND STAFF OF GENERAL SYNOD
Regional Synod of Canada, Synod Executive, Mr. Fred Algera, 1985 Beke Rd. RR#4, Cambridge, ON N1R 5S5
President, The Rev. Bradley Lewis, 475 Riverside Dr., 18th Floor, New York, NY 10115
General Synod Council; Moderator, The Rev. Steven Vander Molen, 475 Riverside Dr., 18th Floor, New York, NY 10115
General Secretary, The Rev. Wesley Granberg-Michaelson, 475 Riverside Dr., 18th Floor, New York, NY 10115; 4500 60th St. S.E., Grand Rapids, MI 49512

Operations and Support, Director & Assistant Secretary, The Rev. Kenneth Bradsell
Global Mission, Director, The Rev. Bruce Menning
Leadership/Revitalization, Director, The Rev. Kenneth Eriks
Church Multiplication/Discipleship, Director, The Rev. Richard Welscott
Finance Services, Treasurer, Ms. Susan Converse

The Reformed Episcopal Church of Canada

The Reformed Episcopal Church is a separate entity. It was established in Canada by an act of Parliament given royal assent on June 2, 1886. It maintains the founding principles of episcopacy (in historic succession from the apostles), Anglican liturgy and Reformed doctrine and evangelical zeal. In practice it continues to recognize the validity of certain nonepiscopal orders of evangelical ministry. The Church has reunited with the Reformed Episcopal Church and is now composed of two Dioceses in this body - the Diocese of Central and Eastern Canada and the Diocese of Western Canada and Alaska.

Headquarters
Box 2532, New Liskeard, ON P0J 1P0 Tel. (705)647-4565 Fax (705)647-1340
Email: fed@nt.nct
Website: www.recus.org
Media Contact, Pres., The Rt. Rev. Michael Fedechko, M. Div., D.D.

Officers
Pres., The Rt. Rev. Michael Fedechko, 320 Armstrong St., Temiskaming Shores, ON P0J 1P0
Vice-Pres., Bob Harrold, St. Catharines, ON.
Sec., Allison Buffet, Hamilton, ON.

BISHOPS
Diocese of Central & Eastern Canada, The Rt. Rev. Michael Fedechko, 320 Armstrong St., Temiskaming Shores, ON P0J 1P0 Tel. (705)647-4565 Fax (705)647-1340
Diocese of Western Canada & Alaska, Rt. Rev. Charles W. Dorrington, 54 Blanchard St., Victoria, BC V8X 4R1 Tel. (604)744-5014 Fax (604)388-5891

Periodicals
The Messenger

Reinland Mennonite Church

This group was founded in 1958 when 10 ministers and approximately 600 members separated from the Sommerfelder Mennonite Church. In 1968, four ministers and about 200 members migrated to Bolivia. The church has work in five communities in Manitoba and one in Ontario

Headquarters
Bishop William H. Friesen, P.O. Box 96, Rosenfeld, MB R0G 1X0 Tel. (204)324-6339

Media Contact, Deacon, Henry Wiebe, Box 2587, Winkler, MB R6W 4C3 Tel. (204)325-8487

Reorganized Church of Jesus Christ of Latter Day Saints—please see Community of Christ

The Roman Catholic Church in Canada

The largest single body of Christians in Canada, the Roman Catholic Church is under the spiritual leadership of His Holiness the Pope. Catholicism in Canada dates back to 1534, when the first Mass was celebrated on the Gaspé Peninsula on July 7, by a priest accompanying Jacques Cartier. Catholicism had been implanted earlier by fishermen and sailors from Europe. Priests came to Acadia as early as 1604. Traces of a regular colony go back to 1608 when Champlain settled in Quebec City. The Récollets (1615), followed by the Jesuits (1625) and the Sulpicians (1657), began the missions among the native population. The first official Roman document relative to the Canadian missions dates from March 20, 1618. Bishop François de Montmorency-Laval, the first bishop, arrived in Quebec in 1659. The church developed in the East, but not until 1818 did systematic missionary work begin in western Canada.

In the latter 1700s, English-speaking Roman Catholics, mainly from Ireland and Scotland, began to arrive in Canada's Atlantic provinces. After 1815 Irish Catholics settled in large numbers in what is now Ontario. The Irish potato famine of 1847 greatly increased that population in all parts of eastern Canada.

By the 1850s the Catholic Church in both English- and French-speaking Canada had begun to erect new dioceses and found many religious communities. These communities did educational, medical and charitable work among their own people as well as among Canada's native peoples. By the 1890s large numbers of non-English and non-French-speaking Catholics had settled in Canada, especially in the Western provinces. In the 20th century the pastoral horizons have continued to expand to meet the needs of what has now become a very multicultural church.

The Canadian Conference of Catholic Bishops is the national association of the Latin and Eastern Catholic Bishops of Canada. Its main offices are in Ottawa, Ontario.

CANADIAN ORGANIZATION

Conférence des évêques catholiques du Canada - Canadian Conference of Catholic Bishops, 2500 Don Reid Drive, Ottawa, ON k1H 2J2, Tel. (613)241-9461, Fax (613)241-9048, cecc@cccb.ca, website:www.cccb.ca

Headquarters

Media Contact, Mr. Gérald Baril, gbaril@cecc.ca Tel. (613)241-9461 cecc@cccb.ca

Officers

General Secretariat of the Canadian Conference of Catholic Bishops
General Secretary: Msgr. Mario Paquette, P.H.
Associate General Secretaries: vacant (French Sector); Mr. Bede Hubbard (English Sector)

EXECUTIVE COMMITTEE

Pres., Most Rev. V. James Weisgerber; Vice-Pres., Most Rev. Pierre Morissette; Co-Treas., Most Rev. Richard Smith and Most Rev. V. Paul-André Durocher

EPISCOPAL COMMISSIONS—NATIONAL LEVEL

Justice and Peace: Most Rev. Brendan O'Brien
Doctrine: Most Rev. Most Rev. Michael Miller, C.S.B.
Christian Unity, Religious Relations with the Jews, and Interfaith Dialogue: Most Rev. Martin Veillette

EPISCOPAL COMMISSIONS— SECTOR LEVEL

Christian Education; Most Rev. Richard Smith
Liturgie et sacrements: Most Rev. Louis Dicaire
Liturgy: Most Rev. Albert LeGatt

NATIONAL COMMITTEES

Canon Law: Most Rev. Peter Hundt
Relations with Catholic Movements and Associations: Most Rev. Pierre-André Fournier
Communications: Most Rev. Pierre Morissette
Government Relations: Most Rev. V. James Weisgerber

OFFICES

Justice, Paix et Missions – Justice Peace and Missions, Mr. François Poitras, Dir.
Communications: Mr. Gérald Baril, Dir.
Droit canonique—inter-rites-Canon Law—Inter-rite: Msgr. Mario Paquette, P.H. Secr.
Éditions-Publications, Dr. Vicki Bennett, Dir.
Liturgie-Liturgy -: M. Gaëtan Baillargeon, Dir. (French Sector); Rev. William Burke, Dir. (English Sector)
National Office of Religious Education: Ms. Joanne Chafe, Dir.
Relations ecclésiales et doctrine – Ecclesial Relations and Doctrine: Mr. Jonas Abromaitis
Tribunal d'appel du Canada - The Canadian Appeal Tribunal: Msgr. Alan McCormack, P.H., Vicaire judiciaire-Judicial Vicar

REGIONAL EPISCOPAL ASSEMBLIES

Atlantic Episcopal Assembly - Assemblée des évêques de l'Atlantique: Pres., Most Rev. François Thibodeau, C.J.M.; Vice Pres., Most Rev. Martin William Currie and Most Claude Champagne, O.M.I.; Secretary-Treasurer, Fr. Léo Grégoire, I.V. Dei, Tel. (506)735-5578, Fax (506)735-4271
Assemblée des évêques catholiques du Québec: Pres., Most Martin Veillette; Vice Prés., Most

Jean Gagnon; Secrétaire général, M. Bertrand Ouellet, Tel. (514)274-4323, Fax (514)274-4383
Ontario Conference of Catholic Bishops - Conférence des évêques catholiques de l'Ontario: Pres., Most Rev. Thomas Collins, Vice Pres., Most Rev. Anthony Daniels; Secretary-Treasurer, Mr. Luciano Piovesan; Tel. (416)923-1423, Fax (416)923-1509
Assembly of Western Catholic Bishops - Assemblée des évêques catholiques de l'Ouest Pres., Most Rev. Daniel Bohan; Vice Pres., Most Rev. Larence Huculak, O.S.B.M.; Sec.-Treasurer, Rt. Rev. Peter Novecosky, O.S.B.; Tel. (306)682-1788, Fax (306) 682-1766 MILITARY ORDINARIATE-ORDINARIAT MILITAIRE
Bishop, Most Rev. Donald J. Theriault, Military Ordinariate of Canada, Canadian Forces Support Unit (Ottawa), Uplands Site Building 469, Ottawa, ON K1A 0K2, Tel. (613)990-7824, Fax (613)991-1056
Canadian Religious Conference, Sec. Gen., Sr. Margaret Toner, SCIC., 4135, rue de Rouen, Montréal, Québec H1V 1G5, Tel. (514)259-0856, Fax (514)259-0857
Organisme catholique pour la vie et la famille/ Catholic Organization for Life and Family, co-directors: Ms. Michèle Boulva, Tel. (613)241-9461, Fax (613)241-9048, mboulva@colf.ca

Periodicals
Foi et Culture (Bulletin natl. de liturgie)

Romanian Orthodox Church in America (Canadian Parishes)

The first Romanian Orthodox immigrants in Canada called for Orthodox priests from their native country of Romania. Between 1902 and 1914, they organized the first Romanian parish communities and built Orthodox churches in different cities and farming regions of western Canada (Alberta, Saskatchewan, Manitoba) as well as in the eastern part (Ontario and Quebec).

In 1929, the Romanian Orthodox parishes from Canada joined with those of the United States in a Congress held in Detroit, Michigan, and asked the Holy Synod of the Romanian Orthodox Church of Romania to establish a Romanian Orthodox Missionary Episcopate in America. The first Bishop, Policarp (Morushca), was elected and consecrated by the Holy Synod of the Romanian Orthodox Church and came to the United States in 1935. He established his headquarters in Detroit with jurisdiction over all the Romanian Orthodox parishes in the United States and Canada.

In 1950, the Romanian Orthodox Church in America (i.e. the Romanian Orthodox Missionary Episcopate in America) was granted administrative autonomy by the Holy Synod of the Romanian Orthodox Church of Romania, and only doctrinal and canonical ties remain with this latter body.

In 1974 the Holy Synod of the Romanian Orthodox Church of Romania recognized and approved the elevation of the Episcopate to the rank of the Romanian Orthodox Archdiocese in America and Canada and completed the administrative autonomy.

Headquarters
Romanian Orthodox Archdiocese in the Americas, 5410 N. Newland Ave., Chicago, IL 60656 USA

Officers
Archbishop, Most Rev. Nicolae Condrea,5410 N. Newland Ave., Chicago, IL 60656 USA Tel. (773)774-1677, Fax (773)774-1805, Email: archnicolae@aol.com
Secretary, V. Rev. Fr. Nicholas Apostola, 44 Midland St. Worchester, MA 01602-4217, Tel. (508)845-0088, Fax (508)752-8180

Periodicals
Credinta - The Faith

The Romanian Orthodox Episcopate of America (Jackson, MI)

This body of Eastern Orthodox Christians of Romanian descent is part of the Autocephalous Orthodox Church in America. For complete description and listing of officers, please see chapter 3, "Religious Bodies in the United States."

Headquarters
2535 Grey Tower Rd., Jackson, MI 49201 Tel. (517)522-4800
Email: chancery@roea.org
Website: www.roca.org
Mailing Address, P.O. Box 309, Grass Lake, MI 49240-0309
Media Contact, Ed.-Sec., Rev. Archdeacon David Oancea, P.O. Box 185, Grass Lake, MI 49240-0185 Tel. (517)522-3656

Officers
Ruling Hierarch, Most. Rev. Archbishop Nathaniel Popp
Dean of All Canada, Very Rev. Daniel Nenson, 2855 Helmsing St., Regina, SK S4V 0W7 Tel. (306)761-2379

Periodicals
Solia - The Herald; Good News- Buna Vestire (in Canada only)

Russian Orthodox Church—please see the Patriarchal Parishes of the Russian Orthodox Church in Canada.

The Salvation Army in Canada

The Salvation Army, an evangelical branch of the Christian Church, is an international movement founded in 1865 in London, England. The ministry of Salvationists, consisting of clergy (officers) and laity, comes from a commitment to Jesus Christ and is revealed in practical service that is offered without discrimination.

The Salvation Army began its work in Canada in 1882 and has grown to become the largest non-governmental direct provider of social services in the country. The Salvation Army gives hope and support to vulnerable people today and everyday in 400 communities across Canada and 115 countries around the world. The Salvation Army offers practical assistance for children and families, often tending to the basic necessities of life, provides shelter for homeless people and rehabilitation for people who have lost control of their lives to an addiction.

Headquarters
2 Overlea Blvd., Toronto, ON M4H 1P4 Tel. (416)425-2111
Media Contact, Andrew Burditt, Tel. (416)422-6208 Fax (416)422-6217
E-mail: andrew_burditt@can.salvationarmy.org
Website: www.SalvationArmy.ca

Officers
Territorial Commander, Commissioner William W. Francis
Territorial President, Women's Organizations, Commissioner Marilyn Francis
Chief Secretary, Lt.-Colonel Donald J. Copple
Secretary for Personnel, Major Jean Moulton
Secretary for Business Administrtaion, Major Neil Watt
Financial Secretary, Paul Goodyear
Secretary for Program, Lt.-Colonel David Hiscock
Secretary for Public Realtions and Development, Graham Moore
Property Secretary, Major Pearce Samson
Social Services Secretary, Mary Ellen Eberlin

Periodicals
Salvationist; Faith & Friends

Serbian Orthodox Church in the U.S.A. and Canada, Diocese of Canada

The Serbian Orthodox Church is an organic part of the Eastern Orthodox Church. As a local church it received its autocephaly from Constantinople in A.D. 1219. The Patriarchal seat of the church today is in Belgrade, Yugoslavia. In 1921, a Serbian Orthodox Diocese in the United States of America and Canada was organized. In 1963, it was reorganized into three dioceses, and in 1983 a fourth diocese was created for the Canadian part of the church. The Serbian Orthodox Church is in absolute doctrinal unity with all other local Orthodox Churches.

Headquarters
7470 McNiven Rd., RR 3, Campbellville, ON L0P 1B0 Tel. (905)878-0043 Fax (905)878-1909
Email: vladika@istocnik.com
Website: www. istocnim.com
Media Contact, Rt. Rev. Georgije

Officers
Serbian Orthodox Bishop of Canada, Rt. Rev. Georgije
Dean of Western Deanery, V. Rev. Drago Knezevic, 12936 - 112th St., Edmonton, AB T5E 6J1, Tel. (780)454-6513
Dean of Eastern Deanery, V. Rev. Zivorad Subotic, 351 Mellville Ave., Westmount, QC H3Z 2Y7 Tel. + Fax (514)931-6664

Periodicals
Istocnik, Herald of the Serbian Orthodox Church—Canadian Diocese

Seventh-day Adventist Church in Canada

The Seventh-day Adventist Church in Canada is part of the worldwide Seventh-day Adventist Church with headquarters in Silver Spring, Maryland (See "Religious Bodies in the United States" section of this *Yearbook* for a fuller description.) The Seventh-day Adventist Church in Canada was organized in 1901 and reorganized in 1932.

Headquarters
1148 King Street East, Oshawa, ON L1H 1H8 Tel. (905)433-0011 Fax (905)433-0982
Media Contact, Nilton D. Amorim

Officers
Pres., Daniel R. Jackson
Sec., Nilton D. Amorim
Treas., John Ramsay

DEPARTMENTS
Undertreasurer, Joyce Jones
Education, Dennis Marshall
Family Ministries, Hebert Valiame
Trust Services,
ADRA Canada

Periodicals
Canadian Adventist Messenger

Southern Baptists—please see Canadian Convention of Southern Baptists

Syriac Orthodox Church of Antioch

The Syriac Orthodox Church professes the faith of the first three ecumenical councils of Nicaea, Constantinople and Ephesus and numbers faithful in the Middle East, India, the Americas, Europe and Australia. It traces its origin to the Patriarchate established in Antioch by St. Peter the Apostle and is under the supreme ecclesiastical jurisdiction of His Holiness the Syrian Orthodox Patriarch of Antioch and All the East, now residing in Damascus, Syria.

The Archdiocese of the Syrian Orthodox Church in the U.S. and Canada was formally established in 1957. In 1995, the Archdiocese of North America was divided into three separate Patriarchal Vicariates, including one for Canada.

The first Syrian Orthodox faithful came to Canada in the 1890s and formed the first Canadian parish in Sherbrooke, Quebec. Today five official parishes of the Archdiocese exist in Canada—two in Quebec and three in Ontario. There is also an official mission congregation in Calgary, Alberta and Ottawa, Ontario.

Headquarters
Archdiocese of Canada, The New Archdiocesan Centre, 4375 Henri-Bourassa Ouest, St.-Laurent, Quebec H4L 1A5, Canada Tel. (514)334-6993 Fax (514)334-8233

Officers
Archbishop Mor Timotheos Aphrem Aboodi

Ukrainian Orthodox Church of Canada

Toward the end of the 19th century many Ukrainian immigrants settled in Canada. In 1918, a group of these pioneers established the Ukrainian Orthodox Church of Canada (UOCC), today the largest Ukrainian Orthodox Church beyond the borders of Ukraine. In 1990, the UOCC entered into a eucharistic communion with the Ecumenical Patriarchate of Constantinople (Istanbul).

Headquarters
Ukrainian Orthodox Church of Canada, Office of the Consistory, 9 St. Johns Ave., Winnipeg, MB R2W 1G8 Tel. (204)586-3093 Fax (204)582-5241
Email: consistory@uocc.ca
Website: www. uocc.ca
Media Contacts, Rev. Fr. Gene Maximiuk, 9st. John's Ave., Winnipeg, MB R2W 1G8, Tel. (204)586-3093 Fax (204)582-5241; Ms. M. Zurek, 9 St. Johns Ave., Winnipeg, MB R2W 1G8 Tel. (204)586-3093 Fax (204)582-5241

Officers
Primate, Most Rev. Metropolitan John (Stinka), 9 St. Johns Ave., Winnipeg, MB R2W 1G8 Tel. (204)586-3093 Fax (204)582-5241
Chair of the Presidium, Very Rev. Bohdan Hladio

Periodicals
Visnyk-The Herald-Le Messager (newspaper)
Ridna Nyva (almanac-annual)

Union d'Eglises Baptistes Françaises au Canada

Baptist churches in French Canada first came into being through the labors of two missionaries from Switzerland, Rev. Louis Roussy and Mme. Henriette Feller, who arrived in Canada in 1835. The earliest church was organized in Grande Ligne (now St.-Blaise), Quebec in 1838.

By 1900 there were 7 churches in the province of Quebec and 13 French-language Baptist churches in the New England states. The leadership was totally French Canadian.

By 1960, the process of Americanization had caused the disappearance of the French Baptist churches in the New England states. During the 1960s, Quebec as a society, began rapidly changing in all its facets, education, politics, social values and structures. Mission, evangelism and church growth once again flourished. In 1969, in response to the new conditions, the Grande Ligne Mission passed control of its work to the newly formed Union of French Baptist Churches in Canada, which then included 8 churches. By 2005 the French Canadian Baptist movement had grown to include 34 congregations present in three provinces: Quebec, New Brunswick, and Ontario.

The Union d'Églises Baptistes Françaises au Canada is a member body of the Canadian Baptist Ministries and thus is affiliated with the Baptist World Alliance.

Headquarters
2285 Avenue Papineau, Montreal, QC H2K 4J5 Tel. (514)526-6643 Fax (514)526-9269
Media Contact, Gen. Sec., Rev. Roland Grimard

Officers
Sec. Gen., Rev. Roland Grimard

Periodicals
www.UnionBaptiste.com (Internet)

Union of Spiritual Communities of Christ (Orthodox Doukhobors in Canada)

The Doukhobors are Canadians of Russian origin living primarily in the western provinces of Canada, but their beginnings in Russia are unknown. The name "Doukhobors," or "Spirit Wrestlers," was given them in derision by the Russian Orthodox clergy in Russia as far back as 1785. The Doukhobors were persecuted by the church for rejecting Orthodoxy, and following the counsel of their leader, Peter V. Verigin, earned the wrath of the Tsarist government by destroying all of their weapons and adopting pacifism in 1895. In 1899 the Tsarist government allowed 8,000 Doukhobors to leave Russia in response to an international uproar over their persecution by the church and state. They made their way to Canada with the assistance of Count Leo Tolstoy, who saw in these people the living embodiment of his philosophy, the Religious Society of Friends, commonly known as Quakers and other people of good will. Originally settled in Saskatchewan, by 1911 the majority followed Verigin to Bristish Columbia because of government efforts to assimilate them.

The teaching of the Doukhobors is penetrated with the Gospel spirit of love. Worshiping God in the spirit, they affirm that the outward church and all that is performed in it and concerns it has no importance for them; the church is where two or three are gathered together, united in the name of Christ. They do not believe in icon worship or in intermediaries between themselves and God. Their spiritual teachings are founded on ancient tradition, which they call the "Book of Life," because it lives in their memory and hearts. In this book are psalms composed by their elders and leaders, partly formed out of the contents of the Bible partly out of their historical experience. These are committed to memory by each succeeding generation. Doukhobors observe complete pacifism and non-violence, are lacto-vegetarians, and attempt to maintain a communal lifestyle.

The majority of Canadian Doukhobors were reorganized in 1938 by Peter P. Verigin, son of P.V. Verigin, shortly before his death, into the Union of Spiritual Communities of Chris to distinguish themselves from a radical off shoot who call themselves Sons of Freedom, and whose embrace of nudity and depradations has been sensationalized by the media and has stigmatized all Doukhobors. Today the USCC is governed by Trustees elected from member communities and administered by an elected Executive Committee headed by Honourary Chairman, John J. Verigin, CM OBC. The USCC executes the will and protects the interests of its member communities and its members living beyond south central British Columbia where the USCC is headquartered. The USCC is the largest organization of Doukhobors and maintains relations with other Doukhobor groups across Canada, in the USA, the Russian Federation, the Ukraine, and Georgia. The USCC also cooperates with other non governmental organizations working non violently to promote peace and justice, and respect for human didgnity and ecological integrity.

Headquarters
USCC Central Office, Box 760, Grand Forks, BC V0H 1H0 Tel. (250)442-8252 Fax (250)442-3433

Media Contact, John J. Verigin, Sr.

Officers
Hon. Chmn. of the Exec. Comm., John J. Verigin, Sr.

Chpsn., Fred Bojey

Periodicals
ISKRA

United Brethren Church in Canada

Founded in 1767 in Lancaster County, Pennsylvania, missionaries came to Canada about 1850. The first class was held in Kitchener in 1855, and the first building was erected in Port Elgin in 1867.

The Church of the United Brethren in Christ had its beginning with Philip William Otterbein and Martin Boehm, who were leaders in the revivalistic movement in Pennsylvania and Maryland during the late 1760s.

Headquarters
302 Lake St., Huntington, IN 46750 Tel. (219)356-2312 Fax (219)356-4730

GENERAL OFFICERS
Pres., Rev. Brian Magnus, 120 Fife Rd., Guelph, ON N1H 6Y2 Tel. (519)836-0180

Treas., Brian Winger, 2233 Hurontario St., Apt. 916, Mississauga, ON L5A 2E9 Tel. (905)275-8140

The United Church of Canada

The United Church of Canada was formed on June 10, 1925, through the union of the Methodist Church, Canada, the Congregational Union of Canada, the Council of Local Union Churches and 70 percent of the Presbyterian Church in Canada. The union culminated years of negotiation between the churches, all of which had integral associations with the development and history of the nation.

In fulfillment of its mandate to be a uniting as well as a United Church, the denomination has been enriched by other unions during its history. The Wesleyan Methodist Church of Bermuda joined in 1930. On January 1, 1968, the Canada Conference of the Evangelical United Brethren became part of The United Church of Canada. At various times, congregations of other Christian communions have also become congregations of the United Church.

The United Church of Canada is a full member of the World Methodist Council, the World Alliance of Reformed Churches (Presbyterian and Congregational), and the Canadian and World Councils of Churches. The United Church is the largest Protestant denomination in Canada.

NATIONAL OFFICES
General Council Office, 3250 Bloor St. W., Ste. 300, Toronto, ON M8X 2Y4 Tel. (416)231-5931 Fax (416)231-3103, 1-(800)268-3781

Media Contact, Communications Officer, Mary-Frances Denis

GENERAL COUNCIL
Mod., Rt. Rev. David W. Giuliano

Gen. Sec., Nora M. Sanders

GENERAL COUNCIL MINISTERS
Planning Processes, Janet McDonald Programs for Mission & Ministry, Rev. Bruce Gregersen

Racial and Gender Justice, Kim Uyede-Kai

Regional Relations, Rev. Carol L. Hancock

Resources for Mission & Ministry, Ian S. Fraser

Archivist, Nicole Vonk

ADMINISTRATIVE UNITS (EXECUTIVE MINISTERS)
Ethnic Ministries, Exec. Min., Rev. Michael Blair

Congregational, Educational and Community Ministries, Exec. Min., Rev. Harry Oussoren

Financial Services, Exec. Officer, Ron Olsen

Financial Stewardship, Exec. Min., Rev. William Steadman

Information Technology Services, Exec. Officer, Vanda Orsini

Justice, Global & Ecumenical Relations, Exec. Min., Omega C. Bula

Ministries in French, Exec. Min., Rev. Pierre Goldberger

Ministry & Employment Policies & Services, Exec. Min., Michael Burke

Resource Production and Distribution, Exec. Min., Dan Benson

CONFERENCE EXECUTIVE SECRETARIES
Alberta and Northwest, Rev. Lynn I. Maki, 9911-48 Ave., NW, Edmonton, AB T6E 5V6 Tel.

(780)435-3995 Fax (780)438-3317, Email: coffice@anwconf.com

All Native Circle, Speaker, Cheryl Jourdain, 367 Selkirk Ave., Winnipeg, MB R2W 2M3 Tel. (204)582-5518 Fax (204)582-6649, Email: allnative@mts.net

Bay of Quinte, Rev. Wendy Bulloch, P.O. Box 700, 67 Mill St., Frankford, ON K0K 2C0 Tel. (613)398-1051 Fax (613)398-8894, E-mail,officeadmin@bayofquinteconference.ca

British Columbia, Rev. Douglas Goodwin, 4383 Rumble St., Burnaby, BC V5J 2A2 Tel. (604)431-0434 Fax (604)431-0439, Email: bcconf@bc.united-church.ca

Hamilton, Rev. Fred Monteith, Box 100, Carlisle, ON L0R 1H0 Tel. (905)659-3343 Fax (905)659-7766, Email: office@hamconf.org

London, Rev. David Woodall, 747 Hyde Park Rd., Ste 116, London, ON N6H 3S3 Tel. (519)672-1930 Fax (519)439-2800, Email: lonconf@execulink.com

Manitoba and Northwestern Ontario, Rev. Bruce Faurschou, 1470 Willson Place, Winnipeg, MB R3T 3N9 Tel. (204)233-8911 Fax (204)233-3289, Email: office@confmnwo.mb.ca

Manitou, Rev. William Kunder, 319 McKenzie Ave., North Bay, ON P1B 7E3 Tel. (705)474-3350 Fax (705)497-3597, Email: office@manitouconference.ca

Maritime, Rev. Catherine H. Gaw, 32 York St., Sackville, NB E4L 4R4 Tel. (506)536-1334 Fax (506)536-2900, Email: info@marconf.ca

Montreal and Ottawa, Rev. Rosemary Lambie, 225-50 Ave., Lachine, QC H8T 2T7 Tel. (514)634-7015 Fax (514)634-2489, Email: lachine@istar.ca

Newfoundland and Labrador, Rev. William G. Bartlett, 320 Elizabeth Ave., St. John's, NL A1B 1T9 Tel. (709)754-0386 Fax (709)754-8336, Email: unitedchurch@nfld.net

Saskatchewan, Joan McConnell, 418 A McDonald St., Regina, SK S4N 6E1 Tel. (306)721-3311 Fax (306)721-3171, Email: ucskco@sasktel.net

Toronto, Rev. David W. Allen, 65 Mayall Ave., Downsview, ON M3L 1E7 Tel. (416)241-2677 Fax (416)241-2689, Email: office@toronto conference.ca

Periodicals

United Church Observer; Mandate; Aujourd'hui Credo

United Pentecostal Church in Canada

This body, which is affiliated with the United Pentecostal Church, International, with headquarters in Hazelwood, Missouri, accepts the Bible standard of full salvation, which is repentance, baptism by immersion in the name of the Lord Jesus Christ for the remission of sins and the baptism of the Holy Ghost, with the initial signs of speaking in tongues as the Spirit gives utterance. Other tenets of faith include the Oneness of God in Christ, holiness, divine healing and the second coming of Jesus Christ.

Headquarters

United Pentecostal Church Intl., 8855 Dunn Rd., Hazelwood, MO 63042 Tel. (314)837-7300 Fax (314)837-4503

Media Contact, Gen. Sec.-Treas., Rev. C. M. Becton

DISTRICT SUPERINTENDENTS

Atlantic, Rev. Harry Lewis, P.O. Box 1046, Perth Andover, NB E0J 1V0

British Columbia, Rev. Paul V. Reynolds, 13447-112th Ave., Surrey, BC V3R 2E7

Canadian Plains, Rev. Johnny King, 615 Northmount Dr., NW, Calgary, AB T2K 3J6

Central Canadian, Rev. Clifford Heaslip, 4215 Roblin Blvd., Winnipeg, MB R3R 0E8

Newfoundland, Jack Cunningham

Nova Scotia, Superintendent, Rev. John D. Mean, P.O. Box 2183, D.E.P.S., Dartmouth, NS B2W 3Y2

Ontario, Rev. Carl H. Stephenson, 63 Castlegrove Blvd., Don Mills, ON M3A 1L3

Universal Fellowship of Metropolitan Community Churches

The Universal Fellowship of Metropolitan Community Churches is a Christian church which directs a special ministry within, and on behalf of, the gay and lesbian community. Involvement, however, is not exclusively limited to gays and lesbians; U.F.M.C.C. tries to stress its openness to all people and does not call itself a "gay church."

Founded in 1968 in Los Angeles by the Rev. Troy Perry, the U.F.M.C.C. has over 300 member congregations worldwide. Congregations are in Vancouver, Edmonton, Windsor, London, Toronto, Ottawa (2), Guelph, Fredericton, Winnipeg, Halifax, Barrie and Belleville.

Theologically, the Metropolitan Community Churches stand within the mainstream of Christian doctrine, being "ecumenical" or "interdenominational" in stance (albeit a "denomination" in their own right).

The Metropolitan Community Churches are characterized by their belief that the love of God is a gift, freely offered to all people, regardless of sexual orientation and that no incompatibility exists between human sexuality and the Christian faith.

The Metropolitan Community Churches in Canada were founded in Toronto in 1973 by the Rev. Robert Wolfe.

Headquarters

Media Contact: The Rev.Cheryl Meyer, 135 Simpson Ave., Totonto, ON M4K 1A4

The Wesleyan Church of Canada

This group is the Canadian portion of The Wesleyan Church which consists of the Atlantic

205

and Central Canada districts. The Central Canada District of the former Wesleyan Methodist Church of America was organized at Winchester, Ontario, in 1889 and the Atlantic District was founded in 1888 as the Alliance of the Reformed Baptist Church, which merged with the Wesleyan Methodist Church in July, 1966.

The Wesleyan Methodist Church and the Pilgrim Holiness Church merged in June, 1968, to become The Wesleyan Church. The doctrine is evangelical and Wesleyan Arminian and stresses holiness beliefs. For more details, consult the U.S. listing under The Wesleyan Church.

Headquarters

The Wesleyan Church Intl. Center, P.O. Box 50434, Indianapolis, IN 46250-0434

Media Contact, Dist. Supt., Central Canada, Rev. Donald E. Hodgins, 17 Saint paul St., Belleview, ON K8N 1A4, Tel. (613)966-7527 Fax (613)968-6190

DISTRICT SUPERINTENDENTS

Central Canada, Rev. Donald E. Hodgins, 17 Saint paul St., Belleview, ON K8N 1A4,
Email: ccd@on.aibn.com

Atlantic, Rev. Dr. H. C. Wilson, 1600 Main st., Ste. 216, Moncton, NB E1E 1G5
Email: ncwilson@nbnet.nb.ca

Periodicals

Central Canada; The Clarion

Religious Bodies in Canada Arranged by Families

The following list of religious bodies appearing in the Directory Section of the Yearbook shows the "families," or related clusters into which Canadian religious bodies can be grouped. For example, there are many communions that can be grouped under the heading "Baptist" for historical and theological reasons. It should not be assumed, however, that all denominations under one family heading are necessarily consistent in belief or practice. The family clusters tend to represent historical factors more often than theological or practical ones. These family categories provide one of the major pitfalls when compiling church statistics because there is often a tendency to combine the statistics by "families" for analytical and comparative purposes. Such combined totals are deeply flawed, even though they are often used as variables for sociological analysis. The arrangement by families offered here is intended only as a general guide for conceptual organization when viewing the broad sweep of Canadian religious culture.

Religious bodies that cannot be categorized under family headings appear alphabetically and are not indented in the following list.

The Anglican Church of Canada
Apostolic Christian Church (Nazarene)
Armenian Evangelical Church
Associated Gospel Churches

Baptist Bodies
Association of Regular Baptist Churches (Canada)
Baptist Convention of Ontario and Quebec
Baptist General Conference of Canada
Baptist Union of Western Canada
Canadian Baptist Ministries
Canadian Convention of Southern Baptists
Convention of Atlantic Baptist Churches
The Fellowship of Evangelical Baptist Churches in Canada
Free Will Baptists
North American Baptist Conference
Union d'Eglises Baptistes Françaises au Canada

Brethren in Christ Church, Canadian Conference
Canadian District of the Moravian Church in America, Northern Province
Canadian Evangelical Christian Churches
Canadian Yearly Meeting of the Religious Society of Friends
Christ Catholic Church International
Christian Brethren (also known as Plymouth Brethren)
Christian and Missionary Alliance in Canada
Church of God (Anderson, Ind.)
Church of the Nazarene in Canada

Churches of Christ-Christian Churches
Christian Church (Disciples of Christ) in Canada
Christian Churches / Churches of Christ
Churches of Christ in Canada

Congregational Christian Churches in Canada

Eastern Orthodox Churches
The Antiochian Orthodox Christian Archdiocese of North America
Greek Orthodox Metropolis of Toronto (Canada)
Orthodox Church in America (Archdiocese of Canada)
Orthodox Church in America (Canada Section)
Patriarchal Parishes of the Russian Orthodox Church in Canada
Romanian Orthodox Church in America (Canada)
The Romanian Orthodox Episcopate of America (Jackson, MI)
Serbian Orthodox Church in the U.S.A. and Canada, Diocese of Canada
Ukrainian Orthodox Church of Canada

The Evangelical Covenant Church of Canada
Evangelical Free Church of Canada
The Evangelical Missionary Church of Canada
General Church of the New Jerusalem
Jehovah's Witnesses

Latter Day Saints (Mormons)
The Church of Jesus Christ of Latter Day Saints in Canada
Community of Christ

Lutheran Bodies
Church of the Lutheran Brethren
The Estonian Evangelical Lutheran Church Abroad
Evangelical Lutheran Church in Canada
Lutheran Church—Canada

Mennonite Bodies
Canadian Conference of Mennonite Brethren Churches
Church of God in Christ (Mennonite)

207

The Evangelical Mennonite Conference
Evangelical Mennonite Mission Conference
Mennonite Church Canada
Old Order Amish Church
Reinland Mennonite Church

Methodist Bodies

British Methodist Episcopal Church of
Canada
Free Methodist Church in Canada
Independent Holiness Church
The Wesleyan Church of Canada

The Christ Catholic Church International
The Old Catholic Church of Canada
Open Bible Faith Fellowship of Canada

Oriental Orthodox Churches

Armenian Holy Apostolic Church - Canadian
Diocese
The Coptic Orthodox Church in Canada
Syriac Orthodox Church of Antioch

Pentecostal Bodies

The Apostolic Church in Canada
Apostolic Church of Pentecost of Canada Inc.
The Bible Holiness Movement
Canadian Assemblies of God (formerly The
Italian Pentecostal Church of Canada)
Church of God (Cleveland, Tenn.)
The Church of God of Prophecy in Canada
East
Elim Fellowship Canada
Foursquare Gospel Church of Canada
General Conference of the Canadian
Assemblies of God
Independent Assemblies of God International
(Canada)
The Pentecostal Assemblies of Canada
Pentecostal Assemblies of Newfoundland
United Pentecostal Church in Canada

Reformed Bodies

Canadian and American Reformed Churches
Christian Reformed Church in North America
Presbyterian Church in America (Canadian
Section)
Presbyterian Church in Canada
Reformed Church in Canada

The Reformed Episcopal Church of Canada
The Roman Catholic Church in Canada
The Salvation Army in Canada
Seventh-day Adventist Church in Canada
Union of Spiritual Communities of Christ
(Orthodox Doukhobors in Canada)
United Brethren Church in Canada
The United Church of Canada
Universal Fellowship of Metropolitan
Community Churches

5. Sources of Religion-Related Research

I. Directory of Selected Research Organizations

The editorial office of the *Yearbook of American & Canadian Churches* receives innumerable requests for data about churches, religious organizations, attendance patterns, and comparative religion concerns. Sometimes we are able to furnish the requested data, but more often we refer the inquirer to other research colleagues in the field. We are always interested in and aided by such requests, and we find ourselves informed by each question.

In response to such inquiries, the "Sources in Religion-Related Research" directory was initiated in the 1999 edition of the *Yearbook* In addition to asking each organization to provide a brief overall description, each was also asked to indicate any special research foci (i.e. denominational, congregational, interfaith, gender, etc.). Further, each organization is asked to identify the sociological, methodological, or theological approaches that serve to guide their research, and to describe any current or recent research projects. Lastly, we asked for a list of recurrent publications. Below the organizations' responses to these questions are reported as clearly and completely as is possible. Contact information appears just beneath the title of each organization. In most cases, the organization's website provides very detailed information about current research projects.

Numerous other research centers in the area of American religious life, each with specific areas of concern, conduct timely and significant research. We hope that readers will find utility in this directory and we invite them to identify additional sources by email: yearbook@ncccusa.org or by Fax: (212) 870-2817.

American Academy of Religion (AAR)

AAR Executive Office
825 Houston Mill Rd., Ste. 300
Atlanta, GA 30329
Tel. (404)727-7920
Fax (404)727-7959
Email: aar@aarweb.org
Website: www.aarweb.org
President: Dr. Diana Eck
Exec. Dir.: Dr. John Fitzmier

The AAR is the major learned society and professional association for scholars whose object of study is religion. Its mission— in a world where religion plays so central a role in social, political and economic events, as well as in the lives of communities and individuals— is to meet a critical need for ongoing reflection upon and understanding of religious traditions, issues, questions and values. As a learned society and professional association of teachers and research scholars, the American Academy of Religion has over 8500 members who teach in some 1,500 colleges, universities, seminaries, and schools in North America and abroad. The Academy is dedicated to furthering knowledge of religion and religious institutions in all their forms and manifestations. This is accomplished through Academy-wide and regional conferences and meetings, publications, programs, and membership services. Within a context of free inquiry and critical assessment, the Academy welcomes all disciplined reflection on religion— both from within and outside of communities of belief and practice— and seeks to enhance its broad public understanding.

The AAR's annual meeting, over 8,000 scholars gather to share research and collaborate on scholarly projects. The annual meeting sessions are grouped into over 70 program units, each representing an ongoing community of scholars who are collectively engaged in pursuing knowledge about a specific religious tradition or a specific aspect of religion. In addition, the AAR's ten regional organizations sponsor smaller annual meetings that are similar in structure to the Academy-wide meeting. All of the world's major religious traditions, as well as indigenous and historical religions, are explored in the work of AAR members.

Current or Recent Research

Currently, for example, the AAR offers Teaching Workshops for both junior and senior scholars. It is organizing efforts to gather data on the field to facilitate departmental planning and funding. A full explanation of the many current research projects is available on the AAR website, which is listed above.

Periodicals
The Journal of the American Academy of Religion is the scholarly periodical of the AAR. In addition, the AAR publishes a quarterly newsletter, *Religious Studies News, AAR Edition.*

Association of Religion Data Archives (ARDA)

Department of Sociology
The Pennsylvania State University
211 Oswald Tower
University Park, PA 16802-6207
Tel. (814)865-6258
Fax (814)863-7216
Email: arda@pop.psu.edu
Website: www.TheARDA.com
Director: Dr. Roger Finke
    The ARDA allows you to interactively explore the highest quality data on American and international religion using online features for generating national profiles, maps, church membership overviews, denominational heritage trees, tables, charts, and other summary reports. Nearly 500 data files are available for online preview and most can be downloaded for additional review. The ARDA (www.theARDA.com) is supported by the Lilly Endowment and the John Templeton Foundation and is housed in the Social Science Research Institute at the Pennsylvania State University. All services are provided free of charge.

Association of Theological Schools (ATS)

10 Summit Park Dr.
Pittsburgh, PA 15275-1103
Tel. (412)788-6505
Fax (412)788-6510
Email: ats@ats.edu
Website: www.ats.edu
Exec. Dir.: Daniel O. Aleshire
Dir. of Communications and Membership Services: Eliza Smith Brown
    The mission of The Association of Theological Schools in the United States and Canada (ATS) is to promote the improvement and enhancement of theological schools to the benefit of communities of faith and the broader public. The Association seeks to fulfill this mission by engaging in four core areas of work, (1) accreditation, (2) leadership education for administrative officers and faculty, (3) development of theological education, which involves the study of critical issues in theological education, and (4) communications and data.
    The Association is a membership organization of approximately 250 graduate schools of theology, including Protestant, Roman Catholic, and Orthodox schools, both freestanding seminaries and university-related divinity schools. A full list of members is available on the above website.
    Targeted areas of the Association's work currently include Theological Schools and the Church, the Character and Assessment of Learning for Religious Vocation, Race and Ethnicity in Theological Education, Women in Leadership in Theological Education, and Technology and Educational Practices.

Current or Recent Research
    The ATS project on Theological Schools and the Church has three goals that, together, will provide a perspective about theological schools' relationships with ecclesial bodies and prescriptions for strengthening them. The goals are (1) to cultivate a broad-based conversation about the institutional relationships between theological schools and church bodies, (2) to define the current patterns of relationship between seminaries and their respective communities of faith, and (3) to develop proposals for strengthening and renewing institutional relationships that benefit both the church and theological schools.
    A project on Technology and Educational Practices is identifying best practices in the use of educational technology in theological education, conducting educational events that provide information about and skill development in the use of educational technology, and creating resources about education and technology for use by theological schools.

Periodicals
    Fact Book on Theological Education is published annually and provides statistical data on the member institutions. The Association publishes a journal, *Theological Education*, bi-annually, a bimonthly newsletter entitled *Colloquy*, and the formal institutional documents of the Association entitled *Bulletin*, part 2 of which is the ATS membership list.

SOURCES

Auburn Theological Seminary

3041 Broadway
New York, NY 10027
Tel. (212)662-4315
Fax (212)663-5214
Email: cste@auburnsem.org; krh@auburnsem.org; slm@auburnsem.org
Website: www.auburnsem.org
President: The Rev. Dr. Katharine R. Henderson
Associate Director, CSTE: Dr. Sharon L. Miller

Auburn Theological Seminary's mission is to strengthen religious leadership. It carries out its mission through programs of non-degree theological education for clergy and laity; through programs for Presbyterian students enrolled at its partner institution, Union Seminary in New York City; and by conducting research on theological education at its Center for the Study of Theological Education. Auburn was founded in 1818 in Auburn, New York; it is currently located on Union Seminary's campus.

Auburn Seminary is related by covenant agreement with Presbyterian Church (U.S.A.), but most of its programs are ecumenical, and many have a multi-faith focus. The Center for the Study of Theological Education includes rabbinical schools and Protestant and Roman Catholic seminaries and divinity schools in its studies.

Research is conducted using a variety of methods, including survey and ethnographic research, structured interview and documentary research, research reports on surveys and case studies. Reports of findings are frequently published with accompanying information on the history of the issue being studied and with theological commentaries written from a variety of perspectives.

Current or Recent Research

"Great Expectations: Fund-raising Prospects for Theological School" (August 2009) looks the challenges and opportunities that theological schools face in fund-raising. Analysis of data from schools in the U.S. and Canada show the growth, and in some cases decline, of donations over the last twenty years. Schools are increasingly dependent on donations from individuals and finding and befriending these donors has become central to a school's mission and survival. Using data from schools that have engaged in capital campaigns, some parameters are given that may be helpful in setting goals for fund-raising. Factors that contribute to a school's successful fund-raising are also included in this report.

"Leadership That Works," a research project nearing completion, analyzes survey and interview data from theological school presidents, their senior administrative teams and board chairs. How can a board ensure success for a new president and how can a president optimally use the first few years of his or her new presidency, are some of the questions researched in this study.

Periodicals

Auburn Studies, an occasional bulletin in which the Center publishes its research results. Research reports are also available on Auburn's website (listed above).

The Barna Group, Ltd.

1957 Eastman Ave., Suite B
Ventura, CA 93003
Tel. (805)658-8885
Fax (805)658-7298
Email: barna@barna.org
Website: www.barna.org
President: George Barna
President: David Kinnaman

The Barna Group conducts primary research related to cultural change, people's lifestyles, values, attitudes, beliefs and religious practices.

Its vision is to provide current accurate and reliable information, in bite-sized pieces and at reasonable costs, to its clients to facilitate strategic decisions. Barna also produces many research-based books, reports, and ministry tools to help churches understand the national context of ministry. The organization works with churches from all Christian denominations.

It conducts projects based upon existing needs in the Church at-large, or for its clients specifically. Methodologically, The Barna Group uses both qualitative approaches (focus groups, depth interviews) and quantitative approaches (cross-sectional surveys, longitudinal studies, panel research).

Data collection methods include telephone surveys, mail surveys, in-person interviews, on-line surveys, self-administered surveys, focus groups.

211

Current or Recent Research

The Barna Group conducts more than 50 studies each year, covering a broad range of topics. Some of the recent non-proprietary studies completed are focused on understanding the state of the Church; the habits of highly

effective churches; worship efficacy; the unchurched; strategies and techniques for developing lay leaders; understanding effective discipleship processes; pastoral profiles; beliefs, behaviors and core attitudes of ministry donors; Biblical knowledge, and many others.

Periodicals

The Barna Group offers a free bi-weekly report, *The Barna Update*, on current information related to faith matters from its national non-proprietary research. This information is free to those who register for it at the website (listed above).

Center for Applied Research in the Apostolate (CARA)
Georgetown University
Washington, DC 20057
Tel. (202) 687-8080
Fax (202) 687-8083
Email: cara@georgetown.edu
Website: www.georgetown.edu/research/cara/index.html
Executive Director: Mary E. Bendyna, RSM, Ph.D.
Sr. Research Associate: Mary Gautier

CARA-the Center for Applied Research in the Apostolate is a not-for-profit research organization of the Roman Catholic Church. It operates on the premise that not only theological principles but also findings of the social sciences must be the basis for pastoral care.

CARA's mission since its founding in 1964 has been "To discover, promote, and apply modern techniques and scientific informational resources for practical use in a coordinated and effective approach to the Church's social and religious mission in the modern world, at home and overseas."

CARA performs a wide range of research studies and consulting services. Since its roots are Roman Catholic, many of its studies are done for dioceses, religious orders, parishes, and the United States Conference of Catholic Bishops. Interdenominational studies are also performed. Publishes The CARA Report, a research newsletter on Catholic Church related topics, four times a year and The Catholic Ministry Formation Directory, a guide and statistical compilation of enrollments for Catholic seminaries, diaconate formation programs, and lay ministry formation programs.

Periodicals
The Catholic Ministry Formation Directory

Center for the Study of Religion and American Culture
Indiana University
Purdue University at Indianapolis
425 University Blvd, Room 341
Indianapolis, IN 46202-5140
Tel. (317)274-8409
Fax (317)278-3354
Email: pgoff@iupui.edu
Website: www.iupui.edu/~raac
Director: Dr. Phillip Goff
Program Coordinator: Rebecca Vasko

The Center for the Study of Religion and American Culture is a research and public outreach institute devoted to the promotion of the understanding of the relation between religion and other features of American culture. Research methods are both inter-disciplinary and multi-disciplinary. Established in 1989, the Center is based in the School of Liberal Arts and Indiana University-Purdue University at Indianapolis. Center activities include national conferences and symposia, commissioned books, essays, bibliographies, and research projects, fellowships for younger scholars, data based communication about developments in the field of American religion, a newsletter devoted to the promotion of Center activities, and the semi-annual scholarly periodical, Religion and American Culture, A Journal of Interpretation.

Current or Recent Research

The Center is presently overseeing two intiatives. The "Young Scholars in American Religion Program" is a multi-year project to assist early-career scholars in developing their teaching skills

SOURCES

and research agendas. The "Centers and Institutes Project," meanwhile, brings together those organizations dedicated to the academic study of religion in the U.S. in order to discuss common problems and solutions, as well as to identify areas for cooperative efforts. The work of these various centers and institutes will be highlighted in future issues of the "Newsletter from the Center for the Study of Religion and American Culture" and the Center's reception at the annual meeting of the American Academy of Religion.

We continue to explore other areas of potential research in the relation between religion and other aspects of American culture. As these projects materialize, they will be announced on this website and in the "Newsletter."

Periodicals
Religion and American Culture, A Journal of Interpretation. Center books include the series, *"The Public Expressions of Religion in America."*

empty tomb, inc.
301 North Fourth Street
P.O. Box 2404
Champaign, IL 61825-2404
Tel. (217)356-9519
Fax (217)356-2344
Email: research@emptytomb.org
Website: www.emptytomb.org
CEO: John L. Ronsvalle
Exec.Vice-Pres.: Sylvia Ronsvalle

empty tomb, inc. is a Christian research and service organization. On a local level, it coordinates direct services to people in need in cooperation with area congregations. On a national level, it studies church member giving patterns of historically Christian churches, including Roman Catholic, mainline and evangelical Protestant, Anabaptist, Pentecostal, Orthodox, and fundamentalist communions. empty tomb publishes the annual State of Church Giving series. Also, empty tomb offers a mission funding incentive program, Mission Match, in an effort to help reverse the negative giving trends indicated by national data.

Current or Recent Research
Current research monitors and analyzes church member giving patterns, and is published in The State of Church Giving series produced by empty tomb, inc.

Periodicals
The State of Church Giving series is an annual publication. It considers denominational giving data, analysis of giving and membership trends, and other estimates of charitable giving. Each edition has featured a special focus chapter, which discusses giving issues relevant to church giving patterns. Past *State of Church Giving* special focus chapters are posted on the www.emptytomb.org website.

The Hartford Institute for Religion Research of Hartford Seminary
Hartford Seminary
77 Sherman Street
Hartford, CT 06105
Tel. (860)509-9543
Fax (860)509-9551
Email: hirr@hartsem.edu
Website: www.hirr.hartsem.edu
Director of Research: Dr. David A. Roozen

The Hartford Institute for Religion Research of Hartford Seminary was established in 1981, formalizing a research program initiated by the Seminary in 1974. Until recently it was known as The Center for Social and Religious Research. The Institute's work is guided by a disciplined understanding of the interrelationship between (a) the inner life and resources of American religious institutions and (b) the possibilities and limits placed on those institutions by the social and cultural context into which God has called them.

Its twenty-one year record of rigorous, policy-relevant research, anticipation of emerging issues, commitment to the creative dissemination of learning, and strong connections to both theological education and the church has earned the Institute an international reputation as an important bridge between the scholarly community and the practice of ministry.

Current or Recent Research

Some of the titles of current projects at the Institute are, "Organizing Religious Work for the 21st Century, Exploring 'Denominationalism;'" "Cooperative Congregational Studies Project;" "Congregational Consulting Services;" "New England Religion Discussion Society (NERDS);" "Congregational Studies Team." Descriptions of these programs are available on the Institute's website, listed above.

Periodicals

Praxis is Hartford Seminary's magazine, which focuses on the activities and faculty of the Seminary.

Institute for Ecumenical & Cultural Research

14027 Fruit Farm Road
PO Box 2000
Collegeville, MN 56321-2000
Tel. (320)363-3366
Fax (320)363-3313
Email: iecr@iecr.org; mbanken@iecr.org
Website: www.iecr.org
Exec. Dir.: Dr. Don B. Ottenhoff

The Institute for Ecumenical and Cultural Research brings together well-trained, creative, articulate men and women for careful thought and dialogue in a place of inquiry and prayer. The Resident scholars Program welcomes researchers and their families for either individual semesters or for an entire academic year. Resident scholars work on their own projects but meet once a week for seminars, and have other occasions for conversation. Each scholar presents a public lecture. Ecumenism happens at the Institute as people come to know one another in community. The Institute is an independent corporation, but shares in the Benedictine and academic life of Saint John's Abbey and University, and of nearby Saint Benedict's Monastery and the College of Saint Benedict. In the summer the Institute uses its facilities for invitational consultations on subjects considered by the Board of Directors to be of special ecumenical interest.

In the Resident Scholars Program, the subjects of research are determined by the interests of the applicants who are invited to come by the Admissions Committee. While most of the work tends to be in traditional theological areas, we encourage people in all fields to consider applying, both because ecumenism is of concern across the spectrum of disciplines, and because the term "cultural" in our title extends our reach beyond theology and religious studies. In particular cases, work done here may have a denominational, congregational, or interfaith focus, but the Institute does not prescribe or delimit, in any narrow way, what is appropriate.

Current or Recent Research

Recent summer consultations have had the following titles, "Ecumenical Formation: The Heart of the Matter";"Igniting Biblical Imagination." Among subjects dealt with in earlier years are " Prayer in the Ecumenical Movement"; "Virtues for an Ecumenical Heart"; "The Price of Disunity"; "Living Faithfully in North America Today"; "Orthodox at Home in North America"; "transmitting Tradition to Children and Young People"; "The Nature of Christian Hope"; "Women and the Church"; Jewish and Christian Relatedness to Scripture"; "Confessing Christian Faith in a Pluralistic Society."

Periodicals

Ecumenical People, Programs, Papers is an bi-annual newsletter containing brief sketches of resident scholars, reports on Institute programs, and, in nearly every issue, an"An Occasional Paper" on a subject of ecumenical interest. The newsletter is free.

Institute for the Study of American Evangelicals (ISAE)

ISAE, Wheaton College
Wheaton, IL 60187
Tel. (630)752-5437
Fax (630)752-5516
Email: isae@wheaton.edu
Website: www.isae@wheaton.edu
Director: Dr. Edith Blumhofer
Associate Director: Larry Eskridge

Founded in 1982, the Institute for the Study of American Evangelicals is a center for research and functions as a program of Wheaton College. The purpose of the ISAE is to encourage and support research on evangelical Christianity in the United States and Canada. The institute seeks to help evangelicals develop a mature understanding of their own heritage and to inform others

214

about evangelicals' historical significance and contemporary role. For the most part, the ISAE focuses on historical research, with input from scholars across a number of disciplines in the humanities and the social sciences.

Current or Recent Research
An edited volume of papers from a 2005 conference, Holding on to the Faith: Confessional Traditions in America was published late last year by University Press of America. Edited by Dr. Douglas A. Sweeney and Dr. Charles Hambrick-Stowe,the book is part of a Lilly Endowment grant on the role of Confessional Traditions in American Christianity. Currently the Institute is involved in a project funded by the Lilly Endowment that examines changes in American Protestant missions in the century since the great Edinburgh Missions Conference of 1910. A 6-part ISAE-backed DVD video study curriculum entitled "People of Faith: the History of the American Church" is nearing completion and should be on the market by early 2010.

Periodicals
The Evangelical Studies Bulletin (ESB) is designed to aid both the scholar and the layman in his or her education and research of evangelicalism. Issued quarterly, the bulletin contains articles, book reviews, notices, a calendar of events, and bibliographic information on the latest dissertations, articles and books related to the study of evangelicals.

Institute for the Study of American Religion
P.O. Box 90709
Santa Barbara, CA 93190-0709
Tel. (805)967-7721
Email: jgordon@linkline.com
Website: www.americanreligion.org
Director: Dr. J. Gordon Melton
Associate Director: Dr. James Beverley
The Institute for the Study of American Religion was founded in 1968 in Evanston, Illinois as a religious studies research facility with a particular focus upon the smaller religions of the United States. Those groups that it has concentrated upon have been known under a variety of labels including sect, cult, minority religion, alternative religion, non-conventional religion, spiritual movement, and new religious movement.
In the 1970s the Institute extended its attention to Canada and in the 1990s developed an even more global focus. In 1985, the institute moved to its present location in Santa Barbara, California. Over the years the institute built a large collection of both primary and secondary materials on the religious groups and movements it studied. In 1985 this collection of more than 40,000 volumes and thousands of periodicals and archival materials was deposited with the Davidson Library at the University of California in Santa Barbara. The reference material exists today as the American Religions Collection and is open to scholars and the interested public. The institute continues to support the collection with donations of additional materials.

Current or Recent Research
Today the institute has two main foci. It monitors all of the religious denominations, organizations, and movements functioning in North America and regularly publishes reports drawing from that activity in a series of reference books. The most important of these reference books is the Encyclopedia of American Religions (Detroit, Gale Group, 7th edition, 2002).
Among the most called for information is factual data on the many new and more controversial religious movements, which are popularly labeled as "cults." The institute's second focus developed out of its more recent refocusing on the international scene, provoked by the international life of most of the religious groups which it has studied in previous decades.

J.M. Dawson Institute of Church-State Studies at Baylor University
P.O. Box 97308
Waco, TX 76798-7308
Tel. (254)710-1510
Fax (254)710-1571
Email: derek_davis@baylor.edu
Website: www.baylor.edu/~Church_State
Director: Dr. Derek Davis
Baylor University established the J.M. Dawson Institute of Church-State Studies in 1957, so named in honor of an outstanding alumnus, an ardent advocate of religious liberty, and a

SOURCES

215

distinguished author of publications on church and state. The Institute is the oldest and most well-established facility of its kind located in a university setting. It is exclusively devoted to research in the broad field of church and state and the advancement of religious liberty around the world.

From its inception in 1957, the stated purpose of the Institute has been to stimulate academic interest and encourage research and publication in the broad area of church-state relations. In carrying out its statement of purpose, the Institute has sought to honor a threefold commitment, to be interfaith, interdisciplinary, and international.

Current or Recent Research

Some current research includes, Government persecution of minority religions in Europe; original intent of Founding Fathers regarding religion and public life; Christian Right views on political activism; conservative versus moderate Baptist views on church-state relations; role of civil religion in America; international treaties and religious liberty.

Periodicals

Journal of Church and State is the only scholarly journal expressly devoted to church-state relations.

The Louisville Institute

1044 Alta Vista Road
Louisville, KY 40205-1798
Tel. (502) 992-9341
Fax (502) 894-2286
Email: jlewis@louisville-institute.org
Website: www.louisville-institute.org
Exec. Dir.: Dr. James W. Lewis

The Louisville Institute is a Lilly Endowment-funded program for the study of American religion based at the Louisville Presbyterian Seminary. The distinctive mission of the Louisville Institute is to enrich the religious life of American Christians and to encourage the revitalization of their institutions by bringing together those who lead religious institutions with those who study them, so that the work of each might inform and strengthen the other. The Louisville Institute offers funding through six grant programs to serve three strategic constituencies: pastors, younger scholars, and researchers and scholars for the broader church. These programs also seek to advance our understanding of three important issues: Christian faith and life, pastoral leadership, and religious institutions. Although many of these grants support research projects, an increasing number of them support other types of projects that contribute to the work of the Louisville Institute.

Current or Recent Research

Please see the Louisville Institute website (listed above) for lists of recent grants made by the Louisville Institute.

Periodicals

"Intersections" newsletter

The Pluralism Project

Harvard University
1531 Cambridge St.
Cambridge, MA 02139
Tel. (617)496-2481
Fax (617)496-2428
Email: staff@pluralism.org
Website: www.pluralsm.org
Director: Dr. Diana L. Eck
Assistant Manager: Kathryn Lohre

The Pluralism Project was developed by Dr. Diana L. Eck at Harvard University to study and document the growing religious diversity of the United States, with a special view to its new immigrant religious communities. The religious landscape of the U.S. has radically changed in the past forty years; in light of these changes, how Americans of all faiths begin to engage with one another in shaping a positive pluralism is one of the most important questions American society faces in the years ahead. In addressing these phenomena, the Project has four goals: 1) To document and better understand the changing contours of American religious demography, focusing especially on those cities and towns where the new plurality has been most evident and discerning the ways in which this plurality is both visible and invisible in American public life. 2) To study the religious communities themselves ¬ their temples, mosques, gurudwaras and retreat centers, their informal networks and emerging institutions, their forms of adaptation and religious education in the American context, their encounter with the other religious traditions of our common society, and their encounter with civic institutions. 3) To explore the ramifications and implications of America's new plurality through case studies of particular cities and towns, looking at the response of Christian and Jewish communities to their new neighbors; the development of interfaith councils and networks; the new theological and pastoral questions that emerge from the pluralistic context; and the recasting of traditional church-state issues in a wider context. 4.) To discern, in light of this work, the emerging meanings of religious "pluralism," both for religious communities and for public institutions, and to consider the real challenges and opportunities of a public commitment to pluralism in the light of the new religious contours of America.

The Pluralism Project has the most comprehensive archive anywhere of the print materials of America's new immigrant religious communities, including newsletters, serial publications, anniversary programs, handbooks, prayer books, calendars, and educational materials donated directly by centers. The Project files also include numerous research papers, profiles of centers, and information on events, all available at www.pluralism.org.

The Pluralism Project On-Line Directory maintains an extensive directory of religious centers in the United States. At present, this directory exists in a searchable database, with listings of over six thousand centers across the U.S.

Current or Recent Research

The Pluralism Project produced a CD-ROM, "On Common Ground- World Religions in America," to present some of the wide range of work that had emerged from three years of research. Numerous affiliate research reports from a wide network of university professors and students are available on their website. Religious Diversity News summarizes news stories on pressing issues in the United States including most minority faiths, with a companion International News; both of these resources are available online in searchable databases, with archives back to 1997. In 2005 the Pluralism Project released, "Acting on Faith: Women's New Religious Activism," available on VHS and DVD. "World Religions in Boston: A Guide to Communities and Resources," is an online resource that profiles many of the diverse religions centers in the Boston area. Current research includes The Interfaith Initiative, The City Hall Initiative, The Women's Initiative, and The International Initiative. One can subscribe to their monthly e-newsletter online.

SOURCES

217

II. Directory of Selected Faith Communities in the USA

Compiling a directory of faith communities is an arduous but rewarding task in religiously plural America. In part, because the very self-understanding and definition of community varies so greatly from tradition to tradition. In order to present a reasonably parallel and well-balanced listing of organizations for each faith, care must be taken not to impose categories or terms from one's own universe of understanding upon other contexts. The very terms, "church," "membership," "denomination," and "hierarchy", which are essential constructs of certain Christian universes of understanding, are rendered meaningless when applied to other faith groups.

Further, it is important to remember that many religious communities lack a centralized organization that speaks for the whole. Often, this lack of centralization reflects the existence of several distinct forms or branches of the religion. In some instances, different ethnic groups immigrating to the U.S., bring with them a distinctive form of their religion, which is particular to their culture of origin. In other cases, plural forms of a faith exist resulting from theological, political, or economic differences. Still other faith groups may be more tightly organized, but the religious center that provides guidance in matters of faith and, perhaps, even organizational discipline may not be in the United States. Hence, the organizations before us are not necessarily religious hierarchical organizations, but are often groups assembled for other purposes that are associated with a particular faith group, or subdivision of that faith group. Caution is advised in regarding these entries as one might regard a "church headquarters."

The compilation of any directory relies upon the existence of some common organizational structure within all the entities listed. Yet, when compiling a directory of faith groups, it cannot be assumed such organizational parallels exist. Oblique ways must be found to adequately represent individual faith groups. The many religious communities in the United States are associated with myriad organizations of all different types. Some of these are primarily places of worship; others are organizations seeking to represent either the religious community as a whole or some particular constituency within it. Others are community centers; some are educational groups; some are organizations particularly for women or youths; and some are political action groups. Still others are peace organizations or relief organizations. That said, a directory of this sort cannot include an exhaustive list of organizations for each faith group nationwide. The omission of any particular organization or branch of any of the major faith groups listed does not reflect a deliberate attempt to homogenize the rich pluralities that exist within faith groups. Instead, the listings that follow are intended to provide the interested reader with a few initial contacts within each religious community, in alphabetical order within the tradition.

Despite the above cautions, this directory provides a rich resource for readers and researchers who wish to learn more about other faith groups. The agencies listed here consist of organizations of importance within the communities they represent, and serve as excellent introductory points of contact with those communities.

In some cases, these religious communities are in a state of flux; the Internet is an excellent way to keep contact with changing religious organizations. There is a plethora of information available about nearly all religious traditions online, but sites vary widely in their accuracy and reliability. Nearly any Internet search engine will provide extensive links to information about specific religious traditions.

For directory information about national Interfaith organizations in the United States, please see Directory 1, "U.S. Cooperative Organizations". For directory information on local Interfaith organizations, please see Directory 6, "U.S. Regional and Local Ecumenical Bodies."

BAHÁ'Í FAITH

The Bahá'í Faith arose in 19th-century Persia, and refers to followers of Mirza Hussein Ali Nuri, whom they call Baha'ullah (Arabic for Glory of God). In 1863, Bahá'u'lláh proclaimed himself to be the Manifestation of God for the present age. His coming had been heralded in 1844 by Mirza Ali Muhammad, also known as the Báb (the Door) whom Bahá'ís consider a Manifestation of God as well. Shortly afterward there was a severe persecution. The Báb was executed in 1850; Bahá'u'lláh died in exile, under house arrest in Acre, Palestine, in 1892. Bahá'ís believe in Progressive Revelation. Thus, as the manifestation of God for the present age, Bahá'u'lláh is considered to be the most recent in a lineage of messengers which includes Abraham, Krishna, the Buddha, Zarathustra, Jesus, and Muhammad. The oneness of God, the oneness of religion, and the oneness of humanity (with stress on racial and gender equality) are key principles of the Bahá'í Faith. Bahá'u'lláh's son Abd-al-Baha organized the religion's sacred texts, and established its system of representative governance through consensus, collaboration, and consultation. This includes the Universal House of Justice (the supreme administrative body, which meets in Haifa, Israel), National Spiritual Assemblies, and Local Spiritual Assemblies.

The Baha'i National Center of the U.S.A. and,
The National Spiritual Assembly of the Bahà'ìs of the United States
1233 Central Street
Evanston, IL 60201
Tel. (847)733-3559/3400 Fax (847)733-3578
Website: www.bahai.usa
    The home of the National Spiritual Assembly of the Bahá'ís of the United States the center is an official source of information about the Bahá'í Faith, resources on many issues (such as peace, justice, economic development, racial unity, and education), and networking with Bahá'í spiritual assemblies throughout the world, of which there are more than 1700 in the U.S.A.

BUDDHISM

    Buddhism is a Western term for the many and varied expressions of practices based on the teachings of Siddhartha Gautama, who lived in northern India c. 563-483 B.C.E.. Called the Buddha (the Enlightened One) by his followers, Siddhartha proposed a Middle Way between self-indulgence and extreme Hindu asceticism. Central to Buddhist teaching are the Four Noble Truths: that life inevitably involves suffering; that the origin of suffering is desire; that suffering can be eradicated by extinguishing desire; and that the way to accomplish this is to follow the Noble Eightfold Path of morality, concentration, and wisdom. Buddhists "take refuge" in the Triple Gem: the Buddha, the dhamma (his teachings), and the sangha (the community). Buddhism has two major branches. Theravada (Way of the Elders) which defines the sangha primarily as the community of ascetics. Mahayana (Great Vehicle) defines the sangha as all Buddhists, and includes the many schools Pure Land, Zen (Ch'an), and Tibetan Buddhism. Vajrayana (Diamond Vehicle) is a rigorous form of Mahayana associated frequently (but not exclusively) with Tibetan practice. Distinctive Western eclectic forms have emerged in recent decades. While there is much variation, Buddhist practice is characterized by meditation, chanting, and emphasis on compassion. Although most practice-groups and temples function autonomously and some are affiliated with a particular teacher or movement, there are continuing local or regional attempts to bridge philosophical differences.

American Buddhist Association
4524 N. Richmond Street
Chicago, IL 60625
Tel: (773)583-5794
Contact person: Richard Brandon (Zenyo)
Email: brightdawn_1@juno.org
Website: www.awakenedone.org
    Founded in 1955 for the study and propagation of Buddhism and to encourage the understanding and application of Buddhist principles in the general American public, this organization's roots are in Japanese Buddhism (Jodo Shinshu and Zen), but is now independent and nonsectarian. It publishes books, pamphlets, and audio-visual materials, sponsors seminars, and acts as a resource center.

American Buddhist Congress
3835 E. Thousand Oaks Blvd., Ste. 450
Westlake Village, CA 91362
Tel. (877)7BUDDHA, (877)728-3342
Email: BuddhistCongress@adelphia.net
Website: www.americanbuddhistcongress.org
    Founded in 1987 to bring together individuals and organizations of various Buddhist traditions, denominations, and ethnic backgrounds, this organization is dedicated to developing an "American" Buddhism which, while paying respect and acknowledging its debt to Buddhist traditions of other cultures, seeks to synthesize American values and traditions with the basic Buddhism of the *tripitaka* (scripture) without the linguistic and cultural aspects which are not understood or confusing to most Americans.

Buddhist Churches of America
1710 Octavia St.
San Francisco, CA 94109
Tel. (415)776-5600
Fax (415)771-6293

219

Email: bcahq@pacbell.net
Website: buddhistchurchesofamerica.org
Founded in 1899, this is a national headquarters and resource center for temples in the Japanese Shin (Pure Land) tradition. It also serves as a regional center of the World Fellowship of Buddhists

Buddhist Council of the Midwest

1812 Washington Street
Evanston, IL 60202
Tel. (847)869-5806
Fax (847)869-5806
Email: infor@buddhistcouncilmidwest.org
Website: www.buddhistcouncilmidwest.org
Incorporated as a non-profit religious organization in 1987, the Buddhist Council of the Midwest includes 95 Buddhist groups in Chicago and the Midwest area. Its purpose is to foster the learning and practice of Buddhism; to represent the Midwest Buddhist community in matters affecting its membership; and to pool resources and coordinate efforts by its membership to create an atmosphere of fellowship and cooperation.

Buddhist Council of the Northwest

1530 184th Ave NE
Bellevue, WA 98008
Tel: (425)442-0986
Fax: (425)643-2490
Email: info@buddhistcouncilnw.org
Website: www.buddhistcouncilnw.org
Founded in 2002, the Buddhist Council of the Northwest is a non-profit organization formed to pool resources and coordinate efforts by its membership. It serves as a consultant to and advocate for Buddhist temples, study groups, and individuals on matters of cultural, legal, and government concern related to the preservation and promotion of the Buddha Dhamma (teaching) in the Pacific Northwest, with special focus on the Asian-American Buddhist temples and communities, and realizing and respecting the diversity of Buddhist traditions within the Pacific Northwest. It initiates and supports religious, cultural or social welfare project which will help to disseminate the spirit of the Buddha Dhamma, and works ecumenically with over religious groups.

The Buddhist Peace Fellowship

P.O. Box 3470
Berkeley, CA 94703
Tel. (510)655-6169
Fax (510)655-1369
Website: www.bpf.org
Founded in 1978, the Buddhist Peace Fellowship's purpose is to serve as a catalyst for socially engaged Buddhism, striving for peace where there is conflict, promoting communication and cooperation among Buddhist *sanghas*, and seeking to alleviate suffering wherever possible. BPF's programs, publications, and practice groups link Buddhist teachings of wisdom and compassion with progressive social change.

Insight Meditation Society

1230 Pleasant St.
Barre, MA 01005
Tel: (978)355-4378
Email: RC@dharma.org
Website: www.dharma.org
Dedicated to *Vipassana* (insight meditation), a practice associated with Theravada Buddhism, this is a loosely associated network of groups, including major centers in New York, Washington DC, Seattle, San Francisco, Los Angeles, and Boston, and smaller centers and practice groups in many other cities and towns.

New York Buddhist Council

c/o Staten Island Buddhist Vihara
115 John Street

Staten Island, NY 10302
Tel: (718)556-2051
Email: sibv.org
Website: www.newyorkbuddhistcouncil.com
An umbrella organization bringing together the leaders of New York City's Buddhist organizations across traditions and ethnicities.

Soka Gakkai International-USA
National Headquarters
606 Wilshire Blvd.
Santa Monica, CA 90401
Tel: (310)260-8900
Fax: (310)260-8917
Website: www.sgi-usa.org
An American Buddhist association that promotes world peace and individual happiness based on the teachings of the Nichiren school of Mahayana Buddhism. Its members reflect a cross section of our diverse American society, representing a broad range of ethnic and social backgrounds.

Texas Buddhist Council
6007 Spindle Dr.
Houston, TX 77086
Tel. (281)445-5773
A regional coordinating body and advocacy agency for Buddhists of all traditions, it seeks to unify Buddhist practitioners across Texas by increasing communication between temples, study groups, and individuals from various schools and by providing opportunities for mutually beneficial interaction. It also strives to bring Buddhist teachings into the Texas mainstream through education and opportunities for social service.

Unified Buddhist Church, Inc.
c/o Blue Cliff Monastery
Address: 3 Mindfulness Rd
Pine Bush
New York 12566
Phone: (845) 733-4959
Email: office@bluecliffmonastery.org
Website: www.bluecliffmonastery.org
This organization of Thich Nhat Hanh and his Sangha (network of practitioners and practice-groups) in the United States of America is also known as the Community of Mindful Living.

Won Buddhism of America Headquarters
143-42 Cherry Avenue
Flushing, NY 11355
Tel: (718)762-4103
Email: info@wonbuddist.org
Won Buddhism is a Korean reform movement with many non-Korean adherents and an abiding commitment to promoting interreligious understanding. While this is the seat of the U.S. branch of the Won movement, English-speakers may find it easier to contact the Manhattan temple, 431 East 57th Street, New York, NY 10022, Tel: (212) 750-2773

HINDUISM

Hinduism is a western term for Sanatana Dharma (Eternal Law), the various streams of practice, ancient texts, and theological traditions associated with the Indian subcontinent. Hindus worship Brahman (Ultimate Reality) which is both the formless Absolute and the divine-as-personal. Hindus fall into schools of devotion to particular forms of the ultimate-as-personal: Vaishnavites (devotees of Vishnu, known also through his avatars [manifestations] such as Rama and Krishna), Shaivites (devotees of Shiva), and devotees of the Parashakti, the Divine Feminine (embodied variously as Durga, Parvati, Kali, and more). Other deities may be regarded as subordinate to, or as personifications of various functions of, the ultimate-as-personal. In the U.S.A., an ecumenical Hindu theology which sees all deities as pointers to the one Brahman, and emphasizes the non-duality of all things is also prevalent.

Hindus agree for the most part on notions of karma and reincarnation, but fall into various philosophical schools of thought regarding the nature of the divine-human relationship. Yoga can take the form of intellectual or physical discipline, selfless service, or devotional practices. Most Hindus acknowledge the authority of the Vedas, but some pay more attention to the Bhaghavad-Gita, the Yoga Sutras of Patanjali, or the writings of the founding guru of their movement. Most North American mandirs (temples) are autonomous, but some are affiliated with a national or international movement.

American Hindus Against Defamation

P.O. Box 611
Inselin,NJ 08830
Tel. (858)866-9661
Email: director_ahad@vhp-america.org
Website: http://www.hindunet.org/ahad
Director, Mr. Ajay Shah

An organization devoted to defending Hindus from stereotyping and discriminatory or defamatory acts or speech.

Bochasanwasi Shri Akshar Purushottam Swaminarayan Sanstha (B.A.P.S.)

BAPS Swaminarayan Sanstha
81 Suttons Lane
Piscattaway, NJ 08854-5723
Tel. (732)777-1414
Email: baps.org
Fax (732)777-1616
Website: www.swaminarayan.org

B.A.P.S. is a reform movement within the Vaishnava Visishtadvaita tradition. This North American headquarters serves about 50 temples in US & Canada.

Council of Hindu Temples of North America

Sri Siva Vishnu Temple
6905 Cipriano Road
Lanham, MD 20706
Tel. (301) 552-3335
Email: info@councilofhindutemples.org
Website: www.councilofhindutemples.org
President: Dr. Siva Subramanian

The council is an independent association of autonomous temples and Hindu religious organizations which promotes the establishment of Hindu temples, encourages interfaith dialogue, and aids in instruction in Indian languages and culture.

The International Society for Krishna Consciousness (ISKCON)

26 Second Avenue,
New York, NY 10003
Tel. (212)253-6182
Email: nycpandit@gmail.com

A modern expression of Vaishnavite belief and practice established by A. C. Bhaktivedanta Swami (called Prabhubapa by devotees), ISKCON is one of many Indian spiritual movements planted in North America during the 20th century. The Second Avenue temple, which dates from 1966, was the movement's first in the U.S.

Vedanta Society of New York

34 West 71st Street
New York, NY 10023
Tel. (212)877-9197, (212)873-7439
Fax: (212) 877-9198
Email: Vedantany@yahoo.com
Website: www.vedanta-newyork.org

Founded in 1894, Vedanta Society of New York is the first Vedanta Center in the West, and has been joined by many other such centers. The various centers of the Vedanta Society are affiliates of the worldwide network of the Ramakrishna Order, headquartered in Belur Math, India. Adherents follow the teachings and example of Sri Ramakrishna (1836-1886), his wife and spiritual companion Holy Mother Sri Sarada Devi (1853-1920), and Ramakrishna's chief disciple Swami Vivekananda.

ISLAM

Islam dates to 7th-century Arabia and the Prophet Muhammad's receipt of the Qur'an. The word *islam* means submission, and is related linguistically to *salaam,* the Arabic word for peace. A Muslim is one who practices Islam by following the Qur'an and the Prophet's *sunna* (example). Muslims consider the Qur'an (in its original Arabic) to be God's speech. They place great emphasis on *tawhid* (God's absolute oneness and its implications). They use the Arabic word Allah for God, stressing that it refers to God as worshiped by Jews and Christians as well. Muslims are to maintain Five Pillars of practice. The first of these is *iman,* the profession of faith called the *shahadah,* which states "There is no God but God, and Muhammad is his prophet." The second, *salah* is the ritual prayer, done five times a day, facing Mecca. Third, is *zakah,* the returning of a portion of one's wealth to the community annually. Fourth, is *swam,* the fasting from dawn to dusk during the holy month of Ramadan. Fifth, is *Hajj,* the pilgrimage to Mecca once in one's lifetime (health and means permitting). Early in its history, Islam split into two branches, Sunni and Shi'ah (and several subgroups of the latter) which differ on some matters of belief and practice, and notions of transmission of authority.

The Islamic Society of North America (ISNA)
P.O. Box 38
Plainfield, IN 46168
Tel. (317)839-8157
Fax (317)839-1840
Website: http://www.isna.net/
President: Dr. Ingrid Mattson; Sec. Gen.: Dr. Munner Fareed
    The Islamic Society of North America grew out of the Muslim Students Association and is one of the oldest national Muslim organizations in the United States. It has a varied program primarily serving the Muslim community, but also seeks to promote relations between Muslims and non-Muslims. It has a speakers' bureau, film loans, library assistance program, and several other services. It has also has a number of publications. Its annual convention during Labor Day weekend usually in Chicago attracts over 35,000 participants.

Council for American-Islamic Relations (CAIR)
453 New Jersey Ave. SE
Washington, DC 20003-4034
Tel. (202)488-8787
Fax (202)488-0833
Email: info@cair.com
Website: www.cair.com
    CAIR's mission is to enhance understanding of Islam, encourage dialogue, protect civil liberties, empower American Muslims and build coalitions that promote justice and mutual understanding.

Islamic Circle of North America (ICNA)
166-26 89th Avenue
Jamaica, NY 11432
Tel. (718)658-1199
Fax (718)658-1255
Website: www.icna.org
    A non-ethnic, non-sectarian grassroots organization with a varied program of education and support for Muslims. Its subsidiary, ICNA Relief, provides humanitarian aid wherever it is needed.

The Mosque Cares (Ministry of Imam W. Deen Mohammed)
P.O. Box 1061
Calumet City, IL 60409
Tel. (708)798-6750
Fax (708)798-6827
Email: WdMinistry@aol.com
Website: www.themosquecares.com
    Also known as the American Society of Muslims, this is the headquarters of the community in association with the leadership of W. D. Mohammed.

SOURCES

223

Muslim American Society
6408 Edsal Road Alexandria, VA 22312
Tel. (703)642-6165 Fax (703)998-6526
Email for General Information: communication@masonline.org
Email for Inquiries by non-Muslims: sg@masnet.org
Website: www.masnet.org

Founded in 1992, this is a charitable, religious, social, cultural, and educational, not-for-profit organization. It is a pioneering Islamic organization, an Islamic revival, and reform movement that uplifts the individual, family, and society. This organization is not to be confused with the ministry of W. D. Mohammad, which once used this name.

Muslim Peace Fellowship
PO Box 271
Nyack, New York 10960 USA
Tel. (845)358-4601
Fax (845)358-4924
Email: mpf@mpfweb.org
Website: www.forusa.org

The Muslim Peace Fellowship (*Ansar as-Salam*) is a network of peace and justice-oriented Muslims of all backgrounds who are dedicated to making the beauty of Islam evident in the world.

Muslim Public Affairs Council (MPAC)
3010 Wilshire Blvd. Ste. 217
Los Angeles, CA 90010
Tel. (213)383-3443
Fax (213)383-9674
Email: mpac-contact@mpac.org
Website: www.mpac.org
Exec. Dir. Salam Al-Marayati

MPAC seeks to establish a vibrant Maerican Msulim community that will enrich American society through promoting the Islamic values of mercy, justice, peace, human dignity, freedom and equality for all.

JAINISM

Jainism is an ancient Indian religion based on the notion that, periodically, humanity is blessed with a series of twenty-four *tirthankaras* (crossing-makers)—great spiritual leaders who attain infinite knowledge; revive a way of life that is based on the principles of non-harming, non-attachment, and openmindedness, and directed by right knowledge, right faith, and right conduct; establish an order of renunciates; and assist in the liberation of countless other human beings from the cycle of reincarnation. Vardhamana (599–527 B.C.E.), a contemporary of the Buddha, was the twenty-fourth and last *tirthankara* for the current eon, and is known as Mahavira (Great Hero). His sermons provide the core of Jain scriptures, the Agam Sutras, but Jainism's two main branches differ over the exact contents. Jainism stresses asceticism. Digambara (sky-clad) monks renounce all clothing; Svetambara (white-clad) monks and nuns wear simple, white robes. Both branches may use *murtis* (images) of *tirthankaras* in devotional practice, but Digambara *murtis* will be plainer. The doctrine of *ahimsa* (non-harming) leads to strict vegetarianism, avoidance of animal products of any kind, and avoidance of interpersonal conflicts. Mahatma Gandhi was influenced greatly by Jain teachings.

JAINA: Federation of Jain Associations in North America
P.O. Box 700
Getzville, NY 14068
Tel. (716)636-5342
Email: jainahq@jaina.org
Website: www.jaina.org

An umbrella organization linking local U.S. and Canadian Jain associations. It seeks to promote Jain principles and better understanding of Jainism. It also engages in humanitarian work.

Siddhachalam International Mahavira Jain Mission
65 Mud Pond Road
Blairstown, NJ 07825
Tel. (908)362-9793, (908)362-5487
Fax (908)362-9649
Email: presidentimjm@gmail.com
Website: www.siddhachalam.org
>Founded by Acharya Shri Shushil Kumarji in 1983, this resident community for monks, nuns, laymen, and laywomen is described as the first Jain pilgrimage site outside India. It promotes *ahimsa* for world peace, vegetarianism, and nonviolence to animals; and is headquarters for the International Jain Mission, the World Fellowship of Religions, and the World Jain Congress.

JUDAISM
Judaism is one of the world's oldest religions, encompassing a rich and complex tradition that has evolved over centuries and has given rise to, or influenced, other major world traditions. Numerous expressions of Judaism have always coexisted with one another, as they do today. The central concern shared by all is to live in relation to God and to follow God's will. Jews understand themselves to be in covenant with God, who is the one transcendent God, Creator of the Universe. God revealed the Torah to the people of Israel as his way of life. History brought the Jewish people into contact with many cultures and civilizations, contacts that continuously transformed the nature of their worship, the understanding of God's law, and even their conceptualization of peoplehood. At the time of the second Diaspora, or great migration of Jews throughout the Middle East, North Africa, and Europe at the beginning of the common era, was the rise of the Rabbinical Tradition, with its emphasis on the study of scripture. Today's Judaism has grown out of these roots. In the 19th century, Reform Judaism arose in Europe and the United States as one Jewish response to modernity. Conservative Judaism and Reconstructionism are branches of Jewish practice that first developed in America. Orthodox Judaism also has a number of modern forms.

ALEPH Administrative Office
7000 Lincoln Drive #B2
Philadelphia, PA 19119-3046
Email: aleph-info@aleph.org
Website: www.aleph.org
Exec. Dir., Ms. Debra Kolodny
>A core institution of the Jewish Renewal movement dedicated to the Jewish people's sacred purpose of partnership with the Divine in the inseparable tasks of healing the world and healing our hearts.

The American Jewish Committee
P.O. Box 705
New York, NY 10150
Tel. (212)751-4000
Fax (212)891-1492
Email: pr@ajc.org
Website: www.ajc.org
Exec. Dir., David A. Harris
>Founded in 1906, The AJC protects the rights and freedoms of Jews world-wide; combats bigotry and anti-Semitism and promotes democracy and human rights for all. It is an independent community-relations organization, with strong interest in interreligious relations and public-policy advocacy. The AJC publishes the *American Jewish Yearbook*, and *Commentary magazine*.

The Anti-Defamation League of B'nai B'rith
823 United Nations Plaza
New York, NY 10017
Tel. (212)885-7707
Fax (212)867-9406
Website: www.adl.org
National Dir., Abraham H. Foxman
>Since 1913, the Anti-Defamation League has been involved in combating and documenting anti-Semitism. It also works to secure fair treatment for all citizens through law, education and community relations.

Jewish Council for Public Affairs

116 East 27th St.10th Floor
New York, NY 10016
Tel. (212)684-6950
Fax (212)686-1353
Email: contactus@thejcpa.org
Website: www.jewishpublicaffairs.org

This national coordinating body for the field of Jewish community relations comprises 13 national and 122 local Jewish communal agencies. Through the Council's work, and in its collaboration with other religious groups, its constituent agencies work on public policy issues, both international and domestic.

Jewish Reconstructionist Federation

Beit Devora, 101 Greenwood Avenue Suite 430
Jenkintown, PA 19046
Tel. (215)885-5601
Fax:(215)885-5603
Email: info@jrf.org
Website: www.jrf.org

Fosters the establishment and ongoing life of Reconstructionist congregations and fellowship groups. Publishes *The Reconstructionist* and other materials. Rabbis who relate to this branch of Judaism are often members of the Reconstructionist Rabbinical Association.

Religious Action Center of Reform Judaism

2027 Massachusetts Ave. NW
At Kivie Kaplan Way
Washington, DC 20036
Tel. (202)387-2800
Fax (202)667-9070
Website: www.rac.org
Exec. Dir., Rabbi David Saperstein

The Religious Action Center pursues social justice and religious liberty by mobilizing the American Jewish community and serving as its advocate in the capitol of the United States.

The Union of Orthodox Jewish Congregations of America

11 Broadway
New York, NY 10004-1003
Tel. (212)563-4000
Fax (212)564-9058
Website: www.ou.org
Exec. Vice-Pres., Rabbi Steven Weil

The national central body of Orthodox synagogues since 1898, providing kashrut supervision, women's and youth organizations, and a variety of educational, religious and public policy programs and activities. Publishers of *Jewish Action* magazine and other materials. The Rabbinical Council of America is the related organization for Orthodox Rabbis.

Union of Reform Judaism

633 Third Ave.
New York, NY 10017
Tel. (212)650-4000
Email: urj@urj.org
Website: www.urj.org
Pres., Rabbi Eric H. Yoffie

The central congregational body of Reform Judaism, founded in 1873. It serves approx. 875 affiliated temples and its members through religious, educational, cultural and administrative programs. Women's Men's and Youth organizations. *Reform Judaism* is one of its publications. The Central Conference of American Rabbis is the affiliated rabbinical body.

The United Synagogue of Conservative Judaism

820 Second Avenue.
New York, NY 10017-7800

Tel. (212)533-7800
Fax (212)353-9439
Website: www.uscj.org
Exec. Vice-Pres., Rabbi Steven Wernick
   The International organization of 800 congregations, founded in 1913. Provides religious, educational, youth, community and administrative programming. Publishes *United Synagogue Review* and other materials. The Rabbinical Assembly is the association of Conservative Rabbis.

NATIVE AMERICAN TRADITIONAL SPIRITUALITY

   Native American spirituality is difficult to define or categorize because it varies so greatly across the continent. Further, it is deeply entwined with elements of nature which are associated with different geographical regions. For example, while Plains Indians possess a spiritual relationship with the buffalo, Indigenous Peoples from the Northwest share a similar relationship with salmon. Hence, the character of Native American spirituality is dependent, to some extent, on the surrounding geography and its incumbent ecosystems. Despite this great variety, there are some similarities which allow us to consider the many Native American forms of spirituality together: Contrary to popular belief, Native American peoples are monotheistic; they do not worship the sun or buffalo or salmon, but rather understand that these elements of nature are gifts from the "Great Mystery," and are parts of it. Today, while still working toward religious freedom in the United States, Native Americans are also struggling to protect sacred sites, which they consider to be comparable to "churches." But since these sites are actually part of the land, not man-made structures, many are constantly under attack for the natural resources they contain. Such exploitation of these resources is an offense to the Native American sense of spirituality, which views resources like timber, oil, and gold, as gifts from the Great Mystery. The struggle to protect and respect these sacred sites is a universal and essential part of Native American spirituality.

National Congress of American Indians (NCAI)
1516 P Street NW
Washington, DC 20005
Tel. (202)466-7767
Fax (202)466-7797
Email: ncia@ncia.org
Website: www.ncai.org
Exec. Dir., Jacqueline Johnson-Pata
   The National Congress of American Indians (NCAI), founded in 1944, is the oldest, largest and most representative national Indian organization serving the needs of a broad membership of American Indian and Alaska Native governments. NCAI stresses the need for unity and cooperation among tribal governments and people for the security and protection of treaty and sovereign rights. As the preeminent national Indian organization, NCAI is organized as a representative congress aiming for consensus on national priority issues.
   The NCAI website contains links for a directory of Indian nations in the continental U.S. and Alaska as well as a directory of tribal governments. There are also links to other Native American websites.

Native American Rights Fund (NARF)
1506 Broadway
Boulder, CO 80302-6296
Tel. (303)447-8760
Fax (303)433-7776
Website: www.narf.org
Exec. Dir., John Echohawk
   The Native American Rights Fund is the non-profit legal organization devoted to defending and promoting the legal rights of the Indian people. NARF attorneys, most of whom are Native Americans, defend tribes who otherwise cannot bear the financial burden of obtaining justice in the courts of the United States. The NARF mission statement outlines five areas of concentration: 1) Preservation of tribal existence; 2) Protection of tribal natural resources; 3) Promotion of human rights; 4) Accountability of government; 5) Development of Indian law.

SOURCES

SIKHISM

Sikhism was founded by Guru Nanak during the 15th and 16th centuries C.E. in the state of Punjab in northwestern India. Nanak was greatly influenced by the teachings of Kabir, a Muslim who became deeply inspired by Hindu philosophies. Kabir's poems called for a synthesis between Islam and Hinduism. In the footsteps of Kabir's wisdom, Nanak drew upon elements of Bhakti Hinduism and Sufi Islam: He stressed the existence of a universal, single God, who transcends religious distinctions. Union with God is accomplished through meditation and surrender to the divine will. Nanak also called for the belief in reincarnation, karma, and also the cyclical destruction and recreation of the universe. However, he rejected the caste system, the devotion to divine incarnations, priesthood, idol worship, all of which were elements of the Hindu tradition. Nanak was the first of ten *gurus*, or teachers. The fourth guru, built the Golden Temple in Amritsar, the Sikh religious center. The fifth guru compiled the *Adi Granth*, a sort of hymn-book of spiritual authority. All male sikhs are initiated into the religious brotherhood called the *Khalsa*. Members of this order vow never to cut their beard or hair, to wear special pants, to wear an iron bangle as an amulet against evil, to carry a steel dagger, and a comb.

Sikh American Heritage Organization (SAHO)

P.O. Box 63
Wayne, IL 60184-0063
Tel. (630)377-5893
Fax (630)377-5893
Email: SikhAmerican@aol.com

    Promotes and fosters fellowship with the American mainstream and minority communities while maintaining Sikh values, heritage, and identity; participates in Asian American events, interfaith programs, community affairs, social services, and other civic activities.

Sikh American Legal Defense and Education Fund (SALDEF)

1413 K Street
5th Floor
Washington, DC 20005
Tel. (202)393-2700
Fax (202)318-4433
Website: www.saldef.org

    Formerly Sikh Mediawatch and Research Task Force (SMART), SALDEF is a national civil rights and educational organization which provides legal assistance, educational outreach, legislative advocacy, and media relations

Sikh Coalition

40 Exchange Place, Suite 728
New York, N.Y. 10005
Tel. (212)655-3095, ext. 83
Email: info@sikhcoalition.org
Website: www.sikhcoalition.org
Exec. Dir., Sapreet Kaur

    Founded in response to bias attacks following the September 11, 2001, Sikh Coalition defends civil rights and liberties, educates the broader community about Sikhs and diversity, promotes local community empowerment, and fosters civic engagement amongst Sikh Americans.

Sikh Foundation

580 College Avenue
Palo Alto, CA 94306
Tel. (650)494-7454
Fax (650)494-3316
Email: info@sikhfoundation.org
Website: www.sikhfoundation.org

    Founded in 1967 to promote the heritage and future of Sikhism, the Sikh Foundation's sponsors academic courses, conferences and chairs of Sikh studies at leading universities in the West; promotes Sikh art exhibitions and the establishing permanent Sikh art galleries at major museums worldwide; and works to provide the community with highest quality of educational products on Sikhism.

Sikh Research Institute
P.O. Box 690504
San Antonio, TX 78269-0504
Tel. (210)582-3371
Fax (469)324-2954
Email: info@sikhri.org
Website: www.sikhri.org
   The goals of this organization are leadership enhancement, community revival, and facilitation of connections between various Sikh organizations. It is active in interfaith work, and education of Americans about Sikhism.

World Sikh Council – America Region
P.O. Box 3635,
Columbus, Ohio 43210
Tel. (614)210-0591
Fax (419)535-6794
Email: contact@worldsikhcouncil.org
Website: www.worldsikhcouncil.org
Secretary General, Anahat Kaur
   A national unit of the World Sikh Council, WSC-AR is a representative and elected body of Sikh Gurudwaras and institutions in the US. Its members include 31 Gurudwaras (Sikh places of worship) and 6 other Sikh institutions across the nation. Its mission is to promote Sikh interests at the national and international level focusing on issues of advocacy, education, and well-being of humankind

ZOROASTRIANISM
   The western name for "The Good Religion" based on the teachings of the Prophet Zarathustra, who lived sometime between 1200 and 550 B.C.E., in what is now Iran. Zoroastrians from India are often called Parsis (Parsees). Zoroastrians worship Ahura Mazda (Wise Lord): the one God, the uncreated, immanent and transcendent source of all that is good, true, and beautiful, for whom the only appropriate symbol is fire. Zoroastrians fall into two streams: traditionalists, for whom all ancient Zoroastrian texts are scripture; and progressives, for whom only the Gathas (the oldest texts) have authority. The two streams differ sharply in beliefs and practices. There are also informal denominations according to which of several Zoroastrian calendars one prefers.

Federation of Zoroastrian Associations of North America (FEZANA)
8615 Meadowbrook Drive
Burr Ridge, IL 60527
Tel/Fax. (630)468-2705
Email: admin@fezana.org
Website: www.fezana.org
President, Dr. Bomi Patel
   A coordinating organization for Zoroastrian Associations of North America.

6. United States Regional and Local Ecumenical Bodies

One of the many ways Christians and Christian churches relate to one another locally and regionally is through ecumenical bodies. The membership in these ecumenical organizations is diverse. Historically, councils of churches were formed primarily by Protestants, but many local and regional organizations now include Orthodox and Roman Catholics. Many are made up of congregations or judicatory units of churches. Some have a membership base of individuals. Others foster cooperation between ministerial groups, community ministries, coalitions, or church agencies. While "council of churches" is a term still commonly used to describe this form of cooperation, other terms such as "conference of churches," "ecumenical councils," "churches united," "metropolitan ministries," are coming into use. Ecumenical organizations that are national in scope are listed in Directory 1, "United States Cooperative Organizations."

An increasing number of ecumenical bodies have been exploring ways to strengthen the interreligious aspect of life in the context of religious pluralism in the U.S. today. Some organizations in this listing are fully interfaith agencies primarily through the inclusion of Jewish congregations in their membership. Other organizations nurture partnerships with a broader base of religious groups in their communities, especially in the areas of public policy and interreligious dialogue.

This list does not include all local and regional ecumenical and interfaith organizations in existence today. The terms regional and local are relative, making identification somewhat ambiguous. Regional councils may cover sections of large states or cross-state borders. Local councils may be made up of several counties, towns, or clusters of congregations. State councils or state-level ecumenical contacts exist in 45 of the 50 states. These state-level or multi-state organizations are marked with an "*." The organizations are listed alphabetically by state.

ALABAMA

Greater Birmingham Ministries

2304 12th Ave. N, Birmingham, AL 35234-3111, Tel. (205)326-6821, Fax (205)252-8458
Email: robert@gbm.org
Website: www.gbm.org
Media Contact, Robert Montgomery
Exec. Dir., Scott Douglas
Economic Justice, Co-Chpsn., Helen Holdefer, Betty Likis
Direct Services, Chpsn., Patty Warren
Faith in Community, Chpsn., Patricia Ross
Finance & Fund-Raising, Chpsn., Richard Ambrose
Pres., Tom Forsee
Treas., Helen Tibbs Wilson
Major Activities: Direct Service Ministries (Food, Utilities, Rent and Nutrition Education, Shelter); Alabama Arise (Statewide legislative network focusing on low income issues); Economic Justice Issues (Low Income Housing and Advocacy, Health Care, Community Development, Jobs Creation, Public Transportation); Faith in Community Ministries (Interchurch Forum, Interpreting and Organizing, Bible Study)

Interfaith Mission Service

701 Andrew Jackson Way NE, Huntsville, AL 35801-3504, Tel. (256)536-2401, Fax (256)536-2284
Email: ims@hiwaay.net
Media Contact,
Exec. Dir., Susan J. Smith

Pres., Richard C. Titus
Major Activities: Foodline & Food Pantry; Local FEMA Committee; Ministry Development; Clergy Luncheon; Workshops; Response to Community Needs; Information and Referral; Interfaith Understanding; Christian Unity; Homeless Needs; School Readiness Screenings

ALASKA

Alaska Christian Conference

P.O. Box 112944, Anchorage, AK 99511, Tel. 907)240-6154, Fax (907)349-3426
Email: jim56@gci.net
Website: www.ak-acc.org
Media Contact, Rev. James Stephens
Pres., Chaplain James Stephens (Retired) (Disciple), 1231 Surray Circle #A, Anchorage, Alaska 99515; Cell# 907-240-6154; Email: jim56@gci.net
Vice-Pres., Bert Hall (American Baptist), 1320 N. Ivy Circle, Wasilla, AK 99654; Tel. 907-355-3568; Email: Rahall@mtaonline.net
Sec., Phyllis Sullivan (United Methodist), 1725 Tillicum, Wasilla, AK 99654; Cell# 907-232-2634; Email: phyllisfs@juno.com
Treas., Phyllis Sullivan, (United Methodist), 1725 Tillicum, Wasilla, AK 99654; Cell# 907-232-2634; Email: phyllisfs@juno.com
Special Asst. Web Master, Rev. David Blanchette, 1100 Pullman Drive, Wasilla, AK 99654; wwww. Ak-acc.org; Cell# 907-232-2634; Email: revdavid@gci.net
Special Asst. RurAL CAP Rep., Rev. David Fison, 6800 O'Malley Road, Anchorage, Alaska 99516, Tel. 907-346-2975 (Home).

Major Activities: Legislative & Social Concerns; Resources and Continuing Education; New Ecumenical Ministries; Communication; Alcoholism (Education & Prevention); Family Violence (Education & Prevention); Native Issues; Ecumenical-Theological Dialogue; HIV-AIDS Education and Ministry; Criminal Justice.

ARIZONA

Arizona Ecumenical Council*
4423 N. 24th St., Ste. 750, Phoenix, AZ 85016, Tel. (602)468-3818, Fax (602)468-3311
Email: aec@aecunity.net
Website: www.aecunity.net
Media Contact, Exec. Dir., Rev. Jan Olav Flaaten, Tel. (602)468-3818, Fax (602)468-3311, Cell (602)670-1594
Exec. Dir., The Rev. Jan Olav Flaaten
President: Bishop Minerva Carcano, United Methodist Church
Vice-President: Bishop Kirk Smith, Episcopal Diocese of Arizona
Secretary: Dr. Tamera Zivic, W.H.E.A.T.
Treasurer: Ed Davis, Evangelical Lutheran Church in America
Past President: Fr. Michael Diskin, Roman Catholic Dioese of Phoenix
Major Activities: Facilitating collaboration among the 20 judicatories for Theological Dialogue, Services of Prayer, Public Policy and Social Justice, Church Leadership School (called Survival School), Local Ecumenism (encouraging and being a resource for local ecumenical groupings), Earth Care Commission (presents annual "Caring for Creation" conference), Arizonans for the Protection of Exploited Children and Adults (APECA), Disaster Relief, Non-Violence Education for Youth, Souper-Bowl

ARKANSAS

Arkansas Interfaith Conference*
P.O. Box 151, Scott, AR 72142, Tel. (501)961-2626
Email: aicark@aol.com
Media Contact, Conf. Exec., Mimi Dortch
Conf. Exec., Mimi Dortch
Pres., Rev. Steve Copley. 6701 JFK Blvd., N. Little Rock, AR. 72116 (Methodist)
Sec., Imam John Hasan. P.O.Box 1607, Little Rock, AR 72203. (Muslim)
Treas., Jim Davis, Box 7239, Little Rock, AR 72217 (Catholic)
Major Activities: Institutional Ministry; Interfaith Executives' Advisory Council; Interfaith Relations; Church Women United; Our House-Shelter; Legislative Liaison; Ecumenical Choir Camp; Tornado Disaster Relief; Camp for Jonesboro School Children Massacre; Welfare Reform Work; Med Center Chaplaincy; Peace Service

CALIFORNIA

California Council of Churches-California Church Impact*
2715 K Street, Suite D, Sacramento, CA 95816, Tel. (916)488-7300, Fax (916)488-7310
Email: cccinfo@calchurches.org
Website: www.calchurches.org
Media Contact, Exec. Dir., The Rev. Rick Schlosser
Exec. Dir., The Rev. Rick Schlosser
Major Activities: Monitoring State Legislation; California IMPACT Network; Legislative Principles; Food Policy Advocacy; Family Welfare Issues; Health; Church-State Issues; Violence Prevention; Child Care Program-Capacity Coordinator to Increase Quality Child Care within California for the Working Poor; Building Bridges of Understanding: An Interfaith Response to Septerber 11.

The Council of Churches of Santa Clara County
1710 Moorpark Avenue, San Jose, CA 95128, Tel. (408)297-2660, Fax (408)297-2661
Email: councilofchurches@sbcglobal.net
Website: www.councilofchurches-scc.org
Media Contact, Co-executive Directors: Rev. Margo Tenold, Rev. Diana Gibson
Chair, Board of Directors, Rev. Jerry Fox
Major Activities: Social Education-Action; Ecumenical and Interfaith Witness; Affordable Housing; Environmental Ministry; Family-Children; Convalescent Hospital Ministries; Gay Ministry; Strengthening Congregations for Ministry

The Ecumenical Council of Pasadena Area Churches
P.O. Box 41125, 444 E. Washington Blvd., Pasadena, CA 91114-8125, Tel. (626)797-2402, Fax (626)797-735
Email: ecpac@prodigy.net
Media Contact,
Exec. Dir., Rev. Frank B. Clark
Major Activities: Christian Education; Community Worship; Community Concerns; Christian Unity; Ethnic Ministries; Hunger; Peace; Food, Clothing Assistance for the Poor; Emergency Shelter

Ecumenical Council of San Diego County
3530 Camino del Rio North, # 301, San Diego, CA 92108, Tel. (619)238-0649, Fax (619) 238-1526
Email: info@ecsd.org
Website: www.ecsd.org
Media Contact,
Exec. Dir. Vacant
Pres. Red. Dr. Richard Freeman
Treas., Rev. Tim Tiffany

Major Activities: Interfaith Shelter Network-Rational Shelter and El Nido Transitional Living Program; Emerging Issues; Faith Order & Witness; Worship & Celebration; Ecumenical Tribute Dinner; Advent Prayer Breakfast; Seminars and Workshops; Continuing Education for clergy and laypersons;Inter-Religious Council.

Fresno Metro Ministry
1055 N. Van Ness, Ste. H, Fresno, CA 93728, Tel. (559)485-1416, Fax (559)485-9109
Email: metromin@fresnometmin.org
Website: www.fresnometmin.org
Media Contact, Exec. Dir., Richard P. Yanes
Exec. Dir., Richard P. Yanes
Pres., Tony Gonzalez
Major Activities: Hunger Relief & Nutrition Advocacy; Cultural Diversity and Anti-Racism; Health Care Advocacy; Environmental Health and Quality; Access and Public Health; Public Education Concerns; Children's Needs; Air Quality; Ecumenical & Interfaith Celebrations & Cooperation; Youth Needs; Community Network Building; Human Services Facilitation; Anti-Poverty Efforts; Low-Income and Immigrant Leadership Development related to public policies

Inland Valley Council of Churches
1753 N. Park Ave., Pomona, CA 91768, Tel. (909)622-3806, Fax (909)622-0484
Email: toiucc@verizon.net
Website: www.hope-partners.com
Media Contact, Dir. of Dev., Fran Robertson
Pres., Scott Williams
Acting Exec. Dir., Wytske G. Visser
Sec., Alfonso Villanueva
Treas., Rebecca Ewing
Major Activities: Advocacy and Education for Social Justice; Ecumenical Celebrations; Hunger Advocacy; Emergency Food and Shelter Assistance; Farmer's Market; Affordable Housing

Interfaith Council of Contra Costa County
1543 Sunnyvale Ave., Walnut Creek, CA 94596, Tel. (925)933-6030, Fax (925)952-4554
Email: eye4cee@aol.com
Media Contact,
Chaplains, The Rev. Charles Tinsley
Pres., Rev. Steve Harms, Rabi Raphael Asher
Treas., Myrdell Dybdal
Major Activities: Youth Chaplaincies, Community Education, Interfaith Cooperation; Social Justice, Winter Shelter

Interfaith Service Bureau
2212 K. St., Sacramento, CA 95816-4923, Tel. (916)456-3815, Fax (916)456-3816
Email: isbdexter@aol.com
Media Contact, Exec. Dir., Dexter McNamara
Executive Dir., Dexter McNamara
Pres., Richard Montgomery

Vice-Pres., Lloyd Hanson
Major Activities: Religious and Racial Cooperation and Understanding; Welfare Reform Concerns; Refugee Resettlement & Support; Religious Cable Television; Violence Prevention; Graffiti Abatement

Marin Interfaith Council
1510 5th Avenue, San Rafael, CA 94901-1807, Tel. (415)456-9657, Fax (415)456-6959
Email: admin@marinifc.org
Website: www.marinifc.org
Media Contact, Exec. Dir., Rev. Carol Hovis
Exec. Dir., Rev. Carol Hovis
Major Activities: Interfaith Dialogue; Education; Advocacy; Convening; Interfaith Worship Services & Commemorations

Northern California Interreligious Conference
534 22nd St., Oakland, CA 94612, Tel. (510)433-0822, Fax (510)433-0813
Email: NCIC@igc.org
Website: ncic.home.igc.org
Media Contact, Pres., Rev. Phil Lawson
Exec. Dir., Catherine Coleman
Pres., Rev. Phil Lawson
Vice-Pres., Esther Ho
Sec., Robert Forsberg
Major Activities: Peace with Justice Commission; Interreligious Relationships Commission; Public Policy Advocacy; Welfare Reform, Founding member of California Council of Churches and of California Interfaith Power and Light; Soul of Justice, a spiritual and leadership concepts interactive performance troupe of teens and young adults; death penalty moratorium; video produced for sale for congregations-organizations to study legal, theological and social implications of marriage and same gender marriage, widening our circle of religious groups participating; a cooperating circle of URL.

San Fernando Valley Interfaith Council
10824 Topanga Canyon Blvd., No. 7, Chatsworth, CA 91311, Tel. (818)718-6460, Fax (818)718-0734
Email: info@vic-LA.org
Website: www.vic-LA.org
Media Contact, Comm. Coord., Eileen Killoren, ext. 3002
Pres., Barry Smedberg; Ext. 3011
Chair, Board of Dir., Earl Fagin, Esq.
Major Activities: Seniors Multi-Purpose Centers; Nutrition & Services; Meals to Homebound; Meals on Wheels; Interfaith Reporter; Interfaith Relations; Social Adult Day Care; Hunger-Homelessness; Volunteer Care-Givers; Clergy Gatherings; Food Pantries and Outreach; Social Concerns; Aging; Hunger; Human Relations; Immigration Services; Self-Sufficiency Program for Section 8 Families

South Coast Interfaith Council
759 Linden Ave., Long Beach, CA 90813, Tel. (562)983-1665, Fax (562)983-8812
Email: scic@charterinternet.com
Website: www.SCInterfaith.org
Media Contact, Exec. Dir., Milia Islam-Majeed
STAFF
Exec. Dir., Milia Islam-Majeed President, Rev. Duane Moret Farmers' Markets, Rev. Dale Whitney
Centro Shalom, Amelia Nieto
Good Samaritan Counseling Center, Dr. William Scar
Major Activities: Farmers' Markets; CROP Hunger Walks; Church
Athletic Leagues; Community Action; Easter Sunrise Worships; Interreligious
Dialogue; Justice Advocacy; Martin Luther King, Jr. Celebration; Violence
Prevention; Long Beach Interfaith Clergy; Publishing Area Religious Directories, Crop Hunger, Walks, Counseling services

Southern California Ecumenical Council
195 So. Hill Ave., Pasadena, CA 91106, Tel. (626)578-6371, Fax (626)578-6358
Email: scec1@scec1.net
Website: www.scec1.net
Media Contact, Exec. Dir., Rev. Albert G. Cohen
Exec. Dir., The Rev. Albert G. Cohen
Pres., Mrs. Lucy Guernsey
Treas., The Rev. Larry Hixon
Sec., Fr. Arshag Khatchadourian
Vice Pres. The Rev. Dr. Gwynne Guibord
Second Vice Pres., Carol Kostura
Members at Large, The Rev.Dr. Dagmar Grefe, Pr. Kenny Bowen, Fr. Alexei Smith
Faith and Order Chair, The Rev Dr. Tamara Rodenberg
Past Pres., The Rev. Dr. Paul Lance
Major Activities: Consultation with the regional religious sector concerning the well being and spiritual vitality of this most diverse and challenging area

Westside Interfaith Council
P.O. Box 1402, Santa Monica, CA 90406, Tel. (310)394-1518, Fax (310)576-1895
Media Contact, Rev. Janet A. Bregar
Exec. Dir., Rev. Janet A. Bregar
Major Activities: Meals on Wheels; Community Religious Services; Convalescent Hospital Chaplaincy; Homeless Partnership; Hunger & Shelter Coalition

COLORADO

Colorado Council of Churches*
3690 Cherry Creek S. Dr., Denver, CO 80209, Tel. (303)825-4910, Fax (303)744-8605
Email: jryan@COchurches.org

Website: www.Cochurches.org
Media Contact, Council Exec., Rev. Dr. James R. Ryan
Pres., Rev. Andrew Simpson
Staff Assoc, Dori Wilson
Major Activities: Addressing issues of Christian Unity, Justice, and Environment

Interfaith Council of Boulder
3700 Baseline Rd., Boulder, CO 80303, Tel. (303)494-8094
Media Contact, Pres., Stan Grotegut, 810 Kalma Ave., Boulder, CO 80304 Tel. (303)443-2291
Pres., Stan Grotegut
Major Activities: Interfaith Dialogue and Programs; Thanksgiving Worship Services; Food for the Hungry; Share-A-Gift; Monthly Newsletter

CONNECTICUT

Association of Religious Communities
325 Main St., Danbury, CT 06810, Tel. (203)792-9450, Fax (203)792-9452
Email: arc325@sbcglobal.net
Media Contact, Exec. Dir., Rev. Phyllis J. Leopold
Exec. Dir., Rev. Phyllis J. Leopold
Pres., The Rev. Angelo S. Arrando
Major Activities: Refugee Resettlement; Family Counseling; Family Violence Prevention; Affordable Housing, Inter-Faith Dialogue, Racial Justice

The Capitol Region Conference of Churches
60 Lorrain St., Hartford, CT 06105, Tel. (860)236-1295, Fax (860)236-8071
Email: crcc@conferenceofchurches.org
Website: www.conferenceofchurches.org
Media Contact, Exec. Dir., Rev. Shelley Copeland
Exec. Dir., The Rev. Shelley Copeland
Pastoral Care & Training, Dir., The Rev. Kathleen Davis
Aging Project, Dir., Barbara Malcolm
Community Organizer, Joseph Wasserman
Broadcast Ministry Consultant, Ivor T. Hugh
Pres., Mr. David O. White
Major Activities: Organizing for Peace and Justice; Aging; Legislative Action; Cooperative Broadcast Ministry; Ecumenical Cooperation; Interfaith Reconciliation; Chaplaincies; Low-Income Senior Empowerment; Anti-Racism Education

Center City Churches
40 Pratt Street, Ste. 210, Hartford, CT 06103-1601, Tel. (860)728-3201, Fax (860)549-8550
Email: info@centercitychurches.org
Website: www.centercitychurches.org
Media Contact, Exec. Dir., Paul C. Christie

233

Exec. Dir., Paul C. Christie
Pres., Jeannette L. Brown
Treas., Rusty Spears
Major Activities: Senior Services; Family
Resource Center; Food Pantry; Assistance &
Advocacy; After School Tutoring and Arts
Enrichment; Summer Day Camp; Housing for
persons with AIDS; Community Soup Kitchen

Christian Community Action
168 Davenport Ave., New Haven, CT 06519, Tel.
(203)777-7848, Fax (203)777-7848
Email: cca@ccahelping.org
Website: www.ccahelping.org
Media Contact, Exec. Dir., The Rev. Bonita
Grubbs
Exec. Dir., The Rev. Bonita Grubbs
Major Activities: Emergency Food Program;
Used Furniture & Clothing; Security and Fuel;
Emergency Housing for Families; Advocacy;
Transitional Housing for Families

Christian Conference of Connecticut*
60 Lorraine St., Hartford, CT 06105, Tel.
(860)236-4281, Fax (860)236-9977
Email: ctchurches@comcast.net
Website: www.ctchurches.org
Media Contact, Exec. Dir., Vacant
Exec. Dir., Vacant
Pres., The Rt. Rev. Andrew D. Smith
Vice Pres., The Most Rev. Michael R. Cote
Sec., The Rev. Dr. Sandra Olsen
Treas., Ms. Alberta Hoagland
Major Activities: Communications; Institutional
Ministries; Connecticut Ecumenical Small
Church Project; Ecumenical Forum; Faith &
Order; Social Concerns; Public Policy; Peace
and Justice Convocation; Restorative Justice &
Death Penalty; Interreligious Dialogue ; Anti—
Nuclear Activities; Problem Gambling; Jewish-
Christian Dialogue, Muslim-Christian Dialogue

The Council of Churches of Greater Bridgeport, Inc.
1100 Boston Avenue, Bldg. 5 A, Bridgeport, CT
06610, Tel. (203)334-1121, Fax (203)367-8113
Email: ccgb@ccgb.org
Website: www.ccgb.org
Media Contact, President & CEO, Rev. Dr. Brian
R. Bodt
President & CEO., Rev. Dr. Brian R. Bodt
Chairman, Carl Johnson
Vice Chair, Fr. Demetrios Racachinas
Sec., Valzie Peterkin
Treas., Phil Norgren
Major Activities: Youth in Crisis; Youth In Crisis
Hotline, Responses & Safe Places; Host Home
Shelter Care; Criminal Justice Services for Ex-
offenders; Jail Ministry; Hunger Outreach and
Networking; Ecumenical & Inter-Religious
Relations, Prayer and Celebration; Covenantal
Ministries; Homework Help; Summer
Programs; Race Relations-Bridge Building

Council of Churches and Synagogues of Southwestern Connecticut
461 Glenbrook Rd, Stamford, CT 06901, Tel.
(203)348-2800, Fax (203)358-0627
Email: council@flvax.ferg.lib.ct.us
Website: www.interfaithcouncil.org
Media Contact, Comm. Ofc., Lois Alcosser
Exec. Dir., Jack Penfield, Interim Director
Major Activities: Partnership Against Hunger;
The Food Bank of Lower Fairfield County;
Friendly Visitors and Friendly Shoppers;
Senior Neighborhood Support Services;
Christmas in April; Interfaith Programming;
Prison Visitation; Friendship House; Help a
Neighbor; Operation Fuel; Teaching Place

Greater Waterbury Interfaith Ministries, Inc.
16 Church St, Waterbury, CT 06702, Tel.
(203)756-7831, Fax (203)419-0024
Media Contact, Exec. Dir., Carroll E. Brown
Exec. Dir., Carroll E. Brown
Pres., The Rev. Dr. James G. Bradley
Major Activities: Emergency Food Program;
Emergency Fuel Program; Soup Kitchen;
Ecumenical Worship; Christmas Toy Sale;
Annual Hunger Walk

Manchester Area Conference of Churches
P.O. Box 3804, Manchester, CT 06045-3804, Tel.
(860)647-8003, Fax (860) 646-9631
Email: bstafford@macc-ct.org
Website: www.macc-ct.org
Media Contact, Exec. Dir., Beth Stafford
Exec. Dir., Beth Stafford
Pres., Rev. Carol Gregory
Vice Pres., Ed Sutton
Sec., Dough Mantz
Treas., Dave Russell
Major Activities: Provision of Basic Needs (Food,
Fuel, Clothing, Furniture); Emergency Aid
Assistance; Emergency Shelter; Soup Kitchen;
Reentry Assistance to Sex-Offenders; Pastoral
Care in Local Institutions; Interfaith Day Camp;
Advocacy for the Poor; Ecumenical Education
and Worship

New Britain Area Conference of Churches (NEWBRACC)
830 Corbin Ave., New Britain, CT 06052, Tel.
(860)229-3751, Fax (860)223-3445
Media Contact, Acting Exec. Dir., Rev. Teresa A.
Hughes
Acting Exec. Dir., The Rev. Teresa A. Hughes
Pastoral Care-Chaplaincy, The Rev. Ron Smith;
The Rev. Will Baumgartner
Pres., The Rev. Charles Tillet
Treas., Dierdre Elloian
Major Activities: Worship; Social Concerns;

Emergency Food Bank Support; Communications-Mass Media; Hospital; Elderly Programming; Homelessness and Hunger Programs; Telephone Ministry

DELAWARE

The Christian Council of Delaware and Maryland's Eastern Shore*
2020 N. Tatnall Street, Wilmington, DE 19802, Tel. (302)-656-5441, Fax
Website: www.DeMdSynod.org
Media Contact, Pres., Bishop Wayne P. Wright, Diocese of Delaware, 2020 N. Tatnall Street, Wilmington, DE 19802
Pres., Bishop Wayne P. Wright, Diocese of Delaware, 2020 N. Tatnall Street, Wilmington, DE 19802
Major Activities: Exploring Common Theological, Ecclesiastical and Community Concerns; Racism; Prisons

DISTRICT OF COLUMBIA

The Council of Churches of Greater Washington
5 Thomas Circle N.W., Washington, DC 20005, Tel. (202)722-9240, Fax (202)722-9240
Media Contact, Exec. Dir., The Rev. Rodger Hall Reed, Sr.
Pres., The Rev. Lewis Anthony
Exec. Dir., The Rev. Rodger Hall Reed, Sr.
Program Officer, Daniel M. Thompson
Major Activities: Promotion of Christian Unity-Ecumenical Prayer & Worship; Coordination of Community Ministries; Summer Youth Employment; Summer Camping-Inner City Youth; Supports wide variety of social justice concerns

InterFaith Conference of Metropolitan Washington
1426 Ninth St., NW, Washington, DC 20001-3344, Tel. (202)234-6300, Fax (202)234-6303
Email: ifc@ifcmw.org
Website: www.ifcmw.org
Media Contact, Exec. Dir., Rev. Dr. Clark Lobenstine
Exec. Dir., Rev. Dr. Clark Lobenstine
Admn. Sec., Judy Bond
Pres., Mrs. Carole Miller
1st Vice-Pres., Siva Subramanian, M.D.
Chpsn., Rev. Dr. Robert Maddo
Sec., Mrs. Iris Lav
Treas., Sheikh Bassam Estwani
Major Activities: Helps end hunger, homelessness, and racism. Strengthens families and youth and deepens understanding by bringing together 10 world religions to build a just, compassionate community in metropolitan Washington D.C.

FLORIDA

Christian Service Center for Central Florida, Inc.
808 W. Central Blvd., Orlando, FL 32805-1809, Tel. (407)425-2523, Fax (407)425-9513
Website: www.christianservicecenter.org
Media Contact, Exec. Dir., Robert F. Stuart
Exec. Dir., Robert F. Stuart
Family Emergency Services, Dir.,Rev. Haggeo Gautier
Fresh Start, Dir., Rev. Haggeo Gautier
Dir. of Mktg.,
Pres., Dr. Bryan Fulwider
Treas., Peter Reinert
Sec., Terry Bitner
Major Activities: Provision of Basic Needs (food, clothing, shelter); Emergency Assistance; Noon-time Meals; Collection and Distribution of Used Clothing; Shelter & Training for Homeless; Children After-School and Summer Programs

Florida Council of Churches*
3838 West Cypress Street, Tampa, FL 33607, Tel. (813)876-7660, Fax (813)435-3239
Email: rmeyer@floridachurches.org
Website: www.floridachurches.org
Media Contact, Exec. Dir., Rev. Russell L. Meyer
Exec. Dir., The Rev. Russell L. Meyer President, Bishop Charles Leigh
Vice President, Bishop Onell Soto
Treasurer, Lynda Mack, CPA
Dean, College of Judicatory Leaders, Bishop Timothy Whitaker
Major Activities: Justice and Peace; Disaster Response; Legislation & Public Policy; Local Ecumenism; Farmworker Ministry; Cherishing the Creation (Environmental Stewardship); Missional Identity

GEORGIA

Georgia Christian Council*
P.O. Box 7193 (2370 Vineville Ave.), Macon, GA 31209-7193, Tel. (478)743-2085, Fax (478)743-2085
Email: GAChristiancouncil@alltel.net
Media Contact, Exec. Dir., Rev. Leland C. Collins
Exec. Dir., Rev. Leland C. Collins
Pres., Bishop B. Michael Watson, 3370 Vineville, Ave., Suite 101, Macon, GA 31204
Sec., Dr. Willis Moore, 5312 W. Mountain St., Suite 200, Stone Mountain, GA 30083-2073
Major Activities: Local Ecumenical Support and Resourcing; Legislation; Rural Development; Racial Justice; Networking for Migrant Coalition; Aging Coalition; GA To GA With Love; Medical Care; Prison Chaplaincy; Training for Church Development; Souper Bowl; Disaster Relief;

235

Clustering; Development of Local Ecumenism; Prison Ministry; Hunger Advocacy; Family Advocacy; Developing Discipleship

The Regional Council of Churches of Atlanta

100 Edgewood Avenue, Suite 812, Atlanta, GA 30303, Tel. (404)523-5554 x 231, Fax (404)523-7330
Email: info@rccatl.org
Website: www.rccatl.org
Media Contact,
Pres., Dr. Robert Franklin
Vice-Pres., Mr. Steve Brown
Vice-Pres., Dr. R. Alan Culpepper
Vice-Pres., Rev. Tim McDonald
Sec., Dr. C.P. Huang
Treas., Ms. Dorothy James
Exec. Dir., Roy Craft
Assoc. Dir., Ethel Ware Carter
Major Activities: Forums of ecumenical interests; promotional collaboration and communication across denominational lines; and across geographical areas of Atlanta, interfaith work, coalition building.

IDAHO

The Regional Council for Christian Ministry, Inc.

237 N. Water, Idaho Falls, ID 83403, Tel. (208)524-9935
Email: rccm@tumcif.org
Media Contact,
Exec. Sec., Daniel Sene
Major Activities: Island Park Ministry; Community Food Bank; Community Observances; F.I.S.H.

ILLINOIS

Churches United of the Quad City Area

630 9th St., Rock Island, IL 61201, Tel. (309)786-6494, Fax (309)786-5916
Email: mjones@churchesunited.net
Website: www.churchesunited.net
Media Contact, Exec. Dir., Rev. Ronald Quay
Exec. Dir., Ronald Quay
Program Manager, Anne E. Wachal
Shelter Manager, Kit Miller
Financial Manager, Melanie Jones
Major Activities: Jail Ministry; Hunger Projects; Minority Enablement; Criminal Justice; Radio-TV; Peace; Local Church Development; Living Wage; Women's Shelter

Community Renewal Society

332 South Michigan Ave. Suite 500, Chicago, IL 60604, Tel. (312)673-3835, Fax (312) 427-6130
Email: jnewman@communityrenewalsociety.org
Website: www.communityrenewalsociety.org

Media Contact, Exec. Dir., Dr. Calvin S. Morris, PhD

Contact Ministries of Springfield

1100 E. Adams, Springfield, IL 62703, Tel. (217)753-3939, Fax (217)753-8643
Email: rtarrcm@springnetl.com
Media Contact, Exec. Dir., Rita Tarr
Exec. Dir., Rita Tarr
Major Activities: Information; Referral and Advocacy; Ecumenical Coordination; Low Income Housing Referral; Food Pantry Coordination; Prescription & Travel Emergency; Low Income Budget Counseling; 24 hours on call; Emergency Shelter On-site Women with Children

Evanston Ecumenical Action Council

P.O. Box 1414, Evanston, IL 60204, Tel. (847)475-1150, Fax (847)475-2526
Website: members.aol.com/eeachome/eeac.html
Media Contact, Comm. Chpsn., Ken Wylie
Dir. Hospitality Cntr. for the Homeless, Sue Murphy
Co-Pres., The Rev. Ted Miller; The Rev. Hardist Lane
Treas., Caroline Frowe
Major Activities: Interchurch Communication and Education; Peace and Justice Ministries; Coordinated Social Action; Soup Kitchens; Multi-Purpose Hospitality Center for the Homeless; Worship and Renewal, Racial Reconciliation, Youthwork

Greater Chicago Broadcast Ministries

112 E. Chestnut St., Chicago, IL 60611-2014, Tel. (312)988-9001, Fax (312)988-9004
Email: gcbm@ameritech.net
Website: gcbm.org
Media Contact, Exec. Dir., Lydia Talbot
Pres., Bd. of Dir., Rev. Phil Blackwell
Exec. Dir., Lydia Talbot
Major Activities: Television, Interfaith-Ecumenical Development; Social-Justice Concerns

The Hyde Park & Kenwood Interfaith Council

5745 S. Blackstone Ave., Chicago, IL 60637, Tel. (773)752-1911, Fax (773)752-2676
Media Contact, Exec. Dir., Lesley M. Radius
Exec. Dir., Lesley M. Radius
Pres., The Rev. David Grainger
Sec., Barbara Krell
Major Activities: Interfaith Work; Hunger Projects; Community Development

Illinois Conference of Churches*

522 East Monroe, Ste. 208, Springfield, IL 62701, Tel. (217)522-7099, Fax (217)522-7105
Email: adminstaff@ilconfchurches.org
Website: ilconfchurches.org

236

Media Contact, Exec. Dir., Rev. David A. Anderson, Email davidanderson@ilconfchurches.org

Exec. Dir., Rev. David A. Anderson

Assoc. Dir., vacant

Pres., Rev. Donald E. Mason

Major Activities: Ecumenical Education and Dialogue; Public Policy Education and Advocacy.

Oak Park-River Forest Community of Congregations

P.O. Box 3365, Oak Park, IL 60303-3365, Tel. (708)386-8802, Fax (708)386-1399

Website: http://lgrossman.comcomcong.htm

Media Contact, The Rev. Marguerite Rourke

Admn. Sec.,

Pres., The Rev. Marguerite Rourke

Treas., The Rev. Dwight Bailey

Major Activities: Community Affairs; Ecumenical-Interfaith Affairs; Youth Education; FOOD PANTRY; Senior Citizens Worship Services; Interfaith Thanksgiving Services; Good Friday Services; Literacy Training; CROP-CWS Hunger Walkathon; Work with Homeless Through PADS (Public Action to Deliver Shelter; Diversity Education; Walk-in Ministry

Peoria Friendship House of Christian Service

800 N.E. Madison Ave., Peoria, IL 61603, Tel. (309)671-5200, Fax (309)671-5206

Media Contact, Exec. Dir., Beverly Isom

Pres. of Bd., David Dadds

Major Activities: Children's After-School; Teen Programs; Recreational Leagues; Senior Citizens Activities; Emergency Food-Clothing Distribution; Emergency Payments for Prescriptions, Rent, Utilities; Community Outreach; Economic Development; Neighborhood Empowerment; GED Classes; Family Literacy; Mother's Group; Welfare to Work Programs

INDIANA

The Associated Churches of Fort Wayne & Allen County, Inc.

602 E. Wayne St., Fort Wayne, IN 46802, Tel. (260)-422-3528, Fax (260)-422-6721

Email: associatedchurches@comcast.net

Website: www.associatedchurches.org

Media Contact, Exec. Dir., Rev. Roger Reece

Exec. Dir., Rev. Roger Reece

Administrative Assistant, Elaine Williamson

Foodbank- Director, John Lassen; Isaac Nickleson;Gordon Matoon

Dir. of Prog. Development & Mission Outreach, Theresa Tracey

Dir. of Weekday Religious Education, Kathy Rolf

Pres., Rev. Richard Hartman, 3923 Nottingham Dr., Fort Wayne, IN 46815

Treas., Mary Jo Mikulski

Major Activities: Weekday Religious Ed.; Baby's Closet; Hunger Walk; Food Bank System; Peace & Justice Commission; Welfare Reform; Endowment Development; Child Care Advocacy; Advocates Inc.

Christian Ministries of Delaware County

401 E. Main St., Muncie, IN 47305, Tel. (317)288-0601, Fax (317)282-4522

Email: christianministries@netzero.net

Website: www.christianministries.ws

Media Contact, Exec. Dir., Becki Clock

Exec. Dir., Becki Clock

Pres., David Abrams

Treas., Joan McKee

Major Activities: Baby Care Program; Youth Ministry at Detention Center; Community Church Festivals; Food Pantry; Emergency Assistance; CROP Walk; Social Justice; Family Life Education; Homeless Shelter (sleeping room only); Clothing and household items available free; workshops for low income clients; homeless apartments available- short stays only at no cost; provide programs and workshops for pastors and churches in community; work with schools sponsoring programs.

Church Community Services

629 S. 3rd Street, Elkhart, IN 46516-3241, Tel. (574)295-3673, Fax (574)295-5593

Email: ccs6293rd@aol.com

Website: www.soupofsuccess.com

Media Contact,

Exec. Director, Dean Preheim-Bartel

Major Activities: Financial Assistance for Emergencies; Food Pantry; Information and Referral; Clothing Referral; Rent Assistance; Utility Assistance; Medication Vouchers; Transportation Vouchers; Job and Life Skills Training Program for Women

The Church Federation of Greater Indianapolis, Inc.

1100 W. 42nd St., Ste. 345, Indianapolis, IN 46208, Tel. (317)926-5371, Fax (317)926-5371

Email: churches@churchfederationindy.org

Website: www.churchfederationindy.org

Media Contact, Pres., Rev. Alan Goertemiller

Exec. Dir., Rev. Dr. Angelique Walker-Smith

Pres., Rev. Alan Goertemiller

Treas., Hugh Moore

Major Activities: Founded in 1912 (John 17: 20-23), Benevolence Ministry-C.R.O.P. (Church World Service); Sacred Conversations (Racial Reconciliation); Clergy ID Badge Program; Community Organizing; Faith and Fathers Juvenile Prison Ministry; Hispanic-Latino Forum; Faith and Education Initiative; Centennial Committee; Project Reconnect: Church and Neighborhood Partnership; Greater Indianapolis Prayer Network to Stop the

237

Violence-Ecumenical Project for Reconciliation and Healing; IndyFaith.Com/net/org; TV Broadcasts; Interfaith Hunger Network; Caring Churches Network; Indianapolis Prayer Breakfast (Partnership).

Indiana Partners for Christian Unity and Mission

P.O. Box 88790, Indianapolis, IN 46208-0790, Tel. (800)746-2310, Fax (315)292-5990
Email: INDUnity@aol.com
Website: www.ipcum.org
Media Contact, Rev. Janet Wanner
Executive Dir., The Rev. Dennis Frische-Mouri
Pres., The Rev. Janet Wanner
Treas., Mrs. Marilyn Moffett
Major Activities: Initiating dialogue on issues of social concern by organizing conferences on the death penalty, racism, welfare reform and violence; facilitating communication through an electronic newsletter and web site; promoting the National Day of Prayer and the Week of Prayer for Christian Unity; and advancing Churches Uniting in Christ.

Interfaith Community Council, Inc.

702 E. Market St., New Albany, IN 47150, Tel. (812)948-9248, Fax (812)948-9249
Email: icc@digicove.com
Website: www.interfaithinc.org
Media Contact, Exec. Dir., Houston Thompson
Exec. Dir., Houston Thompson
Programs - Emergency Assistance
RSVP, Dir., Ceil Sperzel
Major Activities: Emergency Assistance; Retired Senior Volunteer Program; New Clothing and Toy Drives; Emergency Food Distribution; Homeless Prevention; Kids' Café; Youth Development Services

Kentuckiana Interfaith Community (see listing under Kentucky)

Lafayette Urban Ministry

525 N. 4th St., Lafayette, IN 47901, Tel. (317)423-2691, Fax (317)423-2693
Media Contact, Exec. Dir., Joseph Micon
Exec. Dir., Joseph Micon
Advocate Coord., Rebecca Smith
Public Policy Coord., Harry Brown
Pres., John Wilson
Major Activities: Social Justice Ministries with and among the Poor

United Religious Community of St. Joseph County

2015 Western Ave., Suite 101, South Bend, IN 46629, Tel. (574)282-2397, Fax (574)282-8014
Email: urc@urcsjc.org
Website: www.urcsjc.org
Media Contact, Exec. Dir., William J. Wassner

Exec. Dir., William J. Wassner
Pres.,Rabbi Michael Friesllow
Refugee Program Director, Carol McDonnell
Victim Impact Panel Director, Marchell Wesaw
Advocacy Centers Director, Marchell Wesaw
Major Activities: Religious Understanding; Interfaith-Ecumenical Education; Interfaith Newsletter "Torch"; CROP Walk; On-site Prayer Ministry; Peacemaker Awards; Hunger Education; Housing and Homelessness Issues; Clergy Education and Support; Refugee Resettlement; Victim Assistance; Advocacy for the Needy; Family Justice Center (Partner addressing chaplaincy), Housing Project for Grandparents raising Grandchildren

Weekday Christian Education

713 N. 2nd Ave., Evansville, IN 47710, Tel. (812)425-3524, Fax (812)425-3525
Email: eacc1@hotmail.com
Media Contact, Weekday Executive Director, Donna K. Carr
Weekday Exec. Dir., Donna K. Carr
Pres., Jean Hartman
V. Pres., Robert Glenn
Sec., Ellen Berberich
Treas., Mary Jane Hudascek
Major Activities: Food Pantry System; Weekday Christian Education

Wellspring Interfaith Social Services, Inc. (previously West Central Neighborhood Ministry, Inc.)

1316 Broadway, Fort Wayne, IN 46802-3304, Tel. (219)422-6618, Fax (219)422-9319
Email: fzirille@wellspringinterfaith.org
Media Contact, Exec. Dir., Francis M. Zirille
Exec. Dir., Francis M. Zirille
Ofc. Mgr., J. R. Stopperich
Neighborhood Services Dir., Carol Salge
Senior Citizens Dir., Gayle Mann
Youth Director, Lois Ehinger
Major Activities: After-school Programs; Teen Drop-In Center; Summer Day Camp; Summer Overnight Camp; Information and Referral Services; Food Pantry; Nutrition Program for Senior Citizens; Senior Citizens Activities; Tutoring; Developmental Services for Families & Senior Citizens; Parent Club

IOWA

Churches United, Inc.

1035 3rd Ave., Suite 202, Cedar Rapids, IA 52403-2463, Tel. (319)366-7163, Fax (319)366-7163
Email: churchesunited@yahoo.com
Website: www.churchesunitedcr.org
Media Contact, Exec. Dir., Darci Morin
Exec. Dir., Darci Morin
Pres., Rev. David Loy
Treas., Ellen Bruckner

Major Activities: Communication-resource center for member churches; Community Information and Referral; Ecumenical City-wide Celebrations; Restorative Justice programs

Des Moines Area Religious Council
3816 36th St., Ste. 202, Des Moines, IA 50310, Tel. (515)277-6969, Fax (515)274-8389
Email: info@dmreligious.org
Website: dmreligious.org
Media Contact, Exec. Dir., Forrest Harms
Exec. Dir., Forrest Harms
Pres., James Swanstrom
Pres. Elect, Faith Ferre
Treas., Leonara Waller
Major Activities: Education; Social Initiatives Advocacy; Mission;
Emergency Food Pantry; Ministry to Widowed; Child Care Assistance,
Compassion in Action, Cross-cultural

Ecumenical Ministries of Iowa (EMI)*
P.O. Box 41487, Des Moines, IA 50311, Tel. (515)274-2278, Fax (515)274-2278
Email: emofiowa@aol.com
Website: www.iowachurches.org
Media Contact, Comm. Coord., Mary Swalla Holmes
Exec. Dir., Rev. Sarai Schnucker Beck
Major Activities: Facilitating the denomination-s'cooperative agenda of resourcing local expression of the church; Assess needs & develop responses through Justice and Unity Commissions

Iowa Religious Media Services*
3116 104th Street, Urbandale, IA 50322-3818, Tel. (515)277-2920, Fax (515)277-0842
Email: questions@irms.org
Website: www.irms.org
Media Contact, Exec. Dir., Sharon E. Strohmaier
Exec. Dir., Sharon E. Strohmaier
Major Activities: Media Library for Churches in 7 Denominations in the Midwest; Provide Video Production Services for Churches, Non-profit & Educational organizations; will rent media to churches in the continental U.S. (details on the website)

KANSAS

Cross-Lines Cooperative Council
736 Shawnee Ave., Kansas City, KS 66105, Tel. (913)281-3388, Fax (913)281-2344
Email: theresa@cross-lines.org
Website: www.cross-lines.org
Media Contact, Dir. of Public Relations & Marketing, Theresa Swartwood
Exec. Dir., Roberta Lindbeck
Dir.of Emergency Services, Carey Sterrett
Major Activities: Emergency Assistance; Hunger Relief; Community Garden/Nutrition Project;

Thrift Store; Highlight Programs such as Prom Attire Distribution, School Supplies; Christmas Store

Inter-Faith Ministries-Wichita
829 N. Market, Wichita, KS 67214-3519, Tel. (316)264-9303, Fax (316)264-2233
Email: smuyskens@ifmnet.org
Website: www.ifmnet.org
Media Contact, Exec. Dir., Sam Muyskens
Exec. Dir., Rev. Sam Muyskens
Adm. Asst.- Kathy Freed
ASAP Haiti, Dir. Bonnie Chadick
Homeless and Housing Services, Dir., Sandy Swank
Special Projects, Dir., Ashley Davis
Development, Dir., Karen Dobbin
Campaign to End Childhood Hunger, Karole Bradford
Community Ministry/Restorative Justice/Family Group Conferencing/Racial Justice Coord., Jeannine Little
Faith in Action, Coord., Richard Hanley
GoZones! Dir., Johanna Wilson
Major Activities: Communications; Urban Education; Inter-religious Understanding; Community Needs and Issues; Theology and Worship; Hunger; Family Life; Multi-Cultural Concerns

Kansas Ecumenical Ministries*
5833 SW 29th St., Topeka, KS 66614-2499, Tel. (785)272-9531
Email: LK331@aol.com
Media Contact, Exec. Dir., Rev. Linda Kemp
Pres., Rev. Charles Claycomb
Vice Pres., Rev. Rebecca New
Sec., Rev. Lee Lever
Exec. Dir., Rev. Linda Kemp
Pres., Rev. Charles Claycomb
Vice Pres., Rev. Rebecca New
Sec., Rev. Lee Lever
Major Activities: State Council of Churches; Legislative Activities; Program Facilitation and Coordination; Education; Mother-to-Mother Program; Rural Concerns; Hate group monitoring; Children & Families; Faith and Order

KENTUCKY

Eastern Area Community Ministries
P.O. Box 43049, Louisville, KY 40253-0049, Tel. (502)244-6141, Fax (502)254-5141
Email: easternacm@cs.com
Media Contact, Acting Exec. Dir., Sharon Eckler
Acting Exec. Dir., Sharon Eckler
Board Pres., Rev. Elwood Sturtevant
Board Sec., Mary Stephens
Board Treas., Homer Lacy, Jr.
Youth and Family Services,Rachael Elrod
Older Adult Services, Associate Program Dir., Joni Snyder
Neighborhood Visitor Program, Acting Prog. Dir., Jane Parker

239

Major Activities: Emergency Assistance; Clothes Closet; Meals on Wheels; Community Worship Services; Good Start for Kids; Juvenile Court Diversion; Community Development; Transient Fund; Ministerial Association; Juvenile Court Diversion

Fern Creek-Highview United Ministries

7502 Tangelo Dr., Louisvlle, KY 40228, Tel. (502)239-7407, Fax (502)239-7454
Email: FernCreek.Ministries@crnky.org
Media Contact, Exec. Dir., Kay Sanders, 7502 Tangelo Dr., Louisville, KY 40228 Tel. (502)239-7407
Exec. Dir., Kay Sanders
Pres., David Pooler
Major Activities: Ecumenically supported social service agency providing services to the community, including Emergency Financial Assistance, Food-Clothing, Health Aid Equipment Loans, Information-Referral, Advocacy, Checks; Holiday Programs, Life Skills Training; Mentoring; Case Management; Adult Day-Care Program

Hazard-Perry County Community Ministries, Inc.

P.O. Box 1506, Hazard, KY 41702-1506, Tel. (606)436-0051, Fax (606)436-0071
Media Contact, Gerry Feamster-Roll
Exec. Dir., Gerry Feamster-Roll
Chpsn., Sarah Hughes
V. Chpsn., Susan Duff
Sec., Virginia Campbell
Treas., Margaret Adams
Major Activities: Food Pantry-Crisis Aid Program; Day Care; Summer Day Camp; After-school Program; Christmas Tree; Family Support Center; Adult Day Care; Transitional Housing

Highlands Community Ministries

1140 Cherokee Rd., Louisville, KY 40204, Tel. (502)451-3695, Fax (502)451-3609
Email: hcmexecu@hotmail.com
Website: www.hcmlou.org
Media Contact, Exec. Dir., Stan Esterle
Exec. Dir., Stan Esterle
Major Activities: Welfare Assistance; Children Day Care; Adult DayHealth Care; Social Services for Elderly; Housing for Elderly and Handicapped; Ecumenical Programs; Interfaith Programs; Community Classes; Activities for Children; Neighborhood and Business organization

Kentuckiana Interfaith Community

P.O. Box 7128, Louisville, KY 40257, Tel. (502)587-6265, Fax (502)451-9827
Email: churchoffice@salemucc.com
Website: www.neighborhoodlink.com/org/kic

Media Contact, Exec. Dir., Rev. Douglas Fowler
Pres., Ron Gaddie
Vice-Pres., Laura Metzger
Treas., Charles Hawkins
Major Activities: Christian-Jewish, Islamic, Bahai Ministries in KY, Southern IN; Consensus Advocacy; Interfaith Dialogue; Community Hunger Walk; Racial Justice Forums; Network for Neighborhood-based Ministries; Hunger & Racial Justice Commission; Faith Channel- Cable TV Station, Horizon News Paper; Police-Comm. Relations Task Force; Ecumenical Strategic Planning; Networking with Seminaries & Religious-Affiliated Institutions

Kentucky Council of Churches*

1500 Leestown Rd., Suite 108, Lexington, KY 40511, Tel. (859)269-7715, Fax (859)269-1240
Email: kcc@kycouncilofchurches.org
Website: www.kycouncilofchurches.org
Media Contact, Exec. Dir., Nancy Jo Kemper
Exec. Dir., The Rev. Dr. Nancy Jo Kemper
Pres., The Rev. Ron Gaddie
Kentucky Interchurch Disaster Recovery Program Coodinator., Mr. Harper Davis
Director Associate for Local Ecumenism, The Rev. W. Chris Benham Skidmore
Major Activities: Christian Unity; Public Policy; Justice; Disaster Response; Peace Issues; Anti-Racism; Health Care Issues; Local Ecumenism; Rural Land-Farm Issues; Gambling; Capital Punishment

Ministries United South Central Louisville (M.U.S.C.L., Inc.)

1207 Hart Avenue, Louisville, KY 42013, Tel. (502)363-9087, Fax (502)363-9087
Media Contact, Exec. Dir., Rev. Antonio (Tony) Aja, M.Div., Tel. (502)363-2383, Email Tony_Aja@pcusa.org
Ex. Dir., Rev. Antonio (Tony) Aja, M.Div.
Airport Relocation Ombudsman, Rev. Phillip Garrett, M.Div. Tel. (502)361-2706; E-mail, philombud@aol.com
Senior Adults Programs, Dir., Mrs. Jeannine Blakeman, BSSW
Emergency Assistance, Dir., Mr. Michael Hundley
Low-Income Coord., Ms. Wanda Irvio
Youth Services, Dir., The Rev. Bill Sanders, M.Div.
Volunteers Coord., Mrs. Carol Stemmle
Major Activities:

Northern Kentucky Interfaith Commission, Inc.

901 York St., P.O. Box 72296, Newport, KY 41072-0296, Tel. (859)581-2237, Fax (859)261-6041
Website: www.nkyinterfaith.com
Media Contact, Exec. Dir., Rev. James A. Bishop
Pres., Mr. Paul Whalen

Sec., Ms.Cordelia Koplow
Treas., Mr. John Wilgus
Admin. Asst., Pat McDermott
Major Activities: Understanding Faiths; Meeting Spiritual and Human Needs; Enabling Churches to Greater Ministry

Paducah Cooperative Ministry
402 Legion Drive, Paducah, KY 42003, Tel. (270)442-6795, Fax (270)442-6812
Email: pcministry@hcis.net
Website: www.paducahcooperativeministry.org
Media Contact, Dir., Heidi Suhrheinrich
Dir., Heidi Suhrheinrich
Chairman., Don Barger
Vice-Chpsn., Rev. David Comperry
Major Activities: Programs for Hungry, Elderly, Poor, Homeless, Handicapped, Undereducated

St. Matthews Area Ministries
201 Biltmore Rd., Louisville, KY 40207, Tel. (502)893-0205, Fax (502)893-0206
Email: danglane@stman.com
Website: www.stmam.com
Media Contact, Exec. Dir., Dan G. Lane
Exec. Dir., Dan G. Lane
Child Care, Dir., Julie Abbott
Dir. Assoc., Danette Baker
Major Activities: Child Care; Emergency Assistance (Financial +); Family Services; Divorce Family Transition Sessions (F.I.T.); Early Essentials for Infants/Toddlers; Case Management; Counseling; Information & Referral; Meals on Wheels; Medical Equipment Loan; Early Essentials For Infants/Toddlers; School Supplies Program; Financial/Budgeting Classes; Families in Transition (Divorce Sessions For Families); Volunteer Organization Active in Disaster (St. MAM V.O.A.D.).

South East Associated Ministries (SEAM)
6500 Six Mile Ln., Ste.A, Louisville, KY 40218, Tel. (502)499-9350
Media Contact, Mary Beth Helton
Exec. Dir., Mary Beth Helton
Life Skills Center, Dir., Robert Davis
Youth Services, Dir., Bill Jewel
Pres., David Ehresman
Treas., Bill Trusty
Major Activities: Emergency Food, Clothing and Financial Assistance; Life Skills Center (Programs of Prevention and Case Management and Self-Sufficiency Through Education, Empowerment, Support Groups, etc.); Bloodmobile; Ecumenical Education and Worship; Juvenile Court Diversion; TEEN Court; Teen Crime & the Community

South Louisville Community Ministries
Peterson Social Services Center,4803 Southside Dr., Louisville, KY 40214, Tel. (502)367-6445, Fax (502)361-4668

Email: slcm@slcm.org
Website: www.slcm.org
Media Contact, Exec. Dir., J. Michael Jupin
Bd. Chair., Rev. Michelle Elfers
Bd. Vice-Chair., Craig Oeswein
Bd. Treas., Greg Greenwood
Exec. Dir., Rev. J. Michael Jupin
Major Activities: Food, Clothing & Financial Assistance; Home Delivered Meals; Ecumenical Worship; Affordable Housing; Adult Day Care; Dare to Care Kids Café

LOUISIANA

Greater New Orleans Federation of Churches
4640 S. Carrollton Ave, Suite 2B, New Orleans, LA 70119-6077, Tel. (504)488-8788, Fax (504)488-8823
Media Contact,
Exec. Dir., The Rev. J. Richard Randels
Major Activities: Information and Referral; Food Distribution(FEMA); Forward Together TV Program; Sponsors seminars for pastors (e.g. church growth, clergy taxes,etc.); Police Chaplaincy; Fire Chaplaincy

Interfaith Federation of Greater Baton Rouge
3112 Convention St., Baton Rouge, LA 70815, Tel. (225)267-5600, Fax (225)267-5100
Email: director@ifedgbr.com
Website: www.ifedgbr.com
Media Contact, Exec. Dir., Rev. Jeff Day
Exec. Dir., Rev. Jeff Day
Admn. Asst., Ashley Griffin
Pres., Rev. Amy Mercer
Pres.-Elect, Joyce Robinson
Treas., Melvin Davis
Major Activities: Combating Hunger; Interfaith Relations; Interfaith Concert; Race Relations; Interfaith Caregivers (Faith in Action)

Louisiana Interchurch Conference*
527 North Boulevard, Fourth Floor, Baton Rouge, LA 70802, Tel. (225)344-0134, Fax (225)927-7
Email: lainterchurch@aol.com
Website: www.lainterchurch.org
Media Contact, Exec. Dir., Rev. C. Dana Krutz
Exec. Dir., Rev. C. Dana Krutz
Pres., Mr. Hugh R. Straub
Major Activities: Ecumenical Dialogue; Prison Reform; Liaison with State Agencies; Institutional Chaplains; Racism; Environmental; Public Policy Advocacy

MAINE

Maine Council of Churches*
19 Pleasant Ave., Portland, ME 04103, Tel. (207)772-1918, Fax (207)772-2947
Email: info@mainecouncilofchurches.org

241

Website: www.mainecouncilofchurches.org
Media Contact, Comm. Dir., Karen Caouette
Exec. Dir., Thomas C. Ewell
Assoc. Dir., Douglas Cruger
Admin. Asst., Sandra Buzzell
Pres., Br. Francis Blouin
Treas., Rev. Richard Swan
Major Activities: Criminal Justice Reform/ Restorative Justice; Economic Justice; Environmental Justice; Peace Issues; Civil Rights

MARYLAND

Central Maryland Ecumenical Council*

Cathedral House, 4 E. University Pkwy., Baltimore, MD 21218, Tel. (410)467-6194, Fax (410)554-6387
Email: cmec@bcpl.net
Media Contact, Exec. Dir., Martha Young
Pres., The Rev. Iris Farabee-Lewis
Major Activities: Interchurch Communications and Collaboration; Information Systems; Ecu-menical Relations; Urban Mission and Advocacy; Staff for Judicatory Leadership Council; Commission on Dialogue; Commission on Church & Society; Commission on Admin. & Dev.; Ecumenical Choral Concerts; Ecumenical Worship Services

The Christian Council of Delaware and Maryland's Eastern Shore (see listing under Delaware)

Community Ministries of Rockville

114 West Montgomery Ave., Rockville, MD 20850, Tel. (301)762-8682, Fax (301)762-2939
Email: asaenz@cmrocks.org
Media Contact, Managing Dir., Agnes Saenz
Exec. Dir. & Comm. Min., Mansfield M. Kaseman
Managing Dir., Agnes Aaenz
Major Activities: Shelter Care; Emergency Assistance; Elderly Home Care; Affordable Housing; Political Advocacy; Community Education; Education to Recent Immigrants

Community Ministry of Montgomery County

114 West Montgomery Ave., Rockville, MD 20850, Tel. (301)762-8682, Fax (301)762-2939
Media Contact, Exec. Dir., Rebecca Wagner
Exec. Dir., Rebecca Wagner
Major Activities: Interfaith Clothing Center; Emergency Assistance Coalition; The Advocacy Function; Information and Referral Services; Friends in Action; The Thanksgiving Hunger Drive; Thanksgiving in February; Community Based Shelter

MASSACHUSETTS

Attleboro Area Council of Churches, Inc.

7 North Main St., Ste. 200, Attleboro, MA 02703, Tel. (508)222-2933, Fax (508)222-2008
Email: director@attleborocouncilofchurches.org
Website: www.attleborocouncilofchurches.org
Media Contact, Executive Director, Dot Embree
Executive Director, Dot Embree Exec. Adm., Kathleen Trowbridge
Pamela Tarallo, Food n Friends Coordinator (foodnfriends@attleborocouncilofchurches.org)
Susan Smith, Homes with Heart Case Manager (casemanager1@attleborocouncilofchurches.org)
Steve Wright, Homes with Heart Assistant Case Manager (casemanager2@attleborocouncilofchurches.org)
Patti Sparrow, Administrative Assistant (office@attleborocouncilofchurches.org)
Bill MacLagan, Assistant Chaplain
Pres., Rev. Ruth Shaver, Minister of Christian Ed. And Family Life, Second Congregational Ch.,
Treas., Mr. Richard Shaw, 70 Stanson Dr., N. Attleboro, MA 02760
Major Activities: Hospital Chaplaincy; personal Growth-Skill Workshops; Ecumenical Worship; Interfaith Worship; Media Resource Center; Referral Center; Communications-Publications; Community Social Action; Food'n Friends Kitchens; Nursing Home Volunteer Visitation Program; Clergy Fellowship-Learning Events

The Cape Cod Council of Churches, Inc.

P.O. Box 758, Hyannis, MA 02601, Tel. (508)775-5073, Fax (508)775-5077
Email: capecodcouncil@verizon.net
Media Contact, Exec. Dir., Diane Casey-Lee
Pres., Rev. Dr. Philip Mitchell Vice Pres., Marilyn Lariviere Treasurer, Al Grorud Corp. Secretary, Shirley Lamson
Major Activities: Human Services; Social Witness; Spirituality; Ecumenism; Interfaith Relations

Cooperative Metropolitan Ministries

474 Centre St., Newton, MA 02458, Tel. (617)244-3650, Fax (617)630-9172
Email: info@coopmet.org
Website: www.coopmet.org
Media Contact, Exec. Dir., Alexander Levering Kern
Exec. Dir., Alexander Levering Kern
Bd. Pres., Rev. Anne Rousseau
Major Activities: Low Income; Suburban-Urban Bridges; Racial and Economic Justice, Leadership Training, Interfaith Dialogue, Poverty, Violence Prevention, Religious Intolerance

Council of Churches of Greater Springfield

39 Oakland St., Springfield, MA 01108, Tel. (413)733-2149, Fax (413)733-9817
Media Contact, Asst. to Dir., Andrea Skeene
Exec. Dir., Rev. Dr. David F. Hunter
Community Min., Dir. Don A. Washington
Pres., The Rev. Dr. David Hunter
Treas., John Pearson, Esq
Major Activities: Advocacy; Emergency Fuel Fund; Peace and Justice Division; Community Ministry; Hospital and Jail Chaplaincies; Pastoral Service; Crisis Counseling; Christian Social Relations; Relief Collections; Ecumenical and Interfaith Relations; Church-Community Projects and Community Dialogues; Publication, "Knowing My Neighbor- Religious Beliefs and Traditions at Times of Death"

Greater Lawrence Council of Churches

95 E. Haverhill Street, Lawrence, MA 01841, Tel. 978-686-4012, Fax 978-689-2006
Email: davidedwards@conversent.net
Website: greater-lawrence-churches.org
Media Contact, Exec. Dir., David Edwards
Exec. Dir., David Edwards
Pres., Jane Barlow
Vice-Pres., Rev. Dr. Richard Haley
Admn. Asst., Barbara Payson
Major Activities: Ecumenical Worship; Radio Ministry; Hospital and Nursing Home Chaplaincy; Afterschool Children's Program; Vacation Bible School, Interfaith care givers of Greater Lawrence

Inter-Church Council of Greater New Bedford

412 County St., New Bedford, MA 02740-5096, Tel. (508)993-6242, Fax (508)991-3158
Email: administration@inter-churchcouncil.org
Website: www.inter-churchcouncil.org
Media Contact, Min., Rev. Edward R. Dufresne, Ph.D.
Exec. Min., Rev. Edward R. Dufresne, Ph.D.
Pres., The Rev. David Lima
Treas., George Mock
Major Activities: Counseling; Spiritual Direction; Chaplaincy; Housing for Elderly and Disabled; Urban Affairs; Community Spiritual Leadership; Parish Nurse Ministry; Accounting and Spiritual Care for the Developmentally Challenged; Ecumenical and Interfaith Ministries; Advocacy for the Homeless; Support for Urban Schhol District; Opposition to Expanded Gambling

Massachusetts Commission on Christian Unity

82 Luce St, Lowell, MA 01852, Tel. (978)453-5423, Fax (978)453-5423
Email: kgordonwhite@msn.com

Media Contact, Exec. Dir., Rev. K. Gordon White
Exec. Sec., Rev. K. Gordon White
Pres., Rev. Fr. Edward O'Flaherty, Ecumenical Officer, Roman Catholic Archdiocese of Boston
Major Activities: Faith and Order Dialogue with Church Judicatories; Guidelines & Pastoral Directives for Inter-Church Marriages; Guidelines for Celebrating Baptism in an Ecumenical Context

Massachusetts Council of Churches*

14 Beacon St., Suite 416, Boston, MA 02108, Tel. (617)523-2771, Fax (617)523-1483
Email: council@masscouncilofchurches.org
Website: www.masscouncilofchurches.org
Media Contact, Dir., Rev. Jack Johnson
Exec. Dir., The Rev. Jack Johnson
Assoc. Dir., Ms. Laura Everett
Pres., Mr. Richard Harter
Vice-Pres., The Rev. Joel Matthew Anderle
Sec., The Rev. Karen Coleman
Treas., The Rev. Kenneth G. Y. Grant
Major Activities: Christian Unity; Education and Evangelism; Social Justice & Individual Rights; Ecumenical Worship; Services and Resources for Individuals and Churches

Worcester County Ecumenical Council

128 Providence Street, Worcester, MA 01604-5432, Tel. (508)757-8385, Fax (508)795-7704
Email: wcec@verizon.net
Media Contact, Exec. Dir., Rev. Allyson D. Platt
The Rev. Allyson D. Platt, Email: wcec.Allyson@verizon.net
Pres., Mrs. Fran Langille
Major Activities: Ecumenical worship and dialogue networking congregations together in partnerships of mission, education and spiritual renewal. Clusters of Churches; Ecumenical Worship and Dialogue; Interfaith Activities; Resource Connection for Churches; Group Purchasing Consortium

MICHIGAN

Bay Area Ecumenical Forum

103 E. Midland St., Bay City, MI 48706, Tel. (989)686-1360, Fax (989)686-0178
Email: wpccares@sbclogal.net
Website: www.wpcbc.org
Media Contact, Jena Windiate
Major Activities: Ecumenical Worship; Community Issues; Christian Unity; Education; CROP Walk

Berrien County Association of Churches

275 Pipestone, Benton Harbor, MI 49022, Tel. (616)926-0030, Fax (616)926-2159*51
Email: bcac_cweb@sbcglobal.net

Website: www.berrienchurches.org
Media Contact, Sec., Mary Ann Hinz
Pres., Rev. George Lawton
Dir., Street Ministry, The Rev. Yvonne Hester
Major Activities: Street Ministry; CROP Walk; Community Issues; Fellowship; Christian Unity; Hospital Chaplaincy Program; Publish Annual County Church Directory and Monthly Newsletter; Resource Guide for Helping Needy; Distribution of Worship Opportunity— Brochure for Tourists

Grand Rapids Area Center for Ecumenism (GRACE)

207 East Fulton, Grand Rapids, MI 49503-3210, Tel. (616)774-2042, Fax (616)774-2883
Email: dbaak@graceoffice.org
Website: www.graceoffice.org
Media Contact, Rev. David P. Baak
Leadership Team: Rev. David P. Baak; Lisa H. Mitchell; Rev. David G. May
Major Activities: AIDS Care Network; Volunteer Transportation; Hunger Walk ; Education; Christian Unity Worship (Ecumenical Lecture, Christian Unity Worship Events, Interfaith Dialogue Conference); (Affiliate, FISH for My People-transportation); Racial Justice Institute; West Michigan Call to Renewal (Response to Poverty Advocacy); Publications (Grace In~Site); Faith In Motion (Mass Transit and Land Use); Restorative Justice Coalition

Greater Flint Council of Churches

310 E. Third St., Suite 600, Flint, MI 48502, Tel. (810)238-3691, Fax (810)238-4463
Email: gfcc1929@aol.com
Media Contact, Coord., Mrs. Constance D. Neely Barbara Spaulding Westcott, Publicity Chairperson
President, Overseer Bernadel L. Jefferson
Major Activities: Christian Education; Christian Unity; Christian Missions; Nursing Home Visitor; Church in Society; American Bible Society Materials; Interfaith Dialogue; Church Teacher Exchange Sunday; Directory of Area Faiths and Clergy; Thanksgiving & Easter Sunrise Services; CROP Walks

The Jackson County Interfaith Council

425 Oakwood, P.O. Box 156, Clarklake, MI 49234-0156, Tel. (517)529-9721
Media Contact, Exec. Dir., -vacant-
Exec. Dir., - vacant-
Major Activities: Chaplaincy at Institutions and Senior Citizens Residences; Martin L. King, Jr. Day Celebrations; Ecumenical Council Representation; Radio and TV Programs; Food Pantry; Interreligious Events; Clergy Directory

The Metropolitan Christian Council: Detroit-Windsor

28 W. Adams, Suite 320, Detroit, MI 48226, Tel. (313)962-0340, Fax (313)962-9044

Email: councilweb@aol.com
Website: users.aol.com/councilweb
Media Contact, Rev. Richard Singleton
Exec. Dir., Rev. Richard Singleton
Meals for Shut-ins, Prog. Dir., John Simpson; Admin. Asst., Mrs. Elaine Kisner
Web Calendar Supervisor, Mr. Gerald Morgan
Major Activities: Theological and Social Concerns; Ecumenical Worship; Educational Services; Electronic Media; Print Media; Meals for Shut-Ins; Summer Feeding Program

Muskegon County Cooperating Churches

1095 Third St., Suite 10, Muskegon, MI 49441-1976, Tel. (231)727-6000, Fax (231)727-0841
Media Contact, Prog. Coord., Delphine Hogston
President: Ron Nyenhuis
Major Activities: Local Faith Community Information Source, Racial Reconciliation, Dialogue, & Healing; Multiracial Family Support; Ecumenical Worship; Faith News TV Ministry; CROP Walk Against Hunger; Jewish-Christian Dialogue; Environmental Issues, Social Justice Issues, Pastoral Support, Homeless Sheltering, Second Harvest Gleaners Food Trucks, Mentoring School Children
SUBSIDIARY ORGANIZATION
Interfaith Hospitality Network in Muskegon
Media Contact: Delphine Hogston
Major Activities: Helping congregations shelter homeless families
Community Connects Choir
Media Contact: Darlene Collett
Major Activities: Winter Holiday Concert. Intentionally interracial, intergenerational, ecumenical singing blending gospel and traditional music. Supports other diverse music opportunities for the community.

MINNESOTA

Arrowhead Interfaith Council*

102 W. 2nd St., Duluth, MN 55802, Tel. (218)722-7166
Email: president@arrowheadinterfaith.org
Website: www.arrowheadinterfaith.org
Media Contact, President - Rev. Erik Nordgren
President - Rev. Erik Nordgren
Vice-President - Rev. Sharon Osborn
Co-Secretary - Liana Salima Rael Swenson
Treasurer - Gary Wise
Major Activities: InterFaith Dialogue; Joint Religious Legislative Coalition; Corrections Chaplaincy; Human Justice and Community Concerns; Community Seminars; Children's Concerns

Community Emergency Assistance Program (CEAP)

6840 78th Ave N, Brooklyn Park, MN 55445, Tel. (763)566-9600, Fax (763)566-9604

244

Email: smklein@isd.net
Website: www.ceap.homestead.com
Media Contact, Exec. Dir., Stephen Klein
Exec. Dir., Stephen Klein
Major Activities: Provision of Basic Needs
(Food, Clothing); Emergency Financial
Assistance for Shelter; Home Delivered
Meals; Chore Services and Homemaking
Assistance; Family Loan Program; Volunteer
Services

Greater Minneapolis Council of Churches

1001 E. Lake St., P.O. Box 7509, Minneapolis,
MN 55407-0509, Tel. (612)721-8687, Fax
(612)276-1534
Email: info@gmcc.org
Website: www.gmcc.org
Media Contact, Dir. of Communications, Randy
Miranda
President and CEO, Rev. Dr. Gary B. Reierson
Email: reierson@gmcc.org
Chair, Ann Merrill
Treas., Mervin Winston
Senior Vice President & Exec. Dir., Division
Indian Work, Noya Woodrich Advancement
Vice President, Tracy Elftmann
Finance & Administration, Vice President and
CFO, Peter Lee
Program Development, Exec. Dir., Bruce Bjork
Minnesota FoodShare, Dir., Barbara Thell
HandyWorks, Dir., Megan Nolan-Elliasen
Clinical Pastoral Education, Dir., Rev. Dr. Susan
Allers Hatlie
Div. of Indian Work, Youth Leadership
Development Program, Dir., Louise Matson
Div. of Indian Work Health Services, Dir.,
George Spears
Div. of Indian Work Strengthening Family
Circles, Dir., Suzanne Tibbetts Young
Div. of Indian Work Healing Spirit Program,
Dir., Kirk Crowshoe
Urban Immersion Service Retreats, - Dir.,
Gennae Falconer
Metro Paint-A-Thon, Dir., Deidre Pope
Discover Parent Groups, Coord., Sandra Vaughn-
Kelly
Community Justice Project, Co-Dirs., Rev. Brian
Herron, Rev. Hillary Freeman
Center for Families, Exec. Dir., Sara Nelson-
Pallmeyer
Project Preserve, Coord., Deborah Easter
Compassion Captial Fund, Program Manager,
Bridget Ryan
Families Forward, Coord., LaDonna White
Major Activities: Indian Work (Emergency
Assistance, Youth Leadership, Self-sufficiency,
Indian parents, Healing Spirit Program (Foster
Care), Supportive Housing, Health Services,
Winter Clothing Distribution, Food Shelf and
Family Violence Program; Minnesota Food-
Share; Metro Paint-A-Thon and HandyWorks;
Clinical Pastoral Education (in supportive

housing and community settings), Social
Justice Advocacy; Urban Immersion Service
Retreats; Welfare Reform; Economic Self-
Sufficiency; Discover Parent Groups;
Compassion Capital Fund; Center for Families
(Immigrant and Refugee Services); Community
Health Promotion; Correctional Aftercare

The Joint Religious Legislative Coalition

122 W. Franklin Ave., Ste 315, Minneapolis, MN
55404, Tel. (612)870-3670, Fax (612)870-3671
Email: info@jrlc.org
Website: www.jrlc.org
Media Contact, Exec. Dir., Brian A. Rusche
Exec. Dir., Brian A. Rusche
Board Chair, Rev. Christopher Morton
Major Activities: Lobbying at State Legislature;
Researching Social Justice Issues and
Preparing Position Statements; Organizing
Grassroots Citizen's Lobby, Social Justice
Advocacy.

Mall Area Religious Council (MARC)

Mall of America, 7200 York Avenue South, #416,
Edina, MN 55435-4406, Tel. (952)831-0447
Email: jchell@manrol.com
Website: www.meaningstore.org
Media Contact, Rev. John Chell, Executive
Director
Major Activities:

Metropolitan Interfaith Council on Affordable Housing (MICAH)

122 W. Franklin Ave., #310, Minneapolis, MN
55404, Tel. (612)871-8980, Fax (612)871-
2634
Email: info@micah.org
Website: www.micah.org
Media Contact, Interim Exec. Dir., Shelley
Jacobson
Interim Ex. Dir., Shelley Jacobson
Congregational Organizer, Jodi Nelson, Renee
Lundgren, John Slade, Cheryl Wilson
Sec., B. Aaron Parker
Pres., Jean Mac Farland
Treas., Barbara Brooks
Past Pres., Rev. Nancy L. Anderson
Major Activities: The Metropolitan Interfaith
Council on Affordable Housing, MICAH, seeks
to live out the prophetic vision that calls us "to
do justice, to love mercy and to walk humbly
with God." (Micah 6:8). We envision a metro-
politan area where everyone without exception
has a safe, decent and affordable home.
MICAH will realize this vision through organizing congregations of faith and community
partners to change the political climate and public policies so that all communities preserve and
build affordable housing. MICAH's faith-based
organizing creates power that produces results.
During the past five years MICAH: Mobilized

245

congregations to build community support for 1,348 affordable homes for families with very low incomes. Increased investment in affordable housing by leading successful campaigns for housing trust funds in Minneapolis, Anoka and Hennepin counties. Twenty-seven (27) comprehensive land use plans have been strangthened to reduce regulatory barriers to affordable housing.

Minnesota Council of Churches*

122 W. Franklin Ave., Rm. 100, Minneapolis, MN 55404, Tel. (612)870-3600, Fax (612)870-3622

Email: mcc@mnchurches.org

Website: www.mnchurches.org

Media Contact, Exec. Dir., Rev. Peg Chemberlin, Email: peg.chemberlin@mnchurches.org

Exec. Dir., Rev. Peg Chemberlin, Enail: peg.chemberlin@mnchurches.org

Unity & Relationships, Organizer, Gail Anderson, Email: gail.anderson@mnchurches.org

Refugee Services, Dir., Rachele King, Email: rachele.king@mnchurches.org

Communications, Emily Jarrett Hughes, Email: emily.jarretthughes@mnchurches.org

Finance & Facilities, Dir., Douglas Swanson, Email: doug.swanson@mnchurches.org

Joint Religious Legislative Coalition, Research Dir. & Admn. Asst., Julie Anderson Smith

Joint Religious Legislative Coalition, Exec., Brian A. Rusche

Pres. Bishop Sally Dyck

Major Activities: Minnesota Church Center, Rural Life-Ag Crisis; Racial Reconciliation; Indian Ministry; Legislative Advocacy; Refugee Services; Service to Newly Legalized-Undocumented persons; Unity & Relationships, Sexual Exploitation within the Religious Community; Jewish-Christian Relations; Muslim-Christian Relations; Hindu-Christian Relations; Minnesota Foodshare; A Minnesota Without Poverty, Healthy Homes Healthy Congregations

Saint Paul Area Council of Churches

1671 Summit Ave, St. Paul, MN 55105, Tel. (651)646-8805, Fax (651)646-6866

Email: info@spacc.org

Website: www.spacc.org

Media Contact, Lee Erickson, Communications Director

Exec. Dir., The Rev. Grant Abbott

Dir. of Development, Kristi Anderson

Congregations in Community, Lucy Zanders Congregations in Community Organizer, Laurel Severns Guntzel Congregations in Community Organizer, Inspired to Serve, Megan Paul-Cook

Project Spirit, Dir., Darcel Hill

Project Home, Dir., Sara Liegl

Dept. of Indian Work, Dir., Sharon Romano

Pres. of the Board, Rev. M. Susan Peterson

Treas., Mr. Ezekiel Jackson

Sec., Stella Lundquist

Major Activities: Education and Advocacy Regarding Children and Poverty; Assistance to Churches Developing Children's Parenting Care Services; Ecumenical Encounters and Activities; Indian Ministries; Leadership in Forming Cooperative Ministries for Children and Youth; After School Tutoring; Interfaith Youth Service project engaging young people in effective service-learning that increases interfaith cooperation, contributes to healthy development, and enriches community life; Assistance to Congregations; Training Programs in Anti-racism; Shelters for homeless

Tri-Council Coordinating Commission

122 W. Franklin, Rm. 100, Minneapolis, MN 55404, Tel. (612)871-0229, Fax (612)870-3622

Email: naja@gmcc.org

Website: www.gmcc.org/tcc.html

Media Contact, Co.-Dir., R. James Addington, Assoc. Rev. Carmen Valenzuela

Exec. Cmte.: The Rev. Peg Chemberlin, The Rev. Gary Reierson and The Rev. Thomas Duke

Major Activities: Anti-Racism training and organizational consultation; Institutional anti-racism team development and coaching; training and coaching of anti-racism trainers and organizers (in cooperation with corss roads ministry)

MISSISSIPPI

Mississippi Religious Leadership Conference*

P.O. Box 68123, Jackson, MS 39286-8123, Tel. (601)924-7430, Fax (601)924-7430

Email: mrlc@netdoor.com

Media Contact, Exec. Dir., Rev. Paul Griffin Jones, II, Th.D., PhD.

Exec. Dir.,The Rev. Paul Griffin Jones, II, Th.D., PhD.

Chair, Bishop Duncan Gray, III

Treas., The Rev. Jim White

Major Activities: Cooperation among Religious Leaders; Lay-Clergy Retreats; Social Concerns Seminars; Disaster Task Force; Advocacy for Disadvantaged

MISSOURI

Council of Churches of the Ozarks

P.O. Box 3947, Springfield, MO 65808-3947, Tel. (417)862-3586, Fax (417)862-2129

Email: ccozarks@ccozarks.org

Website: www.ccozarks.org

Media Contact, Comm. Dir., Susan Jackson

Exec. Dir., Dr. David W. Hockensmith, Jr.

Chief Operating Officer, Julie Guillebeau

Major Activities: Ministerial Alliance; Child

Care Food Program-FDA Food Program; Child Care Resource & Referral; Connections Handyman Service; Crosslines-Food and Clothing Pantry; Daybreak Adult Day Care Center; Long-Term Care Ombudsman Programs; Ozarks Food Harvest; Retired and Senior Volunteer Program; Sigma House-Treatment Center for Alcohol and Drug Abuse; Therapeutic Riding of the Ozarks

Interfaith Community Services
200 Cherokee St., P.O. Box 4038, St. Joseph, MO 64504-0038, Tel. (816)238-4511, Fax (816)238-3274
Email: rsharp@inter.serv.org
Website: www.inter-serv.org
Media Contact, Exec. Dir., David G. Howery
Exec. Dir., David G. Howery Dir. of Operations, Randy Sharp
Major Activities: Child Development; Neighborhood Family Services; Immigration Services; Retired Senior Volunteer Program; Nutrition Program; Mobile Meals; Southside Youth Program; Church and Community; Housing Development; Homemaker Services to Elderly; Emergency Food, Rent, Utilities; AIDS Assistance; Family Respite; Family and Individual Casework

Interfaith Partnership of Metropolitan St. Louis
4144 Lindell Blvd Ste 221, St Louis, MO 63108, Tel. (314)531-4784, Fax (314)531-4785
Email: bdrodriguez@faithbeyondwalls.org
Website: http://www.interfaithpartnership.org/
Media Contact, Director of Service Learning and Projects, Mandy Ellis
Cabinet Chair, Cynthis Holmes
President, Rev. Dr. Dieter Heinzl
Executive Director, Beth Damsgaard-Rodriguez
Major Activities: Speaking out with a concerted faith voice on public issues
Celebrating our diversity encouraging respect for our faith traditions through interfaith dialogue, service projects, health initiatives and health care advocacy.
Projects that promote bridge building across racial, religious, and cultural divides, and health promotion through congregational health initiatives.

MONTANA

Montana Association of Churches*
25 South Ewing, Ste 408, Helena, MT 59601, Tel. (406)449-6010, Fax (406)449-6657
Email: montanachurches@earthlink.net
Website: www.montana-churches.org
Media Contact, Exec Dir.: The Rev. Dr. Brady J. Vardemann
Exec Dir.: The Rev. Dr. Brady J. Vardemann
Pres., Fr. Jay Peterson, Box 1399, Great Falls, MT 59403

President Elect: Dr. Walter Gulick, 2018 12th Street West, Billings, MT 59102
Treas., The Rev. Barbara Archer, 2210 Pryor Lane, Billings, MT 59102
Sec., The Rev. Kama Morton, P.O. Box 115, Choteau, MT 59422
Major Activities: Christian Unity; Lay Ministries Institute; Junior Citizen Camp; Montana Christian Advocates Network; Renewing the Public Church; Partnership For Rural Life; Health Ministries.

NEBRASKA

Interchurch Ministries of Nebraska*
215 Centennial Mall S., Suite 300, Lincoln, NE 68508-1888, Tel. (402)476-3391, Fax (402)202-2005
Email: im50427@winstream.net
Website: www.interchurchministries.org
Media Contact, Exec., Mrs. Marilyn P. Mecham
Pres., Rev. Roddy Dunkerson
Treas., Mr. Barry Hemmerling
Exec., Mrs. Marilyn Mecham
Adm. Asst., Sharon K. Kalcik
Major Activities: Planning and Development; Indian Ministry; Rural Church Strategy; United Ministries in Higher Education; Disaster Response; Rural Response Hotline; Health Ministry; Peace with Justice; Angel Connection; Domestic Violence Program; Social Ministries; Nurturing & Enhancing the Spiritual Tapestry, Ministry to Returning Military Persons and their Families

Lincoln Interfaith Council
140 S. 27th St., Ste. B, Lincoln, NE 68510-1301, Tel. (402)474-3017, Fax (402)475-3262
Email: mail@lincolninterfaith.org
Website: www.lincolninterfaith.org
Media Contact, Doug Boyd
Interim Coordinator, Kim Beyer Nelson
Pres., Sue Howe
Vice-Pres., Gene Crump
Sec., Stephanie Dohner
Treas.,Terri Lee
Major Activities: MLK, Jr. Observance; Week of Prayer Christian Unity; Festival of Faith & Culture; Holocaust Memorial Observance; Citizens Against Racism & Discrimination; Community organization; Multi-Faith & Multi-Cultural Training; New Clergy Orientation; Directory of Clergy, Congregations & Religious Resources; Multi-Faith Planning Calendar Publication

NEW HAMPSHIRE

New Hampshire Council of Churches*
140 Sheep Davis Road, Ste. 1, Pembroke, NH 03275, Tel. (603)224-1352, Fax (603)224-9161

247

Email: churches@nhchurches.org
Website: www.nhchurches.org
Media Contact, Exec. Dir., David Lamarre-Vincent, P.O. Box 1087, Concord, NH 03302-1087 Tel. (603)224-1352 Fax (603)224-9161, Email david@nhchurches.org
Pres., The Rev. David Yasenka, Triumphant Cross ELCA, 171 Zion's Hill Rd, Salem, NH 03079
Treas., Mr. Alvah Chisholm
Major Activities: Statewide Ecumenical Work For Christian Unity, Interfaith Understanding, and Social Justice

NEW JERSEY

Bergen County Council of Churches
58 James Street, Bergenfield, NJ 07621, Tel. (201)384-7505, Fax (201)384-2585
Email: bergenccc@hotmail.com
Website: www.bergenccc.org
Media Contact, Pres., Rev. Dr. Stephen T. Giordano, Clinton Avenue Reformed Church, Clinton Ave. & James St., Bergenfield, NJ 07621 Tel. (201)384-2454 Fax (201)384-2585
Exec. Sec., Anne Annunziato
Major Activities: Ecumenical and Religious Institute; Brotherhood-Sisterhood Breakfast; Center for Food Action; Homeless Aid; Operation Santa Claus; Aging Services; Boy & Girl Scouts; Easter Dawn Services; Music; Youth; Ecumenical Representation; Support of Chaplains in Jails & Hospitals; Faith & Values Online project www.njfaithandvalues.org; Welfare into Workplace

Ecclesia
700 West State St., Trenton, NJ 08618, Tel. (609)394-9229, Fax (609)394-8231
Email: team@teamtrenton.org
Media Contact, Sec., Mrs. Tina Swan
Pres., Rev. Joseph P. Ravenell
Campus Chaplains- Rev. Nancy Schulter; Rev. Robert Wittin, Rev. Richard Kocses
Major Activities: Racial Justice; Children & Youth Ministries; Advocacy; CROP Walk; Ecumenical Worship; Hospital Chaplaincy; Church Women United; Campus Chaplaincy; Congregational Empowerment; Prison Chaplaincy; Substance Abuse Ministry Training

Metropolitan Ecumenical Ministry
525 Orange St., Newark, NJ 07107, Tel. (973)485-8100, Fax (973)485-1165
Media Contact, Consultant, Rev. M. L. Emory
Exec. Dir., C. Stephen Jones
Major Activities: Community Advocacy (education, housing, environment); Church Mission Assistance; Community and Clergy Leadership Development; Economic Development; Affordable Housing

Metropolitan Ecumenical Ministry Community Development Corp.
525 Orange St., Newark, NJ 07107, Tel. (973)481-3100, Fax (201)481-7883
Email: memcdc@juno.com
Media Contact,
Exec. Dir., Jacqueline Jones
Major Activities: Housing Development; Neighborhood Revitalization; Commercial-Small Business Development; Economic Development; Community Development; Credit Union; Home Ownership Counseling; Credit Repair; Mortgage Approval; Technical Assitance To Congregations

New Jersey Council of Churches*
176 W. State St., Trenton, NJ 08608, Tel. (609)396-9546, Fax (609)396-7646
Media Contact, Public Policy Dir., Joan Diefenbach, Esq.
Pres., Rev. Jack Johnson
Sec., Beverly McNally
Treas., Marge Christie
Major Activities: Racial Justice; Children's Issues; Theological Unity; Ethics Public Forums; Advocacy; Economic Justice

NEW MEXICO

Faith Community Assistance Center
P.O. Box 15517, Santa Fe, NM 87592, Tel. (505)438-4782, Fax (505)473-5637
Media Contact, Barbara A. Robinson
Major Activities: Faith Community Assistance Center; providing emergency assistance to the poor; Interfaith Dialogues-Celebrations-Visitations; Peace Projects; Understanding Hispanic Heritage; Newsletter

New Mexico Conference of Churches*
336 N Camino del Pueblo, P O Box 606, Bernalillo, NM 87004-0606, Tel. (505)867-2956, Fax (505)867-6379
Email: nmcc@nmchurches.org
Website: www.nmchurches.org
Media Contact, Exec. Dir., Rev. Barbara E Dua
Pres., Dr. Robert S. Turner
Treas., Robert Sandoval
Exec. Dir., Rev. Dr. Barbara E. Dua
Major Activities: Affordable Housing; Social Justice Coalitions; Spiritual Life & Ministries

NEW YORK

Brooklyn Council of Churches
125 Ft. Greene Place, Brooklyn, NY 11217, Tel. (718)625-5851, Fax (718)522-1231
Media Contact, Dir., Charles Henze
Program Dir., Charles Henze (Deacon)
Pres., The Rev. James H. Eggleston
Treas., The Rev. Charles H. Straut , Jr.

Major Activities: Education Workshops; Food Pantries; Hospital and Nursing Home Chaplaincy; Church Women United; Legislative Concerns; Directory of Churches; Ecumenical Dialogue

Broome County Council of Churches, Inc.
William H. Stanton Center, 3 Otseningo St., Binghamton, NY 13903, Tel. (607)724-9130, Fax (607)724-9148
Email: mfrick@broomecouncil.net
Website: www.broomecouncil.net
Media Contact, Rev. Dr. Murray Frick
Exec. Dir., Rev. Dr. Murray Frick
Exec. Asst., Brigitte Stella
Hospital Chaplains, Betty Pomeroy; Rev. David Rockwell
Jail Chaplain, Rev. Cris Mogenson
Aging Ministry Coord., Linda McColgin
CHOW Prog. Coord., Wendy Primavera
Pres., Dr. Thomas Kelly
Treas., Rey Hull
Caregiver Program Coord., Joanne Kays
Community and Donor Relations, Dir., Dr. Murray Frick
Major Activities: Hospital and Jail Chaplains; Youth and Aging Ministries; Broome Bounty (Food Rescue Program); Emergency Hunger & Advocacy Program; Faith & Family Values; Ecumenical Worship and Fellowship; Media; Community Affairs; Peace with Justice; Day by Day Marriage Prep Program; Interfaith Coalition; Interfaith Volunteer Caregiver Program

Capital Area Council of Churches, Inc.
646 State St., Albany, NY 12203-1217, Tel. (518)462-5450, Fax (518)462-5450
Email: capareacc@aol.com
Website: www.capareacc.org
Media Contact, Admin. Director, Kitt Jackson
Exec. Dir., Rev. John U. Miller
Admn. Dir., Kitt Jackson
Pres., Rev. Paul Rees-Rohrbacher
Treas., William Hedberg
Major Activities: CROP Walk; Jail and Court Ministries; Martin Luther King Memorial Service and Scholarship Fund; Emergency Shelter for the Homeless; Campus Ministry; Ecumenical Dialogue; Forums on Social Concerns; Peace and Justice Education; Inter-Faith Programs; Legislative Concerns; Comm. Thanksgiving Day and Good Friday Services; Annual Ecumenical Musical Celebration

Capital Region Ecumenical Organization (CREO)
102 Arrow Wood Place, Malta, NY 12020, Tel. (518)729-0278, Fax (518)382-7505
Email: mishamarvel@gmail.com
Media Contact, Coord., Misha Marvel

Ian Leet, President (RCA)
Barbara DiTommaso, Vice President (RC)
Kay Victorson, Treasurer (ELCA)
Ms. Kitt Jackson, Secretary (RCA)
Misha Marvel, Coordinator (RCA/ELCA)
Major Activities: Promote Cooperation-Coordination Among Member Judicatories and Ecumenical Organizations in the Capital Region in Urban Ministries, Social Action.

Chautaugua County Rural Ministry
127 Central Ave., P.O. Box 362, Dunkirk, NY 14048, Tel. (716)366-1787, Fax (716)366-1787
Email: ccrm@netsync.net
Website: www.ccrm.netsync.net
Media Contact,
Exec. Dir., Kathleen Peterson
Major Activities: Chautaugua County Food Bank; Collection-Distribution of Furniture, Clothing, & Appliances; Homeless Services; Advocacy for the Poor; Soup Kitchen; Emergency Food Pantry; Thrift Store

Concerned Ecumenical Ministry to the Upper West Side
286 Lafayette Ave., Buffalo, NY 14213, Tel. (716)882-2442, Fax (716)882-2477
Email: information@cembuffalo.org
Website: www.cembuffalo.org
Media Contact, Exec. Dir., The Rev. Catherine Rieley-Goddard
Pres., Mr. Peter Hogan
Major Activities: Community Center Serving Youth, Families, Seniors and the Hungry

Cortland County Council of Churches, Inc.
7 Calvert St., Cortland, NY 13045, Tel. (607)753-1002, Fax (607)758-8780
Email: cortlandchurches@gmail.com
Media Contact, Office Mgr., Joy Niswender
Exec. Dir., The Rev. Donald M. Wilcox
Major Activities: College Campus Ministry; Hospital Chaplaincy; Nursing Home Ministry; Newspaper Column; Interfaith Relationships; Hunger Relief; CWS; Crop Walk; Leadership Education; Community Issues; Mental Health Chaplaincy; Grief Support; Jail Ministry

Council of Churches of Chemung County, Inc.
1009 Maple Ave., Elmira, NY 14901, Tel. (607)733-4374, Fax (607)734-2294
Email: ecumenic2000@yahoo.com
Media Contact, Exec. Dir., Joan Geldmacher, Tel. (607)734-7622
Exec. Dir., Joan Geldmacher
Pres., Rev. Ann Taylor, 115 Dewitt, Elmira, NY 14901
Major Activities: CWS Collection; CROP Walk; UNICEF; Institutional Chaplaincies; Radio,

249

Easter Dawn Service; Communications Network; Produce & Distribute Complete Church Directories; Representation on Community Boards and Agencies; Ecumenical Services; Interfaith Coalition; Taskforce on Children & Families; Compeer; Interfaith Hospitality Center

Council of Churches of the City of New York

475 Riverside Dr., Rm. 727, New York, NY 10115, Tel. (212)870-1020, Fax (212)870-1025
Email: cccny@cccny.net
Website: www.cccny.net
Media Contact, Exec. Dir., Rev. Jimmy Seong G. Lim
Exec. Dir., Rev. Jimmy Seong G. Lim
Pres., The Rev. A. R. Bernard, Sr.
1st Vice-Pres., Mr. G. Morris Gurley, Esq.
2nd Vice-Pres., The Rev. Arabella Meadows-Rogers
3rd Vice-Pres., Bishop Norman N. Quick
Sec., The Rev. N. J. "Skip" L'Heureux
Treas., The Rev. Dr. Adolfo Carrion, Sr.
Major Activities: Clergy Training, Radio & TV; Pastoral Care; Christ for the World Chapel, Kennedy International Airport; Coordination and Strategic Planning; Interfaith Coordinator, Religious Conferences; Interfaith Commission of Religious Leaders; Referral & Advocacy; Youth Development; Directory of Churches and Database Available

Dutchess County Interfaith Council, Inc.

9 Vassar St., Poughkeepsie, NY 12601, Tel. (845)471-7333, Fax (845)471-5253
Email: dic@bestweb.net
Website: www.dutchessinterfaithcouncil.org
Media Contact, Exec. Dir., The Rev. Philip Carr-Harris
Exec. Dir., The Rev. Philip Carr-Harris
Pres., Rabbi Paul Golumb
Treas., Amy Harding King
Major Activities: CROP Hunger Walk; Interfaith Music Festival; Public Worship Events; Interfaith Story Circles; Oil Purchase Group; Tour Of Houses Of Worship; Weekly Radio Program; Racial Unity Work; Poverty Forums

Genesee County Churches United, Inc.

P.O. Box 547, Batavia, NY 14021, Tel. (716) 343-6763
Media Contact, Pres.,Captain Leonard Boynton, Salvation Army, 529 East Main St., Batavia, NY 14020 Tel. (716)343-6284
Pres., James Woodruff
Exec. Sec., Cheryl Talone
Chaplain, The Rev. Peter Miller
Major Activities: Jail Ministry; Food Pantries; Serve Needy Families; Radio Ministry; Pulpit

Exchange; Community Thanksgiving; Ecumenical Services at County Fair

Genesee-Orleans Ministry of Concern

Arnold Gregory Memorial Complex, Suite 271
243 South Main St., Albion, NY 14411, Tel. (585)589-9210, Fax (585)589-9617
Email: gomoc1@rochester.rr.com
Media Contact, Exec. Dir., Malika Hill
Exec. Dir., Malika Hill
Pres., John W. Cebula, Esq.
Vice Pres., Rev. Joseph Fifagrowicz
Sec., Jane Balbick
Treas., Mary Grace Demarse
Major Activities: Advocacy Services for the Disadvantaged, Homeless, Ill, Incarcerated and Victims of Family Violence; Emergency Food, Shelter, Utilities, Medicines, just Friends (a mentoring program for children), Parenting Program, Furniture Program.

Greater Rochester Community of Churches

2 Riverside St., Rochester, NY 14613-1222, Tel. (585)254-2570, Fax (585)254-6551
Email: grcc1@frontiernet.net
Website: www.grcc.org
Media Contact, Executive Director, Marie E. Gibson
Dr. Marvin K. Mich, President
Rev. Debbie Grohman, VP for Program and Discipleship
Robert Crystal, VP for Organization
Rev. William Wilkinson, VP for Social Justice Ministry
Alberta Moss, Secretary
Kenneth Anderson, Treasurer
Elizabeth LeValley SSJ, Officer-at-Large
Major Activities: Faith-based information-resources for the greater Rochester area; Social Justice Ministry; Anti-Racism and Peace initiatives; Ecumenical Worship; Interfaith Health Care Coalition; Commission on Christian Jewish Relations, Commission on Christian Muslim Relations, Faith in Action Celebration; Rochester's Religious Community Directory.

InterFaith Works of Central New York

3049 E. Genesee St., Syracuse, NY 13224, Tel. (315)449-3552, Fax (315)449-3103
Email: mbowles@interfaithworkscny.org
Website: www.interfaithworkscny.org
Media Contact, Dir. of Advancement, Ms. Sarah Beth Lardie
Executive Dir., Dr. James B. Wiggins
Pres., Mr. Dennis R. Baldwin
CFO, John Ashby
Director for Resource Development, Ms. Sarah Beth Lardie
Spiritual Care Program Director, The Rev. Roberta Yackel

Center for New Americans, Dir., Ms. Hope Wallis
Senior Companion Prog., Dir., Mr. Larry Crinnin
Covenanat Housing Prog., Dir., Ms. Marilyn Woyciesjes
Community Wide Dialogue on Racism, Beth Broadway
InterFaith Works News, Ed., Ms. Sarah Beth Lardie
Major Activities: Pastoral Ministries; Community Ministries; Interrreligious and Ecumenical Relations; Diversity Education; Worship; Community Advocacy and Planning

The Long Island Council of Churches

1644 Denton Green, Hempstead, NY 11550, Tel. (516)565-0290, Fax (516)565-0291
Email: licchemp@aol.com
Website: www.ncccusa.org/ecmin/licc
Media Contact, Exec. Dir., Thomas W. Goodhue
Exec. Dir., Rev. Thomas W. Goodhue
Pastoral Care, Dir., Rev. Richard Lehman
Community Resources Dir., Alric Kennedy, Tel. (516)565-0390 ext. 204
Nassau County Ofc., Social Services Sec., Yolanda Murray
Suffolk County Ofc., Food Program & Family Support, Carolyn Gumbs, Tel: (631)727-2210
Major Activities: Pastoral Care in Jails; Emergency Food; Family Support & Advocacy; Advocacy for Peace & Justice; Church World Service; Multifaith Education; Clergy-Laity Training; Newsletter; Church Directory; AIDS Interfaith of Long Island

Network of Religious Communities

1272 Delaware Ave., Buffalo, NY 14209-2496, Tel. (716)882-4793, Fax (716)882-3797
Email: nrc@religiousnet.org
Website: www.ReligiousNet.org
Media Contact, Exec. Dir., CEO, Rev. Dr. G. Stanford Bratton
Exec. Dir. & CEO, The Rev. Dr. G. Stanford Bratton
Associate Executive., The Rev. Francis X. Mazur (Ecumenical Officer, Diocese of Buffalo-Roman Catholic)
Co-Presidents, Marlene Clickman (Judaism); Rev. Dr. Kenneth Neal, Western NY Churches in Covenant (Disciples of Christ/United Church of Christ)
Immediate Past President, Rev. Frances Manly, Unitarian/Universalist
Vice-Pres. For Outreach, Deacon James Anderson, National Baptist
Vice-Pres. For Administration, Rev. Merle Showers, Niagara Frontier District, United Methodist Church
Vice-Pres. For Finance, Dr. ViJay Chakravarthy (Hindu Cultural Society)
Vice-Pres. For Program, Dr. Douglas Bunker, Church of Jesus Christ of Latter Day Saints

Secretary, Ms. Susan Dayton, Church of Jesus Christ of Latter Day Saints
Treasurer, Dr. Nasir Khan, Ahmadiyya Muslim Community
Chpsn., Interreligious Concerns, Dr. Othman Shibly, Islamic Society of the Niagara Frontier
Chpsn., Personnel, The Rev. Tim Ashton, Unitarian/Universalist
Chpsn., Membership, The Rev. Jeff Carter (Pentecostal)
Chpsn., Christian Concerns, The Rev. Robert Grimm (United Church of Christ)
Chpsn., Communications, Mr Faizan Haq,Islamic Cultural Association WNY
Chpsn., Riefler Enablement Fund, Rev. Charles Bang (Evangelical Lutheran Church in America)
Chpsn., Public Issues, Ms Judy Metzger, Episcopal Diocese of WNY
Chpsn., Religious Leaders Forum, The Rev. Paul Litwin (Chancelor, Diocese of Buffalo - Roman Catholic)
Chpsn., Church Women United, Ms. Norma Roscover (Presbytery WNY)

STAFF (Other than Executive Directors)
Financial/office administrator, Ms. Bonnie Jehle
Church Women United Coordinator, Ms. Sally Giordano
Food For All, Coordinator, Ms. Kelly Kowalski
Nutrition Outreach, Marlyn Moore
Major Activities: Regionwide Interreligious Conversation, Hunger Advocacy, Food Distribution, Food Stamp Promotion and coordination, Roll Call Against Racism, Ecumenical and Interreligious Relations and Celebrations, Radio-TV Broadcast and Production (3 TV and 2 weekly radio Programs), Indigenous Women's Initiative, Church Women United, Festivals of Faiths, Community Development, Yom Hashoah Commemoration Service, Aids Memorial Service, Police-Community Relations, CROP Walks, Interfaith Thanksgiving Service. Spirituality and End of Life Care Training for Medical Students, Spirituality and Health Initiative, U.S.-Canadian Border Policy and enforcement issues, Legal action against opening of Casino in Buffalo Area.

New York State Council of Churches, Inc.*

18 Computer Dr. West, Suite 107, Albany, NY 12205, Tel. (518)436-9319, Fax (518)427-6705
Email: nyscoc@nycap.rr.com
Website: www.nyscoc.org
Media Contact, Ms. Mary Lu Bowen
Executive Dir., Ms. Mary Lu Bowen
Pres., The Rev. Dr. Clint McCoy
Vice Pres., Bishop Marie C. Jerge
Corp. Sec., The Rev. Dr. Jon Norton
Treas., The Rev. Dr. John Hiemstra
Convener of Collegium, Linda Chidsey

STAFF:
Coordinator of Chaplaincy Services, Ms. Damaris McGuire
Public Policy Consultant, The Rev. Daniel Hahn
Communications Consultant, The Rev. Daniel Hahn
Admin. Asst., Sylvenia F. Cochran Book Keeper, Charlene Schaffer
Major Activities: State Chaplaincy; Public Policy Advocacy in the following areas, Anti-Racism; Campaign Reform; Criminal Justice System Reform; Disability; Ecomomic-Social Justice; Environmental; Health care; Homelessness-Shelter; Hunger-Food; Immigrant Issues; Public Education; Rural Issues; Substance Abuse; Violence; Women's Issues; Peace

The Niagara Council of Churches Inc.

St. Paul UMC, 723 Seventh St., Niagara Falls, NY 14301, Tel. (716)285-7505
Media Contact, Pres., Nessie S. Bloomquist, 7120 Laur Rd., Niagara Falls, NY 14304 Tel. (716)297-0698 Fax (716)298-1193
Exec. Dir., Ruby Babb
Pres., Nessie S. Bloomquist
Treas., Shirley Bathurst
Trustees Chpsn., The Rev. Vincent Mattoni, 834 19th St., Niagara Falls, NY 14304
Major Activities: Ecumenical Worship; Bible Study; Christian Ed. & Social Concerns; Church Women United; Evangelism & Mission; Institutional Min. Youth Activities; Hymn Festival; Week of Prayer for Christian Unity; CWS Projects; Audio-Visual Library; UNICEF; Food Pantries and Kitchens; Community Missions, Inc.; Political Refugees; Eco-Justice Task Force; Migrant-Rural Ministries; Interfaith Coalition on Energy

Queens Federation of Churches

86-17 105th St., Richmond Hill, NY 11418-1597, Tel. (718)847-6764, Fax (718)847-7392
Email: qfc@queenschurches.org
Website: www.queenschurches.org
Media Contact, The Rev. N. J. L'Heureux, Jr.
Exec. Dir., The Rev. N. J. L'Heureux, Jr.
York College Chaplain, The Rev. Dr. Henrietta Fullard
Pres., Shirley K. Ford, Rev Lois B. Stewart
Treas., Annie Lee Phillips
Major Activities: Queens Interfaith Hunger Network—Emergency Food Service; York College Campus Ministry; Scouting & Youth Ministry; Christian Education Workshops; Plan-ning and Strategy; Church Women United; Com-munity Consultations; Seminars for Church Leaders; Online Directory of Congregations; Christian Relations (Prot-RC); Chaplaincies; Public Policy Issues; N.Y.S. Interfaith Commis-sion on Landmarking of Religious Property; "The Nexus of Queens" (online, weekly newspaper)

Rural Migrant Ministry

P.O. Box 4757, Poughkeepsie, NY 12602, Tel. (845)485-8627, Fax (845)485-1963
Email: rmmhope3@aol.com
Website: ruralmigrantministry.org
Media Contact, Exec. Dir., Rev. Richard Witt
Exec. Dir., The Rev. Richard Witt
Pres., Melinda Trotti
Major Activities: Serving the Rural Poor and Migrants Through a Ministry of Advocacy & Empowerment; Youth Program; Latino Committee; Organization and Advocacy with and for Rural Poor and Migrant Farm Workers

Schenectady Inner City Ministry

930 Albany St., Schenectady, NY 12307-1514, Tel. (518)374-2683, Fax (518)382-1871
Email: INFORMATION@SICM.US
Website: www.sicm.us
Media Contact, Janet Mattis
Urban Agent, Rev. Phillip N. Grigsby
Business Manager, Barbara Bieniek
Emergency Food, Gail Van Vallenburgh
Pres., John Held
Damien Center, Daniel Butterworth
Summer Food, Crystal Hamelink
Housing Task Force, Rev. Phil Grigsby
Spiritually Sound and Physically Fit, Rev. Phillip Grugsby Safe Parks and Eligible Playgrounds, Rev. Dr. Van I. W. Stuart Healthy Homes and Healthy People, Nancy Peterson
Major Activities: Food Security; Advocacy; Housing; Neighborhood and Economic Issues; Ecumenical Worship and Fellowship; Community Research; Education in Congregations on Faith Responses to Social Concerns; Legislative Advocacy; CROP Walk; HIV-AIDS Ministry; Summer Lunch for Youth; Study Circles Initiative on Embracing Diversity; Community Crisis Nework; Housing Services and Advocacy; Youth Initiative; After-School Program; Committee for Social Justice; Theological Center; Computer for Kids; Faith Based Nutrition and Wellness; Environmental Justice

Southeast Ecumenical Ministry

25 Westminster Rd., Rochester, NY 14607, Tel. (585)271-5350, Fax (585)271-8526
Email: sem@frontiernet.net
Media Contact, Laurie Jenkins
Dir., Laurie Jenkins
Pres., Ronald K. Fox
Major Activities: Transportation of Elderly & Disabled; Emergency Food Cupboard for Case Managers to access for their clients; Supplemental Nutrition Program for seniors;Community Health and Pharmacy Partnership (CHAPP).

Staten Island Council of Churches

2187 Victory Blvd., Staten Island, NY 10314, Tel. (718)761-6782
Email: sicoc@verizon.net

252

Media Contact, Pres., Rev. Virginia Kaada, 2187 Victory Blvd., Staten Island, NY 10314 Tel. (718)761-6782
Pres., The Rev. Virginia Kaada
Exec. Sec., Rebekah A. Ellis
Major Activities: Congregational Support & Outreach; Education & Pastoral Care; Ecumenical & Interfaith Witness; Social Witness

Troy Area United Ministries
392 Second St., Troy, NY 12180, Tel. (518)274-5920, Fax (518)271-1909
Email: info@TAUM.org
Website: www.taum.org
Media Contact, Exec. Dir., Rev. Donna Elia
Pres., Rev. Arthur Hagy Jr.
Chaplain, R.P.I. And Russel Sage, Rev. Beth Illingworth
Damien Center, Dir., Terri Conhue
Furniture Program, Dir., Michael Barrett
Major Activities: College Ministry; CROP Walk; Homeless and Housing Concerns; Community Worship Celebrations; Racial Relations; Furniture Program; Damien Center of Troy Hospitality for persons with HIV-AIDS; Computer Ministries; Youth Ministry

Wainwright House
260 Stuyvesant Ave., Rye, NY 10580, Tel. (914)967-6080, Fax (914)967-6114
Email: frandavies@wainwright.org
Website: www.wainwright.org
Media Contact, Exec. Dir., Fran Davies
Exec. Dir., Fran Davies
Pres., Robert Laughlin
Vice-Pres., Michael Standen
Major Activities: Educational Programs, Retreat and Conference Center; Intellectual, Psychological, Physical and Spiritual Growth; Healing and Health

NORTH CAROLINA

Asheville-Buncombe Community Christian Ministry (ABCCM)
30 Cumberland Ave., Asheville, NC 28801, Tel. (828)259-5300, Fax (828)259-5923
Email: srogers@abccm.org
Website: www.abccm.org
Media Contact, Exec. Dir., Rev. Scott Rogers, Fax (828)259-5323
Exec. Dir., The Rev. Scott Rogers
Pres., Stephen Williamson
Major Activities: Crisis Ministry; Jail-Prison Ministry; Shelter Ministry; Medical Ministry

Greensboro Urban Ministry
305 West Lee St., Greensboro, NC 27406, Tel. (910)271-5959, Fax (910)271-5920
Email: Guministry@aol.com
Website: www.greensboro.com/gum
Media Contact, Exec. Dir., Rev. Mike Aiken
Exec. Dir., The Rev. Mike Aiken

Major Activities: Emergency Financial Assistance; Emergency Housing; Hunger Relief; Inter-Faith and Inter-Racial Understanding; Justice Ministry; Chaplaincy with the Poor

North Carolina Council of Churches*
Methodist Bldg., 1307 Glenwood Ave., Suite 156, Raleigh, NC 27605-3256, Tel. (919)828-6501, Fax (919)828-9697
Email: nccofc@nccouncilofchurches.org
Website: www.nccouncilofchurches.org
Media Contact, Comm. Assoc., Aleta Payne
Exec. Dir., The Rev. J. George Reed
Program Associate, Steve Smith
Program Associate, Denise Long
Program Associate, Barbara Zelter
Communications Associate, Aleta Payne
Health Program Associate, Dr. Gordon DeFriese
Pres., The Rev. Michael Cogsdale, 806 College Ave., Lenoir, NC 28645
Treas., Dr. James W. Ferree, 168 Brook Landing Drive Winston-Salem, NC 27106
Climate Connection Associate, Alice Boyd
Program Associates, Jason Jenkins, Rollin Russell
Major Activities: Health Care Justice; Christian Unity; Legislative Program; Farmworker Ministry; Rural Crisis; Racial and Ethnic Justice; Climate Change; Public Education; Economic Justice; Peace

NORTH DAKOTA

North Dakota Conference of Churches*
9195 70th Avenue, SE, Ashley, ND 58413-9600, Tel. (701)647-2063
Email: exe_sec.ndcc@yahoo.com
Website: ndconference.org
Media Contact, Exec. Sec., Renee Gopal
Pres., Bishop Paul Zipfel
Vice Pres. I, Dr. Wade Schemmel
Vice Pres. II, Grace Wisthoff
Treas., The Rev. Michael Hicken
Secretary, Bishop Duane Danielson
Major Activities: Rural Life Ministry; Faith and Order; North Dakota 101; Victims & Offenders Ministry; Rural Life Convocation; Restorative Justice

OHIO

Akron Area Association of Churches
800 East Market Street, Akron, OH 44305-2424, Tel. (330)535-3112, Fax (330)374-5041
Email: akronchurches@earthlink.net
Website: www.triple-ac.org
Media Contact, Exec. Dir., Chloe Ann Kriska
Bd. of Trustees, Pres., Rev. Dr. J. Wayman Butts
Vice-Pres., The Rev. Mark Frey
Sec., Dale Kline

253

Treas., Ms. Sherrie Petrochuk

Major Activities: Messiah Sing; Interfaith Council; Newsletters; Resource Center; Community Worship; Training of Local Church Leadership; Radio Programs; Clergy and Lay Fellowship Luncheons; Neighborhood Development; Community Outreach; Church Interracial Partnerships; Pastor Peer Group Program; Advocacy, Social Justice

Alliance of Churches

470 E. Broadway, Alliance, OH 44601, Tel. (330)821-6648, Fax (330)821-7288

Email: dcarter@fbcalliance.org

Media Contact, Dir., Lisa A. Oyster

Dir., Lisa A. Oyster

Pres., Rev. Bud Hoffman

Treas., Betty Rush

Major Activities: Christian Education; Community Relations & Service; Ecumenical Worship; Community Ministry; Peacemaking; Medical Transportation for Anyone Needing It; Emergency Financial Assistance

Churchpeople for Change and Reconciliation

Box 488, Lima, OH 45802-0488, Tel. (419)224-2086, Fax (419)224-2086

Media Contact, Exec. Dir., The Rev. Darwin Ralston

Exec. Dir., The Rev. Darwin Ralston

Major Activities: Developing Agencies for Minorities, Poor, Alienated and Despairing; Our Daily Bread Soup Kitchen

Council of Christian Communions of Greater Cincinnati

7030 Reading Road

Suite 642, Cincinnati, OH 45237, Tel. (513)351-6789, Fax (513)458-2252

Email: joellengrady@zoomtown.com

Website: www.cccgc.org

Media Contact, Exec. Dir., Joellen W. Grady

Exec. Dir., Joellen W. Grady

Justice Chaplaincy, Assoc. Dir., Rev. Jack Marsh

Educ., Assoc., Lillie D. Bibb

Pres., Rev. Damon Lynch III

Major Activities: Christian Unity & Interfaith Cooperation; Justice Chaplaincies; Police-Clergy Team; Adult and Juvenile Jail Chaplains; Religious Education

Greater Dayton Christian Connections

601 W. Riverview Ave., Dayton, OH 45406, Tel. (937)227-9485, Fax (937)227-9407

Email: gdcc@Christianconnections.org

Website: www.christianconnections.org

Media Contact, Exec. Dir., Rev. Darryl Fairchild

Exec. Dir., Rev. Darryl Fairchild

Major Activities: Ecumenical and Interfaith Dialogue; Peace Making; Environmental Justice; Racial Reconciliation; Pastoral Leadership Resources; Ministry Recruitment and Placement; Communication

Mahoning Valley Association of Churches

30 W. Front St., Youngstown, OH 44503, Tel. (330)744-8946, Fax (330)774-0018

Email: mvac@onecom.com

Media Contact, Exec. Dir., Elsie L. Dursi

Exec. Dir., Elsie L. Dursi

Pres., Rev. Joyce Lawson

Treas., Carol Williams

Major Activities: Communications; Christian Education; Ecumenism; Social Action; Advocacy

Metropolitan Area Church Council

760 E. Broad St., Columbus, OH 43205, Tel. (614)461-7103, Fax (614)280-0352

Email: church_council@yahoo.com

Media Contact, Exec. Dir., Alvin Hadley

President: The Rev. Melvin Richardson

Vice-Pres.: The Rev. Ken Coy

Secretary: Ms. Margaret Stansbery

Treasurer: Mr. Brian Shaffer

Exec. Dir.:Alvin Hadley

Major Activities: Newspaper; Published nine times annually; Annual Living Faiths Awards; Quarterly Racial unity Services; Clergy Hospital Indentification Badges; Community Computer Center; Social Concerns relating to human needs in our community; Older Adult ministries; Collaborations to facilitate unity among religious denominations.

Metropolitan Area Religious Coalition of Cincinnati

632 Vine Street, Suite 606, Cincinnati, OH 45202-2423, Tel. (513)721-4843, Fax (513) 721-4891

Email: marcc@fuse.net

Website: www.marcconline.com

Media Contact, Dir., Margaret A. Fox

Pres., Mr. William K. Woods

Dir., Rev. Duane Holm

Major Activities: Local social policy decisions chosen annually: 2008 - Collaborative Agreement/Justice Reform, Public Education

Ohio Council of Churches*

6230 Busch Blvd., Ste 430, Columbus, OH 43229-1879, Tel. (614)885-9590, Fax (614) 885-6097

Email: mail@ohcouncilchs.org

Website: www.ohcouncilchs.org

Media Contact,

Exec. Dir., The Rev. Rebecca J. Tollefson

Public Policy, Dir., Tom Smith

Major Activities: Economic & Social Justice; Ecumenical Relations; Health Care Reform; Theological Dialogue; Education; Environmental Stewardship, Anti-Gambling

Pike County Outreach Council
107-9 West Second Street, Waverly, OH 45690,
Tel. (740)941-4348
Email: pikecountyoutreachcouncil@yahoo.com
Website: www.pikecountyoutreach.com
Dir., Judy Dixon
Major Activities: Emergency Service Program;
Self Help Groups; Homeless Shelter, Food
Pantry

Toledo Area Ministries
444 Floyd St., Toledo, OH 43620, Tel. (419)242-
7401, Fax (419)242-7404
Email: santhony@tamohio.org
Website: www.tamohio.org
Media Contact, Executive Director, Rev. Stephen
D. Anthony
Major Activities: Ecumenical Relations;
Interfaith Relations; Food Program; Housing
Program; Social Action-Public Education;
Urban Ministry; Youth Leadership; Elimi-
nation of Discrimination

Tuscarawas County Council for Church and Community
1458 5th St. NW, New Philadelphia, OH 44663,
Tel. (330)343-6012, Fax (330)343-9845
Email: mooredj3@neohio.twebe.com
Website: www.tyeonline.net
Media Contact, Donna J. Moore
Exec. Dir., Donna J. Moore
Pres., Mrs. Agnes Swigart, 2514 Denise Dr NE,
New Philadelphia, OH 44663
Treas., James Barnhouse, 120 N. Broadway,
New Philadelphia, OH 44663
Major Activities: Human Services; Legislative
Concerns; Home Improvements; Character
Counts; Abstinence Education; Youth Boosters;
Emergency Assistance

West Side Ecumenical Ministry
5209 Detroit Ave, Cleveland, OH 44102, Tel.
(216)651-2037, Fax (216)651-4145
Email: Eotero@wsem.org
Website: www.wsem.org
Media Contact, Dir. of Marketing and Public
Relations, Kami L. Marquardt
Pres., & CEO, Judith Peters
Chief Operation Officer, Adam Roth
Major Activities: WSEM is dedicated to serving urban low-income families by providing
programs that encourage self-sufficiency.
Three food pantries and outreach centers, a
job-training program, early childhood,
preschool, and school-age child care, crisis
intervention, counseling, youth services, a
theatre education program and a senior nutrition program are among the services available. WSEM serves more than 56,000 children, families, and individuals annually with
a staffing of more than 300 employees and
3,200 volunteers.

OKLAHOMA

Oklahoma Conference of Churches*
301 Northwest 36th St., Oklahoma City, OK
73118, Tel. (405)525-2928, Fax (405)525-2636
Email: okchurches@okchurches.org
Website: www.okchurches.org
Media Contact, Joanne Kurklin, Email:
joanne.kurklin@okchurches.org
Exec. Dir., Joanne Kurklin
Pres., The Rev. Dr. Rockford Johnson
Major Activities: Christian Unity Issues;
Community Building Among Members; Rural
Community Care; Children's Advocacy; Day
at the Legislature; Impact; Criminal Justice;
Hunger & Poverty; Legislative Advocacy;
Aging; Women's Issues; Interfaith Coalition
and Activities

Tulsa Metropolitan Ministry
221 S. Nogales, Tulsa, OK 74127, Tel. (918)582-
3147, Fax (918)582-3159
Email: tummtulsa@aol.com
Website: www.TUMM.org
Media Contact, Exec. Dir., The Rev. James W.
Mishler
Exec. Dir., The Rev. James W. Mishler
Pres., The Rev. Marlin Lavanhar
Treas., Virginia Katz
Major Activities: Religious Understanding;
Legislative Issues; Christian Unity; Criminal
and Justice Issues; Committee against Racism;
Disability Awareness; Directory of Metropolitan
Religious Community; Airport Interfaith
Chapel; Native American Issues.

OREGON

Ecumenical Ministries of Oregon*
0245 S.W. Bancroft St., Ste. B, Portland, OR
97239, Tel. (503)221-1054, Fax (503)223-
7007
Email: emo@emoregon.org
Website: www.emoregon.org
Media Contact, Dir. of Development &
Communications, Carla Starrett Bigg
Exec. Dir., David A. Leslie
Finance and Administrative Services, Dir., Gary
B. Logsdon
Development & Communications, Carla Starrett
Bigg
Community Ministries, Lowen Berman
Sponsors Organized to Assist Refugees, Vesna
Vila
Russian Oregon Social Services, Yelena Hansen
Portland International Community School, Skip
Adams
Public Policy Dir., Kevin Finney
Interfaith Network for Earth Concerns, Jenny
Holmes
HIV Day Center, Lowen Berman
Shared Housing, Barbara Stone

255

Northeast Emergency Food Program, John Elizade

President, The Rev. Lowell Greathouse

Major Activities: Ecumenical Ministries of Oregon is a statewide association of Christian denominations—including Protestant, Roman Catholic and Orthodox bodies—congregations, ecumenical organizations and interfaith partners working together to improve the lives of Oregonians through community ministry programs, ecumenical and interreligious dialogue, environmental ministry and public policy advocacy.

PENNSYLVANIA

Allegheny Valley Association of Churches

1913 Freeport Rd., Natrona Heights, PA 15065, Tel. (724)226-0606, Fax (724)226-3197

Email: avac@avaoc.org

Website: www.avaoc.org

Media Contact, Exec. Dir., Karen Snair

Exec. Dir., Karen Snair

Pres., The Rev. Dr. W. James Legge

1st Vice President: The Rev James Gascoine

2nd Vice President: Mrs. Darlene Benn

Secretary: The Rev. Stephen Smalley

Treasurer: Mrs. Libby Grimm

Major Activities: Ecumenical Services; Dial-a-Devotion; Walk for Hunger; Food Bank; Emergency Aid; Cross-on-the-Hill; AVAC Hospitality Network for Homeless Families; Senior Citizen Housing-Pine Ridge Heights Senior Complex, AVAC Chaplaincy Program; Summer Camp for Children, Case Management, Faith-in-Action

Christian Associates of Southwest Pennsylvania

204 37th St., Suite 201, Pittsburgh, PA 15201, Tel. (412)688-9070, Fax (412)688-9091

Email: info@casp.org

Website: www.casp.org

Media Contact, Dir. of Television Ministry, Monica Kao

Exec., Dir., Rev. Dr. Donald B. Green

Chair of Council, Rev. Dr. Wayne Yost

Pres., Board of Delegates, Rev. Dr. Eric Brown

Executive Administrative Asst., Tracy Ritchie

Director of Television Ministry, Monica Kao

Television Studio Director, George Salopek

Director of Jail Chaplaincy Services, Chaplain Lynn Yeso Protestant Chaplain- Shuman Youth Detention Center, Rev. Floyd Palmer

Protestant Chaplains, Rev. Dallas Brown and Rev. Shawn Drummond

Catholic Chaplain, Fr. Malcolm McDonald Jail Administrative Assistant, Karen Mack

Major Activities: Jail Chaplaincy; Youth-Incarceration Chaplaincies; Theological Dialogue-Religious Education; Religious Leadership Forum; Christian Associates Television (CATV); The Call...Newsletter; Media Ministries Internet ministry; Indigent Burial program; Interfaith Dialogue; Disaster Preparedness and Response, Pre and Post Release Program for Jail Inmates

Christian Churches United of the Tri-County Area

413 South 19th St.

P.O. Box 60750, Harrisburg, PA 17106-0750, Tel. (717)230-9550, Fax (717)230-9554

Email: ccuhbg@aol.com

Website: www.ccuhbg.org

Media Contact, Exec. Dir., Jacqueline P. Rucker

Exec. Dir., Jacqueline P. Rucker

Pres., Wendi Taylor

Treas., Joseph J Fielder

Vice-Pres., Rev. Dr. Thomas Johnston

Sec., Mary P. Hafer

HELP & LaCasa Ministries, John Scarpato, Program Director, P.O. Box 60750, Harrisburg, PA 17106-0750 Tel. (717)238-2851 Fax (717)238-1916

Major Activities: Volunteer Ministries to Prisons; HELP (Housing, Rent, Food, Medication, Transportation, Home Heating, Clothing); La Casa de Amistad (The House of Friendship) Social Services; Prison Chaplaincy; Susquehanna Harbor Safe Haven (Homeless Shelter)

Christians United in Beaver County

1098 Third St., Beaver, PA 15009, Tel. (724)774-1446, Fax (724)774-1446

Email: cubc@access995.com

Media Contact, Exec. Sec., Lois L. Smith

Exec. Sec., Lois L. Smith

Chaplains- The Rev. Dennis Ugoletti; The Rev. Anthony Massey; The Rev. Arthur Peters; John Pusateri, Rev. Bertha Lay

Pres., Mrs. Delores Tisdale, 1021-5th Street, New Brighton, PA. 15066

Treas., Mr. Richard Puryear, 2 McCabe Street, Sewickley, PA. 15143

Major Activities: Christian Education; Evangelism; Social Action; Church Women United; United Church Men; Ecumenism; Hospital, Detention Home and Jail Ministry, Behavioral Health Clinic.

East End Cooperative Ministry

250 N. Highland Ave., Pittsburgh, PA 15206, Tel. (412)361-5549, Fax (412)361-0151

Email: eecm@eecm.org

Website: www.eecm.org

Media Contact, Exec. Dir., Myrna Zelenitz

Exec. Dir., Myrna Zelenitz

Ass. Dir., Rev. Darnell Leonard

Major Activities: Food Pantry; Soup Kitchen; Men's Emergency Shelter; Drop-In Shelter for Homeless; Meals on Wheels; Information and Referral; Programs for Children and Youth; Bridge Housing Program for Men and PennFree Housing for Women in Recovery

Ecumenical Conference of Greater Altoona

P.O. Box 771, Altoona, PA 16693, Tel. (814)942-0512, Fax (814)942-0512
Email: ecumenaltoona@charter.net
Media Contact, Exec. Dir., Susanna M. Tomlinson
Pres., Eillen Becker
Major Activities: Religious Education; Workshops; Ecumenical Activities; Religious Christmas Parade; Campus Ministry; Community Concerns; Peace Forum; Religious Education for Mentally Challenged, and Interfaith Committee

Hanover Area Council of Churches

136 Carlisle St., Hanover, PA 17331-2406, Tel. (717)633-6353, Fax (717)633-1992
Email: opsmanhacc@netrax.net
Website: www.hanoverareacouncilofchurches.org
Operations Manager, Carol Hinkle
Major Activities: Meals on Wheels, Provide a Lunch Program, Fresh Air Program, Clothing Bank, Hospital Chaplaincy Services; Congregational & Interfaith Relations, Public Ecumenical Programs and Services, State Park Chaplaincy Services & Children's Program; Compeer; Faith at Work; CROP Walk; Stolte Scholarship Fund; Community Needs; Cold Weather Shelter; AA

Inter-Church Ministries of Erie County

2216 Peach St., Erie, PA 16502, Tel. (814)454-2411, Fax (814)454-2412
Email: icm@icmeriecounty.com
Website: www.icmeriecounty.com
Pres., The Rev. Dr. Andrew Harvey
Treas., Mary C. Stewart
Major Activities: Local Ecumenism; Social Ministry; Continuing Education; North West Pennsylvania Conference of Bishops and Judicatory Execs.; Theological Dialogue; Coats for Kids; Voucher Program for Emergency Assistance; Worship; Advocacy

Lancaster County Council of Churches

344 N. Marshall St., Lancaster, PA 17602, Tel. (717)291-2261, Fax (717)291-2261
Email: office@lccouncilofchurches.org
Website: www.lccouncilofchurches.org
Media Contact, Interim Exec. Dir., Kenneth Trauger
Pres.: Steve Mentzer
Service Ministry Interim Director: Doug Hopwood
Major Activities: Social Ministries

Lebanon County Christian Ministries

250 S. 7th St., P.O. Box 654, Lebanon, PA 17042, Tel. (717)274-2601, Fax (717)274-1361
Email: info@lccm.us
Media Contact, Exec. Dir., Lillian Morales
Exec. Dir., Lillian Morales
Noon Meals Coord., Wenda Dinatale
Major Activities: H.O.P.E. (Helping Our People in Emergencies); Food & Clothing Bank; Free Meal Program; Commodity Distribution Program; Ecumenical Events

Lehigh County Conference of Churches

534 Chew St., Allentown, PA 18102, Tel. (610)433-6421, Fax (610)433-6421
Email: lccc@lcconfchurch.org
Website: www.lcconfchurch.org
Media Contact, Dir. of Dev., Ira Faro
Exec. Dir., The Rev. Dr. Christine L. Nelson
Pres., Ms. Joanne Gantz-Jalowiecki
1st Vice-Pres.,The Rev. Thomas Thomas
Sec., Mrs. Eunice Schermerhorn
Treas., Mr. Nelson Rabenold
Major Activities: Social Concerns and Action; Clergy Dialogues; Daybreak Drop-In-Center for Mental Health Adults; Soup Kitchen; Housing Advocacy Program; Pathways (Referral to Social Services); Street Ministry via Linkage; Homelessness Prevention; Pharmaceutical Assistance; Campbell Christian-Unity lecture; Clothing Distribution; Aspires Mentoring Program; Ecumenical & Interfaith Services; Homeless Supportive Services; CROPWalk

Lewisburg Council of Churches

5. S. Asper Place, Lewisburg, PA 17837, Tel. (570)524-2834
Media Contact, Guy Temple
139 Iron Cave Lane
Lewisburg, PA 17837
(570)-524-4877
President, Mrs. Gail Pepper, First Baptist Church, 51 S. 3rd St, Lewisburg, PA 17837; Tel. (570)524-7438
Treasurer, Mrs. Jan Temple, 139 Iron Cave Lane, Lewisburg, PA 17837; Tel. (570)524-4877
Major Activities: Supplementary and Emergency Food Pantries; Clothing Bank; CROP Walk; Week of Prayer for Christian Unity; Soup & Scripture Lenten Series; 3-hour Good Friday Service; Human Services Directory; Transient-Homeless Aid

Metropolitan Christian Council of Philadelphia

1501 Cherry St., Philadelphia, PA 19102-1429, Tel. (215)563-7854, Fax (215)563-6849
Email: geiger@mccp.org
Website: www.mccp.org
Media Contact, Assoc. Communications, Nancy L. Nolde

257

Exec. Dir., Rev. C. Edward Geiger
Assoc. Communications, Nancy L. Nolde
Office Mgr., Joan G. Shipman
Pres., Rev. Steven B. Laurence
First Vice-Pres., Rev. G. Daniel Jones
Treas., A. Louis Denton, Esq.
Major Activities: Congregational Clusters; Public Policy Advocacy; Communication; Theological Dialogue (Christian & Interfaith); Women's Issues

North Hills Youth Ministry Counseling Center
802 McKnight Park Dr., Pittsburgh, PA 15237, Tel. (412)366-1300, Fax (412)366-1333
Email: nhym@nhymcc.org
Website: www.nhymcc.org
Media Contact, Exec. Dir., Rev. Ronald B. Barnes
Exec. Dir., Ronald B. Barnes
Major Activities: Elementary, Junior and Senior High School Individual and Family Counseling; Elementary Age Youth Early Intervention Counseling; Educational Programming for Churches and Schools; Youth Advocacy; Parent Education; Marital Counseling; Tutoring for Elementary, Junior and Senior High Students; Healthy Communities-Healthy Youth Training and workshops based on Search Institutes (out of Mineapolis, MN); 40 Assets

Northside Common Ministries
P.O. Box 99861, Pittsburgh, PA 15233, Tel. (412)323-1163, Fax (412)323-1749
Email: NCM@city-net.com
Media Contact, Exec. Dir., Janet E. Holtz
Exec. Dir., Janet E. Holtz
Major Activities: Pleasant Valley Shelter for Homeless Men; Advocacy around Hunger, Housing, Poverty, and Racial Issues; Community Food Pantry and Service Center; Supportive Housing

Northwest Interfaith Movement
6757 Greene St., Philadelphia, PA 19119, Tel. (215)843-5600, Fax (215)843-2755
Email: jejohnson@nim-phila.org
Website: www.nim-phila.org
Media Contact, Exec. Dir., Rabbi George M. Stern
Exec. Dir., Rabbi George M. Stern
Chpsn., Judy Weinstein
Long Term Care Program, Dir., Donald Carlin
Neighborhood Child Care Resource Prog., Dir., Leslie S. Eslinger
Major Activities: Resources amd Technical Assistance for Child Care Programs; Conflict Mediation and Support for Nursing and Boarding Home Residents

Pennsylvania Conference on Interchurch Cooperation*
P.O. Box 2835, 223 North St., Harrisburg, PA 17105, Tel. (717)238-9613, Fax (717)238-1473

Email: staff@pacatholic.org
Website: www.pacatholic.org/ecumenism
Media Contact, Carolyn Astfalk
Co-Staff, Dr. Robert J. O'Hara, Jr., Rev. Gary Harke
Co-Chpsns., Bishop Joseph Martino; Bishop Donald Main.
Major Activities: Theological Consultation; Social Concerns; Public Policy; Conferences and Seminars

The Pennsylvania Council of Churches*
900 S. Arlington Ave., Ste. 100, Harrisburg, PA 17109-5089, Tel. (717)545-4761, Fax (717)545-4765
Email: pcc@pachurches.org
Website: www.pachurches.org
Media Contact, Exec. Dir.,The Rev. Gary L. Harke
Exec. Dir., The Rev. Gary L. Harke
Dir. of Public Advocacy, The Rev. Sandra L. Strauss
Dir. of Finance & Facilities, Janet A. Gulick
Pres., The Rev. Dr. Marjorie Coons-Torn
Vice-Pres., Bishop Gregory R. Pile
Sec., The Rev. Lavette Paige
Treas., Mr. David Hoffman, CPA
Major Activities: Inter-church dialogue; trade association activities; faith and order; seasonal farmworker ministry; trucker-traveler ministry; public policy advocacy and education; leisure ministry; conferences and continuing education events; disaster response

Project of Easton, Inc.
330 Ferry St., Easton, PA 18042, Tel. (215)258-4361, Fax 610)258.7502
Email: jkomisor@projecteaston.org
Pres., Dr. John H. Updegrove
Vice-Pres. Public Relations, Rev. Charles E. Staples
Vice-Pres. Operations, Don Follett
Sec., Rosemary Reese
Treas., Steve Barsony
Exec. Dir., Maryellen Shuman
Major Activities: Food Bank; Adult Literacy Program; English as a Second Language; Children's Programs; Parents as Student Support; CROP Walk; Interfaith Council; Family Literacy; Emergency Assistance; Even Start Family Literacy

Reading Berks Conference of Churches
519 Elm St., P.O.Box 957, Reading, PA 19603, Tel. (610)375-6108, Fax (610)375-6205
Email: rdgbrkscc@comcast.net
Website: www.readingberksconferenceof churches.com
Media Contact, Exec. Dir., Rev. Calvin Kurtz
Admin Asst., Donna Boyajcan
Exec. Dir., Rev. Calvin Kurtz

Pres., John Roland
Treas., William Maslo
Major Activities: Institutional Ministry; Social Action; CROP Walk for Hunger; Emergency Assistance; Prison Chaplaincy; Hospital Chaplaincy; Interchurch-Intercultural Services; Children & Youth Ministry; Healthy Family & Marriage Initiatives; Lazarus Project

South Hills Interfaith Ministries
1900 Sleepy Hollow Rd., South Park, PA 15129, Tel. (412)854-9120, Fax (412)854-9123
Website: www.shimcenters.org
Media Contact, Exec. Dir., Jerry Ellis
Prog. Dir., Director of Youth Programs, Sarah Henkel
Psychological Services, Don Zandier
Family Assistance Coordinator, Harry Dietz
Business Mgr., Amy Puglisi
Volunteer Coordinator, Barbara Houston
Major Activities: Basic Human Needs; Community Organization and Development; Inter-Faith Cooperation; Personal Growth; At-Risk Youth Development; Women in Transition; Elderly Support; After School Homework Club; Early Childhood Program (Pre-School); Interfaith Educational Programs & Observances

United Churches of Lycoming County
202 E. Third St., Williamsport, PA 17701, Tel. (570)322-1110, Fax (570)326-4572
Email: uclc@sunlink.net
Website: www.uclc.org
Media Contact, Exec. Dir., Rev. Gwen Nelson Bernstine
Exec. Dir., Rev. Gwen Nelson Bernstine
Ofc. Sec., Linda Winter
Pres., Rev. Maurice C. Frontz III, 324 South Howard Street, South Williamsport PA 17702
Treas., Mrs. Madeline Bird, 407 South Market Street, Muncy PA17756
Shepherd of the Streets, Rev. Dr. J. Morris Smith, 669 Center Street., Williamsport, PA 17701
Ecumenism, Dir., Rev. Maurice C. Frontz, 324 Howard Street, South Williamsport, PA 17702
Educ. Ministries, Dir., Mr. James Foran, 711 Edwin Street, Williamsport PA 17701
Institutional Ministry, Dir., Pastor Constance Waugh, 4570 Rt 87 Hwy, Williamsport PA 17701
Radio-TV, Dir., Rev. Dr. James Behrens, 1971 Lycoming Creek Rd., Williamsport, PA 17701
Prison Ministry, Dir., Mrs. Evadna Cline, 3336 West Fourth St., Williamsport, PA 17701
Christian Social Concerns, Dir., Pastor Kathy Behrens, 21 Casey Drive, Williamsport APA 17701
Major Activities: Ecumenism; Educational Ministries; Church Women United; Church World Service
and CROP; Prison Ministry; Radio-TV; Nursing Homes; Fuel Bank; Food Pantry;

Family Life; Shepherd of the Streets Urban Ministry; Peace Concerns; Housing Initiative; Interfaith Dialogue, Youth Ministry, Campus Ministry

Wilkinsburg Community Ministry
710 Mulberry St., Pittsburgh, PA 15221, Tel. (412)241-8072, Fax (412)241-8315
Email: wcm15221@juno.com
Website: trfn.clpgh.org/wcm
Media Contact, Dir., Rev. Vivian Lovingood
Acting Dir., Elizabeth Mulvaney, MSW, LSW
Pres. of Bd., Glenna Wilson, MSW, LSW
Major Activities: Hunger Ministry;Summer Reading Camp; Teen-Moms Infant Care; Meals on Wheels; Church Camp Scholarships; Utility Assistance; Clothing-Furniture Assistance; Case Management for Elderly Homebound Persons and Families, Soup Kitchen

Wyoming Valley Council of Churches
70 Lockhart St., Wilkes-Barre, PA 18702, Tel. (570)825-8543
Media Contact, Exec. Dir., Beth Titus
Exec. Dir., Beth Titus
Ofc. Sec., Sandra Karrott
Pres., Very Rev. Joseph Martin
Treas., Rev. Dr. Robert Zanicky
Major Activities: Nursing Home Chaplaincy; Hospital Referral Service; CROP Hunger Walk; Pastoral Care Ministries; Clergy Retreats and Seminars; Meals on Wheels Fuel Service; Citizen's Voice articles

York County Council of Churches
P.O. Box 1865, York, PA 17405-1865, Tel. (717)854-9504, Fax (717)843-5295
Email: ycccoffice@yccchurches.org
Website: www.yccchurches.org
Media Contact, Ryan Sttler, Chariman of P.R. Comm.
Pres., Rev. Patrick Rooney
Vice Pres., Major Darren Mudge
Exec. Dir., Rev. Guy W. Dunham
Major Activities: Educational Development; Spiritual Growth and Renewal; Worship and Witness; Congregational Resourcing; Outreach and Mission

RHODE ISLAND

The Rhode Island State Council of Churches*
100 Niantic Avenue Suite 101, Providence, RI 02907, Tel. (401)461-5558, Fax (401)461-5233
Email: riscc@councilofchurchesri.org
Website: www.councilof churchesri.org
Media Contact, Exec. Minister, Dr. Donald C. Anderson
Exec. Min., Dr. Donald C. Anderson
Admn. Asst., Dolores Taylor
Pres., Rev. Matthew Kai

259

Treas., George Weavill
Major Activities: Urban Ministries; Institutional Chaplaincy; Advocacy-Justice & Service; Legislative Liaison; Faith & Order; Community Network; Campus Ministries; Prison Ministry

SOUTH CAROLINA

South Carolina Christian Action Council, Inc.*
P.O. Drawer 3248, Columbia, SC 29230, Tel. (803)786-7115
Email: sccouncil@sccouncil.net
Website: www.sccouncil.net
Media Contact, Exec. Minister, Rev. Brenda Kneece
Exec. Minister, The Rev. Brenda Kneece
Pres., The Rev. Dr. Joseph Darby, AME Pastor
Secretary, The Rev. Terry Brooks, CBF
Treasurer, The Rev. Dr. Carl Evans, UMC
President Elect: Mrs. Melissa (Missie) Walker
Past President, Mrs. Debbie Dantzler, Attorney, CBF
Major Activities: Advocacy and Ecumenism; Continuing Education; Interfaith Dialogue; Citizenship and Public Affairs; Publications; Race Relations; Child Advocacy; Faith and Health; Environmental Stewardship

United Ministries
606 Pendleton St., Greenville, SC 29601, Tel. (864)232-6463, Fax (864)370-3518
Email: info@united-ministries.org
Website: www.united-ministries.org
Media Contact, Exec. Dir., Rev. Beth Templeton
Exec. Dir., The Rev. Beth Templeton
Pres., Nancy Orders Smith
Vice-Pres., Anne Ellefson
Sec., Becky Bouton
Treas., Lan Nix
Major Activities: Assistance with rent, utilities, prescriptions, food, heat; Place of Hope (A day shelter for people who are homeless); Assistance with getting and keeping jobs; A GED program for adults; Case Management as part of all activities, College assistance with books and scholarships.

SOUTH DAKOTA

Association of Christian Churches of South Dakota*
100 S. Spring Ave., Suite 106, Sioux Falls, SD 57104-3626, Tel. (605)334-1980
Email: office@accsd.org
Website: www.accsd.org
Media Contact, Gene E. Miller, 100 S. Spring Ave., Sioux Falls, SD 57104 Tel. (605)334-1980
Pres., Bd. of Directors, Ms. Ann Smith
Major Activities: Ecumenical Forums; Continuing Education for Clergy; Legislative Information;

Resourcing Local Ecumenism; Native American Issues; Ecumenical Fields Ministries; Rural Economic Development; Children at Risk

TENNESSEE

Metropolitan Inter Faith Association (MIFA)
P.O. Box 3130, Memphis, TN 38173-0130, Tel. (901)527-0208, Fax (901)527-3202
Website: www.mifa.org
Media Contact, Vice President, Public Relations, Elizabeth Garrett
Exec. Dir., Margaret Craddock
Major Activities: Emergency Services (Rent, Utility, Food, Clothing Assistance); Home-Delivered Meals and Senior Support Services; Youth Services; Homeless Programs

Tennessee Association of Churches*
103 Oak St., Ashland City, TN 37015, Tel. (615)792-4631
Ecumenical Admn., -vacant-
Pres., Rev. Steve Mosley
Treas., Paul Milliken
Major Activities: Faith and Order; Christian Unity; Social Concern Ministries; Governmental Concerns; Governor's Prayer Breakfast

Volunteer Ministry Center
103 South Gay St., Knoxville, TN 37902, Tel. (423)524-3926, Fax (423)524-7065
Media Contact, Exec. Dir., Angelia Moon
Exec. Dir., Angelia Moon
Pres., David Leech
Vice-Pres., John Moxham
Treas., Doug Thompson
Major Activities: Homeless Program; Food Line; Crisis Referral Program; Subsidized Apartment Program; Counselling Program; Parenting Education for Single Parents

TEXAS

Austin Area Interreligious Ministries
701 Tillery St., Ste. 8, Austin, TX 78705, Tel. (512)386-9145, Fax (512)385-1430
Email: aaim@ammaustin.org
Website: www.ammaustin.org
Media Contact, Chief Executive Officer, Tom Spencer
Exec. Dir., Susan Wills
Pres., Rev. Mel Waxler
Treas., Anita Maxwell
Major Activities: Youth at Risk Mentoring; Housing Rehabilitation; Broadcast Ministry; Interfaith Dialogues; Family Issues; Homeless Issues; Hunger Issues; Racial Reconciliation, ESL

Border Association for Refugees from Central America (BARCA), Inc.
P.O. Box 1725, Edinburg, TX 78540, Tel. (956)631-7447, Fax (956)631-7447
Email: barcainc@aol.com
Media Contact, Exec. Dir., Ninfa Ochoa-Krueger
Exec. Dir, Ninfa Ochoa-Krueger
Outreach Services, Dir., Juanita Ledesma
Major Activities: Direct assistance and referral service to Newly Arrived Indigent Immigrants & Refugees; Medical and Other Emergency Aid; Special Services to Children; Speakers on Refugee and Immigrant Concerns for Church; School and other social service agencies and Groups; Orientation, Advocacy and Legal Services for Immigrants and Refugees

Corpus Christi Metro Ministries
1919 Leopard St., P.O. Box 4899, Corpus Christi, TX 78469-4899, Tel. (361)887-0151, Fax (361)887-7900
Email: edseeger@ccmetrominstries.com
Website: www.ccmetroministries.com
Media Contact, Exec. Dir., The Reverend Robert G. Trache
Exec. Dir., The Reverend Robert G. Trache, Email; btrache@ccmetroministries.com
Admn. Dir., Ginger Flewelling-Leeds
Volunteer Dir., Ann Cox
Fin. Coord., Sue McCown
Loaves & Fishes Dir., Ray Gomez
Emergency Services Mgr., Ann Cox
Employment Dir., Larry Curtis
Health and Human Services, Dir., Ann Cox
Major Activities: Clothing Distribution, Employment Assistance, Healthcare, Homelessness/Shelter, and Hunger/Food Programs.

East Dallas Cooperative Parish
P.O. Box 720305, Dallas, TX 75372-0305, Tel. (214)823-9149, Fax (214)823-2015
Email: edcp@swbell.net
Media Contact, Exec. Dir., Nancy Jellinek
Pres., Debbie Thorpe
Major Activities: Emergency Food, Clothing, Job Bank; Medical Clinic; Legal Clinic, Tutorial Education; Home Companion Service; Pre-School Education; Hispanic Ministry; Activity Center for Low Income Older Adults; Pastoral Counseling; English Language Ministry, Pre-GED program

Greater Dallas Community of Churches
624 N. Good-Latimer #100, Dallas, TX 75204-5818, Tel. (214)824-8680, Fax (214)824-8726
Email: gdcc@churchcommunity.org
Media Contact, Exec. Dir., Rev. Elzie Odom
Exec. Dir., Rev. Elzie Odom
Assoc. Dirs.,

AmeriCorps-Building Blocks Dir., Venita Allen-Kent
Development Vice Pres., Charlotte Coyle
Pres.,Richard Selby
Treas., John Rutzler
Major Activities: Interdenominational, Interfaith and Interracial Understanding and Joint Work; AmeriCorps-Building Blocks (Direct Service to Develop Inner City Children, Youth & Families); Summer Food & Reading; Hunger; Peacemaking; Public Policy; Social Justice; Faith & Life; Children's Health Outreach; Child Advocacy; Dismantaling Racism

Interfaith Ministries for Greater Houston
3217 Montrose Blvd., Houston, TX 77006, Tel. (713)522-3955, Fax (713)520-4663
Media Contact, Exec. Dir., Betty P. Taylor
Exec. Dir., Betty P. Taylor
Pres., Charles R. Erickson
Development, Dir., Sharon Ervine
Assoc. Exec. Dir., Larry Norton
Treas., Fort D. Flowers, Jr.
Sec., Darlene Alexander
Major Activities: Community Concerns, Hunger; Older Adults; Families; Youth; Child Abuse; Refugee Services; Congregational Relations and Development; Social Service Programs, Refugee Services; Hunger Coalition; Youth Victim Witness; Family Connection; Meals on Wheels; Senior Health; RSVP; Foster Grandparents

North Dallas Shared Ministries
2530 Glenda Ln., #500, Dallas, TX 75229, Tel. (214)620-8696, Fax (214)620-0433
Media Contact, Exec. Dir., J. Dwayne Martin
Exec. Dir., J. Dwayne Martin
Pres., vacant
Major Activities: Emergency Assistance; Job Counseling; ESL

Northside Inter-Church Agency (NICA)
1600 Circle Park Blvd., Fort Worth, TX 76106-8943, Tel. (817)626-1102, Fax (817)626-9043
Email: nicaagency@sbcglobal.net
Website: www.nicaagency.org
Media Contact, Exec. Dir., Connie Nahoolewa
Exec. Dir., Connie Nahoolewa
Major Activities: Food; Clothing; Counseling; Information and Referral; Furniture and Household Items; Nutrition Education; Employment Services; Thanksgiving Basket Program; "Last Resort" Christmas Program; Community Networking; Ecumenical Worship Services; Volunteer Training; Newsletter; Senior Home Repairs; School Clothing Program; Advocacy; GED Preparation; Literacy; Computer Training; English as a Second Language

San Antonio Community of Congregations

1101 W. Woodlawn, San Antonio, TX 78201, Tel. (210)733-9159, Fax (210)733-5780
Email: sacommchurches@sbcglobal.net
Website: www.sacoc.info
Media Contact, Exec. Dir., Mrs. Jeanne Goodlin
Exec. Dir., Mrs. Jeanne Goodlin
Pres., Rev. Mike Cave
Major Activities: Infant Formula Program for "at risk" infants; Social Issues; Disaster Recovery; Marriage Education; Environmental Concerns; Sponsor annual CROP Walk for Hunger; Peace and Anti-Violence Initiatives

San Antonio Urban Ministries

535 Bandera Rd., San Antonio, TX 78228, Tel. (210) 431-6466, Fax (210) 431-6470
Email: administration@saum.org
Media Contact, Sue Kelly
Exec. Dir., Sue Kelly
Pres., Rev. Leslie Ellison
Major Activities: Homes for Discharged Mental Patients; After School Care for Latch Key Children; Christian Based Community Ministry

Southeast Area Churches (SEARCH)

P.O. Box 51256, Fort Worth, TX 76105, Tel. (817)531-2211
Exec. Dir., Dorothy Anderson-Develrow
Major Activities: Emergency Assistance; Advocacy; Information and Referral; Community Worship; School Supplies; Direct Aid to Low Income and Elderly

Tarrant Area Community of Churches

P.O. Box 11471, Fort Worth, TX 76110-0471, Tel. (817)534-1790, Fax (817)534-1995
Email: revkm@flash.net
Pres., Regina Taylor
Treas., Don Hoak
Exec. Dir., Dr. Kenneth W. McIntosh
Major Activities: Eldercare Program; Children's Sabbath Sponsorship; Week of Prayer for Christian Unity; CROP Walk for Hunger Relief; Community Issues Forums; Family Pathfinders

Texas Conference of Churches*

1033 La Posada, Ste. 125, Austin, TX 78752, Tel. (512)451-0991, Fax (512)451-5348
Email: tcc@txconfchurches.org
Website: www.txconfchurches.org
Media Contact, Comm. and Web Services, Caryn Wontor
Exec. Dir., Rev. Dr. George P. Bithos
Dir. of Business Administration, Caryn Wontor
Pres., Rev. Dr. T. Randall Smith

Major Activities: Faith & Order; Related Ecumenism; Christian-Jewish Relations; Church and Society Issues

United Board of Missions

1701 Bluebonnet Ave., P.O. Box 3856, Port Arthur, TX 77643-3856, Tel. (409)982-9412, Fax (409)985-3668
Media Contact, Admin. Asst., Carolyn Schwarr
Exec. Dir., Clark Moore
Pres., Glenda McCoy
Major Activities: Emergency Assistance (Food and Clothing, Rent and Utility, Medical, Dental, Transportation); Share a Toy at Christmas; Counseling; Back to School Clothing Assistance; Information and Referral; Hearing Aid Bank; Meals on Wheels; Super Pantry; Energy Conservation Programs; Job Bank Assistance to Local Residents Only

VERMONT

Vermont Ecumenical Council and Bible Society*

P.O. Box 728, Richmond, VT 05477, Tel. (802)434 -7307, Fax (802) 434-7306
Email: info@vecbs.org
Website: www.vecbs.org
Media Contact, Admin. Asst., Betsy Hardy
Exec. Officer, Dr. Linda Howe
Pres., The Rev. Robert Athas
Vice-Pres., Mr. Chistopher McCandles
Treas., Mrs. Mary Margaret Hamlin
Major Activities: Christian Unity; Bible Distribution; Social Justice; Committee on Faith and Order; Committee on Peace, Justice and the Integrity of Creation; Committee on Prayer and Worship

VIRGINIA

Virginia Council of Churches, Inc.*

1214 W. Graham Rd., Richmond, VA 23220-1409, Tel. (804)321-3300, Fax (804)329-5066
Email: barton@vacouncilofchurches.org
Website: www.vacouncilofchurches.org
Media Contact, Gen. Min., Rev. Jonathan Barton
President, The Rev. Tom Joyce Vice President, The Rev. Jim Parke
Treasurer, Vacant Secretary, Ms. Betty Altic Gen. Min., The Rev. Jonathan Barton Migrant Head Start, Dir., The Rev. Victor Gomez
Refugee Resettlement, Dir., The Rev. Richard D. Cline
Campus Ministry Forum, Coord., The Rev. Steve Darr
Major Activities: Faith and Order; Network Building & Coordination; Ecumenical Communications; Justice and Legislative Concerns; Educational Development; Rural Concerns; Refugee Resettlement; Migrant

262

Ministries and Migrant Head Start; Disaster Coordination; Infant Mortality Prevention

WASHINGTON

Associated Ministries of Tacoma-Pierce County

1224 South I St., Tacoma, WA 98405-5021, Tel. (253)383-3056, Fax (253)383-2672
Email: info@associatedministries.org
Website: www. associatedministries.org
Media Contact, Exec. Dir., Rev. David T. Alger
Dir. of Communications, Judy Jones
Pres., Rev. Arne Bergland
Vice-Pres., Danna Clancy
Sec., Connie Robey
Treas., Jeff Cunningham
Exec. Dir., Rev. David T. Alger
Deputy Dir., Diane Powers
Dir. of Mental Health Chaplaincy, Terry Mattock
Dir. of Project Interdependence, Valorie Crout
Dir. of Paint Tacoma-Pierce Beautiful, Sallie Shawl
Dir. of Development, Stephanie Paige Barnett
Dir. of Hilltop Action Coalition, Jeanie Peterson
Director of Communication and Education, Judy Jones
Program Manager of Pierce County Asset Building Coalition, Barbara Gorzinski
Major Activities: County-wide Hunger Walk; Hunger Awareness; Economic Justice; Religious Education; Social Service Program Advocacy; Communication and Networking of Churches; Housing; Paint Tacoma-Pierce Beautiful; Mental Health Chaplaincy; Theological Dialogue; Welfare to Work Mentoring; Hilltop Action Coalition; Compeer; Homelessness; Youth Ministry; Ecumenical Formation; Interfaith Roundtable, Domestic Violence Chaplain, Asset Building Coalition; Family Emergency Fund

Church Council of Greater Seattle

4 Nickerson Street, Seattle, WA 98109-1699, Tel. (206)525-1213, Fax (206)525-1218
Email: info@thechurchcouncil.org
Website: www.thechurchcouncil.org
Media Contact, Exec. Dir.,The Rev. Dr. Sanford Brown
Executive Dir., The Rev. Dr. Sanford Brown
Emergency Feeding Prog., Dir., Arthur Lee
Friend to Friend, Dir., Marilyn Soderquist
Youth Chaplaincy Program, Dir., Chaplain Rev. Benny Wright
The Sharehouse, Dir., Michal Nortness
The Homelessness Project, Dir., Nancy Dorman
Mission for Music & Healing, Dir., Susan Gallaher & Esther "Little Dove" John
Sound Youth-AmeriCorps, Dir., Cat Koehn
Academy of Religious Broadcasting, Dir., Rev. J. Graley Taylor
Board Chair,Verlene Jones
Board Treas., The Rev. Jeb Parr

Board Secretary, Susan Segall
Editor, The Source, Tricia Schug
Seattle Youth Garden Works, Dir.,Conner Sharpe
SW King County Mental Health Ministry, Dir., The Rev. Stephen Jones
JOY Initiative, Prog. Dir., Rick Jump
St. Petersburg- Seattle Sister Churches Program Chair, Nigel Taber-Hamilton
Asia Pacific Task Force, Contact Person, Akio Yanagihara
Self-Managed Housing Programs, Dir., Misti Uptain
Cuba Friendshipment Committee, Chair, Monica Zapeda
Palestinian Concerns Task Force, Chair, Constance Trowbridge
Interfaith Network of Concern for the People of Iraq, Chair, The Rev. Rich Gamble & Andrew Fung
Major Activities: Children; Youth & Families; Hunger Relief; Global Peace and Justice; Housing and Homelessness; Pastoral Care; Services for the Aging; Public Witness; Interfaith and Ecumenical Relations; Publisher of the The Source, monthly ecumenical newspaper

FaithTrust Institute

2400 N. 45th St, Suite 10, Seattle, WA 98103, Tel. (206)634-1903, Fax (206)634-0115
Email: info@faithtrustinstitute.org
Website: www.faithtrustinstitute.org
Media Contact, Ko-Eun Kim
Executive Director, Rev. Kathryn J. Johnson, kjohnson@faithtrustinstitute.org
Founder & Senior Analyst, Rev. Dr. Marie M. Fortune, mfortune@faithtrustinstitute.org
Director of Training & Education, Rev. Thelma Burgonio-Watson, burgonio@faithtrustinstitute.org
Director of the Jewish Program, Rabbi Cindy Enger, cenger@faithtrustinstitute.org
Clearinghouse Coordinator, Dinah Hall, dhall@faithtrustinstitute.org
Finance Director, Marion J. Ward
Major Activities: Training - Domestic Violence, Healthy teen relationships, Child Abuse, Sexual Abuse by Clergy and Religious Leaders, Sexual Violence Consultation - Expertise to develop policies to address and prevent sexual abuse by clergy, guidance on integrating issues of sexual and domestic violence into religious education Educational Materials - multicultural and multifaith educational materials, extensive resource catalog includes videos, books and curricula

The Interfaith Association of Snohomish County

2301 Hoyt, P.O. Box 12824, Everett, WA 98206, Tel. (206)252-6672
Email: admin@.tiasccom
Website: www.tiasc.com
Media Contact, Exec. Dir., Janet Pope

263

Exec. Dir., Janet Pope
Pres., William Comfort
Major Activities: Housing and Shelter;
Economic Justice; Hunger; Interfaith Worship
and Collaboration

Interfaith Council
1620 N. Monroe, Spokane, WA 99205, Tel.
(509)329-1410, Fax (509)329-1409
Email: info@interfaithnw.org
Website: www.interfaithnw.org
Media Contact, Dir.,Kateri Caron
Director: Kateri Caron
Board President: Stephen Rorie
Vice President: Elliot Fabric
Sec., Rev. Dr. Richard Erhardt
Major Activities: Camp PEACE; Multi-Cultural
Human Relations; High School Youth Camp;
Eastern Washington Legislative Conference;
CROP Walk; Interfaith Thanksgiving
Worship; Easter Sunrise Service; Dir. of
Churches & Community Agencies; Circle of
Caring (for Women in Domestic Violence);
Guatemala Dialogues

Interfaith Works
P.O. Box 1221, Olympia, WA 98507, Tel.
(360)357-7224
Email: InterfaithWorks@comcast.net
Website: www.interfaith-works.org
Media Contact, Exec. Dir., Kathy Erlandson
Exec. Dir., Kathy Erlandson
Pres., Jim Fulton
Treas., Paddy Mackin
Major Activities: Interfaith Relations; Social and
Health Concerns; Community Action; Social
Justice

Northwest Harvest-E. M. M.
P.O. Box 12272, Seattle, WA 98102, Tel.
(206)625-0755, Fax (206)625-7518
Email: nharvest@blarg.net
Website: www. northwestharvest.org
Media Contact, Comm. Affairs Dir., Ellen Hansen
Exec. Dir., Ruth M. Velozo
Chpsn., Patricia Barcott
Major Activities: Northwest Harvest (Statewide
Hunger Response); Cherry Street Food Bank
(Community Hunger Response); Northwest
Infants Corner (Special Nutritional Products
for Infants and Babies)

Washington Association of
Churches*
419 Occidental Ave. S., Ste. 201, Seattle, WA
98104-2886, Tel. (206)625-9790, Fax
(206)625-9791
Email: wac@thewac.org
Website: www.thewac.org
Media Contact, John C. Boonstra, Email boon-
stra@thewac.org
Exec. Min., Rev. John C. Boonstra, boonstra@
thewac.org

Director for Operations, Bette Schneider,
schneider@thewac.org
Major Activities: Faith and Order; Ecumenical
Dialogue; Justice Advocacy; Confronting
Poverty; Hunger Action; Legislation;
Denomi-national Ecumenical Coordination;
Theological Formation; Leadership Deve-
lopment; Immigrant Rights Advocacy; Racial
Justice Advocacy; International Solidarity;
Environmental Justice Advocacy; Tax Justice
Advocacy; Congregation Public Policy
Organizing

WEST VIRGINIA

Greater Fairmont Council of
Churches
P.O. Box 108, Fairmont, WV 26554, Tel.
(304)367-0962
Media Contact, Pres., Rev. Jeremiah Jasper
President, Rev. Jeremiah Jasper
Major Activities: Community Ecumenical
Services; Youth and Adult Sports Leagues;
CROP Walk Sponsor; Weekly Radio
Broadcasts

West Virginia Council of
Churches*
2207 Washington St. E., Charleston, WV 25311-
2218, Tel. (304)344-3141, Fax (304)342-1506
Email: wvcc@wvcc.org
Website: www.wvcc.org
Media Contact, Exec. Dir., The Rev. Dennis D.
Sparks, Tel. (304)344-3141; Email:
dsparks@wvcc.org
Assoc. Dir., Cheryl A. Ingraham, Tel. (304)344-
31cheryli@wvcc.org
Pres., Monsignor Fredrick Annie, Diocese of
Wheeling - Charleston, Tel. (304)233-0880
Vice Pres., Bishop Ernest Lgyht, WV
Conference of the United Methodist Church,
Tel. (304)344-8330
Treas., Rev. Dr. William "Bill" Wilson, WV
Conference of the United Methodist Church,
Tel. (304)244-8331
Sec.,Rev. Brian O'Donnel SJ, Wheeling Jesuit
University, Tel. (304)243-6242
Major Activities: Disaster Response; Faith and
Order; Family Concerns; Inter-Faith
Relations; Peace and Justice; Government
Concerns; Support Services Network

WISCONSIN

Christian Youth Council
1715-52nd St., Kenosha, WI 53140, Tel.
(262)654-6200 x120, Fax (414)652-4461
Media Contact, Exec. Dir., Steven L. Nelson
Exec. Dir., Steven L. Nelson
Sports Dir., Jerry Tappen
Outreach Dir., Linda Osborne
Accountant, Debbie Cutts

Class Director, Jill Cox
Pres. & Chmn. of Board, Lon Knoedler
Gang Prevention Dir., Sam Sauceda
Major Activities: Leisure Time Ministry;
Institutional Ministries; Ecumenical
Committee; Social Concerns; Outreach
Sports(with a Christian Philosophy)

Interfaith Conference of Greater Milwaukee

1442 N. Farwell Ave., Ste. 200, Milwaukee, WI
53202, Tel. (414)276-9050, Fax (414)276-
8442
Email: IFCGM@aol.com
Media Contact, Exec. Dir., Marcus White
Chpsn., Rev. Velma Smith
First Vice-Chair, Archbishop Rembert G.
Weakland
Second Vice-Chair, Rev. Charles Graves
Sec., Paula Simon
Treas., The Rev. Mary Ann Neevel
Exec. Dir., Marcus White
Consultant in Communications, Rev. Robert P.
Seater
Major Activities: Economic Issues; Racism,
CROP Walk; Public Policy; Suburban and
Urban Partnerships; TV Programming; Peace
and International Issues Committee; Annual
Membership Luncheon; Religion Diversity;
Restorative Justice

Madison-area Urban Ministry

2300 S. Park St. # 5, Madison, WI 53713, Tel.
(608)256-0906, Fax (608)256-4387
Email: mum@emum.org
Website: www.emum.org
Media Contact, Office Mgr., Linda Ketcham
Exec. Dir., Linda Ketcham
Major Activities: Community Projects;
Dialogue-Forums; Prisoner Re-Entry

Wisconsin Council of Churches*

750 Windsor St. Ste. 301, Sun Prairie, WI 53590-
2149, Tel. (608)837-3108, Fax (608)837-3038
Email: wcoc@wichurches.org
Website: www.wichurches.org
Media Contact,
Exec. Dir., Exec. Dir., Scott D. Anderson
Public Policy Coordinator, Dr. Peter Bakken
Coordinator for Local Ecumenism, The Rev.
Kenneth Pennings
Pres., Bishop James Justman
Treas., Dr. Robert Bock
Accountant, Rick Fluechtling
Coordinator for Program Support Services, Mr.
Christopher Marceil
Major Activities: Anti-racism, Christian
Education, Domestic Violence, Economic/
Social Justice, Environmental, Faith & Order,
Healthcare, Housing/ Homelessness/Shelter,
Hunger/Food Programs, Immigrant Services,
Public Education, Rural Issues, Theology &
Worship

WYOMING

Wyoming Association of Churches*

1131 13th St., Suite 210, Cody, WY 82414, Tel.
(307)527-7026, Fax (307)527-4737
Email: wychurches@wyoming.com
Website: www.wyomingassociationofchurches.org
Media Contact, The Rev. Warren Murphy,
Director
Dir., Rev. Warren Murphy
Chair, The Rev. Tim Trippel
Treasurer, Maia Rose
Admin. Assistant, Rose Hackett
Major Activities: Alternatives to Violence;
Beyond Tolerance; Malicious Harrasment;
Domestic Violence; Empowering the Poor
and Oppressed; Peace and Justice; Public
Health Issues; Welfare Reform; Anti-Death
Penalty, Community Networking Facili-
tation, Environmental Justice

Index of Select Programs for U.S. Regional and Local Ecumenical Bodies

For many years the Yearbook of American & Canadian Churches has published the previous chapter, The Directory of U.S. Regional and Local Ecumenical Bodies. Each entry of that directory contains a brief description of the diverse programs offered by each agency. However, researchers, pastors, service organizations and theological seminaries often inquire about specific programs and which agencies carry out such programs. In response we have created this chapter, which indexes the various regional and local ecumenical agencies by twenty-five different program areas. These program areas are the twenty-five that have been the most frequent subjects of inquiry in our office. We have collected this program information directly from these organizations by means of a simple response form. There is an enormous diversity of ministries and missions conducted by these diverse organizations. Most organizations pursue several kinds of programs at once. However, some of these may focus their efforts most especially on only one of their programs; their other programs may be less well developed than their specialty. Consequently, the extent to which any of these ministries is a priority for any particular organization cannot be inferred from this list. For detailed information about the nature and extent of any particular ministry, the reader is urged to contact the organization directly using the directory of "U.S. Regional and Local Ecumenical Bodies," which is found in the pages just prior to this index.

AIDS/HIV Programs

Arizona Ecumenical Council—Phoenix, AZ
Center City Churches—Hartford, CT
Christian Churches United of the Tri-County Area—Harrisburg, PA
The Council of Churches of Santa Clara County—San Jose, CA
East Dallas Cooperative Parish—Dallas, TX
Ecumenical Ministries of Oregon—Portland, OR
Grand Rapids Area Center for Ecumenism (GRACE)—Grand Rapids, MI
Greater Chicago Broadcast Ministries—Chicago, IL
Interfaith Community Services—St. Joseph, MO
Interfaith Federation of Greater Baton Rouge—Baton Rouge, LA
Metropolitan Ecumenical Ministry—Newark, NJ
Network of Religious Communities—Buffalo, NY
The Regional Council of Churches of Atlanta—Atlanta, GA
Schenectady Inner City Ministry—Schenectady, NY
Southeast Ecumenical Ministry—Rochester, NY
Troy Area United Ministries—Troy, NY
Wyoming Valley Council of Churches—Wilkes-Barre, PA
York County Council of Churches—York, PA

Anti-Gambling Programs

The Associated Churches of Fort Wayne & Allen County, Inc.—Fort Wayne, IN
Associated Ministries of Tacoma-Pierce County—Tacoma, WA
Association of Christian Churches of South Dakota.—Sioux Falls, SD
The Cape Cod Council of Churches, Inc.—Hyannis, MA
Christian Associates of Southwest Pennsylvania—Pittsburgh, PA

Ecumenical Ministries of Iowa (EMI)—Des Moines, IA
Genesee County Churches United, Inc.—Batavia, NY
Greater Chicago Broadcast Ministries—Chicago, IL
Greater Lawrence Council of Churches—Lawrence, MA
The Joint Religious Legislative Coalition—Minneapolis, MN
Kentuckiana Interfaith Community—Louisville, KY
Kentucky Council of Churches—Lexington, KY
Mahoning Valley Association of Churches—Youngstown, OH
Massachusetts Council of Churches—Boston, MA
Mississippi Religious Leadership Conference—Jackson, MS
Montana Association of Churches—Helena, MT
Network of Religious Communities—Buffalo, NY
New Mexico Conference of Churches—Bernalillo, NM
The Pennsylvania Council of Churches—Harrisburg, PA
Texas Conference of Churches—Austin, TX
United Churches of Lycoming County—Williamsport, PA
Washington Association of Churches—Seattle, WA
West Virginia Council of Churches—Charleston, WV
Worcester County Ecumenical Council—Worcester, MA
Wyoming Association of Churches—Cody, WY

Anti-Racism Programs

Akron Area Association of Churches—Akron, OH
Arizona Ecumenical Council—Phoenix, AZ
Associated Ministries of Tacoma-Pierce County—Tacoma, WA

266

Association of Christian Churches of South Dakota—Souix Falls, SD

Association of Religious Communities—Danbury, CT

Austin Area Interreligious Ministries—Austin, TX

Broome County Council of Churches, Inc.—Binghamton, NY

The Capitol Region Conference of Churches—Hartford, CT

Christian Associates of Southwest Pennsylvania—Pittsburg, PA

Christian Ministries of Delaware County—Muncie, IN

The Church Federation of Greater Indianapolis, Inc.—Indianapolis, IN

Colorado Council of Churches—Denver, CO

Community Emergency Assistance Program (CEAP)—Brooklyn Park, MN

Cooperative Metropolitan Ministries—Newton, MA

Council of Churches of the City of New York—New York, NY

The Council of Churches of Greater Bridgeport, Inc.—Bridgeport, CT

The Council of Churches of Santa Clara County—San Jose, CA

Council of Churches and Synagogues of Southwestern Connecticut—Stamford, CT

Dutchess County Interfaith Council, Inc.—Poughkeepsie, NY

East Dallas Cooperative Parish—Dallas, TX

Ecclesia—Trenton, NJ

Ecumenical Conference of Greater Altoona—Altoona, PA

Evanston Ecumenical Action Council—Evanston, IL

Faith Community Assistance Center Santa Fe, NM

FaithTrust Institute—Seattle, WA

Fresno Metro Ministry—Fresno, CA

Georgia Christian Council—Macon, GA

Grand Rapids Area Center for Ecumenism (GRACE)—Grand Rapids, MI

Greater Birmingham Ministries—Birmingham, AL

Greater Chicago Broadcast Ministries—Chicago, IL

Greater Dallas Community of Churches—Dallas, TX

Greater Dayton Christian Connections—Dayton, OH

Greater Minneapolis Council of Churches—Minneapolis, MN

Greater Rochester Community of Churches—Rochester, NY

Greensboro Urban Ministry—Greensboro, NC

Illinois Conference of Churches—Springfield, IL

Indiana Partners for Christian Unity and Mission—Indianapolis, IN

Inter-Church Council of Greater New Bedford—New Bedford, MA

Interfaith Conference of Greater Milwaukee—Milwaukee, WI

InterFaith Conference of Metropolitan Washington—Washington, DC

Interfaith Council—Spokane, WA

Interfaith Federation of Greater Baton Rouge—Baton Rouge, LA

Inter-Faith Ministries-Wichita—Wichita, KS

Interfaith Mission Service—Huntsville, AL

Interfaith Service Bureau—Sacramento, CA

InterFaith Works of Central New York—Syracuse, NY

The Joint Religious Legislative Coalition—Minneapolis, MN

Kansas Ecumenical Ministries—Topeka, KS

Kentuckiana Interfaith Community—Louisville, KY

Kentucky Council of Churches—Lexington, KY

Lincoln Interfaith Council—Lincoln, NE

The Long Island Council of Churches—Hempstead, NY

Louisiana Interchurch Conference—Baton Rouge, LA

Madison-area Urban Ministry—Madison, WI

Mahoning Valley Association of Churches—Youngstown, OH

Massachusetts Council of Churches—Boston, MA

The Metropolitan Christian Council: Detroit-Windsor—Detroit, MI

Metropolitan Christian Council of Philadelphia—Philadelphia, PA

Metropolitan Ecumenical Ministry—Newark, NJ

Metropolitan Interfaith Council on Affordable Housing (MICAH)—Minneapolis, MN

Minnesota Council of Churches—Minneapolis, MN

Mississippi Religious Leadership Conference—Jackson, MS

Montana Association of Churches—Helena, MT

Network of Religious Communities—Buffalo, NY

New Britain Area Conference of Churches (NEWBRACC)—New Britain, CT

New Hampshire Council of Churches—Pembroke, NH

New Mexico Conference of Churches—Bernalillo, NM

North Carolina Council of Churches—Raleigh, NC

Northern California Interreligious Conference—Oakland, CA

Northside Common Ministries—Pittsburgh, PA

Oklahoma Conference of Churches—Oklahoma City, OK

The Regional Council of Churches of Atlanta—Atlanta, GA

St. Matthews Area Ministries—Louisville, KY

Saint Paul Area Council of Churches—St. Paul, MN

South Carolina Christian Action Council, Inc.—Columbia, SC

South Hills Interfaith Ministries—South Park, PA

Tarrant Area Community of Churches—Fort Worth, TX

Texas Conference of Churches—Austin, TX

Tri-Council Coordinating Commission—Minneapolis, MN

267

Troy Area United Ministries—Troy, NY
Tulsa Metropolitan Ministry—Tulsa, OK
United Churches of Lycoming County—
Williamsport, PA
Vermont Ecumenical Council and Bible
Society—Richmond, VT
Virginia Council of Churches, Inc.—Richmond,
VA
Wainwright House—Rye, NY
Washington Association of Churches—Seattle,
WA
West Virginia Council of Churches—Charleston,
WV
Wisconsin Council of Churches—Sun Prairie, WI
Wyoming Association of Churches—Cody, WY

Christian Education Programs

Akron Area Association of Churches—Akron,
OH
Arizona Ecumenical Council—Phoenix, AZ
Arkansas Interfaith Conference—Scott, AR
The Associated Churches of Fort Wayne & Allen
County, Inc.—Fort Wayne, IN
Associated Ministries of Tacoma-Pierce
County—Tacoma, WA
Attleboro Area Council of Churches, Inc.—
Attleboro, MA
Berrien County Association of Churches—
Benton Harbor, MI
Brooklyn Council of Churches—Brooklyn, NY
Christian Ministries of Delaware County—
Muncie, IN
Christians United in Beaver County—Beaver,
PA
Colorado Council of Churches—Denver, CO
The Council of Churches of Santa Clara
County—San Jose, CA
Council of Churches and Synagogues of
Southwestern Connecticut—Stamford, CT
East Dallas Cooperative Parish—Dallas, TX
Ecclesia—Trenton, NJ
Ecumenical Conference of Greater Altoona—
Altoona, PA
Ecumenical Council of San Diego County—San
Diego, CA
FaithTrust Institute—Seattle, WA
Georgia Christian Council—Macon, GA
Grand Rapids Area Center for Ecumenism
(GRACE)—Grand Rapids, MI
Greater Chicago Broadcast Ministries—
Chicago, IL
Greater Dayton Christian Connections—Dayton,
OH
Greater Fairmont Council of Churches—
Fairmont, WV
Greater Flint Council of Churches—Flint, MI
Greater Lawrence Council of Churches—
Lawrence, MA
Greater New Orleans Federation of Churches—
New Orleans, LA
Greensboro Urban Ministry—Greensboro, NC
Inter-Church Council of Greater New Bedford—
New Bedford, MA
Iowa Religious Media Services—Urbandale, IA

InterFaith Works of Central New York—
Syracuse, NY
Iowa Religious Media Services—Urbandale, IA
Marin Interfaith Council—San Rafael, CA
The Metropolitan Christian Council: Detroit-
Windsor—Detroit, MI
Metropolitan Christian Council of
Philadelphia—Philadelphia, PA
Metropolitan Ecumenical Ministry—Newark, NJ
Montana Association of Churches—Helena, MT
New Britain Area Conference of Churches
(NEWBRACC)—New Britain, CT
New Hampshire Council of Churches—
Pembroke, NH
New Mexico Conference of Churches—
Bernalillo, NM
Northern Kentucky Interfaith Commission,
Inc.—Newport, KY
Oklahoma Conference of Churches—Oklahoma
City, OK
Peoria Friendship House of Christian Service—
Peoria, IL
Reading Berks Conference of Churches—
Reading, PA
The Regional Council of Churches of Atlanta—
Atlanta, GA
San Antonio Community of Congregations—San
Antonio, TX
Staten Island Council of Churches—Staten
Island, NY
Tarrant Area Community of Churches—Fort
Worth, TX
Texas Conference of Churches—Austin, TX
Troy Area United Ministries—Troy, NY
United Churches of Lycoming County—
Williamsport, PA
Wainwright House—Rye, NY
Weekday Christain Education—Evansville, IN
Wisconsin Council of Churches—Sun Prairie,
WI
Wyoming Association of Churches—Cody, WY
Wyoming Valley Council of Churches—Wilkes-
Barre, PA

Clothing Distribution Programs

Asheville-Buncombe Community Christian
Ministry (ABCCM)—Asheville, NC
Associated Ministries of Tacoma-Pierce
County—Tacoma, WA
Attleboro Area Council of Churches, Inc.—
Attleboro, MA
The Cape Cod Council of Churches, Inc.—
Hyannis, MA
Chautauqua County Rural Ministry—Dunkirk,
NY
Christian Ministries of Delaware County—
Muncie, IN
Christian Service Center for Central Florida,
Inc.—Orlando, FL
Community Emergency Assistance Program
(CEAP)—Brooklyn Park, MN
Community Ministry of Montgomery County—
Rockville, MD
Contact Ministries of Springfield—Springfield, IL

268

Cooperative Metropolitan Ministries—Newton, MA

Corpus Christi Metro Ministries—Corpus Christi, TX

Council of Churches of the Ozarks—Springfield, MO

Cross-Lines Cooperative Council—Kansas City, KS

East Dallas Cooperative Parish—Dallas, TX

Eastern Area Community Ministries—Louisville, KY

The Ecumenical Council of Pasadena Area Churches—Pasadena, CA

Ecumenical Ministries of Oregon—Portland,OR

Evanston Ecumenical Action Council—Evanston, IL

Fern Creek-Highview United Ministries—Louisvlle, KY

Greater Birmingham Ministries—Birmingham, AL

Greater Fairmont Council of Churches—Fairmont, WV

Greater Lawrence Council of Churches—Lawrence, MA

Greater Minneapolis Council of Churches—Minneapolis, MN

Greensboro Urban Ministry—Greensboro, NC

Hanover Area Council of Churches—Hanover, PA

Highlands Community Ministries—Louisville, KY

Inter-Church Ministries of Erie County—Erie, PA

Interfaith Community Services—St. Joseph, MO

Lebanon County Christian Ministries—Lebanon, PA

Lewisburg Council of Churches—Lewisburg, PA

Madison-area Urban Ministry—Madison, WI

Metropolitan Ecumenical Ministry—Newark, NJ

New Mexico Conference of Churches—Bernalillo, NM

Northside Inter-Church Agency (NICA)—Fort Worth, TX

Peoria Friendship House of Christian Service—Peoria, IL

Reading Berks Conference of Churches—Reading, PA

St. Matthews Area Ministries—Louisville, KY

Saint Paul Area Council of Churches—St. Paul, MN

South East Associated Ministries (SEAM)—Louisville, KY

South Hills Interfaith Ministries—South Park, PA

Tuscarawas County Council for Church and Community—New Philadelphia, OH

West Side Ecumenical Ministry—Cleveland, OH

Wilkinsburg Community Ministry—Pittsburgh, PA

CROP Walks

Akron Area Association of Churches—Akron, OH

Asheville-Buncombe Community Christian Ministry (ABCCM)—Asheville, NC

Associated Ministries of Tacoma-Pierce County—Tacoma, WA

Attleboro Area Council of Churches, Inc.—Attleboro, MA

Austin Area Interreligious Ministries—Austin, TX

Berrien County Association of Churches—Benton Harbor, MI

Broome County Council of Churches, Inc.—Binghamton, NY

Capital Area Council of Churches, Inc.—Albany, NY

Chautaugua County Rural Ministry—Dunkirk, NY

Christian Ministries of Delaware County—Muncie, IN

Christian Service Center for Central Florida, Inc.—Orlando, FL

Church Community Services—Elkhart, IN

Churches United, Inc.—Cedar Rapids, IA

Churches United of the Quad City Area—Rock Island, IL

Community Emergency Assistance Program (CEAP)—Brooklyn Park, MN

The Council of Churches of Greater Bridgeport, Inc.—

Council of Churches of Greater Springfield—Springfield, MA

The Council of Churches of Santa Clara County—San Jose, CA

Dutchess County Interfaith Council, Inc.—Poughkeepsie, NY

East Dallas Cooperative Parish—Dallas, TX

East End Cooperative Ministry—Pittsburgh, PA

Ecclesia—Trenton, NJ

The Ecumenical Council of Pasadena Area Churches—Pasadena, CA

Ecumenical Ministries of Oregon—Portland, OR

Evanston Ecumenical Action Council—Evanston, IL

Greater Dayton Christian Connections—Dayton, OH

Greater Fairmont Council of Churches—Fairmont, WV

Greater Flint Council of Churches—Flint, MI

Greater Waterbury Interfaith Ministries, Inc.—Waterbury, CT

Greensboro Urban Ministry—Greensboro, NC

Hanover Area Council of Churches—Hanover, PA

Inter-Church Ministries of Erie County—Erie, PA

Interfaith Conference of Greater Milwaukee—Milwaukee, WI

Interfaith Council—Spokane, WA

Interfaith Council of Contra Costa County—Walnut Creek, CA

Inter-Faith Ministries-Wichita—Wichita, KS

Interfaith Works—Olympia, WA

Lebanon County Christian Ministries—Lebanon, PA

Lewisburg Council of Churches—Lewisburg, PA

The Long Island Council of Churches—Hempstead, NY

Mahoning Valley Association of Churches—Youngstown, OH

Marin Interfaith Council—San Rafael, CA

The Metropolitan Christian Council: Detroit-Windsor—Detroit, MI

Metropolitan Ecumenical Ministry—Newark, NJ

Muskegon County Cooperating Churches—Muskegon, MI

Network of Religious Communities—Buffalo, NY

New Mexico Conference of Churches—Bernalillo, NM

Northside Inter-Church Agency (NICA)—Fort Worth, TX

Oak Park-River Forest Community of Congregations—Oak Park, IL

Peoria Friendship House of Christian Service—Peoria, IL

Pike County Outreach Council—Waverly, OH

Reading Berks Conference of Churches—Reading, PA

Saint Paul Area Council of Churches—St. Paul, MN

San Antonio Community of Congregations—San Antonio, TX

San Fernando Valley Interfaith Council—Chatsworth, CA

Schenectady Inner City Ministry—Schenectady, NY

South Coast Interfaith Council—Long Beach, CA

Staten Island Council of Churches—Staten Island, NY

Tarrant Area Community of Churches—Fort Worth, TX

Troy Area United Ministries—Troy, NY

Tuscarawas County Council for Church and Community—New Philadelphia, OH

United Churches of Lycoming County—Williamsport, PA

United Religious Community of St. Joseph County—South Bend, IN

Virginia Council of Churches, Inc.—Richmond, VA

Weekday Christain Education—Evansville, IN

Wilkinsburg Community Ministry—Pittsburgh, PA

Worcester County Ecumenical Council—Worcester, MA

Wyoming Association of Churches—Cody, WY

Wyoming Valley Council of Churches—Wilkes-Barre, PA

York County Council of Churches—York, PA

Domestic Violence

Arizona Ecumenical Council—Phoenix, AZ

Asheville-Buncombe Community Christian Ministry (ABCCM)—Asheville, NC

Associated Ministries of Tacoma-Pierce County—Tacoma, WA

Association of Religious Communities—Danbury, CT

Border Association for Refugees from Central America (BARCA), Inc.—Edinburg, TX

Chautaugua County Rural Ministry—Dunkirk, NY

Churches United of the Quad City Area—Rock Island, IL

Colorado Council of Churches—Denver, CO

Contact Ministries of Springfield—Springfield, IL

The Council of Churches of Santa Clara County—San Jose, CA

Dutchess County Interfaith Council, Inc.—Poughkeepsie, NY

The Ecumenical Council of Pasadena Area Churches—Pasadena, CA

Ecumenical Council of San Diego County—San Diego, CA

Ecumenical Ministries of Oregon—Portland, OR

FaithTrust Institute—Seattle, WA

Genesee-Orleans Ministry of Concern—Albion, NY

Greater Chicago Broadcast Ministries—Chicago, IL

Greater Minneapolis Council of Churches—Minneapolis, MN

Indiana Partners for Christian Unity and Mission—Indianapolis, IN

Inter-Church Council of Greater New Bedford—New Bedford, MA

Interchurch Ministries of Nebraska—Lincoln, NE

Interfaith Council—Spokane, WA

Interfaith Service Bureau—Sacramento, CA

The Long Island Council of Churches—Hempstead, NY

The Metropolitan Christian Council: Detroit-Windsor—Detroit, MI

Metropolitan Ecumenical Ministry—Newark, NJ

Metropolitan Inter Faith Association (MIFA)—Memphis, TN

Mississippi Religious Leadership Conference—Jackson, MS

Network of Religious Communities—Buffalo, NY

New Hampshire Council of Churches—Pembroke, NH

New Mexico Conference of Churches—Bernalillo, NM

North Hills Youth Ministry Counseling Center—Pittsburgh, PA

Oklahoma Conference of Churches—Oklahoma City, OK

Peoria Friendship House of Christian Service—Peoria, IL

Saint Paul Area Council of Churches—St. Paul, MN

Southeast Ecumenical Ministry—Rochester, NY

Troy Area United Ministries—Troy, NY

Tulsa Metropolitan Ministry—Tulsa, OK

United Religious Community of St. Joseph County—South Bend, IN

Vermont Ecumenical Council and Bible Society—Richmond, VT

West Side Ecumenical Ministry—Cleveland, OH

Wisconsin Council of Churches—Sun Prairie, WI

Wyoming Association of Churches—Cody, WY

Economic/Social Justice Programs

Arizona Ecumenical Council—Phoenix, AZ

Arkansas Interfaith Conference—Scott, AR

Asheville-Buncombe Community Christian Ministry (ABCCM)—Asheville, NC

The Associated Churches of Fort Wayne & Allen County, Inc.—Fort Wayne, IN

Associated Ministries of Tacoma-Pierce County—Tacoma, WA

Association of Christian Churches of South Dakota—Sioux Falls, SD

Austin Area Interreligious Ministries—Austin, TX

Border Association for Refugees from Central America (BARCA), Inc.—Edinburg, TX

Brooklyn Council of Churches—Brooklyn, NY

Broome County Council of Churches, Inc.—Binghamton, NY

California Council of Churches-California Church Impact—Sacramento, CA

The Cape Cod Council of Churches, Inc.—Hyannis, MA

Capital Area Council of Churches, Inc.—Albany, NY

Capital Region Ecumenical Organization (CREO)—Schenectady, NY

The Capitol Region Conference of Churches—Hartford, CT

Chautauqua County Rural Ministry—Dunkirk, NY

Christian Associates of Southwest Pennsylvania—Pittsburgh, PA

Christian Ministries of Delaware County—Muncie, IN

Christian Service Center for Central Florida, Inc.—Orlando, FL

Church Council of Greater Seattle—Seattle, WA

The Church Federation of Greater Indianapolis, Inc.—Indianapolis, IN

Churches United, Inc.—Cedar Rapids, IA

Colorado Council of Churches—Denver, CO

Community Emergency Assistance Program (CEAP)—Brooklyn Park, MN

Community Ministry of Montgomery County—Rockville, MD

Community Renewal Society—Chicago, IL

Contact Ministries of Springfield—Springfield, IL

Cooperative Metropolitan Ministries—Newton, MA

Council of Churches of the City of New York—New York, NY

Council of Churches of Greater Springfield—Springfield, MA

The Council of Churches of Santa Clara County—San Jose, CA

Eastern Area Community Ministries—Louisville, KY

Ecclesia—Trenton, NJ

Ecumenical Conference of Greater Altoona—Altoona, PA

The Ecumenical Council of Pasadena Area Churches—Pasadena, CA

Ecumenical Council of San Diego County—San Diego, CA

Ecumenical Ministries of Oregon—Portland, OR

Evanston Ecumenical Action Council—Evanston, IL

Faith Community Assistance Center—Santa Fe, NM

Florida Council of Churches—Tampa, FL

Fresno Metro Ministry—Fresno, CA

Grand Rapids Area Center for Ecumenism (GRACE)—Grand Rapids, MI

Greater Birmingham Ministries—Birmingham, AL

Greater Chicago Broadcast Ministries—Chicago, IL

Greater Dallas Community of Churches—Dallas, TX

Greater Dayton Christian Connections—Dayton, OH

Greater Minneapolis Council of Churches—Minneapolis, MN

Greater Rochester Community of Churches—Rochester, NY

Highlands Community Ministries—Louisville, KY

Illinois Conference of Churches—Springfield, IL

Inter-Church Council of Greater New Bedford—New Bedford, MA

Inter-Church Ministries of Erie County—Erie, PA

Interchurch Ministries of Nebraska—Lincoln, NE

Interfaith Community Council, Inc.—New Albany, IN

Interfaith Conference of Greater Milwaukee—Milwaukee, WI

InterFaith Conference of Metropolitan Washington—Washington, DC

Interfaith Council—Spokane, WA

Interfaith Council of Contra Costa County—Walnut Creek, CA

Inter-Faith Ministries-Wichita—Wichita, KS

Interfaith Mission Service—Huntsville, AL

Interfaith Service Bureau—Sacramento, CA

InterFaith Works of Central New York—Syracuse, NY

The Joint Religious Legislative Coalition—Minneapolis, MN

Kansas Ecumenical Ministries—Topeka, KS

Kentuckiana Interfaith Community—Louisville, KY

Kentucky Council of Churches—Lexington, KY

Lincoln Interfaith Council—Lincoln, NE

Louisiana Interchurch Conference—Baton Rouge, LA

Madison-area Urban Ministry—Madison, WI

Mahoning Valley Association of Churches—Youngstown, OH

Maine Council of Churches—Portland, ME

Marin Interfaith Council—San Rafael, CA

Massachusetts Council of Churches—Boston, MA

The Metropolitan Christian Council: Detroit-Windsor—Detroit, MI

Metropolitan Christian Council of Philadelphia—Philadelphia, PA

271

Metropolitan Ecumenical Ministry—Newark, NJ
Metropolitan Inter Faith Association (MIFA)—Memphis, TN
Metropolitan Interfaith Council on Affordable Housing (MICAH)—Minneapolis, MN
Minnesota Council of Churches—Minneapolis, MN
Mississippi Religious Leadership Conference—Jackson, MS
Montana Association of Churches—Helena, MT
Muskegon County Cooperating Churches—Muskegon, MI
New Britain Area Conference of Churches (NEWBRACC)—New Britain, CT
New Hampshire Council of Churches—Pembroke, NH
New Mexico Conference of Churches—Bernalillo, NM
North Carolina Council of Churches—Raleigh, NC
North Dakota Conference of Churches—Ashley, ND
Northern California Interreligious Conference—Oakland, CA
Northside Inter-Church Agency (NICA)—Fort Worth, TX
Northwest Interfaith Movement—Philadelphia, PA
Oak Park-River Forest Community of Congregations—Oak Park, IL
Oklahoma Conference of Churches—Oklahoma City, OK
Pennsylvania Conference on Interchurch Cooperation—Harrisburg, PA
The Pennsylvania Council of Churches—Harrisburg, PA
Peoria Friendship House of Christian Service—Peoria, IL
Queens Federation of Churches—Richmond Hill, NY
The Regional Council of Churches of Atlanta—Atlanta, GA
Rural Migrant Ministry—Poughkeepsie, NY
St. Matthews Area Ministries—Louisville, KY
San Antonio Community of Congregations—San Antonio, TX
San Fernando Valley Interfaith Council—Chatsworth, CA
Schenectady Inner City Ministry—Schenectady, NY
South Carolina Christian Action Council, Inc.—Columbia, SC
South East Associated Ministries (SEAM)—Louisville, KY
Southern California Ecumenical Council—Pasadena, CA
Tarrant Area Community of Churches—Fort Worth, TX
Texas Conference of Churches—Austin, TX
Troy Area United Ministries—Troy, NY
United Churches of Lycoming County—Williamsport, PA
United Religious Community of St. Joseph County—South Bend, IN

Vermont Ecumenical Council and Bible Society—Richmond, VT
Wainwright House—Rye, NY
Washington Association of Churches—Seattle, WA
West Virginia Council of Churches—Charleston, WV
Wilkinsburg Community Ministry—Pittsburgh, PA
Wyoming Association of Churches—Cody, WY

Employment Assistance Programs

Asheville-Buncombe Community Christian Ministry (ABCCM)—Asheville, NC
Chautaugua County Rural Ministry—Dunkirk, NY
Christian Community Action—New Haven, CT
Community Emergency Assistance Program (CEAP)—Brooklyn Park, MN
Contact Ministries of Springfield—Springfield, IL
Corpus Christi Metro Ministries—Corpus Christi, TX
East Dallas Cooperative Parish—Dallas, TX
East End Cooperative Ministry—Pittsburgh, PA
Eastern Area Community Ministries—Louisville, KY
Ecumenical Ministries of Oregon—Portland, OR
Evanston Ecumenical Action Council—Evanston, IL
Fern Creek-Highview United Ministries—Louisvlle, KY
Genesee-Orleans Ministry of Concern—Albion, NY
Greater Chicago Broadcast Ministries—Chicago, IL
Greater Dallas Community of Churches—Dallas, TX
Greater Minneapolis Council of Churches—Minneapolis, MN
Greensboro Urban Ministry—Greensboro, NC
Kentuckiana Interfaith Community—Louisville, KY
Madison-area Urban Ministry—Madison, WI
Metropolitan Ecumenical Ministry—Newark, NJ
Minnesota Council of Churches—Minneapolis, MN
Network of Religious Communities—Buffalo, NY
Northside Inter-Church Agency (NICA)—Fort Worth, TX
Peoria Friendship House of Christian Service—Peoria, IL
St. Matthews Area Ministries—Louisville, KY
Schenectady Inner City Ministry—Schenectady, NY
South East Associated Ministries (SEAM)—Louisville, KY
Southeast Ecumenical Ministry—Rochester, NY
United Ministries—Greenville, SC
West Side Ecumenical Ministry—Cleveland, OH

Environmental Programs

Akron Area Association of Churches—Akron, OH
Arizona Ecumenical Council—Phoenix, AZ

California Council of Churches-California Church Impact—Sacramento, CA
The Cape Cod Council of Churches, Inc.—Hyannis, MA
The Capitol Region Conference of Churches—Hartford, CT
Christian Associates of Southwest Pennsylvania—Pittsburgh, PA
Colorado Council of Churches—Denver, CO
The Council of Churches of Santa Clara County—San Jose, CA
Ecumenical Ministries of Iowa (EMI)—Des Moines, IA
Ecumenical Ministries of Oregon—Portland, OR
Florida Council of Churches—Tampa, FL
Fresno Metro Ministry—Fresno, CA
Georgia Christian Council—Macon, GA
Greater Chicago Broadcast Ministries—Chicago, IL
Greater Dayton Christian Connections—Dayton, OH
Inter-Church Council of Greater New Bedford—New Bedford, MA
Interfaith Conference of Greater Milwaukee—Milwaukee, WI
InterFaith Conference of Metropolitan Washington—Washington, DC
Interfaith Council of Contra Costa County—Walnut Creek, CA
Interfaith Mission Service—Huntsville, AL
Kentucky Council of Churches—Lexington, KY
Louisiana Interchurch Conference—Baton Rouge, LA
Maine Council of Churches—Portland, ME
Massachusetts Council of Churches—Boston, MA
The Metropolitan Christian Council: Detroit-Windsor—Detroit, MI
Metropolitan Christian Council of Philadelphia—Philadelphia, PA
Metropolitan Ecumenical Ministry—Newark, NJ
Minnesota Council of Churches—Minneapolis, MN
Mississippi Religious Leadership Conference—Jackson, MS
Montana Association of Churches—Helena, MT
Muskegon County Cooperating Churches—Muskegon, MI
Network of Religious Communities—Buffalo, NY
New Hampshire Council of Churches—Pembroke, NH
New Mexico Conference of Churches—Bernalillo, NM
North Carolina Council of Churches—Raleigh, NC
Northern California Interreligious Conference—Oakland, CA
Oklahoma Conference of Churches—Oklahoma City, OK
The Pennsylvania Council of Churches—Harrisburg, PA
The Regional Council of Churches of Atlanta—Atlanta, GA
San Antonio Community of Congregations—San Antonio, TX

Schenectady Inner City Ministry—Schenectady, NY
South Coast Interfaith Council—Long Beach, CA
South Carolina Christian Action Council, Inc.—Columbia, SC
South Coast Interfaith Council—Long Beach, CA
Southern California Ecumenical Council—Pasadena, CA
United Churches of Lycoming County—Williamsport, PA
Vermont Ecumenical Council and Bible Society—Richmond, VT
Washington Association of Churches—Seattle, WA
West Virginia Council of Churches—Charleston, WV
Wisconsin Council of Churches—Sun Prairie, WI
Wyoming Association of Churches—Cody, WY

Faith and Order Programs

Akron Area Association of Churches—Akron, OH
Arizona Ecumenical Council—Phoenix, AZ
The Associated Churches of Fort Wayne & Allen County, Inc.—Fort Wayne, IN
Associated Ministries of Tacoma-Pierce County—Tacoma, WA
Association of Christian Churches of South Dakota—Sioux Falls, SD
The Cape Cod Council of Churches, Inc.—Hyannis, MA
Capital Area Council of Churches, Inc.—Albany, NY
Capital Region Ecumenical Organization (CREO)—Schenectady, NY
Christian Associates of Southwest Pennsylvania—Pittsburgh, PA
Church Council of Greater Seattle—Seattle, WA
The Church Federation of Greater Indianapolis, Inc.—Indianapolis, IN
Churches United, Inc.—Cedar Rapids, IA
Churches United of the Quad City Area—Rock Island, IL
Colorado Council of Churches—Denver, CO
Council of Churches of the City of New York—New York, NY
The Council of Churches of Greater Bridgeport—Bridgeport, CT
Council of Churches of Greater Springfield—Springfield, MA
The Council of Churches of Santa Clara County—San Jose, CA
Council of Churches and Synagogues of Southwestern Connecticut—Stamford, CT
East Dallas Cooperative Parish—Dallas, TX
Ecclesia—Trenton, NJ
Ecumenical Council of San Diego County—San Diego, CA
Ecumenical Ministries of Iowa (EMI)—Des Moines, IA
Ecumenical Ministries of Oregon—Portland, OR
Florida Council of Churches—Tampa, FL

273

Georgia Christian Council—Macon, GA
Greater Chicago Broadcast Ministries—Chicago, IL
Greater Dallas Community of Churches—Dallas, TX
Greater Dayton Christian Connections—Dayton, OH
Greater Lawrence Council of Churches—Lawrence, MA
Greater New Orleans Federation of Churches—New Orleans, LA
Greater Waterbury Interfaith Ministries, Inc.—Waterbury, CT
Illinois Conference of Churches—Springfield, IL
Inter-Church Council of Greater New Bedford—New Bedford, MA
Interchurch Ministries of Nebraska—Lincoln, NE
InterFaith Conference of Metropolitan Washington—Washington, DC
InterFaith Works of Central New York—Syracuse, NY
Kansas Ecumenical Ministries—Topeka, KS
Kentuckiana Interfaith Community—Louisville, KY
Kentucky Council of Churches—Lexington, KY
Louisiana Interchurch Conference—Baton Rouge, LA
Mahoning Valley Association of Churches—Youngstown, OH
The Metropolitan Christian Council: Detroit-Windsor—Detroit, MI
Metropolitan Christian Council of Philadelphia—Philadelphia, PA
Metropolitan Ecumenical Ministry—Newark, NJ
Minnesota Council of Churches—Minneapolis, MN
Montana Association of Churches—Helena, MT
Network of Religious Communities—Buffalo, NY
New Britain Area Conference of Churches (NEWBRACC)—New Britain, CT
New Hampshire Council of Churches—Pembroke, NH
New Mexico Conference of Churches—Bernalillo, NM
North Carolina Council of Churches—Raleigh, NC
North Dakota Conference of Churches—Ashley, ND
Northern California Interreligious Conference—Oakland, CA
Northern Kentucky Interfaith Commission, Inc.—Newport, KY
Ohio Council of Churches—Columbus, OH
Oklahoma Conference of Churches—Oklahoma City, OK
The Pennsylvania Council of Churches—Harrisburg, PA
Queens Federation of Churches—Richmond Hill, NY
San Antonio Community of Congregations—San Antonio, TX

South Carolina Christian Action Council, Inc.—Columbia, SC
Southern California Ecumenical Council—Pasadena, CA
Texas Conference of Churches—Austin, TX
Troy Area United Ministries—Troy, NY
Tulsa Metropolitan Ministry—Tulsa, OK
United Churches of Lycoming County—Williamsport, PA
United Religious Community of St. Joseph County—South Bend, IN
Vermont Ecumenical Council and Bible Society—Richmond, VT
Virginia Council of Churches, Inc.—Richmond, VA
Wainwright House—Rye, NY
Washington Association of Churches—Seattle, WA
Weekday Christain Education—Evansville, IN
West Virginia Council of Churches—Charleston, WV
Wisconsin Council of Churches—Sun Prairie, WI
Wyoming Valley Council of Churches—Wilkes-Barre, PA

Health Care Issues

Asheville-Buncombe Community Christian Ministry (ABCCM)—Asheville, NC
California Council of Churches-California Church Impact—Sacramento, CA
Capital Region Ecumenical Organization (CREO)—Malta NY
Christian Associates of Southwest Pennsylvania—Pittsburg, PA
Christian Churches United of the Tri-County Area—Harrisburg, PA
Churchpeople for Change and Reconciliation—Lima, OH
Colorado Council of Churches-Denver, CO
Community Ministries of Rockville—Rockville, MD
Community Renewal Society—Chicago, IL
Corpus Christi Metro Ministries—Corpus Christi, TX
Council of Churches of the City of New York—New York, NY
The Council of Churches of Santa Clara County—San Jose, CA
East Dallas Cooperative Parish—Dallas, TX
Eastern Area Community Ministries—Louisville, KY
Ecumenical Ministries of Iowa (EMI)—Des Moines, IA
Fresno Metro Ministry—Fresno, CA
Greater Chicago Broadcast Ministries—Chicago, IL
Greater Rochester Community of Churches—Rochester, NY
Greensboro Urban Ministry—Greensboro, NC
Highlands Community Ministries—Louisville, KY
Inter-Church Council of Greater New Bedford—New Bedford, MA

Interfaith Conference of Greater Milwaukee—Milwaukee, WI
Interfaith Council of Contra Costa County—Walnut Creek, CA
Interfaith Federation of Greater Baton Rouge—Baton Rouge, LA
Madison-area Urban Ministry—Madison, WI
The Metropolitan Christian Council: Detroit-Windsor—Detroit, MI
Metropolitan Ecumenical Ministry—Newark, NJ
Metropolitan Ecumenical Ministry Community Development Corp.—Newark, NJ
Mississippi Religious Leadership Conference—Jackson, MS
Montana Association of Churches—Helena, MT
Network of Religious Communities—Buffalo, NY
New Hampshire Council of Churches—Pembroke, NH
New Mexico Conference of Churches—Bernalillo, NM
North Carolina Council of Churches—Raleigh, NC
Oklahoma Conference of Churches—Oklahoma City, OK
The Pennsylvania Council of Churches—Harrisburg, PA
Peoria Friendship House of Christian Service—Peoria, IL
Pike County Outreach Council—Waverly, OH
The Regional Council of Churches of Atlanta—Atlanta, GA
Saint Paul Area Council of Churches—St. Paul, MN
Schenectady Inner City Ministry—Schenectady, NY
South Carolina Christian Action Council, Inc.—Columbia, SC
Southeast Ecumenical Ministry—Rochester, NY
Tarrant Area Community of Churches—Fort Worth, TX
Tuscarawas County Council for Church and Community—New Philadelphia, OH
United Churches of Lycoming County—Williamsport, PA
United Religious Community of St. Joseph County—South Bend, IN
Washington Association of Churches—Seattle, WA
West Virginia Council of Churches—Charleston, WV
Wyoming Association of Churches—Cody, WY

Homelessness/Shelter Programs

Allegheny Valley Association of Churches—Natrona Heights, PA
Arkansas Interfaith Conference—Scott, AR
Asheville-Buncombe Community Christian Ministry (ABCCM)—Asheville, NC
Associated Ministries of Tacoma-Pierce County—Tacoma, WA
Attleboro Area Council of Churches, Inc.—Attleboro, MA
Austin Area Interreligious Ministries—Austin, TX

Border Association for Refugees from Central America (BARCA), Inc.—Edinburg, TX
The Cape Cod Council of Churches, Inc.—Hyannis, MA
Capital Area Council of Churches, Inc.—Albany, NY
The Capitol Region Conference of Churches—Hartford, CT
Center City Churches—Hartford, CT
Chautauqua County Rural Ministry—Dunkirk, NY
Christian Associates of Southwest Pennsylvania—Pittsburgh, PA
Christian Churches United of the Tri-County Area—Harrisburg, PA
Christian Community Action—New Haven, CT
Christian Ministries of Delaware County—Muncie, IN
Christian Service Center for Central Florida, Inc.—Orlando, FL
Church Council of Greater Seattle—Seattle, WA
Churches United, Inc.—Cedar Rapids, IA
Churches United of the Quad City Area—Rock Island, IL
Colorado Council of Churches—Denver, CO
Community Emergency Assistance Program (CEAP)—Brooklyn Park, MN
Community Ministries of Rockville—Rockville, MD
Community Ministry of Montgomery County—Rockville, MD
Community Renewal Society—Chicago, IL
Contact Ministries of Springfield—Springfield, IL
Cooperative Metropolitan Ministries—Newton, MA
Corpus Christi Metro Ministries—Corpus Christi, TX
Council of Churches of the City of New York—New York, NY
Council of Churches of Greater Springfield—Springfield, MA
The Council of Churches of Santa Clara County—San Jose, CA
East End Cooperative Ministry—Pittsburgh, PA
The Ecumenical Council of Pasadena Area Churches—Pasadena, CA
Ecumenical Council of San Diego County—San Diego, CA
Ecumenical Ministries—Fulton, MO
Ecumenical Ministries of Oregon—Portland, OR
Evanston Ecumenical Action Council—Evanston, IL
Faith Community Assistance Center—Santa Fe, NM
Genesee-Orleans Ministry of Concern—Albion, NY
Grand Rapids Area Center for Ecumenism (GRACE)—Grand Rapids, MI
Greater Chicago Broadcast Ministries—Chicago, IL
Greater Minneapolis Council of Churches—Minneapolis, MN
Greensboro Urban Ministry—Greensboro, NC

Hanover Area Council of Churches—Hanover, PA

Highlands Community Ministries—Louisville, KY

Inter-Church Ministries of Erie County—Erie, PA

Interfaith Community Council, Inc.—New Albany, IN

Interfaith Community Services—St. Joseph, MO

Interfaith Conference of Greater Milwaukee—Milwaukee, WI

InterFaith Conference of Metropolitan Washington—Washington, DC

Interfaith Council of Contra Costa County—Walnut Creek, CA

Inter-Faith Ministries-Wichita—Wichita, KS

Interfaith Mission Service—Huntsville, AL

Interfaith Works—Olympia, WA

InterFaith Works of Central New York—Syracuse, NY

Lewisburg Council of Churches—Lewisburg, PA

The Long Island Council of Churches—Hempstead, NY

Madison-area Urban Ministry—Madison, WI

Maine Council of Churches—Portland, ME

Marin Interfaith Council—San Rafael, CA

Metropolitan Ecumenical Ministry—Newark, NJ

Metropolitan Inter Faith Association (MIFA)—Memphis, TN

Metropolitan Interfaith Council on Affordable Housing (MICAH)—Minneapolis, MN

Minnesota Council of Churches—Minneapolis, MN

Mississippi Religious Leadership Conference—Jackson, MS

Montana Association of Churches—Helena, MT

New Britain Area Conference of Churches (NEWBRACC)—New Britain, CT

New Hampshire Council of Churches—Pembroke, NH

New Mexico Conference of Churches—Bernalillo, NM

North Carolina Council of Churches—Raleigh, NC

Northside Common Ministries—Pittsburgh, PA

Northside Inter-Church Agency (NICA)—Fort Worth, TX

Oklahoma Conference of Churches—Oklahoma City, OK

Paducah Cooperative Ministry—Paducah, KY

Peoria Friendship House of Christian Service—Peoria, IL

Pike County Outreach Council—Waverly, OH

Reading Berks Conference of Churches—Reading, PA

The Regional Council of Churches of Atlanta—Atlanta, GA

St. Matthews Area Ministries—Louisvilee, KY

Saint Paul Area Council of Churches—St. Paul, MN

Schenectady Inner City Ministry—Schenectady, NY

Tarrant Area Community of Churches—Fort Worth, TX

Troy Area United Ministries—Troy, NY

Tuscarawas County Council for Church and Community—New Philadelphia, OH

United Ministries—Greenville, SC

United Religious Community of St. Joseph County—South Bend, IN

Wisconsin Council of Churches—Sun Prairie, WI

Wyoming Valley Council of Churches—Wilkes-Barre, PA

Hunger/Food Program

Allegheny Valley Association of Churches—Natrona Heights, PA

Arkansas Interfaith Conference—Scott, AR

Asheville-Buncombe Community Christian Ministry (ABCCM)—Asheville, NC

The Associated Churches of Fort Wayne & Allen County, Inc.—Fort Wayne, IN

Associated Ministries of Tacoma-Pierce County—Tacoma, WA

Attleboro Area Council of Churches, Inc.—Attleboro, MA

Austin Area Interreligious Ministries—Austin, TX

Border Association for Refugees from Central America (BARCA), Inc.—Edinburg, TX

Brooklyn Council of Churches—Brooklyn, NY

Broome County Council of Churches, Inc.—Binghamton, NY

California Council of Churches-California Church Impact—Sacramento, CA

The Cape Cod Council of Churches, Inc.—Hyannis, MA

Capital Region Ecumenical Organization (CREO)—Malta,NY

Center City Churches—Hartford, CT

Chautauqua County Rural Ministry—Dunkirk, NY

Christian Churches United of the Tri-County Area—Harrisburg, PA

Christian Community Action—New Haven, CT

Christian Ministries of Delaware County—Muncie, IN

Christian Service Center for Central Florida, Inc.—Orlando, FL

Church Community Services—Elkhart, IN

Church Council of Greater Seattle—Seattle, WA

The Church Federation of Greater Indianapolis, Inc.—Indianapolis, IN

Churches United of the Quad City Area—Rock Island, IL

Colorado Council of Churches—Denver, CO

Community Emergency Assistance Program (CEAP)—Brooklyn Park, MN

Community Ministry of Montgomery County—Rockville, MD

Concerned Ecumenical Ministry to the Upper West Side—Buffalo, NY

Contact Ministries of Springfield—Springfield, IL

Corpus Christi Metro Ministries—Corpus Christi, TX

Council of Churches of the City of New York—New York, NY

The Council of Churches of Greater Bridgeport—Bridgeport, CT

277

Immigration Issues

Interfaith Dialogue/Relationships

278

Community Ministries of Rockville—Rockville, MD

Community Ministry of Montgomery County—Rockville, MD

Community Renewal Society—Chicago, IL

Cooperative Metropolitan Ministries—Newton, MA

Council of Churches of Chemung County, Inc.—Elmira, NY

Council of Churches of the City of New York—New York, NY

Council of Churches of Greater Springfield—Springfield, MA

The Council of Churches of Santa Clara County—San Jose, CA

Council of Churches and Synagogues of Southwestern Connecticut—Stamford, CT

Des Moines Area Religious Council—Des Moines, IA

Dutchess County Interfaith Council, Inc.—Poughkeepsie, NY

East Dallas Cooperative Parish—Dallas, TX

Eastern Area Community Ministries—Louisville, KY

Ecclesia—Trenton, NJ

Ecumenical Conference of Greater Altoona—Altoona, PA

The Ecumenical Council of Pasadena Area Churches—Pasadena, CA

Ecumenical Council of San Diego County—San Diego, CA

Ecumenical Ministries of Iowa (EMI)—Des Moines, IA

Ecumenical Ministries of Oregon—Portland, OR

Evanston Ecumenical Action Council—Evanston, IL

Faith Community Assistance Center—Santa Fe, NM

FaithTrust Institute—Seattle, WA

Florida Council of Churches—Tampa, FL

Fresno Metro Ministry—Fresno, CA

Georgia Christian Council—Macon, GA

Grand Rapids Area Center for Ecumenism (GRACE)—Grand Rapids, MI

Greater Birmingham Ministries—Birmingham, AL

Greater Chicago Broadcast Ministries—Chicago, IL

Greater Dallas Community of Churches—Dallas, TX

Greater Dayton Christian Connections—Dayton, OH

Greater Flint Council of Churches—Flint, MI

Greater Lawrence Council of Churches—Lawrence, MA

Greater New Orleans Federation of Churches—New Orleans, LA

Greater Rochester Community of Churches—Rochester, NY

Greater Waterbury Interfaith Ministries, Inc.—Waterbury, CT

Greensboro Urban Ministry—Greensboro, NC

Highlands Community Ministries—Louisville, KY

Inter-Church Council of Greater New Bedford—New Bedford, MA

Inter-Church Ministries of Erie County—Erie, PA

Interchurch Ministries of Nebraska—Lincoln, NE

Interfaith Community Services—St. Joseph, MO

Interfaith Conference of Greater Milwaukee—Milwaukee, WI

InterFaith Conference of Metropolitan Washington—Washington, DC

Interfaith Council—Spokane, WA

Interfaith Council of Contra Costa County—Walnut Creek, CA

Interfaith Federation of Greater Baton Rouge—Baton Rouge, LA

Inter-Faith Ministries-Wichita—Wichita, KS

Interfaith Mission Service—Huntsville, AL

Interfaith Service Bureau—Sacramento, CA

Interfaith Works—Olympia, WA

InterFaith Works of Central New York—Syracuse, NY

The Joint Religious Legislative Coalition—Minneapolis, MN

Kentuckiana Interfaith Community—Louisville, KY

Lewisburg Council of Churches—Lewisburg, PA

Lincoln Interfaith Council—Lincoln, NE

The Long Island Council of Churches—Hempstead, NY

Louisiana Interchurch Conference—Baton Rouge, LA

Madison-area Urban Ministry—Madison, WI

Mahoning Valley Association of Churches—Youngstown, OH

Maine Council of Churches—Portland, ME

Marin Interfaith Council—San Rafael, CA

Massachusetts Council of Churches—Boston, MA

The Metropolitan Christian Council: Detroit-Windsor—Detroit, MI

Metropolitan Christian Council of Philadelphia—Philadelphia, PA

Metropolitan Ecumenical Ministry—Newark, NJ

Metropolitan Interfaith Council on Affordable Housing (MICAH)—Minneapolis, MN

Minnesota Council of Churches—Minneapolis, MN

Mississippi Religious Leadership Conference—Jackson, MS

Montana Association of Churches—Helena, MT

Muskegon County Cooperating Churches—Muskegon, MI

Network of Religious Communities—Buffalo, NY

New Britain Area Conference of Churches (NEWBRACC)—New Britain, CT

New Hampshire Council of Churches—Pembroke, NH

New Mexico Conference of Churches—Bernalillo, NM

North Dakota Conference of Churches—Ashley, ND

279

Northern California Interreligious Conference—
Oakland, CA
Northern Kentucky Interfaith Commission,
Inc.—Newport, KY
Northwest Interfaith Movement—Philadelphia,
PA
Oak Park-River Forest Community of
Congregations—Oak Park, IL
Oklahoma Conference of Churches—Oklahoma
City, OK
Pennsylvania Conference on Interchurch
Cooperation—Harrisburg, PA
The Pennsylvania Council of Churches—
Harrisburg, PA
Peoria Friendship House of Christian Service—
Peoria, IL
Reading Berks Conference of Churches—
Reading, PA
The Regional Council of Churches of Atlanta—
Atlanta, GA
St. Matthews Area Ministries—Louisville, KY
Saint Paul Area Council of Churches—St. Paul,
MN
San Antonio Community of Congregations—San
Antonio, TX
San Fernando Valley Interfaith Council—
Chatsworth, CA
South Carolina Christian Action Council, Inc.—
Columbia, SC
South Coast Interfaith Council—Long Beach,
CA
South Hills Interfaith Ministries—South Park,
PA
Staten Island Council of Churches—Staten
Island, NY
Texas Conference of Churches—Austin, TX
Troy Area United Ministries—Troy, NY
Tulsa Metropolitan Ministry—Tulsa, OK
Tuscarawas County Council for Church and
Community—New Philadelphia, OH
United Churches of Lycoming County—
Williamsport, PA
United Religious Community of St. Joseph
County—South Bend, IN
Vermont Ecumenical Council and Bible
Society—Richmond, VT
Wainwright House—Rye, NY
Washington Association of Churches—Seattle,
WA
West Side Ecumenical Ministry—Cleveland, OH
Worcester County Ecumenical Council—
Worcester, MA
Wyoming Valley Council of Churches—Wilkes-
Barre, PA

Peace Advocacy

Arkansas Interfaith Conference—Scott, AR
The Associated Churches of Fort Wayne & Allen
County, Inc.—Fort Wayne, IN
Associated Ministries of Tacoma-Pierce
County—Tacoma, WA
Association of Christian Churches of South
Dakota—Sioux Falls, SD
Border Association for Refugees from Central
America (BARCA), Inc.—Edinburg, TX

The Cape Cod Council of Churches, Inc.—
Hyannis, MA
Capital Area Council of Churches, Inc.—Albany,
NY
Church Council of Greater Seattle—Seattle, WA
The Church Federation of Greater Indianapolis,
Inc.—Indianapolis, IN
Churches United of the Quad City Area—Rock
Island, IL
Community Renewal Society—Chicago, IL
Council of Churches of the City of New York—
New York, NY
Council of Churches of Greater Springfield—
Springfield, MA
The Council of Churches of Santa Clara
County—San Jose, CA
Ecumenical Conference of Greater Altoona—
Altoona, PA
Ecumenical Ministries of Iowa (EMI)—Des
Moines, IA
Ecumenical Ministries of Oregon—Portland, OR
Greater Chicago Broadcast Ministries—
Chicago, IL
Greater Dallas Community of Churches—
Dallas, TX
Greater Rochester Community of Churches—
Rochester, NY
Interchurch Ministries of Nebraska—Lincoln, NE
Interfaith Council of Contra Costa County—
Walnut Creek, CA
InterFaith Works of Central New York—
Syracuse, NY
Interfaith Works—Olympia, WA
Kentuckiana Interfaith Community—Louisville,
KY
Lincoln Interfaith Council—Lincoln, NE
Madison-area Urban Ministry—Madison, WI
Marin Interfaith Council—San Rafael, CA
Montana Association of Churches—Helena, MT
Network of Religious Communities—Buffalo,
NY
New Mexico Conference of Churches—
Bernalillo, NM
North Carolina Council of Churches—Raleigh,
NC
Ohio Council of Churches—Columbus, OH
Oklahoma Conference of Churches—Oklahoma
City, OK
The Pennsylvania Council of Churches—
Harrisburg, PA
The Regional Council of Churches of Atlanta—
Atlanta, GA
San Fernando Valley Interfaith Council—
Chatsworth, CA
South Carolina Christian Action Council, Inc.—
Columbia, SC
Southern California Ecumenical Council—
Pasadena, CA
Staten Island Council of Churches—Staten
Island, NY
Texas Conference of Churches—Austin, TX
Tulsa Metropolitan Ministry—Tulsa, OK
United Religious Community of St. Joseph
County—South Bend, IN

Vermont Ecumenical Council and Bible Society—Richmond, VT

Washington Association of Churches—Seattle, WA

West Virginia Council of Churches—Charleston, WV

Worcester County Ecumenical Council—Worcester, MA

Wyoming Association of Churches—Cody, WY

Prison Chaplaincy

Akron Area Association of Churches—Akron, OH

Asheville-Buncombe Community Christian Ministry (ABCCM)—Asheville, NC

Berrien County Association of Churches—Benton Harbor, MI

Broome County Council of Churches, Inc.—Binghamton, NY

The Cape Cod Council of Churches, Inc.—Hyannis, MA

Capital Area Council of Churches, Inc.—Albany, NY

Christian Associates of Southwest Pennsylvania—Pittsburgh, PA

Christian Churches United of the Tri-County Area—Harrisburg, PA

Christians United in Beaver County—Beaver, PA

Church Council of Greater Seattle—Seattle, WA

The Church Federation of Greater Indianapolis, Inc.—Indianapolis, IN

Churches United of the Quad City Area—Rock Island, IL

Churchpeople for Change and Reconciliation—Lima, OH

Community Renewal Society—Chicago, IL

Council of Christian Communions of Greater Cincinnati—Cincinnati, OH

Council of Churches of the City of New York—New York, NY

The Council of Churches of Greater Bridgeport, Inc.—Bridgeport, CT

Council of Churches of Greater Springfield—Springfield, MA

The Council of Churches of Santa Clara County—San Jose, CA

Ecclesia—Trenton, NJ

Genesee County Churches United, Inc.—Batavia, NY

Greater Chicago Broadcast Ministries—Chicago, IL

Inter-Church Ministries of Erie County—Erie, PA

Interfaith Council of Contra Costa County—Walnut Creek, CA

The Long Island Council of Churches—Hempstead, NY

Louisiana Interchurch Conference—Baton Rouge, LA

Maine Council of Churches—Portland, ME

Montana Association of Churches—Helena, MT

New Hampshire Council of Churches—Pembroke, NH

New Mexico Conference of Churches—Bernalillo, NM

Reading Berks Conference of Churches—Reading, PA

United Churches of Lycoming County—Williamsport, PA

United Religious Community of St. Joseph County—South Bend, IN

Weekday Christain Education—Evansville, IN

York County Council of Churches—York, PA

Programs with/for Persons with Disabilities

Associated Ministries of Tacoma-Pierce County—Tacoma, WA

Christian Ministries of Delaware County—Muncie, IN

Greater Chicago Broadcast Ministries—Chicago, IL

Greater Minneapolis Council of Churches—Minneapolis, MN

Inter-Church Council of Greater New Bedford—New Bedford, MA

Inter-Faith Ministries-Wichita—Wichita, KS

InterFaith Works of Central New York—Syracuse, NY

Massachusetts Council of Churches—Boston, MA

Metropolitan Ecumenical Ministry—Newark, NJ

New Hampshire Council of Churches—Pembroke, NH

Reading Berks Conference of Churches—Reading, PA

Southeast Ecumenical Ministry—Rochester, NY

Public Education

Akron Area Association of Churches—Akron, OH

Arizona Ecumenical Council—Phoenix, AZ

The Associated Churches of Fort Wayne & Allen County, Inc.—Fort Wayne, IN

Associated Ministries of Tacoma-Pierce County—Tacoma, WA

Austin Area Interreligious Ministries—Austin, TX

Border Association for Refugees from Central America (BARCA), Inc.—Edinburg, TX

California Council of Churches-California Church Impact—Sacramento, CA

The Cape Cod Council of Churches, Inc.—Hyannis, MA

Center City Churches—Hartford, CT

Christian Ministries of Delaware County—Muncie, IN

The Church Federation of Greater Indianapolis, Inc.—Indianapolis, IN

Colorado Council of Churches—Denver, CO

Community Emergency Assistance Program (CEAP)—Brooklyn Park, MN

Community Ministries of Rockville—Rockville, MD

Community Ministry of Montgomery County—Rockville, MD

Community Renewal Society—Chicago, IL

Concerned Ecumenical Ministry to the Upper West Side—Buffalo, NY

Contact Ministries of Springfield—Springfield, IL

Council of Churches of the City of New York—New York, NY

Council of Churches of Greater Springfield—Springfield, MA

Evanston Ecumenical Action Council—Evanston, IL

Greater Birmingham Ministries—Birmingham, AL

Greater Chicago Broadcast Ministries—Chicago, IL

Greater Fairmont Council of Churches—Fairmont, WV

Greater Waterbury Interfaith Ministries, Inc.—Waterbury, CT

Inter-Church Council of Greater New Bedford—New Bedford, MA

Interfaith Conference of Greater Milwaukee—Milwaukee, WI

InterFaith Conference of Metropolitan Washington—Washington, DC

Interfaith Council—Spokane, WA

Interfaith Federation of Greater Baton Rouge—Baton Rouge, LA

InterFaith Works of Central New York—Syracuse, NY

The Joint Religious Legislative Coalition—Minneapolis, MN

Louisiana Interchurch Conference—Baton Rouge, LA

Madison-area Urban Ministry—Madison, WI

Maine Council of Churches—Portland, ME

Metropolitan Christian Council of Philadelphia—Philadelphia, PA

Metropolitan Ecumenical Ministry—Newark, NJ

Metropolitan Interfaith Council on Affordable Housing (MICAH)—Minneapolis, MN

Mississippi Religious Leadership Conference—Jackson, MS

Network of Religious Communities—Buffalo, NY

New Hampshire Council of Churches—Pembroke, NH

New Mexico Conference of Churches—Bernalillo, NM

North Carolina Council of Churches—Raleigh, NC

Oak Park-River Forest Community of Congregations—Oak Park, IL

Oklahoma Conference of Churches—Oklahoma City, OK

The Pennsylvania Council of Churches—Harrisburg, PA

Peoria Friendship House of Christian Service—Peoria, IL

South Carolina Christian Action Council, Inc.—Columbia, SC

Tarrant Area Community of Churches—Fort Worth, TX

Tuscarawas County Council for Church and Community—New Philadelphia, OH

United Religious Community of St. Joseph County—South Bend, IN

Washington Association of Churches—Seattle, WA

Refugee Assistance Programs

Association of Religious Communities—Danbury, CT

Austin Area Interreligious Ministries—Austin, TX

Border Association for Refugees from Central America (BARCA), Inc.—Edinburg, TX

The Capitol Region Conference of Churches—Hartford, CT

Community Emergency Assistance Program (CEAP)—Brooklyn Park, MN

Ecumenical Ministries of Oregon—Portland, OR

Greater Chicago Broadcast Ministries—Chicago, IL

Greater Minneapolis Council of Churches—Minneapolis, MN

Interfaith Service Bureau—Sacramento, CA

InterFaith Works of Central New York—Syracuse, NY

Kentuckiana Interfaith Community—Louisville, KY

Metropolitan Ecumenical Ministry—Newark, NJ

Minnesota Council of Churches—Minneapolis, MN

Network of Religious Communities—Buffalo, NY

The Regional Council of Churches of Atlanta—Atlanta, GA

United Religious Community of St. Joseph County—South Bend, IN

Rural Issues

Alaska Christian Conference—Fairbanks, AK

Association of Christian Churches of South Dakota—Sioux Falls, SD

Berrien County Association of Churches—Benton Harbor, MI

Border Association for Refugees from Central America (BARCA), Inc.—Edinburg, TX

Chautaugua County Rural Ministry—Dunkirk, NY

Christian Associates of Southwest Pennsylvania—Pittsburgh, PA

Ecumenical Ministries of Iowa (EMI)—Des Moines, IA

Ecumenical Ministries of Oregon—Portland, OR

Georgia Christian Council—Macon, GA

Greater Minneapolis Council of Churches—Minneapolis, MN

Interchurch Ministries of Nebraska—Lincoln, NE

Interfaith Conference of Greater Milwaukee—Milwaukee, WI

Kansas Ecumenical Ministries—Topeka, KS

Kentucky Council of Churches—Lexington, KY

Louisiana Interchurch Conference—Baton Rouge, LA

Minnesota Council of Churches—Minneapolis, MN

Mississippi Religious Leadership Conference—Jackson, MS
Montana Association of Churches—Helena, MT
New Mexico Conference of Churches—Bernalillo, NM
North Carolina Council of Churches—Raleigh, NC
North Dakota Conference of Churches—Ashley, ND
Oklahoma Conference of Churches—Oklahoma City, OK
Pike County Outreach Council—Waverly, OH
Reading Berks Conference of Churches—Reading, PA
United Churches of Lycoming County—Williamsport, PA
United Religious Community of St. Joseph County—South Bend, IN
West Virginia Council of Churches—Charleston, WV
Wisconsin Council of Churches—Sun Prairie, WI
Wyoming Association of Churches—Cody, WY

Senior Citizen Programs

Allegheny Valley Association of Churches—Natrona Heights, PA
Associated Ministries of Tacoma-Pierce County—Tacoma, WA
Attleboro Area Council of Churches, Inc.—Attleboro, MA
The Capitol Region Conference of Churches—Hartford, CT
Center City Churches—Hartford, CT
Christian Ministries of Delaware County—Muncie, IN
Church Council of Greater Seattle—Seattle, WA
Community Emergency Assistance Program (CEAP)—Brooklyn Park, MN
Community Ministries of Rockville—Rockville, MD
Community Renewal Society—Chicago, IL
Concerned Ecumenical Ministry to the Upper West Side—Buffalo, NY
Council of Churches of Greater Springfield—Springfield, MA
Council of Churches of the Ozarks—Springfield, MO
Council of Churches and Synagogues of Southwestern Connecticut—Stamford, CT
Cross-Lines Cooperative Council—Kansas City, KS
East Dallas Cooperative Parish—Dallas, TX
East End Cooperative Ministry—Pittsburgh, PA
Eastern Area Community Ministries—Louisville, KY
Fern Creek-Highview United Ministries—Louisvlle, KY
Florida Council of Churches—Tampa, FL
Georgia Christian Council—Macon, GA
Greater Chicago Broadcast Ministries—Chicago, IL
Greater Lawrence Council of Churches—Lawrence, MA
Greater Minneapolis Council of Churches—Minneapolis, MN

Highlands Community Ministries—Louisville, KY
Inter-Church Council of Greater New Bedford—New Bedford, MA
Interfaith Community Council, Inc.—New Albany, IN
Interfaith Community Services—St. Joseph, MO
Interfaith Council of Contra Costa County—Walnut Creek, CA
Interfaith Federation of Greater Baton Rouge—Baton Rouge, LA
Inter-Faith Ministries-Wichita—Wichita, KS
InterFaith Works of Central New York—Syracuse, NY
The Long Island Council of Churches—Hempstead, NY
Louisiana Interchurch Conference—Baton Rouge, LA
Metropolitan Ecumenical Ministry—Newark, NJ
Metropolitan Inter Faith Association (MIFA)—Memphis, TN
Mississippi Religious Leadership Conference—Jackson, MS
Montana Association of Churches—Helena, MT
New Hampshire Council of Churches—Pembroke, NH
New Mexico Conference of Churches—Bernalillo, NM
Northside Inter-Church Agency (NICA)—Fort Worth, TX
Northwest Interfaith Movement—Philadelphia, PA
Oklahoma Conference of Churches—Oklahoma City, OK
Paducah Cooperative Ministry—Paducah, KY
Peoria Friendship House of Christian Service—Peoria, IL
St. Matthews Area Ministries—Louisville, KY
San Fernando Valley Interfaith Council—Chatsworth, CA
South Hills Interfaith Ministries—South Park, PA
South Louisville Community Ministries—Louisville, KY
Southeast Ecumenical Ministry—Rochester, NY
Tarrant Area Community of Churches—Fort Worth, TX
Troy Area United Ministries—Troy, NY
Tuscarawas County Council for Church and Community—New Philadelphia, OH
United Religious Community of St. Joseph County—South Bend, IN
Wainwright House—Rye, NY
Wellspring Interfaith Social Services, Inc. (previously West Central Neighborhood Ministry, Inc.)—Fort Wayne, IN
West Side Ecumenical Ministry—Cleveland, OH
Wilkinsburg Community Ministry—Pittsburgh, PA

Substance Abuse Programs

Community Ministries of Rockville—Rockville, MD
Corpus Christi Metro Ministries—Corpus Christi, TX

283

Council of Churches of the Ozarks—Springfield, MO

East End Cooperative Ministry—Pittsburgh, PA

Ecumenical Ministries of Iowa (EMI)—Des Moines, IA

Evanston Ecumenical Action Council—Evanston, IL

Greater Chicago Broadcast Ministries—Chicago, IL

Greater Minneapolis Council of Churches—Minneapolis, MN

Greensboro Urban Ministry—Greensboro, NC

Hanover Area Council of Churches—Hanover, PA

The Metropolitan Christian Council: Detroit-Windsor—Detroit, MI

Metropolitan Ecumenical Ministry—Newark, NJ

Metropolitan Ecumenical Ministry Community Development Corp.—Newark, NJ

Mississippi Religious Leadership Conference—Jackson, MS

Montana Association of Churches—Helena, MT

Muskegon County Cooperating Churches—Muskegon, MI

New Hampshire Council of Churches—Pembroke, NH

North Hills Youth Ministry Counseling Center—Pittsburgh, PA

Pike County Outreach Council—Waverly, OH

Southeast Ecumenical Ministry—Rochester, NY

United Religious Community of St. Joseph County—South Bend, IN

West Side Ecumenical Ministry—Cleveland, OH

West Virginia Council of Churches—Charleston, WV

Wyoming Association of Churches—Cody, WY

Theology and Worship Programs

Akron Area Association of Churches—Akron, OH

Allegheny Valley Association of Churches—Natrona Heights, PA

Arizona Ecumenical Council—Phoenix, AZ

Arkansas Interfaith Conference—Scott, AR

The Associated Churches of Fort Wayne & Allen County, Inc.—Fort Wayne, IN

Associated Ministries of Tacoma-Pierce County—Tacoma, WA

Association of Christian Churches of South Dakota—Sioux Falls, SD

Attleboro Area Council of Churches, Inc.—Attleboro, MA

Brooklyn Council of Churches—Brooklyn, NY

Broome County Council of Churches, Inc.—Binghamton, NY

The Cape Cod Council of Churches, Inc.—Hyannis, MA

Capital Area Council of Churches, Inc.—Albany, NY

Capital Region Ecumenical Organization (CREO)—Malta, NY

Christian Associates of Southwest Pennsylvania—Pittsburgh, PA

Christian Churches United of the Tri-County Area—Harrisburg, PA

Christians United in Beaver County—Beaver, PA

Church Council of Greater Seattle—Seattle, WA

The Church Federation of Greater Indianapolis, Inc.—Indianapolis, IN

Churches United of the Quad City Area—Rock Island, IL

Colorado Council of Churches—Denver, CO

Council of Churches of the City of New York—New York, NY

The Council of Churches of Santa Clara County—San Jose, CA

Council of Churches and Synagogues of Southwestern Connecticut—Stamford, CT

Dutchess County Interfaith Council, Inc.—Poughkeepsie, NY

East Dallas Cooperative Parish—Dallas, TX

The Ecumenical Council of Pasadena Area Churches—Pasadena, CA

Ecumenical Council of San Diego County—San Diego, CA

Ecumenical Ministries of Iowa (EMI)—Des Moines, IA

Ecumenical Ministries of Oregon—Portland, OR

FaithTrust Institute—Seattle, WA

Florida Council of Churches—Tampa, FL

Georgia Christian Council—Macon, GA

Grand Rapids Area Center for Ecumenism (GRACE)—Grand Rapids, MI

Greater Chicago Broadcast Ministries—Chicago, IL

Greater Dallas Community of Churches—Dallas, TX

Greater Dayton Christian Connections—Dayton, OH

Greater Fairmont Council of Churches—Fairmont, WV

Greater Lawrence Council of Churches—Lawrence, MA

Greater New Orleans Federation of Churches—New Orleans, LA

Greater Rochester Community of Churches—Rochester, NY

Greensboro Urban Ministry—Greensboro, NC

Illinois Conference of Churches—Springfield, IL

Inter-Church Council of Greater New Bedford—New Bedford, MA

Inter-Church Ministries of Erie County—Erie, PA

Interchurch Ministries of Nebraska—Lincoln, NE

Interfaith Council—Spokane, WA

Interfaith Mission Service—Huntsville, AL

InterFaith Works of Central New York—Syracuse, NY

Kentuckiana Interfaith Community—Louisville, KY

The Long Island Council of Churches—Hempstead, NY

Mahoning Valley Association of Churches—Youngstown, OH

The Metropolitan Christian Council: Detroit-Windsor—Detroit, MI

Metropolitan Christian Council of Philadelphia—Philadelphia, PA

Metropolitan Ecumenical Ministry—Newark, NJ
Montana Association of Churches—Helena, MT
Muskegon County Cooperating Churches—Muskegon, MI
New Britain Area Conference of Churches (NEWBRACC)—New Britain, CT
New Hampshire Council of Churches—Pembroke, NH
New Mexico Conference of Churches—Bernalillo, NM
North Carolina Council of Churches—Raleigh, NC
Northern Kentucky Interfaith Commission, Inc.—Newport, KY
Oak Park-River Forest Community of Congregations—Oak Park, IL
Oklahoma Conference of Churches—Oklahoma City, OK
The Pennsylvania Council of Churches—Harrisburg, PA
Reading Berks Conference of Churches—Reading, PA
The Regional Council for Christian Ministry, Inc.—Idaho Falls, ID
The Regional Council of Churches of Atlanta—Atlanta, GA
The Rhode Island State Council of Churches—Providence, RI
San Antonio Community of Congregations—San Antonio, TX
Schenectady Inner City Ministry—Schenectady, NY
South East Associated Ministries (SEAM)—Louisville, KY
Tarrant Area Community of Churches—Fort Worth, TX
Texas Conference of Churches—Austin, TX
Troy Area United Ministries—Troy, NY
United Churches of Lycoming County—Williamsport, PA
United Religious Community of St. Joseph County—South Bend, IN
Vermont Ecumenical Council and Bible Society—Richmond, VT
Wainwright House—Rye, NY
Washington Association of Churches—Seattle, WA
Wisconsin Council of Churches—Sun Prairie, WI
Worcester County Ecumenical Council—Worcester, MA
York County Council of Churches—York, PA

Women

Associated Ministries of Tacoma-Pierce County—Tacoma, WA
California Council of Churches-California Church Impact—Sacramento, CA
Chautaugua County Rural Ministry—Dunkirk, NY
Christian Ministries of Delaware County—Muncie, IN
Church Community Services—Elkhart, IN
Community Ministries of Rockville—Rockville, MD

Council of Churches of the City of New York—New York, NY
The Council of Churches of Santa Clara County—San Jose, CA
East Dallas Cooperative Parish—Dallas, TX
Ecumenical Council of San Diego County—San Diego, CA
FaithTrust Institute—Seattle, WA
Genesee-Orleans Ministry of Concern—Albion, NY
Georgia Christian Council—Macon, GA
Greater Birmingham Ministries—Birmingham, AL
Greater Chicago Broadcast Ministries—Chicago, IL
Greater Dallas Community of Churches—Dallas, TX
Inter-Church Council of Greater New Bedford—New Bedford, MA
Interfaith Community Services—St. Joseph, MO
Interfaith Council—Spokane, WA
InterFaith Works of Central New York—Syracuse, NY
Madison-area Urban Ministry—Madison, WI
The Metropolitan Christian Council: Detroit-Windsor—Detroit, MI
Metropolitan Christian Council of Philadelphia—Philadelphia, PA
Metropolitan Ecumenical Ministry—Newark, NJ
Mississippi Religious Leadership Conference—Jackson, MS
Montana Association of Churches—Helena, MT
Network of Religious Communities—Buffalo, NY
New Mexico Conference of Churches—Bernalillo, NM
Oklahoma Conference of Churches—Oklahoma City, OK
Peoria Friendship House of Christian Service—Peoria, IL
The Regional Council of Churches of Atlanta—Atlanta, GA
South Hills Interfaith Ministries—South Park, PA
Wainwright House—Rye, NY
West Side Ecumenical Ministry—Cleveland, OH
Wyoming Association of Churches—Cody, WY

Youth

Arizona Ecumenical Council—Phoenix, AZ
Associated Ministries of Tacoma-Pierce County—Tacoma, WA
Austin Area Interreligious Ministries—Austin, TX
The Cape Cod Council of Churches, Inc.—Hyannis, MA
Center City Churches—Hartford, CT
Christian Ministries of Delaware County—Muncie, IN
The Church Federation of Greater Indianapolis, Inc.—Indianapolis, IN
Churches United of the Quad City Area—Rock Island, IL
Concerned Ecumenical Ministry to the Upper West Side—Buffalo, NY

285

7. Canadian Regional and Local Ecumenical Bodies

Most of the organizations listed below are councils of churches in which churches participate officially, whether at the parish or judicatory level. They operate at the city, metropolitan area, or county level. Parish clusters within urban areas are not included.

Canadian local ecumenical bodies operate without paid staff, with the exception of a few which have part-time staff. In most cases, the name and address of the president or chairperson is listed. As these offices change from year to year, some of the information may be out of date by the time the Yearbook of American and Canadian Churches is published.

ALBERTA

Calgary Council of Churches
120 17th Ave., Calgary, AB T2S 2T2 Tel. (403) 218 - 5521
Media Contact: Fr. James Hagel
Email: ecumenism@rcdiocese-calgary.ab.ca

Calgary Inter-Faith Community Action Association
2405 Macleod Trail SW, Calgary, AB T2G 2P3 Tel. (403)262-5171
Media Contact: J. McGrath
Email: jmcgrath@shawcable.com
Website: www.calgary-interfaith.ab.ca

BRITISH COLUMBIA

Greater Victoria Council of Churches
St. Alban's Church, 1468 Ryan St. at Balmont, Victoria, BC V8R 2X1
Media Contact: Rev. Edwin Taylor

Multifaith Action Society of British Columbia
5 - 305 West 41st Ave., Vancouver, BC V5Y 2S5 Tel. (604)321-1302 Fax (604)321-1370
Media Contact: Nancy A. Chiavario
Email: admin@multifaithaction.org
Website: www.multifaithaction.org

Vancouver Council of Churches
700 Kingsway, Vancouver, BC V5V 3C1 Tel. (604)420-0761
Media Contact: Murray Moerman

MANITOBA

Association of Christian Churches in Manitoba
150 de la Cathedrale Ave., Winnipeg, MB R2H 0H6 Tel. (204)237-9851*

NEW BRUNSWICK

Atlantic Ecumenical Council of Churches
170 Daniel Ave., Saint John, NB E2K 4S7 Tel. (506)538-2491

Media Contact: Rev. Rufus Onyewuchi
Email: mknowles@ ns.sympatico.ca

First Miramichi Inter-Church Council
Doaktown, NB E0C 1G0
Media Contact: Ellen Robinson

Moncton Area Council of Churches
135 Mount Royal Blvd., Moncton, NB E1E 2V5 Tel. (506)382-7725
Media Contact: Rev. Donald Routledge

NEWFOUNDLAND

St. John's Area Council of Churches
31 Hazelwood Cres., St. John's, NF A1E 6B3 Tel. (709)579-0536
Media Contact: Rev. Canon Ralph Billard
Email: ralphbillard@nl.rogers.com

NOVA SCOTIA

Atlantic Ecumenical Council of Churches
Box 637, 90 Victoria St., Amherst, NS B4H 4B4 Tel. (902)864-1834
Media Contact: Rev. Dr. Chris Coffin
Email: jhtye@isn.net

Bridgewater Inter-Church Council
30 Parkdale Ave., Bridgewater, NS B4V 1L8
Media Contact: Wilson Jones
Email: wjones@ns.sympatico.ca

Cornwallis District Inter-Church Council
Centreville, RR 2, Kings County, NS B0T 1J0
Media Contact: Mr. Tom Regan

Industrial Cape Breton Council of Churches
24 Huron Ave., Sydney Mines, NS B1S 1V2
Media Contact: Rev. Karen Ralph

Kentville Council of Churches
325-325 Main St., Kentville, NS B4N 1C5
Media Contact: Rev. Canon S.J.P. Davies

Lunenburg Queens BA Association
66 Hillside Dr., RR 4, Bridgewater, NS B4V 2W3 Tel. 902-543-3328
Media Contact: Mrs. Nilda Chute
Email: n-chute@ns.sympatico.ca

Mahone Bay Interchurch Council
RR 1, Blockhouse, NS B0J 1E0
Media Contact: Patricia Joudrey

Pictou Council of Churches
P.O. Box 70, Pictou, NS B0K 1H0
Media Contact: Rev. D.J. Murphy

Queens County Association of Churches
Box 537, Liverpool, NS B0T 1K6
Media Contact: Mr. Donald Burns

ONTARIO

Burlington Inter-Church Council
425 Breckenwood, Burlington, ON L7L 2J6
Media Contact: Mr. Fred Townsend
Email: eandbwheeler@sympatico.ca

Christian Leadership Council of Downtown Toronto
40 Homewood Ave. #509, Toronto, ON M4Y 2K2
Media Contact: Ken Bhagan

Ecumenical Committee
76 Eastern Ave., Sault Ste. Marie, ON P6A 4R2
Media Contact: Rev. William B. Kidd

Glengarry-Prescott-Russell Christian Council
St. Eugene's, Prescott, ON K0B 1P0
Media Contact: Rev. G. Labrosse

The Greater Toronto Council of Christian Churches
1155 Yonge St., Toronto, ON M4T 1W2 Tel. (416) 934 - 3400 ext. 344
Media Contact: Father Damian MacPherson
Email: dmacpherson@archtoronto.org

Ignace Council of Churches
Box 5, 205 Pine St., Ignace, ON P0T 1H0

Inter Church Council of Burlington
P.O. Box 62120, Burlington Mall R.P.O., Burlington, ON L7R 4K2 Tel. (905)333-0515
Media Contact: Rev. Moe Anderson
Email: webmaster@iccb.ca
Website: www.iccb.ca

Kitchener-Waterloo Council of Churches
53 Allen St. E., Waterloo, ON N2J 1J3
Media Contact: Rev. Clarence Hauser, CR

London Inter-City Faith Team
United Church, 711 Colbourne St., London, ON N6A 3Z4
Media Contact: David Carouthers

Massey Inter-Church Council
Box 238, Massey, ON P0P 1P0 Tel. (705)865-2202
Media Contact: Rev. Brian Sonnenburg

Ottowa Christian Council of the Capital Area
1247 Kilborn Ave., Ottowa, ON K1H 6K9

St. Catharines & District Clergy Fellowship
663 Vince St., St. Catharines, ON L2M 3V8
Media Contact: Rev. Victor Munro

Spadina-Bloor Interchurch Council
Bathurst St. United Church, 427 Bloor St. W., Toronto, ON M5S 1X7
Media Contact: Rev. Frances Combes

Stratford & District Council of Churches
202 Erie St., Stratford, ON N5A 2M8
Media Contact: Rev. Ted Heinze

Thorold Inter-Faith Council
1 Dunn St., St. Catharines, ON L2T 1P3

Thunder Bay Council of Churches
1800 Moodie St. E., Thunder Bay, ON P7E 4Z2
Media Contact: Rev. Richard Darling

PRINCE EDWARD ISLAND

Atlantic Ecumenical Council
Immaculate Conception Church, St. Louis, PEI C0B 1Z0 Tel. (902)963-2202 or (902)882-2610
Media Contact: Rev. Arthur J. Pendergast

Summerside Christian Council
P.O. Box 1551, Summerside, PEI C1N 4K4
Media Contact: Ms. A. Kathleen Miller

QUEBEC

Action des Chrétiens pour l'Abolition de la Torture
15 rue de Castelnau Ouest, Montréal, QC H2R 2W3 Tel. (514)890-6169
Media Contact: Raoul Lincourt
Email: info@acatcanada.org
Website: www.acatcanada.org

AGAPÉ Deux-Montagnes
1002 chemin d'Oka, Deux-Montagnes, QC J7R 1L7 Tel. (450)473-9877
Media Contact: Donald Tremblay

Canadian Centre for Ecumenism
2065 Sherbrooke St. West, Montreal, QC H3H
1G6 Tel. (514) 937-9176
Media Contact: Dr. Stuart Brown, Director
Email: ccocce@oecumenisme.ca

Centre Emmaüs
Centre de spiritualité des Églisesd'Orient, 3774
chemin Queen-Mary, 3e étage, Montréal, QC
H3V 1A6 Tel. (514)276-2144
Email: centre-emmaus@hotmail.com
Website: www.centre-emmaus.qc.ca

Christian-Jewish Dialogue of Montreal
c/oTemple Emanu-El-Beth Sholom, 4100
Sherbrooke St. West, Westmount, QC H3Z
1A5 Tel. (514)937-3575 or (514)937-3708
Media Contact: Rev. Ihor Kutash
Email: rabbi@templemontreal.ca

Comité Québécois du Dialogue musulman-chrétien
1640 rueSt. Hubert, Montréal, QC H2L 3Z3 Tel.
(514)849-1167 Fax (514)284-2034
Media Contact: RP Gilles Barrette
Email: gilbar1945@yahoo.ca
Website: www.interreligion.com

Direction Chrétienne
1450 rue City Councillors, bureau 520,
Montréal, QC H3A 2E6 Tel. (514)878-3035
Fax (514)878-8048
Media Contact: Rev. Glenn Smith
Email: info@direction.ca
Website: www.direction.ca

Hemmingford Ecumenical Committee
Box 300, Hemmingford, QC J0L 1H0
Media Contact: Catherine Priest

Interfaith Council of Montréal
2065 Sherbrooke West, Montréal, QC H3H 1G6
Tel. (514) 937-9176 Fax (514) 937-4986
Media Contact: Mandit Singh, President
Email: info@oikoumene.ca
Website: www.oikoumene.ca

Montreal Association for the Blind Foundation
7000 Sherbrooke St. W., Montréal, QC H4B 1R3
Tel. (514)489-8201 Fax (514)489-3477
Media Contact: Rev. Dr. John A. Simms
Email: info@mab.ca
Website: www.mab.ca

Radio Ville-Marie
Radio religieuse, 505 avenue de Mont-Cassin,
Montréal, QC H3L 1W7 Tel. (514)382-3913
or (877)668-6601 Fax (514)858-0965
Email: cira@radiovm.com
Website: www.radiovm.com

Réseau Oecuménique Justice et Paix
114 Secc. D., Montréal, QC H3K 3B9 Tel.
(514)937-2683 Fax (514)937-2683
Media Contact: Jean-Luc Djigo
Email: info@justicepaix.org
Website: www.justicepaix.org

Réseau Oecuménique du Québec (Quebec Ecumenical Network)
le Centre canadien d'oecuménisme en assure le
secretariat, 2065 rue Sherbrooke ouest,
Montréal, QC H3H 1G6 Tel. (514)937-9176
Fax (514)937-4986
Media Contact: Friends
Email: ccocce@oecumenisme.ca
Website: www.oecumenisme.ca

The St. Bruno Ecumenical Group
Holy Trinity Anglican Church, 140 Beaumont St.
East, St. Bruno, QC J3V 5L9 Tel. (450)653-
4531

UNITAS
Centre oecuménique de meditation chrétienne et
de spiritualité, 1950 rue St. Antoine Ouest,
Montréal, QC H3J 1A5 Tel. (514)485-0009
Media Contact: Friends
Email: info@unitasmeditation.ca
Website: www.unitasmeditation.ca

SASKATCHEWAN

Humboldt Clergy Council
Box 1989, Humboldt, SK S0K 2A0
Media Contact: Fr. Leo Hinz, OSB

Melville Association of Churches
Box 878, Melville, SK S0A 2P0 Tel. (306)
728-5081
Media Contact: Catherine Gaw

Prairie Centre for Ecumenism
600 45th Street W., Saskatoon, SK S7L 5W9 Tel.
(306)653-1633 Fax (306)653-1821
Media Contact: Rev. Dr. Jan Bigland-Pritchard,
Director
Email: pce@ecumenism.net
Website: www.ecumenism.net

Regina Council of Churches
2660 Albert St, Regina, SK S4P 2V9 Tel.
(306)545-3375
Media Contact: Joan Galvin
Email: jegalvin@saskatel.net

8. Theological Seminaries and Bible Colleges in the United States

The following list includes theological seminaries, Bible colleges and departments in colleges and universities in which ministerial training is given. Many denominations have additional programs.

Inclusion in or exclusion from this list implies no judgment about the quality or accreditation of any institution. Those schools that are members of the Association of Theological Schools are marked with a (‡). Those schools that are accredited by the Transnational Association of Christian Colleges and Schools are marked with a (†). Additional information about enrollment in ATS member schools can be found in the "Trends in Seminary Enrollment" section of chapter III. Information about TRACS and ATS can be found in the United States Cooperative Organizations section of chapter II.

Each of the listings include when available: the institution name, denominational sponsor, location, the president or dean of the institution, telephone and fax numbers and email and website addresses.

Abilene Christian University Graduate School of Theology‡ (Churches of Christ), Jack R. Reese, Dean, College of Biblical Studies, ACU Box 29422; 1850 N. Judge Ely Boulevard, CBS Room 297, Abilene, TX 79699-9422 Tel. (325)674-3700 Fax (325)674-6180
Email: thompson@bible.acu.edu
Website: www.acu.edu/GST

Alaska Bible College (Nondenominational), Nick Ringger, President, P.O. Box 289, Glennallen, AK 99588 Tel. (907)822-3201 Fax (907)822-5027
Email: info@akbible.edu
Website: www.akbible.edu

Alliance Theological Seminary‡ (The Christian and Missionary Alliance), Michael G. Scales, President, 350 N. Highland Ave., Nyack, NY 10960-1416 Tel. (845)353-2020 Fax (845)727-3002
Email: Emily.Wilkins@nyack.edu
Website: www.alliance.edu

American Baptist College (National Baptist Convention USA, Inc.), Dr. Forrest E. Harris, Sr., President, 1800 Baptist World Center Dr., Nashville, TN 37207 Tel. (615)256-1463 Fax (615)226-7855
Email: jwright@abcnash.edu
Website: www.abcnash.edu

American Baptist Seminary of the West‡ (American Baptist Churches in the USA), Keith A. Russell, President, 2606 Dwight Way, Berkeley, CA 94704-3029 Tel. (510)841-1905 Fax (510)841-2446
Email: krussell@absw.edu
Website: www.absw.edu

Anderson University School of Theology‡ (Church of God (Anderson, Ind.)), James L. Edwards, President, 1100 East Fifth Street, Anderson, IN 46012-3495 Tel. (765)641-4032 Fax (765)641-3851
Email: dlneidert@anderson.edu
Website: www.anderson.edu/academics/sot

Andover Newton Theological School‡ (American Baptist Churches in the USA; United Church of Christ), Nick Carter, President, 210 Herrick Rd., Newton Centre, MA 02459 Tel. (617)964-1100 Fax (617)558-9785
Email: admissions@ants.edu
Website: www.ants.edu

Apex School of Theology (Interdenominational), Dr. Joseph E. Perkins, President, 5104 Revere Road, Durham, NC 27713 Tel. (919) 572-1625 Fax (919) 572-1762
Email: info@apexsot.edu
Website: www.apexsot.edu

Appalachian Bible College (Nondenominational), Daniel L. Anderson, President, P.O. Box ABC, Bradley, WV 25818 Tel. (304)877-6428 Fax (304)877-5082
Email: abc@abc.edu,
Website: www.abc.edu

Aquinas Institute of Theology‡ (Catholic Church), The Rev. Charles E. Bouchard, O.P., President, 3642 Lindell Blvd., St. Louis, MO 63108-3396 Tel. (314)977-3882 Fax (314)977-7225
Email: aquinas@slu.edu
Website: www.ai.edu

Arlington Baptist College (Baptist), David Bryant, President, 3001 W. Division, Arlington, TX 76012-3425 Tel. (817)461-8741 Fax (817)274-1138
Email: info@abconline.org
Website: www.abconline.edu

Asbury Theological Seminary‡ (Inter/Multidenominational), Jeffrey E Greenway, President, 204 N. Lexington Ave., Wilmore, KY 40390-1199 Tel. (859)858-3581
Website: www.asburyseminary.edu

Ashland Theological Seminary‡ (Brethren Church (Ashland, Ohio)), John C. Shultz, President, 910 Center St., Ashland, OH 44805 Tel. (419)289-5161 Fax (419)289-5969
Email: jshultz@ashland.edu
Website: www.ashland.edu/seminary

290

Assemblies of God Theological Seminary‡ (Assemblies of God), Byron D. Klaus, President, 1435 North Glenstone Avenue, Springfield, MO 65802-2131 Tel. (417)268-1000 Fax (417)268-1001
Email: agts@agseminary.edu
Website: www.agts.edu

Associated Mennonite Biblical Seminary‡ (Mennonite Church; General Conference Mennonite Church), J. Nelson Kraybill, President, 3003 Benham Ave., Elkhart, IN 46517-1999 Tel. (574)295-3726 Fax (574)295-0092
Email: nkraybill@ambs.edu
Website: www.ambs.edu

Athenaeum of Ohio‡ (The Catholic Church), Edward P. Smith, President and Rector, 6616 Beechmont Ave., Cincinnati, OH 45230-2091 Tel. (513)231-2223 Fax (513)231-3254
Email: atheathenaeum.edu
Website: www.athenaeum.edu

Atlanta Christian College (Christian Churches and Churches of Christ), R. Edwin Groover, President, 2605 Ben Hill Rd., East Point, GA 30344 Tel. (404)761-8861 Fax (404)669-2024
Email: admissions@acc.edu
Website: www.acc.edu

Austin Presbyterian Theological Seminary‡ (Presbyterian Church (U.S.A.)), Theodore J. Wardlaw, President, 100 E. 27th St., Austin, TX 78705-5797 Tel. (512)472-6736 Fax (512)479-0738
Email: admissions@austinseminary.edu
Website: www.austinseminary.edu

Bakke Graduate University of Ministry† (Non-Denominational), Brad Smith, President, 1013 Eighth Ave, Suite 401, Seattle, WA 98104 Tel. (206) 264-9100 Fax (206)624-8828
Email: bgu@bgu.edu
Website: www.bgu.edu

Bangor Theological Seminary‡ (United Church of Christ; Ecumenical; Interfaith), Kent J. Ulery, President, Two College Circle, PO Box 411 and 159 State Street, Portland ME 04101, Bangor, ME 04402-0411 Tel. (207)942-6781 Fax (207)942-4914
Email: mhuddy@bts.edu
Website: www.bts.edu

Baptist Bible College (Baptist Bible Fellowship International), Jim Edge, President, 628 E. Kearney, Springfield, MO 65803 Tel. (417)268-6060 Fax (417)268-6694
Email: info@baptist.edu
Website: www.baptist.edu

Baptist Bible College and Seminary (Baptist), Jim Jeffery, President, 538 Venard Rd., Clarks Summit, PA 18411 Tel. (570)586-2400 Fax (570)586-1753
Email: bbc@bbc.edu
Website: www.bbc.edu

Baptist Missionary Association Theological Seminary‡ (Baptist Missionary Association of America), Charley Holmes, President, 1530 E. Pine St., Jacksonville, TX 75766 Tel. (903)586-2501 Fax (903)586-0378
Email: bmatsem@bmats.edu
Website: www.bmats.edu

Baptist Theological Seminary at Richmond‡ (Cooperative Baptist Fellowship), Thomas H. Graves, President, 3400 Brook Rd., Richmond, VA 23227 Tel. (804)355-8135 Fax (804)355-8182
Email: tgraves@btsr.edu
Website: www.btsr.edu

Barclay College (Interdenominational), Maurice G. Chandler, President, 607 N Kingman, Haviland, KS 67059 Tel. (620)862-5252 Fax (620)862-5403
Email: carju@barclaycollege.edu
Website: www.barclaycollege.edu

Barry University Department of Theology and Philosophy‡, Mark E. Wedig, Chair of the Department of Theology and Philosophy, 11300 Northeast Second Avenue, Miami Shores, FL 33161-6695 Tel. (305)899-3469 Fax (305)899-3385
Email: theology@mail.barry.edu
Website: www.barry.edu/TheologyPhilosophy /default

Bay Ridge Christian College (Church of God (Anderson, Ind.)), Dr. Verda Beach, President, P.O. Box 726, Kendleton, TX 77451 Tel. (979)532-3982 Fax (979)532-4352
Email: brccampus@wcnet.net
Website: brcconline.org

Beacon College & Graduate School† (Non-Denominational), Dr. John Durden, Dean, 6003 Veterans Parkway, Columbus, GA 31909 Tel. (706)323-5364 Fax (706)323-3236
Email: beacon@beacon.edu
Website: www.beacon.edu

Beeson Divinity School of Samford University‡ (Inter/Multidenominational), Timothy George, Dean, 800 Lakeshore Dr., Birmingham, AL 35229-2252 Tel. (205)726-2991 Fax (205)726-2260
Email: JTPrince@samford.edu
Website: www.beesondivinity.com

Berkeley Divinity School‡ (Episcopal Church), Joseph H. Britton, Dean, 409 Prospect Street, New Haven, CT 06511 Tel. (203)432-9285, or -9290 Fax (203)432-9353
Email: joseph.britton@yale.edu
Website: www.yale.edu/berkeleydivinity

Bethany Lutheran Theological Seminary (Evangelical Lutheran Synod), G. R. Schmeling, President, 6 Browns Court, Mankato, MN 56001 Tel. (507)344-7354 Fax (507)344-7426
Email: gschmeli@blc.edu
Website: www.blts.edu

291

Bethany Theological Seminary‡ (Church of the Brethren), Ruthann K. Johansen, President, 615 National Rd. W., Richmond, IN 47374 Tel. (765)983-1800 Fax (765)983-1840
Email: president@bethanyseminary.edu
Website: www.bethanyseminary.edu

Bethel Seminary of Bethel University‡ (Coverge Worldwide (Baptist General Conference)), James Barnes III, President, 3949 Bethel Dr., St. Paul, MN 55112 Tel. (651)638-6180 Fax (651)638-6002
Email: c-pfingsten@bethel.edu
Website: www.bethel.edu

Beulah Heights Bible College† (The International Pentecostal Church of Christ), Dr. Benson M. Karanja, Ed. D., President, 892 Berne St. SE, Atlanta, GA 30316 Tel. (404)627-2681 Fax (404)627-0702
Email: Benson.Karanja@beulah.org
Website: www.beulah.org

Bexley Hall Seminary‡ (Episcopal Church), John R. Kevern, President and Dean, 583 Sheridan Avenue, Columbus, OH 43209-2325 Tel. (614)231-3095 Fax (614)231-3236
Email: bexleyhall@bexley.edu
Website: www.bexley.edu

Bible Church of Christ Theological Institute (Nondenominational), Roy Bryant, Sr., President, 1358 Morris Ave., Bronx, NY 10456-1402 Tel. (718)588-2284 Fax (718)992-5597
Email: info@thebiblechurchofchrist.org
Website: www.thebiblechurchofchrist.org

Biblical Theological Seminary‡ (Inter/Multidenominational), David G. Dunbar, President, 200 N. Main St., Hatfield, PA 19440 Tel. (215)368-5000 Fax (215)368-2301
Email: president@biblical.edu
Website: www.biblical.edu

Blessed John XXIII National Seminary‡ (Catholic Church), Francis D. Kelly, Rector, 558 South Avenue, Weston, MA 02493-2699 Tel. (781)899-5500 Fax (781)899-9057
Email: seminary@blessedjohnxxiii.edu
Website: www.blessedjohnxxiii.edu

Boise Bible College (Christian Churches and Churches of Christ), Dr. Charles A. Crane, President, 8695 Marigold St., Boise, ID 83714 Tel. (208)376-7731 Fax (208)376-7743
Email: boisebible@boisebible.edu
Website: www.boisebible.edu

Boston Baptist College† (Baptist), Rev. David Melton, President, 950 Metropolitan Avenue, Boston, MA 02136 Tel. (617)364-3510 Fax (617)364-0723
Email: mail@boston.edu/gsnavely@boston.edu
Website: www.boston.edu

Boston College School of Theology and Ministry (Catholic Church), Richard Clifford, S.J., Dean, 140 Commonwealth Avenue, Chestnut Hill, MA 02467-3800, Tel. (617)552-6501 or (800)487-1167
Email: STMadmissions@bc.edu
Website: www.bc.edu/schools/stm/

Boston University School of Theology‡ (The United Methodist Church), Ray L. Hart, Dean, 745 Commonwealth Ave., Boston, MA 02215 Tel. (617)353-3050 Fax (617)353-3061
Website: www.bu.edu/STH

Brite Divinity School, Texas Christian University‡ (Christian Church (Disciples of Christ)), Newell Williams, President, TCU Box 298130, Ft. Worth, TX 76129-0002 Tel. (817)257-7575 Fax (817)257-7305
Email: k.winter@tcu.edu
Website: www.brite.tcu.edu

Byzantine Catholic Seminary of SS. Cyril and Methodius‡ (Byzantine Catholic Archeparchy of Pittsburgh), John G. Petro, Rector, 3605 Perrysville Ave., Pittsburgh, PA 15214 Tel. (412)321-8383 Fax (412)321-9936
Email: m.andrako@verizon.net
Website: www.byzcathsem.org

California Christian College† (Free Will Baptist), Wendell Walley, President, 4881 E. University Avenue, Fresno, CA 93703 Tel. (559)251-4215 Fax (559)251-4231
Email: cccregistrar@sbcglobal.net
Website: www.calchristiancollege.org

Calvary Bible College and Calvary Theological Seminary (Independent Fundamental Churches of America, International), Elwood H. Chipchase, D.Min., D.D., President, 15800 Calvary Rd., Kansas City, MO 64147-1341 Tel. (800)326-3960 Fax (816)331-4474
Email: president@calvary.edu
Website: www.calvary.edu

Calvin Theological Seminary‡ (Christian Reformed Church in North America), The Rev. Cornelius Plantinga, Jr., Ph.D., President, 3233 Burton St. S.E., Grand Rapids, MI 49546-4387 Tel. (616)957-6036; (616)957-6044 Fax (616)957-8621
Email: sempres@calvinseminary.edu
Website: www.calvinseminary.edu

Campbell University Divinity School‡ (Baptist State Convention of North Carolina), Michael G. Cogdill, Dean, 116 T. T. Lanier Street PO Drawer 4050, Buies Creek, NC 27506 Tel. (910)893-1830 Fax (910)893-1835
Email: cogdill@campbell.edu
Website: www.campbell.edu/divinity

Candler School of Theology of Emory University‡ (The United Methodist Church), Jan Love, Dean, 500 Kilgo Circle N.E., Emory Univ., Atlanta, GA 30322 Tel. (404)727-6324 Fax (404)727-3182
Email: candler@emory.edu
Website: www.emory.edu/candler

Capital Bible Seminary‡ (Nondenominational), Larry A. Mercer, President, 6511 Princess Garden Parkway, Lanham, MD 20706 Tel. (301)552-1400 Fax (301)614-1024
Email: bfox@bible.edu
Website: www.bible.edu

Carolina Evangelical Divinity School‡ (Religious Society of Friends), Frank P. Scurry, President, P.O. Box 7841, High Point, NC 27265 Tel. (336)882-3370 Fax (336)882-3370
Email: fscurry@ceds.edu
Website: www.ceds.edu

Catholic Theological Union at Chicago‡ (Catholic Church), Donald Senior, C.P., President, 5401 S. Cornell Ave., Chicago, IL 60615-5664 Tel. (773)371-5400 Fax (773)324-8490
Email: donald@ctu.edu
Website: www.ctu.edu

Catholic University of America School of Theology and Religious Studies‡ (Catholic Church), Rev. Msgr. Kevin W. Irwin, Dean, 620 Michigan Avenue NE, Washington, DC 20064 Tel. (202)319-5683 Fax (202)319-4967
Email: cua-deansrs@cua.edu
Website: www.trs.cua.edu

Central Baptist College (Baptist Missionary Association of Arkansas), Terry Kimbrow, President, 1501 College Ave., Conway, AR 72032 Tel. (501)329-6872 Fax (501)329-2941
Email: TKimbrow@cbc.edu
Website: www.cbc.edu

Central Baptist Theological Seminary‡ (Baptist), The Rev. Dr. Molly T. Marshall, President, 6601 Monticello Road, Shawnee, KS 66226-3513 Tel. (913)667-5700 Fax (913)371-8110
Email: kansascity@cbts.edu
Website: www.cbts.edu

Central Baptist Theological Seminary in Indiana (National Baptist Convention USA, Inc.), Dr. Robert Lee, President-Dean, 1535 Dr. A. J. Brown Ave. N., Indianapolis, IN 46202 Tel. (317)636-6622
Email: henriettabrown@webtv.net

Central Bible College (Assemblies of God), In Transition, President, 3000 N. Grant Ave., Springfield, MO 65803 Tel. (417)833-2551 Fax (417)833-5141
Email: info@cbcag.edu
Website: www.cbcag.edu

Central Christian College of the Bible (Christian Churches and Churches of Christ), Ronald L. Oakes, D.Min, President, 911 E. Urbandale Dr., Moberly, MO 65270-1997 Tel. (660)263-3900 Fax (660)263-3936
Email: president@cccb.edu
Website: www.cccb.edu

Central Indian Bible College (Assemblies of God), M George Kallappa, President, P.O. Box 550, Mobridge, SD 57601 Tel. (605)845-7801 Fax (605)845-7744

Chapman Seminary of Oakland City University‡ (General Association of General Baptists), Ray G. Barber, President, 138 Lucretia Street, Oakland City, IN 47660 Tel. (812)749-4781 Fax (812)749-1233
Email: bbenson@oak.edu
Website: www.oak.edu

Chicago Theological Seminary‡ (United Church of Christ), Susan Brooks Thistlethwaite, President, 5757 South University Ave., Chicago, IL 60637-1507 Tel. (773)752-5757 Fax (773)752-5925
Email: sthistle@ctschicago.edu, lredmond@ctschicago.edu
Website: www.ctschicago.edu

Christ the King Seminary‡ (Catholic Church), Rev. Peter J. Drilling, President and Rector, 711 Knox Rd., P.O. Box 607, East Aurora, NY 14052-0607 Tel. (716)652-8900 Fax (716)652-8903
Email: pdrilling@cks.edu
Website: www.cks.edu

Christ the Savior Seminary (The American Carpatho-Russian Orthodox Greek Catholic Church), Nicholas Smisko, President, 225 Chandler Ave., Johnstown, PA 15906 Tel. (814)539-0116 Fax (814)536-4699
Email: csseminary@atlanticbb.net
Website: www.acrod.org/seminary

Christian Life College† (Non-Denominational), Harry Schmidt, President, 400 E. Gregory Street, Mount Prospect, IL 60056 Tel. (847)259-1840 Fax (847)259-3888
Email: admissions@christianlifecollege.edu
Website: www.christianlifecollege.edu

Christian Theological Seminary‡ (Christian Church (Disciples of Christ)), Dr. Edward L. Wheeler, President, 1000 W. 42nd St., Indianapolis, IN 46208-3301 Tel. (317)924-1331 Fax (317)923-1961
Email: wheeler@cts.edu
Website: www.cts.edu

Christian Witness Theological Seminary‡ (Nondenominational), Rev. David A. Cheung, President, 1040 Oak Grove Rd., Concord, CA 94518 Tel. (925)676-5002 Fax (925)676-5220
Email: admin@cwts.edu
Website: cwts.edu

Church Divinity School of the Pacific‡ (Episcopal Church), Donn F. Morgan, President, 2451 Ridge Rd., Berkeley, CA 94709-1217 Tel. (510)204-0700 Fax (510)644-0712
Email: jrobinson@cdsp.edu
Website: www.cdsp.edu

Church of God Theological Seminary‡ (Church of God (Cleveland, Tenn.)), Steven J. Land, President, P.O. Box 3330, Cleveland, TN 37320-3330 Tel. (423)478-1131 Fax (423)478-7711
Email: tgilbert@cogts.edu
Website: www.cogts.edu

293

Cincinnati Bible Seminary of Cincinnati Christian University‡ (Christian Churches and Churches of Christ), David M. Faust, President, 2700 Glenway Ave., Cincinnati, OH 45204-3200 Tel. (513)244-8120, (513)244-8100, 800-949-4228 Fax (513)244-8434 Email: judy.pratt@ccuniversity.edu/ linda.palmerccuniversity.edu Website: www.CCuniversity.edu

Circleville Bible College (Churches of Christ in Christian Union), John Conley, President, P.O. Box 458, Circleville, OH 43113 Tel. (740)474-8896 Fax (740)477-7755 Email: stolbert@biblecollege.edu Website: www.biblecollege.edu

Claremont School of Theology‡ (The United Methodist Church), Jerry D. Campbell, President, 1325 N. College Ave., Claremont, CA 91711-3199 Tel. (909)447-2500 Fax (909) 621-3437 Email: jcampbell@cst.edu Website: www.cst.edu

Clear Creek Baptist Bible College (Southern Baptist Convention), President Bill Whittaker, President, 300 Clear Creek Rd., Pineville, KY 40977 Tel. (606)337-3196 Fax (606)337-2372 Email: ccbbc@ccbbc.edu Website: www.ccbbc.edu

Clinton Junior College† (African Methodist Episcopal Zion Church), Dr. Elaine Johnson Copeland, President, 1029 Crawford Road, Rock Hill, SC 29730 Tel. (803)327-7402 Fax (803)327-3261 Email: ecopeland@clintonjrcollege.org Website: www.clintonjrcollege.org

Colegio Biblico Pentecostal de Puerto Rico (Church of God (Cleveland, Tenn.)), Dr. Ildefonso Caraballo, President, P.O. Box 901, Saint Just, PR 00978 Tel. (787)761-0640 Fax (787)748-9228 Email: ildefonso@cbp.edu Website: www.cbp.edu

Colgate Rochester Crozer Divinity School‡ (American Baptist Churches in the USA), Eugene C. Bay, President, 1100 S. Goodman St., Rochester, NY 14620 Tel. (585)271-1320 Fax (585)271-8013 Email: thalbrooks@crcds.edu Website: www.crcds.edu

Colorado Christian University (Nondenominational), Larry R. Donnithorne, President, 180 S. Garrison St., Lakewood, CO 80226 Tel. (303)202-0100 Fax (303)274-7560 Email: dlong@ccu.edu Website: www.ccu.edu

Columbia International University Seminary & School of Missions‡ (Multidenominational), William H. Jones, President, PO Box 3122, Columbia, SC 29230-3122 Tel. (803) 754-4100 Fax (803)786-4209 Email: publicrelations@ciu.edu Website: www.ciu.edu

Columbia Theological Seminary‡ (Presbyterian Church (U.S.A.)), Laura S. Mendenhall, President, 701 Columbia Dr., P.O. Box 520, Decatur, GA 30031 Tel. (404)378-8821 Fax (404)377-9696 Email: MendenhallL@CTSnet.edu Website: www.CTSnet.edu

Concordia Seminary‡ (The Lutheran Church-Missouri Synod), Dale A. Meyer, President, 801 Seminary Place, St. Louis, MO 63105 Tel. (314)505-7010 Fax (314)505-7002 Email: bartelta@csl.edu Website: www.csl.edu

Concordia Theological Seminary‡ (The Lutheran Church-Missouri Synod), Dean O. Wenthe, President, 6600 N. Clinton St., Ft. Wayne, IN 46825-4996 Tel. (260)452-2100 Fax (260)452-2121 Email: wenthedo@mail.ctsfw.edu Website: www.ctsfw.edu

Covenant Theological Seminary‡ (Prebyterian Church in America), Dr. Bryan Chapell, President, 12330 Conway Rd., St. Louis, MO 63141-8697 Tel. (314)434-4044 Fax (314)434-4819 Email: kathy.woodward@covenantseminary.edu Website: www.covenantseminary.edu

Cranmer Seminary (The Episcopal Orthodox Church; The Anglican Rite Synod in the Americas; The Orthodox Anglican Communion), The Most Rev. Scott E. McLaughlin, D.D., Ph.D., President, 901 English Rd., High Point, NC 27262 Tel. (336)885-6032 Fax (336)885-6021 Email: seminaryinfo@orthodoxanglican.net Website: orthodoxanglican.net; divinityschool.org

Criswell Center for Biblical Studies (Southern Baptist Convention), President, 4010 Gaston Ave., Dallas, TX 75246 Tel. (214)821-5433 Fax (214)818-1320 Email: jjohnson@criswell.edu Website: www.criswell.edu

Crossroads College (Christian Churches and Churches of Christ - Non-denominational), Michael Kilgallin, President, 920 Mayowood Rd. S.W., Rochester, MN 55902 Tel. (507)288-4563 Fax (507)288-9046 Email: academic@crossroadscollege.edu Website: www.crossroadscollege.edu

Crown College (The Christian and Missionary Alliance), Rick Man, President, 8700 College View Dr., St. Bonifacius, MN 55375-9001 Tel. (952)446-4100 Fax (952)446-4149 Email: crown@crown.edu Website: www.crown.edu

Cummins Theological Seminary (Reformed Episcopal Church), James C. West, President, 705 S. Main St., Summerville, SC 29483 Tel. (843)873-3451 Fax (843)875-6200
Email: jcw121@aol.com,
canon_moock@prodigy.net
Website: www.recus.org

Dallas Christian College (Christian Churches and Churches of Christ), Dustin "Dusty" Rubeck, President, 2700 Christian Pkwy, Dallas, TX 75234 Tel. (972)241-3371 Fax (972)241-8021
Email: dcc@dallas.edu
Website: www.dallas.edu

Dallas Theological Seminary‡ (Inter/Multidenominational), Dr. Mark L. Bailey, President, 3909 Swiss Ave., Dallas, TX 75204 Tel. (214)824-3094 Fax (214)841-3625
Email: kgrassmick@dts.edu
Website: www.dts.edu

Davis College (Practical Bible College) (Independent Baptist), Dr. George Miller, President, 400 Riverside Drive, Johnson City, NY 13790 Tel. (607)729-1581 Fax (607)729-2962
Website: www.davisny.edu

Denver Seminary‡ (Nondenominational), Mark S. Young, PhD, President, 6399 S. Santa Fe Drive, Littleton, CO 80120 Tel. (303)761-2482 Fax (303)761-8060
Email: info@denverseminary.edu
Website: www.denverseminary.edu

The Disciples Divinity House of the University of Chicago (Christian Church (Disciples of Christ)), Dr. Kristine A. Culp, Dean, 1156 E. 57th St., Chicago, IL 60637-1536 Tel. (773)643-4411 Fax (773)643-4413
Email: ddh.uchicago.admin@attglobal.net
Website: ddh.uchicago.edu

Dominican House of Studies‡ (Catholic Church), Dwight Reginald Whitt, O.P., President, 487 Michigan Ave. N.E., Washington, DC 20017-1585 Tel. (202)529-5300 Fax (202)636-1700
Email: assistant@dhs.edu
Website: www.dhs.edu

Dominican School of Philosophy and Theology‡ (Catholic Church), Michael Sweeney, President, 2401 Ridge Rd., Berkeley, CA 94709 Tel. (510)849-2030 Fax (510)849-1372
Email: msweeney@dspt.edu
Website: www.dspt.edu

Dominican Study Center of the Caribbean‡ (Catholic Church), Rev. Fr. Dr. Félix Struik, O.P., Regent of the Center, Apartado Postal 1968, Bayamon, PR 00960-1968 Tel. (787)787-1826 Fax (787)798-2712
Email: fstruik@cedocpr.org
Website: www.cedocpr.org

Drew University Theological School‡ (The United Methodist Church), Maxine C. Beach, Vice President and Dean, 36 Madison Ave., Madison, NJ 07940-4010 Tel. (973)408-3258 Fax (973)408-3534
Email: miannuzzi@drew.edu
Website: www.drew.edu/theo

Duke University Divinity School‡ (The United Methodist Church), L. Gregory Jones, Dean, Box 90968, Durham, NC 27708-0968 Tel. (888)462-3853 Fax (919)660-3535
Email: admissions@div.duke.edu
Website: www.divinity.duke.edu

Earlham School of Religion‡ (Interdenominational-Friends), Jay Wade Marshall, Dean, 228 College Ave., Richmond, IN 47374 Tel. (800)432-1377 Fax (765)983-1688
Email: esr@earlham.edu
Website: www.esr.earlham.edu

Eastern Mennonite Seminary of Eastern Mennonite University‡ (Mennonite Church), Ervin Stutzman, Dean, 1200 Park Road, Harrisonburg, VA 22802 Tel. (540)432-4260 Fax (540)432-4598
Email: swartlej@emu.edu
Website: www.emu.edu/seminary

Ecumenical Theological Seminary‡ (Inter/Multidenominational), Marsha Foster Boyd, President, 2930 Woodward Ave., Detroit, MI 48201 Tel. (313)831-5200 Fax (313)831-1353
Email: lhannum@etseminary.edu
Website: www.etseminary.edu

Eden Theological Seminary† (United Church of Christ), David M. Greenhaw, President, 475 E. Lockwood Ave., St. Louis, MO 63119-3192 Tel. (314)961-3627 Fax (314)918-2626
Email: dgreenhaw@eden.edu
Website: www.eden.edu

Emmanuel School of Religion‡ (Christian Churches and Churches of Christ), Michael L. Sweeney, President, One Walker Dr., Johnson City, TN 37601-9438 Tel. (423)926-1186 Fax (423)926-6198
Email: sweeneym@esr.edu
Website: www.esr.edu

Emmaus Bible College (Christian Brethren (also known as Plymouth Brethren)), Kenneth Alan Daughters, President, 2570 Asbury Rd., Dubuque, IA 52001 Tel. (563)588-8000 Fax (563)588-1216
Email: info@emmaus.edu
Website: www.emmaus.edu

Episcopal Divinity School‡ (Episcopal Church), The Rev. Dr Randall Chase, Acting President and Dean, 99 Brattle St., Cambridge, MA 02138-3494 Tel. (617)868-1511 Fax (617)864-5385
Email: rchase@eds.edu
Website: www.eds.edu

Erskine Theological Seminary‡ (Associate Reformed Presbyterian Church (General Synod)), Dr. Randall T. Ruble, President, PO Box 668, Due West, SC 29639 Tel. (864)379-8833 Fax (864)379-2171
Email: ruble@erskine.edu
Website: www.erskineseminary.org

Eugene Bible College (Open Bible Churches, Inc.), David Cole, President, 2155 Bailey Hill Rd., Eugene, OR 97405 Tel. (541)485-1780 Fax (541)343-5801
Email: davidcole@ebc.edu
Website: www.ebc.edu

Evangelical Theological Seminary‡ (The Evangelical Congregational Church), Dennis P. Hollinger, President, 121 S. College St., Myerstown, PA 17067 Tel. (717)866-5775 Fax (717)866-4667
Email: dhollinger@evangelical.edu
Website: www.evangelical.edu

Evangelical Seminary of Puerto Rico‡ (Inter/Multidenominational), Sergio Ojeda-Carcamo, President, Ponce de Leon Avenue 776, San Juan, PR 00925 Tel. (787)763-6700 Fax (787)751-0847
Email: meperez@se-pr.org
Website: www.seminarioevangelicopr.org

Faith Baptist Bible College and Theological Seminary, James D. Maxwell III, President, 1900 N.W. 4th St., Ankeny, IA 50023 Tel. (515)964-0601 Fax (515)964-1638
Email: stet@faith.edu
Website: www.faith.edu

Faith Evangelical Lutheran Seminary† (Conservative Lutheran Association), R. H. Redal, President, 3504 N. Pearl St., Tacoma, WA 98407 Tel. (253)752-2020/(888)777-7675 Fax (206)759-1790
Email: fsinfo@faithseminary.edu
Website: www.faithseminary.edu

Florida Center for Theological Studies‡ (Inter/Multidenominational), Patrick H. O'Neill, President, 111 NE First St., Eighth Floor, Miami, FL 33132 Tel. (305)379-3777 Fax (305)379-1006
Email: budrew@fcts.edu
Website: www.fcfts.org

Florida Christian College (Christian Churches and Churches of Christ), A. Wayne Lowen, President, 1011 Bill Beck Blvd., Kissimmee, FL 34744 Tel. (407)847-8966 Fax (407)847-3925
Email: fcc@fcc.edu
Website: www.fcc.edu

Franciscan School of Theology‡ (Catholic Church), Mario DiCicco, President, 1712 Euclid Ave., Berkeley, CA 94709 Tel. (510)848-5232 Fax (510)549-9466
Email: mdicicco@fst.edu
Website: www.fst.edu

Free Will Baptist Bible College (National Association of Free Will Baptists), J. Matthew Pinson, President, 3606 West End Ave., Nashville, TN 37205 Tel. (615)383-1340 Fax (615)269-6028
Email: president@fwbbc.edu
Website: www.fwbcc.edu

Fuller Theological Seminary‡ (Multidenominational), Richard J. Mouw, President, 135 N. Oakland Ave., Pasadena, CA 91182 Tel. (626)584-5200 Fax (626)795-8767
Email: lguernse@fuller.edu
Website: www.fuller.edu

Garrett-Evangelical Theological Seminary‡ (The United Methodist Church), Philip A. Amerson, President, 2121 Sheridan Rd., Evanston, IL 60201-3298 Tel. (847)866-3900 Fax (847)866-3957
Email: seminary@garrett.edu
Website: www.garrett.edu

The General Theological Seminary‡ (Episcopal Church), Ward B. Ewing, Dean and President, 175 Ninth Ave., New York, NY 10011-4977 Tel. (212)243-5150 Fax (212)647-0294
Email: ewing@gts.edu
Website: www.gts.edu

George Fox Evangelical Seminary‡ (Inter/Multidenominational), Charles Conniry Jr, Vice President & Dean, 12753 SW 68th Ave., Portland, OR 97223 Tel. (503)554-6150 Fax (503)554-6155
Email: seminary@georgefox.edu
Website: www.seminary.georgefox.edu

George Mercer Jr. Memorial School of Theology (Episcopal Church), The Right Reverend Johncy Itty, D.D. PhD, Interim Director, 65 Fourth St., Garden City, NY 11530 Tel. (516)248-4800 Fax (516)248-4883
Email: merceroffice@dioceseli.org
Website: www.mercerschool.org

George W. Truett Theological Seminary of Baylor University‡ (Baptist General Convention of Texas), David E. Garland, Dean, One Bear Place # 97126, Waco, TX 76798-7126 Tel. (254)710-3755 Fax (254)710-3753
Email: Nancy_Floyd@Baylor.edu
Website: www.truettseminary.net

God's Bible School and College (Nondenominational), Dr. Michael Avery, President, 1810 Young St., Cincinnati, OH 45202 Tel. (513)721-7944 Fax (513)721-3971
Email: president@gbs.edu
Website: www.gbs.edu

Golden Gate Baptist Theological Seminary‡ (Southern Baptist Convention), Jeff Iorg, President, 201 Seminary Dr., Mill Valley, CA 94941-3197 Tel. (415)380-1300 Fax (415)380-1302
Email: seminary@ggbts.edu
Website: www.ggbts.edu

Gonzaga University Department of Religious Studies (Catholic Church), Pat McCormick, Dept. Head, Spokane, WA 99258-0001 Tel. (509)328-6782 Fax (509)323-5718 Email: McCormick@Gonzaga.edu Website: www.gonzaga.edu

Gordon-Conwell Theological Seminary‡ (Inter/Multidenominational), James Emery White, President, 130 Essex St., South Hamilton, MA 01982 Tel. (978)468-7111 Fax (978)468-6691 Email: info@gcts.edu Website: www.gordonconwell.edu

Grace Bible College (Grace Gospel Fellowship), Kenneth B. Kemper, President, P.O. Box 910, Grand Rapids, MI 49509 Tel. (616)538-2330 Fax (616)538-0599 Email: info@gbcol.edu Website: www.gbcol.edu

Grace Theological Seminary‡ (Fellowship of Grace Brethren Churches), Ronald E. Manahan, President, 200 Seminary Dr., Winona Lake, IN 46590-1294 Tel. (574)372-5100 Fax (574)372-5139 Email: rmanahan@grace.edu Website: www.grace.edu

Grace University (Interdenominational), Dr. James Eckman, President, 1311 South 9th St., Omaha, NE 68108 Tel. (402)449-2809 Fax (402)341-9587 Email: jofast@graceu.edu Website: www.graceuniversity.edu

Graduate Theological Foundation (Interdenominational/Interfaith), John Morgan, Ph.D., D.Sc., Psy.D., President, Dodge House, 415 Lincoln Way East, Mishawaka, IN 46544 Tel. (800) 423-5983, (574) 255-3642 Fax (574) 255-7520 Email: info@gtfeducation.org Website: www.gtfeducation.org

Graduate Theological Union‡ (Inter-denominational), James A. Donahue, President, 2400 Ridge Rd., Berkeley, CA 94709-1212 Tel. (510)649-2400 Fax (510)649-1417 Email: president@gtu.edu Website: www.gtu.edu

Grand Rapids Theological Seminary of Cornerstone University‡ (Non-Denominational), Douglas L. Fagerstrom, 1001 East Beltline NE, Grand Rapids, MI 49525-5897 Tel. (616)222-1422 Fax (616)222-1502 Email: grts@cornerstone.edu Website: www.grts.cornerstone.edu

Great Lakes Christian College (Christian Churches and Churches of Christ), Larry Carter, President, 6211 W. Willow Hwy., Lansing, MI 48917 Tel. (517)321-0242 Fax (517)321-5902 Email: lcarter@glcc.edu Website: www.glcc.edu

Greenville College (Free Methodist Church of North America), Dr. Larry Linamen, President, 315 E. College Ave., P.O. Box 159, Greenville, IL 62246 Tel. (618)664-2800 Fax (618)664-1748 Website: www.greenville.edu

Haggard Graduate School of Theology at Azusa Pacific University‡ (Interdenominational), David W. Wright, President, 901 E. Alosta, P.O. Box 7000, Azusa, CA 91702-7000 Tel. (845)969-3434 Fax (845)969-7180 Email: ezone@apu.edu Website: www.apu.edu/theology

Harding University Graduate School of Religion‡ (Churches of Christ), Evertt W. Huffard, Executive Director, 1000 Cherry Rd., Memphis, TN 38117-5499 Tel. (901)761-1352 Fax (901)761-1358 Email: dean@hugsr.edu Website: www.hugsr.edu

Hartford Seminary‡ (Interdenominational), Heidi Hadsell, President, 77 Sherman St., Hartford, CT 06105-2260 Tel. (860)509-9500 Fax (860)509-9509 Email: info@hartsem.edu Website: www.hartsem.edu

Harvard University Divinity School‡ (Multidenominational/Multireligious), Professor William A. Graham, Dean, 45 Francis Ave., Cambridge, MA 02138 Tel. (617)495-4513 Fax (617)496-8026 Email: suzanne_rom@harvard.edu Website: www.hds.harvard.edu

Hebrew Union College-Jewish Institute of Religion (Jewish), Rabbi David Ellenson, President, 3077 University Ave., Los Angeles, CA 90007 Tel. (213)749-3424 Fax (213)747-6128 Email: presoff@huc.edu Website: www.huc.edu

Hebrew Union College - Jewish Institute of Religion, NY (Reform Judaism), Rabbi David Ellenson, Ph.D., President, 1 W. 4th St., New York, NY 10012 Tel. (212)674-5300 Fax (212)533-0129 Email: presoff@huc.edu/jrosensaft@huc.edu Website: www.huc.edu

Heritage Bible College† (Pentecostal Free Will Baptist), Dr. Elvin R. Butts, President, 1747 Bud Hawkins Road, PO Box 1628, Dunn, NC 28335 Tel. (910)892-3178 Fax (910)892-1809 Email: generalinfo@heritagebiblecollege.org Website: www.heritagebiblecollege.org

Hillsdale Free Will Baptist College† (Free Will Baptist), Carl Cheshier, President, PO Box 7208, Moore, OK 73153-1208 Tel. (405)912-9000 Fax (405)912-9050 Email: hillsdale@hc.edu Website: www.hc.edu

297

Hobe Sound Bible College (Nondenominational), P. Daniel Stetler, President, P.O. Box 1065, Hobe Sound, FL 33475 Tel. (407)546-5534 Fax (407)545-1421
Email: lavernegagnon@hsbc.edu
Website: www.hsbc.edu

Holy Cross Greek Orthodox School of Theology‡ (Greek Orthodox Archdiocese of America), Rev. Nicholas C. Triantafilou, President, 50 Goddard Ave., Brookline, MA 02445-7495 Tel. (617)731-3500 Fax (617)850-1460
Email: admissions@hchc.edu/jbakas@hchc.edu
Website: www.hchc.edu

Holy Trinity Orthodox Seminary (The Russian Orthodox Church Outside of Russia), Archbishop Laurus Skurla, President, P.O. Box 36, Jordanville, NY 13361 Tel. (315)858-0945 Fax (315)858-0945
Email: info@hts.edu
Website: www.hts.edu

Hood Theological Seminary‡ (African Methodist Episcopal Zion Church), Albert J.D. Aymer, President, 1810 Lutheran Synod Drive, Salisbury, NC 28144 Tel. (704)636-7611 Fax (704)636-7699
Email: pwells@hoodseminary.edu
Website: www.hoodseminary.edu

Hope International University (Christian Churches and Churches of Christ), Dr. John Derry, President, 2500 E. Nutwood Ave., Fullerton, CA 92831-3104 Tel. (714)879-3901 Fax (714)681-7451
Email: slcarter@hiu.edu
Website: www.hiu.edu

Houston Graduate School of Theology‡ (Friends/Nondenominational), Keith A. Jenkins, President, 2501 Central Parkway, Suite A-19, Houston, TX 77092- Tel. (713)942-9505 Fax (713)942-9506
Email: hgst@hgst.edu
Website: www.hgst.edu

Howard University School of Divinity‡ (Nondenominational), Alton B. Pollard III, Dean, 1400 Shepherd St. N.E., Washington, DC 20017 Tel. (202)806-0500 Fax (202)806-0711
Email: apollard@howard.edu
Website: www.divinity.howard.edu

Huntington University, Graduate School of Christian Ministries (Church of the United Brethren in Christ), Blair Dowden, President, 2303 College Ave., Huntington, IN 46750 Tel. (260)359-4039 Fax (260)359-4126
Email: gscm@huntington.edu
Website: www.huntington.edu/gscm

Iliff School of Theology‡ (The United Methodist Church), David Trickett, President, 2201 S. University Blvd., Denver, CO 80210-4798 Tel. (303)744-1287 Fax (303)777-3387
Email: dgtrickett@iliff.edu
Website: www.iliff.edu

Immaculate Conception Seminary Seton Hall University‡ (Catholic Church), Rev. Msgr. Robert F. Coleman, J. C. D., Rector and Dean, 400 S. Orange Ave., South Orange, NJ 07079 Tel. (973)761-9575 Fax (973)761-9577
Email: theology@shu.edu
Website: www.theology.shu.edu

Indiana Wesleyan University (The Wesleyan Church), James Barnes, President, 4201 S. Washington, Marion, IN 46953-4974 Tel. (765)674-6901 Fax (765)677-2465
Email: james.barnes@indwes.edu
Website: www.indwes.edu

Institute for Creation Research Graduate School (Non-Denominational), Dr. John Morris, President, 10946 Woodside Avenue North, Santee, CA 92071 Tel. (619)448-0900 Fax (619)448-3469
Email: kcumming@icr.edu; jkriege@icr.org
Website: www.icr.org

Inter-American Adventist Theological Seminary‡ (Seventh-day Adventist), Jaime Castrejon, PhD, President, PO Box 830518, Miami, FL 33283 Tel. (305)403-4575 Fax (305)403-4646
Email: castrejon@interamerica.org
Website: www.interamerica.org

Interdenominational Theological Center‡ (Interdenominational), Dr. Michael A. Battle, President, 700 Martin Luther King, Jr. Dr. S.W., Atlanta, GA 30314-4143 Tel. (404)527-7702 Fax (404)527-7770
Email: info@itc.edu
Website: www.itc.edu

International Baptist College† (Baptist), Pastor David Brock, President, 2211 West Germann Rd, Chandler, AZ 85286 Tel. (480)838-7070 Fax (480)505-3299
Email: info@ibconline.edu
Website: www.tri-citybaptist.org

International College & Graduate School (Non-Denominational), Dr. Rick Stinton, President, 20 Dowsett Avenue, Honolulu, HI 96817 Tel. (808)595-4247 Fax (808)595-4779
Email: icgs@hawaii.rr.com
Website: www.icgshawaii.org

International Theological Seminary‡ (Nondenominational), Seenam Kim, President, 3215-3225 N. Tyler Ave., El Monte, CA 91731 Tel. (626)448-0023 Fax (626)350-6343
Email: dean@itsla.edu
Website: www.itsla.edu

James and Carolyn McAfee School of Theology of Mercer University‡ (Cooperative Baptist Fellowship), R. Alan Culpepper, Dean of the School of Theology, 3001 Mercer University Drive, Atlanta, GA 30341-4115 Tel. (678)547-6470 Fax (678)547-6478
Email: culpepper_ra@mercer.edu
Website: theology.mercer.edu

Jesuit School of Theology of Santa Clara University‡ (Catholic Church), Kevin F. Burke, Acting President, 1735 LeRoy Ave., Berkeley, CA 94709-1193 Tel. (510)549-5000 Fax (510)841-8536
Email: cdodson@jstb.edu
Website: www.jstb.edu

Jewish Theological Seminary of America (Jewish), Ismar Schorsch, President, 3080 Broadway, New York, NY 10027-4649 Tel. (212)678-8000 Fax (212)678-8947
Email: webmaster@jtsa.edu
Website: www.jtsa.edu

The John Leland Center for Theological Studies‡ (Baptist), Mark Olson, President, 1301 N. Hartford St., Arlington, VA 22201 Tel. (703)812-4757 Fax (703)812-4764
Email: jwilletts@johnlelandcenter.edu
Website: www.johnlelandcenter.edu

John Wesley College (Interdenominational), Brian C. Donley, President, 2314 N. Centennial St., High Point, NC 27265 Tel. (336)889-2262 Fax (336)889-2261
Email: admissions@johnwesley.edu
Website: www.johnwesley.edu

Johnson Bible College (Christian Churches and Churches of Christ), Gary E. Weedman, President, 7900 Johnson Dr., Knoxville, TN 37998 Tel. (865)573-4517 Fax (865)251-2336
Email: tnice@jbc.edu
Website: www.jbc.edu

Kansas City College and Bible School (Church of God (Holiness)), Gayle Woods, President, 7401 Metcalf Ave., Overland Park, KS 66204 Tel. (913)722-0272 Fax (913)722-2135
Email: pastorchad@eldochurch.com
Website: www.kccbs.edu

Kenrick-Glennon Seminary‡ (Catholic Church), Ted L. Wojcicki, President-Rector, 5200 Glennon Dr., St. Louis, MO 63119-4399 Tel. (314)792-6100 Fax (314)792-6500
Email: wojcicki@kenrick.edu
Website: www.kenrick.edu

Kentucky Christian University (Christian Churches and Churches of Christ), Keith P. Keeran, Ph.D., President, 100 Academic Parkway, Grayson, KY 41143 Tel. (606)474-3000 Fax (606)474-3155
Email: TLW@kcu.edu
Website: www.kcu.edu

Kentucky Mountain Bible College (Interdenominational), Philip Speas, President, Box 10, Vancleve, KY 41385 Tel. (606)666-5000 Fax (606)666-7744

King's College and Seminary† (Non-Denominational), Paul G. Chappell, Ph.D., Chief Academic Officer, 14800 Sherman Way, Van Nuys, CA 91405 Tel. (818)779-8040 Fax (818)779-8241
Email: admissions@kingsseminary.edu
Website: www.kingsseminary.edu / www.kingscollege.edu

Knox Theological Seminary‡ (Presbyterian Church in America), R. Fowler White, Administrator and Dean of the Faculty, 5554 North Federal Highway, Fort Lauderdale, FL 33308 Tel. (954)771-0376 Fax (954)351-3343
Email: knox@crpc.org
Website: www.knoxseminary.org

Kuyper College (Interdenominational), Nicholas V. Kroeze, President, 3333 East Beltline N.E., Grand Rapids, MI 49525-9749 Tel. (616)222-3000 Fax (616)988-3608
Email: jheyboer@kuyper.edu
Website: www.kuyper.edu

La Sierra University School of Religion‡ (Seventh-day Adventist Church), Randal R. Wisbey, President, 4500 Riverwalk Parkway, Riverside, CA 92515-8247 Tel. (951)785-2041 Fax (951)785-2199
Email: religion@lasierra.edu
Website: www.lasierra.edu/religion

Lancaster Bible College (Nondenominational), Peter W. Teague, President, 901 Eden Road, Lancaster, PA 17601 Tel. (717)560-8278 Fax (717)560-8260
Email: president@lbc.edu
Website: www.lbc.edu

Lancaster Theological Seminary‡ (United Church of Christ), Rev. Dr. Riess W. Potterveld, President, 555 W. James St., Lancaster, PA 17603-2897 Tel. (717)393-0654 Fax (717)393-4254
Email: seminary@lancasterseminary.edu
Website: www.lancasterseminary.edu

Lexington Theological Seminary‡ (Christian Church (Disciples of Christ)), R. Robert Cueni, President, 631 S. Limestone St., Lexington, KY 40508 Tel. (859)252-0361 Fax (859)281-6042
Email: rlowery@lextheo.edu
Website: www.lextheo.edu

Liberty Theological Seminary and Graduate School (Independent Baptist), Dr. Ergun Caner, Dean, 1971 University Blvd., Lynchburg, VA 24502-2269 Tel. (434)592-4140 Fax (434)522-0415
Email: ecaner@liberty.edu
Website: www.liberty.edu/Academics/Religion/Seminary

Liberty University (Baptist), Dr. John Borek, President, 1971 University Boulevard, Lynchburg, VA 24502 Tel. (434)582-2000 Fax (434)582-2304
Email: admissions@liberty.edu
Website: www.liberty.edu

Life Pacific College (International Church of the Foursquare Gospel), Dan R. Stewart, President, 1100 Covina Blvd., San Dimas, CA 91773 Tel. (909)599-5433 Fax (909)599-6690
Email: info@lifepacific.edu
Website: www.lifepacific.edu

299

Lincoln Christian College and Seminary of Lincoln Christian University‡ (Christian Churches and Churches of Christ), Keith H. Ray, President, 100 Campus View Dr., Lincoln, IL 62656 Tel. (217)732-3168 ext.2354 Fax (217)732-5718 Email: ttanner@lccs.edu Website: www.lccs.edu

Lipscomb University College of Bible and Ministry‡ (Churches of Christ), Terry Briley, Dean, 3901 Granny White Pike, Nashville, TN 37204-3951 Tel. (615)279-6051 Fax (615)279-6052 Email: audrey.everson@lipscomb.edu Website: www.lipscomb.edu

Logos Evangelical Seminary‡ (Evangelical Formosan Church), Felix Liu, President, 9358 Telstar Ave., El Monte, CA 91731 Tel. (626)571-5110 Fax (626)571-5119 Email: logos@les.edu Website: www.logos-seminary.edu

Logsdon Seminary of Logsdson School of Theology of Hardin-Simmons University‡ (Baptist General Convention of Texas), Thomas Brisco, Dean, P.O. Box 16235, Abilene, TX 79698-6235 Tel. (325)670-1287 Fax (325)670-1406 Email: tbrisco@hsutx.edu Website: www.hsutx.edu/academics/logsdon

Louisville Presbyterian Theological Seminary‡ (Presbyterian Church (U.S.A.)), Dean K. Thompson, President, 1044 Alta Vista Rd., Louisville, KY 40205 Tel. (502)895-3411 Fax (502)895-1096 Email: dthompson@lpts.edu Website: www.lpts.edu

Loyola Marymount University Department of Theological Studies‡ (Catholic Church), Jeffrey S. Siker, Chair, One LMU Drive, Los Angeles, CA 90045-2659 Tel. (310)338-7670 Fax (310)338-1947 Email: jsiker@lmu.edu Website: bellarmine.lmu.edu/theology

Loyola University Chicago Institute of Pastoral Studies (Catholic Church), Robert A. Ludwig, Director, 820 N. Michigan Ave., Chicago, IL 60611 Tel. (312)915-7400 Fax (312)915-7410 Email: rludwig@luc.edu Website: www.luc.edu/depts/ips

Luther Rice Bible College & Seminary† (Baptist), Dr. James Flanagan, President, 3038 Evans Mill Road, Lithonia, GA 30038 Tel. (770)484-1204 Fax (770)484-1155 Email: lrs@lrs.edu Website: www.lrs.edu

Luther Seminary‡ (Evangelical Lutheran Church in America), Richard H. Bliese, President, 2481 Como Ave., St. Paul, MN 55108 Tel. (651)641-3456 Fax (651)641-3425 Email: admissions@luthersem.edu Website: www.luthersem.edu

Lutheran Bible Institute in California (Intersynodical Lutheran), Samuel Giesy, Acting President, 5321 University Dr., Ste. G, Irvine, CA 92612-2942 Tel. (949)262-9222, (800)261-5242 Fax (949)262-0283 Email: info@lbic.org Website: www.lbic.org

Lutheran Brethren Seminary (Church of the Lutheran Brethren of America), David Veum, D. Min, President, 815 W. Vernon, Fergus Falls, MN 56537 Tel. (218)739-3375 Fax (218)739-1259 Email: clb@clba.org Website: www.clba.org

Lutheran School of Theology at Chicago‡ (Evangelical Lutheran Church in America), James Kenneth Echols, President, 1100 E. 55th St., Chicago, IL 60615-5199 Tel. (773)256-0700 Fax (773)256-0782 Email: jechols@lstc.edu Website: www.lstc.edu

Lutheran Theological Seminary at Gettysburg‡ (Evangelical Lutheran Church in America), The Rev. Michael L. Cooper-White, President, 61 Seminary Ridge, Gettysburg, PA 17325-1795 Tel. (717)334-6286 Fax (717)334-3469 Email: ctroyer@ltsg.edu Website: www.ltsg.edu

Lutheran Theological Seminary at Philadelphia‡ (Evangelical Lutheran Church in America), Philip D.W. Krey, President, 7301 Germantown Ave., Philadelphia, PA 19119 Tel. (215)248-4616 Fax (215)248-4577 Email: mtairy@ltsp.edu Website: www.ltsp.edu

Lutheran Theological Southern Seminary‡ (Evangelical Lutheran Church in America), Marcus J. Miller, President, 4201 North Main St., Columbia, SC 29203 Tel. (803)786-5150 Fax (803)786-6499 Email: Mmiller@ltss.edu Website: www.ltss.edu

M. Christopher White School of Divinity of Gardner-Webb University‡ (Baptist State Convention of North Carolina), Robert W. Canoy, Dean, 110 N. Main Street, Noel Hall, Boiling Springs, NC 28017 Tel. (704)406-4400 Fax (704)406-3935 Email: rcanoy@gardner-webb.edu Website: www.divinity.gardner-webb.edu

Manhattan Christian College (Christian Churches and Churches of Christ), Jolene Rupe, Secretary, Institutional Advancement, 1415 Anderson Ave., Manhattan, KS 66502 Tel. (785)539-3571 Fax (785)539-0832 Email: jrupe@mccks.edu Website: www.mccks.edu

Maple Springs Baptist Bible College and Seminary† (Non-Denominational), Dr. Larry W. Jordan, President, 4130 Belt Road, Capital Heights, MD 20743 Tel. (301)736-3631 Fax (301)735-6507
Email: larry.jordan@msbbcs.edu
Website: www.msbbcs.edu

Mars Hill Graduate School‡† (Non-Denominational), Dr. Dan Allander, President, 2525 - 220th Street, Bothell, WA 98021 Tel. (425)415-0505 Fax (425)806-5599
Email: info@mhgs.edu
Website: www.mhgs.net

McCormick Theological Seminary‡ (Presbyterian Church (U.S.A.)), Cynthia M. Campbell, President, 5460 S. University Ave., Chicago, IL 60615-5108 Tel. (773)947-6300 Fax (773)288-2612
Email: ccampbell@mccormick.edu
Website: www.mccormick.edu

Meadville Lombard Theological School‡ (Unitarian Universalist), Lee Barker, President, 5701 S. Woodlawn Ave., Chicago, IL 60637 Tel. (773)256-3000 Fax (773)753-1323
Email: LBarker@meadville.edu
Website: www.meadville.edu

Memphis Theological Seminary‡ (Cumberland Presbyterian Church), Daniel J Earheart-Brown, President, 168 E. Parkway S at Union, Memphis, TN 38104-4395 Tel. (901)458-8232 Fax (901)452-4051
Email: jebrown@memphisseminary.edu
Website: www.memphisseminary.edu

Mennonite Brethren Biblical Seminary‡ (General Conference of Mennonite Brethren Churches), Jim Holm, President, 4824 E. Butler Ave. (at Chestnut Ave.), Fresno, CA 93727-5097 Tel. (559)251-8628 Fax (559)251-7212
Email: fresno@mbseminary.edu
Website: www.mbseminary.edu

Messenger College† (Pentecostal Church of God), Tiffany Stump, Dir. of Admissions, 300 E. 50th Street, Joplin, MO 64804 Tel. (417)624-7070 Fax (417)624-5070
Email: info@messengercollege.edu
Website: www.messengercollege.edu

Methodist Theological School in Ohio‡ (The United Methodist Church), Jay Rundell, President, 3081 Columbus Pike, P.O. Box 8004, Delaware, OH 43015-8004 Tel. (740)363-1146 Fax (740)362-3135
Email: jrundell@mtso.edu
Website: www.mtso.edu

Michigan Theological Seminary‡† (Non-Denominational), Bruce W. Fong, President, 41550 E. Ann Arbor Trail, Plymouth, MI 48170-4308 Tel. (734)207-9581 Fax (734)207-9582
Email: admissions@mts.edu
Website: www.mts.edu

Mid-America Christian University (The Church of God - Anderson, IN), Dr. John D. Fozard, President, 3500 S.W. 119th St., Oklahoma City, OK 73170 Tel. (405)691-3800 Fax (405)692-3165
Email: info@macu.edu
Website: www.macu.edu

Mid-America Reformed Seminary‡† (Inter/Multidenominational), Cornelius P. Venema, President, 229 Seminary Drive, Dyer, IN 46311 Tel. (219)864-2400 Fax (219)864-2410
Email: info@midamerica.edu
Website: www.midamerica.edu

Mid-Atlantic Christian University (Christian Churches and Churches of Christ), D. Clay Perkins, Ph.D., President, 715 N. Poindexter St, Elizabeth City, NC 27909-4054 Tel. (252)334-2070 Fax (252)334-2071
Email: clay.perkins@macuniversity.edu
Website: www.macuniversity.edu

Midwest University† (Interdenominational), Dr. James Song, President, 851 Parr Road, Wentzville, MO 63385 Tel. (636) 327-4645 Fax (636) 327-4715
Email: usa@midwest.edu
Website: www.midwest.edu

Midwestern Baptist Theological Seminary‡ (Southern Baptist Convention), Dr. R. Philip Roberts, President, 5001 N. Oak Trafficway, Kansas City, MO 64118 Tel. (816)414-3700 Fax (816)414-3799
Email: president@mbts.edu
Website: www.mbts.edu

Moody Bible Institute (Interdenominational), Michael J. Easley, President, 820 N. La Salle Blvd., Chicago, IL 60610 Tel. (312)329-4000 Fax (312)329-4109
Email: pr@moody.edu
Website: www.moody.edu

Moravian Theological Seminary‡ (Moravian Church in America (Unitas Fratrum)), Christopher M. Thomforde, President, 1200 Main St., Bethlehem, PA 18018 Tel. (610)861-1516 Fax (610)861-1569
Email: seminary@moravian.edu
Website: www.moravianseminary.edu

Moreau Seminary (Congregation of Holy Cross) (Catholic Church), Rev. Wilson Miscamble, C.S.C., President, Moreau Seminary, University of Notre Dame, Notre Dame, IN 46556 Tel. (574)631-7735 Fax (574)631-9233
Email: vocation.1@nd.edu
Website: www.vocation.nd.edu

Morehouse School of Religion (Interdenominational Baptist), William T. Perkins, President, 645 Beckwith St. S.W., Atlanta, GA 30314 Tel. (404)527-7777 Fax (404)681-1005
Website: www.itc.edu

301

Mount Angel Seminary‡ (Catholic Church), Very Rev. Fr. Richard Paperini, President Rector, St. Benedict, OR 97373 Tel. (503)845-3951 Fax (503)845-3126
Email: seminary@mountangelabbey.org
Website: www.mountangelabbey.org/seminary

Mt. St. Mary's Seminary‡ (Catholic Church), Steven P. Rohlfs, Rector, 16300 Old Emmitsburg Rd., Emmitsburg, MD 21727-7797 Tel. (301)447-5295 Fax (301)447-5636
Email: rhoades@msmary.edu
Website: www.msmary.edu

Mt. St. Mary's Seminary of the West (Catholic Church), Gerald R. Haemmerle, President, 6616 Beechmont Ave., Cincinnati, OH 45230 Tel. (513)231-2223 Fax (513)231-3254
Email: jhaemmer@mtsm.org
Website: mtsm.org

Multnomah Biblical Seminary‡ (Multnomah Biblical Seminary), Dr. Daniel R. Lockwood, President, 8435 N.E. Glisan St., Portland, OR 97220 Tel. (503)255-0332 Fax (503)251-6701
Email: dlockwood@multnomah.edu
Website: www.multnomah.edu

The University of St. Mary of the Lake/ Mundelein Seminary‡ (The Catholic Church), Dennis J. Lyle, Rector-President, 1000 E. Maple, Mundelein, IL 60060-1174 Tel. (847)566-6401 Fax (847)566-7330
Email: rector@usml.edu
Website: www.usml.edu

Nashotah House (Theological Seminary)‡ (Episcopal Church), Robert S. Munday, President and Dean, 2777 Mission Rd., Nashotah, WI 53058-9793 Tel. (262)646-6500 Fax (262)646-6504
Email: smills@nashotah.edu
Website: www.nashotah.edu

Nazarene Bible College (Church of the Nazarene), Hiram Sanders, President, 1111 Academy Park Loop, Colorado Springs, CO 80910-3704 Tel. (719)884-5000 Fax (719)884-5199
Email: info@nbc.edu
Website: www.nbc.edu

Nazarene Theological Seminary‡ (Church of the Nazarene), Ron Benefiel, President, 1700 E. Meyer Blvd., Kansas City, MO 64131-1246 Tel. (816)333-6254 Fax (816)333-6271
Email: lneely@nts.edu
Website: www.nts.edu

Nebraska Christian College (Christian Churches and Churches of Christ), Richard D. Milliken, President, 1800 Syracuse Ave., Norfolk, NE 68701-2458 Tel. (402)379-5000 Fax (402)391-5100
Email: info@nechristian.edu
Website: www.nechristian.edu

New Brunswick Theological Seminary‡ (Reformed Church in America), Gregg A. Mast, President, 17 Seminary Pl., New Brunswick, NJ 08901-1196 Tel. (732)247-5241 Fax (732)247-5412
Email: gmast@nbts.edu
Website: www.nbts.edu

New Orleans Baptist Theological Seminary‡ (Southern Baptist Convention), Charles S. Kelley, President, 3939 Gentilly Blvd., New Orleans, LA 70126 Tel. (504)282-4455 Fax (504)816-8023
Email: nobts@nobts.edu
Website: www.nobts.edu

New York Theological Seminary‡ (Inter/Multi-denominational), Dale T. Irvin, President, 475 Riverside Drive, Ste. 500, New York, NY 10115 Tel. (212)870-1250 Fax (212)870-1236
Email: drhgaston@nyts.edu
Website: www.nyts.edu

North Central Bible College (Assemblies of God), Gordon L. Anderson, President, 910 Elliot Ave. S., Minneapolis, MN 55404 Tel. (612)332-3491 Fax (612)343-4778
Email: INFO@NCBC.EDU
Website: www.NCBC.EDU

North Park Theological Seminary‡ (The Evangelical Covenant Church), John E. Phelan Jr., President and Dean, 3225 W. Foster Ave., Chicago, IL 60625 Tel. (773)244-6214 Fax (773)244-6244
Email: jphelan@northpark.edu
Website: www.northpark.edu

Northeastern Seminary at Roberts Wesleyan College‡ (Nondenominational), John A. Martin, President, 2265 Westside Dr., Rochester, NY 14624-1977 Tel. (585)594-6800 Fax (585)594-6801
Email: seminary@roberts.edu
Website: www.nes.edu

Northern Baptist Theological Seminary‡ (American Baptist Churches in the USA), Dr. Alister Brown, President, 660 E. Butterfield Rd., Lombard, IL 60148-5698 Tel. (630)620-2100 Fax (630)620-2194
Email: abrown@northern.seminary.edu
Website: www.seminary.edu

Northwest Baptist Seminary†‡ (Baptist), Dr. Mark Wagner, President, 4301 N. Stevens, Tacoma, WA 98407 Tel. (253)759-6104 Fax (253)759-3299
Email: nbs@nbs.edu
Website: www.nbs.edu

Northwest College (Assemblies of God), Don H. Argue, Ed.D., President, 5520 108th Ave. N.E., P.O. Box 579, Kirkland, WA 98083-0579 Tel. (425)822-8266 Fax (425)827-0148
Email: receptionist@NorthwestU.edu
Website: www.nwcollege.edu

Notre Dame Seminary‡ (Catholic Church), Patrick J. Williams, M. Div., M.S., President and Rector, 2901 S. Carrollton Ave., New Orleans, LA 70118-4391 Tel. (504)866-7426 Fax (504)866-3119
Email: pjwilliams@nds.edu
Website: www.nds.edu

Oak Hills Christian College (Interdenominational), Dr. Steven Hostetter, Provost, 1600 Oak Hills Rd. S.W., Bemidji, MN 56601 Tel. (218)751-8670 Fax (218)751-8825
Email: dclausen@oakhills.edu
Website: www.oakhills.edu

Oblate School of Theology‡ (Catholic Church), Ronald Rolheiser, President, 285 Oblate Dr., San Antonio, TX 78216-6693 Tel. (210)341-1366 Fax (210)341-4519
Email: oblate@connecti.com
Website: www.ost.edu

Oral Roberts University School of Theology‡ (Inter/Multidenominational), Dr. Thomson K. Mathew, Dean, 7777 S. Lewis Ave., Tulsa, OK 74171 Tel. (918)495-7016 Fax (918)495-6259
Email: jcope@oru.edu
Website: www.oru.edu

Ozark Christian College (Christian Churches and Churches of Christ), Matt Proctor, President, 1111 N. Main St., Joplin, MO 64801 Tel. (417)624-2518 Fax (417)624-0090
Email: pres@occ.edu
Website: www.occ.edu

Pacific Islands Bible College†, The Rev. David L. Owen, President, PO Box 22619, GMF, GU 96921 Tel. (671) 734-1812 Fax (671) 734-1813
Email: GuamCampus@pibc.edu; ChuukCampus@pibc.edu
Website: www.pibc.edu

Pacific Lutheran Theological Seminary‡ (Evangelical Lutheran Church in America), Phyllis Anderson, President, 2770 Marin Ave., Berkeley, CA 94708-1530 Tel. (510)524-5264 Fax (510)524-2408
Email: president@plts.edu
Website: www.plts.edu

Pacific School of Religion‡ (Inter/Multidenominational), William McKinney, President, 1798 Scenic Ave., Berkeley, CA 94709 Tel. (510)848-0528 Fax (510)845-8948
Email: wmckinney@psr.edu
Website: www.psr.edu

Palmer Theological Seminary‡ (American Baptist Churches in the USA), Wallace C. Smith, President, 6 Lancaster Ave., Wynnewood, PA 19096 Tel. (610)896-5000 Fax (610)649-3834
Email: sempres@eastern.edu
Website: www.ebts.edu

Payne Theological Seminary‡ (African Methodist Episcopal Church), Leah Gaskin Fitchue, Ed.D., President, P.O. Box 474, 1230 Wilberforce-Clifton Rd., Wilberforce, OH 45384-0474 Tel. (937)376-2946 Fax (937)376-3330
Email: LFitchue@payne.edu
Website: www.payne.edu

Pentecostal Theological Seminary (Church of God), Steve J. Land, President, PO Box 3330, Cleveland, TN 37320-3330, Tel. (423)478-1131
Website: www.cogts.edu/

Pepperdine University (Churches of Christ), Dr. Randall Chesnutt, Chair of Religion Division, Religion Division, Malibu, CA 90263-4352 Tel. (310)506-4352 Fax (310)317-7271
Email: randall.chesnutt@pepperdine.edu
Website: pepperdine.edu/religion

Perkins School of Theology (Southern Methodist University)‡ (The United Methodist Church), William B. Lawrence, Dean, PO Box 750133, Dallas, TX 75275-0133 Tel. (214)768-2335 Fax (214)768-2117
Email: Rcox@smu.edu
Website: www.smu.edu/perkins

Philadelphia Biblical University (Nondenominational), Todd J. Williams, President, 200 Manor Ave., Langhorne, PA 19047-2990 Tel. (215)752-5800 Fax (215)702-4341
Email: president@pbu.edu
Website: www.pbu.edu

Phillips Theological Seminary‡ (Christian Church (Disciples of Christ)), Gary Peluso-Verdend, President, 901 North Mingo Road, Tulsa, OK 74116 Tel. (918)610-8303 Fax (918)610-8404
Email: linda.ford@ptstulsa.edu
Website: www.ptstulsa.edu

Phoenix Seminary‡ (Nondenominational), Dr. Darryl DelHousaye, President, 4222 E. Thomas Road, Ste 400, Phoenix, AZ 85018-Tel. (602)850-8000 Fax (602)850-8080
Email: ddel@ps.edu
Website: www.phoenixseminary.edu

Piedmont Baptist College† (Baptist (Independent)), Charles W. Petitt, President, 716 Franklin St., Winston-Salem, NC 27101 Tel. (336)725-8344 Fax (336)725-5522
Email: admissions@pbc.edu
Website: www.pbc.edu

Pittsburgh Theological Seminary‡ (Presbyterian Church (U.S.A.)), William J. Carl III, President, 616 N. Highland Ave., Pittsburgh, PA 15206 Tel. (412)362-5610 Fax (412)363-3260
Email: calian@pts.edu
Website: www.pts.edu

Pontifical College Josephinum‡ (Catholic Church), Msgr. Paul J. Langsfeld, Rector and President, 7625 N. High St., Columbus, OH 43235 Tel. (614)885-5585 Fax (614)885-2307
Email: plangsfeld@pcj.edu
Website: www.pcj.edu

Pope John XXIII National Seminary (Catholic Church), Francis D. Kelly, President, 558 South Ave., Weston, MA 02193 Tel. (617)899-5500 Fax (617)899-9057
Email: seminary@blessedjohnxxiii.edu
Website: www.blessedjohnxxiii.edu

Princeton Theological Seminary‡ (Presbyterian Church (U.S.A.)), Iain R. Torrance, President, P.O. Box 821, Princeton, NJ 08542-0803 Tel. (609)921-8300 Fax (609)924-2973
Email: comm-pub@ptsem.edu
Website: www.ptsem.edu

Puget Sound Christian College (Christian Churches and Churches of Christ), Randy J. Bridges, Ph.D., President, P.O. Box 13108, Everett, WA 98206-3108 Tel. (425)257-3090 Fax (425)258-1488
Email: president@pscc.edu
Website: www.pscc.edu

Rabbi Isaac Elchanan Theological Seminary (Jewish), Dr. Norman Lamm, President, 2540 Amsterdam Ave., New York, NY 10033 Tel. (212)960-5344 Fax (212)960-0061
Email: amlevin@ymail.yu.edu
Website: www.yu.edu/riets

Reconstructionist Rabbinical College (Jewish), Dan Ehrenkrantz, President, 1299 Church Rd, Wyncote, PA 19095 Tel. (215)576-0800 Fax (215)576-6143
Email: admissions@rrc.edu
Website: www.rrc.edu

Reformed Episcopal Seminary‡ (Reformed Episcopal Church), Wayne A. Headman, President, 826 Second Ave., Blue Bell, PA 19422-1257 Tel. (610)292-9852 Fax (610)292-9853
Email: wayne.headman@reseminary.edu
Website: www.reseminary.edu

Reformed Presbyterian Theological Seminary‡ (Reformed Presbyterian Church of North America), Jerry F. O'Neill, President, 7418 Penn Ave., Pittsburgh, PA 15208-2594 Tel. (412)731-8690 Fax (412)731-4834
Email: info@rpts.edu
Website: www.rpts.edu

Reformed Theological Seminary‡ (Inter/Multidenominational), Dr. Robert C. Cannada, Jr., President, 5422 Clinton Blvd., Jackson, MS 39209-3099 Tel. (601)923-1600 Fax (601)923-1654
Email: rts.orlando@rts.edu
Website: www.rts.edu

Regent University School of Divinity‡ (Nondenominational/Evangelical), Michael Palmer, Dean, 1000 Regent University Dr, Virginia Beach, VA 23464-9870 Fax (757)226-4597
Email: mpalmer@regent.edu
Website: www.regent.edu/acad/schdiv

Sacred Heart Major Seminary‡ (Catholic Church), Very Rev. Msgr. Jeffrey M. Monforton, President, 2701 Chicago Blvd., Detroit, MI 48206 Tel. (313)883-8501 Fax (313)868-6440
Email: Information@shms.edu
Website: www.shmsonline.org

Sacred Heart School of Theology‡ (Catholic Church), Very Rev. Thomas Knoebel, Acting President-Rector, P.O. Box 429, Hales Corners, WI 53130-0429 Tel. (414)425-8300 Fax (414)529-6999
Email: rector@shst.edu
Website: www.shst.edu

St. Bernard's School of Theology and Ministry‡ (Catholic Church), Patricia A. Schoelles, President, 120 French Road, Rochester, NY 14618 Tel. (585)271-3657 Fax (585)271-2045
Email: pschoelles@sbi.edu
Website: www.stbernards.edu

St. Charles Borromeo Seminary‡ (Catholic Church), Rev. Msgr. Joseph G. Prior, M.Div., M.A., S.S.L., S.T.D., President and Rector, 100 East Wynnewood Rd., Wynnewood, PA 19096-3001 Tel. (610)667-3394 Fax (610)667-0452
Email: developmentscs@adphila.org
Website: www.scs.edu

St. Francis Seminary‡ (Catholic Church), Very Rev.Donald J. Hying, Rector, 3257 S. Lake Dr., St. Francis, WI 53235 Tel. (414)747-6404 Fax (414)747-6442
Email: mwitczak@sfs.edu
Website: www.sfs.edu

St. John Vianney Theological Seminary‡ (Catholic Church), Michael Glenn, Rector, 1300 S. Steele St., Denver, CO 80210-2599 Tel. (303)282-3427 Fax (303)282-3453
Website: www.sjvdenver.com

St. John's Seminary‡ (Catholic Church), John Farren, Rector and President, 127 Lake St., Brighton, MA 02135 Tel. (617)254-2610 Fax (617)787-2336
Email: Reverend_John_L_Sullivan@rcab.org
Website: www.sjs.edu

St. John's Seminary‡ (Catholic Church), Monsignor Helmut Hefner, Rector and President, 5012 Seminary Rd., Camarillo, CA 93012-2598 Tel. (805)482-2755 Fax (805)482-0637
Email: helmut@stjohnsem.edu
Website: www.stjohnsem.edu

St. John's University, School of Theology - Seminary‡ (Catholic Church), William J. Cahoy, Dean, Box 7288, Collegeville, MN 56321-7288 Tel. (320)363-2622 Fax (320)363-3145
Email: bduffy@csbsju.edu
Website: www.csbsju.edu/sot

St. Joseph's Seminary‡ (Catholic Church), Peter G. Finn, President, 201 Seminary Ave., Yonkers, NY 10704 Tel. (914)968-6200 Fax (914)968-7912
Email: sjsirs@aol.com
Website: www.ny-archdiocese.org/pastoral/seminary.cfm

St. Louis Christian College (Christian Churches and Churches of Christ), Dr. Guthrie Veech, President, 1360 Grandview Dr., Florissant, MO 63033 Tel. (314)837-6777 Fax (314)837-8291 Email: agall@slcconline.edu Website: www.slcconline.edu

St. Mary Seminary and Graduate School of Theology‡ (Catholic Church), Thomas W. Tifft, President, 28700 Euclid Ave., Wickliffe, OH 44092-2585 Tel. (440)943-7600 Fax (440)943-7577 Email: mal@dioceseofcleveland.org Website: www.stmarysem.edu

St. Mary's Seminary (Catholic Church), Very Rev. Brendan Cahill, Rector, 9845 Memorial Dr., Houston, TX 77024-3498 Tel. (713)686-4345 Fax (713)681-7550 Email: cahillb@stthom.edu Website: www.diocese-gal-hou.org/education_stmarysseminary

St. Mary's Seminary and University‡ (Catholic Church), Thomas Hurst, President and Rector, 5400 Roland Ave., Baltimore, MD 21210 Tel. (410)864-4000 Fax (410)864-4278 Email: thurst@stmarys.edu Website: www.stmarys.edu

Saint Meinrad School of Theology‡ (Catholic Church), Fr. Denis Robinson, OSB, President, 200 Hill Drive, St. Meinrad, IN 47577 Tel. (812)357-6611 Fax (812)357-6964 Email: theology@saintmeinrad.edu Website: www.saintmeinrad.edu

St. Patrick's Seminary and University‡ (Catholic Church), James L. McKearney, President and Rector, 320 Middlefield Rd., Menlo Park, CA 94025 Tel. (650)325-5621 Fax (650)322-0997 Email: jennifer@stpatricksseminary.org Website: www.stpatricksseminary.org

Saint Paul School of Theology‡ (The United Methodist Church), Myron F. McCoy, President, 5123 Truman Rd., Kansas City, MO 64127-2499 Tel. (816)483-9600 Fax (816)483-9605 Email: spst@spst.edu Website: www.spst.edu

St. Paul Seminary School of Divinity of the University of St. Thomas‡ (Catholic Church), The Rev. Aloysius R. Callaghan, Rector and Vice-President, 2260 Summit Ave., St. Paul, MN 55105 Tel. (651)962-5050 Fax (651)962-5790 Email: jlubel@stthomas.edu Website: www.stthomas.edu/spssod

St. Petersburg Theological Seminary† (Inter/Multidenominational), Dr. Myron P. Miller, President, 10830 Navajo Dr., St. Petersburg, FL 33708 Tel. (727)399-0276 Fax (727)399-1324 Email: sptseminary@tampabay.rr.com Website: www.sptseminary.edu

St. Tikhon's Orthodox Theological Seminary‡ (The Orthodox Church in America), Bishop Tikhon (Mollard), Rector, President, Box 130, St. Tikhon's Rd., South Canaan, PA 18459-0130 Tel. (570)937-4411 Fax (570)937-3100 Email: info@stots.edu (General Information) fr.michael@stots.edu (Dean's Office) admissions@stots.edu (Admissions) acadean@stots.edu (Academic Dean) Website: www.stots.edu

St. Vincent de Paul Regional Seminary‡ (Catholic Church), Msgr. Keith R. Brennan, Rector and President, 10701 South Military Trail, Boynton Beach, FL 33436-4899 Tel. (561)732-4424 Fax (561)737-2205 Email: Kbrennan@svdp.edu Website: www.svdp.edu

St. Vincent Seminary‡ (Catholic Church), Very Rev. Kurt Belsole, O.S.B., Rector, 300 Fraser Purchase Rd., Latrobe, PA 15650-2690 Tel. (724)537-4592 Fax (724)532-5052 Email: kurt.belsole@email.stvincent.edu Website: benedictine.stvincent.edu/seminary

St. Vladimir's Orthodox Theological Seminary‡ (The Orthodox Church in America), John Behr, Dean, 575 Scarsdale Rd., Crestwood, NY 10707-1699 Tel. (914)961-8313 Fax (914)961-4507 Email: info@svots.edu Website: www.svots.edu

SS. Cyril and Methodius Seminary‡ (Catholic Church), Very Rev. Charles G Kosanke, Rector, 3535 Indian Trail, Orchard Lake, MI 48324-1623 Tel. (248)683-0310 Fax (248)738-6735 Email: info@sscms.edu Website: www.sscms.edu

Samuel DeWitt Proctor School of Theology of Virginia Union University‡ (American Baptist Churches in the USA, National Baptist Convention, Progressive National Baptist Convention), Dr. John W. Kinney, Dean, 1500 North Lombardy Street, Richmond, VA 23330 Tel. (804)257-5715 Fax (804)342-3911 Email: JWKinney@vuu.edu Website: www.vuu.edu

San Diego Christian College (Southern Baptist), 2100 Greenfield Drive, El Cajon, CA 92019 Tel. (619)441-2200 Fax (619)440-0209 Email: chcadm@christianheritage.edu Website: www.christianheritage.edu

San Francisco Theological Seminary‡ (Presbyterian Church (U.S.A.)), Rev. Dr. Philip W. Butin, President, 105 Seminary Rd., San Anselmo, CA 94960 Tel. (415)451-2800 Fax (415)451-2811 Email: sftsinfo@sfts.edu Website: www.sfts.edu

Savonarola Theological Seminary (Polish National Catholic Church of America), Most Rev. Robert M. Nemkovich, Prime Bishop,

Rector, 1031 Cedar Ave., Scranton, PA 18505 Tel. (570)346-2188
Email: BpNemko@aol.com

Seabury-Western Theological Seminary‡ (Episcopal Church), The Very Rev. Gary Hall, Dean and President, 2122 Sheridan Rd., Evanston, IL 60201-2976 Tel. (847)328-9300 Fax (847)328-9624
Email: seabury@seabury.edu
Website: www.seabury.edu

Seattle University School of Theology and Ministry‡ (Catholic Church and 10 Mainline Protestant Denominations and Associations), Mark S Markuly, Dean, 901 12th Avenue, PO Box 222000, Seattle, WA 98122-1090 Tel. (206)296-5330 Fax (206)296-5329
Email: sueh@seattleu.edu
Website: www.seattleu.edu/stm

Seminario Evangelico de Puerto Rico (Interdenominational), Samuel Pagán, President, 776 Ponce de León Ave., San Juan, PR 00925 Tel. (787)763-6700 Fax (787)751-0847
Email: drspagan@icepr.com, jvaldes@tld.net
Website: netministries.org/see/charmin/CM01399

Seminary of the Immaculate Conception‡ (Catholic Church), Msgr. Francis J. Schneider, J.C.D., Rector/President, 440 West Neck Rd., Huntington, NY 11743 Tel. (631)423-0483 Fax (631)423-2346
Email: eluckstone@icseminary.edu
Website: www.icseminary.edu

Seminary of the Southwest‡ (Episcopal Church), Titus L. Presler, Dean and President, P.O. Box 2247, Austin, TX 78768-2247 Tel. (512)472-4133 Fax (512)472-3098
Email: salexander@etss.edu
Website: www.etss.edu

Seventh-day Adventist Theological Seminary of Andrews University‡ (Seventh-Day Adventist Church), Dennis Fortin, Dean, Andrews University, Berrien Springs, MI 49104-1500 Tel. (269)471-3537 Fax (269)471-6202
Email: seminary@andrews.edu
Website: www.andrews.edu/sem

Seventh Day Baptist School of Ministry (Seventh Day Baptist General Conference USA and Canada Ltd.), Gordon P. Lawton, Dean of School of Ministry, 3120 Kennedy Rd., P.O. Box 1678, Janesville, WI 53547 Tel. (608)752-5055 Fax (608)752-7711
Email: dean@sdbministry.org
Website: www.sdbministry.org

Shasta Bible College and Graduate School† (Baptist), Dr. David Nicholas, President, 2951 Goodwater Avenue, Redding, CA 96002 Tel. (530)221-4275 Fax (530)221-6929
Email: sbcadm@shasta.edu
Website: www.shasta.edu

Shaw University Divinity School‡ (General Baptist State Convention, N.C.; American Baptist Churches), James T. Roberson, Jr., Dean, PO Box 2090, Raleigh, NC 27602 Tel. (919)546-8569 Fax (919)546-8571
Email: JTRob@ShawU.edu
Website: www.shawuniversity.edu

Simpson College (The Christian and Missionary Alliance), James M. Grant, President, 2211 College View Dr., Redding, CA 96003 Tel. (916)224-5600 Fax (916)224-5608
Email: rerickson@simpsonuniversity.edu
Website: www.simpsonuniversity.edu

Sioux Falls Seminary‡ (North American Baptist Conference), G. Michael Hagan, President, 2100 S. Summit Avenue, Sioux Falls, SD 57105-2729 Tel. (605)336-6588 Fax (605)335-9090
Email: info@sfseminary.edu
Website: www.sfseminary.edu

Southeastern Baptist College (Baptist Missionary Association of America), Dr. Medrick Savell, President, 4229 Highway 15N, Laurel, MS 39440 Tel. (601)426-6346 Fax (601)426-6347
Email: info@southeasternbaptist.edu
Website: www.southeasternbaptist.edu

Southeastern Baptist Theological Seminary‡ (Southern Baptist Convention), Daniel L. Akin, President, PO Box 1889, Wake Forest, NC 27588-1889 Tel. (919)556-3101 Fax (919)556-8550
Email: president@sebts.edu
Website: www.sebts.edu

Southeastern Bible College (Interdenominational), Dr. Don Hawkins, President, 2545 Valleyvale Rd., Birmingham, AL 35244 Tel. (205)408-7073 or (205)970-9200 Fax (205)970-9207
Email: President@sebc.edu
Website: www.sebc.edu

Southeastern University (Assemblies of God), Mark Rutland, President, 1000 Longfellow Blvd., Lakeland, FL 33801 Tel. (863)667-5000 Fax (863)667-5200
Email: info@seuniversity.edu
Website: www.seuniversity.edu

Southern Baptist Theological Seminary‡ (Southern Baptist Convention), R. Albert Mohler, Jr., President, 2825 Lexington Rd., Louisville, KY 40280- Tel. (502)897-4011 Fax (502)899-1770
Email: communications@sbts.edu
Website: www.sbts.edu

Southern California Seminary (Southern Baptist Convention), Dr. Gary F. Coombs, President, 2075 East Madison Avenue, El Cajon, CA 92019 Tel. (619)442-9841 or (619)590-2128 Fax (619)442-4510

Email: eherrelko@socalsem.edu
Website: www.socalsem.edu

Southern Evangelical Seminary† (Interdenominational), Dr. Norman Geisler, President, 3000 Tilley Morris Road, Matthews, NC 28104 Tel. (704)847-5600 Fax (704)845-1747
Email: ses@ses.edu
Website: www.ses.edu

Southern Methodist College† (Southern Methodist Church), The Rev. Gary Briden, President, 541 Broughton Street, PO Box 1027, Orangeburg, SC 29116-1027 Tel. (803)534-7826 Fax (803)534-7827
Email: smcinfo@smcollege.edu
Website: www.smcollege.edu

Southern Wesleyan University (The Wesleyan Church), President David J. Spittal, President, 907 Wesleyan Dr., P.O. Box 1020, Central, SC 29630-1020 Tel. (864)644-5000 Fax (864)644-5900
Email: dspittal@swu.edu
Website: www.swu.edu

Southwestern Assemblies of God University (Assemblies of God), Kermit S. Bridges, President, 1200 Sycamore St., Waxahachie, TX 75165 Tel. (972)937-4010 Fax (972)923-0488
Email: president@sagu.edu
Website: www.sagu.edu

Southwestern Baptist Theological Seminary‡ (Southern Baptist Convention), Paige Patterson, President, 2001 W. Seminary Dr., Fort Worth, TX 76115 Tel. (817)923-1921 Fax (817)923-0610
Email: PresidentsOffice@swbts.edu
Website: www.swbts.edu

Southwestern College (Conservative Baptist Association of America), Brent D. Garrison, President, 2625 E. Cactus Rd., Phoenix, AZ 85032 Tel. (602)992-6101 Fax (602)404-2159
Email: swc@swcaz.edu
Website: www.southwesterncollege.edu

Starr King School for the Ministry‡ (Unitarian Universalist Association), Rebecca Parker, President, 2441 LeConte Ave., Berkeley, CA 94709 Tel. (510)845-6232 Fax (510)845-6273
Email: rparker@sksm.edu;
starrking@sksm.edu
Website: www.sksm.edu

Swedenborgian House of Studies at the Pacific School of Religion (The Swedenborgian Church), Dr. James F. Lawrence, Dean, 1798 Scenic Ave., Berkeley, CA 94709 Tel. (510)849-8228 Fax (510)849-8296
Email: jlawrence@shs.psr.edu
Website: www.shs.psr.edu

Talbot School of Theology of Biola University‡ (Inter/Multidenominational), Dr. Barry H. Corey, President, 13800 Biola Ave., La Mirada, CA 90639-0001 Tel. (562)903-4816 Fax (562)903-4759
Email: talbot.receptionist@biola.edu
Website: www.talbot.edu

Temple Baptist Seminary† (Interdenominational), Dr. Barkev Trachian, President, 1815 Union Ave., Chattanooga, TN 37404 Tel. (423)493-4221 Fax (423)493-4471
Email: tbsinfo@templebaptistseminary.edu
Website: www.templebaptistseminary.edu

Tennessee Temple University†, President, 1815 Union Avenue, Chattanooga, TN 37404 Tel. (423)493-4202 Fax (423)493-4114
Email: ttuinfo@tntemple.edu
Website: www.tntemple.edu

Theological School of the Protestant Reformed Churches (Protestant Reformed Churches in America), Barrett L. Gritters, President, 4949 Ivanrest Ave., Grandville, MI 49418 Tel. (616)531-1490 Fax (616)531-3033
Email: doezema@prca.org
Website: www.prca.org/seminary

Toccoa Falls College (The Christian and Missionary Alliance), Dr. W. Wayne Gardner, President, P.O. Box 800777, Toccoa Falls, GA 30598 Tel. (706)886-6831 Fax (706)282-6005
Email: president@tfc.edu
Website: www.tfc.edu

Trevecca Nazarene University (Church of the Nazarene), Dan Boone, President, 333 Murfreesboro Rd., Nashville, TN 37210-2877 Tel. (615)248-1200 Fax (615)248-7728
Email: atwining@trevecca.edu
Website: www.trevecca.edu

Trinity Baptist College† (Baptist), Tom Messer, Pastor, 800 Hammond Boulevard, Jacksonville, FL 32221 Tel. (904)596-2400 Fax (904)596-2531
Email: trinity@tbc.edu
Website: www.tbc.edu

Trinity Bible College (Assemblies of God), Dennis D. Niles, President, 50 S. 6th Ave., Ellendale, ND 58436 Tel. (701)349-3621, (800)523-1603 Fax (701)349-5443
Email: president@trinitybiblecollege.edu
Website: www.trinitybiblecollege.edu

Trinity College of Florida (Nondenominational), Mark T. O'Farrell, President, 2430 Welbilt Blvd., Trinity, FL 34655-4401 Tel. (727)376-6911 Fax (727)376-0781
Email: admissions@trinitycollege.edu
Website: www.trinitycollege.edu

Trinity Episcopal School for Ministry‡ (Episcopal Church), The Very Rev. Dr. Paul F.M. Zahl, Dean and President, 311 Eleventh St., Ambridge, PA 15003 Tel. (724)266-3838 Fax (724)266-4617
Email: tesm@tesm.edu
Website: www.tesm.edu

Trinity Evangelical Divinity School of Trinity International University‡ (Evangelical Free Church of America), Jeanette Hsieh, Interim President, 2065 Half Day Rd., Deerfield, IL 60015 Tel. (847) 945-8800 Fax (847)317-8141
Email: gwaybrig@tiu.edu
Website: www.tiu.edu/divinity

Trinity Lutheran College (Interdenominational-Lutheran), John M. Stamm, Ph.D., President, 4221 - 228th Ave., S.E., Issaquah, WA 98029-9299 Tel. (425)392-0400 Fax (425)392-0404
Email: info@tlc.edu, sconner@tlc.edu
Website: www.tlc.edu

Trinity Lutheran Seminary‡ (Evangelical Lutheran Church in America), Mark R. Ramseth, President, 2199 East Main Street, Columbus, OH 43209-2334 Tel. (614)235-4136 Fax (614)238-0263
Email: mramseth@TrinityLutheranSeminary.edu
Website: www.TrinityLutheranSeminary.edu

Turner School of Theology of Amridge University‡ (Churches of Christ), Dr. Rex A. Turner, Jr., President, 1200 Taylor Rd., Montgomery, AL 36117-3553 Tel. (334)387-3877 Fax (334)387-3878
Email: rexturner@regionsuniversity.edu
Website: www.regionsuniversity.edu

Union Theological Seminary‡ (Inter/Multidenominational), Serene Jones, President, 3041 Broadway at 121st Street, New York, NY 10027-0003 Tel. (212)662-7100 Fax (212)280-1440
Email: spak@uts.columbia.edu
Website: www.utsnyc.edu

Union Theological Seminary and Presbyterian School of Christian Education (Union-PSCE)‡ (Presbyterian Church (U.S.A.)), Brian K. Blount, President, 3401 Brook Rd., Richmond, VA 23227 Tel. (800)229-2990 Fax (804)355-3919
Email: gbirch@union-psce.edu
Website: www.union-psce.edu

United Theological Seminary‡ (The United Methodist Church), Dr. Wendy J. Deichmann Edwards, President, 4501 Denlinger Rd, Dayton, OH 45426 Tel. (937)529-2201 Fax (937)592-2345
Email: utscom@united.edu
Website: www.united.edu

United Theological Seminary of the Twin Cities‡ (United Church of Christ), Mary E. McNamara, President, 3000 Fifth St. N.W., New Brighton, MN 55112 Tel. (651)633-4311 Fax (651)633-4315
Email: info@unitedseminary.edu
Website: www.unitedseminary-mn.org

University of Chicago Divinity School‡ (Interdenominational), Richard A. Rosengarten, Dean, 1025 E. 58th St., Chicago, IL 60637 Tel. (773)702-8221 Fax (773)702-6048
Email: raroseng@midway.uchicago.edu
Website: www.uchicago.edu/divinity

University of Dubuque Theological Seminary‡ (Presbyterian Church (U.S.A.)), Jeffrey Bullock, President, 2000 University Ave., Dubuque, IA 52001-5099 Tel. (563)589-3122 Fax (563)589-3110
Email: udtsadms@dbq.edu
Website: www.UDTSeminary.net

University of Notre Dame Department of Theology‡ (Catholic Church), John C. Cavadini, Department Chair, 130 Malloy Hall, Notre Dame, IN 46556-5639 Tel. (574)631-6662 Fax (574)631-4291
Email: Cavadini.1@nd.edu
Website: www.nd.edu/†theo

University of St. Mary of the Lake Mundelein Seminary‡ (Catholic Church), Dennis J. Lyle, Rector and President, 1000 E. Maple Avenue, Mundelein, IL 60060-1174 Tel. (847)566-6401 Fax (847)566-7330
Email: rectort@usml.edu
Website: www.usml.edu

University of St. Thomas School of Theology‡ (Catholic Church), Sandra Magie, Dean, 9845 Memorial Dr., Houston, TX 77024 Tel. (713)686-4345 Fax (713)683-8673
Email: sms@stthom.edu
Website: www.stthom.edu/stmary

University of the South School of Theology‡ (Episcopal Church), The Very Rev. William S. Stafford, Ph.D. D.D, Dean, 335 Tennessee Ave., Sewanee, TN 37383-0001 Tel. (800)722-1974 Fax (931)598-1412
Email: theology@sewanee.edu
Website: www.theology.sewanee.edu

Urshan Graduate School of Theology‡ (United Pentecostal Church International), David Bernard, President, 704 Howdershell Road, Florissant, MO 63031 Tel. (314) 921-9290 Fax (314) 921-9203
Email: info@ugst.org
Website: www.ugst.org

Valley Forge Christian College (Assemblies of God), Don Meyer, President, 1401 Charlestown Rd., Phoenixville, PA 19460 Tel. (610)935-0450 Fax (610)935-9353
Email: admissions@vfcc.edu
Website: www.vfcc.edu

Vanderbilt University Divinity School‡ (Inter/Multidenominational), James Hudnut-Beumler, Dean, 411 21st Av. So., Nashville, TN 37240 Tel. (615)322-2776 Fax (615)343-9957
Email: james.hudnut-beumler@vanderbilt.edu
Website: divinity.lib.vanderbilt.edu/vds/vds-home

Vennard College (Interdenominational), Dr. Bruce Moyer, President, Box 29, University Park, IA 52595 Tel. (641)673-8391 Fax (641)673-8365
Email: bruce.moyer@vennard.edu
Website: www.vennard.edu

308

Virginia Theological Seminary ‡ (Episcopal Church), Ian Markham, President, 3737 Seminary Rd., Alexandria, VA 22304 Tel. (703)370-6600 Fax (703)370-6234 Email: mhorne@vts.edu Website: www.vts.edu

Virginia Union University (School of Theology) (American Baptist Churches in the USA, National Baptist Convention, USA, Inc., Progressive National Baptist Convention, Inc.), Dr. John W. Kinney, Dean, 1500 N. Lombardy St., Richmond, VA 23220 Tel. (804)257-5715 Fax (804)342-3911 Email: JWKinney@vuu.edu Website: www.vuu.edu/theology

Wake Forest University Divinity School‡ (Inter/Multidenominational), Bill J. Leonard, Dean, P.O. Box 7719 Reynolda Station, Winston-Salem, NC 27109-7719 Tel. (336)758-3957 Fax (336)758-4316 Email: leonahj@wfu.edu Website: www.wfu.edu

Walla Walla College (School of Theology) (Seventh-day Adventist Church), Dr. Jon Dybdahl, President, 204 S. College Ave., College Place, WA 99324-1198 Tel. (509)527-2194 Fax (509)527-2253 Email: dybdjo@wwc.edu Website: www.wwc.edu

Wartburg Theological Seminary‡ (Evangelical Lutheran Church in America), Duane H. Larson, President, 333 Wartburg Pl., P.O. Box 5004, Dubuque, IA 52004-5004 Tel. (563)589-0200 Fax (563)589-0333 Email: mailbox@wartburgseminary.edu Website: www.wartburgseminary.edu

Washington Baptist Theological Seminary of Washington Baptist University‡ (Baptist), Jacob S. Shin, President, 4300 Evergreen Lane, Annandale, VA 22003 Tel. (703)333-5904 Fax (703)333-5906 Email: info@wbcs.edu Website: www.wbcs.edu

Washington Theological Consortium (Nondenominational), The Rev. John W. Crossin, O.S.F.S., Executive Director, 487 Michigan Ave. N.E., Washington, DC 20017 Tel. (202)832-2675 Fax (202)526-0818 Email: wtc@washtheocon.org Website: www.washtheocon.org

Washington Theological Union‡ (Catholic Church), Louis Iasiello, President, 6896 Laurel St. N.W., Washington, DC 20012-2016 Tel. (202)726-8800 Fax (202)726-1716 Email: welch@wtu.edu Website: www.wtu.edu

Wesley Biblical Seminary‡ (Interdenominational), Ronald E. Smith, President, P.O. Box 9938, Jackson, MS 39286-0938 Tel. (601)366-8880 Fax (601)366-8832

Email: rsmith@wbs.edu Website: www.wbs.edu

Wesley Theological Seminary‡ (The United Methodist Church), David F. McAllister-Wilson, President, 4500 Massachusetts Ave. N.W., Washington, DC 20016-5690 Tel. (800)885-8600 or (800)882-4987 Fax (202)885-8605 Email: caldridge@wesleysem.edu Website: www.Wesleysem.edu

Western Seminary‡ (Conservative Baptist Association of America), Randal R. Roberts, President, 5511 S.E. Hawthorne Blvd., Portland, OR 97215 Tel. (877) 517-1800 or (503) 517-1800 Fax (503)517-1801 Email: admiss@westernseminary.edu Website: www.westernseminary.edu

Western Theological Seminary‡ (Reformed Church in America), Dennis N. Voskuil, President, 101 E. 13th St., Holland, MI 49423 Tel. (616)392-8555 Fax (616)392-7717 Email: dennis@westernsem.edu Website: www.westernsem.edu

Westminster Theological Seminary‡ (various Reformed), Peter A. Lillback, President, Chestnut Hill, P.O. Box 27009, Philadelphia, PA 19118 Tel. (215)887-5511 Fax (215)887-5404 Email: admissions@wts.edu Website: www.wts.edu

Westminster Seminary in California‡ (Nondenominational), W. Robert Godfrey, President, 1725 Bear Valley Pkwy, Escondido, CA 92027-4128 Tel. (760)480-8474 Fax (760)480-0252 Email: info@wscal.edu Website: www.wscal.edu

William Jessup University (Christian Churches and Churches of Christ), Bryce L. Jessup, D.D., President, 333 Sunset Blvd., Rocklin, CA 95765 Tel. (916)577-2210 Fax 916-577-2213 Email: bjessup@jessup.edu Website: www.jessup.edu

William Tyndale College (Interdenominational), Robert E. Hagerty, President, 35700 W. Twelve Mile Rd., Farmington Hills, MI 48331 Tel. (248)553-7200 Fax (248)553-5963 Website: www.williamtyndale.edu

Williamson Christian College† (Non-Denominational), Dr. Ken Oosting, President, 200 Seaboard Lane, Franklin, TN 37067 Tel. (615)771-7821 Fax (615)771-7810 Email: info@williamsoncc.edu Website: www.williamsoncc.edu

Winebrenner Theological Seminary‡ (Churches of God, General Conference), David E. Draper, President, 950 N. Main Street, Findlay, OH 45840 Tel. (419)434 4200 Fax (419)434 4267 Email: wts@winebrenner.edu Website: www.winebrenner.edu

US SEMINARIES

309

Wisconsin Lutheran Seminary (Wisconsin Evangelical Lutheran Synod), Paul O. Wendland, President, 11831 N. Seminary Dr., 65W, Mequon, WI 53092-1597 Tel. (262)242-8100 Fax (262)242-8110
Email: president@wls.wels.net
Website: www.wls.wels.net

Word of Life Bible Institute† (Non-Denominational), Dr. Joe Jordan, Chancellor, PO Box 129, 4200 Glendale Road, Pottersville, NY 12860 Tel. (518)494-4723 Fax (518)494-7474
Email: admissions@wol.org
Website: www.wol.org

World Mission University (Inter/Multidenominational), Dong Sun Lim, President, 500 Shatto Place, Suite 600, Los Angeles, CA 90020, Tel. (213)385-2322
Website: www.wmu.edu

Yale University Divinity School‡ (Inter/Multidenominational), Harold W. Attridge, Dean, 409 Prospect Sreet, New Haven, CT 06511-2167 Tel. (203)432-5303 Fax (203)432-7475
Email: divinity.admissions@yale.edu
Website: www.yale.edu/divinity

9. Theological Seminaries and Bible Colleges in Canada

The following list includes theological seminaries and departments in colleges and universities in which ministerial training is provided. Many denominations have additional programs. The list has been developed from direct correspondence with the institutions. Inclusion in or exclusion from this list implies no judgment about the quality or accreditation of any institution. Those schools that are members of the Association of Theological Schools are marked with a (‡). Each of the listings include: the institution name, denominational sponsor when appropriate, location, the president or dean, telephone and fax numbers when known and email and website addresses when available.

Acadia Divinity College‡ (Convention of the Atlantic Baptist Church), Dr. Harry G. Gardner, Principal and Dean of the Faculty of Theology, 31 Horton Street, Wolfville, NS B4P 2R6 Tel. (866)875-8975 (902)585-2210 Fax (902)585-2233
Email: adcinfo@acadiau.ca
Website: adc.acadiau.ca

Alberta Bible College (Christian Churches and Churches of Christ in Canada), Ronald A. Fraser, President, 635 Northmount Dr. NW, Calgary, AB T2K 3J6 Tel. (877)542-9492 (403)282-2994 Fax (403)282-3084
Email: generalinquiries@abc-ca.org
Website: www.abc-ca.org

Ambrose Seminary of Ambrose University College‡ (Christian and Missionary Alliance in Canada), Dr. George Durance, President, 833-4th Avenue SW #630, Calgary, AB T2P 3T5 Tel. (403)410-2000 Fax (403)571-2556
Information: Info@aun-nuc.ca; President: gdurance@auc-nuc.ca
Website: www.auc-nuc.ca

Ambrose University College (Church of the Nazarene Canada), Riley Coulter, President, 610, 833 4th Ave. SW, Calgary, AB T2P 3T5 Tel. (403)571-2550 Fax (403)571-2556
Email: wcampbell@auc-nuc.ca
Website: www.auc-nuc.ca

Arthur Turner Training School (The Anglican Church of Canada), Principal, Principal, Box 378, Pangnirtung, NU X0A 0R0 Tel. (867)873-5432 Fax (867)473-8375
Email: diocese@arcticnet.org

Associated Canadian Theological Schools of Trinity Western University‡ (Baptist General Conference of Canada, Evangelical Free Church of Canada, The Fellowship of Evangelical Baptist Churches in Canada, Christian and Missionary Alliance, Canadian Conference of Mennonite Brethren Churches), Dr. Phil Zylla, Principal, 7600 Glover Rd., Langley, BC V2Y 1Y1 Tel. (888)468-6898 (604)513-2044 Fax (604)513-2045
Email: acts@twu.ca
Website: www.acts.twu.ca

Atlantic School of Theology‡ (Tridenominational (Anglican Church of Canada, Roman Catholic Church, and United Church of Canada), The Rev. Canon Eric Beresford, President, 660 Francklyn St., Halifax, NS B3H 3B5 Tel. (902)423-6801 Fax (902)492-4048
Email: academicoffice@astheology.ns.ca
Website: www.astheology.ns.ca

Baptist Leadership Training School (Canadian Baptist Ministries), Hugh Fraser, President, 4330 16th St. S.W., Calgary, AB T2T 4H9 Tel. (403)243-3770 Fax (403)287-1930
Email: blts@imag.net
Website: www.yet.ca

Bethany Bible College-Canada (The Wesleyan Church), Dr. Arthur W. Maxwell, President, 26 Western St., Sussex, NB E4E 1E6 Tel. (506)432-4400 Fax (506)432-4425
Email: president@bbc.ca
Website: www.bbc.ca

Bethany College (Canadian Conference of Mennonite Brethren Churches (Saskatchewan and Alberta Conferences)), Rick McCorkindale, Academic Dean, President, Box 160, Hepburn, Saskatchewan S0K 1Z0 Tel. (306)947-2175 Fax (306)947-4229
Email: info@bethany.sk.ca
Website: www.bethany.sk.ca

Briercrest Seminary‡ (Interdenominational), Dwayne Uglem, President, 510 College Dr., Caronport, SK S0H 0S0 Tel. (800)667-5199 Fax (306)756-5500
Email: admissions@briercrest.ca
Website: www.briercrest.ca

Canadian Lutheran Bible Institute (Lutheran), Pastor Harold Rust, President, 4837 52A St., Camrose, AB T4V 1W5 Tel. (780)672-4454 Fax (780)672-4455
Email: clbi@clbi.edu
Website: www.clbi.edu

Canadian Mennonite University (Mennonite Brethren Churches, Mennonite Church Canada), Gerald Gerbrandt, President, 500 Shaftesbury Blvd, Winnipeg, MB R3P 2N2 Tel. (204)487-3300 Fax (204)487-3858
Email: reception@cmu.ca
Website: www.cmu.ca

311

Canadian Southern Baptist Seminary‡ (Canadian Convention of Southern Baptists), G. Richard Blackaby, President, 200 Seminary View, Cochrane, AB T4C 2G1 Tel. (877)922-2727 (403)932-6622 Fax (403)932-7049 Email: csbs@compuserve.com Website: www.csbs.edu

Carey Theological College‡ (Canadian Baptists of Western Canada), Brian F. Stelck, President, 5920 Iona Drive, Vancouver, BC V6T 1J6 Tel. (604)224-4308 Fax (604)224-5014 Email: info@careycentre.com Website: www.careycentre.com

Centre for Christian Studies (The Anglican Church of Canada, The United Church of Canada), Megan McKenzie, Principal, 60 Maryland, Winnipeg, MB R3G 1K7 Tel. (204)783-4490 Fax (204)786-3012 Email: mmckenzie@ccsonline.ca Website: www.ccsonline.ca

College Biblique Québec (The Pentecostal Assemblies of Canada), William Raccah, President, 740 Lebourgneuf, Ste. 100, Ancienne Lorette, QC G2J 1E2 Tel. (418)622-7552 Fax (418)622-1470 Email: mlecompte@ibq-canada.org Website: http://www.ibq-canada.org/

Collège Dominicain de Philosophie et de Théologie (The Roman Catholic Church in Canada), Gabor Csepregi, President, 96 Avenue Empress, Ottawa, ON K1R 7G3 Tel. (613)233-5696 ext. 206 Fax (613)233-6064 Email: service.accueil@collegedominicain.ca Website: www.collegedominicain.ca

College of Emmanuel and St. Chad (The Anglican Church of Canada), The Rev. Dr. William (Bill) Richards, Principal, 114 Seminary Crescent, Saskatoon, SK S7N 0X3 Tel. (306)975-3753 Fax (306)934-2683 Email: emmanuel.stchad@usask.ca Website: www.usask.ca/stu/emmanuel

Columbia Bible College (BC Conference of Mennonite Brethren Churches & Mennonite Church in BC), Dr. Ron Penner, President, 2940 Clearbrook Rd., Abbotsford, BC V2T 2Z8 Tel. (604)853-3358 Fax (604)853-3063 Email: info@columbiabc.edu Website: www.columbiabc.edu

Concordia Lutheran Seminary‡ (Lutheran Church-Canada), Manfred Zeuch, President, 7040 Ada Blvd., Edmonton, AB T5B 4E3 Tel. (780)474-1468 Fax (780)479-3067 Email: info@concordiasem.ab.ca Website: www.concordiasem.ab.ca

Concordia Lutheran Theological Seminary‡ (Lutheran Church-Canada), Thomas Winger, President, 470 Glenridge Ave., St. Catharines, ON L2T 4C3 Tel. (905)688-2362 Fax (905)688-9744 Email: concordia@brocku.ca Website: www.brocku.ca/concordiaseminary

Ecole de Theologie Evangelique de Montreal (Canadian Conference of Mennonite Brethren Churches), Annie Brosseau, President, 4824, ch. de la Cote-des-Neiges, Suite 301, Montreal, QC H3V 1G4 Tel. (514)331-0878 Fax (514)331-0879 Email: info@etem.ca Website: www.etem.ca

Emmanuel Bible College (The Evangelical Missionary Church of Canada), Thomas E. Dow, President, 100 Fergus Ave., Kitchener, ON N2A 2H2 Tel. (519)894-8900 Fax (519)894-5331 Email: admin@ebcollege.on.ca Website: www.ebcollege.on.ca

Emmanuel College of Victoria University‡ (The United Church of Canada), The Rev. Dr. Mark G. Toulouse, Principal, 75 Queens Park Crescent East, Toronto, ON M5S 1K7 Tel. (416)585-4539 Fax (416)585-4516 Email: ec.office@utoronto.ca Website: vicu.utoronto.ca

Eston College (Apostolic Church of Pentecost of Canada Inc.), Rev. Lauren E. Miller, President, Box 579, Eston, SK S0L 1A0 Tel. (306)962-3621 Fax (306)962-3810 Email: fgbi@fgbi.sk.ca Website: fgbi.sk.ca

Faculté De Théologie Évangélique (Interdenominational), Amar Djaballah, President, 2285 Avenue Papineau, Montréal, QC H2K 4J5 Tel. (514)526-2003 Fax (514)526-6887 Email: reg@fteacadia.ca Website: www.fteacadia.ca

Faith Alive Bible College (Nondenominational), David Pierce, Dean, 637 University Dr., Saskatoon, SK S7N 0H8 Tel. (306)652-2230 Fax (306)665-1125 Email: info@fabc.ca Website: www.fabc.ca

Gardner College, A Centre for Christian Studies (Church of God (Anderson, Ind.)), Donnalyn Froese, President, 4707 56th St., Camrose, AB T4V 2C4 Tel. (780)672-0171 Fax (780)672-2465 Email: info@gardnercollege.org Website: www.gardnercollege.org

Grand Seminaire de Montréal (The Roman Catholic Church in Canada), Charles Langlois, P.S.S., Rector, 2065, Sherbrooke Ouest, Montréal, QC H3H 1G6 Tel. (514)935-1169 Fax (514)935-5497 Email: Information Generale, info@gsdm.qc.ca OR Bibliotheque, biblio@gsdm.qc.ca Website: www.gsdm.qc.ca

Great Lakes Bible College (Churches of Christ in Canada), Mr. J. Arthur Ford, President, 470 Glenelm Crescent, Waterloo, ON N2L 5C8 Tel. (519)884-4310 Fax (519)884-4412

Email: learn@glbc.on.ca
Website: www.glbc.on.ca

Heritage Theological Seminary‡, Marvin R. Brubacher, President, 175 Holiday Inn Dr., Cambridge, ON N3C 3T2 Tel. (519)651-2869 or 800-465-1961 Fax (519)651-2870 Email: discover@heritageseminary.net Website: www.DiscoverHeritage.ca

Horizon College and Seminary, Affiliated College of the University of Saskatchewan (The Pentecostal Assemblies of Canada), D. Munk, Academic Dean, 1303 Jackson Ave., Saskatoon, SK S7H 2M9 Tel. (306)374-6655/(879)374-6655/(877)374-6655 Fax (306)373-6968 Email: admissions@horizon.edu Website: www.horizon.edu

Huron University College Faculty of Theology‡ (The Anglican Church of Canada), Dr. Ramona Lumpkin, Principal, 1349 Western Rd., London, ON N6G 1H3 Tel. (519)438-7224 Fax (519)438-9981 Email: huron@uwo.ca Website: www.huronuc.on.ca

Institut Biblique Beree (The Pentecostal Assemblies of Canada), André L. Gagnon, President, 1711 Est Boul. Henri-Bourassa, Montréal, QC H2C 1J5 Tel. (514)385-4238 Fax (514)385-4238 Email: mlecompte@ibq-canada.org Website: http://www.ibq-canada.org

Institut Périchorèse Atelier d'iconographie, Michèle Lévesque, Director, 3774 Chemin Queen Mary - Suite 309, Montréal, QC H3V 1A6 Tel. 514-510-0579 Email: perichorese.icones@videotron.ca Website: www.perichorese-icones.org

Institute for Christian Studies (Nondenominational), Harry Fernhout, President, 229 College St., Suite 200, Toronto, ON M5T 1R4 Tel. (416)979-2331 or 1 (888)326-5347 Fax (416) 979-2332 Email: info@icscanada.edu Website: www.icscanada.edu

International Bible College (Church of God (Cleveland, Tenn.)), Cheryl Busse, President, 401 Trinity La., Moose Jaw, SK S6H 0E3 Tel. (306)692-4041 Fax (306)692-7968 Email: ibc@cofg.net Website: www.ibc.cofg.net

Key-Way-Tin Bible Institute (Nondenominational), Jon Siebert, Interim Administrator, Site 633 Comp 8 RR1, Lac La Biche, AB T0A 2C1 Tel. (780)623-4565 Fax (780)623-1788 Email: kbi@telus.net Website: www.keywaytinbibleinstitute.org

Knox College‡ (The Presbyterian Church in Canada), J. Dorcas Gordon, Principal, 59 St. George St., Toronto, ON M5S 2E6 Tel.

(416)978-4500 Fax (416)971-2133 Email: knox.college@utoronto.ca Website: www.utoronto.ca/knox

Living Faith Bible College (Fellowship of Christian Assemblies (Canada)), Paul Reich, M.A, President, Box 100, Caroline, AB T0M 0M0 Tel. (403)722-2225, (800)838-2975 Fax (403)722-2459 Email: office@lfbc.net Website: www.lfbc.net

Lutheran Theological Seminary‡ (Evangelical Lutheran Church in Canada), Kevin A. Ogilvie, President, 114 Seminary Crescent, Saskatoon, SK S7N 0X3 Tel. (306)966-7850 Fax (306)966-7852 Email: lutheran.seminary@usask.ca Website: www.usask.ca/stu/luther

Maritime Christian College (Christian Churches and Churches of Christ), Fred C. Osborne, President, 503 University Ave., Charlottetown, PE C1A 7Z4 Tel. (902)628-8887 Fax (902)892-3959 Email: registrar@maritimechristiancollege.pe.ca Website: www.maritimechristiancollege.pe.ca

Master's College and Seminary (The Pentecostal Assemblies of Canada), Rev. David Hazzard, President, 3080 Yonge St., Box 70, Suite 3040, Toronto, ON M4N 3N1 Tel. (416)482-2224 Fax (416)482-7004 Email: info@mcs.edu Website: www.mcs.edu

McGill University Faculty of Religious Studies‡ (Interdenominational), B. Barry Levy, Dean, 3520 University St., Montréal, QC H3A 2A7 Tel. (514)398-4125 Fax (514)398-6665 Email: web.relgstud@mcgill.ca Website: www.mcgill.ca/religiousstudies

McMaster Divinity College‡ (Baptist Convention of Ontario and Quebec (BCOQ)), Stanley E. Porter, Principal/Dean, 1280 Main St. West, Hamilton, ON L8S 4K1 Tel. (905)525-9140x24401 Fax (905)577-4782 Email: divinity@mcmaster.ca Website: www.macdiv.ca

Millar College of the Bible (Interdenominational), A. Brian Atmore, President, Box 25, Pambrun, SK S0N 1W0 Tel. (306)582-2033 Fax (306)582-2027 Email: info@millarcollege.ca Website: www.millarcollege.ca

Montreal Diocesan Theological CollegeTrue (The Anglican Church of Canada), Bishop of Montreal, President, 3473 University St., Montreal, QC H3A 2A8 Tel. (514)849-3004 Fax (514)849-4113 Email: diocoll@netrover.com Website: www.dio-mdtc.ca

Montreal School of Theology‡ (Inter/Multidenominational), Dr. John Simons, Administrative Officer, 3475 University St., Montréal, QC H3A 2A8 Tel. (514)849-8511 Fax (514)849-4113
Email: info@mst-etm.ca
Website: www.mst-etm.ca

Mount Carmel Bible School (Transdenominational), Wayne Tomalty, President, 4725 106 Ave., Edmonton, AB T6A 1E7 Tel. (780)465-3015 Toll-free 1(800) 561-6443 Fax (780)466-2485
Email: mail@mountcarmel.net
Website: www.mountcarmel.net

Newman Theological College‡ (The Catholic Church in Canada), M. Bryn Kulmatycki, PhD, President, #172, 2257 Premier Way, Sherwood Park, AB T8H 2M8 Tel. (780)467-5858 Fax (780)467-8733
Email: maria.saulnier@newman.edu
Website: www.newman.edu

Nipawin Bible Institute (Interdenominational), Mr. Wes Fehr, Acting President, Box 1986, Nipawin, SK S0E 1E0 Tel. (306)862-5095 Fax (306)862-3651
Email: info@nipawin.org
Website: www.nipawin.org

Northwest Baptist Theological College and Seminary (The Fellowship of Evangelical Baptist Churches of Canada), Dr. Larry Perkins, President, 7600 Glover Rd., Langley, BC V2Y 1Y1 Tel. (604)888-7592 Fax (604)513-8511
Email: larry@nbseminary.com
Website: www.nbseminary.com

Ontario Christian Seminary (Christian Churches and Churches of Christ in Canada), James R. Cormode, President, 260 High Park Ave., Toronto, ON M6P 3J9 Tel. (416)769-7115 Fax (416)769-7047

Pacific Life Bible College (Foursquare), Rob Buzza, President, 15030 66 A Ave., Surrey, BC V3S 2A5 Tel. (604)597-9082 Fax (604)597-9090
Email: plbc@pacificlife.edu
Website: www.pacificlife.edu

Parole de Vie Bethel/Word of Life Bethel (Nondenominational), Mark Strout, Director, 1175, ch. Thomas - Woodward, Sherbrooke, QC J1M 0B4 Tel. (819)823-8435 Fax (819)823-2468
Email: quebec@pdvb.org
Website: www.pdvb.org

Peace River Bible Institute (Interdenominational), Waldie Neufeld, President, Box 99, Sexsmith, AB T0H 3C0 Tel. (780)568-3962 Fax (780)568-4431
Email: prbi@prbi.edu
Website: www.prbi.edu

Prairie Graduate School (Interdenominational), Dr. Charlotte Kinvig Bates, Co-President, 330 6th Ave., Three Hills, AB T0M 2N0 Tel. (403) 443-5511 Fax (403)443-5540
Email: prairie@prairie.edu
Website: www.pbi.ab.ca

The Presbyterian College, Montreal‡ (Presbyterian Church in Canada), John Vissers, Principal, 3495 University St., Montreal, QC H3A 2A8 Tel. (514)288-5256 Fax (514)288-8072
Email: info@presbyteriancollege.ca
Website: www.presbyteriancollege.ca

Providence College and Theological Seminary (Inter/Multidenominational), August H. Konkel, President, 10 College Crescent, Otterburne, MB R0A 1G0 Tel. (204)433-7488 Fax (204)433-7158
Email: info@prov.ca
Website: www.prov.ca

Queens College Faculty of Theology‡ (The Anglican Church of Canada), John Mellis, President, 210 Prince Philip Dr., Suite 3000, St. Johns, NL A1B 3R6 Tel. (709)753-0116 Fax (709)753-1214
Email: queens@mun.ca
Website: www.mun.ca/queens

Queen's Theological College‡ (The United Church of Canada), M. Jean Stairs, Principal, Room 212 Theological Hall, Kingston, ON K7L 3N6 Tel. (613)533-2110 Fax (613)533-6879
Email: theology@queensu.ca
Website: www.queensu.ca/theology

Reformed Episcopal Theological College (Reformed Episcopal Church of Canada), Rt. Rev. Michael Fedechko, President, 320 Armstrong St., Box 2532, New Liskeard, ON P0J 1P0 Tel. (705)647-4565 Fax (705)647-4565
Email: fed@nt.net
Website: www.retcc.com

Reformed Episcopal Theological College (The Reformed Episcopal Church of Canada), Rt. Rev. Michael Fedechko, President, PO Box 2532, Hwy 11 North, New Liskeard, ON P0J 1P0 Tel. (705)647-4565 Fax (705)647-4565
Email: fed@nt.net
Website: www.retcc.com

Regent College‡ (Interdenominational), Rod Wilson, PhD, President, 5800 University Blvd., Vancouver, BC V6T 2E4 Tel. (800)663-8664 or (604)224-3245 Fax (604)224-3097
Email: administration@regent-college.edu
Website: www.regent-college.edu

Regis College‡ (The Roman Catholic Church in Canada), Joseph G. Schner, S.J, President, 100 Wellesley St. West, Toronto, ON M5S 2Z5 Tel. (416)922-5474 Fax (416)922-2898
Email: regis.registrar@utoronto.ca
Website: www.regiscollege.ca

Rocky Mountain College, Centre for Biblical Studies (The Evangelical Missionary Church of Canada), Gordon Dirks, President, 4039

Brentwood Rd. NW, Calgary, AB T2L 1L1 Tel. (403)284-5100 Fax (403)220-9567 Email: admissions@rockymountaincollege.ca Website: www.rockymountaincollege.ca

St. Andrew's College‡ (The United Church of Canada), Rev. Lorne Calvert, Principal, 1121 College Dr., Saskatoon, SK S7N 0W3 Tel. (306)966-8970; (877)644-8970 Fax (306)966-8981 Email: lorne.calvert@usask.ca Website: www.standrews.ca

St. Augustine's Seminary of Toronto‡ (The Roman Catholic Church in Canada), Rev. Msgr. A. Robert Nusca, President and Rector, 2661 Kingston Rd., Toronto, ON M1M 1M3 Tel. (416)261-7207 Fax (416)261-2529 Email: info@staugustines.on.ca Website: www.staugustines.on.ca

St. John's College, Univ. of Manitoba, Faculty of Theology (The Anglican Church of Canada), Dr. Janet A. Hoskins, Warden & Vice Chancellor, 92 Dysart Rd., Winnipeg, MB R3T 2M5 Tel. (204)474-8531 Fax (204)474-7610 Email: stjohns_college@umanitoba.ca Website: www.umanitoba.ca/colleges/st_johns

Saint Paul University, Faculty of Theology (The Roman Catholic Church), Fr. Andrea Spatafora, Ph.D., Dean, 223 Main St., Ottawa, ON K1S 1C4 Tel. (613)236-1393 x. 2247 Fax (613)751-4016 Email: fquesnel@ustpaul.ca Website: www.ustpaul.ca

St. Peter's Seminary‡ (The Roman Catholic Church in Canada), William T. McGrattan, Rector, 1040 Waterloo St. North, London, ON N6A 3Y1 Tel. (519)432-1824 Fax (519)432-0964 Email: jslawik@uwo.ca Website: www.stpetersseminary.ca

St. Stephen's CollegeUniversity of Alberta‡ (The United Church of Canada), Dr. Earle Sharam, President, 8810 112th St., Edmonton, AB T6G 2J6 Tel. (800)661-4956 Fax (780)433-8875 Email: westema@ualberta.ca Website: www.ststephenscollege.ca

Salvation Army College for Officer Training (The Salvation Army in Canada), Wayne N. Pritchett, Principal, 2130 Bayview Ave., North York, ON M4N 3K6 Tel. (416)481-6131 Fax (416)481-6810; (416)481-2895 (Library) Email: sandra_rice@can.salvationarmy.org; ray_harris@can.salvationarmy.org

The Salvation Army William and Catherine Booth College (The Salvation Army in Canada), Dr. Jonathan S. Raymond, President, 447 Webb Pl., Winnipeg, MB R3B 2P2 Tel. (204)947-6701 Fax (204)942-3856 Email: wcbc@boothcollege.ca Website: www.boothcollege.ca

Steinbach Bible College (Mennonite), Rob Reimer, President, 50 PTH 12 N, Steinbach, MB R5G 1T4 Tel. (204)326-6451 Fax (204) 326-6908 Email: info@sbcollege.ca Website: www.sbcollege.ca

Summit Pacific College (The Pentecostal Assemblies of Canada), David Demchuk, President, Box 1700, Abbotsford, BC V2S 7E7 Tel. (604)853-7491 Fax (604)853-8951 Email: pr@summitpacific.ca Website: www.summitpacific.ca

Taylor College of Mission and Evangelism (Non-Denominational), Reed Fleming, Director of Formation, 105 Mountain View Drive, Saint John, NB E2J 5B5 Tel. (866)693-8975 Fax (506)657-8217 Email: reed.fleming@taylorcollege.ca Website: www.taylorcollege.ca

Taylor University College and Seminary‡ (North American Baptist Conference), Dr. Marvin L. Dewey, President, 11525-23 Ave., Edmonton, AB T6J 4T3 Tel. (780)431-5200 Fax (780)436-9416 Email: marvin.dewey@taylor-edu.ca Website: www.taylor-edu.ca

Theological College of the Canadian Reformed Churches (Canadian and American Reformed Churches), Dr. G. H. Visscher, President, 110 West 27th St., Hamilton, ON L9C 5A1 Tel. (905)575-3688 Fax (905)575-0799 Email: theocollege@seminary.canrc.org Website: www.theologicalcollege.ca

Toronto Baptist Seminary and Bible College (Baptist), Dr. Glendon G. Thompson, President, 130 Gerrard St., E., Toronto, ON M5A 3T4 Tel. (416)925-3263 Fax (416)925-8305 Email: inquiry@tbs.edu Website: www.tbs.edu

Toronto School of Theology‡ (Inter/Multidenominational), Alan Hayes, Director, 47 Queens Park Crescent E., Toronto, ON M5S 2C3 Tel. (416)978-4039 Fax (416)978-7821 Email: alan.hayes@utoronto.ca Website: www.tst.edu

Trinity College Faculty of Divinity‡ (The Anglican Church of Canada), David Neelands, Dean, 6 Hoskin Ave., Toronto, ON M5S 1H8 Tel. (416)978-2133 Fax (416)978-4949 Email: divinity@trinity.utoronto.ca Website: www.trinity.utoronto.ca/divinity

Tyndale University College & Seminary‡ (Transdenominational), Dr. Brian C. Stiller, President, 25 Ballyconnor Ct., Toronto, ON M2M 4B3 Tel. (416)226-6380 Fax (416)226-9464 Email: info@tyndale.ca Website: www.tyndale.ca

United Theological College/Le Séminaire Uni (The United Church of Canada), Rev. Philip Joudrey, President, 3521 rue Université, Montréal, QC H3A 2A9 Tel. (514)849-2042 Fax (514)849-8634
Email: admin@utc.ca
Website: www.utc.ca

Université Laval, Faculté de Théologie et de Sciences Religieuses (The Roman Catholic Church in Canada), Marc Pelchat, Doyen, Pavillon Felix-Antoine Savard, 2325 Rue Des Bibliotheques, Hocal 846, Quebec, QC G1V 0A6 Tel. (418)656-3576 Fax (418)656-3273
Email: ftsr@ftsr.ulaval.ca
Website: www.ftsr.ulaval.ca

Université de Montréal, Faculté de théologie et de sciences des religion (The Roman Catholic Church in Canada), Jean Duhaime Doyen, President, C. P. 6128 Succ. Centre Ville, Montréal, QC H3C 3J7 Tel. (514)343-7160 Fax (514)343-5738
Email: ftsr@umontreal.ca
Website: www.ftsr.umontreal.ca

Université de Sherbrooke, Faculté de theologié, d'éthique et de philosophie (The Roman Catholic Church in Canada), Jean-François Malherbe, President, 1111, rue Saint-Charles Ouest, Tourquest - Bureau 310, Longueuil, QC J4K 5G4 Tel. (450)670-7157 Fax (450)670-1959
Email: jf.malherbe@sympatico.ca
Website: www.usherb.ca/longueuil

University of St. Michael's College Faculty of Theology‡ (Roman Catholic Church), Rev. Dr. Mario O. D'Souza, C.S.B., Dean, 81 St. Mary St., Toronto, ON M5S 1J4 Tel. (416)926-7140 Fax (416)926-7294
Email: usmctheology.registrar@utoronto.ca
Website: www.utoronto.ca/stmikes

The University of Winnipeg Faculty of Theology‡ (Multi-denominational and the United Church of Canada), James T. Christie, Dean, 515 Portage Ave., Winnipeg, MB R3B 2E9 Tel. (204)786-9390 Fax (204)772-2584
Email: theology@uwinnipeg.ca
Website: www.theology/uwinnipeg.ca

Vancouver School of Theology‡ (Inter/Multidenominational), Rev. Dr. Wendy Fletcher, Principal, 6000 Iona Dr., Vancouver, BC V6T 1L4 Tel. 1-(866)822-9031 Fax (604)822-9212
Email: vstinfo@vst.edu
Website: www.vst.edu

Vanguard College (The Pentecostal Assemblies of Canada), Stephen Hertzog, President, 12140 103 St., Edmonton, AB T5G 2J9 Tel. (780)452-0808 Fax (780)452-5803
Email: info@vanguardcollege.com
Website: www.vanguardcollege.com

Waterloo Lutheran Seminary‡ (Evangelical Lutheran Church in Canada), David Pfrimmer, Principal Dean, 75 University Ave. W., Waterloo, ON N2L 3C5 Tel. (519)884-1970 Fax (519)725-2434
Email: seminary@wlu.ca
Website: www.seminary.wlu.ca

Western Christian College (Churches of Christ in Canada), Kevin Vance, President, 100-4400 4th Ave., Regina, SK S4T 0H8 Tel. (306)545-1515 Fax (306)352-2198
Email: president@westernchristian.ca
Website: www.westernchristian.ca

Wycliffe College‡ (The Anglican Church of Canada), Rev. Canon. Dr. George R. Sumner, Jr., Principal, 5 Hoskin Ave., Toronto, ON M5S 1H7 Tel. (416)946-3535 Fax (416)946-3545
Email: info@wycliffe.utoronto.ca
Website: www.wycliffecollege.ca

10. Religious Periodicals in the United States

This directory lists publications primarily of the organizations listed in Directory 3, "Religious Bodies in the United States." Some independent publications are also listed. The list does not include all publications prepared by religious bodies, and not all the publications listed here are necessarily the official publication of a particular church. Regional publications and newsletters are not included. A more extensive list of religious periodicals published in the United States can be found in *Gale Directory of Publications and Broadcast Media* (Gale Research, Inc., P.O. Box 33477, Detroit MI 48232-5477).

Each entry in this directory contains: the title of the periodical, frequency of publication, religious affiliation, editor's name, address, telephone and fax number and e-mail and website addresses when available. The frequency of publication, which appears in parenthesis after the name of the publication is represented by a "D" for daily, "W" for weekly; "M" for monthly; "Q" for quarterly; "Y" for yearly, "I" for Internet.

21st Century Christian (M) Churches of Christ, M. Norvel Young and Prentice A. Meador, Jr., Box 40304, Nashville, TN 37204 Tel. (800)331-5991 Fax (615)385-5915 Email: eric@nafwb.org

Action (6-Y) Churches of Christ, John D. Reese, P.O. Box 2169, Cedar Park, TX 78630-2169 Tel. (512)345-8191 Fax (512)401-8265 Email: wbsinfo@wbschool.org Website: www.wbschool.org

Adra Today (Q) Seventh-day Adventist Church, Beth Schaefer, 12501 Old Columbia Pike, Silver Spring, MD 20904-6600 Tel. (301)680-6355 Fax (301)680-6370 Email: 74617.2105@compuserve.com Website: www.adra.org

The Adult Quarterly (Q) Associate Reformed Presbyterian Church (General Synod), The Rev. William B. Evans, PhD, P.O. Box 275, Due West, SC 29639 Tel. (864)379-8896 Email: wbevans@erskine.edu

Advent Christian News (M) Advent Christian Church, Rev. Keith D. Wheaton, P.O. Box 23152, Charlotte, NC 28227 Tel. (704)545-6161 Fax (704)573-0712 Email: Acpub@Adventchristian.org

The Adventist Chaplain (Q) Seventh-day Adventist Church, Deena Bartel-Wagner - Editor, Adventist Chaplaincy Ministries, General Conference of Seventh-day Adventists, 12501 Old Columbia Pike, Silver Spring, MD 20904-6600 Tel. (301)680-6780 Fax (301)680-6783 Email: acm@gc.adventist.org Website: www.adventistchaplains.org

Adventist Review (3-M) Seventh-day Adventist Church, W. G. Johnsson, 12501 Old Columbia Pike, Silver Spring, MD 20904-6600 Tel. (301)680-6560 Fax (301)680-6638 Email: letters@adventistreview.org Website: www.adventistreview.org

Adventist World (M) Seventh-day Adventist Church, William G. Johnson, 12501 Old Columbia Pike, Silver Spring, MD 20904-6600 Tel. (301)680-6560 Fax (301)680-6638

Agape Magazine (bi-M) Coptic Orthodox Church, Bishop Serapion, P.O.Box 4960, Diamond Bar, CA 91765 Tel. (909)865-8378 Fax (909)865-8348 Email: agape@lacopts.org Website: lacopts.org

Alive Now (bi-M) The United Methodist Church, JoyAnn Miller (Interim), P.O. Box 340004, Nashville, TN 37203-0004 Tel. (615)340-7218 Email: alivenow@upperroom.org Website: www.alivenow.org

The Allegheny Wesleyan Methodist (M) The Allegheny Wesleyan Methodist Connection (Original Allegheny Conference), William Cope, P.O. Box 357, Salem, OH 44460 Tel. (330)337-9376 Fax (330)337-9700 Email: awmc@juno.com

Alliance Life (M) The Christian and Missionary Alliance, Mark Failing, P.O. Box 35000, Colorado Springs, CO 80935 Tel. (719)599-5999 Fax (719)599-8234 Email: alife@cmalliance.org Website: www.alliancelife.org

The A.M.E. Christian Recorder (bi-W) African Methodist Episcopal Church, Dr. Calvin H. Sydnor, III, 500 Eighth Ave. South, Nashville, TN 37203-4181

American Baptist Quarterly (Q) American Baptist Churches in the USA, Dr. Robert E. Johnson, P.O. Box 851, Valley Forge, PA 19482-0851 Tel. (610)768-2269 Fax (610)768-2266 Email: dbvanbro@abc-usa.org Website: www.cbts.edu/rejohnsonweb/ABQuarterly

American Baptists In Mission (Q) American Baptist Churches in the USA, Richard W. Schramm, P.O. Box 851, Valley Forge, PA 19482-0851 Tel. (610)768-2077 Fax (610)768-2320
Email: richard.schramm@abc-usa.org
Website: www.abc-usa.org

American Bible Society Record (Q) Nondenominational, Liz Smith, 1865 Broadway, New York, NY 10023-7505 Tel. (212)408-1367 Fax (212)582-7245
Email: absrecord@americanbible.org
Website: www.americanbible.org

The Anchor of Faith (M) The Anglican Orthodox Church, The Most Rev. Jerry L. Ogles, Anglican Orthodox Church, P.O. Box 128, Statesville, NC 28687-0128 Tel. (704)873-8365 Fax (704)873-5359
Email: aocusa@energyunited.net
Website: www.anglicanorthodoxchurch.org

Annual Catholic Directory, The (Y) The Catholic Church, Michelle Laque Johnson, 222 N. 17th St., Philadelphia, PA 19103 Tel. (215)587-3660 Fax (215)587-3979

El Aposento Alto (bi-M) The United Methodist Church, Carmen Gaud, P.O. Box 340004, Nashville, TN 37203-0004 Tel. (615)340-7253 Fax (615)340-7267
Email: ElAposentoAlto@upperroom.org
Website: www.upperroom.org

The Armenian Church (2-Y) Diocese of the Armenian Church of America, Arpie McQueen, 630 Second Avenue, New York, NY 10016 Tel. (212)686-0710 Fax (212) 779-3558
Email: tac@armeniandiocese.org
Website: www.armenianchurch.org

Around the Fellowship (M) Universal Fellowship of Metropolitan Community Churches, Director of Communications: James N. Birkitt, Jr., 8704 Santa Monica Blvd, 2nd Fl., West Hollywood, CA 90069-4548 Tel. (310)360-8640 Fax (310)360-8680
Email: info@mccchurch.org
Website: www.mccchurch.org

The Associate Reformed Presbyterian (M) Associate Reformed Presbyterian Church (General Synod), Mrs. Sabrina M. Cooper, One Cleveland St., Greenville, SC 29601 Tel. (864)232-8297 Fax (864)271-3729
Email: arpmaged@arpsynod.org
Website: www.arpmagazine.org

Attack, A Magazine for Christian Men (Q) National Association of Free Will Baptists, James E. Vallance, P.O. Box 5002, Antioch, TN 37011-5002 Tel. (615)731-4950 Fax (615)731-0771

Awake! (M) Jehovah's Witnesses, Watch Tower Society, 25 Columbia Heights, Brooklyn, NY 11201-2483 Tel. (718)560-5000
Website: watchtower.org

The Banner (M) Christian Reformed Church in North America, Robert DeMoor, 2850 Kalamazoo Ave., S.E., Grand Rapids, MI 49560 Tel. (616)224-0732 Fax (616)224-0834
Email: editorial@thebanner.org
Website: www.thebanner.org

The Banner of Truth (M) Netherlands Reformed Congregations, J. den Hoed, 1113 Bridgeview Dr., Lynden, WA 98264 Tel. (360)354-4203 Fax (360)354-7565

The Baptist Bible Tribune (M) Baptist Bible Fellowship International, Mike Randall, P.O. Box 309, Springfield, MO 65801-0309 Tel. (417)831-3996 Fax (417)831-1470
Email: editors@tribune.org
Website: www.tribune.org

Baptist Bulletin (M) General Association of Regular Baptist Churches, Sr Editor: Norman A. Olson, 1300 N. Meacham Rd., Schaumburg, IL 60173-4806 Tel. (847)843-1600 Fax (847) 843-3757
Email: baptistbulletin@garbc.org
Website: www.garbc.org

Baptist History and Heritage Society (3-Y) Baptist, Pamela R. Durso, P.O. Box 728, Brentwood, TN 37021-0728 Tel. (615)371-7937 Fax (615)371-7939
Email: pdurso@tnbaptist.org
Website: www.baptisthistory.org

Baptist Peacemaker (Q) Baptist, Katie Cook, 4800 Wedgewood Dr., Charlotte, NC 28210 Tel. (704)521-6051 Fax (704)521-6053
Email: bpfna@bpfna.org
Website: www.bpfna.org

The Baptist Preacher (bi-M) Baptist Bible Fellowship International, Mike Randall, P.O. Box 309 HSJ, Springfield, MO 65801 Tel. (417)831-3996 Fax (417)831-1470
Email: editors@tribune.org
Website: www.tribune.org

The Baptist Preacher's Journal (Q) Baptist Bible Fellowship International, Keith Bassham, P.O. Box 309, Springfield, MO 65801 Tel. (417)831-3996 Fax (417)831-1470
Email: editor@tribune.org
Website: tribune.org

Baptist Witness (M) Primitive Baptists, Lasserre Bradley, Jr., P.O. Box 17037, Cincinnati, OH 45217 Tel. (513)821-7289 Fax (513)821-7303
Email: bbh45217@aol.com
Website: www.BaptistBibleHour.org

318

BGC World (8-Y) Baptist General Conference, Bob Putman, 2002 S. Arlington Heights Rd., Arlington Heights, IL 60005 Tel. (847)228-0200 Fax (847)228-5376 Email: bgcworld@bgcworld.org Website: www.bgcworld.org

The Bible Advocate (8-Y) The Church of God (Seventh Day), Denver, CO, Calvin Burrell, P.O. Box 33677, Denver, CO 80233 Tel. (303)452-7973 Fax (303)452-0657 Email: bibleadvocate@cog7.org Website: www.cog7.org/BA

The Brethren Evangelist (4-6-Y) The Brethren Church, 524 College Ave., Ashland, OH 44805 Tel. (419)289-1708 Fax (419)281-0450 Email: brethren@brethrenchurch.org Website: www.brethrenchurch.org

Brethren Journal (10-Y) Unity of the Brethren, Rev. Milton Maly, 6703 FM 2502, Brenham, TX 77833-9803 Tel. (409)830-8762 Website: www.unityofthebrethren.org

Brethren Life and Thought (Q) Church of the Brethren, Karen Garrett, Bethany Seminary, 615 National Road West, Richmond, IN 47374-4019 Tel. (765)983-1811 Fax (765)983-1840 Email: gardnca@bethanyseminary.edu Website: www.bethanyseminary.edu/?page=blt

The Bridegroom's Messenger (bi-M) The International Pentecostal Church of Christ, Janice Boyce, 121 W. Hunters Trail, Elizabeth City, NC 27909 Tel. (919)338-3003 Fax (919)338-3003

The Burning Bush (Q) The Metropolitan Church Association, Inc. (Wesleyan), Rev. Gary Bowell, The Metropolitan Church Assoc., 2425 West Ramsey Ave, Milwaukee, WI 53221-4907 Tel. (414)282-8539 Email: metrochurch assn@wi.rr.com Website: www.TheMCA.net

Call to Unity: Resourcing the Church for Ecumenical Ministry (bi-M) Christian Church (Disciples of Christ), Robert K. Welsh, P.O. Box 1986, Indianapolis, IN 46206-1986 Tel. (317)713-2586 Fax (317)713-2588 Email: rwelsh@ccu.disciples.org Website: www.disciples.org/ccu

Calvary Messenger (M) Beachy Amish Mennonite Churches, Paul L. Miller, 7809 Soul Herren Road, Partridge, KS 67566 Tel. (620)567-2286 Fax (620)567-2286 Email: paullmiller@btsskynet.com

Caring (Q) Assemblies of God, Owen Wilkie, Gospel Publishing House, 1445 N. Boonville Ave., Springfield, MO 65802 Tel. (417)862-2781 Fax (417)862-0503 Email: benevolences@ag.org Website: www.benevolences.ag.org

Cathedral Age (Q) Interdenominational, Craig W. Stapert, Washington National Cathedral, 3101 Wisconsin Ave., NW, Washington, DC 20016-5098 Tel. (202)537-5681 Fax (202)364-6600 Email: cathedral_age@cathedral.org Website: www.cathedralage.org

Catholic Chronicle (2nd & 4th Sundays) The Catholic Church, Angela Kessler, 1933 Spielbusch Avenue, Toledo, OH 43604-5360 Tel. (419)244-6711 ext. 138 Fax (419)244-0468 Email: ccnews@toledodiocese.org Website: www.catholicchronicle.org

Catholic Digest (M) The Catholic Church, Dan Connors, P.O. Box 6015, New London, CT 06320 Tel. (800)321-0411 Fax (860)536-5600 Email: dconnors@catholicdigest.com Website: www.CatholicDigest.org

Catholic Herald (Milwaukee) (W) The Catholic Church, Brian T. Olszewski, 3501 S. Lake Dr., St. Francis, WI 53235-0913 Tel. (414)769-3500 Fax (414)769-3468 Email: chnonline@archmil.org Website: www.chnonline.org

Catholic Light (17-Y) The Catholic Church, William R. Genello, 300 Wyoming Ave., Scranton, PA 18503 Tel. (570)207-2229 Fax (570)207-2271 Email: william-genello@dioceseofscranton.org Website: www.dioceseofscranton.org

The Catholic Peace Voice (bi-M) The Catholic Church, Dave Robinson, 532 W. 8th Street, Erie, PA 16502 Tel. (814)453-4955 Fax (814)452-4784 Email: info@paxchristiusa.org Website: www.paxchristiusa.org

The Catholic Review (W) The Catholic Church, Daniel L. Medinger - Associate Publisher, P.O. Box 777, Baltimore, MD 21203 Tel. (443)524-3150 Fax (443)524-3155 Email: mail@catholicreview.org Website: www.catholicreview.org

Catholic Standard and Times (W) The Catholic Church, Michelle Laque Johnson, 222 N. 17th St., Philadelphia, PA 19103 Tel. (215)587-3660 Fax (215)587-3979 Email: standard@adphila.org Website: www.cst-phl.com

The Catholic Worker (7-Y) The Catholic Church, Joanne Kennedy, Tanya Thevialt & Matt Vogel, Managing Editors, 36 E. First St., New York, NY 10003 Tel. (212)777-9617

Cela Biedrs (bi-M) The Latvian Evangelical Lutheran Church in America, Vieturs Bambans, 7630 S.W. 26th Ave., Portland, OR 97219 Tel. (503)781-6724 Email: celabiedrs@yahoo.com/ celabiedrs@lelba.org Website: www.lelba.org

Celebration: An Ecumenical Worship Resource (M) Interdenominational, Patrick Marrin, 115 East Armor Blvd., Kansas City, MO 64111 Tel. (816)531-0538 Fax (816)968-2291
Email: patmarrin@aol.com
Website: www.ncrpub.com

The Challenge (Q) The Bible Church of Christ, Inc., A.M. Jones, 1358 Morris Ave., Bronx, NY 10456 Tel. (718)588-2284 Fax (718)992-5597
Website: www.thebiblechurchofchrist.org

Charisma (M) Nondenominational, J. Lee Grady, 600 Rinehart Rd., Lake Mary, FL 32746 Tel. (407)333-0600 Fax (407)333-7133
Email: grady@strang.com
Website: www.charismamag.com

The Children's Friend (Braille) (Q) Seventh-day Adventist Church, Bert Williams, Christian Record Services for the Blind, P.O. Box 6097, Lincoln, NE 68506 Tel. (402)488-0981 Fax (402)488-7582
Email: editorial@christianrecord.org
Website: www.christianrecord.org

Christadelphian Advocate (M) Christadelphians, James I. Millay, 27 Delphian Road, Springfield, VT 05156-9335 Tel. (802)885.2316 Fax (802)885.2319
Email: jimillay@vermontel.net
Website: www.christadelphian-advocate.org

Christadelphian Tidings (M) Christadelphians, Donald H. Styles, 42076 Hartford Dr., Canton, MI 48187 Tel. (313)844-2426 Fax (313)844-8304

The Christian Baptist (Q) Primitive Baptists, Elder S. T. Tolley, P.O. Box 68, Atwood, TN 38220 Tel. (901)662-7417
Email: cbl@aeneas.net

Christian Bible Teacher (Q) Churches of Christ, Bob Connel, P.O. Box 7385, Ft. Worth, TX 76111 Tel. (817)838-2644 Fax (817)838-2644

The Christian Century (bi-W) Nondenominational, John Buchanan, 104 South Michigan Ave. Suite 700, Chicago, IL 60603 Tel. (312)263-7510 Fax (312)263-7540
Email: main@christiancentury.org
Website: www.christiancentury.org

The Christian Chronicle (M) Churches of Christ, Lynn McMillon, P.O. Box 11000, Oklahoma City, OK 73136-1100 Tel. (405)425-5070 Fax (405)425-5076
Website: www.christianchronicle.org

The Christian Community (8-Y) International Council of Community Churches, Rev. Michael E. Livingston, 21116 Washington Pkwy., Frankfort, IL 60423 Tel. (815)464-5690 Fax (815)464-5692

Email: ICCC60423@sbcglobal.net
Website: icccusa.com

The Christian Contender (M) Mennonite Church, James Boll, Box 3, Highway 172, Crockett, KY 41413 Tel. (606)522-4348 Fax (606)522-4896

The Christian Index (M) Christian Methodist Episcopal Church, Dr. Kenneth E. Jones, P.O. Box 431, Fairfield, AL 35064 Tel. (205)929-1410 Fax (205)744-0010
Email: goodoc@aol.com
Website: www.c-m-e.org

Christian Journal (Q) Churches of Christ, J.E. Snelson, P.O. Box 7385, Ft. Worth, TX 76111 Tel. (817)838-2644

Christian Leader (M) U.S. Conference of Mennonite Brethren Churches, Connie Faber, P.O. Box 220, Hillsboro, KS 67063 Tel. (316)947-5543 Fax (316)947-3266
Email: chleader@southwind.net

Christian Monthly (M) Apostolic Lutheran Church of America, Linda Mattson, P.O. Box 220, Yamhill, OR 97148 Tel. (360)687-6493 Fax (503)662-5909
Email: christianm@apostolic-lutheran.org
Website: www.Apostolic-Lutheran.org

Christian Record (Braille) (Q) Seventh-day Adventist Church, Bert Williams, Christian Record Services for the Blind, P.O. Box 6097, Lincoln, NE 68506 Tel. (402)488-0981 Fax (402)488-7582
Email: editorial@christianrecord.org
Website: www.christianrecord.org

Christian Record Talking Magazine (Audio) (Q) Seventh-day Adventist Church, Bert Williams, Christian Record Services for the Blind, P. O. Box 6097, Lincoln, NE 68506 Tel. 402-488-0981
Email: editorial@christianrecord.org
Website: http://www.christianrecord.org

The Christian Science Journal (M) Church of Christ, Scientist, Mary M. Trammell, Editor in Chief; William G. Dawley, Editor, One Norway St., Boston, MA 02115-3195 Tel. (617)450-2000 Fax (617)450-2930
Email: trammellm@csps.com OR dawleyw@csps.com
Website: www.csjournal.com

The Christian Science Monitor (D & W) Church of Christ, Scientist, David T. Cook, One Norway St., Boston, MA 02115 Tel. (617)450-2000 Fax (617)450-7575
Website: www.csmonitor.com

Christian Science Quarterly Bible Lessons (M & Q) First Church of Christ, Scientist, Joan Mashman, Operations Manager, 210 Massachusetts Ave, P.O. Box 20, Boston, MA 02115 Tel. (617)450-2651 Fax (617)450-2203 Email: service@csps.com Website: www.BibleLesson.com

Christian Science Sentinel (W) Church of Christ, Scientist, Mary M. Trammell, Editor in Chief; William G. Dawley, Editor, One Norway St., Boston, MA 02115-3195 Tel. (617)450-2000 Fax (617)450-2930 Email: sentinel@csps.com/ trammellm@csps.com (the Editor) Website: www.cssentinel.com

Christian Standard (W) Christian Churches and Churches of Christ, Mark A. Taylor, 8121 Hamilton Ave., Cincinnati, OH 45231 Tel. (513)931-4050 Fax (513)931-0950 Email: christianstd@standardpub.com Website: www.christianstandard.com

The Christian Union Witness (M, except Jy-Ag) Christian Union, Joseph Cunningham, P.O. Box 361, Greenfield, OH 45123 Tel. (937)981-2760 Fax (937)981-2760 Email: ohiocu@bright.net Website: christianunionbright.net

Christian Woman (bi-M) Churches of Christ, Sandra Humphrey, Box 150, Nashville, TN 37202 Tel. (615)254-8781 Fax (615)254-7411

The Church Advocate (Q) Churches of God, General Conference, Rachel L. Foreman, P.O. Box 926, 700 E. Melrose Ave., Findlay, OH 45839 Tel. (419)424-1961 Fax (419) 424-3433 Email: communications@cggc.org Website: www.cggc.org

Church of God Evangel (M) Church of God (Cleveland, Tenn.), James E. Cossey, P.O. Box 2250, Cleveland, TN 37320 Tel. (423)478-7592 Fax (423)478-7616 Email: editor@pathwaypress.org Website: www.pathwaypress.org

The Church Herald (11-Y) Reformed Church in America, Christina Van Eyl, 4500 60th St. SE, Grand Rapids, MI 49512 Tel. (616)698-7071 Email: herald@rca.org Website: herald.rca.org

Church History: Studies in Christianity and Culture (Q) Scholarly, John Corrigan, Amanda Porterfield, Florida State Univesity, Dept of Religion, M05 Dodd Hall, Tallahassee, FL 32306-1520 Tel. (850)644-9038 Fax (850)644-7225 Email: church-history@admin.fsu.edu Website: www.churchhistory.org/church history.html

The Church Messenger (bi-W) The American Carpatho-Russian Orthodox Greek Catholic Church, V. Rev. Michael Rosco, 145 Broad St., Perth Amboy, NJ 08861 Tel. (732)826-4442

Email: mrosco2@excite.com Website: www.acrod.org/news/messenger1.html

Church School Herald (Q) African Methodist Episcopal Zion Church, Ms. Mary A. Love, P.O. Box 26769, Charlotte, NC 28221-6769 Tel. (704)599-4630 ext. 324 Fax (704)688-2548 Email: MaLove@amezhqtr.org

Church & Society Magazine (bi-M) Presbyterian Church (U.S.A.), Rev. Dr. Bobbi Wells Hargleroad, 100 Witherspoon St., Louisville, KY 40202-1396 Tel. (502)569-5810 Fax (502)569-8116 Email: c-s@ctr.pcusa.org Website: www.pcusa.org/churchsociety

Churchwoman (Q) Interdenominational, Annie Llamoso-Songco, 475 Riverside Dr., Suite 500, New York, NY 10115 Tel. (212)870-3339 Fax (212)870-2338 Email: allamoso@churchwomen.org Website: www.churchwomen.org

Circuit Rider (bi-M) The United Methodist Church, Jill S. Reddig, 201 Eighth Ave. S, Nashville, TN 37203 Tel. (615)749-6538 Fax (615)749-6061 Email: jreddig@umpublishing.org Website: www.circuitrider.com

Clarion Herald (W/45-Y) The Catholic Church, Peter P. Finney, Jr., P.O. Box 53247, 1000 Howard Ave. Suite 400, New Orleans, LA 70153 Tel. (504)596-3035 Fax (504)596-3020 Email: clarionherald@clarionherald.org Website: www.clarionherald.org

Clergy Comminique (2-Y) International Council of Community Churches, Virginia Leopold, 21116 Washington Pky., Frankfort, IL 60423-3112 Tel. (815)464-5690 Fax (815)464-5692 Email: iccc60423@aol.com Website: icccusa.com

The Clergy Journal (9-Y) Nondenominational, Sharon L. Firle, Managing Editor & Clyde J. Steckel, Executive Editor, 6160 Carmen Avenue E, Inver Grove Heights, MN 55076-4422 Tel. (800)328-0200 Fax (651)457-4617 Email: editor@logostaff.com Website: www.logosproductions.com

Club Connection (Q) Assemblies of God, Debby Seler, 1445 Boonville Ave., Springfield, MO 65802-1894 Tel. (417)862-2781 Fax (417)862-0503 Email: clubconnection@ag.org Website: www.missionettes.ag.org

CoLaborer (bi-M) National Association of Free Will Baptists, Sarah Fletcher, Women Nationally Active for Christ, P.O. Box 5002, Antioch, TN 37011-5002 Tel. (615)731-6812 Fax (615)731-0771 Email: wnac@nafwb.org

College and University Dialogue (3-Y) Seventh-day Adventist Church, John M. Fowler, 12501 Old Columbia Pike, Silver Spring, MD 20904-6600 Tel. Fax (301)622-9627 Website: dialogue.adventist.org

Collegiate Quarterly (Q) Seventh-day Adventist Church, Lyndelle Brower Chiomenti, 12501 Old Columbia Pike, Silver Spring, MD 20904 Tel. (301)680-6160 Fax (301)680-6155

Columbia (M) The Catholic Church, Tim S. Hickey, One Columbus Plaza, New Haven, CT 06510 Tel. (203)752-4398 Fax (203)752-4109 Email: info@kofc.org Website: www.kofc.org

The Commission (2-Y) International Mission Board, Southern Baptist Convention, Michael Chute, Box 6767, Richmond, VA 23230-6767 Tel. (804)219-1373 Fax (804)219-1410 Email: commission@imb.org Website: www.tconline.org

Common Lot (Q) United Church of Christ, Martha J. Hunter, 700 Prospect Ave., Cleveland, OH 44115 Tel. (216)736-2150 Fax (216)736-2156

Commonweal (bi-W) The Catholic Church, Paul Baumann, 475 Riverside Drive, Rm 405, New York, NY 10115 Tel. (212)662-4200 Fax (212)662-4183 Email: editors@commonwealmagazine.org Website: www.commonwealmagazine.org

Communion (bi-M) Church of God (Anderson, Indiana), Arthur Kelly, P.O. Box 2420, 1201 E. 5th Street, Anderson, IN 46018-2420 Tel. (765)642-0256 Fax (765)652-5652 Email: AKelly@chog.org Website: chog.org/news/communion.asp

The Congregationalist (5-Y) National Association Congregational Christian Churches, Rev. James E. Eaton, 87 Broadway, Norwich, CT 06360 Tel. (860)889-1363 Fax (860)887-5715 Email: jeaton@unitedcongregational.org Website: www.congregationalist.org

Connections (M) Alliance of Baptists, Sue Harper Poss, 1328 16th St. N.W., Washington, DC 20036 Tel. (202)745-7609 Fax (202)745-0023 Email: editor@allianceofbaptists.org Website: www.allianceofbaptists.org

Conqueror (bi-M) United Pentecostal Church International, Shay Mann, 8855 Dunn Rd., Hazelwood, MO 63042 Tel. (314)837-7300 Fax (314)837-4503 Email: smann@upci.org Website: www.pentecostalyouth.org

Context (M) Nondenominational, Martin Marty, 205 W. Monroe St., Chicago, IL 60606-5013 Tel. (312)236-7782 Fax (312)236-8207

Email: editors@uscatholic.org Website: www.contextonline.org

Covenant (Q) Presbyterian Church in America, Jackie Fogas, Covenant Theological Seminary, 12330 Conway Road, St. Louis, MO 63141 Tel. (314)434-4044 Fax (314)434-4819 Email: covenantmagazine@covenant seminary.edu Website: www.convenantseminary.edu

Cook Partners (bi-M) Nondenominational online magazine on Christian publishing worldwide, Kim A. Pettit, 4050 Lee Vance View Drive, Colorado Springs, CO 80918 Tel. (719)536-0100 Fax (719)536-3266 Email: kim.pettit@cookinternational.org Website: www.cookinterntional.org/ www.cook-partners.org

Cornerstone Connections (Q) Seventh-day Adventist Church, Gary B. Swanson, 12501 Old Columbia Pike, Silver Spring, MD 20904 Tel. (301)680-6160 Fax (301)680-6155

The Covenant Companion (M) Evangelical Covenant Church, Donald L. Meyer, Editor; Jane K. Swanson-Nystrom, Managing Editor, 5101 N. Francisco Ave., Chicago, IL 60625 Tel. (773)906-3328 Fax (773)784-4366 Email: communication@covchurch.org Website: www.covchurch.org/cov/companion

Covenant Home Altar (Q) Evangelical Covenant Church, Jane K. Swanson-Nystrom, 5101 N. Francisco Ave., Chicago, IL 60625 Tel. (773)784-3000 Fax (773)784-4366 Email: communication@covchurch.org Website: www.covchurch.org

Covenant Quarterly (Q) Evangelical Covenant Church, Paul E. Koptak, 3225 W. Foster Ave., Chicago, IL 60625-4895 Tel. (773)244-6242 Email: info@covenantbookstore.com

The Covenanter Witness (11-Y) Reformed Presbyterian Church of North America, Drew Gordon and Lynne Gordon, 7408 Penn Ave., Pittsburgh, PA 15208 Tel. (412)241-0436 Fax (412)731-8861 Email: info@psalms4u.com Website: www.psalms4u.com

Credinta—The Faith (Q) The Romanian Orthodox Church in America, V. Rev. Archim. Dr. Vasile Vasilac, 45-03 48th Ave., Woodside, Queens, NY 11377 Tel. (313)893-8390

The Cumberland Presbyterian (11-Y) Cumberland Presbyterian Church, Patricia P. White, Cumberland Presbyterian Church, 1978 Union Ave., Memphis, TN 38104 Tel. (615)731-5556 Email: cpmag@comcast.net Website: www.cumberland.org/cpmag/

Currents in Theology and Mission (bi-M) Evangelical Lutheran Church in America, Ralph W. Klein, 1100 E. 55th St., Chicago, IL 60615 Tel. (773)256-0751 Fax (773)256-0782 Email: currents@lstc.edu Website: www.lstc.edu/pub_peo/pub/currents.html

Cutting Edge (Q) Association of Vineyard Churches, Jeff Bailey, 2495 Howard St., Evanston, IL 60202 Tel. (847)328-4544 Fax (847)328-5153 Email: cuttingedge@vineyardusa.org Website: www.vineyardusa.org/publications/newsletters/cutting_edge

Decision (11-Y) Nondenominational, Bob Paulson, 1 Billy Graham Parkway, Charlotte, NC 28201-0001 Tel. (704)401-2432 Fax (704)401-3009 Email: decision@bgea.org Website: www.decisionmag.org

DisciplesWorld (10-Y) Christian Church (Disciples of Christ) in the United States and Canada, Verity A. Jones, 6325 N. Guilford Ave Suite 213, Indianapolis, IN 46220 Tel. (317)375-8846 Fax (317)375-8849 Email: info@disciplesworld.com Website: www.disciplesworld.com

EcuLink (Occasional) Interdenominational, Philip E. Jenks, 475 Riverside Drive, 8th Floor, New York, NY 10115-0050 Tel. (212)870-2227 Fax (212)870-2030 Email: pjenks@councilofchurches.org Website: www.councilofchurches.org

Ecumenical Trends (M) The Catholic Church, Rev. James Loughran, SA, Graymoor Ecumenical & Interreligious Institute, PO Box 300, Garrison, NY 10524-0300 Tel. (845)424-3671 ext. 3303 Fax (845)424-2163 Email: jlgeii@aol.com Website: www.geii.org

Eleventh Hour Messenger (bi-M) Wesleyan Holiness Association of Churches, John Brewer, 11411 N US Hwy 27, Fountain City, IN 47341-9757 Tel. (317)584-3199

Encounter (Audio) (Q) Seventh-day Adventist Church, Bert Williams, Christian Record Services for the Blind, P. O. Box 6097, Lincoln, NE 68506 Tel. 402-488-0981 Fax (402)488-7582 Email: editorial@christianrecord.org Website: www.christianrecord.org

Enrichment: A Journal for Pentecostal Ministry (Q) Assemblies of God, Gary Allen; Rick Knoth, Managing Editor, 1445 N. Boonville Ave., Springfield, MO 65802 Tel. (417)862-2781 Fax (417)862-0416 Email: rKnoth@ag.org Website: www.enrichmentjournal.ag.org

The Ensign (M) The Church of Jesus Christ of Latter-day Saints, Don L. Searle, Managing Editor, 50 E North Temple Street, Room 2420, Salt Lake City, UT 84150 Tel. (801)240-2950 Fax (801)240-2270 Email: ensign@ldschurch.org Website: www.magazines.lds.org

Episcopal Life (M) The Episcopal Church, Jerrold Hames, 815 Second Ave., New York, NY 10017-4503 Tel. (800)334-7626 Fax (212)949-8059 Email: jhames@episcopalchurch.org Website: www.episcopal-life.org

Equip (bi-M) Presbyterian Church in America, Dr. Charles Dunahoo, 1700 N. Brown Road Ste. 102, Lawrenceville, GA 30043 Tel. (678)825-1100 Fax (678)825.1101 Email: cep@pcanet.org Website: pcanet.org

The Evangel (bi-M) American Association of Lutheran Churches, The, Rev. Charles D. Eidum, 801 W. 106th St, Suite 203, Minneapolis, MN 55420-5603 Tel. (952)884-7784 Fax (952)884-7894 Email: aa2taalc@aol.com Website: www.taalc.com

The Evangel (Q) The Evangelical Church Alliance, Dr. Henry A. (Hank) Roso, 205 W. Broadway, P. O. Box 9, Bradley, IL 60915 Tel. (815)937-0720 Fax (815)937-0001 Email: info@ecainternatinal.org Website: www.ecainternational.org

The Evangelical Advocate (bi-M) Churches of Christ in Christian Union, Ralph Hux, P.O. Box 30, Circleville, OH 43113 Tel. (740)474-8856 Fax (740)477-7766 Email: doc@cccuhg.org Website: www.cccuhq.org

Evangelical Beacon (bi-M) The Evangelical Free Church of America, Ms. Carol Madison, 901 East 78th St., Minneapolis, MN 55420-1300 Tel. (877)293-5653 Fax (952)853-8488 Email: beacon@efca.org Website: www.efca.org

Evangelical Challenge (Q) The Evangelical Church, Shirley Roehl, 9421 West River Road, Minneapolis, MN 55444 Tel. (763)424-2589 Fax (763)424-9230 Email: ecdenom@usfamily.net Website: www.theevangelicalchurch.org

The Evangelist (W) The Roman Catholic Church, James Breig, 40 N. Main Ave., Albany, NY 12203 Tel. (518)453-6688 Fax (518)453-8448 Email: james.breig@rcda.org Website: www.evangelist.org

Explorations (Q) Nondenominational, Irvin J. Borowsky, 321 Chestnut Street, 4th Floor, Philadelphia, PA 19106-2779 Tel. (215)925-2800 Fax (215)925-3800 Email: aii@interfaith-scholars.org

Extension (M) The Catholic Church, Bradley Collins, Editor, 150 S. Wacker Drive, 20th Floor, Chicago, IL 60606 Tel. (312)236-7240 Fax (312)236-5276
Email: magazine@catholic-extension.org
Website: www.catholic-extension.org

Faith & Fellowship (M) Church of the Lutheran Brethren of America, Bruce Stumbo, P.O. Box 655, Fergus Falls, MN 56538 Tel. (218)736-7357 Fax (218)736-2200
Email: ffpress@clba.org
Website: www.faithandfellowship.org

Faith in Action (I) The United Methodist Church, vacant, 100 Maryland Ave. NE, Washington, DC 20002 Tel. (202)488-5621 Fax (202)488-1617
Website: www.umc-gbcs.org/site/c.frLJK2PKL qF/b.2798475/k.7A8F/ Faith_in_Action.htm

Faith-Life (bi-M) Lutheran, Pastor Marcus Albrecht, 2107 N. Alexander St., Appleton, WI 54911 Tel. (920)733-1839 Fax (920)733-4834
Email: malbrecht@milwpc.com

FEConnections (Q) Fellowship of Evangelical Churches, Ron Habegger, 1420 Kerrway Ct., Fort Wayne, IN 46805 Tel. (260)423-3649 Fax (260)420-1905
Email: FECministries@aol.com
Website: www.fecministries.org

Fellowship (bi-M) Interfaith, Ethan Vesely-Flad, Box 271, Nyack, NY 10960-0271 Tel. (845)358-4601 Fax (845)358-4924
Email: fellowship@forusa.org
Website: www.forusa.org

Fellowship Focus (bi-M) Fellowship of Evangelical Bible Churches, Sharon K. Berg, 3339 N 109th Plz, Omaha, NE 68164-2908 Tel. (402)965-3860 Fax (402)965-3871
Email: fellowshipfocus@febcministries.org
Website: www.febcministries.org

Fellowship News (M) Bible Fellowship Church, Carol Snyder, 3000 Fellowship Drive, Whitehall, PA 18052-3343 Tel. (877) 795-1212 Fax (215)536-2120
Email: ccsnyder@supernet.com
Website: www.bfc.org

Fellowship Tidings (Q) Full Gospel Fellowship of Churches and Ministers International, Cynthia Mattox, 1000 N. Beltline Road, Irving, TX 75061 Tel. (214)492-1254 Fax (214)492-1736
Email: FGFCMI@aol.com
Website: www.fgfcmi.org

FGConnections (2-Y) Friends General Conference, Lucy Duncan, Deborah Fisch, 1216 Arch Street 2B, Philadelphia, PA 19107 Tel. (215)561-1700 Fax (215)561-0759
Email: connections@fgcquaker.org
Website: www.fgcquaker.org/fgconnections

Firm Foundation (M) Churches of Christ, H. A. Dobbs, P.O. Box 690192, Houston, TX 77269-0192 Tel. (713)469-3102 Fax (713)469-7115
Email: had@worldnet.att.net

First Things: A Monthly Journal of Religion & Public Life (10-Y) Interdenominational, Richard J. Neuhaus, 156 Fifth Ave., Ste. 400, New York, NY 10010 Tel. (212)627-1985 Fax (212)627-2184
Email: ft@firstthings.com
Website: www.firstthings.com

The Flaming Sword (M) Bible Holiness Church, Susan Davolt, 10th St. & College Ave., Independence, KS 67301 Tel. (316)331-2580 Fax (316)331-2580

For God and Country (Q) Seventh-Day Adventist Church, Deena Bartel-Wagner - Editor; Gary R. Councell - Executive Editor, Adventist Chaplaincy Ministries. General Conference of Seventh-day Adventists, 12501 Old Columbia Pike, Silver Spring, MD 20904-6600

Foresee (bi-M) Conservative Congregational Christian Conference, Richard & Shirley Leonard, 8941 Highway 5, Lake Elmo, Lake Elmo, MN 55042 Tel. (651)739-1474 Fax (651)739-0750
Email: dmjohnson@ccccusa.com
Website: www.ccccusa.com

Forum Letter (M) Independent, Intra-Lutheran (companion publication to the quarterly, Lutheran Forum), Pastor Richard O. Johnson, Peace Lutheran Church, P. O. Box 1394, Grass Valley, CA 95945 Tel. (530)273-9631 Fax (530)274-2772
Email: roj@nccn.net
Website: www.alpb.org

Forward (Q) United Pentecostal Church International, Rev. J. L. Hall, 8855 Dunn Rd., Hazelwood, MO 63042 Tel. (314)837-7300 Fax (314)837-4503
Email: info@upci.org
Website: www.upci.org

Forward in Christ (M) Wisconsin Evangelical Lutheran Synod, Rev. John A. Braun, 2929 N. Mayfair Rd., Milwaukee, WI 53222 Tel. (414)256-3210 Fax (414)256-3862
Email: fic@sab.wels.net
Website: www.wels.net

Foursquare World Advance (Q w/a bonus issue) International Church of the Foursquare Gospel, Dr. Ron Williams, P.O. Box 26902, 1910 W. Sunset Blvd., Ste 400, Los Angeles, CA 90026-0176 Tel. (213)989-4230 Fax (213)989-4544
Email: comm@foursquare.org
Website: www.advancemagazine.org

Free Will Baptist Gem (M) National Association of Free Will Baptists, Gary Fry, P.O. Box 991/ 100 E. Commercial Street, Lebanon, MO 65530 Tel. (417)532-9131 Fax (417)588-7911 Email: gwfry@webound.com

Friend Magazine (M) The Church of Jesus Christ of Latter-day Saints, Vivian Paulsen, 50 E South Temple Street, 24th Fl, Salt Lake City, UT 84150 Tel. (801)240-2210 Fax (801)240-2270

Friends Bulletin (10-Y) Religious Society of Friends, Anthony Manousos, 3223 Danaha St., Torrance, CA 90505 Tel. (310)-325-3581 Email: friendsbul@aol.com Website: www.westernquaker.net

Friends Journal (M) Religious Society of Friends, Susan Corson-Finnerty, Publisher & Exec. Editor, 1216 Arch St., 2A, Philadelphia, PA 19107-2835 Tel. (215)563-8629 Fax (215)568-1377 Email: info@friendsjournal.org Website: www.friendsjournal.org

The Friends Voice (3-Y) Evangelical Friends International—North America Region, Dr. Becky Towne, Sr. Editor, Dr. Kathy Roblyer, Assoc. Editor, 2748 E. Pikes Peak Ave, Colorado Springs, CO 80909 Tel. (719)632-5721 (800)351-2973 Email: thevoice@evangelicalfriends.org Website: evangelicalfriends.org

Front Line (3-Y) Conservative Baptist Association of America, Al Russell, P.O. Box 58, Long Prairie, MN 56347 Tel. (320)732-8072 Fax (509)356-7112 Email: chaplruss@earthlink.net Website: www.cbchaplains.net

Full Gospel Ministries Outreach Report (Q) Full Gospel Assemblies International, Simeon Strauser, P.O. Box 1230, Coatsville, PA 19320 Tel. (610)857-2357 Fax (610)857-3109

The Gem (W) Churches of God, General Conference, Rachel Foreman, P.O. Box 926, Findlay, OH 45839 Tel. (419)424-1961 Fax (419)424-3433 Email: communications@cggc.org Website: www.cggc.org

God's Field (bi-W, except Dec.) Polish National Catholic Church of America and Canada, Rev. Anthony Mikovsky (English) and Rt. Rev. Casimir Grotnik (Polish), 1006 Pittston Ave., Scranton, PA 18505-4109 Tel. (570)346-9131 Fax (570)346-2188 Email: GodsField@adelphia.net Website: www.pncc.org

Good News - Buna Vestire (Q) The Romanian Orthodox Episcopate of America, The Romanian Orthodox Deanery of Canada, 11400 88St. SE, Regina, SK S4V 0W7 Tel. (403)203-7033 Fax (306)525-9650

Email: fatherlupu@shaw.ca Website: www.romanianorthodoxdeanery.org

Gospel Advocate (M) Churches of Christ, Neil W. Anderson, 1006 Elm Hill Pike, Nashville, TN 37202 Tel. (615)254-8781 Fax (615)254-7411 Email: info@gospeladvocate.com Website: www.gospeladvocate.com

The Gospel Herald (M) Church of God, Mountain Assembly, Inc., Scott Isham, P.O. Box 157, Jellico, TN 37762 Tel. (423)784-8260 Fax (423)784-3258 Email: cgmahdq@jellico.com Website: www.cgmahdq.org

The Gospel Light (2-Y) The Bible Church of Christ, Inc., Carole Crenshaw, 1358 Morris Ave., Bronx, NY 10456 Tel. (718)588-2284 Fax (718)992-5597 Website: www.thebiblechurchofchrist.org

The Gospel Messenger (M) Congregational Holiness Church, Inc., Rev. Danny K. Jones, Congregational Holiness Church, 3888 Fayetteville Highway, Griffin, GA 30223 Tel. (770-228-4833 Fax (770-228-1177 Email: messenger@CHChurch.com Website: www.CHChurch.com

The Gospel Truth (bi-Y) Church of the Living God, C.W.F.F., Robert D. Tyler, 430 Forest Avenue, Cincinnati, OH 45229 Tel. (513)569-5660 Fax (513)569-5661 Email: national@ctlycwff.org Website: www.ctlgcwff.org

Grow Magazine (Q) Church of the Nazarene, Jim Dorsey, 6401 The Paseo, Kansas City, MO 64131 Tel. (816)333-7000 ext. 2828 Fax (816)523-1872 Email: jdorsey@nazarene.org Website: www.growmagazine.org

Guide (W) Seventh-day Adventist Church, Randy Fishell, 55 W. Oak Ridge Dr., Hagerstown, MD 21740 Tel. (301)393-4037 Fax (301)393-4055 Email: guide@rhpa.org Website: www.guidemagazine.org

The Handmaiden (Q) The Antiochian Orthodox Christian Archdiocese of North America, Virginia Nieuwsma, P.O. Box 76, Ben Lomond, CA 95005-0076 Tel. (831)336-5118 Fax (831)336-8882 Email: czell@conciliarpress.com Website: www.conciliarpress.com

The Happy Harvester (M) Church of God of Prophecy, Diane Pace, P.O. Box 2910, Cleveland, TN 37320-2910 Tel. (423)559-5435 Fax (423)559-5444 Email: JoDiPace@wingnet.net

Herald (M) Community of Christ, Editorial Board, 1001 W. Walnut, Independence, MO 64050 Tel. (816)833-1000 Fax (816)521-3043 Email: Herald@cofochrist.org Website: www.heraldhouse.org or www.cofchrist.org

The Herald of Christian Science (M. & Q) Church of Christ, Scientist, Mary M. Trammell, Editor-in-Chief, The Christian Science Publishing Society, One Norway St., Boston, MA 02115-3195 Tel. (617)450-2000 Fax (617)450-2930 Email: trammellm@csps.com or herald@csps.com Website: www.csherald.com

Heritage (Y) Assemblies of God, Darrin Rodgers, 1445 Boonville Ave., Springfield, MO 65802 Tel. (417)862-1447 Ext. 4400 Fax (417)862-6203 Email: drodgers@ag.org Website: www.agheritage.org

High Adventure (Q) Assemblies of God, John M. Hicks, Gospel Publishing House, 1445 N. Boonville Ave., Springfield, MO 65802-1894 Tel. (417)862-2781 Fax (417)831-8230 Email: rangers@ag.org Website: www.royalrangers.ag.org

Higher Way (Q) Apostolic Faith Mission of Portland, Oregon, Darrel D. Lee, 6615 S.E. 52nd Ave., Portland, OR 97206 Tel. (503)777-1741 Fax (503)777-1743 Email: kbarrett@apostolicfaith.org Website: www.apostolicfaith.org

Holiness Today (bi-M) Church of the Nazarene, David J. Felter, 6401 The Paseo, Kansas City, MO 64131 Tel. (816)333-7000 Fax (816) 333-1748 Email: HolinessToday@nazarene.org Website: www.holinesstoday.com

Homiletic and Pastoral Review (M) The Roman Catholic Church, Kenneth Baker, 50 S Franklin Tpk, P. O. Box 297, Ramsey, NJ 07446 Tel. (201)236-9336

Horizons (M) Christian Churches and Churches of Christ, Leah Ellison Bradley, Susan Jackson Dowd, 100 Witherspoon St, Louisville, KY 40202-1396 Tel. (505)569-5368 Fax (502) 569-8085 Email: msa@missionservices.org Website: www.missionservices.org

Horizons (7-Y) Presbyterian Church (U.S.A.), Leah Ellison Bradley, Susan Jackson Dowd, Presbyterian Women, 100 Witherspoon St., Louisville, KY 40202-1396 Tel. (502)569-5368 Fax (502)569-8085 Email: lbradley@ctr.pcusa.org Website: www.pcusa.org/horizons

Ignite Your Faith (9-Y) Nondenominational, Christopher Lutes, 465 Gunderson Dr., Carol Stream, IL 60188 Tel. (630)260-6200 Fax (630)480-2004 Email: iyf@igniteyourfaith.com Website: www.igniteyourfaith.com

The Inclusive Pulpit (Y) International Council of Community Churches, Larry and Carolyn Dipboye, 21116 Washington Pky., Frankfort, IL 60423-3112 Tel. (815)464-5690 Fax (815)464-5692 Email: iccc60423@aol.com Website: icccusa.com

Insight Into (bi-M) Netherlands Reformed Congregations, Mr. Schipper, 4732 E. C Avenue, Kalamazoo, MI 49004 Tel. (269)349-9448

International Bulletin of Missionary Research (Q) Nondenominational, Jonathan J. Bonk, Overseas Ministries Study Center, 490 Prospect St., New Haven, CT 06511-2196 Tel. (203)624-6672 Fax (203)865-2857 Email: ibmr@OMSC.org Website: www.OMSC.org; www.DACB.org

Interpretation: A Journal of Bible and Theology (Q) Ecumenical, Co - Editors, James Brashler and Sam Balentine, 3401 Brook Rd., Richmond, VA 23227 Tel. (804)278-4296 Fax (804)278-4208 Email: email@interpretation.org Website: www.interpretation.org

el Intérprete (bi-M) The United Methodist Church, Amanda M. Bachus, Director/Editor, Spanish Resources, United Methodist Communications, P.O. Box 320, Nashville, TN 37202-0320 Tel. (615)742-5113 Fax (615) 742-5460 Email: abachus@umcom.org Website: www.interpretermagazine.org; www.noticias.umc.org

Interpreter (6-Y) The United Methodist Church, Kathy Noble, United Methodist Communications, P.O. Box 320, Nashville, TN 37202-0320 Tel. (615)742-5441 Fax (615)742-5469 Email: knoble@umcom.org Website: www.interpretermagazine.org

IPHC Experience (bi-M) International Pentecostal Holiness Church, Shirley Spencer, P.O. Box 12609, Oklahoma City, OK 73157 Tel. (405)787-7110 Fax (405)789-3957 Website: www.iphc.org/wms

John Three Sixteen (Q) Bible Holiness Church, Mary Cunningham, 10th St. & College Ave., Independence, KS 67301 Tel. (316)331-2580 Fax (316)331-2580

Journal of Adventist Education (5-Y) Seventh-day Adventist Church, Beverly J. Robinson-

Rumble, 12501 Old Columbia Pike, Silver Spring, MD 20904-6600 Tel. (301)680-5075 / (301)680-5069 Fax (301)622-9627 Email: rumbleb@gc.adventist.org goffc@gc.adventist.org Website: education.gc.adventist.org/jae

Journal of the American Academy of Religion (Q) Nondenominational, Charles T. Mathewes, Department of Religous Studies, University of Virginia, P. O. Box 400126, Charlottesville, VA 22904-4126 Email: jaar@virginia.edu Website: www.aarweb.org

Journal of Christian Education (Q) African Methodist Episcopal Church, Kenneth H. Hill, 500 Eighth Ave., S., Nashville, TN 37203 Tel. (615)242-1420 Fax (615)726-1866 Email: cedoffice@ameced.com Website: www.ameced.com

Journal of Ecumenical Studies (Q) Interdenominational/Interfaith, Leonard Swidler, Temple Univ. (022-38), 1114 West Berks St.- Anderson #511, Philadelphia, PA 19122-6090 Tel. (215)204-7714 Fax (215)204-4569 Email: nkrody@temple.edu Website: ecumene.org/jes

The Journal of Pastoral Care & Counseling (Q) Nondenominational, Orlo Strunk, Jr., 1068 Harbor Dr., SW, Calabash, NC 28467 Tel. (910)579-5084 Fax (910)579-5084 Email: jpcp@jpcp.org Website: www.jpcp.org

Journal of Presbyterian History (bi-Y) Presbyterian Church (U.S.A.), James H. Moorhead; Frederick J. Heuser, Jr., 425 Lombard St., Philadelphia, PA 19147 Tel. (215)627-1852 Fax (215)627-0509 Email: jph@history.pcusa.org Website: www.history.pcusa.org

Journal From the Radical Reformation (bi-Y) Church of God General Conference (Morrow, GA), Kent Ross and Anthony Buzzard, Sr. Editors, Box 100,000, Morrow, GA 30260-7000 Tel. (404)362-0052 Fax (404) 362-9307 Email: info@abc-coggc.org Website: www.abc-coggc.org

Journal of Theology (Q) Church of the Lutheran Confession, Prof. Steve Sippert, Immanuel Lutheran College, 501 Grover Rd., Eau Claire, WI 54701-7199 Tel. (715)832-9936 Fax (715)836-6634 Email: ilcgreekprof@yahoo.com Website: www.clcpub/clc/clc.html

The Joyful Noiseletter (10-Y) Interdenominational, Cal Samra, P.O. Box 895, Portage, MI 49081-0895 Tel. (616)324-0990 Fax (616) 324-3984 Email: joyfulnz@aol.com Website: www.joyfulnoiseletter.com

Judaism (Q) Jewish (American Jewish Conference), Rabbi Shammai Engelmayer, 15 E. 84th St., New York, NY 10028 Tel. (212)879-4500 Fax (212)249-3672 Email: judaism@ajcongress.org Website: humwww.ucsc.edu/judaism/ judaism.html

Key Lay Notes (2-Y) International Council of Community Churches, Phil Smith, 21116 Washington Pky., Frankfort, IL 60423-3112 Tel. (815)464-5690 Fax (815)464-5692 Email: iccc60423@aol.com Website: icccusa.com

The Lantern (bi-M) National Baptist Convention of America, Inc., Robert Jeffrey, 1320 Pierre Avenue, Shreveport, LA 71103 Tel. (318)221-3701 Fax (318)222-7512

Leadership: A Practical Journal for Church Leaders (Q) Nondenominational, Marshall Shelley, 465 Gundersen Dr., Carol Stream, IL 60188 Tel. (630)260-6200 Fax (630)260-0114 Email: LJeditor@leadershipjournal.net Website: www.Leadershipjournal.net

Learning and Living (Q) Netherlands Reformed Congregations, David Engelsma, 1000 Ball, Northeast, Grandrapids, MI 49505 Tel. (616) 458-4367 Fax (616)458-8532 Email: engelsma@plymouthchristian.put. k12.mi.us

Liberty (bi-M) Seventh-day Adventist Church, Clifford R. Goldstein, 12501 Old Columbia Pike, Silver Spring, MD 20904 Tel. (301)680-6691 Fax (301)680-6695

Lifeglow, Large Print (6-Y) Seventh-day Adventist Church, Bert Williams, Christian Record Services for the Blind, P.O. Box 6097, Lincoln, NE 68506 Tel. (402)488-0981 Fax (402)488-7582 Email: editorial@christianrecord.org Website: www.christianrecord.org

Light and Life Magazine (bi-M) Free Methodist Church, Douglas M. Newton, P.O. Box 535002, Indianapolis, IN 46253-5002 Tel. (317)244-3660 Email: llmeditor@fmcna.org Website: www.freemethodistchurch.org

Liguorian (10-Y) The Catholic Church, William J. Parker, C.SS.R., 1 Liguori Dr., Liguori, MO 63057 Tel. (636)464-2500 Fax (636)464-8449 Email: liguorianeditor@liguori.org Website: www.liguorian.org

Listen (Sep–May) Seventh-day Adventist Church, Céleste Walker, 55 W. Oak Ridge Dr., Hagerstown, MD 21740 Tel. (301)393-4082 Fax (301)393-4055
Email: listen@healthconnection.org
Website: www.listenmagazine.org

Living Orthodoxy (bi-M) The Russian Orthodox Church Outside of Russia, Fr. Gregory Williams, 1180 Orthodox Way, Liberty, TN 37095 Tel. (615)536-5239 Fax (615)536-5945
Email: info@sjkp.org
Website: www.sjkp.org

The Long Island Catholic (W) The Roman Catholic Church, Richard Hinshaw, P.O. Box 9000, 200 W Centennial Ave Suite 201, Roosevelt, NY 11575 Tel. (516)594-1000 Fax (516)594-1092
Website: www.licatholic.org

The Lookout (W) Christian Churches and Churches of Christ, Shawn McMullen, 8121 Hamilton Ave., Cincinnati, OH 45231 Tel. (513)931-4050 Fax (513)931-0950
Email: lookout@standardpub.com
Website: www.lookoutmag.com

Lumicon Digital Productions (I) Independent, Protestant, Rev. Dr. Tom Boomershine, UMR Communications, P.O. Box 660275, Dallas, TX 75266-0275 Tel. (214)630-6495 Fax (214)630-0079
Email: tboom@umr.org
Website: www.lumicon.org

The Lutheran (M) Evangelical Lutheran Church in America, Daniel J. Lehmann, 8765 W. Higgins Rd., Chicago, IL 60631-4183 Tel. (773)380-2540 Fax (773)380-2751
Email: lutheran@elca.org
Website: www.thelutheran.org

The Lutheran Ambassador (16-Y) The Association of Free Lutheran Congregations, Craig Johnson, 575 34th Street, Astoria, OR 97103 Tel. (541)687-8643 Fax (541)683-8496
Email: cjohnson@efn.org

The Lutheran Educator (Q) Wisconsin Evangelical Lutheran Synod, Prof. Jack N. Minch, Martin Luther College, 1995 Luther Ct., New Ulm, MN 56073 Tel. (507)354-8221 Fax (507)354-8225
Email: lutheraneducator@mlc-wels.edu

Lutheran Forum (Q) Interdenominational Lutheran, Ronald B. Bagnall, 207 Hillcrest Ave., Trenton, NJ 08618 Tel. (856)696-0417

The Lutheran Layman (bi-M) The Lutheran Church—Missouri Synod, Gerald Perschbacher, 660 Mason Ridge Center Dr, St. Louis, MO 63141-8557 Tel. (314)317-4100 Fax (314)317-4295

Lutheran Partners (bi-M) Evangelical Lutheran Church in America, William A. Decker, 8765 W. Higgins Rd., Chicago, IL 60631-4101 Tel. (773)380-2884 Fax (773)380-2829
Email: lutheran.partners@elca.org
Website: www.elca.org/lutheranpartners

Lutheran Sentinel (M) Evangelical Lutheran Synod, Theodore Gullixson, 5530 Englewood Dr., Madison, WI 53705 Tel. (641)585-1683 Fax (641)585-1683
Email: Theodore Gullixson

Lutheran Spokesman (M) Church of the Lutheran Confession, Rev. Paul Fleischer, 1741 E. 22nd St., Cheyenne, WY 82001 Tel. (307)638-8006
Email: paulgf@qwest.net
Website: www.lutheranspokeman.org

Lutheran Synod Quarterly (Q) Evangelical Lutheran Synod, G.R. Schmeling, Bethany Lutheran Theological Semi, 6 Browns Ct., Mankato, MN 56001 Tel. (507)344-7855 Fax (507)344-7426
Email: elsynod@blc.edu
Website: www.blts.edu

The Lutheran Witness (M) The Lutheran Church—Missouri Synod, James Heine, 1333 S. Kirkwood Road, St. Louis, MO 63122-7295 Tel. (314)965-9000 Fax (314)966-1126
Email: lutheran.witness@lcms.org
Website: www.lcms.org/witness

Lutheran Woman Today (10-Y) Evangelical Lutheran Church in America, Kate Sprutta Elliott, Women of the ELCA, 8765 W. Higgins Rd., Chicago, IL 60631-4101 Tel. (773)380-2730 Fax (773)380-2419
Email: lwt@elca.org
Website: www.lutheranwomantoday.org

Lyceum Spotlight (10-Y) National Spiritualist Association of Churches, Rev. Cosie Allen, 1418 Hall St., Grand Rapids, MI 49506 Tel. (616)241-2761 Fax (616)241-4703
Email: cosie@dnx.net
Website: www.nsac.org/spotlight

Magyar Egyhaz—Magyar Church (Q) Hungarian Reformed Church in America, Stephen Szabo, 464 Forest Ave., Paramus, NJ 07652 Tel. (201)262-2338 Fax (845)359-5771

Mar Thoma Messenger (Q) Mar Thoma Syrian Church of India, Eapen Daniel, 2320 S. Merrick Ave, Merrick, NY 11566 Tel. (516)377-3311 Fax (516)377-3322
Email: marthoma@aol.com

Maranatha (Q) Advent Christian Church, John Roller, P.O. Box 23152, Charlotte, NC 28227 Tel. (704)545-6161 Fax (704)573-0712
Email: jroller@acgc.us
Website: www.acgc.us

Marriage Partnership (I) Nondenominational, Ginger Kolbaba, 465 Gundersen Dr., Carol Stream, IL 60188 Tel. (630)260-6200 Fax (630)260-0114
Email: mp@marriagepartnership.com
Website: www.marriagepartnership.com

Mature Years (Q) The United Methodist Church, Marvin W. Cropsey, 201 Eighth Ave. S, Nashville, TN 37202 Tel. (615)749-6292 Fax (615)749-6512
Email: matureyears@umpublishing.org

The Mennonite (24-Y) Mennonite Church USA, Everett J. Thomas, 1700 S. Main St., Goshen, IN 46526 Tel. (574)535-6051 Fax (574)535-6050
Email: editor@themennonite.org
Website: www.themennonite.org

Mennonite Historical Bulletin (Q) Mennonite Church USA, Susan Fisher Miller, 1700 South Main St., Goshen, IN 46526 Tel. (574)535-7477 Fax (574)535-7756
Email: archives@goshen.edu
Website: www.MennoniteUSA.org/history

Mennonite Quarterly Review (Q) Mennonite Church, John D. Roth, 1700 S. Main St., Goshen, IN 46526 Tel. (574)535-7433 Fax (574)535-7438
Email: MQR@goshen.edu
Website: www.goshen.edu/mgr

Message (bi-M) Seventh-day Adventist Church, Dr. Ron C. Smith, Review and Herald Publishing Association, 55 West Oak Ridge Dr., Hagerstown, MD 21740 Tel. (301)393-4099 Fax 301-393-4103
Email: pharris@rhpa.org OR ronsmith@rhpa.org
Website: MESSAGEMAGAZINE.org

Message of the Open Bible (bi-M) Open Bible Standard Churches, Inc., Andrea Johnson, 2020 Bell Ave., Des Moines, IA 50315-1096 Tel. (515)288-6761 Fax (515)288-2510
Email: message@openbible.org
Website: www.openbible.org

Messenger (11-Y) Church of the Brethren, Walt Wiltschek, 1451 Dundee Ave., Elgin, IL 60120 Tel. (847)742-5100 Fax (847)742-1407
Email: messenger@brethren.org

The Messenger (M) The Swedenborgian Church, Patte LeVan, Central Office, 11 Higland Ave, Newton Ville, Julian, MA 02460 Tel. (760)765-2915
Email: messengerpwl@ixpres.com
Website: www.swedenborg.org

The Messenger (M) Pentecostal Free Will Baptist Church, Inc., Patte Levan, P.O. Box 1568, Dunn, NC 28335 Tel. (910)892-4161 Fax (910)892-6876
Email: messengerpwl@ixpres.com

Messenger of Truth (bi-W) Church of God in Christ (Mennonite), Gladwin Koehn, P.O. Box 230, Moundridge, KS 67107 Tel. (620)345-2532 Fax (620)345-2582
Email: gospelpublishers@cogicm.org

Methodist History (Q) The United Methodist Church, Robert J. Williams, P.O. Box 127, Madison, NJ 07940 Tel. (973)408-3189 Fax (973)408-3909
Email: rwilliams@gcah.org
Website: www.gcah.org

Ministry (M) Seventh-day Adventist Church, Nikolaus Satelmajer, 12501 Old Columbia Pike, Silver Spring, MD 20904 Tel. (301)680-6510 Fax (301)680-6502
Email: ministrymagazine@gc.adventist.org

Mission, Adult, and Youth Children's Editions (Q) Seventh-day Adventist Church, Charlotte Ishkanian, 12501 Old Columbia Pike, Silver Spring, MD 20904 Tel. (301)680-6167 Fax (301)680-6155
Email: 74532.2435@compuserve.com

Mission Connection (Q) Wisconsin Evangelical Lutheran Synod, Rev. Gary Baumler, 2929 N. Mayfair Rd., Milwaukee, WI 53222 Tel. (414)256-3210 Fax (414)256-3862
Email: mc@sab.wels.net

Mission Herald (Q) National Baptist Convention, U.S.A., Inc., Dr. Bruce N. Alick, 701 S. 19th Street, Philadelphia, PA 19146 Tel. (215)735-9853 Fax (215)735-1721

Missionary Church Today (Q) Missionary Church, Rev. Thomas Murphy, P.O. Box 9127, Ft. Wayne, IN 46899 Tel. (260)747-2027 Fax (260)747-5331
Email: tommurphy@mcusa.org
Website: www.mcusa.org

The Missionary Messenger (bi-M) Christian Methodist Episcopal Church, Doris F. Boyd, 213 Viking Dr., W., Cordova, TN 38018 Tel. (901)757-1103 Fax (901)751-2104
Email: doris.boyd@williams.com

The Missionary Messenger (bi-M) Cumberland Presbyterian Church, Michael G. Sharpe, 1978 Union Ave., Memphis, TN 38104 Tel. (901)276-9988 Fax (901)276-4578
Email: messenger@cumberland.org
Website: www.cumberland.org/bom/Communication_and_Publication_Unit/Missionary Messenger.htm

Missionary Seer (bi-M) African Methodist Episcopal Zion Church, Rev. Kermit J. DeGraffenreidt, 475 Riverside Dr., Rm. 1935, New York, NY 10115 Tel. (212)870-2952 Fax (212)870-2808
Email: domkd5@aol.com

329

The Missionary Signal (bi-M) Churches of God, General Conference, Rachel Foreman, P.O. Box 926, Findlay, OH 45839 Tel. (419)424-1961 Fax (419)424-3433
Email: communications@cggc.org
Website: cggc.org

Missions Ministry (Q) Progressive National Baptist Convention, Inc., Justus Y. Reeves, 601 50th St. NE, Washington, DC 20019 Tel. (202)396-0558 Fax (202)398-4998
Email: justusreeves@aol.com
Website: www.PNBC.org

The Moravian (10-Y) Moravian Church in North America (Unitas Fratrum), Deanna L. Hollenbach - Dir. Of Communication, Interprovincial Bd. Of Communication, 1021 Center St., P.O. Box 1245, Bethlehem, PA 18016 Tel. (610)867-0593/800-732-0591 Fax (610)866-9223
Email: pubs@mcnp.org
Website: www.moravian.org

The Mother Church (bi-M) Western Diocese of the Armenian Church of North America, Archpriest Fr. Sipan Mekhsian, 3325 N. Glenoaks Blvd., Burbank, CA 91504 Tel. (818)558-7474 Fax (818)558-6333
Email: mgizlechyan@armenianchurchwd.com
Website: www.armenianchurchwd.com

Multiply (Q) Presbyterian Church in America, Fred Marsh, Mission to North America, 1700 North Brown Road, Ste. 101, Lawrenceville, GA 30044 Tel. (678)825-1200 Fax (678)825-1201
Email: mna@pcanet.org
Website: www.pca-mna.org

NABtoday for you (Q) North American Baptist Conference, Lucinda Armas, 1 So 210 Summit Ave., Oakbrook Terrace, IL 60181 Tel. (630)495-2000 Fax (630)495-3301
Email: serve@nabconference.org
Website: www.nabconference.org

NAE Insight (bi-M) Interdenominational, Rev. Richard Cizik, 701 G St SW, WASHINGTON, DC 20024 Tel. (202)789-1011 Fax (202)842-0392
Email: rcizike@nae.net

NAE Washington Insight (Q) Interdenominational, Rev. Richard Cizik, 701 G Street, SW, Washington, DC 20024 Tel. (202)789-1011 Fax (202)842-0392
Email: govaffairs@nae.net
Website: www.nae.net

National Catholic Reporter (44-Y) The Catholic Church, Tom Roberts, P.O. Box 419281, Kansas City, MO 64141 Tel. (816)531-0538 Fax (816)968-2280
Email: editor@natcath.org
Website: www.NCRonline.org

The National Spiritualist Summit (M) National Spiritualist Association of Churches, Rev. Sandra Pfortmiller, 3521 W. Topeka Dr., Glendale, AZ 85308-2325 Tel. (623)581-6686 Fax (623)581-5544
Website: www.nsac.org

Network (Q) Presbyterian Church in America, Susan Fikse, 1600 North Brown Road, Lawrenceville, GA 30047 Tel. (678)823-0004 Fax (678)823-0027
Website: pca.org

New Church Life (M) General Church of the New Jerusalem, Rev. Donald L. Rose, Box 277, Bryn Athyn, PA 19009 Tel. (215)947-6225 ext. 209 Fax (215)938-1871
Email: DonR@BACS-GC.org
Website: www.newchurch.org

New Horizons in the Orthodox Presbyterian Church (11-Y) The Orthodox Presbyterian Church, Danny E. Olinger, 607 N. Easton Rd., Bldg. E, P.O. Box P, Willow Grove, PA 19090-0920 Tel. (215)830-0900 Fax (215)830-0350
Email: olinger.1@opc.org
Website: www.opc.org/

New Oxford Review (11-Y) The Catholic Church, Peter Vree, 1069 Kains Ave., Berkeley, CA 94706 Tel. (510)526-5374 Fax (510)526-3492
Website: www.newoxfordreview.org

New World Outlook (bi-M) Mission Magazine of The United Methodist Church, Christie R. House, 475 Riverside Dr., Rm. 1476, New York, NY 10115 Tel. (212)870-3765 Fax (212)870-3654
Email: NWO@gbgm-umc.org
Website: gbgm-umc.org/now

Newscope (W) The United Methodist Church, Barbara Dick, P.O. Box 801, Nashville, TN 37202 Tel. (800)672-1789 Fax (800)445-8189
Email: umnewscope@umpublishing.org
Website: www.umph.org

Newsline (bi-W, I) Church of the Brethren, Cheryl Brumbaugh-Cayford, 1451 Dundee Ave., Elgin, IL 60120-1694 Tel. (847)742-5100 (800) 323-8039 Fax (847)742-6103
Email: cobnews@brethren.org
Website: http://www.brethren.org/genbd/newsline/index.htm

The North American Catholic (M) North American Old Roman Catholic Church, Theodore J. Remalt, 4154 W. Berteau Ave, Chicago, IL 60641 Tel. (312)685-0461 Fax (312)485-0461
Email: chapelhall@aol.com

The North American Challenge (M) Home Missions Division of The United Pentecostal Church International, Joseph Fiorino, 8855 Dunn Rd., Hazelwood, MO 63042-2299 Tel. (314)837-7300 Fax (314)837-5632

NRB Magazine (9-Y) Nondenominational, Valerie Fraedrich, National Religious Broadcasters, 9510 Technology Drive, Manassas, VA 20110 Tel. (703)330-7000 Fax (703) 330-6996
Email: vfraedrich@nrb.org
Website: www.nrb.org

On Course (bi-M) Assemblies of God, Kristi Arnold and Amber Weigand-Buckley (Interim co-editors), 1445 N. Boonville Ave., Springfield, MO 65802-1894 Tel. (417)862-2781 Fax (417)862-1693
Email: oncourse@ag.org
Website: oncourse.ag.org

On the Line (M) Mennonite Church, Mary C. Meyer, 616 Walnut Ave., Scottdale, PA 15683 Tel. (724)887-8500 Fax (724)887-3111
Email: info@mph.org
Website: www.mph.org/otl

On Mission (Q) Southern Baptist Convention, Carol Pipes, 4200 North Point Pkwy., Alphretta, GA 30202-4174 Tel. (770)410-6394 Fax (770)410-6105
Website: www.onmission.com

ONE Magazine (bi-M) National Association of Free Will Baptists, Eric Thomsen, P.O. Box 5002, Antioch, TN 37011-5002 Tel. 615-731-6812 Fax 615-731-0771
Email: eric@nafwb.org
Website: http://www.onemag.org/plymouth _rock.htm

OnSite (Q) United Pentecostal Church International, Bryan Abernathy, 8855 Dunn Rd., Hazelwood, MO 63042 Tel. (314)837-7300 Fax (314)837-2387
Email: fmmail@upci.org
Website: www.foreignmissions.com

Orthodox America (8-Y) The Russian Orthodox Church Outside of Russia, Mary Mansur, P.O. Box 383, Richfield Springs, NY 13439-0383 Tel. (315)858-1518
Email: info@orthodoxamerica.org
Website: www.orthodoxamerica.org

The Orthodox Church (M) The Orthodox Church in America, Very Rev. John Matusiak, Managing Editor - Very Rev. Leonid Kishkovsky, Editor, Editorial Office, One Wheaton Center #912, Wheaton, IL 60187 Tel. (630)668-3071 Fax (630)668-5712
Email: tocmed@hotmail.com
Website: www.oca.org

Orthodox Family (Q) The Russian Orthodox Church Outside of Russia, George Johnson and Deborah Johnson, P.O. Box 45, Beltsville, MD 20705 Fax (301)890-3552
Email: 1lew@cais.com
Website: www.roca.org/orthodox

Orthodox Life (bi-M) The Russian Orthodox Church Outside of Russia, Fr. Luke, Holy Trinity Monastery, P.O Box 36, Jordanville, NY 13361-0036 Tel. (315)858-0940 Fax (315)858-0505
Email: orthlife@telenet.net

The Orthodox Observer (M) Greek Orthodox Archdiocese of America, Jim Holding (Chryssoulis), 8 E. 79th St., New York, NY 10021 Tel. (212)570-3555 Fax (212)774-0239
Email: observer@goarch.org
Website: www.observer.goarch.org

Orthodox Russia (English translation of Pravoslavnaya Rus) (24-Y) The Russian Orthodox Church Outside of Russia, Archbishop Laurus, Holy Trinity Monastery, P.O. Box 36, Jordanville, NY 13361-0036 Tel. (315)858-0940 Fax (315)858-0505
Email: orthrus@telenet.net

Our Daily Bread (M) The Swedenborgian Church, Lee Woofenden, P.O. Box 396, Bridgewater, MA 02324 Tel. (508)946-1767 Fax (508)946-1757
Email: odb@swedenborg.org
Website: www.swedenborg.org/odb/index.cfm

Our Little Friend (W) Seventh-day Adventist Church, Aileen Andres Sox, P.O. Box 5353, Nampa, ID 83653-5353 Tel. (208)465-2500 Fax (208)465-2531
Email: ailsox@pacificpress.com
Website: www.pacificpress.com

Our Sunday Visitor (W) The Catholic Church, Gerald Korson, 200 Noll Plaza, Huntington, IN 46750 Tel. (219)356-8400
Email: oursunvis@osv.com
Website: www.osv.com

Outreach (6-Y) Armenian Apostolic Church of America, Iris Papazian, 138 E. 39th St., New York, NY 10016 Tel. (212)689-7810 Fax (212)689-7168
Email: info@armenianprelacy.org
Website: www.armenianprelacy.org

The Path of Orthodoxy (Serbian) (M) Serbian Orthodox Church in the U.S.A. and Canada, V. Rev. Nedeljko Lunich, 300 Striker Ave., Joliet, IL 60436 Tel. (815)741-1023 Fax (815)741-1883
Email: nedlunich300@comcast.net

Paul (Q) Netherlands Reformed Congregations, J. Spans, 47 Main Street E., Norwich, ON N0J 1P0 Tel. (519)863-3306 Fax (519)863-2793

Pentecostal Evangel (W) Assemblies of God, Ken Horn, Gospel Publishing House, 1445 N. Boonville Ave., Springfield, MO 65802-1894 Tel. (417)862-2781 Fax (417)862-0416
Email: pe@ag.org
Website: www.pe.ag.org

Pentecostal Evangel, Missions World Edition (M) Assemblies of God, Ken Horn, Gospel Publishing House, 1445 N. Boonville Ave., Springfield, MO 65802 Tel. (417)862-2781 Fax (417)862-0416
Email: pe@ag.org
Website: www.pe.ag.org

The Pentecostal Herald (M) United Pentecostal Church International, Rev. J. L. Hall, 8855 Dunn Rd., Hazelwood, MO 63042 Tel. (314)837-7300 Fax (314)837-4503

Pentecostal Leader (bi-M) The International Pentecostal Church of Christ, Clyde M. Hughes, P.O. Box 439, London, OH 43140 Tel. (740)852-4722 Fax (740)852-0348
Email: hqipcc@aol.com
Website: www.IPCC.CC

The Pentecostal Messenger (M) Pentecostal Church of God (Joplin, MO), John Mallinak, P.O. Box 850, Joplin, MO 64802 Tel. (417)624-7050 Fax (417)624-7102
Email: johnm@pcg.org
Website: www.pcg.org

Perspectives (10-Y) Reformed Church in America, James Bratt, David E. Timmer, Scott Hoezee (co-editors), P.O. Box 1196, Holland, MI 49422-1196 Tel. (616)392-8555 ext. 131 Fax (616)392-7717
Email: perspectives@rca.org
Website: www.perspectivesjournal.org

Perspectives on Science and Christian Faith (Q) Nondenominational, Dr. Roman J. Miller, 4956 Singers Glen Rd., Harrisonburg, VA 22802 Tel. (540)432-4412 Fax (540)432-4488
Email: millerrj@rica.net
Website: www.asa3.org

The Pilot - America's Oldest Catholic Newspaper (W, 49-Y) The Catholic Archdiocese of Boston, Antonio Enrique, 2121 Commonwealth Ave., Brighton, MA 02135 Tel. (617)746-5889 Fax (617)783-2684
Email: editorial@bostonpilot.org
Website: www.rcab.org

Pockets (11-Y) The United Methodist Church, Lynn W. Gilliam, P.O. Box 340004, Nashville, TN 37203-0004 Tel. (615)340-7333 Fax (615)340-7267
Email: pockets@upperroom.org
Website: www.pockets.org

Polka (Q) Polish National Catholic Church of America, Cecelia Lallo, 1127 Frieda St., Dickson City, PA 18519-1304 Tel. (570)489-4364 Fax (570)346-2188

Pravoslavnaya Rus (Russian) (24-Y) The Russian Orthodox Church Outside of Russia, Archbishop Laurus, Holy Trinity Monastery, P.O. Box 36, Jordanville, NY 13361-0036 Tel.

(315)858-0940 Fax (315)858-0505
Email: orthrus@telenet.net

Pravoslavnaya Zhisn (Monthly Supplement to Pravoslavnaya Rus) (M) The Russian Orthodox Church Outside of Russia, Archbishop Laurus, Holy Trinity Monastery, P.O. Box 36, Jordanville, NY 13361-0036 Tel. (315)858-0940 Fax (315)858-0505
Email: Orthrus@telenet.net

Preacher's Magazine (3-Y) Church of the Nazarene, Jeren Rowell and David Busic, 6401 Paseo Blvd, Kansas City, MO 64131-1213
Website: www.nph.com/nphweb/html/pmol/index.htm

Presbyterian News Service "The News" (bi-M) Presbyterian Church (U.S.A.), Jerry L. Van-Marter, 100 Witherspoon St., Rm. 5418, Louisville, KY 40202 Tel. (502)569-5493 Fax (502)569-8073
Email: JVanMart@ctr.pcusa.org
Website: www.pcusa.org/pcnews

Presbyterian Outlook (43-Y) Presbyterian Church (U.S.A.), Rev. Dr. Jack Haberer, 2112 W. Labaurnum Ave., Suite 109, Richmond, VA 23227 Tel. (800)446-6008 Fax (804)353-6369
Email: jhaberer@pres-outlook.com
Website: www.pres-outlook.com

Presbyterians Today (10-Y) Presbyterian Church (U.S.A.), Eva Stimson, 100 Witherspoon St., Louisville, KY 40202-1396 Tel. (502)569-5637 Fax (502)569-8632
Email: today@pcusa.org
Website: www.pcusa.org/today

Primary Source (Q) American Baptist Historical Society, Deborah Van Broekhoven, P.O. Box 851, Valley Forge, PA 19482-0851 Fax (610)768-2266
Email: dbvanbro@abc-usa.org
Website: www.abc-usa.org/abhs

Primary Treasure (W) Seventh-day Adventist Church, Aileen Andres Sox, P.O. Box 5353, Nampa, ID 83653-5353 Tel. (208)465-2500 Fax (208)465-2531
Email: ailsox@pacificpress.com
Website: www.pacificpress.com

Priority (M) Missionary Church, Dr. Thomas Murphy, P.O. Box 9127, Ft. Wayne, IN 46899 Tel. (260)747-2027 Fax (260)747-5331
Email: mcdenomusa@aol.com
Website: mcusa.org

Pulse (M) The Church of God (Seventh Day), Denver, CO, Jamie Stroupe, P.O. Box 33677, 330 W. 152nd Ave., Denver, CO 80233 Tel. (303)452-7973 Fax (303)452-0657
Email: offices@cog7.org
Website: cog7.org

Purpose (M. in weekly parts) Mennonite Church Canada and Mennonite Church USA, James E. Horsch, 616 Walnut Ave., Scottdale, PA 15683 Tel. (724)887-8500 Fax (724)887-3111 Email: horsch@mph.org Website: www.mph.org

PYM News (5-Y) Philadelphia Yearly Meeting of the Religious Society of Friends, Allen R. Reeder, 1515 Cherry St., Philadelphia, PA 19102-1479 Tel. (215)241-7000 Fax (215)241-7045 Email: news@pym.org Website: www.pym.org

Quaker Life (6-Y) Friends United Meeting, Patricia Edwards-Konic, 101 Quaker Hill Dr., Richmond, IN 47374-1980 Tel. (765)962-7573 Fax (765)966-1293 Email: QuakerLife@fum.org Website: www.fum.org

Quarterly Review, A.M.E. Zion (Q) African Methodist Episcopal Zion Church, Rev. James D. Armstrong, P.O. Box 33247, Charlotte, NC 28233 Tel. (704)599-4630 Fax (704)688-2544 Email: jaarmstrong@amezhqtr.org

Reflections (bi-M) United Pentecostal Church International, Melissa Anderson, 8855 Dunn Rd, Hazelwood, MO 63042 Tel. (918)371-2659 Fax (918)371-6320 Email: manderson@tums.org Website: www.upci.org/ladies

Reformed Worship (Q) Christian Reformed Chuch in North America, Rev. Joyce Borger, 2850 Kalamazoo Ave. SE, Grand Rapids, MI 49560-0001 Tel. (800)777-7270 Fax (616)224-0834 Email: info@reformedworship.org Website: www.reformedworship.org

Rejoice! (Q) Mennonite Church, Byron Rempel-Burkholder, 600 Shaftesbury Blvd., Winnipeg, MB R3P 0M4 Tel. (204)488-0610 Fax (204)831-5675 Email: byronrb@mpn.org Website: www.mpn.org/rejoice

Rejoice! (Q) Mennonite & Mennonite Brethren Church, Philip Wiebe, 3052 Kurt Dr. NW, Salem, OR 97304-1053 Tel. (503)585-4458 Fax (503)585-4458

Report From The Capital (10-Y) Baptist Joint Committee, Jeff Huett, 200 Maryland Ave. NE, Washington, DC 20002-5797 Tel. (202)544-4226 Fax (202)544-2094 Email: jhuett@bjconline.org Website: www.bjconline.org

Reporter (M) The Lutheran Church—Missouri Synod, Joe Isenhower Jr., Managing Editor, 1333 S. Kirkwood Rd., St. Louis, MO 63122-7295 Tel. (314)996-9000 Fax (314)966-1126 Email: vicki.biggs@lcms.org Website: vicki.biggs@lcms.org

Reporter Interactive (D) Independent, Protestant, Cynthia B. Astle, UMR Communications, P.O. Box 660275, Dallas, TX 75266-0275 Tel. (214)630-6495 Fax (214)630-0079 Email: news@umr.org Website: www.lumicon.org

The Rescue Herald (3-Y) American Rescue Workers, Deborah La Valla, 24 Carriage House, Enfield, CT 06082 Tel. (860)741-0727 Email: deb@arwus.com Website: www.arwus.com

Response (M) The United Methodist Church, Dana Jones, 475 Riverside Dr., Room 1356, New York, NY 10115 Tel. (212)870-3755 Fax (212)870-3940

The Restitution Herald and Church of God Progress Journal (bi-M) Church of God General Conference (Oregon, Ill. & Morrow GA), Tim Jones, Box 100,000, Morrow, GA 30260 Tel. (504)362-0052 Fax (404)362-9307 Email: info@abc-coggc.org Website: www.abc-coggc.org

Restoration Herald (M) Christian Churches and Churches of Christ, H. Lee Mason, 7133 Central Parks Blvd., Mason, OH 45040 Tel. (513)229-8000 Fax (513)229-8003 Email: thecra@aol.com Website: www.thecra.org

Restoration Quarterly (Q) Churches of Christ, James W. Thompson, Box 28227, Abilene, TX 79699-8227 Tel. (915)674-3781 Fax (915)674-3776 Email: rq@bible.acu.edu Website: www.rq.acu.edu

Review for Religious (Q) The Catholic Church, David L. Fleming, S.J., 3601 Lindell Blvd., St. Louis, MO 63108 Tel. (314)663-4160 Fax (314)633-4611 Email: review@slu.edu Website: www.reviewforreligious.org

Review of Religious Research (Q) Nondenominational, Patricia Wittberg, Sociology Department, Indiana University Purdue University, Indianapolis, IN 46202 Tel. (317)274-4478 Fax (317)278-3654 Email: pwittber@iupui.edu Website: rra.hartsem.edu

Road to Emmaus (Q) Orthodox Christian, Nun Nectaria, 1516 N. Delaware, Indianapolis, IN 46202 Tel. (317)631-1344 Fax (317)637-1897 Email: csb@indy.net Website: www.roadtoemmaus.net

Rocky Mountain Christian (M) Churches of Christ, Ron L. Carter, P.O. Box 803, Eastlake, CO 80614-0803. Tel. (719)598-4197 Fax (719)528-1549 Email: rmcnews@pcisys.net

Sabbath Recorder (M) Seventh Day Baptist General Conference, USA and Canada, Rev. Kevin J. Butler, 3120 Kennedy Rd., P.O. Box 1678, Janesville, WI 53547 Tel. (608)752-5055 Fax (608)752-7711
Email: editor@seventhdaybaptist.org
Website: www.seventhdaybaptist.org

Sabbath School Leadership (M) Seventh-day Adventist Church, Faith Crumbly, Review and Herald Publishing Assoc., 55 W. Oak Ridge Dr., Hagerstown, MD 21740 Tel. (301)393-4090 Fax (301)393-4055
Email: sabbathschoolleadership@rhpa.org
Website: www.rhpa.org

Saint Anthony Messenger (M) The Catholic Church, Fr. Pat McCloskey, O.F.M., St. Anthony Messenger Editorial, Dept., 28 W. Liberty St., Cincinnati, OH 45202 Tel. (513) 241-5615 Fax (513)241-0399
Email: StAnthony@AmericanCatholic.org
Website: www.AmericanCatholic.org

Saint Willibrord Journal (Q) Christ Catholic Church, The Rev. Monsignor Charles E. Harrison, P.O. Box 271751, Houston, TX 77277-1751 Tel. (713)515-8206 Fax (713)622-5311
Website: www.christcatholic.org

Saints Herald (M) Community of Christ, Linda Booth, The Herald Publishing House, P.O. Box 390, Independence, MO 64051-0390 Tel. (816)521-3015 Fax (816)521-3066
Email: Herald@CofChrist.org
Website: www.heraldhouse.org

SBC Life (10-Y) Southern Baptist Convention, John Revell, Executive Editor: Kenyn Cureton, VP for Convention Relations, 901 Commerce St., Nashville, TN 37203 Tel. (615) 244-2355 Fax (615)782-8684
Email: jrevell@sbc.net
Website: sbc.net

The Schwenkfeldian (3-Y) The Schwenkfelder Church, Gerald Heebner, 105 Seminary Street, Pennsburg, PA 18073 Tel. (215)679-3103 Fax (215)679-8175
Email: info@schwenfelder.com
Website: www.schwenkfelder.com

Searching Together (Q) Sovereign Grace Believers, Jon Zens, Box 548, St. Croix Falls, WI 54024 Tel. (651)465-6516 Fax (651) 465-5101
Email: jzens@searchingtogether.org
Website: www.searchingtogether.org

The Secret Place (Q) American Baptist Churches USA, Kathleen Hayes, Senior Editor, P.O. Box 851, Valley Forge, PA 19482-0851 Tel. (610)768-2434 Fax (610)768-2441
Email: thesecretplace@abc-usa.org
Website: www.judsonpress.com

Seeds for the Parish (bi-M) Evangelical Lutheran Church in America, Janice Rizzo, 8765 W. Higgins Rd., Chicago, IL 60631 Tel. (773)380-2949/(800)638-3522 Fax (773) 380-2406
Email: Janice.Rizzo@elca.org
Website: www.elca.org/seeds

Shalom! (Q) Brethren in Christ Church, Harriet Bicksler, P.O. Box A, Grantham, PA 17027 Tel. (717)697-2634
Email: bickhouse@aol.com
Website: www.bic-church.org/connect/publications/Shalom/default.asp

Shiloh's Messenger of Wisdom (M) Israelite House of David, William Robertson, P.O. Box 1067, Benton Harbor, MI 49023

The Shofar Apostolic Catholic Church, Myra Calahan, 7813 N. Nebraska Ave., Tampa, FL 33604 Tel. (813)238-6060
Email: Bishop-Chuck@apostoliccatholic-church.com
Website: www.ApostolicCatholicChurch.com

Signs of the Times (M) Seventh-day Adventist Church, Marvin Moore, P.O. Box 5353, Nampa, ID 83653-5353 Tel. (208)465-2577 Fax (208)465-2531
Website: www.signstimes.com

The Silver Lining (M) Apostolic Christian Churches of America, Bruce Leman, R.R. 2, Box 50, Roanoke, IL 61561-9625 Tel. (309)923-7777 Fax (309)923-7359

Social Questions Bulletin (bi-M) The United Methodist Church, Rev. Kathryn J. Johnson, 212 East Capitol St., NE, Washington, DC 20003 Tel. (202)546-8806 Fax (202)546-6811
Email: mfsa@mfsaweb.org
Website: www.mfsaweb.org

Sojourners (M) Ecumenical, Jim Wallis, 3333 14th Street NW, Suite 200, Washington, DC 20010 Tel. (202)328-8842 Fax (202)328-8757
Email: sojourners@sojo.net
Website: www.sojo.net

Solia Calendar (Y) The Romanian Orthodox Episcopate of America, The Department of Publications of the Romanian Orthodox Episcopate of America, P.O. Box 185, Grass Lake, MI 49240-0185 Tel. (517)522-4800 Fax (517)522-5907
Email: solia@roea.org
Website: roea.org

Solia - The Herald (M) The Romanian Orthodox Episcopate of America, Rev. Archdeacon David Oancea, P.O. Box 185, Grass Lake, MI 49240-0185 Tel. (517)522-3656 Fax (517)522-5907
Email: solia@roea.org
Website: www.roea.org

Sound of Grace (Q) Sovereign Grace Believers, 5317 Wye Creek Dr, Frederick, MD 21703-6938

334

The **Southern Methodist** (bi-M) Southern Methodist Church, Thomas M. Owens, Sr., P.O. Box 39, Orangeburg, SC 29116-0039 Tel. (803)534-9853 Fax (803)535-3881 Email: foundry@bellsouth.net

Spirit (Q) Volunteers of America, Arthur Smith and Denis N. Baker, 1809 Carrollton Ave, New Orleans, LA 70118-2829 Tel. (504)897-1731

The **Spiritual Sword** (Q) Churches of Christ, Alan E. Highers, 1511 Getwell Rd., Memphis, TN 38111 Tel. (901)743-0464 Fax (901)743-2197 Email: getwellcc@aol.com Website: www.getwellchurchofchrist.org

The **Standard Bearer** (21-Y) Protestant Reformed Churches in America, Russell J. Dykstra, 4949 Ivanrest Ave. SW, Grandville, MI 49418 Tel. (616)531-1490 Fax (616)531-3033 Email: dykstra@prca.org Website: www.rfpa.org/sb.asp

The **Star of Zion** (bi-W) African Methodist Episcopal Zion Church, Mr. Mike Lisby, P.O. Box 26770, Charlotte, NC 28221-6770 Tel. (704)599-4630 ext.318 Fax (704)688-2546 Email: service@starofzion.org Website: www.starofzion.org

The **Student (Braille & Cassette)** (M) Seventh-day Adventist Church, Bert Williams, Christian Record Services for the Blind, P.O. Box 6097, Lincoln, NE 68506-0097 Tel. (402)488-0981 Fax (402)488-7582 Email: editorial@christianrecord.org Website: www.christianrecord.org

Sunday (Q) Interdenominational, Timothy A. Norton, 2930 Flowers Rd., S., Atlanta, GA 30341-5532 Tel. (770)936-5376 Fax (770)936-5385 Email: tnorton@ldausa.org Website: www.sundayonline.org

The **Tablet** (W) The Catholic Church, Ed Wilkinson, 310 Prospect Park West, Brooklyn, NY 11215 Tel. (718)965-7333 Fax (718)965-7337 Email: TheTablet@aol.com Website: http://www.dioceseofbrooklyn.org/tablet/contact/index.html

Theology Digest (Q) The Catholic Church, Bernhard Asen, Rosemary Jermann (co-editors), 3800 Lindell Blvd., St. Louis, MO 63108 Tel. (314)977-3410 Fax (314)977-3704 Email: thdigest@slu.edu

Theology Today (Q) Nondenominational, James F. Kay, Reviews Editor: Gordon S. Mikoski, P.O. Box 821, Princeton, NJ 08542-0803 Tel. (609)497-7714 Fax (609)497-1826 Email: theology.today@ptsem.edu Website: theologytoday.ptsem.edu

These Days (Q) Interdenominational, Vince Patton, 100 Witherspoon St., Louisville, KY 40202-1396 Tel. (502)569-5080 Fax (502)569-5113 Website: www.ppcpub.com

The **Three-Fold Vision** (M) Apostolic Faith Mission Church of God, Alice Walker, 156 Walker Street, Munford, AL 36268 Tel. (256)358-9763 Email: alicemtwalker@aol.com

Timbrel: The Publication for Mennonite Women The (bi-M) Mennonite Church Canada and USA, Laurie Oswald Robinson, 420 SE Richland Ave., Corvallis, Newton, OR 97333 Tel. (316) 283-5100 Email: timbrel@mennonitewomenUSA.org Website: www.mennonitewomenusa.org

Today's Christian (bi-M) Nondenominational, Ed Gilbreath, 465 Gundersen Dr., Carol Stream, IL 60188 Tel. (630)260-6200 Fax (630)480-2004 Email: tceditor@todays-christian.com Website: www.todays-christian.com

Today's Christian Woman (bi-M) Nondenominational, Jane Johnson Struck, 465 Gundersen Dr., Carol Stream, IL 60188 Tel. (630)260-6200 Fax (630)260 0114 Email: TCWedit@christianitytoday.com Website: www.todayschristianwoman.com

Tomorrow Magazine (Q) American Baptist Churches in the USA, Sara E. Hopkins, 475 Riverside Dr., Room 1700, New York, NY 10115-0049 Tel. (800)986-6222 Fax (800)986-6782

The **Tover of St. Cassian** (bi-M) Apostolic Episcopal Church, Rev. Stacy C. Douglas MA, MTh, Society of St. Cassian; c/o S.C. Douglas, P.O.Box 5016, Athens, GA 30604 Tel. (917)373-4036 Email: apostolic.episcopal@gmail.com Website: www.apostolic-episcopal.org

Truth (Q) Grace Gospel Fellowship, Phil Cereghino, 2125 Martindale SW, Grand Rapids, MI 49509 Tel. (616)247-1999 Fax (616)241-2542 Email: ggfinc@aol.com Website: www.ggfusa.org

Truth Magazine (bi-W) Churches of Christ, Mike Willis, Box 9670, Bowling Green, KY 42102 Tel. (800)428-0121 Website: truthmagazine.com

Ubique (Q) The Liberal Catholic Church— Province of the United States, Mrs. Erin S.W. Satterlee, 2033 22nd Ave. #302, Greeley, CO 80631 Email: ubiquetlcc@fastmail.fm Website: www.TheLCC.org

335

Ukrainian Orthodox Herald Ukrainian Orthodox Church of America (Ecumenical Patriarchate), Rev. Dr. Anthony Ugolnik, P.O. Box 774, Allentown, PA 18105

Ukrainian Orthodox Word (M) Ukrainian Orthodox Church of the USA, Heiromonk Daniel (Zelinskyy), P.O. Box 495, South Bound Brook, NJ 08880 Tel. (732) 356-0090 Fax (732)356-5556
Email: FatherVZ@aol.com
Website: www.uocofusa.org

UMR Communications, Inc. (W, bi-W) Independent, Protestant, Robin Russell, P.O. Box 660275, Dallas, TX 75266-0275 Tel. (214)630-6495 Fax (214)630-0079
Email: rrussell@umr.org
Website: www.umr.org
www.reporterinteractive.org (news site)
www.lumicon.org

United Church News (10-Y) United Church of Christ, W. Evan Golder, 700 Prospect Ave., Cleveland, OH 44115 Tel. (216)736-2218 Fax (216)736-2223
Email: goldere@ucc.org
Website: www.ucc.org

The United Methodist Reporter (W) Independent, Protestant, Cynthia B. Astle, UMR Communications, P.O. Box 660275, Dallas, TX 75266-0275 Tel. (214)630-6495 Fax (214)630-0079
Email: news@umr.org
Website: www.umr.org

United Methodists in Service (Korean) (6-Y) The United Methodist Church (Korean), Keihwan Ryoo, UMCom, P. O. Box 320, Nashville, TN 37202-0320 Tel. 615-742-5400 Fax 615-742-5469
Email: kumc@umcom.org
Website: http://www.koreanumc.org/

UOL Bulletin (Ukrainian Orthodox League Bulletin) (7-Y) Ukrainian Orthodox Church of the USA, Dr. Stephen Sivulich, 206 Christopher Circle, Pittsburgh, PA 15205 Tel. (412)276-1140
Email: ssivulich1@juno.com
Website: www.uocofusa.org

The Upper Room (bi-M) The United Methodist Church, Steven D. Bryant, P.O. Box 340004, Nashville, TN 37203-0004 Tel. (877)899-2780 Fax (615)340-7289
Email: sbryant@upperroom.org
Website: www.upperroom.org

U.S. Catholic (M) The Catholic Church, Rev. John Molyneux, 205 W. Monroe St., Chicago, IL 60606 Tel. (312)236-7782 Fax (312)236-8207
Email: editors@uscatholic.org
Website: www.uscatholic.org

UU World (Q) Unitarian Universalist Association of Congregations, Christopher L. Walton, Executive Editor, 25 Beacon St., Boston, MA 02108-2803 Tel. (617)948-6518 Fax (617)742-7025
Email: world@uua.org
Website: www.uuworld.org

Vibrant Life (bi-M) Seventh-day Adventist Church, Heather Quintana, 55 W. Oak Ridge Dr., Hagerstown, MD 21740 Tel. (301)393-4019 Fax (301)393-4055
Email: vibrantlife@rhpa.org
Website: www.vibrantlife.com

Victory (Youth Sunday School/Bible Study Curriculum) (Q) Church of God of Prophecy, David Bryan, P.O. Box 2910, Cleveland, TN 37320-2910 Tel. (423)559-5321 Fax (423)559-5461
Email: david@cogop.org
Website: www.cogop.org

The Vindicator (M) Old German Baptist Brethren Church, Steven L. Bayer, 6952 N. Montgomery Co. Line Rd., Englewood, OH 45322-9748 Tel. (937)884-7531 Fax (937) 884-7531

Vira/Faith (Q) Ukrainian Orthodox Church of the U.S.A., Hieromonk Daniel (Zelinskyy), P.O. Box 495, South Bound Brook, NJ 08880 Tel. (732)356-0090 Fax (732)356-5556
Email: virafaith@aol.com
Website: uocofusa.org

Vista (Q) International Fellowship of Christian Assemblies, Kerrie Evans, 1294 Rutledge Rd., Transfer, PA 16154 Tel. (412)962-3501 Fax (412)962-1766
Email: ifcahq@neohio.twcbc.com
Website: www.ifcaministry.com

Vital Signs (bi-M) Conservative Baptist Association of America (CBAmerica), Rev. Stanley Rieb, 3686 Stagecoach Rd Unit F, Longmot, CO 80504 Tel. (720)283-3030
Email: info@CBAmerica.org
Website: www.CBAmerica.org

The Voice (bi-M) IFCA International, Inc., Les Lofquist, P.O. Box 810, Grandville, MI 49468-0810 Tel. (616)531-1840 Fax (616)531-1814
Email: Voice@ifca.org

The Voice (Q) The Bible Church of Christ, Inc., Montrose Bushrod, 1358 Morris Ave., Bronx, NY 10456 Tel. (718)588-2284 Fax (718)992-5597
Website: www.thebiblechurchofchrist.org

Voice of Mission (Q) African Methodist Episcopal Church, Dr. John W.P. Collier, 1587 Savannah Highway, Ste. A, Charleston, SC 29407 Tel. (843)852-2645 Fax (843)852-2648
Email: gwmame@bellsouth.net
Website: amegobalmissions.com

The War Cry (bi-M) The Salvation Army, Ed Forster, Editor in Chief; Jeff McDonald, Managing Editor, 615 Slaters Lane, Alexandria, VA 22314 Tel. (703)684-5500 Fax (703) 684-5539
Email: war_cry@usn.salvationarmy.org

Watchtower (bi-W) Jehovah's Witnesses, Watch Tower Society, 25 Columbia Heights, Brooklyn, NY 11201-2483 Tel. (718)560-5000 Fax (718)560-8850
Website: www.watchtower.org

Weavings: A Journal of the Christian Spiritual Life (Q) The United Methodist Church, Pamela C. Hawkins, 1908 Grand Avenue, P.O. Box 30004, Nashville, TN 37203-0004 Tel. (615)340-7254 Fax (615)340-7267
Email: weavings@upperroom.org
Website: www.upperroom.org/weavings

Wesleyan Life (Q) The Wesleyan Church, Norman G. Wilson, P.O. Box 50434, Indianapolis, IN 46250-0434 Tel. (317)774-7909 Fax (317) 774-7913
Email: wilsonn@wesleyan.org
Website: www.wesleyan.org

Wesleyan World (Q) The Wesleyan Church, P.O. Box 50434, Indianapolis, IN 46250 Tel. (317)774-7950 Fax (317)774-7958
Email: ghpm@wesleyan.org
Website: www.praygivego.com

The White Wing Messenger (bi-W) Church of God of Prophecy, Virginia E. Chatham, P.O. Box 2970, Cleveland, TN 37320-2970 Tel. (423)559-5129/24 Fax (423)559-5128
Website: www.cogop.org

Window on the World (3-Y) The Evangelical Congregational Church, Rev. Randy Sizemore, 100 W. Park Ave, Myerstown, PA 17067 Tel. (717)866-7584 Fax (717)866-7383
Email: ecglobal@eccenter.com
Website: www.eccenter.com

Wineskins (bi-M) Churches of Christ, Mike Cope and Rubel Shelly, Box 41028, Nashville, TN 37024-1028 Tel. (615)373-5004 Fax (615)373-5006
Email: wineskinsmagazine@msn.com
Website: www.wineskins.org

Wisconsin Lutheran Quarterly (Q) Wisconsin Evangelical Lutheran Synod, John F. Brug, 11831 N. Seminary Dr., Mequon, WI 53092 Tel. (262)242-8139 Fax (262)242-8110
Email: brugj@wls.wels.net
Website: www.wls.wels.net

With: The Magazine for Radical Christian Youth (bi-M) Mennonite Church USA, Carol Duerksen, P.O. Box 347, 722 Main Street, Newton, KS 67114 Tel. (620)367-8432 Fax (620)367-8218

Email: carold@mennoniteusa.org
Website: withonline.org

The Witness (10-Y) Nondenominational, Julie A. Wortman, 7000 Michigan Ave., Detroit, MI 48210 Tel. (313)841-1967 Fax (313)841-1956
Email: office@thewitness.org
Website: www.thewitness.org

Woman to Woman (M) General Association of General Baptists, Carol Lawrence, 100 Stinson Dr., Poplar Bluff, MO 63901 Tel. (573)785-7746 Fax (573)785-0564
Email: wmofc@generalbaptist.com
Website: www.generalbaptist.com

The Woman's Pulpit (Q) Nondenominational, LaVonne Althouse, 14 St. Mark Avenue, Lititz, PA 17543 Tel. (717)626-0463
Email: revla32@.dejazzd.com
Website: www.womenministers.org

Women's Missionary Magazine (9-Y) African Methodist Episcopal Church, Dr. Bettye J. Allen, 17129 Bennett Dr, South Holland, IL 60473 Tel. (708)339-5997 Fax (708)339-5987
Email: bettye1901@aol.com

The Word (10-Y) The Antiochian Orthodox Christian Archdiocese of North America, V. Rev. John Abdalah, 635 Miranda Dr., Pittsburgh, PA 15241-2041 Tel. (412)681-2988 Fax (412)831-5554
Email: frjpa@aol.com
Website: www.antiochian.org

The Worker (Q) Progressive National Baptist Convention, Inc., Mattie A Robinson, 601 50th St. NE, Washington, DC 20019 Tel. (202)398-5343 Fax (202)398-4998
Email: info@pnbc.org
Website: www.pnbc.org

World Parish: International Organ of the World Methodist Council (I, M) Interdenominational Methodist (Christian World Communion of Methodist and WMC-Wesleyan Related Churches), Dr. George Freeman, P.O. Box 518, Lake Junaluska, NC 28745 Tel. (828)456-9432 Fax (828)456-9433
Email: georgefreeman@charter.net
Website: www.worldmethodistcouncil.org

Worldorama (M) Pentecostal Holiness Church, International, Donald Duncan, P.O. Box 12609, Oklahoma City, OK 73157 Tel. (405)787-7110 Fax (405)787-7729
Email: donald@iphc.org

Worship (bi-M) The Catholic Church, R. Kevin Seasoltz, St. John's Abbey, Collegeville, MN 56321 Tel. (320)363-3883 Fax (320)363-3145
Email: kseasoltz@csbsju.edu
Website: www.sja.org/worship

Worship Arts (bi-M) The United Methodist Church, David A Wiltse, P.O. Box 6247, Grand Rapids, MI 49516-6247 Tel. (616)459-4503 Fax (616)459-0191
Email: graphics@iserv.net
Website: www.fummwa.org

Woman's Touch (bi-M) Assemblies of God, Arlene Allen, 1445 N. Boonville Ave., Springfield, MO 65802-1894 Tel. (417)862-2781 Fax (417)862-0503
Email: womanstouch@ag.org
Website: www.womanstouch.ag.org

Youth Ministry Accent (Q) Seventh-day Adventist Church, Vacant, 12501 Old Columbia Pike, Silver Spring, MD 20904-6600 Tel. (301)680-6180 Fax (301)680-6155
Email: 74532.1426@compuserve.com

YPD Newsletter (3-M) African Methodist Episcopal Church, Adrienne A. Morris and Andrea Smith, 327 Washington Avenue, Wyoming, OH 45215 Tel. (513)821-1481 Fax (513)821-3073
Email: amconndri@cs.com
Website: ameypd.org

Zion's Advocate (M) Church of Christ, Gordon McCann, P.O. Box 472, Independence, MO 64051-0472 Tel. (816)796-6255

11. Religious Periodicals in Canada

The religious periodicals below constitute a basic core of important journals and periodicals circulated in Canada. The list does not include all publications prepared by religious bodies, and not all the publications listed here are necessarily the official publication of a particular church. Each entry gives: the title of the periodical, frequency of publication, religious affiliation, editor's name, address, telephone and fax number and email and website addresses when available. The frequency of publication, which appears in parenthesis after the name of the publication, is represented by a "D" for daily, "W" for weekly; "M" for monthly; "Q" for quarterly, "Y" for yearly, "I" for Internet.

The Anglican (10-Y) The Anglican Church of Canada, Stuart Mann, 135 Adelaide St. E., Toronto, ON M5C 1L8 Tel. (416)363-6021 Fax (416)363-7678
Email: smann@toronto.anglican.ca
Website: www.toronto.anglican.ca

Anglican Journal (10-Y) The Anglican Church of Canada, Kristin Jenkins, 80 Hayden St., Toronto, ON M4Y 3G2 Tel. (416)924-9199 x. 306 Fax (416)921-4452
Email: editor@national.anglican.ca
Website: www.anglicanjournal.com

Armenian Evangelical Church Newsletter (bi-M) Armenian Evangelical Church, Rev. Samuel Albarian, 2600 14th Avenue, Markham, ON L3R 3X1 Tel. (905)305-8144 Fax (905)305-8125
Email: aectoronto@yahoo.com

Aujourd'hui Credo (10-Y) The United Church of Canada, David Fines, 1332 Victoria, Longueuil, QC J4V 1L8 Tel. (450)446-7733 Fax (450)466-2664
Email: davidfines@egliseunce.org
Website: www.united-church/credo

The Baptist Horizon (M) Canadian Convention of Southern Baptists, Nancy McGough, 100 Convention Way, Cochrane, AB T4C 2G2 Tel. (403)932-5688 Fax (403)932-4937
Email: office@ccsb.ca

B.C. Fellowship Baptist (Q) The Fellowship of Evangelical Baptist Churches in BC and Yukon, David Horita, #201-26620-56th Ave, Langley, BC V4W 3X5 Tel. (604)607-1192 Fax (604)607-1193
Email: fellowship@shaw.ca
Website: www.bcfellowship.ca

Blackboard Bulletin (10-Y) Old Order Amish Church, Old Order Amish Church, Rt. 4, Aylmer, ON N5H 2R3

Die Botschaft (W) Old Order Amish Church, James Weaver, Brookshire Publishing, Inc., 200 Hazel St., Lancaster, PA 17603 Tel. (717)392-1321 Fax (717)392-2078

The Budget (W) Old Order Amish Church, Fannie Erb-Miller, P.O. Box 249, Sugarcreek, OH 44681 Tel. (330)852-4634 Fax (330)852-4421
Email: budgetnews@aol.com

Cahiers de Spiritualite Ignatienne (3-Y) The Roman Catholic Church in Canada, Etienne Pouliot, 965 Avenue Loius-Fréchette, Québec, QC G1S 4V1 Tel. (418)653-6353 Fax (418)653-1208
Email: cahiersi@centremanrese.org
Website: www.centremanrese.org

Canada Lutheran (8-Y) Evangelical Lutheran Church in Canada, Lucia Carruthers, Editor; Trina Gallop, Editorial Director; Catherine Crivici, Graphic Designer, 302-393 Portage Avenue, Winnipeg, MB R3B 3H6 Tel. (204)984-9150 Toll Free: (888) 786-6707 Fax (204)984-9185
Email: canaluth@elcic.ca
Website: www.elcic.ca/clweb

Canada Update (Q) The Church of God of Prophecy - Eastern Canada Administrative Office, Editor, 5145 Tomken Road, Mississaugh, ON L4W 1P1 Tel. (905)625-1278 Fax (905)625-1316
Website: www.coqop.ca

Canadian Adventist Messenger (12-Y) Seventh-day Adventist Church in Canada, Carolyn Willis, 1148 King St. E., Oshawa, ON L1H 1H8 Tel. (905)433-0011 Fax (905)433-0982
Email: cwillis@sdacc.org
Website: www.sdacc.org

The Canadian Baptist (10-Y) Baptist Convention of Ontario and Quebec, Larry Matthews, 195 The West Mall, Ste.414, Etobicoke, ON M9C 5K1 Tel. (416)622-8600 Fax (416)622-0780
Email: thecb@baptist.ca

The Canadian Friend (bi-M) Canadian Yearly Meeting of the Religious Society of Friends, Anne Marie Zilliacus, 218 Third Ave., Ottawa, ON K1S 2K3 Tel. (613)567-8628 Fax (613)567-1078
Email: zilli@cyberus.ca

The Canadian Lutheran (9-Y) Lutheran Church—Canada, Ida Backman, Interim Editor, 3074 Portage Ave., Winnipeg, MB R3K 0Y2 Tel. (204)895-3433 ext.24 Fax (204)897-4319
Website: www.lutheranchurch.ca

Canadian Mennonite (bi-W) Mennonite Church Canada, Dick Benner, Suite C5, 490 Dutton

Dr., Waterloo, ON N2L 6H7 Tel. (519)884-3810 Fax (519)884-3331
Email: editor@canadianmennonite.org
Website: www.canadianmennonite.org

Canadian Orthodox Messenger (Q) Orthodox Church in America (Canada Section), Nun Sophia (Zion), P.O. Box 179, Spencerville, ON K0E 1X0 Tel. (613)925-0645 Fax (613)925-1521
Email: sophia@ripnet.com

The Catalyst (6-Y) Nondenominational, Karen Diepeveen, Citizens for Public Justice, 501-309 Cooper St., Ottawa, ON K2P 0G5 Tel. (613)232-0275 Fax (613)232-1275
Email: karen@cpj.ca
Website: www.cpj.ca

The Catholic Register (W) The Roman Catholic Church in Canada, Joseph Sinasac, 1155 Yonge St., Ste. 401, Toronto, ON M4Y 1W2 Tel. (416)934-3410 Fax (416)934-3409
Email: editor@catholicregister.org
Website: www.catholicregister.org

The Catholic Times (Montreal) (10-Y) The Roman Catholic Church in Canada, Eric Durocher, 2005 St. Marc St., Montreal, QC H3H 2G8 Tel. (514)937-2301 Fax (514)937-3051

Channels (3-Y) Presbyterian Church in Canada, Calvin Brown Managing Editor, Dal Schindell, Renewal Fellowship, 3819 Bloor St W, Etobicoke, ON M9B 1K7 Tel. (416)233-6581 Fax (416)233-1743
Email: cbbrown@rogers.com
Website: www.presbycan.ca/rfpc

Chinese Herald (bi-M) Canadian Conference of Mennonite Brethren Churches, Joseph Kwan, 8143 Burnlake Drive, Burnaby, BC V5A 3R6 Tel. (604)421-4100 Fax (604)421-4100
Email: chineseherald@mbconf.ca

Church of God Beacon (Q) Church of God (Cleveland, Tenn.), Andrew Binda, P.O. Box 2036, Brampton Commercial Service Center, Brampton, ON L6T 3T0 Tel. (905)793-2213 Fax (905)793-9173
Email: afinda@cogontario.com

Clarion-The Canadian Reformed Magazine (bi-W) Canadian and American Reformed Churches, J. Visscher, One Beghin Ave., Winnipeg, MB R2J 3X5 Tel. (204)663-9000 Fax (204)663-9202
Email: clarionadmin@premierpublishing.ca
Website: premierpublishing.ca

CLBI-Cross Roads (6-Y) Lutheran, Dean J. Rostand, 4837-52A St., Camrose, AB T4V 1W5 Tel. (780)672-4454 Fax (780)672-4455
Email: communications@clbi.edu
Website: www.clbi.edu

The Communicator (3-Y) The Roman Catholic Church in Canada, Editor, Box 2400, London,

ON N6A 4G3 Tel. (519)439-7514 Fax (519)439-0207
Email: info@arccc.ca
Website: arccc.ca/news.htm

Connexions (4-Y) Interdenominational, Ulli Diemer, 489 College St., Ste. 305, Toronto, ON M6G 1A5 Tel. (416)964-1511
Website: www.connexions.org

The Covenant Messenger (Q) The Evangelical Covenant Church of Canada, Doug Wildman, Box 93, Norquay, SK S0A 2V0 Tel. (204)269-3437 Fax (204)269-3584
Email: messengr@escape.ca
Website: www.canadacovenantchurch.org

Crux (Q) Nondenominational, Donald Lewis, Regent College, 5800 University Blvd., Vancouver, BC V6T 2E4 Tel. (604)224-3245 Fax (604)224-3097
Email: crux@regent.college.edu
Website: www.cruxonline.net

Diakonia-A Magazine of Office-Bearers (4-Y) Canadian and American Reformed Churches, J. Visscher, Brookside Publishing, 3911 Mt. Lehman Rd., Abbotsford, BC V4X 2M9 Tel. (604)856-4127 Fax (604)856-6724

The Diary (M) Old Order Amish Church, Don Carpenter, P.O. Box 98, Gordonville, PA 17529 Tel. (717)529-3938 Fax (717)529-3292

Ecumenism-Oecumenisme (Q) Interdenominational, Dr. Stuart E. Brown, 1819 Rene-Levesque Blvd West # 003, Montreal, QC H3H 2PH Tel. (514)937-9176 Fax (514)937-4986
Email: info@oikoumene.ca/mpanz@oikoumene.ca
Website: www.oikoumene.ca

The Edge (Christian Youth Magazine) (10-Y) The Salvation Army in Canada, John McAlister, 2 Overlea Blvd., Toronto, ON M4H 1P4 Tel. (416)422-6116 Fax (416)422-6120
Email: edge@can.salvationarmy.org
Website: www.salvationarmy.ca

Eesti Kirik (Q) The Estonian Evangelical Lutheran Church Abroad, Rev. U. Petersoo, 383 Jarvis St., Toronto, ON M5B 2C7 Tel. (416)925-5465 Fax (416)925-5688

EMMC Recorder (M) Evangelical Mennonite Mission Conference, Lil Goertzen, Box 52059 Niakwa P.O., Winnipeg, MB R2M 5P9 Tel. (204)253-7929 Fax (204)256-7384
Email: info@emmc.ca
Website: www.emmc.ca

En Avant! (12-Y) The Salvation Army in Canada, Marie-Michele Roy, 1655 Rue Richardson, Montreal, PQ H3K 3J7 Tel. (514)288-2848 x 2236 Fax (514)288-4657
Email: enavant@can.salvationarmy.org
Website: www.Salvationarmy.org

Esprit (Q) Evangelical Lutheran Church in Canada (Evangelical Lutheran Women), Catherine Pate, 302-393 Portage Avenue, Winnipeg, MB R3B 3H6 Tel. (204)984-9160 Fax (204)984-9162
Email: esprit@elcic.ca
Website: www.elw.ca

Evangel-The Good News of Jesus Christ (4-Y) Canadian and American Reformed Churches, D. Moes, 21804 52nd Ave., Langley, BC V2Y 1L3 Tel. (604)576-2124 Fax (604)576-2101
Email: canrc@uniserve.com or jvisscher@telus.ca

Evangel Voice-Voce Evangelica (Q) Canadian Assemblies of God, Rev. Daniel Costanza, 140 Woodbridge Ave., Suite 400, Woodbridge, ON L4L 4K9 Tel. (905)850-1578 Fax (905)850-1578
Email: bethel@idirect.com
Website: www.the-ipcc.org

The Evangelical Baptist (4-Y) The Fellowship of Evangelical Baptist Churches in Canada, Dr. John Kaiser, P O Box 457, Guelph, ON N1H 6K9 Tel. (519)821-4830 Fax (519)821-9829
Email: president@fellowship.ca
Website: www.fellowship.ca

Faith & Friends (M) The Salvation Army in Canada, Geoff Moulton, 2 Overlea Blvd., Toronto, ON M4H 1P4 Tel. (416)422-6110 Fax (416)422-6120
Website: faithandfriends.sallynet.org

Faith Today (bi-M) The Evangelical Fellowship of Canada (a cooperative organization of more than 40 Protestant denominations), Gail Reid, M.I.P. Box 3745, Markham, ON L3R 0Y4 Tel. (905)479-5885 Fax (905)479-4742
Email: ft@efc-canada.com
Website: www.faithtoday.ca

Family Life (11-Y) Old Order Amish Church, Joseph Stoll and David Luthy, Old Order Amish Church, Rt. 4, Aylmer, ON N5H 2R3

Family Life Network Newsline (3-Y) Canadian Conference of Mennonite Brethren Churches, Dorothy Siebert, 225 Riverton Ave., Winnipeg, MB R2L 0N1 Tel. (204)667-9576 Fax (204)669-6079
Email: info@fln.ca
Website: www.fln.ca

Fellowship Magazine (4-Y) The United Church of Canada, Rev. Diane Walker, Box 237, Barrie, ON L4M 4T2 Tel. (705)737-0114 or (800)678-2607 Fax (705)737-1086
Email: felmag@csolve.net
Website: www.fellowshipmagazine.org

Foi & Vie (12-Y) The Salvation Army in Canada, Marie-Michele Roy, 1655 Rue Richardson, Montreal, PQ H3K 3J7 Tel. (514)288-2848 ext. 2236 Fax (514)288-4657

Email: Edouard_Hoyer@can.salvationarmy.org
Website: www.SalvationArmy.ca

Glad Tidings (6-Y) Presbyterian Church in Canada, Colleen Wood, Women's Missionary Society, 50 Wynford Dr., Toronto, ON M3C 1J7 Tel. (800)619-7301/(416)441-1111 Fax (416)441-2825
Email: cwood@presbyterian.ca
Website: http://www.wmspcc.ca/gladtidingsA/gladtidings.html

Good Tidings (10-Y) The Pentecostal Assemblies of Newfoundland and Labrador, H. Paul Foster, 57 Thorburn Rd., P.O. Box 8895, Sta. A, St. John's, NL A1B 3T2 Tel. (709)753-6314 Fax (709)753-4945
Email: paon@paon.nf.ca

The Gospel Contact (4-Y) Church of God (Anderson, InD), Editorial Committee, 4717 56th St., Camrose, AB T4V 2C4 Tel. (780)672-0772 Fax (780)672-6888
Email: wcdncog@cable-lynx.net
Website: www.chog.ca

Gospel Herald (M) Churches of Christ in Canada, Wayne Turner and Max E. Craddock, 4904 King St., Beamsville, ON L0R 1B6 Tel. (905)563-7503 Fax (905)563-7503
Email: editorial@gospelherald.org
Website: www.gospelherald.org

The Gospel Standard (M) Nondenominational, Perry F. Rockwood, Box 1660, Halifax, NS B3J 3A1 Tel. (902)423-5540 Fax (902)423-0820

Gospel Tidings (M) Independent Holiness Church, Marilyn E. Votary, 1564 John Quinn Rd., Greely, ON K4P 1J9 Tel. (613)821-2237 Fax (613)821-4663
Email: marilynv@hotmail.com
Website: www.holiness.ca

The Grape Vine (12-Y) Reformed Episcopal Church in Canada, Ingrid Andreller, 626 Blanshard Street, Victoria, BC V8W 3G6 Tel. (250)383-8915 Fax (250)383-8916
Email: office@churchofourlord.org
Website: www.churchofourlord.org

Hallelujah! (bi-M) The Bible Holiness Movement, Wesley H. Wakefield, Box 223, Postal Stn. A, Vancouver, BC V6C 2M3 Tel. (250) 492-3376
Website: http://www.bible-holiness-movement.com/magazine.html

Herold der Wahrheit (M) Old Order Amish Church, Cephas Kauffman, 1827 110th St., Kalona, IA 52247

Horizons (bi-M) The Salvation Army in Canada, 2 Overlea Blvd., Toronto, ON M4H 1P4 Tel. (416)425-6118 Fax (416)422-6120

Insight*Insound*In Touch (6-Y. (Insight); 6-Y. (In Sound); 4-Y. (In Touch)) Interdenominational. Insight (large print newspaper); In Sound (audio magazine); In Touch (braille newspaper), Rebekah Chevalier, Graham Down, John Milton Society for the Blind in Canada, 40 St. Clair Ave. E., Ste. 202, Toronto, ON M4T 1M9 Tel. (416)960-3953 Fax (416)960-3570 Email: admin@jmsblind.ca Website: www.jmsblind.ca

Intercom (Q) The Fellowship of Evangelical Baptist Churches in Canada, Terry D. Cuthbert, 679 Southgate Dr., Suite 100, Guelph, ON N1G 4S2 Tel. (519)821-4830 Fax (519)821-9829 Email: president@fellowship.ca Website: www.fellowship.ca

ISKRA (20-Y) Union of Spiritual Communities of Christ (Orthodox Doukhobors in Canada), Dmitri E. (Jim) Popoff, Box 760, Grand Forks, BC V0H 1H0 Tel. (604)442-8252 Fax (604)442-3433 Email: iskra@sunshinecable.com

Istocnik (4-Y) Serbian Orthodox Church in the U.S.A. and Canada, Diocese of Canada, Very Rev. Ljubomir Rajic, 7470 McNiven Rd., RR 3, Campbellville, ON L0P 1B0 Tel. (905)878-0043 Fax (905)878-1909 Email: vladika@istocnik.com Website: www.istocnik.com

Leader (Q) Mennonite Church USA and Mennonite Church Canada, Sr Editor: Richard A. Kaufman, Editor: Byron Rempel-Burkholder, 600 Shaftesbury Blvd., Winnipeg, MB R3P 0M4 Tel. (204)885-2565 x 179 Fax (204)831-2454 Email: byronrb@mph.org Website: www.leaderonline.org

Leader: Equipping the Missional Congregation (Q) Mennonite Church, Byron Rempel-Burkholder, Faith & Life Resources/Mennonite Publishing Network, 600 Shaftesbury Blvd, Winnipeg, Manitoba R3P 0M4 Tel. (204) 888-6781 ext. 179 Fax (204) 831-5675 Email: byronrb@mph.org

Le Lien (11-Y) Canadian Conference of Mennonite Brethren Churches, Jean Bieri, 4824, ch. de la Cote-des-Neiges, Suite 301, Montreal, QC H3V 1G4 Tel. (514)331-0878 Fax (514)331-0879 Email: info@etem.ca Website: www.etem.ca

Vivre et Celebrer (4-Y) The Roman Catholic Church in Canada, Service des Editions de la CECC, Office national de liturgie, 3530 rue Adam, Montreal, QC H1W 1Y8 Tel. (514)522-4930 Fax (514)522-1557 Email: onl@cecc.ca Website: www.cccb.ca

Mandate (4-Y) The United Church of Canada, Rebekah Chevalier, 3250 Bloor St W., Ste. 300, Toronto, ON M8X 2Y4 Tel. (416)231-5931 Fax (416)231-3103

Email: rchevali@united-church.ca Website: www.united-church.ca/sales/magazines/mandate

The Mantle (M) Independent Assemblies of God International (Canada), Philip Rassmussen, P.O. Box 2130, Laguna Hills, CA 92654-9901 Tel. (514)522-4930 Fax (514)522-1557

Mennonite Brethren Herald (M) Canadian Conference of Mennonite Brethren Churches, Laura Kalmar, 1310 Taylor Ave., Winnipeg, MB R3M 3Z6 Tel. (204)654-5760 Fax (204)654-1865 Email: mbherald@mbconf.ca Website: www.mbherald.com

Mennonite Historian (Q) Canadian Conference of Mennonite Brethren Churches, Mennonite Church Canada, Abe Dueck and Alf Redekopp, Ctr. for Menn. Brethren Studies, 169 Riverton Ave., Winnipeg, MB R2L 2E5 Tel. (204)669-6575 Fax (204)654-1865 Email: adueck@mbconf.ca Website: mbconf.ca/mbstudies

Die Mennonitische Post (bi-M) Mennonite Central Committee Canada, Kennert Giesbrecht, 383 Main St., Steinbach, MB R5G 1S1 Tel. (204)326-6790 Fax (204)326-6302 Email: mennpost@mts.net Website: www.mennonitischepost.com

Mennonitische Rundschau (M) Canadian Conference of Mennonite Brethren Churches, Brigitte Penner; Marianne Dulder, 3-169 Riverton Ave., Winnipeg, MB R2L 2E5 Tel. (204)669-6575 Fax (204)654-1865 Email: MR@mbconf.ca Website: www.mbconf.ca

The Messenger (bi-M) Church of God (in Eastern Canada), Rosemary Krashel, 20625 Winston Churchill Blvd., Alton, ON LON 1AO Tel. (514)938-9994 Email: rosemarykrushel@sympatico.ca

The Messenger (Q) The Reformed Episcopal Church of Canada, Rt. Rev. Michael Fedechko, 320 Armstrong St., New Liskeard, ON P0J 1P0 Tel. (705)647-4565 Fax (705)647-4565 Email: fed@nt.net Website: www.forministry.com/REC-Canada

The Messenger (22-Y) The Evangelical Mennonite Conference, Terry M. Smith, Editor; Rebecca Roman, Assistant Editor, 440 Main Street, Steinbach, MB R5G 1Z5 Tel. (204)326-6401 Fax (204)326-1613 Email: messenger@emconf.ca/ tsmith@emconf.ca Website: www.emconf.ca/Messenger

MinistryMatters (3-Y) The Anglican Church of Canada, Vianney (Sam) Carriere, 80 Hayden St., Toronto, ON M4Y 3G2 Tel. (905)833-6200 Fax (905)833-2116

342

Email: matters@national.anglican.ca
Website: www.ministrymatters.ca

Missions Today (bi-M) Roman Catholic, Paul Coady, Society for the Propagation of the Faith, 3329 Danforth Ave., Scarborough, ON M1L 4T3 Tel. (416)699-7077 or 800-897-8865 Fax (416)699-9019
Email: missions@eda.net
Website: www.eda.net/~missions

Mosaic (Q) Canadian Baptist Ministries, Jennifer Lau, 7185 Millcreek Dr., Mississauga, ON L5N 5R4 Tel. (905)821-3533 Fax (905)826-3441
Email: mosaic@cbmin.org
Website: www.cbmin.org

The New Freeman (W) The Roman Catholic Church in Canada, Margie Traftan, One Bayard Dr., Saint John, NB E2L 3L5 Tel. (506)653-6806 Fax (506)653-6818
Email: tnf@nbnet.nb.ca

News of Québec (3-Y) Christian Brethren (also known as Plymouth Brethren), Richard E. Strout, P.O. Box 1054, Sherbrooke, QC J1H 5L3 Tel. (819)820-1693 Fax (819)821-9287

Orthodox Way (M) Greek Orthodox Metropolis of Toronto (Canada), Orthodox Way Committee, 86 Overlea Blvd., 4th Floor, Toronto, ON M4H 1C6 Tel. (416)429-5757 Fax (416)429-4588
Email: greekomt@on.aibn.com
Website: www.gocanada.org

Passport (3-Y) Interdenominational, Mike Benallick, Briercrest Family of Schools, 510 College Dr., Caronport, SK S0H 0S0 Tel. (306)756-3200 Fax (306)756-3366
Email: passport@briercrest.ca
Website: www.briercrest.ca

Pourastan (bi-M) Armenian Holy Apostolic Church - St. Gregory the Illuminator Armenian Cathedral of Montreal, Editor, 615 Stuart Ave., Outremont, QC H2V 3H2 Tel. (514)279-3066 Fax (514)279-8008
Email: stgreogrychurch@gmail.com
Website: www.armeniancathedral.ca

Prairie Messenger (W) The Roman Catholic Church in Canada, Peter Novecosky, O.S.B., Box 190, 11 College Drive, Muenster, SK S0K 2Y0 Tel. (306)682-1772 Fax (306)682-5285
Email: pm.editor@stpeterspress.ca
Website: www.prairiemessenger.ca

The Presbyterian Message (10-Y) Presbyterian Church in Canada, Janice Carter, 563 Tweedie Brook Rd, Kouchibouguac, NB E4X 1M2 Tel. (506)876-4379
Email: mjcarter@nb.sympatico.ca

Presbyterian Record (11-Y) The Presbyterian Church in Canada, Rev. David Harris, 50 Wynford Dr., Toronto, ON M3C 1J7 Tel. (416)441-1111 Fax (416)441-2825

Email: pcrecord@presbyterian.ca
Website: www.presbyterian.ca/record

Presence (8-Y) The Roman Catholic Church in Canada, Jean-Claude Breton, Presence Magazine Inc., 2715 chemin de la Côte Ste-Catherine, Montreal, QC H3T 1B6 Tel. (514)739-9797 Fax (514)739-1664
Email: presence@presencemag.qc.ca

The Pulse (4-Y) Evangelical Free Church of Canada, Dr. Ron Unruh, Editor-in-Chief; Tracy Morris, Managing Editor, Box 850, LCDI, Langley, BC V8A 8S6 Tel. (604)888-8668 Fax (604)888-3108
Email: efcc@twu.ca
Website: www.efcc.ca

Quaker Concern (3-Y) Canadian Yearly Meeting of the Religious Society of Friends, Jane Orion Smith, 60 Lowther Ave., Toronto, ON M5R 1C7 Tel. (416)920-5213 Fax (416)920-5214
Email: cfsc-office@quaker.ca
Website: www.cfsc.quaker.ca

Reformed Perspective -A Magazine for the Christian Family (M) Canadian and American Reformed Churches and United Reformed Churches in North America, Jon Dykstra, 162 Cambridge Drive, Lynden, WA 98264 Tel. (360)739-7480
Email: editor@reformedperspective.ca
Website: www.reformedperspective.ca

Relations (8-Y) The Roman Catholic Church in Canada, Jean-Marc Biron, 25 Jarry Ouest, Montreal, QC H2P 1S6 Tel. (514)387-2541 Fax (514)387-0206
Email: relations@cjf.qc.ca
Website: www.cjf.qc.ca

RESCUE (bi-M) Association of Gospel Rescue Missions, Philip Rydman, 1045 Swift, N. Kansas City, MO 64116 Tel. (816)471-8020 Fax (816)471-3718
Email: pwydman@agrm.org
Website: www.agrm.org

Revival News (Q) Interdenominational, John McGregor, Canadian Revival Fellowship, Box 584, Regina, SK S4P 3A3 Tel. (306)522-3685 Fax (306)522-3686
Email: crfellowship@accesscomm.ca
Website: www.revivalfellowship.com

Rupert's Land News (10-Y) The Anglican Church of Canada, Irvin J. Kroeker, Anglican Centre, 935 Nesbitt Bay, Winnipeg, MB R3T 1W6 Tel. (204)992-4205 Fax (204)992-4219
Email: rlnews@rupertsland.ca

St. Luke Magazine (M) Christ Catholic Church International, Donald W. Mullan, 4695 St. Lawrence Ave, Niagara Falls, ON L2E 6S8 Tel. (905)354-2329 Fax (905)354-9934
Email: dmullan1@cogeco.ca

Salvationist (M) The Salvation Army in Canada and Bermuda, Geoff Moulton, Managing Editor, 2 Overlea Blvd., Toronto, ON M4H 1P4 Tel. (416)425-2111 Fax (416)422-6120 Email: salvationist@can.salvationarmy.org Website: www.salvationist/CAN/Sarmy.ca

Scarboro Missions (7-Y) The Roman Catholic Church in Canada, Cathy Van Loon, 2685 Kingston Rd., Scarborough, ON M1M 1M4 Tel. (416)261-7135 or 800-260-4815 (In Canada) Fax (416)261-0820 Email: editor@scarboromissions.ca Website: www.scarboromissions.ca

The Shantyman (6-Y) Nondenominational, Ken Godevenos, Editor in Chief; Phil Hood, Managing Editor, 1885 Clements Rd., Unite 226, Pickering, ON L1W 3V4 Tel. (905)686-2030 Fax (905)427-0334 Email: shanty@pathcom.com Website: www.shantymen.org

Sister Triangle (Q) Churches of Christ, Marilyn Muller, P.O. 948, Dauphin, MB R7N 3J5 Tel. (204)638-9812 Fax (204)638-6231 Email: dmmuller@mb.sympatico.ca

SR- Studies in Religion-Sciences religieuses (Q) Nondenominational, Dr. Aaron Hughes, Dept. of Religious Studies, University of Calgary, 2500 University Avenue NW, Calgary, AB T2N 1N4 Tel. (403)220-7063 Email: hugesa@ucalgary.ca Website: http://www.wlupress.wlu.ca

Testimony (M) The Pentecostal Assemblies of Canada, Steve Kennedy, 2450 Milltower Ct., Mississauga, ON L5N 5Z6 Tel. (905)542-7400 Fax (905)542-7313 Email: testimony@PAOC.org

Topic (10-Y) The Anglican Church of Canada, Randy Murray, 580-401 W. Georgia St., Vancouver, BC V6B 5A1 Tel. (604)684-6306 ext. 223 Fax (604)684-7017 Email: rmurray@vancouver.anglican.ca Website: www.vancouver.anglican.ca

United Church Observer (M) The United Church of Canada, Muriel Duncan, 478 Huron St., Toronto, ON M5R 2R3 Tel. (416)960-8500 Fax (416)960-8477 Email: general@ucobserver.org Website: www.ucobserver.org

La Vie Chretienne (French) (M) Presbyterian Church in Canada, Jean Porret, PO Box 272, Suzz. Rosemont, Montreal, QC H1X 3B8 Tel. (514)737-4168

La Vie des Communautes religieuses (5-Y) The Roman Catholic Church in Canada, Religious Communities (Consortium), 251 St-Jean-Baptiste, Nicolet, QC J3T 1X9 Tel. (819)293-8736 Fax (819)293-2419 Email: viecr@sogetel.net

Vie Liturgique (6-Y) The Roman Catholic Church in Canada, Jean Grou, 4475, rue Frontenac, Montreal, QC H2H 2S2 Tel. (800)668-2547 Fax (514)278-3030 Email: vieliturgique@ustpaul.ca Website: www.novalis.ca

VIP Communique Foursquare Gospel Church of Canada, Barry Buzza, B307-2099 Lougheed Highway, Port Coquitlam, BC V3S 1A8 Tel. (604)941-8414 Fax (604)941-8415 Email: foursquare@foursquare.ca Website: www.foursquare.ca

Visnyk- The Herald (M) Ukrainian Orthodox Church of Canada, Rev. Fr. Eugene Maximiuk, 9 St. John's Ave., Winnipeg, MB R2W 1G8 Tel. (204)586-3093 x 236 Fax (204)582-5241 Email: visnyk@uocc.ca Website: www.uocc.ca

Word Alive (Q) Nondenominational, Dwayne Janke, Wycliffe Bible Translators of Canada Inc., 4316 10 St. NE, Calgary, AB T2E 6K3 Tel. (403)250-5411 Fax (403)250-2623 Email: editors_wam@wycliffe.ca Website: www.wycliffe.ca

Young Companion (11-Y) Old Order Amish Church, Joseph Stoll and Christian Stoll, Old Order Amish Church, Rt. 4, Aylmer, ON N5H 2R3

12. Church Archives and Historical Records Collections

American and Canadian history is interwoven with the social and cultural experience of religious life and thought. Most repositories of primary research materials in North America will include some documentation on religion and church communities. This directory is not intended to replace standard bibliographic guides to those resources. The intent is to give a new researcher entry to major archival holdings of religious collections and to programs of national scope. In the interest of space, no attempt has been made to list the specific contents of the archives or to include the numerous specialized research libraries of North America. The repositories listed herein are able to re-direct inquirers to significant regional and local church archives, and specialized collections such as those of religious orders, educational and charitable organizations, and personal papers.

Repositories marked with an asterisk (*) are designated by their denomination as the official archives. The reference departments at these archives will assist researchers in locating primary material of geographic or subject focus.

UNITED STATES

Adventist

Adventist World Headquarters: Office of Archives and Statistics, 12501 Old Columbia Pike, Silver Spring, MD 20904-6600, Director: Bert Haloviak, Tel. (301)680-5020, Fax (301)680-5038, Email: haloviakb@gc.adventist.org, Website: ast.gc.adventist.org

Repository of the records created at the world administrative center of the Seventh-day Adventist Church and includes the period from the 1860s to the present.

Aurora University, Aurora University, Charles B. Phillips Library, 347 S. Gladstone, Aurora, IL 60506, Volunteer Curator: David T. Arthur, Tel. (630)844-5437, Fax (630)844-3848, Email: jhuggins@aurora.edu, Website: www.aurora.edu/academics/library/index.html

Advential archival materials on the Millerite/Early Adventist movement (1830-1860); also denominational archives relating to Advent Christian Church, Life and Advent Union, and to a lesser extent, Evangelical Adventists and Age-to-Come Adventists.

Center for Adventist Research, James White Library, Andrews University, 4190 Administration Drive, Berrien Springs, MI 49104-1440, Director: Dr. Merlin D. Burt, Tel. (269)471-3209, Fax (269)471-2646, Email: car@andrews.edu, Website: www.andrews.edu/library/car

Large collection of Seventh-day Adventist material.

Ellen G. White Estate Branch Office, Loma Linda University Library, Department of Archives and Special Collections, 11072 Anderson Street, Loma Linda, CA 92350, Associate Director/Archivist: Lori Curtis, Tel. (909)558-4942, Fax (909)558-0381, Email: archives@llu.edu, whiteestate@llu.edu, Website: www.llu.edu/library/speccoll/index.page

Photographs, sound and video recordings, personal papers, and library pertaining to the Seventh-day Adventist Church.

Ellen G. White Estate, Inc., 12501 Old Columbia Pike, Silver Spring, MD 20904, Archivist: Tim Poirier, Tel. (301)680-6540, Fax (301)680-6559, Email: mail@whiteestate.org, Website: www.whiteestate.org

Records include letters and manuscripts (1840s to 1915), pamphlets and publications, and the White papers.

Assemblies of God

*Flower Pentecostal Heritage Center, 1445 Boonville Ave., Springfield, MO 65802, Director: Darrin Rodgers, Tel. (417)862-1447 ext. 4400, Fax (417)862-6203, Email: archives@ag.org, Website: www.ifphc.org

Official repository for materials related to the Assemblies of God, as well as materials related to the broader Pentecostal and charismatic movements.

Baptist

*American Baptist Historical Society, 3001 Mercer University Dr., Atlanta, GA 30341, Exec. Director: Dr. Deborah B. Van Broekhoven, Reader Services: Betsy Dunbar, Tel. (678) 547-6680, Fax (678) 547-6682, Email: abhs@crcds.edu Website: www.abhsarchives.org

Official archives of the American Baptist Churches, USA and the Baptist World Alliance. Collections also include original manuscripts of Baptist ministers, missionaries and scholars; some original church records; printed reports of national, state and association minutes for over two centuries covering numerous Baptist denominations; serials representing the Baptist worldwide press; books and pamphlets which are by, about, for and against Baptists.

American Baptist-Samuel Colgate Historical Library, See American Baptist Historical Society.

*Seventh-day Baptist Historical Society, 3120 Kennedy Rd., P.O. Box 1678, Janesville, WI 53547, Librarian-Historian: Nicholas J. Kersten, Tel. (608)752-5055, Fax (608)752-7711, Email: sdbhist@seventhdaybaptist.org, Website www.sdbhistory.org

Serves as a depository for records of Seventh-day Baptists, Sabbath and Sabbath-keeping Baptists since the mid-seventeenth century.

*Southern Baptists Historical Library & Archives, 901 Commerce St., Suite 400, Nashville, TN 37203-3630, Director and Archivist: Bill Sumners, Tel. (615)244-0344, Fax (615)782-4821, Email: bill@sbhla.org, Website: www.sbhla.org

Central depository of the Southern Baptist Convention. Materials include official records of denominational agencies; personal papers of denominational leaders; records of related Baptist organizations; and annual proceedings of national and regional bodies.

Primitive Baptist Library of Carthage Illinois, 416 Main St., Carthage, IL 62321, Director of Library: Elder Robert Webb, Tel. (217)357-3723, Fax (217)357-3723, Email: bwebb9@juno.com, Website: www.carthage.lib.il.us/community/churches/primbap/pbl.html

Collects the records of congregations and associations.

Baptist and United Church of Christ

Andover Newton Theological School, Andover Newton Theological School, Franklin Trask Library, 169 Herrick Rd., Newton Centre, MA 02459, Associate Director for Special Collections: Diana Yount, Tel. (617)964-1100 ext.252, Fax (617)467-3051, Email: dyount@ants.edu, Website: www.ants.edu/library

The collections document Baptist, Congregational and United Church history, including personal papers relating to national denominational work and foreign missions, with emphasis on New England Church history.

Brethren in Christ

*Brethren in Christ Historical Library and Archives, One College Avenue, P.O. Box 3002, Grantham, PA 17027, Director: Glen Pierce, Tel. (717)691-6048, Fax (717)691-6042, Email: archives@messiah.edu, Website: www.messiah.edu/archives

Records of general church boards and agencies, regional conferences, congregations and organizations; also includes library, manuscripts, and oral history collection.

Church of the Brethren

*Brethren Historical Library and Archives, 1451 Dundee Ave., Elgin, IL 60120, Librarian/Archivist: Kenneth M. Shaffer, Jr., Tel. (847) 742-5100 ext. 294, Fax (847)742-6103, Email: brethrenarchives@brethren.org, Website: www.brethren.org/genbd/bhla

Archival materials dating from 1800-present relating to the cultural, socio-economic, theological, genealogical, and institutional history of the Church of the Brethren.

Churches of Christ

Center for Restoration Studies, Abilene Christian University, 760 Library Court, P.O. Box 29208, Abilene, TX 79699-9208, Archivist: Dr. Carisse Berryhill, Tel. (325)674-2538, Fax (325)674-2202, Email: carisse.berryhill@acu.edu, Website: www.bible.acu.edu/crs

Archival materials connected with the Stone-Campbell Movement. The chief focus is on the Church of Christ in the twentieth century.

Emmanuel School of Religion Library, One Walker Drive, Johnson City, TN 37601-9438, Director: Thomas E. Stokes, Tel. (423)926-1186, or (423)461-1541, Fax (423)926-6198, Email: library@esr.edu, Website: library.esr.edu

Materials related to the Stone-Campbell/Restoration Movement tradition. Collection includes items from the Christian Church and Churches of Christ, the a cappella Churches of Christ, and the Christian Church (Disciples of Christ).

Churches of God General Conference

*Winebrenner Theological Seminary Library, Winebrenner Theological Seminary, 950 N. Main St., Findlay, OH 45840, Director of Library Services: Margaret Hirschy, Tel. (419)434-4260, Fax (419)434-4267, Email: library@winebrenner.edu, Website: www.winebrenner.edu/?id=85

Archival materials of the Churches of God, General Conference including local conference journals.

Disciples of Christ

Christian Theological Seminary Library, Christian Theological Seminary Library, 1000 W. 42nd St., P.O. Box 88267, Indianapolis, IN 46208, Archives Manager: Don Haymes, Tel. (317)931-2368, Fax (317)931-2363, Email: dhaymes@cts.edu, Website: www.cts.edu/Library

Archival materials dealing with the Disciples of Christ and related movements.

Disciples of Christ

*Disciples of Christ Historical Society, 1101 19th Ave. S, Nashville, TN 37212, Vice-President for Information Technology and Chief

Archivist: Sara Harwell, Tel. (615)327-1444, Fax (615)327-1445, Email: ice@discipleshistory.org Website: www.discipleshistory.org

Collects documents of the Stone-Campbell Movement.

Episcopal

*The Archives of the Episcopal Church, P.O. Box 2247, Austin, TX 78768-2247, Canonical Archivist and Director: Mark J. Duffy, C.A., Tel. (512)472-6816, Fax (512)480-0437, Email: research@episcopalarchives.org, Website: www.episcopalarchives.org

Repository for the official records of the national Church, its corporate bodies and affiliated agencies, personal papers, and some diocesan archives. Contact the Archives for reference to diocesan and parochial church records.

Evangelical and Reformed

*Evangelical and Reformed Historical Society, Lancaster Theological Seminary, 555 W. James St., Lancaster, PA 17603, Archivist: Rev. Richard R. Berg, Tel. (717)290-8734, Fax (717)394-4254, Email: erhs@lancasterseminary.edu, Website: www.erhs.info

Manuscripts and transcriptions of early German Reformed Church (U.S.) 1725-1863; Reformed Church in the United States 1863-1934, and Evangelical and Reformed Church 1934-1957 records of coetus, synods, and classes, pastoral records, and personal papers.

Evangelical Congregational Church

*Archives of the Evangelical Congregational Church, Evangelical School of Theology, Rostad Library, 121 S. College St., Myerstown, PA 17067, Archivist: Terry M. Heisey, Tel. (717)866-5775, Fax (717)866-4667, Email: theisey@evangelical.edu, Website: www.evangelical.edu

Repository of records of the administrative units of the denomination, affiliated organizations, and closed churches. Also collected are records of local congregations and materials related to the United Evangelical Church and the Evangelical Association.

Friends

*Friends Historical Library, Swarthmore College, 500 College Ave., Swarthmore, PA 19081-1399, Curator: Christopher Densmore, Tel. (610)328-8497, Fax (610)690-5728, Email: friends@swarthmore.edu, Website: www.swarthmore.edu/library/friends

Official depository for the records of the Philadelphia, Baltimore, and New York Yearly Meetings. Comprehensive collection of originals and copies of other Quaker meeting archives.

Special Collections-Quaker Collection, Haverford College, 370 Lancaster Ave., Haverford, PA 19041-1392, Manuscripts Librarian, Diana Franzusoff Peterson, Tel. (610)896-1161, Fax (610)896-1102, Email: dfpeters@haverford.edu, Website: www.haverford.edu/library/special

Repository for material relating to the Society of Friends (Quakers), especially to the segment known from 1827 to the mid-20th century as "Orthodox" in the Delaware Valley.

Interdenominational

American Bible Society Library and Archives, 1865 Broadway, New York, NY 10023-9980, Curator: Liana Lupas, Tel. (212)408-1204, Fax (212)408-1526, Email: llupas@americanbible.org, Website: www.americanbible.org/BiblicalHeritage/library.dsp

Core of collections includes founders' documents, minutes, and correspondence related to the worldwide mission of the ABS.

Billy Graham Center Archives, Wheaton College, 500 College Ave., 3rd Floor, Wheaton, IL 60187-5593, Director of Archives: Paul Erickson, Tel. (630)752-5910, Fax (630)752-5916, Email: bgcarc@wheaton.edu, Website: www.wheaton.edu/bgc/archives/archhp1.html

Graduate Theological Union Archives, 2400 Ridge Road, Berkeley, CA 94709, Archivist: Lucinda Glenn, Tel. (510)649-2507, Fax (510)649-2508, Email: lglenn@gtu.edu, Website: www.gtu.edu/library/special-collections

Holy Spirit Research Center, Oral Roberts University, LRC 5E 02, 7777 S. Lewis Ave., Tulsa, OK 74171, Director: Mark E. Roberts, Tel. (918)495-6391, Fax (918)495-6662, Email: mroberts@oru.edu, Website: www.oru.edu/university/library/holyspirit

Pentecostal and Charismatic records, with emphasis on divine healing.

National Council of Churches of Christ Archives, Presbyterian Church (U.S.A.), Presbyterian Historical Society, 425 Lombard St., Philadelphia, PA 19147-1516, Manager: Margery N. Sly, Tel. (215)627-1852, Fax (215)627-0509, Email: refdesk@history.pcusa.org, Website: www.history.pcusa.org

Schomburg Center for Research in Black Culture, 515 Malcolm X Blvd., New York, NY 10037, Manuscripts, Archives, and Rare Books Division, Curator: Diana Lachatanere, Tel. (212)491-2224 Fax (212)491-6067, Email: scmarbref@nypl.org, Website: www.schomburgcenter.org

The Burke Library at Union Theological Seminary, Columbia University, 3041 Broadway, New York, NY 10027, Archivist: Ruth Tonkiss Cameron, Tel. (212)851-5612, Fax (212) 851-5613, Email: archives@uts.columbia.edu, Website: www.columbia.edu/cu/lweb/indiv/burke

The largest theological library in the western hemisphere with extensive rare and antique holdings.

University of Chicago, University of Chicago, Regenstein Library, 1100 E 57th St., Chicago, IL 60537-1502, Bibliographer for Religion and Philosophy:Beth Bidlack, Tel. (773)702-8442, Email: bbidlack@uchicago.edu, Website: www.lib.uchicago.edu/e/su/rel

Yale Divinity School Library, 409 Prospect St., New Haven, CT 06511, Research Services Librarian: Martha Smalley, Tel. (203)432-5290, Fax (203)432-3906, Email: divinity.library@yale.edu, Website: www.library.yale.edu/div

Jewish

American Jewish Historical Society (NY Location), Center for Jewish History, 15 W. 16th St., New York, NY 10011, Director of Library and Archives: Susan Malbin, Tel. (212)294-6160, Fax (212)294-6161, Email: info@ajhs.org, Website: www.ajhs.org

Archival repositories of the Jewish people in America, including significant religious contributions to American life.

American Jewish Historical Society (MA Location), Friedman Memorial Library, 160 Herrick Rd., Newton Centre, MA 02459, Director of Library and Archives: Susan Malbin, Tel. (617)559-8880, Fax (617)559-8881, Email: info@ajhs.org, Website: www.ajhs.org

Archival repositories of the Jewish people in America, including significant religious contributions to American life.

Jacob Rader Marcus Center of the American Jewish Archives, Hebrew Union College, 3101 Clifton Ave., Cincinnati, OH 45220, Senior Archivist: Kevin Proffitt, Tel. (513)221-1875, Fax (513)221-7812, Email: aja@huc.edu, Website: www.americanjewisharchives.org

Materials documenting the Jewish experience in the Western Hemisphere with emphasis on the Reform movement. Included in the collection are congregational and organizational records, personal papers of rabbis and secular leaders, and genealogical materials.

Latter Day Saints

*Archives, Church of Jesus Christ of Latter Day Saints, 50 E. North Temple, Salt Lake City, UT 84150-3800, Director: Steven R. Sorensen, Tel. (801)240-2273, Fax (801)240-6134

Repository of official records of church departments, missions, congregations, and associated organizations. Includes personal papers of church leaders and members.

Family History Library, 35 North West Temple, Salt Lake City, UT 84150-3440, Tel. (801)240-2331, Fax (801)240-1794, Email: fhl@familysearch.org, Website: www.familysearch.org

Primarily microfilmed vital, church, probate, land, census, and military records including local church registers.

Lutheran

*Archives of the Evangelical Lutheran Church in America, 321 Bonnie Lane, Elk Grove Village, IL 60007, Chief Archivist for Management, Reference Services, and Technology: Joel Thoreson, Tel. (847)690-9410, Fax (847)690-9502, Email: archives@elca.org, Website: www.elca.org/archives

Official repository for the churchwide offices of the ELCA and its predecessors. For further information on synod and regional archives, contact the Chicago archives or check the ELCA World Wide Web site. For ELCA college and seminary archives, contact those institutions directly, or consult the ELCA Archives.

*Concordia Historical Institute, Concordia Seminary, 804 Seminary Place, St. Louis, MO 63105, Interim Director: Marvin A. Huggins, Tel. (314)505-7900, Fax (314)505-7901, Email: chi@lutheranhistory.org, Website: www.lutheranhistory.org

Official repository of The Lutheran Church-Missouri Synod. Collects synodical and congregational records, personal papers and records of Lutheran agencies.

Lutheran History Center of the West, 1712 Greentree Dr., Concord, CA, Editor: Duane A. Peterson, Tel. (925)825-2109, Email: duane428@astound.net

Mennonite

Center for Mennonite Brethren Studies, Fresno Pacific University, 1717 S. Chestnut, Fresno, CA 93702, Archivist: Kevin Enns-Rempel, Tel. (559)453-2225, Fax (559)453-2124, Email: kennsrem@fresno.edu, Website: www.fresno.edu/library/cmbs

Official repository for the General Conference of Mennonite Brethren Churches.

*Mennonite Church USA Archives-Goshen, 1700 South Main, Goshen, IN 46526, Director: Rich Preheim, Tel. (574)-523-3080, Fax (574)535-7756, Email: archives@mennoniteusa.org, Website: www.MennoniteUSA.org/History

Repository of the official organizational records of the Mennonite Church and personal papers of leaders and members.

*Mennonite Church USA Archives-North Newton, Bethel College, 300 E. 27th St., North Newton, KS 67117-0531, Archivist and Co-director of Libraries: John D. Thiesen, Tel. (316)284-5304, Fax (316)284-5843, Email: mla@bethelks.edu, Website: www.bethelks.edu/mla/index.php

An official repository for the General Conference Mennonite Church and several other organizations related to the General Conference.

Methodist

B. L. Fisher Library, Asbury Theological Seminary, 204 N. Lexington Ave., Wilmore, KY 40390, Archivist and Special Collections Librarian: Grace Yoder, Tel. (859)858-2352, Fax (859)858-2350, Email: grace_yoder@asburyseminary.edu, Website: www.asbury seminary.edu

Documents the Holiness Movement and evangelical currents in the United Methodist Church. Holdings include records of related associations, camp meetings, personal papers, and periodicals.

Center for Evangelical United Brethren Heritage, United Theological Seminary, 4501 Denlinger Road, Dayton, OH 45426; Assistant Director: Sarah D. Brooks Blair Ph.D., Tel. 937.529.2201 ext. 3400, Fax (866) 841-6265, Email: sblair@united.edu, Website: www.united.edu/eubcenter

Documents predecessor and cognate church bodies of the United Methodist Church including the Evangelical Association, United Brethren in Christ, United Evangelical, Evangelical, Evangelical United Brethren, Evangelical Congregational, and Evangelical of North America.

*General Commission on Archives and History, The United Methodist Church, P.O. Box 127, Madison, NJ 07940, Archivist/Records Administrator: L. Dale Patterson, Tel. (973) 408-3189, Fax (973)408-3909, Email: research@gcah.org, Website: www.gcah.org

Collects administrative and episcopal records, and personal papers of missionaries and leaders. Holds limited genealogical information on ordained ministers. Will direct researchers to local and regional collections of congregational records and information on United Methodism and its predecessors.

*Heritage Hall at Livingstone College, 701 W. Monroe St., Salisbury, NC 28144, Tel. (704) 216-6094, Fax (704)216-6246, Email: hfelton@livingstone.edu, Website: www.living stone.edu

Records of the African Methodist Episcopal Zion Church.

*Office of the Historiographer of the African Methodist Episcopal Church, Department of Research & Scholarship, 500 8th Avenue South, Nashville, Tennessee 37203 Historiographer/Executive Director: Dr. Dennis C. Dickerson, (615)248-0905, Fax (413)597-3673, Email: WhhButller@cs.com

General and annual conference minutes; reports of various departments such as missions and publications; and congregational histories and other local materials. The materials are housed in the office of the historiographer and other designated locations.

Moravian

Moravian Archives-Northern Province, 41 W. Locust St., Bethlehem, PA 18018-2757, Archivist: Dr. Paul Peucker, Tel. (610)866-3255, Fax (610)866-9210, Email: info@moravian churcharchives.org, Website: www.moravian churcharchives.org

Records of the Northern Province of the Moravian Church in America, including affiliated provinces in the Eastern West Indies, Nicaragua, Honduras, Labrador, and Alaska.

Moravian Archives-Southern Province, 457 S. Church St., Winston-Salem, NC 27101, Archivist: C. Daniel Crews, Tel. (336)722-1742, Fax (336)725-4514, Email: moravian archives@mcsp.org, Website: www.moravian archives.org

Repository of the records of the Moravian Church, Southern Province, its congregations, and its members.

Nazarene

*Nazarene Archives, Church of the Nazarene, 17001 Prairie Star Parkway, Lenexa, KS 66220, Archives Manager: Stan Ingersol, Tel. (913)577-0641, Fax (913)577-0848, Email: singersol@nazarene.org, Website: www.nazarene.org/archives

Collections are international in scope, including general and district materials, leaders, agencies, study commissions, congregations, church universities and seminaries world-wide, medical work, and social ministries.

Pentecostal

Center for the Study of Oneness Pentecostalism, 700 Howdershell Road, Florissant, MO 63031, Chair, Historical Committee: J. L. Hall, Tel. (314)838-8858 x2107, Fax (314)838-8848, Email: rjohnston@upci.org, Website: www.upci.org

Collects a variety of Pentecostal archives, primarily the United Pentecostal (Oneness) Branch.

David du Plessis Archives, David Allan Hubbard Library, Fuller Theological Seminary, 135 North Oakland Ave., Pasadena, CA 91182, Archivist: Nancy Gower, Tel. (626)584-5311, Fax (626)584-5613, Email: archive@fuller.edu, Website: www.fuller.edu/library

Collects material related to the Pentecostal and Charismatic movements; also includes material related to Charles Fuller and the Old Fashioned Revival Hour broadcast, Fuller Theological Seminary, and neo-evangelicalism.

*Hal Bernard Dixon Jr. Pentecostal Research Center, 260 11th St. NE, Cleveland, TN 37311, Director: David G. Roebuck, Tel. (423)614-8576, Fax (423)614-8555, Email: dixon_research@leeuniversity.edu, Website: www.cogheritage.org

Official repository of the Church of God (Cleveland, TN). Also collects other Pentecostal and Charismatic materials.

*International Pentecostal Holiness Church Archives and Research Center, P.O. Box 12609, Oklahoma City, OK 73157, Director: Harold D. Hunter, Tel. (405)787-7110 ext. 3132, Fax (405)789-3957, Email: archives@iphc.org, Website: www.pctii.org/arc/archives.html

Official repository for records and publications produced by the international headquarters, conferences, and influential leaders.

Polish National Catholic

*Polish National Catholic Church Commission on History and Archives, 1031 Cedar Ave., Scranton, PA 18505, Chair: Joseph Wieczerzak, Tel. (717)343-0100

Documents pertaining to the Church's national office, parishes, Prime Bishop, leaders, and organizations.

Presbyterian

*Historical Foundation of the Cumberland Presbyterian Church and the Cumberland Presbyterian Church in America, 8207 Traditional Place, Cordova, Tennessee 38016, Director and Archivist: Susan Knight Gore, Tel. (901)276-8602, Fax (901)272-3913, Email: archives@cumberland.org, Website: www.cumberland.org/hfcpc

*Presbyterian Church in America Historical Center, 12330 Conway Rd., St. Louis, MO 63141, Director: Wayne Sparkman, Tel. (314)469-9077, Fax (314)469-9077, Email: wsparkman@pcanet.org, Website: www.pca history.org

Center serves as the official archive of the Presbyterian Church in America. The Center also holds the records of five other Presbytrerian denominations and the manuscript collections of over one hundred individuals connected with these church bodies.

*Presbyterian Historical Society Headquarters, 425 Lombard St., Philadelphia, PA 19147-1516, Deputy Director: Margery N. Sly, Tel. (215)627-1852, Fax (215)627-0509, Email: refdesk@ history.pcusa.org, Website: www.history. pcusa.org

Collects the official records of the Church's national offices and agencies, synods, presbyteries, and some congregations. The Society also houses records of the Church's predecessor denominations, personal papers of prominent Presbyterians, and records of ecumenical organizations. In addition, the Southern Regional Office in Montreat, NC holds local and regional records for the fourteen southern states.

Presbyterian Historical Society Southern Regional Office. See Presbyterian Historical Society Headquarters

Princeton Theological Seminary Libraries, Library Place and Mercer Street, P.O. Box 111, Princeton, NJ 08542-0803, Director of Special Collections: Robert Benedetto, Tel. (609)497-7953, Fax (609)497-1826, Email: special. collections@ptsem.edu, Website: www.library. ptsem.edu/collections

The strengths of the collection are its documentation of the history of the Seminary; American Presbyterianism; English and American Puritanism; Presbyterian missions; hymnology; works by and about Reformed theologians Karl Barth and Abraham Kuyper; and the history of Presbyterians in Korea.

Reformed

*Heritage Hall, Calvin College, 1855 Knollcrest Circle SE, Grand Rapids, MI 49546, Curator of Archives: Richard H. Harms, Tel. (616)957-6313, Fax (616)957-6470, Email: crcarchives@ calvin.edu, Website: www.calvin.edu/hh

Repository of the official records of the Christian Reformed Church in North America, including classes, congregations, and denominational agencies and committees.

Reformed

*Reformed Church Archives, 21 Seminary Place, New Brunswick, NJ 08901-1159, Archivist: Russell Gasero, Tel. (732)246-1779, Fax (732) 249-5412, Email: rgasero@rca.org, Website: www.rca.org/Page.aspx?pid=230

Official repository for denominational records including congregations, classes, synods, missions, and national offices.

Catholic Church

American Catholic History Research Center and University Archives, Catholic University of America, 101 Aquinas Hall, Washington, DC 20064, Archivist: Timothy Meagher, Tel. (202) 319-5065, Fax (202)319-6554, Email: meagher@cua.edu, Website: libraries.cua. edu/achrcua

Department of Special Collections and Archives, John P. Raynor, S.J. Library, Marquette University, P.O. Box 3141, Milwaukee, WI 53201-3141, Department Head and Archivist: Matt Blessing, Tel. (414)288-7256, Fax (414)288-6709, Email: matt.blessing@marquette.edu, Website: www.marquette.edu/ library/collections/ archives

Collection strengths are in the areas of Catholic social action, American missions and missionaries, and other work with Native Americans and African Americans.

United States Catholic Historical Society, 201 Seminary Ave., Yonkers, NY 10704, Tel. (914)337-8381, Fax (914)337-6379, Website: www.uschs.com

University of Notre Dame Archives, 607 Hesburgh Library, Notre Dame, IN 46556, Archivist and Curator of Manuscripts: William Kevin Cawley, Tel. (574)631-6448, Fax (574)631-7980, Email: archives@nd.edu, Website: www.archives.nd.edu
Papers of bishops and prominent Catholics and records of Catholic organizations. Includes parish histories, but few parish records.

Salvation Army
*Salvation Army Archives and Research Center, 615 Slaters Lane, Alexandria, VA 22313, Archivist: Susan Mitchem, Tel. (703)684-5500, Email archives@usn.salvationarmy.org, Website: www.salvationarmy.org
Holds the documents of Salvation Army history, personalities, and events in the United States from 1880.

Swedenborgian
*Swedenborg Library, Bryn Athyn College of the New Church, 2925 College Drive, P.O. Box 740, Bryn Athyn, PA 19009-0740, Director: Carroll C. Odhner, Tel. (267)950-2547, Fax (267)502-2637, Email: carroll.odhner@brynathyn.edu, Website: www.brynathyn.edu/academics/swedenborg-library

Unitarian Universalist
*Andover-Harvard Theological Library, Andover-Harvard Theological Library, Harvard Divinity School, 45 Francis Ave., Cambridge, MA 02138, Curator: Frances O'Donnell, Tel. (617) 496-5153, Fax (617)496-4111, Email: archives@hds.harvard.edu, Website: www.hds.harvard.edu/library
Institutional archives of the Unitarian Universalist Association including the Unitarian Universalist Service Committee; also houses records of many congregations; personal papers of ministers and other individuals.

Meadville-Lombard Theological School Library, Meadville/Lombard Theological School Library, 5701 S. Woodlawn Ave., Chicago, IL 60637, Director: Neil W. Gerdes, Tel. (773)256-3000 ext. 225, Fax (773)256-3008, Email: ngerdes@meadville.edu, Website: www.meadville.edu
Repository for materials relating to Unitarian Universalism in particular and liberal religion in general. Includes personal papers of several noted UU ministers, and church records from many UU churches in the Midwestern USA.

United Church of Christ
Archives of the Evangelical Synod, Eden Theological Seminary, Luhr Library, 475 E. Lockwood Ave., Webster Groves, MO 63119-3192, Sr. Research Consultant: The Reverend Dr. Lowell Zuck, Tel. (314) 252-3140, Email: lzuck@eden.edu, Website: www.eden.edu/EducationalResources/Archives.aspx
Archival records include organization records, personal papers and immigration records.

Congregational Library, Congregational Library, 14 Beacon St., Boston, MA 02108, Archivist: Jessica Steytler, Tel. (617)523-0470, Fax (617) 523-0491, Email: jsteytler@14beacon.org, Website: www.congregationallibrary.org
Documentation on the Congregational, Congregational Christian, Christian, and United Church of Christ throughout the world, including local church records, associations, charitable organizations, and papers of clergy, missionaries and others.

Elon University Library, Belk Library, 2550 Campus Box, Elon, NC 27244, Archivist and Special Collections Librarian: Katie Nash Tel. (336)278-6681, Fax (336)278-6638, Email: knash@elon.edu, Website: www.elon.edu/e-web/library/libraryinfo/archive info.xhtml
Collection of membership records and other archival material on the predecessor churches of the UCC: Christian Church and the Southern Conference of the Christian Church; also maintains records of churches that no longer exist.

*United Church of Christ Archives, 700 Prospect Ave, Cleveland, OH 44115, Archivist: Edward Cade, Tel. (216)736-2111, Email: cadee@ucc.org, Website: www.ucc.org/about-us/archives
Records created in the national setting of the Church since its founding in 1957, including the General Synod, Executive Council, officers, instrumentalities, and bodies created by and/or related to the General Synod.

CANADA

Anglican
*General Synod Archives, 80 Hayden St., Toronto, ON M4Y 3G2, Archivist: Nancy Hurn, Tel. (416)924-9199 ext. 279, Fax (416)968-7983, Email: archives@national.anglican.ca, Website: www.anglican.ca/about/departments/gso/archives
Collects the permanent records of the General Synod, its committees, and its employees. The Archives has a national scope, and provides referral services on local Church records.

Baptist
*Atlantic Baptist Historical Collection of the Acadia University Archives, Vaughan Memorial Library, P.O. Box 4, Wolfville, NS B4P 2R6, Archives and Special Collections Services Assistant: Winnie Bodden, Tel. (902)585-1011, Fax (902)585-1748, Email: archives@acadiau.ca, Website: library.acadiau.ca/archives

351

Records of associations and churches of the United Baptist Convention of the Atlantic Provinces; also personal papers of pastors and missionaries.

Canadian Baptist Archives, McMaster Divinity College, 1280 Main St. W, Hamilton, ON L8S 4K1, Director: Dr. Gordon Heath, Tel. (905)525-9140 ext. 23511, Fax (905)577-4782, Email: gheath@mcmaster.ca, Website: divinity.mcmaster.ca/academics/resources/bap tistArchives

Friends

Canadian Yearly Meeting Archives and Canadian Quaker Archives, Pickering College, 16945 Bayview Ave., New Market, ON L3Y 4X2, Yearly Meeting Archivist: Jane Zavitz-Bond, Tel. (905)895-1700 ext. 247, Fax (905)895-9076, Email: cym-archivist@pickeringcollege.on.ca, or canadianquakerarchives@pickeringcollege.on.ca, Website: www.archives-library.quaker.ca/en/about.html

Holds the extant records for Quakers in Canada beginning with Adolphus in 1798 to the present, including the records of the Canadian Friends Service Committee.

Interdenominational

Canadian Council of Churches Archives, Library and Archives Canada, 395 Wellington, Ottawa, ON K1A 0N3, Tel.(866) 578-7777, Fax(613)995-6274, Email: reference@lac-bac.gc.ca, Website: www. collectionscanada. gc.ca; Genealogical assistance: (613)996-7458

Library and Archives Canada, 395 Wellington, Ottawa, ON K1A 0N3, Librarian and Archivist of Canada: Dr. Daniel J. Caron, Tel. (866)578-7777, Fax (613)995-6274, Email: reference@lac-bac.gc.ca, Website: www.collections canada.gc.ca

Records of interdenominational and ecumenical organizations, missionary societies, denominational churches, parish registers, and papers of prominent clergy.

Jewish

Canadian Jewish Congress Charities Committee National Archives, 1590 Avenue Docteur Penfield, Montreal, QC H3G 1C5, Director of Archives: Janice Rosen, Tel. (514)931-7531 ext.2, Fax (514)931-0548, Email: archives@cjccc.ca, Website: www.cjccc.ca/national_archives

Collects documentation on all aspects of social, political, and cultural history of the Jewish presence in Quebec and Canada.

Lutheran

*Archives of the Evangelical Lutheran Church in Canada, Lutheran Theological Seminary, 114 Seminary Crescent, Saskatoon, Saskatchewan, S7N-0X3 National Secretary: Donald Storch Tel. (306)966 7850, Fax (204)984-9185, Email: dstorch@shaw.ca Website: www.elcic.ca

Official repository for the ELCIC and its predecessor bodies, the Evangelical Lutheran Church of Canada and the Evangelical Lutheran Church of America-Canada Section.

Lutheran Historical Institute, 7100 Ada Blvd., Edmonton, AB T5B 4E4, Archivist: Karen Baron, Tel. (780)474-8156, Fax (780)477-9829, Email: kbaron@lccarchives.com Website: www.lccarchives.ca

Mennonite

*Centre for Mennonite Brethren Studies, 1310 Taylor Ave., Winnipeg, MB R3M 3Z6, Director: Doug Heidebrecht, Archivist: Conrad Stoesz, Tel. (204)669-6575, or (888) 669-6575, Fax (204)654-1865, Email: dheidebrecht@mbconf.ca, or cstoesz@mbconf.ca, Website: www.mbconf.ca/CMBS

Institutional records of the boards and agencies of the Mennonite Brethren Church in Canada with some holdings pertaining to other parts of North America; also personal papers of leaders.

*Mennonite Heritage Centre, Mennonite Church Canada, 600 Shaftesbury Blvd., Winnipeg, MB R3P OM4, Director: Alf Redekopp, Tel. (204)888-6781, Fax (204)831-5675, Email: aredekopp@mennonitechurch.ca, Website: www.mennonitechurch.ca/programs/archives

Institutional records and personal papers of leaders within the Mennonite Community. Holdings include the records of Mennonite Church Canada and its predecessor organizations, individual congregations and related agencies, plus a Mennonite Historical Library in cooperation with Canadian Mennonite University.

Pentecostal

*Pentecostal Assemblies of Canada, 2450 Milltower Court, Mississauga, ON L5N 5Z6, Director of Archives: Marilyn Stroud, Tel. (905)542-7400, Fax (905)542-7313, Email: mstroud@paoc.org, Website: www.paoc.org/archives

Repository of archival records created by the Pentecostal Assemblies of Canada.

Presbyterian

*Presbyterian Church in Canada Archives and Records, 50 Wynford Dr., Toronto, ON M3C 1J7, Archivist/Records Administrator: Kim M. Arnold, Tel. (416)441-1111 ext. 310, Fax (416)441-2825, Email: karnold@ presbyterian.ca, Website: www.presbyterianarchives.ca

Records of the Presbyterian Church in Canada, its officials, ministers, congregations and organizations.

Roman Catholic

Research Centre for the Religious History of Canada, St. Paul University, 223 Main St., Ottawa, ON K1S 1C4, Director:: Pierre Hurtubise, Tel. (613)236-1393 ext. 2270, Fax (613)782-3005, Email: sdlrinfo@ustpaul.ca, Website: www.ustpaul.ca/RCRHC/index_e.asp

Holds 900 linear feet of documents, mainly records on deposit from other institutions; and also guides to many Canadian Catholic archives.

Salvation Army

Salvation Army Archives Canada and Bermuda Territory, 26 Howden Road, Scarborough, ON M1R 3E4, Director: Col. John E. Carew, Tel. (416)285-4344 Fax (416) 285-7763, Email: heritage_centre@can.salvationarmy.org Website: www.heritage.salvationarmy.ca

Records include publications; also financial, personnel, social welfare, and immigration records.

United Church of Canada

*United Church of Canada Central Archives, 3250 Bloor St. West, Suite 300, Toronto, ON M8X 2Y4, General Council Archivist: Nichole Vonk, Central Conferences Archivist: Clay Thibodeau, Tel. (416) 231-7680 ext.3123 Fax (416)231-3103, Email: archives@united-church.ca, Website: www.united-church.ca/local/archives/on

Records of the United Church and its antecedent denominations and local and regional records of the Church in Ontario. Call or view the web page for information on other regional archives.

III

STATISTICAL SECTION

Guide to Statistical Tables

Since questions regarding religious affiliation are no longer a part of the United States Census, the *Yearbook of American & Canadian Churches* is as near an "official" record of denominational statistics as is available.

Because these data represent the most complete annual compilation of church statistics, there is a temptation to expect more than is reasonable. These tables provide the answers to very simple and straightforward questions. Officials in church bodies were asked: "How many members does your organization have?" "How many clergy?" and "How much money does your organization spend?" Each respondent interprets the questions according to the policies of the organization.

Caution should, therefore, be exercised when comparing statistics across denominational lines, comparing statistics from one year to another and adding together statistics from different denominations.

Some particular methodological issues and therefore cautions in interpretation include the following considerations:

1. Definitions of membership, clergy, and other important characteristics differ from religious body to religious body. In this section, ***Full or Confirmed Membership*** refers to those with full communicant status. ***Inclusive Membership*** refers to those who are full communicants or confirmed members plus other members baptized, non-confirmed or non-communicant. Each church determines the age at which a young person is considered a member. Churches also vary in their approaches to statistics. For some, very careful counts are made of members. Other groups only make estimates.

2. Each year the data are collected with the same questions. While most denominations have consistent reporting practices from one year to the next, any change in practices is not noted in the tables. Church mergers and splits can also influence the statistics when they are compared over a number of years. Churches have different reporting schedules and some do not report on a regular basis.

3. The two problems listed above make adding figures from different denominations problematic. However, an additional complication is that individuals who attend two different churches may be included more than once. For example, a person who attends the Church of God in Christ Wednesday evening and an AME service on Sunday morning will likely be included in both counts.

4. Churches were asked to report figures for the full year ending December 31, 2008. Churches actually collect statistics according to their own ecclesial calendars. Data collected consistently from year to year accurately reflect trends over time, irrespective of when customarily collected. Caution should, therefore, be exercised when comparing statistics across denominational lines, comparing statistics from one year to another and adding together statistics from different denominations.

Table 1. Membership Statistics in Canada

Religious Body	Year Reporting	Number of Churches Reporting	Full Communicant or Confirmed Members	Inclusive Membership	Number of Pastors Serving Parishes	Total Number of Clergy	Number of Sunday or Sabbath Schools	Total Enrollment
The Anglican Church of Canada	2007	2,884	641,845	641,845	1,930	3,591	1,633	54,345
The Antiochian Orthodox Christian Archdiocese of North America	2007	18	130,000	130,000	35	36	18	1,605
Apostolic Christian Church (Nazarene)	1985	14		830	49	49		
The Apostolic Church in Canada	2002	20	1,450	1,740	22	28	17	687
Apostolic Church of Pentecost of Canada Inc.	2008	147	26,000	26,000	311	403		
Associated Gospel Churches	2008	146	11,171	11,171	134	267		
Association of Regular Baptist Churches (Canada)	1994	12			8	11		
Baptist Convention of Ontario and Quebec	2008	363	42,513	56,852	309	621		
Baptist General Conference of Canada	1999	103	7,500	14,000	150	240		
The Bible Holiness Movement	2007	29	611	1,298	15	17	25	
Brethren in Christ Church, Canadian Conference	2003		3,287	3,287	81	81		
Canadian and American Reformed Churches	2008	54	9,735	16,843	49	74		
Canadian Baptist Ministries	1996	1,133	129,055	129,055				
Canadian Baptists of Western Canada	2008	158	18,200	18,200	400	550	142	15,432
Canadian Conference of Mennonite Brethren Churches	2007	245	37,751	37,751				
Canadian Convention of Southern Baptists	2007	271	14,297	14,297	250	250	124	4,907
Canadian District of the Moravian Church in America, Northern Province	2008	9	1,006	1,304	9	12	8	341

Table 1. Membership Statistics in Canada *(continued)*

Religious Body	Year Reporting	Number of Churches Reporting	Full Communicant or Confirmed Members	Inclusive Membership	Number of Pastors Serving Parishes	Total Number of Clergy	Number of Sunday or Sabbath Schools	Total Enrollment
Canadian Yearly Meeting of the Religious Society of Friends	2008	24	1,176	1,810			24	84
Christian Brethren (also known as Plymouth Brethren)	2006	580		47,000		250	500	
Christian Church (Disciples of Christ) in Canada	2002	25	1,599	2,631	24	32	23	390
Christian Churches / Churches of Christ	2004	65	5,500	9,500	75	105	60	3,300
Christian and Missionary Alliance in Canada	2005	428	44,852	131,031	1,037	1,381	353	37,681
Christian Reformed Church in North America	2008	250	51,500	78,460	222	378		
Church of God (Anderson, Ind.)	2002	48	3,711	3,711	41	88	37	1,794
Church of God (Cleveland, Tenn.)	2008	144	14,709	14,709	109	368	189	4,043
Church of God in Christ (Mennonite)	2008	55	4,948	4,948	187	201	55	
The Church of God of Prophecy Canada East	2006	26	4,217	4,217	45	93	20	1,769
The Church of Jesus Christ of Latter-Day Saints in Canada	2007	481	164,617	178,102	1,443	1,623	481	125,930
Church of the Lutheran Brethren	2004	8	425	676	10	13	7	336
Church of the Nazarene in Canada	2008	177	13,293	13,354	141	285	133	15,477
Churches of Christ in Canada	2005	149	6,857	6,857	122	122		
Community of Christ	2007	68	8,483	8,483	976	976		
Congregational Christian Churches in Canada		73		7,200	141	184		
Convention of Atlantic Baptist Churches	2006	512	62,070	62,070	297	650		9,878

Table 1. Membership Statistics in Canada (continued)

Religious Body	Year Reporting	Number of Churches Reporting	Full Communicant or Confirmed Members	Inclusive Membership	Number of Pastors Serving Parishes	Total Number of Clergy	Number of Sunday or Sabbath Schools	Total Enrollment
The Coptic Orthodox Church in Canada	2006	24	55,000	55,000	33	33		
The Estonian Evangelical Lutheran Church Abroad	2004	11	4,996	4,996	7	10	4	55
Evangelical Christian Church in Canada	2008	36	665	2,031	89	105	49	5,006
The Evangelical Covenant Church of Canada	2002	21	1,384	1,384	6	25		1,763
Evangelical Free Church of Canada	2004	140	8,441	8,441	199	199		
Evangelical Lutheran Church in Canada	2006	623	174,555	174,555	485	866	447	17,926
Evangelical Mennonite Conference	2006	60	7,455	7,455		57	55	
Evangelical Mennonite Mission Conference	2007	27	5,160	5,160	27	57	27	
The Evangelical Missionary Church of Canada	2007	130	11,322		218	309		
The Fellowship of Evangelical Baptist Churches in Canada	2004	499	71,073		318	348		
Foursquare Gospel Church of Canada	2007	61	3,307	3,307	117	141		860
Free Methodist Church in Canada	2003	149	7,603	7,603	123	223		5,955
Free Will Baptists	1998	10	347		3	4	8	
General Church of the New Jerusalem	2007	3	276	797	5	5	2	59
General Conference of the Canadian Assemblies of God	2008	20			20	26		
Greek Orthodox Metropolis of Toronto (Canada)	2004	76	350,000	350,000	62	73	76	
Independent Assemblies of God International (Canada)	2007	500			750	750		

Table 1. Membership Statistics in in Canada (continued)

Religious Body	Year Reporting	Number of Churches Reporting	Full Communicant or Confirmed Members	Inclusive Membership	Number of Pastors Serving Parishes	Total Number of Clergy	Number of Sunday or Sabbath Schools	Total Enrollment
Independent Holiness Church	1994	5		150	4	10	4	118
Jehovah's Witnesses	2008	1,325	112,092	112,092				
Lutheran Church-Canada	2008	319	53,536	72,116	211	391	233	5,093
Mennonite Church Canada	2008	225	32,000	32,000				
North American Baptist Conference	2008	140	17,222	17,222	130	201	140	
The Old Catholic Church of Canada	2000	4	30	100	4	5		
Old Order Amish Church	1999	24						
Open Bible Faith Fellowship of Canada	2003	75	2,500	9,000	164	256	77	3,900
Orthodox Church in America (Archdiocese of Canada)	2004	68	2,000	10,000	59	73	20	450
Patriarchal Parishes of the Russian Orthodox Church in Canada	2007	24	1,200	3,200	5	6	4	108
The Pentecostal Assemblies of Canada	2007	1,108	66,213	232,000	1,532	2,168	552	23,777
The Pentecostal Assemblies of Newfoundland	2004	128	8,864	26,432	212	308	95	5,770
Presbyterian Church in America (Canadian Section)	2008	21	1,003	1,407	33	33		330
Presbyterian Church in Canada	2008	933	113,104	178,482		1,346	933	19,670
Reformed Church in Canada	2008	40	3,702	5,635	34	73		
The Reformed Episcopal Church of Canada	2007	10	805	1,035	9	12	6	43
Reinland Mennonite Church	2007	6	898	1,922	10	13	5	347
The Roman Catholic Church in Canada	2008	5,109	12,987,637	12,987,637		5,109		

Table 1. Membership Statistics in Canada (continued)

Religious Body	Year Reporting	Number of Churches Reporting	Full Communicant or Confirmed Members	Inclusive Membership	Number of Pastors Serving Parishes	Total Number of Clergy	Number of Sunday or Sabbath Schools	Total Enrollment
Romanian Orthodox Church in America (Canadian Parishes)	2007	26	3,700	8,200	32	36	20	352
The Romanian Orthodox Episcopate of America (Jackson, MI)	2008	23	1,005	1,611	30	32	12	
The Salvation Army in Canada	2007	321	20,935	72,481	567	2,064		
Serbian Orthodox Church in the U.S.A. and Canada, Diocese of Canada	2008	26	10,000	235,000	26	30	15	2,070
Seventh-day Adventist Church in Canada	2008	344	59,354	59,354	197	291	377	31,021
Syriac Orthodox Church of Antioch	1995	5	2,500	2,500	3	4		
Ukrainian Orthodox Church of Canada	2007	273	11,000	32,000	69	93	33	
Union d'Eglises Baptistes Françaises au Canada	2004	34	1,868	1,868	29	40	62	629
United Brethren Church in Canada	2008	12	825	825	12	14	9	447
The United Church of Canada	2006	3,405	558,000	1,358,000	1,484	4,094	2,525	43,400
United Pentecostal Church in Canada	1997	199				340		
Universal Fellowship of Metropolitan Community Churches	1992	12	50	1,500	8	9	1	36
The Wesleyan Church of Canada	2002	89	5,977	6,481	131	201	80	5,306
TOTALS		**25,442**	**16,241,982**	**17,781,533**	**16,079**	**33,405**	**9,720**	**452,490**

Table 2. Membership Statistics in the United States

Religious Body	Year Reporting	Number of Churches Reporting	Full Communicant or Confirmed Members	Inclusive Membership	Number of Pastors Serving Parishes	Total Number of Clergy	Number of Sunday or Sabbath Schools	Total Enrollment
Advent Christian Church	2007	294	23,629	23,629	220	481	285	12,516
African Methodist Episcopal Church*	1999	4,174	1,857,186	2,500,000	7,741	14,428	6,128	303,199
The African Methodist Episcopal Zion Church*	2008	3,393		1,400,000	3,867	4,537	2,765	75,338
Albanian Orthodox Diocese of America	2008	3	2,800	2,800	5	5	2	49
The Allegheny Wesleyan Methodist Connection (Original Allegheny Conference)	2008	102	1,367	1,456	69	158	101	4,200
Alliance of Baptists*	2006	127	65,000	65,000	320	465		
The American Association of Lutheran Churches	2008	70	9,000	16,000	50	120	40	1,635
The American Baptist Association	2000	1,760	275,000	275,000	1,740	1,760		
American Baptist Churches in the U.S.A.*	2008	5,469	1,331,127	1,331,127	3,281	6,308		93,521
The American Carpatho-Russian Orthodox Greek Catholic Church	2008	80	13,721	13,721	74	103	80	
American Evangelical Christian Churches	2006	192	16,000	17,400	192	224	192	
American Rescue Workers	2007	5	3,500	3,500	20	29	6	318
Anglo-Lutheran Catholic Church	2008	11	3,000	3,000	10	12	4	
The Antiochian Orthodox Christian Archdiocese of North America	2007	256	430,000	430,000	480	545	250	21,850
Apostolic Catholic Church	2008	16	5,116	5,736	24	31	10	953
Apostolic Catholic Orthodox Church	2008	11	1,500	8,500	11	26	4	
Apostolic Christian Church (Nazarene)	2008	54	3,527	3,527	202	211	48	1,524

Table 2. Membership Statistics in the United States (continued)

Religious Body	Year Reporting	Number of Churches Reporting	Full Communicant or Confirmed Members	Inclusive Membership	Number of Pastors Serving Parishes	Total Number of Clergy	Number of Sunday or Sabbath Schools	Total Enrollment
Apostolic Christian Churches of America	2008	87	12,900	12,900	332	440	87	6,330
Apostolic Episcopal Church	2006	200	6,200	12,000	250	255		800
Apostolic Faith Mission Church of God	2008		5,200	6,830	41	45	15	3,308
Apostolic Faith Mission of Portland, Oregon	1994	54	4,500	4,500	60	85	54	
Apostolic Orthodox Catholic Church of North America	2005	25	15,900	15,900	40	49		
Armenian Apostolic Church of America	2008	36	350,000	350,000	30	45	25	1,715
Armenian Apostolic Church, Dioceses of America*	2008	63	650,000	650,000	28	56	40	2,552
Assemblies of God	2008	12,377	1,662,632	2,899,702	20,004	34,178	11,297	1,112,602
Associate Reformed Presbyterian Church (General Synod)	2008	296	34,911	39,681	246	449	285	
The Association of Free Lutheran Congregations	2008	274	32,151	43,477	154	249	242	13,043
Association of Independent Evangelical Lutheran Churches	2007	35	6,075	6,318	35	49	23	338
Association of Vineyard Churches	2007	592	188,000	188,000	601	2,495		
Baptist Bible Fellowship International	1997	4,500	1,200,000	1,200,000				
Baptist General Conference	2007	1,071	147,500	147,500		1,066		
Baptist Missionary Association of America	2008	1,287	126,056	126,056	824	3,239	377	28,437
Beachy Amish Mennonite Churches	2008	211	12,062	12,062	284	291		
Berean Fellowship of Churches	2005	56	12,000	12,000				

Table 2. Membership Statistics in the United States *(continued)*

Religious Body	Year Reporting	Number of Churches Reporting	Full Communicant or Confirmed Members	Inclusive Membership	Number of Pastors Serving Parishes	Total Number of Clergy	Number of Sunday or Sabbath Schools	Total Enrollment
The Bible Church of Christ, Inc.	1993	6	4,150	6,850	11	52	6	
Bible Fellowship Church	2008	62	7,621	7,621	69	136	51	4,638
Brethren in Christ Church	2001	232	20,739	20,739	151	295		12,404
Brethren Church (Ashland, Ohio)	2008	116	10,106	10,106	86	181		
Calvary Chapel	2008		9,000	10,000				
The Catholic Church	2008	18,674	68,115,001	68,115,001		57,897		6,576,604
Christ Catholic Church	2005	6	1,797	2,887	7	7	1	23
Christ Community Church (Evangelical-Protestant)	2005	3	1,149	1,819	3	7	1	265
Christian Brethren (also known as Plymouth Brethren)	2006	1,145		86,000		600	1,000	
Christian Church (Disciples of Christ) in the United States and Canada*	2008	3,714	434,008	679,563	3,969	7,103	3,006	169,147
Christian Church of North America, General Council	2003	90	363	363	100	162	90	
Christian Churches and Churches of Christ	1988	5,579	1,071,616	1,071,616	5,525			
The Christian Congregation, Inc.	2004	1,496	122,181	122,181	1,574	1,575	1,347	41,891
Christian Methodist Episcopal Church*	2006	3,500	850,000	850,000	3,106	3,548	2,500	69,368
The Christian and Missionary Alliance	2008	2,018	194,473	425,587	2,800	4,525		
Christian Reformed Church in North America	2008	787	133,000	188,000	685	1,407		
Christian Union	2008	107	3,647	4,014	154	225	102	3,143
Church of the Brethren*	2008	1,049	123,855	123,855	788	1,863	760	28,456

363

Table 2. Membership Statistics in the United States (continued)

Religious Body	Year Reporting	Number of Churches Reporting	Full Communicant or Confirmed Members	Inclusive Membership	Number of Pastors Serving Parishes	Total Number of Clergy	Number of Sunday or Sabbath Schools	Total Enrollment
The Church of Christ (Holiness) U.S.A.	2007	148	11,468	11,468	193	221	148	6,276
Church Communities International	2008	14	997	1,771	32	47		
Church of God (Anderson, Indiana)	2007	2,248	252,905	252,905	5,130	5,992	2,248	115,453
The Church of God in Christ	1991	15,300	5,499,875	5,499,875	28,988	33,593		
Church of God in Christ, Mennonite	2008	146	14,493	14,493	525	565	146	
Church of God (Cleveland, Tennessee)	2008	6,677	1,072,169	1,072,169	4,761	16,667	5,240	295,844
Church of God by Faith, Inc.	2004	149	35,000	35,000	152	235		
Church of God, Mountain Assembly, Inc.	2005	120	7,200	7,200	140		120	11,040
Church of God of Prophecy	2007	1,860	89,674	89,674	4,340	4,340	1,860	64,000
The Church of God (Seventh Day), Denver, Colorado	2008	210	9,000	11,000	100	130	210	
The Church of Illumination	2000	4	1,200	1,200		16	1	216
The Church of Jesus Christ (Bickertonites)	2008	77	2,870	13,975	270	482		
The Church of Jesus Christ of Latter-day Saints	2008	13,363	5,346,808	5,974,041	40,089	44,545	13,363	4,546,992
Church of the Living God (Motto, Christian Workers for Fellowship)	2006	170	42,000	42,000	105	214	65	
Church of the Lutheran Brethren of America	2008	116	9,070	14,752	135	219	113	7,956
Church of the Lutheran Confession	2006	87	6,365	8,390	64	90	67	943
Church of the Nazarene	2008	5,090	636,923	645,048	5,403	9,391	4,664	769,470
Church of the United Brethren in Christ, USA	2008	200	20,500	20,500	160	350		

Table 2. Membership Statistics in the United States *(continued)*

Religious Body	Year Reporting	Number of Churches Reporting	Full Communicant or Confirmed Members	Inclusive Membership	Number of Pastors Serving Parishes	Total Number of Clergy	Number of Sunday or Sabbath Schools	Total Enrollment
Churches of Christ	2006	13,000	1,250,000	1,639,495			10,500	
Churches of Christ in Christian Union	2008	230	11,234	11,234	148	328		8,485
Churches of God, General Conference	2008	322	31,326	31,326	393	545	322	13,826
Community of Christ	2007	935	178,328	178,328		20,420		
Congregational Holiness Church	2005	225	25,000	25,000	225	225		
Conservative Baptist Association of America (CBAmerica)	2006	12,000	200,000	200,000	1,800	2,200		
Conservative Congregational Christian Conference	2008	296	42,149	42,149	297	578	254	12,184
Conservative Lutheran Association	2002	3	852	1,267	8	29	3	120
Coptic Orthodox Church*	2000	100	250,000	300,000	140	145	100	5,500
Cumberland Presbyterian Church	2008	716	78,074	78,592	645	909	650	30,064
Cumberland Presbyterian Church in America	1996	152	15,142	15,142	141	156	152	9,465
The Episcopal Church*	2008	6,964	1,666,202	2,057,292			6,097	227,619
The Estonian Evangelical Lutheran Church	2001	21	3,508	3,508	10	12		
The Evangelical Church	2000	133	12,475	12,475	164	255	125	8,000
The Evangelical Church Alliance	2008		293,375	293,375	2,437	2,437		
The Evangelical Congregational Church	2008	135	18,710	18,710	152	209		
The Evangelical Covenant Church	2006	783	114,283	114,283	1,486	1,833	750	106,022
The Evangelical Free Church of America	2008	1,475	159,166	356,000	1,503	2,201		

Table 2. Membership Statistics in the United States (continued)

Religious Body	Year Reporting	Number of Churches Reporting	Full Communicant or Confirmed Members	Inclusive Membership	Number of Pastors Serving Parishes	Total Number of Clergy	Number of Sunday or Sabbath Schools	Total Enrollment
Evangelical Friends International – North American Region	2008	284	27,844	38,428				
Evangelical Lutheran Church in America*	2008	10,396	3,483,336	4,633,887	8,713	17,660	7,860	691,986
Evangelical Lutheran Synod	2008	130	15,672	19,777	106	166	111	2,450
Evangelical Methodist Church	2005	108	7,348	7,348	101	202	102	4,920
Evangelical Presbyterian Church	2007	207	77,794	89,190	385	608	171	39,153
Fellowship of Evangelical Bible Churches	2008	19	2,197	2,197	15	44	19	1,591
Fellowship of Evangelical Churches	2008	44	6,933	6,933	100	179	44	4,892
Fellowship of Fundamental Bible Churches	2007	20	980	1,760	32	46	20	1,140
Fellowship of Grace Brethren Churches	1997	260	30,371	30,371		564		
Free Methodist Church of North America	2008	991	66,878	75,115		2,055		33,062
Friends General Conference	2002	832	32,000	32,000			400	
Friends United Meeting*	2008	600	36,302	36,302	327	576	273	
Full Gospel Assemblies International	2007	11	2,786	2,786	220		22	
Full Gospel Fellowship of Churches and Ministers International	2007	1,273	430,000	432,632	2,631	3,381		
Fundamental Methodist Church, Inc.	1993	12	682	787	17	22	12	454
General Association of General Baptists	2007	562	46,242	46,242			562	
General Association of Regular Baptist Churches	2007	1,321	132,700	132,700			1,321	
General Church of the New Jerusalem	2006	37	3,519	6,760	34	71		
General Conference of Mennonite Brethren Churches	1996	368	50,915	82,130	590			34,668

Table 2. Membership Statistics in the United States (continued)

Religious Body	Year Reporting	Number of Churches Reporting	Full Communicant or Confirmed Members	Inclusive Membership	Number of Pastors Serving Parishes	Total Number of Clergy	Number of Sunday or Sabbath Schools	Total Enrollment
Grace Gospel Fellowship	1992	128	60,000	60,000	160	196	128	
Greek Orthodox Archdiocese of America*	2006	560	1,500,000	1,500,000	553	840	550	
The Holy Eastern Orthodox Catholic and Apostolic Church in North America, Inc.	2001	17	4,138	4,138	9		17	
Hungarian Reformed Church in America*	2001	27	6,000	6,000	27	30		
Hutterian Brethren	2000	444	36,800	43,000	600	600		
IFCA International, Inc.	1998	659	61,655	61,655			659	57,768
International Church of the Foursquare Gospel	2006	1,875	255,773	353,995	6,738	8,486	1,450	61,000
International Council of Community Churches*	2006	155	73,174	73,174	630	705		
International Fellowship of Bible Churches, Inc	2004	37	677	1,354	54	115	30	
The International Pentecostal Church of Christ	2003	67	2,004	4,961	51	157	48	1,918
International Pentecostal Holiness Church	2008	2,024	265,744	330,054	2,946	4,239		
Jehovah's Witnesses	2008	12,728	1,114,009	1,114,009				
The Korean Presbyterian Church Abroad*	2003	302	38,500	55,000	465	583		17,760
The Latvian Evangelical Lutheran Church in America	2007	60	9,700	10,950	41	61	14	
The Liberal Catholic Church-- Province of the United States of America	2006	21	5,800	5,800	41	44		
The Lutheran Church--Missouri Synod (LCMS)	2008	6,123	1,803,900	2,337,349	5,359	9,010	4,839	417,303
Malankara Orthodox Syrian Church, Diocese of America*	2006	80	30,000	30,000	100	120	77	3,780

Table 2. Membership Statistics in the United States (continued)

Religious Body	Year Reporting	Number of Churches Reporting	Full Communicant or Confirmed Members	Inclusive Membership	Number of Pastors Serving Parishes	Total Number of Clergy	Number of Sunday or Sabbath Schools	Total Enrollment
Mar Thoma Syrian Church of India*	2008	85	26,500	42,000	53	63	65	4,675
Mennonite Church USA	2008		106,172	106,172	1,165	1,879		
The Missionary Church	2008	431	38,206	38,206	362	746		23,656
Moravian Church in America (Northern Province)*	2008	86	16,733	20,983	82	168	80	4,459
National Association of Congregational Christian Churches	2001	432	65,392	65,392	507	650		
National Association of Free Will Baptists	2007	2,369	185,798	185,798		3,915	2,369	106,397
National Baptist Convention of America, Inc.*	2000		3,500,000	3,500,000			9,000	
National Baptist Convention, U.S.A., Inc.*	2004	9,000	5,000,000	5,000,000			9,000	
National Missionary Baptist Convention of America*	1992		2,500,000	2,500,000				
National Organization of the New Apostolic Church of North America	2008	309	38,764	38,764	1,675	1,675	300	3,700
National Primitive Baptist Convention, Inc.	2002	1,565	600,000	600,000				
Netherlands Reformed Congregations	2008	26	4,862	10,080	10	10		
North American Baptist Conference	2006	272	47,150	47,150	296	418	272	
North American Old Roman Catholic Church (Archdiocese of New York)	2008	5	2,750	2,785	4	7	3	15
The Old Catholic Orthodox Church		11	11,000	11,470	29	29		
Old German Baptist Brethren Church	2008	56	6,149	6,149	277	277		
Old Order Amish Church	2001	898	80,820	80,820	3,592	3,617	55	

Table 2. Membership Statistics in the United States (continued)

Religious Body	Year Reporting	Number of Churches Reporting	Full Communicant or Confirmed Members	Inclusive Membership	Number of Pastors Serving Parishes	Total Number of Clergy	Number of Sunday or Sabbath Schools	Total Enrollment
Old Order (Wisler) Mennonite Church	2004	47	7,100	7,100	135	135		
Open Bible Churches	2007	302	45,000	45,000	400	1,026		
The Orthodox Presbyterian Church	2008	268	21,243	29,095		477		12,663
Patriarchal Parishes of the Russian Orthodox Church in the U.S.A.*	2008	31	7,000	17,000	37	63		
Pentecostal Assemblies of the World, Inc.	2006	1,750	1,500,000	1,500,000	4,500	4,500		
Pentecostal Church of God	2008	1,134	44,850	98,579	1,134	1,572		
Pentecostal Fire-Baptized Holiness Church	1996	27	223	223		28	25	400
Philadelphia Yearly Meeting of the Religious Society of Friends*	2008	103	11,511	11,511			80	2,500
Polish National Catholic Church of America*	2008	126	60,000	60,000	103	127		
Presbyterian Church in America	2008	1,672	266,988	335,850	3,562	3,562		110,322
Presbyterian Church (U.S.A.)*	2008	10,751	2,140,165	2,844,952	8,427	21,286	8,370	964,388
Primitive Advent Christian Church	1993	10	345	345	11	11	10	292
Primitive Methodist Church in the U.S.A.	2008	67	3,574	3,915	47	84	61	1,965
Progressive National Baptist Convention, Inc.*	1995	2,000	2,500,000	2,500,000				
Protestant Reformed Churches in America	2008	30	4,396	7,625	27	42	23	
Reformed Catholic Church	2006	100	57,000	57,000	187	227	6	412
Reformed Church in America*	2008	893	157,570	254,485	855	2,101		
Reformed Church in the United States	2002	48	3,258	4,369	42	50	48	951
Reformed Episcopal Church	2008	149	9,342	15,573	168	221		

Table 2. Membership Statistics in the United States *(continued)*

Religious Body	Year Reporting	Number of Churches Reporting	Full Communicant or Confirmed Members	Inclusive Membership	Number of Pastors Serving Parishes	Total Number of Clergy	Number of Sunday or Sabbath Schools	Total Enrollment
Reformed Mennonite Church	2008	8	252	270	33	37		
Reformed Presbyterian Church of North America	2004	80	4,542	6,347	77	147		
Religious Society of Friends (Conservative)	2004	1,200	104,000	104,000				
The Romanian Orthodox Church in America	2008	32	3,200	9,700	33	37	28	562
The Romanian Orthodox Episcopate of America	2006	64	7,135	10,635	116	138		
The Russian Orthodox Church Outside of Russia	2008	190	480,000	480,000	221	269	30	2,642
The Salvation Army	2008	1,252	106,914	512,881	2,504	5,474	1,277	97,012
The Schwenkfelder Church	2008	5	2,300	2,300	6	8	5	
Separate Baptists in Christ	1992	100	8,000	8,000	95	140	100	
Serbian Orthodox Church in the U.S.A. and Canada*	2005	68	67,000	67,000	60	82		
Seventh-day Adventist Church	2008	4,870	1,021,777	1,021,777	2,610	5,150	4,029	240,203
Seventh Day Baptist General Conference, USA and Canada	2006	96	5,200	6,200	60	80		
Southern Baptist Convention	2008	44,848	16,228,438	16,228,438	104,503	121,028	38,481	7,752,794
Southern Methodist Church	2006	101	6,000	6,000	109	158	105	3,774
Sovereign Grace Believers	2002	350	4,000	4,000	450	450	350	
The Swedenborgian Church*	2007	35	1,197	1,608	36	70		
Syriac-Greek Antiochian Orthodox Catholic Church	2008	180	22,700	22,895	195	212	40	1,425

Table 2. Membership Statistics in the United States (continued)

Religious Body	Year Reporting	Number of Churches Reporting	Full Communicant or Confirmed Members	Inclusive Membership	Number of Pastors Serving Parishes	Total Number of Clergy	Number of Sunday or Sabbath Schools	Total Enrollment
Syrian (Syriac) Orthodox Church of Antioch*	2008	32	32,500	32,500	24	25	22	1,585
True Orthodox Church of Greece (Synod of Metropolitan Cyprian), American Exarchate	1999	9	1,095	1,095	18	19		
Ukrainian Orthodox Church of the U.S.A.*	2006	118	30,000	50,000	99	114	67	640
Unitarian Universalist Association of Congregations	2007	1,046	221,476	221,476	1,752	1,752	1,046	56,673
The United Catholic Church, Inc.	2008	16	2,102	3,206	23	36		
United Christian Church	2006	9	280	280	9	15	7	577
United Church of Christ*	2008	5,320	1,111,691	1,111,691	3,919	10,201	4,552	218,816
The United Methodist Church*	2007	34,136	7,853,987	7,853,987	24,238	45,186	54,975	4,854,996
United Pentecostal Church International	2006	4,358		646,304	9,224	9,224		
The United Pentecostal Churches of Christ	2000	62	7,059	7,059	466	483	62	2,289
United Zion Church	2008	14	774	774	17	27	11	490
Unity of the Brethren	1998	27	2,548	3,218	25	39	24	1,442
Universal Catholic Church	2007	3	25	75	3	3		
Universal Fellowship of Metropolitan Community Churches	2006	115	15,666	15,666	293	425		
The Wesleyan Church	2008	1,614	117,147	131,791	2,399	3,761	1,614	
Wisconsin Evangelical Lutheran Synod	2008	1,286	309,116	390,213	1,226	1,832	1,146	34,676
TOTALS		338,713	153,588,962	163,325,722	372,223	607,944	234,889	30,710,878

* National Council of Churches USA member communions.

371

Table 3. Membership Statistics
for the National Council of Churches USA

Religious Body	Year Reporting	Number of Churches Reporting	Inclusive Membership	Number of Pastors Serving Parishes
African Methodist Episcopal Church	1999	4,174	2,500,000	7,741
The African Methodist Episcopal Zion Church	2008	3,393	1,400,000	3,867
Alliance of Baptists	2006	127	65,000	320
American Baptist Churches in the U.S.A.	2008	5,469	1,331,127	3,281
Armenian Apostolic Church, Dioceses of America	2008	63	650,000	28
Christian Church (Disciples of Christ) in the United States and Canada	2008	3,714	679,563	3,969
Christian Methodist Episcopal Church	2006	3,500	850,000	3,106
Church of the Brethren	2008	1,049	123,855	788
Coptic Orthodox Church	2000	100	300,000	140
The Episcopal Church	2008	6,964	2,057,292	
Evangelical Lutheran Church in America	2008	10,396	4,633,887	8,713
Friends United Meeting	2008	600	36,302	327
Greek Orthodox Archdiocese of America	2006	560	1,500,000	553
Hungarian Reformed Church in America	2001	27	6,000	27
International Council of Community Churches	2006	155	73,174	630
The Korean Presbyterian Church Abroad	2003	302	55,000	465
Malankara Orthodox Syrian Church, Diocese of America	2006	80	30,000	100
Mar Thoma Syrian Church of India	2008	85	42,000	53

Table 3. Membership Statistics
for the National Council of Churches USA (*continued*)

Religious Body	Year Reporting	Number of Churches Reporting	Inclusive Membership	Number of Pastors Serving Parishes
Moravian Church in America (Northern Province, Southern Province)	2008	86	20,983	82
National Baptist Convention of America, Inc.	2000		3,500,000	
National Baptist Convention, U.S.A., Inc.	2004	9,000	5,000,000	
National Missionary Baptist Convention of America	1992		2,500,000	
The Orthodox Church in America*	2004	737		824
Patriarchal Parishes of the Russian Orthodox Church in the U.S.A.	2008	31	17,000	37
Philadelphia Yearly Meeting of the Religious Society of Friends	2008	103	11,511	
Polish National Catholic Church of America	2008	126	60,000	103
Presbyterian Church (U.S.A.)	2008	10,751	2,844,952	8,427
Progressive National Baptist Convention, Inc.	1995	2,000	2,500,000	
Reformed Church in America	2008	893	254,485	855
Serbian Orthodox Church in the U.S.A. and Canada	2005	68	67,000	60
The Swedenborgian Church	2007	35	1,608	36
Syrian (Syriac) Orthodox Church of Antioch	2008	32	32,500	24
Ukrainian Orthodox Church of the U.S.A.	2006	118	50,000	99
United Church of Christ	2008	5,320	1,111,691	3,919
The United Methodist Church	2007	34,136	7,853,987	24,238
TOTALS		**104,194**	**42,158,917**	**72,812**

*The Orthodox Church in America is reassessing its methodology for estimating membership.

373

Table 4. Selected Statistics of Church

Religious Body	Year	Full or Confirmed Members	Inclusive Members	TOTAL CONTRIBUTIONS		
				Total Contributions	Per Capita Full or Confirmed Members	Per Capita Inclusive Members
The Apostolic Church in Canada	2002	1,450	1,740	$1,705,737	$1,176.37	$980.31
Armenian Holy Apostolic Church - Canadian Diocese	2007	87,000	87,000	$895,000	$10.29	$10.29
Baptist Convention of Ontario and Quebec	2004	42,513	56,852	$42,120,960	$990.78	$740.89
The Bible Holiness Movement	2007	611	1,298	$164,696	$269.55	$126.88
Canadian Baptists of Western Canada	2008	18,200	18,200	$5,681,170	$312.15	$312.15
Canadian District of the Moravian Church in America, Northern Province	2008	1,006	1,304	$2,450,396	$2,435.78	$1,879.14
Christian Church (Disciples of Christ) in Canada	2002	1,599	2,631	$1,449,009	$906.20	$550.74
Christian and Missionary Alliance in Canada	2005	44,852	131,031	$136,297,640	$3,038.83	$1,040.19
Church of the Lutheran Brethren	2004	425	676	$755,605	$1,777.89	$1,117.76
Church of the Nazarene in Canada	2008	13,293	13,354	$14,820,938	$1,114.94	$1,109.85
Convention of Atlantic Baptist Churches	2006	62,070	62,070	$45,537,677	$733.65	$733.65
Evangelical Christian Church in Canada	2008	665	2,031	$5,608	$8.43	$2.76
Evangelical Lutheran Church in Canada	2002	174,555	174,555	$61,270,705	$351.01	$351.01
The Latvian Evangelical Lutheran Church in America	1995	4,162	4,647	$1,201,332	$288.64	$258.52
North American Baptist Conference	2006	17,222	17,222	$34,886,910	$2,025.72	$2,025.72
The Pentecostal Assemblies of Canada	2007	66,213	232,000	$393,094,226	$5,936.81	$1,694.37
The Pentecostal Assemblies of Newfoundland	2004	8,864	26,432	$5,624,770	$634.56	$212.80
Presbyterian Church in America (Canadian Section)	2008	1,003	1,407	$2,514,778	$2,507.26	$1,787.33
Reformed Church in Canada	2008	3,702	5,635	$7,086,236	$1,914.16	$1,257.54
The Reformed Episcopal Church of Canada	2007	805	1,035	$437,525	$543.51	$422.73
Seventh-day Adventist Church in Canada	2008	59,354	59,354	$97,585,429	$1,644.13	$1,644.13
Union d'Eglises Baptistes Françaises au Canada	2004	1,868	1,868	$888,230	$475.50	$475.50
The United Church of Canada	2006	558,000	1,358,000	$360,225,200	$645.56	$265.26
TOTALS		**1,222,968**	**2,332,458**	**$1,216,699,777**	**$994.87**	**$521.64**

NOTE: Rounding may cause some totals to appear inaccurate.

Finances—Canadian Churches

CONGREGATIONAL FINANCES			BENEVOLENCES			
Total Congregational Contributions	Per Capita Full or Confirmed Members	Per Capita Inclusive Members	Total Benevolences	Per Capita Full or Confirmed Members	Per Capita Inclusive Members	Benevolences as a Percentage of Total Giving
$1,506,104	$1,038.69	$865.58	$199,633	$137.68	$114.73	11.7%
$475,000	$5.46	$5.46	$440,000	$5.06	$5.06	49.2%
$35,540,033	$835.98	$625.13	$6,580,927	$154.80	$115.76	15.6%
$43,330	$70.92	$33.38	$121,346	$198.60	$93.49	73.7%
$566,299	$31.12	$31.12	$5,114,871	$281.04	$281.04	90.0%
$2,329,504	$2,315.61	$1,786.43	$120,892	$120.17	$92.71	0.0%
$1,230,384	$769.47	$467.65	$218,625	$136.73	$83.10	15.1%
$114,235,867	$2,546.95	$871.82	$22,061,773	$491.88	$168.37	16.2%
$605,137	$1,423.85	$895.17	$150,468	$354.04	$222.59	19.9%
$12,112,273	$911.18	$907.01	$2,708,665	$203.77	$202.84	18.3%
$42,389,451	$682.93	$682.93	$3,148,226	$50.72	$50.72	6.9%
$4,056	$6.10	$2.00	$1,764	$2.65	$0.87	31.5%
$52,343,354	$299.87	$299.87	$7,518,028	$43.07	$43.07	12.3%
$1,014,766	$243.82	$218.37	$186,566	$44.83	$40.15	15.5%
$28,670,810	$1,664.78	$1,664.78	$6,216,100	$360.94	$360.94	17.8%
$346,531,783	$5,233.59	$1,493.67	$46,562,443	$703.22	$200.70	11.8%
$3,948,770	$445.48	$149.39	$1,676,000	$189.08	$63.41	29.8%
$2,202,335	$2,195.75	$1,565.27	$312,443	$311.51	$222.06	12.4%
$5,717,691	$1,544.49	$1,014.67	$1,368,545	$369.68	$242.87	19.3%
$432,525	$537.30	$417.90	$5,800	$7.20	$5.60	1.3%
$32,968,504	$555.46	$555.46	$64,616,925	$1,088.67	$1,088.67	66.2%
$430,230	$230.32	$230.32	$458,000	$245.18	$245.18	51.6%
$313,913,000	$562.57	$231.16	$46,312,200	$83.00	$34.10	12.9%
$999,211,206	**$817.04**	**$428.39**	**$216,100,240**	**$176.70**	**$92.65**	**18%**

Table 5. Selected Statistics of Church

Religious Body	Year	Full or Confirmed Members	Inclusive Members	TOTAL CONTRIBUTIONS		
				Total Contributions	Per Capita Full or Confirmed Members	Per Capita Inclusive Members
Albanian Orthodox Diocese of America	2008	2,800	2,800	$96,000	$34.29	$34.29
The Allegheny Wesleyan Methodist Connection (Original Allegheny Conference)	2008	1,367	1,456	$4,756,409	$3,479.45	$3,266.76
American Baptist Churches in the U.S.A.*	2008	1,331,127	1,331,127	$315,128,625	$236.74	$236.74
The Antiochian Orthodox Christian Archdiocese of North America	2007	430,000	430,000	$6,648,954	$15.46	$15.46
Apostolic Catholic Church	2006	5,116	5,736	$192,728	$37.67	$33.60
Apostolic Faith Mission Church of God	2008	5,200	6,830	$1,183,346	$227.57	$173.26
Associate Reformed Presbyterian Church (General Synod)	2008	34,911	39,681	$76,353,565	$2,187.09	$1,924.18
Association of Independent Evangelical Lutheran Churches	2007	6,075	6,318	$14,600	$2.40	$2.31
Baptist Missionary Association of America	2008	126,056	126,056	$73,251,890	$581.11	$581.11
Berean Fellowship of Churches	2000	12,000	12,000	$10,309,605	$859.13	$859.13
Bible Fellowship Church	2008	7,621	7,621	$16,913,298	$2,219.30	$2,219.30
Brethren in Christ Church	2001	20,739	20,739	$36,431,223	$1,756.65	$1,756.65
Brethren Church (Ashland, Ohio)	2008	10,106	10,106	$1,243,735	$123.07	$123.07
Christian Church (Disciples of Christ) in the United States and Canada*	2008	434,008	679,563	$524,213,682	$1,207.84	$771.40
The Christian and Missionary Alliance	2008	194,473	425,587	$466,388,400	$2,398.22	$1,095.87
Christian Union	2008	3,647	4,014	$7,816,278	$2,143.21	$1,947.25
Church of the Brethren*	2008	123,855	123,855	$87,494,968	$706.43	$706.43
The Church of Christ (Holiness) U.S.A.	2007	11,468	11,468	$13,571,278	$1,183.40	$1,183.40
Church of the Lutheran Brethren of America	2008	9,070	14,752	$23,828,096	$2,627.13	$1,615.25
Church of the Lutheran Confession	2003	6,365	8,390	$5,855,961	$920.03	$697.97
Church of the Nazarene	2008	636,923	645,048	$829,801,861	$1,302.83	$1,286.42
Churches of God, General Conference	2008	31,326	31,326	$34,968,971	$1,116.29	$1,116.29
Community of Christ	2007	178,328	178,328	$39,121,403	$219.38	$219.38
Conservative Congregational Christian Conference	2008	42,149	42,149	$72,677,645	$1,724.30	$1,724.30
Cumberland Presbyterian Church	2008	78,074	78,592	$57,646,214	$738.35	$733.49

Finances—United States Churches

CONGREGATIONAL FINANCES			BENEVOLENCES			
Total Congregational Contributions	Per Capita Full or Confirmed Members	Per Capita Inclusive Members	Total Benevolences	Per Capita Full or Confirmed Members	Per Capita Inclusive Members	Benevolences as a Percentage of Total Giving
$86,000	$30.71	$30.71	$10,000	$3.57	$3.57	10%
$3,605,777	$2,637.73	$2,476.49	$1,150,632	$841.72	$790.27	24%
$266,054,814	$199.87	$199.87	$49,073,811	$36.87	$36.87	16%
$3,098,954	$7.21	$7.21	$3,550,000	$8.26	$8.26	53%
$175,260	$34.26	$30.55	$17,468	$3.41	$3.05	9%
$579,120	$111.37	$84.79	$604,226	$116.20	$88.47	51%
$62,983,823	$1,804.13	$1,587.25	$13,369,742	$382.97	$336.93	18%
$2,850	$0.47	$0.45	$11,750	$1.93	$1.86	80%
$49,433,825	$392.16	$392.16	$23,818,065	$188.95	$188.95	33%
$9,277,940	$773.16	$773.16	$1,031,665	$85.97	$85.97	10%
$13,387,979	$1,756.72	$1,756.72	$3,525,319	$462.58	$462.58	21%
$29,566,287	$1,425.64	$1,425.64	$6,864,936	$331.02	$331.02	19%
$447,012	$44.23	$44.23	$796,723	$78.84	$78.84	64%
$479,485,251	$1,104.78	$705.58	$44,728,431	$103.06	$65.82	9%
$398,507,989	$2,049.17	$936.37	$67,880,411	$349.05	$159.50	15%
$2,951,783	$809.37	$735.37	$4,864,495	$1,333.83	$1,211.88	62%
$69,331,885	$559.78	$559.78	$18,163,083	$146.65	$146.65	21%
$12,855,697	$1,121.01	$1,121.01	$715,581	$62.40	$62.40	5%
$21,667,832	$2,388.96	$1,468.81	$2,160,264	$238.18	$146.44	9%
$4,999,122	$785.41	$595.84	$856,839	$134.62	$102.13	15%
$690,867,740	$1,084.70	$1,071.03	$138,934,121	$218.13	$215.39	17%
$28,866,361	$921.48	$921.48	$6,102,610	$194.81	$194.81	17%
$22,270,216	$124.88	$124.88	$16,851,187	$94.50	$94.50	43%
$62,792,643	$1,489.78	$1,489.78	$9,885,002	$234.53	$234.53	14%
$49,052,918	$628.29	$624.15	$8,593,296	$110.07	$109.34	15%

377

Table 5. Selected Statistics of Church

Religious Body	Year	Full or Confirmed Members	Inclusive Members	TOTAL CONTRIBUTIONS		
				Total Contributions	Per Capita Full or Confirmed Members	Per Capita Inclusive Members
Cumberland Presbyterian Church in America	1996	15,142	15,142	$40,408,524	$2,668.64	$2,668.64
The Episcopal Church*	2008	1,666,202	2,057,292	$2,294,941,221	$1,377.35	$1,115.52
The Evangelical Church	2000	12,475	12,475	$15,632,985	$1,253.15	$1,253.15
The Evangelical Congregational Church	2008	18,710	18,710	$18,736,646	$1,001.42	$1,001.42
The Evangelical Covenant Church	2006	114,283	114,283	$291,847,011	$2,553.72	$2,553.72
Evangelical Lutheran Church in America*	2008	3,483,336	4,633,887	$2,764,009,721	$793.50	$596.48
Evangelical Lutheran Synod	2008	15,672	19,777	$15,635,281	$997.66	$790.58
Fellowship of Evangelical Bible Churches	2008	2,197	2,197	$2,965,644	$1,349.86	$1,349.86
Fellowship of Evangelical Churches	2008	6,933	6,933	$24,446,883	$3,526.16	$3,526.16
Free Methodist Church of North America	2008	66,878	75,115	$171,677,077	$2,567.02	$2,285.52
General Association of General Baptists	2007	46,242	46,242	$31,385,133	$678.71	$678.71
General Conference of Mennonite Brethren Churches	1996	50,915	82,130	$65,851,481	$1,293.36	$801.80
International Church of the Foursquare Gospel	2003	255,773	353,995	$533,993,579	$2,087.76	$1,508.48
The International Pentecostal Church of Christ	2002	2,004	4,961	$3,551,761	$1,772.34	$715.94
International Pentecostal Holiness Church	2007	265,744	330,054	$14,928,490	$56.18	$45.23
The Latvian Evangelical Lutheran Church in America	2004	9,700	10,950	$3,934,000	$405.57	$359.27
The Lutheran Church--Missouri Synod (LCMS)	2008	1,803,900	2,337,349	$1,343,086,275	$744.55	$574.62
Mar Thoma Syrian Church of India*	2008	26,500	42,000	$7,639,318	$288.28	$181.89
The Missionary Church	2008	38,206	38,206	$88,233,789	$2,309.42	$2,309.42
Moravian Church in America (Northern Province, Southern Province)*	2008	16,733	20,983	$18,268,105	$1,091.74	$870.61
National Association of Free Will Baptists	2007	185,798	185,798	$131,462,428	$707.56	$707.56
North American Baptist Conference	2006	47,150	47,150	$72,279,470	$1,532.97	$1,532.97
The Orthodox Presbyterian Church	2008	21,243	29,095	$46,035,988	$2,167.11	$1,582.26
Presbyterian Church in America	2008	266,988	335,850	$714,356,133	$2,675.61	$2,127.01
Presbyterian Church (U.S.A.)*	2008	2,140,165	2,844,952	$2,921,571,493	$1,365.12	$1,026.93

Finances—United States Churches (continued)

CONGREGATIONAL FINANCES			BENEVOLENCES			
Total Congregational Contributions	Per Capita Full or Confirmed Members	Per Capita Inclusive Members	Total Benevolences	Per Capita Full or Confirmed Members	Per Capita Inclusive Members	Benevolences as a Percentage of Total Giving
$34,921,064	$2,306.24	$2,306.24	$5,487,460	$362.40	$362.40	14%
$1,963,911,105	$1,178.68	$954.61	$331,030,116	$198.67	$160.91	14%
$12,784,502	$1,024.81	$1,024.81	$2,848,483	$228.34	$228.34	18%
$16,658,718	$890.36	$890.36	$2,077,928	$111.06	$111.06	11%
$266,614,225	$2,332.93	$2,332.93	$25,232,786	$220.79	$220.79	9%
$2,507,117,689	$719.75	$541.04	$256,892,032	$73.75	$55.44	9%
$14,565,105	$929.37	$736.47	$1,070,176	$68.29	$54.11	7%
$2,286,715	$1,040.84	$1,040.84	$678,929	$309.03	$309.03	23%
$22,705,650	$3,275.01	$3,275.01	$1,741,233	$251.15	$251.15	7%
$146,736,387	$2,194.09	$1,953.49	$24,940,690	$372.93	$332.03	15%
$27,179,045	$587.76	$587.76	$4,206,088	$90.96	$90.96	13%
$50,832,814	$998.39	$618.93	$15,018,667	$294.98	$182.86	23%
$490,130,528	$1,916.27	$1,384.57	$43,863,051	$171.49	$123.91	8%
$2,648,634	$1,321.67	$533.89	$903,127	$450.66	$182.05	25%
$5,310,313	$19.98	$16.09	$9,618,177	$36.19	$29.14	64%
$3,473,000	$358.04	$317.17	$461,000	$47.53	$42.10	12%
$1,223,607,882	$678.31	$523.50	$119,478,393	$66.23	$51.12	9%
$2,851,298	$107.60	$67.89	$4,788,020	$180.68	$114.00	63%
$77,967,320	$2,040.71	$2,040.71	$10,266,469	$268.71	$268.71	12%
$17,264,555	$1,031.77	$822.79	$1,003,550	$59.97	$47.83	5%
$105,481,483	$567.72	$567.72	$25,980,945	$139.83	$139.83	20%
$62,175,197	$1,318.67	$1,318.67	$10,104,273	$214.30	$214.30	14%
$39,118,505	$1,841.48	$1,344.51	$6,917,483	$325.64	$237.76	15%
$587,328,486	$2,199.83	$1,748.78	$127,027,647	$475.78	$378.23	18%
$2,542,921,235	$1,188.19	$893.84	$378,650,258	$176.93	$133.10	13%

Table 5. Selected Statistics of Church

Religious Body	Year	Full or Confirmed Members	Inclusive Members	TOTAL CONTRIBUTIONS		
				Total Contributions	Per Capita Full or Confirmed Members	Per Capita Inclusive Members
Primitive Methodist Church in the U.S.A.	2008	3,574	3,915	$5,450,501	$1,525.04	$1,392.21
Reformed Church in America*	2008	157,570	254,485	$329,904,049	$2,093.70	$1,296.36
Reformed Church in the United States	2002	3,258	4,369	$6,241,428	$1,915.72	$1,428.57
Reformed Presbyterian Church of North America	2004	4,542	6,347	$7,129,652	$1,569.72	$1,123.31
The Schwenkfelder Church	2005	2,300	2,300	$1,910,513	$830.66	$830.66
Seventh-day Adventist Church	2008	1,021,777	1,021,777	$1,195,419,795	$1,169.94	$1,169.94
Southern Baptist Convention	2008	16,228,438	16,228,438	$12,121,220,925	$746.91	$746.91
Syriac-Greek Antiochian Orthodox Catholic Church	2008	22,700	22,895	$63,600	$2.80	$2.78
United Church of Christ*	2008	1,111,691	1,111,691	$941,553,040	$846.96	$846.96
The United Methodist Church*	2007	7,853,987	7,853,987	$6,295,942,455	$801.62	$801.62
Unity of the Brethren	1998	2,548	3,218	$165,184	$64.83	$51.33
Universal Fellowship of Metropolitan Community Churches	2006	15,666	15,666	$19,509,664	$1,245.35	$1,245.35
The Wesleyan Church	2008	117,147	131,791	$333,767,545	$2,849.13	$2,532.55
Wisconsin Evangelical Lutheran Synod	2008	309,116	390,213	$321,752,628	$1,040.88	$824.56
TOTALS		**41,176,007**	**44,960,160**	**$35,922,818,150**	**$872.42**	**$798.99**

* National Council of Churches USA member communions
NOTE: Rounding may cause some totals to appear inaccurate.

Summary Statistics

Nation	Number Reporting	Full or Confirmed Members	Inclusive Members	Total Contributions	Per Capita Full or Confirmed Members	Per Capita Inclusive Members
Canada	23	1,222,968	2,332,458	$1,216,699,777	$994.87	$521.64
United States	64	41,176,007	44,960,160	$35,922,818,150	$872.42	$798.99

| CONGREGATIONAL FINANCES | | | BENEVOLENCES | | | |
Total Congregational Contributions	Per Capita Full or Confirmed Members	Per Capita Inclusive Members	Total Benevolences	Per Capita Full or Confirmed Members	Per Capita Inclusive Members	Benevolences as a Percentage of Total Giving
$4,827,828	$1,350.82	$1,233.16	$622,673	$174.22	$159.05	11%
$283,598,231	$1,799.82	$1,114.40	$46,305,818	$293.87	$181.96	14%
$5,309,445	$1,629.66	$1,215.25	$931,983	$286.06	$213.32	15%
$6,447,987	$1,419.64	$1,015.91	$681,665	$150.08	$107.40	10%
$1,682,568	$731.55	$731.55	$227,946	$99.11	$99.11	12%
$321,184,421	$314.34	$314.34	$874,235,374	$855.60	$855.60	73%
$10,762,418,889	$663.18	$663.18	$1,358,802,036	$83.73	$83.73	11%
$39,000	$1.72	$1.70	$26,600	$1.17	$1.16	42%
$869,869,656	$782.47	$782.47	$71,683,884	$64.48	$64.48	8%
$5,080,054,998	$646.81	$646.81	$1,215,887,457	$154.81	$154.81	19%
$51,465	$20.20	$15.99	$113,719	$44.63	$35.34	69%
$19,290,664	$1,231.37	$1,231.37	$219,224	$13.99	$13.99	1%
$291,780,474	$2,490.72	$2,213.96	$41,987,071	$358.41	$318.59	13%
$253,081,873	$818.73	$648.57	$68,670,755	$222.15	$175.98	21%
$30,408,578,031	**$738.50**	**$676.34**	**$5,514,242,844**	**$133.92**	**$122.65**	**15%**

# of Church Finances

Total Congregational Contributions	Per Capita Full or Confirmed Members	Per Capita Inclusive Members	Total Benevolences	Per Capita Full or Confirmed Members	Per Capita Inclusive Members	Benevolences as a Percentage of Total Contributions
$999,211,206	$817.04	$428.39	$216,100,240	$176.70	$92.65	18%
$30,408,578,031	$738.50	$676.34	$5,514,242,844	$133.92	$122.65	15%

STATISTICAL SECTION

Trends in Seminary Enrollment

Data Provided by The Association of Theological Schools (ATS) in the United States and Canada

Table 1: ATS total student enrollment figures include the number of individuals enrolled in degree programs as well as persons enrolled in non-degree programs of study. From Fall 2007 to Fall 2008, the total head count enrollment reported by ATS member schools decreased by 1,778 students, a decrease of 2.2%. This is the third straight year of declines in the 2% range. In the same period, the full-time equivalent (FTE) enrollment decreased by 2,201 students or 4.4%.

Table 1. Number of Member Schools from 1998 to 2008

Year	Number of Schools	Total Enrollment	Canada Head Count	FTE	United States Head Count	FTE	By Membership Accredited	Non-Accredited
1998	237	68,875	5,847	3,683	63,028	40,994	64,412	4,463
1999	237	70,432	6,010	3,224	64,422	41,528	65,674	4,758
2000	243	72,728	5,868	3,251	66,860	44,627	69,850	2,878
2001	243	73,925	6,254	3,342	67,671	45,094	70,942	2,983
2002	244	76,530	6,643	3,512	69,887	44,557	73,615	2,895
2003	243	78,709	6,925	3,653	71,784	46,559	75,660	3,017
2004	251	80,773	7,036	3,597	73,737	48,093	77,513	2,627
2005	251	81,302	6,950	3,523	74,352	48,398	79,083	2,050
2006	253	81,063	6,395	3,205	74,668	47,377	79,618	1,445
2007	253	79,639	5,922	2,991	73,717	46,902	78,050	1,589
2008	252	77,861	5,827	3,081	72,034	44,611	76,333	1,528

Table 2: ATS analyzes enrollment both by the total number of individual students (Head Count) and the equivalent of full-time students (FTE). Full-time equivalency indicates the number of students who would be enrolled if all students were attending on a full-time basis. Decreasing full-time equivalent enrollment as a percentage of head count enrollment over the past ten years indicates an increasing number of part-time students.

Table 2. Head Count and FTE for all Member Schools 1998 to 2008

Year	Head Count	% Change	FTE	% Change	FTE % of Head Count
1998	68,875	5.38	44,678	3.31	64.9%
1999	70,432	2.17	44,845	0.68	63.7%
2000	72,728	3.26	47,876	6.76	65.8%
2001	73,925	1.65	48,435	1.17	65.5%
2002	76,550	3.50	48,130	-0.76	62.8%
2003	78,709	2.82	50,206	4.3	63.8%
2004	80,773	2.62	51,690	2.9	64.1%
2005	81,302	0.65	51,922	0.4	63.9%
2006	81,063	-0.29	50,582	-2.6	62.4%
2007	79,639	-1.76	49,893	-1.36	62.6%
2008	77,861	-2.23	47,692	-4.41	61.3%

Table 3: ATS member schools offer a variety of degree programs. Table 3 displays enrollment by categories of degree programs. The Master of Divinity (MDiv) degree is the normative degree to prepare persons for ordained ministry and for pastoral and religious leadership responsibilities in congregations. Over the past four years, from fall 2005 to fall 2008, the MDiv experienced a 3.4% decrease in the number of students enrolled.

Table 3. Head Count Enrollment by Degree Categories 1998 to 2008

Year	Basic Ministerial Leadership		General Theological Studies	Advanced Ministerial Leadership	Advanced Theological Research	Other
	(M.Div.)	(Non-M.Div.)				
1998	29,263	8,066	7,602	8,641	5,712	9,591
1999	29,842	8,361	7,862	8,743	5,396	10,228
2000	30,427	9,098	8,436	8,758	5,692	10,317
2001	31,128	8,652	8,503	8,790	5,756	11,096
2002	32,005	9,493	8,626	9,209	5,653	11,544
2003	33,287	10,343	8,708	9,213	5,804	11,354
2004	34,096	10,417	9,257	9,435	5,541	11,394
2005	34,505	11,018	9,831	9,330	5,790	10,828
2006	34,442	11,057	9,811	9,366	5,876	10,511
2007	34,123	11,031	9,608	9,411	5,937	9,529
2008	33,319	11,071	9,221	9,554	5,938	8,758

Table 4: In Fall 2008, women constituted 34.5% of the total enrollment in all ATS schools and 31% of the enrollment in the MDiv degree program. When ATS first began gathering enrollment data by gender in 1972, women represented 10% of the total enrollment and 5% of the MDiv enrollment.

Table 4. Women Student Head Count Enrollment 1998 to 2008

Year	Head Count	% Change	FTE % of Head Count
1998	23,176	7.04	33.65%
1999	24,057	3.73	34.16%
2000	25,391	5.55	34.91%
2001	25,999	2.39	35.17%
2002	27,328	5.06	35.70%
2003	27,920	2.19	35.50%
2004	28,875	3.42	36.03%
2005	29,257	1.32	35.98%
2006	27,921	-4.57	34.44%
2007	27,481	-1.58	34.51%
2008	26,870	-2.22	34.51%

Tables 5, 6, 7: Enrollment of North American racial/ethnic students in ATS schools has grown relatively consistently both in overall numbers and as a percent of total enrollment over several decades. African American students were 11.62% of the total enrollment in Fall 2008; Hispanic students, 4.13%; and Pacific/Asian American students, 6.69%. These newest figures show an increase in African American representation, but declines in Asian and Hispanic enrollment.

Table 5. African American Student Head Count Enrollment 1998 to 2008

Year	Number of Students	% Annual Increase	% of Total Enrollment
1998	6,328	9.07	9.19%
1999	6,854	8.31	9.42%
2000	7,161	4.48	9.85%
2001	7,462	4.20	10.09%
2002	8,192	9.78	10.71%
2003	8,144	-0.60	10.30%
2004	8,393	3.06	10.47%
2005	8,946	6.59	12.10%
2006	8,344	-6.73	10.29%
2007	8,839	5.93	11.09%
2008	9,049	2.38	11.62%

Table 6. Hispanic Student Head Count Enrollment 1998 to 2008

Year	Number of Students	% Annual Increase	% of Total Enrollment
1998	2,175	13.58	3.16%
1999	2,256	3.72	3.10%
2000	2,685	19.02	3.69%
2001	2,756	2.64	3.72%
2002	2,449	-11.14	3.20%
2003	2,863	16.9	3.60%
2004	2,842	-0.73	3.54%
2005	2,899	2.00	3.90%
2006	3,104	7.07	3.83%
2007	3,296	6.19	4.12%
2008	3,217	-2.39	4.13%

Table 7. Pacific/Asian American Student Head Count Enrollment 1998 to 2008

Year	Number of Students	% Annual Increase	% of Total Enrollment
1998	4,992	8.95	7.25%
1999	4,932	-1.20	6.78%
2000	5,003	1.44	6.88%
2001	5,021	0.36	6.79%
2002	5,005	-0.32	6.54%
2003	5,499	9.90	7.00%
2004	5,226	-4.96	6.52%
2005	5,189	-7.08	7.00%
2006	5,370	3.49	6.62%
2007	5,524	2.87	6.94%
2008	5,208	-5.72	6.69%

IV
A CALENDAR FOR CHURCH USE
2010-2013

This calendar presents the major days of religious observances for Christians, Jews, Bahá'is, and Muslims; and, within the Christian community, major dates observed by Catholic, Eastern and Oriental Orthodox, Episcopal, and Lutheran churches. Within each of these traditions many other observances, such as saints' days, exist, but only those generally regarded as the most important are listed. Dates of interest to many Protestant communions are also included.

In the Orthodox dates, immovable observances are listed in accordance with the Gregorian calendar. Movable dates (those depending on the date of Easter) often will differ from Western observance, since the date of Easter (Pascha) in the Orthodox communions does not always correlate with the date for Easter of the Western churches. For Orthodox churches that use the old Julian calendar, observances are held thirteen days later than listed here.

Jewish and Muslim holidays begin after sunset the day previous to the date listed in this calendar. For Jews and Muslims, who follow differing lunar calendars, the dates of major observances are translated into Gregorian dates. Since the actual beginning of a new month in the Islamic calendar is determined by the appearance of the new moon, the corresponding dates given here on the Gregorian calendar may vary by geographic location and practice. Following the lunar calendar, Muslim dates fall roughly eleven days earlier each year on the Gregorian calendar. Practice concerning transliteration of the titles of holidays varies widely as well.

(Note: This listing reflects the first full day of holidays extending over two or more days. "C" stands for Catholic; "O" stands for Orthodox; "E" stands for Episcopal; "L" stands for Lutheran; "ECU" stands for Ecumenical.)

Religious Event	2010	2011	2012	2013
New Year's Day (RC-Solemnity of Mary; O-Circumcision of Jesus Christ; E-Feast of Holy Name; L-Naming of Jesus)	Jan 01	Jan 01	Jan 01	Jan 01
Epiphany Sunday (RC)	Jan 03	Jan 02	Jan 08	Jan 06
Epiphany (RC, O, E, L)	Jan 06	Jan 06	Jan 06	Jan 06
Armenian Christmas (O)	Jan 06	Jan 06	Jan 06	Jan 06
First Sunday After Epiphany (Feast of the Baptism of Our Lord) (Christian)	Jan 10	Jan 09	Jan 15	Jan 13
Feast Day of St John the Baptist (Armenian O)	Jan 13	Jan 13	Jan 13	Jan 13
Ecumenical Sunday (ECU)	Jan 17	Jan 16	Jan 15	Jan 20
Week of Prayer for Christian Unity (ECU)	Jan 18	Jan 18	Jan 18	Jan 18
Week of Prayer for Christian Unity, Canada (ECU)	Jan 18	Jan 17	Jan 16	Jan 21
Theophany (Oriental O)	Jan 19	Jan 19	Jan 19	Jan 19
Tu B'Shevat (Jewish)	Jan 30	Jan 20	Feb 08	Jan 26
Presentation of Jesus in the Temple (Candlemas; Purification of the Virgin Mary; O-The Meeting of Our Lord and Savior Jesus Christ) (Christian)	Feb 02	Feb 02	Feb 02	Feb 02
Ash Wednesday (Western Churches)	Feb 17	Mar 09	Feb 22	Feb 13
Brotherhood Week (Interfaith)	Feb 21	Feb 20	Feb 19	Feb 17
Great Lent (First Day of Lent) (O)	Feb 21	Mar 13	Feb 26	Feb 17
Mawlid al-Nabi (Anniversary of the Prophet Muhammed's Birthday) (Muslim)	Feb 26	Feb 15	Feb 04	Jan 24
Purim (Jewish)	Feb 28	Mar 20	Mar 08	Feb 24
Bahá'i Fasting Season begins (19 days) (Bahá'i)	Mar 02	Mar 02	Mar 02	Mar 02
World Day of Prayer (ECU)	Mar 05	Mar 04	Mar 02	Mar 01
Joseph, Husband of Mary (RC, E, L)	Mar 19	Mar 19	Mar 19	Mar 19
Feast of Naw-Ruz (Bahá'i New Year) (Bahá'i)	Mar 21	Mar 21	Mar 21	Mar 21

385

Religious Event	2010	2011	2012	2013
The Annunciation (Christian)	Mar 25	Mar 25	Mar 25	Mar 25
Palm Sunday (O)	Mar 28	Apr 17	Apr 08	Apr 28
Holy Week (Western Churches)	Mar 28	Apr 17	Apr 01	Mar 24
Holy Week (O)	Mar 28	Apr 17	Apr 08	Apr 28
Passover (Pesach) (8 days) (Jewish)	Mar 30	Apr 19	Apr 07	Mar 26
Holy Thursday (O)	Apr 01	Apr 21	Apr 12	May 02
Holy Thursday (Western Churches)	Apr 01	Apr 21	Apr 05	Mar 28
Holy Friday (Good Friday; Burial of Jesus Christ) (O)	Apr 02	Apr 22	Apr 13	May 03
Good Friday (Friday of the Passion of Our Lord) (Western Churches)	Apr 02	Apr 22	Apr 06	Mar 29
Pascha (Orthodox Easter) (O)	Apr 04	Apr 24	Apr 15	May 05
Easter (Western Churches)	Apr 04	Apr 24	Apr 08	Mar 31
Yom Hashoah (Jewish)	Apr 11	May 01	Apr 19	Apr 07
Yom Haatzma'ut (Jewish)	Apr 19	May 09	Apr 26	Apr 15
Feast of Ridvan (Declaration of Baha'u'llah) (12 days) (Bahá'i)	Apr 21	Apr 21	Apr 21	Apr 21
Lag B'Omer (Jewish)	May 02	May 22	May 10	Apr 28
National Day of Prayer (ECU)	May 06	May 05	May 03	May 02
May Friendship Day (ECU)	May 07	May 06	May 04	May 03
Rural Life Sunday (ECU)	May 09	May 08	May 13	May 12
Ascension Thursday (Western Churches)	May 13	Jun 02	May 17	May 09
Ascension Day (O)	May 13	Jun 02	May 24	Jun 13
Shavuot (Pentacost) (2 days) (Jewish)	May 19	Jun 08	May 27	May 15
Pentecost (Whitsunday) (Western Churches)	May 23	Jun 12	May 27	May 19
Pentecost (O)	May 23	Jun 12	Jun 03	Jun 23
Declaration of the Bab (Bahá'i)	May 23	May 23	May 23	May 23
Ascension of Baha'u'llah (Bahá'i)	May 29	May 29	May 29	May 29
Holy Trinity (RC, E, L)	May 30	Jun 19	Jun 03	May 26
Visitation of the Blessed Virgin Mary (RC, E, L)	May 31	May 31	May 31	May 31
Corpus Christi (RC)	Jun 06	Jun 26	Jun 10	Jun 02
Martyrdom of the Bab (Bahá'i)	Jun 09	Jun 09	Jun 09	Jun 09
Sacred Heart of Jesus (RC)	Jun 11	Jul 01	Jun 15	Jun 07
Nativity of St. John the Baptist (RC, E, L)	Jun 24	Jun 24	Jun 24	Jun 24
Saint Peter and Saint Paul, Apostles of Christ (O)	Jun 29	Jun 29	Jun 29	Jun 29
Feast Day of the Twelve Apostles of Christ (O)	Jun 30	Jun 30	Jun 30	Jun 30
Laylat al-Miraj (Ascension of the Prophet) (Muslim)	Jul 09	Jun 29	Jun 17	Jun 06
Tish'a B'Av (Jewish)	Jul 20	Aug 09	Jul 29	Jul 16
Laylat-ul-Bara'h (Night of Forgiveness) (Muslim)	Jul 27	Jul 16	Jul 05	Jun 24
Transfiguration of the Lord (RC, O, E)	Aug 06	Aug 06	Aug 06	Aug 06
Ramadan Begins (First day of the month of Ramadan) (Muslim)	Aug 11	Aug 01	Jul 20	Jul 09
Assumption of the Blessed Virgin Mary (E-Feast of the Blessed Virgin Mary; O-Falling Asleep (Domition) of the Blessed Virgin) (RC, O, E)	Aug 15	Aug 15	Aug 15	Aug 15
Laylat al-Qadr (Night of Destiny, Revelation of the Holy Qur'an) (Muslim)	Sep 06	Aug 27	Aug 15	Aug 04
The Birth of the Blessed Virgin (RC, O)	Sep 08	Sep 08	Sep 08	Sep 08
Rosh Hashanah (New Year) (2 days) (Jewish)	Sep 09	Sep 29	Sep 17	Sep 05
'Id al-Fitr (Festival of the End of Ramadan; First day of the month of Shawwal) (Muslim)	Sep 10	Aug 30	Aug 19	Aug 08
Holy Cross Day (RC-Triumph of the Cross; O-Adoration of the Holy Cross (Christian)	Sep 14	Sep 14	Sep 14	Sep 14
Yom Kippur (Day of Atonement) (Jewish)	Sep 18	Oct 08	Sep 26	Sep 14
Sukkot (Tabernacles) (7 days) (Jewish)	Sep 23	Oct 13	Oct 01	Sep 19
Michaelmas (St. Michael and All Angels) (Christian)	Sep 29	Sep 29	Sep 29	Sep 29

Religious Event	2010	2011	2012	2013
Shmini Atzeret (Solemn Assembly) (Jewish)	Sep 30	Oct 20	Oct 08	Sep 26
Simchat Torah (Rejoicing of the Law) (Jewish)	Oct 01	Oct 21	Oct 09	Sep 27
World Communion Sunday (ECU)	Oct 03	Oct 02	Oct 07	Oct 06
Laity Sunday (ECU)	Oct 10	Oct 09	Oct 14	Oct 13
Thanksgiving Day (Canada) (National)	Oct 11	Oct 10	Oct 08	Oct 14
Birth of the Bab (Bahá'i)	Oct 20	Oct 20	Oct 20	Oct 20
Reformation Sunday (L)	Oct 31	Oct 30	Oct 28	Oct 27
Reformation Day (L)	Oct 31	Oct 31	Oct 31	Oct 31
All Saints Day (RC, E, L)	Nov 01	Nov 01	Nov 01	Nov 01
World Community Day (ECU)	Nov 04	Nov 03	Nov 01	Nov 07
Birth of Baha'u'llah (Bahá'i)	Nov 12	Nov 12	Nov 12	Nov 12
Waqf al-Arafah (Eve of 'Id al-Adha) (Muslim)	Nov 15	Nov 05	Oct 25	Oct 14
'Id al-Adha (Festival of Sacrifice at time of Pilgrimage to Mecca) (Muslim)	Nov 16	Nov 06	Oct 26	Oct 15
Last Sunday After Pentecost (L-Feast of Christ the King) (RC, L)	Nov 21	Nov 20	Nov 25	Nov 24
Thanksgiving Sunday (U.S.) (Christian)	Nov 21	Nov 20	Nov 18	Nov 24
Presentation of the Blessed Virgin Mary in the Temple (Presentation of the Theotokos) (O)	Nov 21	Nov 21	Nov 21	Nov 21
National Bible Week (ECU)	Nov 21	Nov 20	Nov 18	Nov 17
Bible Sunday (ECU)	Nov 21	Nov 20	Nov 18	Nov 17
Thanksgiving Day (U.S.) (National)	Nov 25	Nov 24	Nov 22	Nov 28
The Day of the Covenant (Bahá'i)	Nov 26	Nov 26	Nov 26	Nov 26
Ascension of 'Abdu'l-Baha (Bahá'i)	Nov 28	Nov 28	Nov 28	Nov 28
First Sunday of Advent (Advent Sunday) (Christian)	Nov 28	Nov 27	Dec 02	Dec 01
Feast Day of St. Andrew the Apostle (RC, O, E, L)	Nov 30	Nov 30	Nov 30	Nov 30
Hanukkah (Chanukah, Festival of Lights) (8 days) (Jewish)	Dec 01	Dec 20	Dec 08	Nov 27
Muharram Begins (First Day of the Month of Muharram; Muslim New Year) (Muslim)	Dec 07	Nov 26	Nov 15	Nov 04
Immaculate Conception of the Blessed Virgin Mary (RC)	Dec 08	Dec 08	Dec 08	Dec 08
Ashura' (Martyrdom of Imam Hussein) (Muslim (Shi'a))	Dec 16	Dec 05	Nov 24	Nov 13
Fourth Sunday of Advent (Christmas Sunday) (Christian)	Dec 19	Dec 18	Dec 23	Dec 22
Christmas (Christian Except Armenian)	Dec 25	Dec 25	Dec 25	Dec 25

CALENDAR

387

V

INDEXES

Organizations

INDEX

391

INDEX

INDEX

INDEX

400

Individuals

INDEX

403

INDEX

INDEX

409

INDEX

411

INDEX

413

INDEX

INDEX

417

INDEX

419

INDEX

421

INDEX

423

INDEX

428

430

Notes

Notes

Notes

Notes

Notes

Notes